Clean Code Principles Edition

A Software Practitioner's Handbook

Petri Silen

Clean Code Principles and Patterns, 2nd Edition

A Software Practitioner's Handbook

Petri Silen

ISBN 9798323162925

Tweet This Book!

Please help Petri Silen by spreading the word about this book on Twitter!

The suggested hashtag for this book is #cleancodeprinciplesandpatterns.

Find out what other people are saying about the book by clicking on this link to search for this hashtag on Twitter:

#cleancodeprinciplesandpatterns

Also By Petri Silen

Clean Code Principles And Patterns
Clean Code Principles And Patterns

Contents

CONTENTS

CONTENTS

1: About the Author

Petri Silén is a seasoned software developer working at Nokia Networks in Finland with industry experience of almost 30 years. He has done both frontend and backend development with a solid competence in multiple programming languages, including C++, Java, Python and JavaScript/TypeScript. He started his career at Nokia Telecommunications in 1995. During his first years, he developed a real-time mobile networks analytics product called "Traffica" in C++ for major telecom customers worldwide, including companies like T-Mobile, Orange, Vodafone, and Claro. The initial product was for monitoring a 2G circuit-switched core network and GPRS packet-switched core network. Later, functionality to Traffica was added to cover new network technologies, like 3G circuit-switched and packet core networks, 3G radio networks, and 4G/LTE. He later developed new functionality for Traffica using Java and web technologies, including jQuery and React. During the last few years, he has developed cloud-native containerized microservices with Java and C++ for the next-generation Customer and Networks Insights (CNI) product used by major communications service providers like Verizon, AT&T, USCC, and KDDI. The main application areas he has contributed during the last years include KPI-based real-time alerting, anomaly detection for KPIs, and configurable real-time data exporting.

During his free time, he has developed a data visualization application using React, Redux, TypeScript, and Jakarta EE. He has also developed a security-first cloud-native microservice framework for Node.js in TypeScript. He likes to take care of his Kaapo cat, take walks, play tennis and badminton, ski in the winter, and watch soccer and ice hockey on TV.

2: Introduction

This book teaches you how to write clean code. It presents software design and development principles and patterns in a very practical manner. This book is suitable for both junior and senior developers. Some basic knowledge of programming in Python is required. All examples in this book are presented in Python, except some examples related to frontend code, which are in JavaScript/TypeScript. The content of this book is divided into ten chapters. All Python examples in this book require Python 3.11 or later. This is a book for primarily software developers. For that reason, some topics are not covered exhaustively. This includes topics related to architecture, DevSecOps, E2E, and non-functional testing. Those are topics most relevant to software architects, DevOps specialists and test/QA engineers. I want to cover them in this book because it is always good to have a basic understanding of topics closely related to software development.

This book presents a lot of principles, best practices, and patterns. It can be difficult to grasp them all on a single read, which is not the purpose. You should pick *the most relevant topics for yourself*, embrace them, and try to put them into use in everyday coding. You can always return to the book to learn additional topics. Some principles, patterns, and practices can be subjective and open for debate, but I have only put into this book such principles, patterns, and practices that I have used or would use myself. In the last *Conclusion* chapter, I will list the topics that I consider the most important based on my experience in real-life projects.

The *second chapter* is about *architectural design principles* that enable the development of true cloud-native microservices. The first architectural design principle described is the single responsibility principle, which defines that a piece of software should be responsible for one thing at its abstraction level. Then, a uniform naming principle for microservices, clients, APIs, and libraries is presented. The encapsulation principle defines how each software component should hide its internal state behind a public API. The service aggregation principle is introduced with a detailed explanation of how a higher-level microservice can aggregate lower-level microservices. Architectural patterns like event sourcing, command query responsibility segregation (CQRS), and distributed transactions are discussed. Distributed transactions are covered with examples using the saga orchestration pattern and the saga choreography pattern. You get answers on how to avoid code duplication at the architectural level. The externalized configuration principle describes how service configuration should be handled in modern environments. We discuss the service substitution principle, which states that dependent services a microservice uses should be easily substitutable. The importance of autopilot microservices is discussed from the point of view of statelessness, resiliency, high availability, observability, and automatic scaling. Towards the end of the chapter, there is a discussion about different ways microservices can communicate. Several rules are presented on how to version software components. The chapter ends with discussing why limiting the number of technologies used in a software system is helpful.

The *third chapter* presents *object-oriented design principles*. We start the chapter with object-oriented programming concepts and programming paradigms followed by the SOLID principles: Single responsibility principle, open-closed principle, Liskov's substitution principle, interface segregation principle, and dependency inversion principle. Each SOLID principle is presented with realistic but simple examples. The uniform naming principle defines a uniform way to name interfaces, classes, functions, function pairs, boolean functions (predicates), builder, factory, conversion, and lifecycle methods. The encapsulation principle describes that a class should encapsulate its internal state and how immutability helps ensure state encapsulation. The encapsulation principle also discusses the importance of not leaking an object's internal state out. The object composition principle defines that composition should be preferred over inheritance. Tactical Domain-driven design (DDD) is presented with two real-world examples. All the design patterns from the *GoF's Design Patterns* book are presented with realistic yet straightforward examples. The don't ask, tell principle is presented as a way to avoid the feature envy design smell. The chapter also discusses avoiding primitive obsession and the benefits of using semantically validated function arguments. The chapter ends by presenting the dependency injection principle and avoiding code duplication principle.

The *fourth chapter* is about *coding principles*. The chapter starts with a principle for uniformly naming variables in code. A uniform naming convention is presented for integer, floating-point, boolean, string, enum, and collection variables. Also, a naming convention is defined for maps, pairs, tuples, objects, and callback functions. The uniform source code repository structure principle is presented with examples. Next, the avoid comments principle lists reasons why most comments are unnecessary and defines concrete ways to remove unnecessary comments from the code. The following concrete actions are presented: naming things correctly, returning a named value, return-type aliasing, extracting a constant for a boolean expression, extracting a constant for a complex expression, extracting enumerated values, and extracting a function. The chapter discusses the benefits of using type hints. We discuss the most common refactoring techniques: renaming, extracting a method, extracting a variable, replacing conditionals with polymorphism, introducing a parameter object, and making anemic objects rich objects. The importance of static code analysis is described, and the most popular static code analysis tools are listed. The most common static code analysis issues and the preferred way to correct them are listed. Handling errors and exceptions correctly in code is fundamental and can be easily forgotten or done wrong. This chapter instructs how to handle errors and exceptions and return errors by returning a boolean failure indicator, an optional value, or an error object. The chapter instructs how to adapt code to a wanted error-handling mechanism and handle errors functionally. Ways to avoid off-by-one errors are presented. Readers are instructed on handling situations where some code is copied from a web page found by googling or generated by AI. Advice is given on what data structure is the most appropriate for a given use case. The chapter ends with a discussion about code optimization: when and how to optimize.

The *fifth chapter* is dedicated to *testing principles*. The chapter starts with the introduction of the functional testing pyramid. Then, we present unit testing and instruct how to use test-driven development (TDD) and behavior-driven development for individual functions. We give unit test examples with mocking. When introducing software component integration testing, we discuss behavior-driven development (BDD), acceptance test-driven development (ATDD), and the Gherkin language to specify features formally. Integration test examples are given using Behave and the Postman API development platform. The chapter also discusses the integration testing of UI software components. We end the integration testing section with an example of setting up an integration testing environment using Docker Compose. We give a complete example of applying multiple design approaches (BDD, ATDD, DDD, OOD, and TDD) in a small project. Lastly, the purpose of end-to-end (E2E) testing is discussed with some examples. The chapter ends with a discussion about non-functional testing. The following categories of non-functional testing are covered in more detail: performance testing, stability testing, reliability testing, security testing, stress, and scalability testing.

The *sixth chapter* handles *security principles*. The threat modeling process is introduced, and there is an example of how to conduct threat modeling for a simple API microservice. A full-blown frontend OpenID Connect/OAuth 2.0 authentication and authorization example for a SPA (single-page application) with TypeScript, Vue.js, and Keycloak is implemented. Then, we discuss how authorization by validating a JWT should be handled in the backend. The chapter ends with a discussion of the most important security features: password policy, cryptography, denial-of-service prevention, SQL injection prevention, security configuration, automatic vulnerability scanning, integrity, error handling, audit logging, and input validation.

The *seventh chapter* is about *API design principles*. First, we tackle design principles for frontend-facing APIs. We discuss how to design JSON-based RPC, REST, and GraphQL APIs. Also, subscription-based and real-time APIs are presented with realistic examples using Server-Sent Events (SSE) and the WebSocket protocol. The last part of the chapter discusses inter-microservice API design and event-driven architecture.

gRPC is introduced as a synchronous inter-microservice communication method, and examples of request-only and request-response asynchronous APIs are presented.

The *8th chapter* discusses *databases and related principles*. We cover the following types of databases: relational databases, document databases (MongoDB), key-value databases (Redis), wide-column databases (Cassandra), and search engines. For relational databases, we present how to use object-relational mapping (ORM), define one-to-one, one-to-many and many-to-many relationships, and parameterized SQL queries. Finally, we present three normalization rules for relational databases.

The *9th chapter* presents *concurrent programming principles* regarding threading and thread safety. For thread safety, we present several ways to achieve thread synchronization: locks, atomic variables, and thread-safe collections. We also discuss publishing changes to a shared state and subscribing to them from two different threads.

The *10th chapter* discusses *teamwork principles*. We explain the importance of using an agile framework and discuss the fact that a developer usually never works alone and what that entails. We discuss how to document a software component so that onboarding new developers is quick and easy. Technical debt in software is something that each team should avoid. Some concrete actions to prevent technical debt are presented. Code reviews are something teams should do, and this chapter gives guidance on what to focus on in code reviews. The chapter ends with a discussion of developer roles each team should have and provides hints on enabling a team to develop software as concurrently as possible.

The *11th chapter* is dedicated to *DevSecOps*. DevOps describes practices that integrate software development (Dev) and software operations (Ops). It aims to shorten the software development life cycle through parallelization and automation and provides continuous delivery with high software quality. DevSecOps is a DevOps augmentation where security practices are integrated into the DevOps practices. This chapter presents the phases of the DevOps lifecycle: plan, code, build and test, release, deploy, operate, and monitor. The chapter gives an example of creating a microservice container image and how to specify the deployment of a microservice to a Kubernetes cluster. Also, a complete example of a CI/CD pipeline using GitHub Actions is provided. Guidance on how to implement microservice observability (logging, metrics, alerts) is given with some examples.

3: Architectural Principles and Patterns

This chapter describes architectural principles and patterns for designing clean, modern, cloud-native[1] software systems and applications. Architectural design means designing a software system consisting of multiple software components. This chapter focuses on modern cloud-native microservices, but some principles can be used with a monolithic software architecture[2]. This book does not cover monolithic software architecture design. Still, if you design a monolithic software system, you should consider implementing a so-called modular monolith[3], which is a monolith with modularity: Different functionalities are separated inside the monolith. This modular architecture makes it easier to dismantle the monolith to microservices or extract part(s) of the monolith into microservice(s) if needed later.

Monoliths are not inherently bad. But when we talk about monoliths, people automatically think of that vast legacy system, a so-called big ball of mud. Many legacy monoliths have lousy designs and contain unmodular spaghetti code full of technical debt. But you can create a monolith with minimal technical debt when you create it as modular. This means that different teams can handle the design and implementation of those modules separately. Monolith can be a sustainable alternative for a small company or a startup. They can start with a modular monolith and break it down into two microservices later if needed. A small company has limited resources. Implementing a monolith can save resources. A startup can save time by implementing a monolith first. Developing a monolith can save time compared to microservices because testing, deployment, observability, and transactions are easier to implement. The decision between a modular monolith and microservices architecture is a strategic architectural decision that should be carefully analyzed by the system architect together with the architecture team. So, the benefits and drawbacks of microservices (listed in a later section of this chapter) should be carefully considered. When choosing a microservice architecture, the sizing of each microservice should be done right (right-sizing microservices). This is also an important strategic decision but not always an easy one. You might get it initially wrong, meaning that you later need to combine several microservices into a single larger microservice or split a large microservice into smaller ones.

This book does not solely promote microservices, but as said, modular monolith can be a viable alternative to a microservices architecture in some cases. Even if you are creating a modular monolith, it is good to know microservice design principles so that you can build the modular monolith in such a way that you can split it into microservices if needed in the future. For this reason, it is worth to know the fundamental design principles of microservices.

Cloud-native software is built of loosely coupled scalable, resilient, and observable services that can run in public, private, or hybrid clouds. Cloud-native software utilizes technologies like containers (e.g., Docker), microservices, serverless functions, and container orchestration (e.g., Kubernetes), and it can be automatically deployed using declarative code. Examples in this chapter assume microservices deployed in a Kubernetes environment. Kubernetes is a cloud provider agnostic way of running containerized microservices and has gained massive popularity in recent years. If you are new to Kubernetes, you can familiarize yourself with the most relevant Kubernetes concepts[4].

This chapter discusses the following architectural principles and patterns:

---

[1]https://en.wikipedia.org/wiki/Cloud-native_computing
[2]https://en.wikipedia.org/wiki/Monolithic_application
[3]https://www.kamilgrzybek.com/blog/posts/modular-monolith-primer
[4]https://kubernetes.io/docs/concepts/

- Software hierarchy
- The twelve-factor app
- Single responsibility principle
- Uniform naming principle
- Encapsulation principle
- Service aggregation principle
- High cohesion, low coupling principle
- Library composition principle
- Avoid duplication principle
- Externalized service configuration principle
- Service substitution principle
- Autopilot microservices principle

  - Stateless microservices principle
  - Resilient microservices principle
  - Horizontally autoscaling microservices principle
  - Highly-available microservices principle
  - Observable services principle

- Individually deployable microservices principle
- Inter-service communication patterns
- Strategical domain-driven design principle
- Software versioning principles
- Git version control principle
- Architectural patterns
- Preferred technology stacks principle
- 8 Fallacies of distributed computing

3.1: Software Hierarchy

A *software system* consists of multiple computer programs and anything related to those programs to make them operable, including but not limited to configuration, deployment code, and documentation. A software system is divided into two parts: *the backend* and *the frontend*. Backend software runs on servers, and frontend software runs on client devices like PCs, tablets, and phones. Backend software consists of *services*. Frontend software consists of *clients* that use backend services and *standalone applications* that do not use any backend services. An example of a standalone application is a calculator or a simple text editor. A service is something that provides a specific functionality and is running continuously.

In addition to services, there are a couple of other types of backend programs, namely jobs and cron jobs. In a Kubernetes environment, programs that run once or on-demand are called Jobs[5], and programs that run on a schedule are called CronJobs[6]. Jobs and CronJobs are typically related to services and perform administrative tasks related to a specific service. According to the *single responsibility principle*, the service itself should not perform administrative tasks but should be dedicated to providing a particular service

---

[5]https://kubernetes.io/docs/concepts/workloads/controllers/job/
[6]https://kubernetes.io/docs/concepts/workloads/controllers/cron-jobs/

only, like an *order-service* provides operations on orders. Let's have an example of a job and cron job with the *order-service*: After the *order-service* installation, an *order-db-init-job* could be triggered to initialize the *order-service*'s database, and an *order-db-cleanup-cronjob* could be triggered on a schedule to perform cleanup actions on the *order-service*'s database.

A separate service can be created to control a service's deployment and lifecycle. In a Kubernetes environment, that kind of service is called an operator[7].

A command line interface (CLI) program is an additional program type. CLI programs are typically used for administrative tasks. For example, an *admin-cli* could be created to install and upgrade a software system.

The term *application* is often used to describe a single program designated for a specific purpose. In general, a software application is some software applied to solve a specific problem. From an end user's point of view, all clients are applications. But from a developer's point of view, an application needs both a client and backend service(s) to be functional unless the application is a *standalone application*. In this book, I will use the term application to designate a logical grouping of program(s) and related artifacts, like configuration, to form a functional piece of the software system dedicated to a specific purpose. In my definition, a non-standalone application consists of one or more services and possibly a client or clients to fulfill an end user's need.

Let's say we have a software system for mobile telecom network analytics. That system provides data visualization functionality. We can call the data visualization part of the software system a data visualization application. That application consists of, for example, a web client and two services, one for fetching data and one for configuration. Suppose we also have a generic data ingester microservice in the same software system. That generic data ingester is not an application without some configuration that makes it a specific service that we can call an application. For example, the generic data ingester can have a configuration to ingest raw data from the radio network part of the mobile network. The generic data ingester and the configuration together form an application: a radio network data ingester. Then, there could be another configuration for ingesting raw data from the core network part of the mobile network. That configuration and the generic data ingester make another application: a core network data ingester.

---

[7]https://kubernetes.io/docs/concepts/extend-kubernetes/operator/

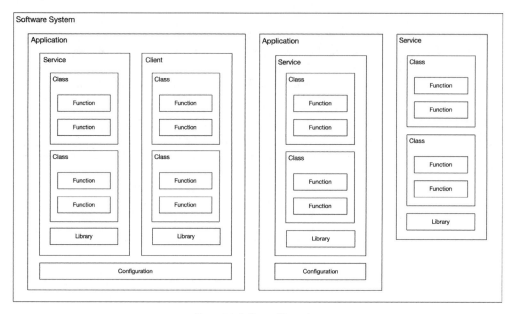

Figure 3.1. Software Hierarchy

Computer programs and *libraries* are *software components*. A *software component* is something that can be individually packaged, tested, and delivered. It consists of one or more classes, and a class consists of one or more functions (class methods). (There are no traditional classes in purely functional languages, but software components consist only of functions.) A computer program can also be composed of one or more libraries and a library can be composed of other libraries.

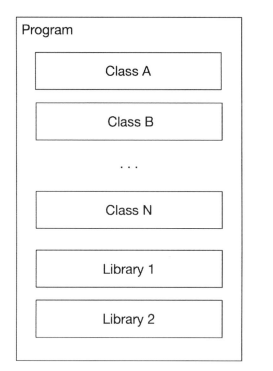 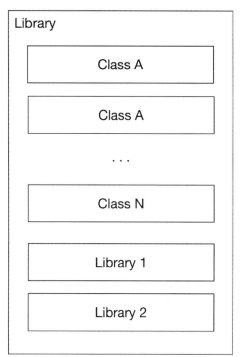

Figure 3.2. Software Components

3.2: The Twelve-Factor App

The twelve-factor app[8] is a methodology for building modern cloud-native microservices.

Below are listed the 12 factors of a cloud-native microservice with short descriptions of each factor. For most of the topics presented here, we will discuss them further and in more detail in later sections of this chapter.

1. **Codebase: One codebase tracked in revision control, many deployments**

There should be one codebase for a microservice stored in a revision control system, like Git. The codebase is not related to deployments. You can make several deployments from the one codebase. There can be *externalized configurations* that can be applied to deployments to make the microservice with one codebase behave differently in different environments.

2. **Dependencies: Explicitly declare and isolate dependencies**

[8]https://12factor.net/

Never rely on implicit system-wide dependencies. Make all your microservice dependencies explicit. Use a software package manager like NPM or Maven to explicitly declare what your microservice needs. Regarding operating system dependencies, declare them in the Dockerfile for a containerized microservice. Use a minimal-size container base image and add only the dependencies you need. If you don't need any operating system dependencies, use a distroless image as the container base image. You should not have anything extra in your container. This will minimize the surface for potential attacks.

3. Configuration: Store configuration in the environment

Configuration is anything that varies between deployments. Never store such configuration information in the microservice source code. Use externalized configuration that is stored in the deployment environment.

4. Backing services: Treat backing services as attached resources

Depending on the deployment environment, the microservice should be able to connect to different backing services. Store the connection information for the backing services in the deployment environment. Never hard-code connection information for backing services in the source code.

5. Build, release, run: Strictly separate build and run stages

For your microservices, implement pipelines for continuous integration (CI), continuous delivery (CD), and continuous deployment (CD). You can combine these stages into a CI/CD pipeline. Each stage is separate and depends on the artifacts produced in the previous stage: continuous integration depends on source code, continuous delivery depends on build artifacts, and continuous deployment depends on release artifacts like a Helm chart and Docker image.

6. Processes: Execute the app as one or more stateless processes

First of all, make your microservice stateless. This allows you to run multiple instances of the microservice easily in parallel (as separate processes).

7. Port binding: Expose services via port binding

Expose your microservice to other microservices via a well-known and fixed hostname and port. The other microservices can then connect to your microservice using the well-known hostname and port combination.

8. Concurrency: Scale out via the process model

Do not scale up; scale out by adding more instances (processes) of your stateless microservice. This approach makes concurrency easy because you don't necessarily need to implement multithreading in your microservice. Correctly implementing multithreading can be complex. You can easily introduce concurrency issues in multithreaded code if you, for example, forget to implement locking when accessing a resource shared by multiple threads. Do not complicate your code with multithreading if it is not needed.

9. Disposability: Maximize robustness with fast startup and graceful shutdown

In a cloud environment, you should be prepared for your microservice instances to go down and then be started again, for example, on a different node. For this reason, make the startup fast and make the shutdown graceful so that no information is lost or left unprocessed upon shutdown. Suppose you have a microservice with an internal queue for processing messages. When a microservice instance receives a shutdown request, it should gracefully shut down by draining the internal queue and processing the messages before termination. Fast startup is critical for containers in a serverless CaaS environment where microservices can be scaled to zero instances when there is no traffic.

10. **Dev/prod parity: Keep development, staging, and production as similar as possible**

Staging and production environments should be identical in every way except the size of the environment. The production environment can be large, but the staging environment does not have to be as big. Do not use different backed services in your development and production environments. For example, don't use a different database in the development environment compared to the production environment. In the development environment, declare your backed services in a Docker Compose file using the same Docker image and version used in the production deployment. Suppose we use MySQL version x.y in production, but the development environment uses MariaDB version z.y. There is now a chance for a situation where a problem in the production environment with the MySQL version x.y cannot be reproduced in the development environment with the MariaDB version x.z.

11. **Logs: Treat logs as event streams**

Microservice developers should only be concerned about writing log entries in a specific format to standard output. The DevOps team will implement the rest of what is needed to collect and store the logs.

12. **Admin processes: Run admin/management tasks as one-off processes**

Do not add administrative tasks to your microservices. Instead, create a separate microservice for each administrative task. Each microservice should be guaranteed a single responsibility. These administrative microservices can then be run on demand or schedule. Examples of administrative tasks are database initialization, database cleanup, and backup. In a Kubernetes environment, you can perform database initialization either in a Helm post-install hook or Pod's init container. Cleanup and backup tasks can be performed using a Kubernetes CronJob.

3.3: Single Responsibility Principle

A software entity should have only a single responsibility at its abstraction level.

A software system at the highest level in the hierarchy should have a single dedicated purpose. For example, there can be an e-commerce or payroll software system. However, there should not be a software system that handles both e-commerce and payroll-related activities. If you were a software vendor and had made an e-commerce software system, selling that to clients wanting an e-commerce solution would be easy. But if you had made a software system encompassing both e-commerce and payroll functionality, it would be hard to sell that to customers wanting only an e-commerce solution because they might already have a payroll software system and, of course, don't want another one.

Let's consider the application level in the software hierarchy. Suppose we have designed a software system for telecom network analytics. This software system is divided into four different applications: Radio network data ingestion, core network data ingestion, data aggregation, and data visualization. Each of these applications has a single dedicated purpose. Suppose we had coupled the data aggregation and visualization applications into a single application. In that case, replacing the data visualization part with a 3rd party application could be difficult. However, when they are separate applications with a well-defined interface, replacing the data visualization application with a 3rd party application would be much easier if needed.

A software component should also have a single dedicated purpose. A service type of software component with a single responsibility is called a *microservice*. For example, in an e-commerce software system, one microservice could be responsible for handling orders and another for handling sales items. Both of those microservices are responsible for one thing only. By default, we should not have a microservice responsible for orders and sales items. That would be against the single responsibility principle because order and sales item handling are different functionalities at the same level of abstraction. Combining two or more functionalities into a single microservice sometimes makes sense. The reason could be that the functionalities firmly belong together, and putting functionalities in a single microservice would diminish the drawbacks of microservices, like needing to use distributed transactions. Thus, the size of a microservice can vary and depends on the abstraction level of the microservice. Some microservices can be small, and others can be larger if they are at a higher level of abstraction. A microservice is always smaller than a monolith and larger than a single function. The higher the level of abstraction the microservice is, the fewer microservice benefits you get. Depending on the software system size and its design, the number of microservices in it can vary from a handful to tens or even hundreds of microservices.

The number of microservices can matter. When you have a lot of microservices, the drawbacks become more prominent, e.g., duplicate DevOps-related code in each microservice's source code repository, observability, troubleshooting, and testing will be more complicated. Running a software system with many small microservices can be more expensive compared to fewer and larger microservices or a monolith. This is because you need to have at least one instance of each microservice running all the time. If you have 500 microservices (you can have additional on-demand microservices, like jobs and cronjobs), there will be 500 instances running. If every microservice requires a minimum of 0.1 vCPU, you need at least 50 vCPUs to run the system when the system load is at the lowest level, e.g., at night. However, you can reduce that cost by using a serverless containers-as-a-service (CaaS) solution. Knative[9] is an open-source serverless CaaS solution that runs on top of Kubernetes. You can define your microservices as Knative *Service* custom resources that automatically scale your microservice in and out. When a microservice is not used for a while, it is automatically scaled to zero instances, and when the microservice is used again, it is scaled out to one or more instances. All of this happens automatically in the background. When you use Knative *Service* custom resources, you don't need to define Kubernetes *Deployment*, *Service*, and *Horizontal Pod Autoscaler* manifests separately. We talk more about these Kubernetes manifests later in this chapter. Consider the earlier example of 500 microservices. Let's say that only 10% of 500 microservices must be running all night. It would mean that Knative can scale 90% of the microservices to zero instances, meaning only five vCPUs are needed at night, reducing the cost to one-tenth.

Let's have an example of an e-commerce software system that consists of the following functionality:

- sales items
- shopping cart
- orders

Let's design how to split the above-described functionality into microservices. When deciding which functionality is put in the same microservice, we should ensure that the requirement of a single responsibility is met and that high functional and non-functional cohesion is achieved. High functional cohesion means

[9]https://knative.dev/docs/

that two functionalities depend on each other and tend to change together. Examples of low functional cohesion would be email sending and shopping cart functionality. Those two functionalities don't depend on each other, and they don't change together. Thus, we should implement email sending and shopping cart functionalities as separate microservices. Non-functional cohesion is related to all non-functional aspects like architecture, technology stack, deployment, scalability, resiliency, availability, observability, etc. We discuss cohesion and coupling more in a later section of this chapter.

We should not put all the e-commerce software system functionality in a single microservice because there is not high non-functional cohesion between sales items-related functionality and the other functionality. The functionality related to sales items should be put into its own microservice that can scale separately because the sales item microservice receives much more traffic than the shopping cart and order services. Also, we should be able to choose appropriate database technology for the sales item microservice. The database engine should be optimized for a high number of reads and a low number of writes. Later, we might realize that the pictures of the sales items should not be stored in the same database as other sales item-related information. We could then introduce a new microservice dedicated to storing/retrieving images of sales items.

Instead of implementing shopping cart and order-related functionality as two separate microservices, we could implement them as a single microservice. This is because shopping cart and order functionalities have high functional cohesion. For example, whenever a new order is placed, the items from the shopping cart should be read and removed. Also, the non-functional cohesion is high. Both services can use the same technology stack and scale together. We eliminate distributed transactions by putting the two functionalities in a single microservice and can use standard database transactions. That simplifies the codebase and testing of the microservice. We should not name the microservice *shopping-cart-and-order-service* because that name does not denote a single responsibility. We should name the microservice using a term on a higher level of abstraction. For example, we could name it *purchase-service* because the microservice is responsible for functionality related to a customer purchasing item(s) from the e-commerce store. In the future, if we notice that the requirement of high functional and non-functional cohesion is no longer met, it is possible to split the *purchase-service* into two separate microservices: *shopping-cart-service* and *order-service*. When you first implement the *purchase-service*, you should put the code related to different subdomains in separate domain-specific source code directories: *shoppingcart* and *order*. It will be easier later to extract those two functionalities into separate microservices.

Right-sizing microservices is not always straightforward, and for this reason, the initial division of a software system into microservices should not be engraved in stone. You can make changes to that in the future if seen as appropriate. You might realize that a particular microservice should be divided into two separate microservices due to different scaling needs, for example. Or you might realize that it is better to couple two or more microservices into a single microservice to avoid complex distributed transactions, for instance.

There are many advantages to microservices:

- Improved productivity

  - You can choose the best-suited programming language and technology stack
  - Microservices are easy to develop in parallel because there will be fewer merge conflicts
  - Developing a monolith can result in more frequent merge conflicts

- Improved resiliency and fault isolation

  - A fault in a single microservice does not bring other microservices down
  - A bug in a monolith can bring the whole monolith down

- Better scalability

  - Stateless microservices can automatically scale horizontally
  - Horizontal scaling of a monolith is complicated or impossible

- Better data security and compliance

  - Each microservice encapsulates its data, which can be accessed via a public API only

- Faster and easier upgrades

  - Upgrading only the changed microservice(s) is enough. There is no need to update the whole monolith every time

- Faster release cycle

  - Build the changed microservice only. There is no need to build the whole monolith when something changes

- Fewer dependencies

  - Lower probability for dependency conflicts

- Enables "open-closed architecture", meaning architecture that is more open for extension and more closed for modification

  - New functionality not related to any existing microservice can be added to a new microservice instead of modifying the current codebase.

The main drawback of microservices is the complexity that a distributed architecture brings. Implementing transactions between microservices requires implementing distributed transactions, which are more complex than standard database transactions. Distributed transactions require more code and testing. You can avoid distributed transactions by placing closely related services in a single microservice whenever possible. Operating and monitoring a microservice-based software system is complicated. Also, testing a distributed system is more challenging than testing a monolith. Development teams should focus on these "problematic" areas by hiring DevOps and test automation specialists.

The *single responsibility principle* is also one of the IDEALS[10] microservice principles.

A library-type software component should also have a single responsibility. Like calling single-responsibility services microservices, we can call a single-responsibility library a *microlibrary*. For example, there could be a library for handling YAML-format content and another for handling XML-format content. We shouldn't try to bundle the handling of both formats into a single library. If we did and needed only the YAML-related functionality, we would also always get the XML-related functionality. Our code would always ship with the XML-related code, even if it was never used. This can introduce unnecessary code bloat. We would also have to take any security patch for the library into use, even if the patch was only for the XML-related functionality we don't use.

---

[10]https://www.infoq.com/articles/microservices-design-ideals/

3.4: Uniform Naming Principle

Use a specific postfix to name different types of software components.

When developing software, you should establish a naming convention for different kinds of software components: Microservices, clients, jobs, operators, command line interfaces (CLIs), and libraries. Next, I present my suggested way of naming different software components.

The preferred naming convention for microservices is *<service's purpose>-service* or *<service's purpose>-svc*. For example: *data-aggregation-service* or *email-sending-svc*. Use the microservice name systematically in different places. For example, use it as the Kubernetes Deployment name and the source code repository name (or directory name in case of a monorepo). It is enough to name your microservices with the *service* postfix instead of a *microservice* postfix because each service should be a microservice by default. So, there would not be any real benefit in naming microservices with the *microservice* postfix. That would make the microservice name longer without any added value.

If you want to be more specific in naming microservices, you can name API microservices with an *api* postfix instead of the more generic *service* postfix, for example, *sales-item-api*. In this book, I am not using the *api* postfix but always use the *service* postfix only.

The preferred naming convention for clients is *<client's purpose>-<client type>-client*, *<client's purpose>-<ui type>-ui* or *<client's purpose>-<app type>-app*. For example: *data-visualization-web-ui*, *data-visualization-mobile-client*, *data-visualization-android-app* or *data-visualization-ios-app*. In this book, I mostly use the *client* postfix because it is the most generic term.

The preferred naming convention for jobs is *<job's purpose>-job*. For example, a job that initializes the database for orders could be named *order-db-init-job*.

The preferred naming convention for cron jobs is *<cron job's purpose>-cronjob*. For example, a cron job that performs order database backup regularly could be named *order-db-backup-cronjob*.

The preferred naming convention for operators is *<operated service>-operator*. For example, an operator for *order-service* could be named *order-service-operator*.

The preferred naming convention for a CLI is *<CLI's purpose>-cli*. For example, a CLI that is used to administer the software system could be named *admin-cli*.

The preferred naming convention for libraries is either *<library's purpose>-lib* or *<library's purpose>-library*. For example: *common-utils-lib* or *common-ui-components-library*.

When using these naming conventions, a clear distinction between a microservice, client, (cron) job, operator, CLI, and library-type software component can be made only by looking at the name. Also, it is easy to recognize if a source code repository contains a microservice, client, (cron) job, operator, CLI, or library.

3.5: Encapsulation Principle

Microservice must encapsulate its internal state behind a public API. Anything behind the public API is considered private to the microservice and cannot be accessed directly by other microservices.

Microservices should define a public API that other microservices use for interfacing. Anything behind the public API is private and inaccessible from other microservices.

While microservices should be made stateless (the *stateless services principle* is discussed later in this chapter), a stateless microservice needs a place to store its state outside the microservice. Typically, the state is stored in a database or a cache. The database is the microservice's internal dependency and should be made private to the microservice, meaning that no other microservice can directly access the database. Access to the database happens indirectly using the microservice's public API.

It is discouraged to allow multiple microservices to share a single database because then there is no control over how each microservice will use the database and what requirements each microservice has for the database. (The architecture where multiple services use a shared database is usually called *service-based architecture* and is different from a microservice architecture.)

It can be possible to share a *physical* database with several microservices if each uses its own *logical* database. This requires that a specific database user is created for each microservice. Each database user can access only one logical database dedicated to a particular microservice. In this way, no microservice can directly access another microservice's data. However, this approach can still pose some problems because the dimensioning requirements of all microservices for the shared physical database must be considered. Also, the deployment responsibility of the shared database must be decided. The shared database could be deployed as a platform or common service as part of the platform or common services deployment, for example.

If a database is shared between microservices, it is called *service-based architecture*, not microservice architecture per se. A service-based architecture's benefit is avoiding complex distributed transactions that the actual microservice architecture would entail. When having a service-based architecture, distributed transactions can be replaced with database transactions. The main problem with this architectural style is that each service is no longer necessarily single-responsibility, which can sometimes be an acceptable trade-off. (e.g. *shopping-cart-service* and *order-service* with a shared database, and creating an order with *order-service* will also read and empty the shopping cart in a single database transaction. Now, the *order-service* is no longer a single-responsibility service because it is doing some work that should be in the *shopping-cart service* in the case of a microservice architecture.

3.6: Service Aggregation Principle

Service on a higher level of abstraction aggregates services on a lower level of abstraction.

Service aggregation happens when one service on a higher level of abstraction aggregates services on a lower level of abstraction.

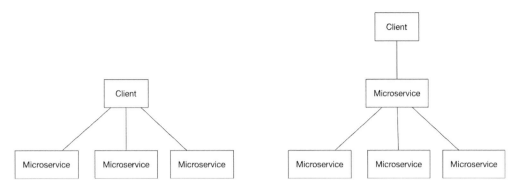

Figure 3.3. Architecture Without and With Service Aggregation

Let's have a service aggregation example with a second-hand e-commerce software system that allows people to sell their products online.

The problem domain of the e-commerce service consists of the following subdomains:

- User account domain

  - Create, modify, and delete a user account
  - View user account with sales items and orders

- Sales item domain

  - Add new sales items, modify, view, and delete sales items

- Shopping cart domain

  - Add/remove sales items to/from a shopping cart, empty a shopping cart
  - View the shopping cart with sales item details

- Order domain

  - Placing orders

    * Ensure payment
    * Create order
    * Remove ordered items from the shopping cart
    * Mark ordered sales items sold
    * Send order confirmation by email

  - View orders with sales item details
  - Update and delete orders

We should not implement all the subdomains in a single *ecommerce-service* because that would be too monolithic. We want to create microservices with a single responsibility. We can use service aggregation. We create a separate lower-level microservice for each subdomain. Then, we create a higher-level *ecommerce-service* microservice that aggregates those lower-level microservices.

We define that our *ecommerce-service* aggregates the following lower-level microservices:

- *user-account-service*

  – Create/Read/Update/Delete user accounts

- *sales-item-service*

  – Create/Read/Update/Delete sales items

- *shopping-cart-service*

  – View a shopping cart, add/remove sales items from a shopping cart, or empty a shopping cart

- *order-service*

  – Create/Read/Update/Delete orders

- *email-notification-service*

  – Send email notifications

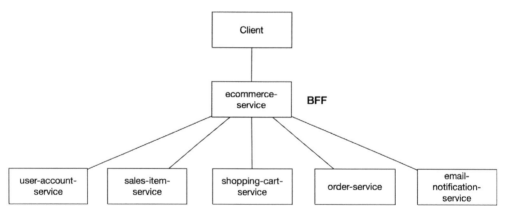

Figure 3.4. Service Aggregation in E-Commerce Software System

Most of the microservices described above can be implemented as REST APIs because they mainly contain basic CRUD (create, read, update, and delete) operations for which a REST API is a good match. We will handle API design in more detail in a later chapter. Let's implement the *sales-item-service* as a REST API using Java and Spring Boot[11].

---

[11]https://spring.io/projects/spring-boot

> Source code for the below example is available here[12].

We will implement the `SalesItemController` class first. It defines API endpoints for creating, getting, updating, and deleting sales items:

Figure 3.5. SalesItemController.java

```java
package com.example.salesitemservice;

import io.swagger.v3.oas.annotations.Operation;
import io.swagger.v3.oas.annotations.tags.Tag;
import org.springframework.beans.factory.annotation.Autowired;
import org.springframework.http.HttpStatus;
import org.springframework.web.bind.annotation.DeleteMapping;
import org.springframework.web.bind.annotation.GetMapping;
import org.springframework.web.bind.annotation.PathVariable;
import org.springframework.web.bind.annotation.PostMapping;
import org.springframework.web.bind.annotation.PutMapping;
import org.springframework.web.bind.annotation.RequestBody;
import org.springframework.web.bind.annotation.RequestMapping;
import org.springframework.web.bind.annotation.RequestParam;
import org.springframework.web.bind.annotation.ResponseStatus;
import org.springframework.web.bind.annotation.RestController;


@RestController
@RequestMapping(SalesItemController.API_ENDPOINT)
@Tag(
  name = "Sales item API",
  description = "Manages sales items"
)
public class SalesItemController {
  public static final String API_ENDPOINT = "/sales-items";
  private final SalesItemService salesItemService;

  @Autowired
  public SalesItemController(final SalesItemService salesItemService) {
    this.salesItemService = salesItemService;
  }

  @PostMapping
  @ResponseStatus(HttpStatus.CREATED)
  @Operation(summary = "Creates new sales item")
  public final SalesItem createSalesItem(
    @RequestBody final InputSalesItem inputSalesItem
  ) {
    return salesItemService.createSalesItem(inputSalesItem);
  }

  @GetMapping
  @ResponseStatus(HttpStatus.OK)
  @Operation(summary = "Gets sales items")
  public final Iterable<SalesItem> getSalesItems() {
    return salesItemService.getSalesItems();
  }

  @GetMapping("/{id}")
  @ResponseStatus(HttpStatus.OK)
  @Operation(summary = "Gets sales item by id")
  public final SalesItem getSalesItemById(
```

[12]https://github.com/pksilen/clean-code-principles-code/tree/main/chapter1/salesitemservice

```
    @PathVariable("id") final Long id
  ) {
    return salesItemService.getSalesItemById(id);
  }

  @GetMapping(params = "userAccountId")
  @ResponseStatus(HttpStatus.OK)
  @Operation(summary = "Gets sales items by user account id")
  public final Iterable<SalesItem> getSalesItemsByUserAccountId(
    @RequestParam("userAccountId") final Long userAccountId
  ) {
    return salesItemService.getSalesItemsByUserAccountId(userAccountId);
  }

  @PutMapping("/{id}")
  @ResponseStatus(HttpStatus.NO_CONTENT)
  @Operation(summary = "Updates a sales item")
  public final void updateSalesItem(
    @PathVariable final Long id,
    @RequestBody final InputSalesItem inputSalesItem
  ) {
    salesItemService.updateSalesItem(id, inputSalesItem);
  }

  @DeleteMapping("/{id}")
  @ResponseStatus(HttpStatus.NO_CONTENT)
  @Operation(summary = "Deletes a sales item by id")
  public final void deleteSalesItemById(
    @PathVariable final Long id
  ) {
    salesItemService.deleteSalesItemById(id);
  }

  @DeleteMapping
  @ResponseStatus(HttpStatus.NO_CONTENT)
  @Operation(summary = "Deletes all sales items")
  public final void deleteSalesItems() {
    salesItemService.deleteSalesItems();
  }
}
```

As we can notice from the above code, the SalesItemController class delegates the actual work to an instance of a class that implements the SalesItemService interface. This is an example of using the *bridge pattern* which is discussed, along with other design patterns, in the next chapter. In the bridge pattern, the controller is just an abstraction of the service, and a class implementing the SalesItemService interface provides a concrete implementation. We can change the service implementation without changing the controller or introduce a different controller, e.g., a GraphQL controller, using the same SalesItemService interface. Only by changing the used controller class could we change the API from a REST API to a GraphQL API. Below is the definition of the SalesItemService interface:

Figure 3.6. SalesItemService.java

```
package com.example.salesitemservice;

public interface SalesItemService {
  SalesItem createSalesItem(InputSalesItem inputSalesItem);
  SalesItem getSalesItemById(Long id);
  Iterable<SalesItem> getSalesItemsByUserAccountId(Long userAccountId);
  Iterable<SalesItem> getSalesItems();
  void updateSalesItem(Long id, InputSalesItem inputSalesItem);
  void deleteSalesItemById(Long id);
  void deleteSalesItems();
}
```

The below `SalesItemServiceImpl` class implements the `SalesItemService` interface. It will interact with a sales item repository to persist, fetch, and delete data to/from a database.

Figure 3.7. SalesItemServiceImpl.java

```java
package com.example.salesitemservice;

import org.springframework.beans.factory.annotation.Autowired;
import org.springframework.stereotype.Service;


@Service
public class SalesItemServiceImpl implements SalesItemService {
  private static final String SALES_ITEM = "Sales item";
  private final SalesItemRepository salesItemRepository;

  @Autowired
  public SalesItemServiceImpl(
    final SalesItemRepository salesItemRepository
  ) {
    this.salesItemRepository = salesItemRepository;
  }

  @Override
  public final SalesItem createSalesItem(
    final InputSalesItem inputSalesItem
  ) {
    final var salesItem = SalesItem.from(inputSalesItem);
    return salesItemRepository.save(salesItem);
  }

  @Override
  public final SalesItem getSalesItemById(final Long id) {
    return salesItemRepository.findById(id)
      .orElseThrow(() ->
        new EntityNotFoundError(SALES_ITEM, id));
  }

  @Override
  public final Iterable<SalesItem> getSalesItemsByUserAccountId(
    final Long userAccountId
  ) {
    return salesItemRepository.findByUserAccountId(userAccountId);
  }

  @Override
  public final Iterable<SalesItem> getSalesItems() {
    return salesItemRepository.findAll();
  }

  @Override
  public final void updateSalesItem(
    final Long id,
    final InputSalesItem inputSalesItem
  ) {
    if (salesItemRepository.existsById(id)) {
      final var salesItem = SalesItem.from(inputSalesItem, id);
      salesItemRepository.save(salesItem);
    } else {
      throw new EntityNotFoundError(SALES_ITEM, id);
    }
  }

  @Override
  public final void deleteSalesItemById(final Long id) {
    if (salesItemRepository.existsById(id)) {
      salesItemRepository.deleteById(id);
    }
  }
}
```

```
@Override
public final void deleteSalesItems() {
  salesItemRepository.deleteAll();
}
}
```

Figure 3.8. EntityNotFoundError.java

```
package com.example.salesitemservice;

import org.springframework.http.HttpStatus;
import org.springframework.web.bind.annotation.ResponseStatus;

@ResponseStatus(HttpStatus.NOT_FOUND)
public class EntityNotFoundError extends RuntimeException {
  EntityNotFoundError(final String entityType, final long id) {
    super(entityType + " entity not found with id " + id);
  }
}
```

The SalesItemRepository interface is defined below. Spring will create an instance of a class implementing that interface and inject it into an instance of the SalesItemServiceImpl class. The SalesItemRepository interface extends Spring's CrudRepository interface, which provides many database access methods by default. It provides the following and more methods: findAll, findById, save, existsById, deleteAll, and deleteById. We need to add only one method to the SalesItemRepository interface: findByUserAccountId. Spring will automatically generate an implementation for the findByUserAccountId method because the method name follows certain conventions of the Spring Data[13] framework. We just need to add the method to the interface, and that's it. We don't have to provide an implementation for the method because Spring will do it for us.

Figure 3.9. SalesItemRepository.java

```
package com.example.salesitemservice;

import org.springframework.data.repository.CrudRepository;
import org.springframework.stereotype.Repository;

@Repository
public interface SalesItemRepository extends
  CrudRepository<SalesItem, Long> {
  Iterable<SalesItem> findByUserAccountId(Long userAccountId);
}
```

Next, we define the SalesItem entity class, which contains properties like name and price. It also includes two methods to convert an instance of the InputSalesItem Data Transfer Object (DTO) class to an instance of the SalesItem class. A DTO is an object that transfers data between a server and a client. I have used the class name InputSalesItem instead of SalesItemDto to describe that a InputSalesItem DTO is an argument for an API endpoint. If some API endpoint returned a special sales item DTO instead of a sales item entity, I would name that DTO class OutputSalesItem instead of SalesItemDto. The terms Input and Output better describe the direction in which a DTO transfers data.

---

[13] https://docs.spring.io/spring-data/jpa/docs/current/reference/html

Figure 3.10. SalesItem.java

```java
package com.example.salesitemservice;

import lombok.AllArgsConstructor;
import lombok.Data;
import lombok.NoArgsConstructor;
import org.modelmapper.ModelMapper;

import jakarta.persistence.Entity;
import jakarta.persistence.GeneratedValue;
import jakarta.persistence.GenerationType;
import jakarta.persistence.Id;
import jakarta.validation.constraints.Max;
import jakarta.validation.constraints.Min;
import jakarta.validation.constraints.NotNull;


@Entity
@Data
@NoArgsConstructor
@AllArgsConstructor
public class SalesItem {
  @Id
  @GeneratedValue(strategy = GenerationType.IDENTITY)
  private Long id;

  private Long userAccountId;

  @NotNull
  private String name;

  @Min(value = 0, message = "Price must be greater than 0")
  @Max(
    value = Integer.MAX_VALUE,
    message = "Price must be <= " + Integer.MAX_VALUE
  )
  private Integer price;

  static SalesItem from(final InputSalesItem inputSalesItem) {
    return new ModelMapper().map(inputSalesItem, SalesItem.class);
  }

  static SalesItem from(
    final InputSalesItem inputSalesItem,
    final Long id
  ) {
    final var salesItem = new ModelMapper().map(inputSalesItem, SalesItem.class);
    salesItem.setId(id);
    return salesItem;
  }
}
```

The below InputSalesItem class contains the same properties as the SalesItem entity class, except the id property. The InputSalesItem DTO class is used when creating a new sales item or updating an existing sales item. When creating a new sales item, the client should not give the' id' property because the microservice will automatically generate it (or the database will, actually, in this case).

Figure 3.11. SalesItemArg.java

```
package com.example.salesitemservice;

import lombok.AllArgsConstructor;
import lombok.Data;
import lombok.NoArgsConstructor;


@Data
@NoArgsConstructor
@AllArgsConstructor
public class InputSalesItem {
  private Long userAccountId;
  private String name;
  private Integer price;
}
```

Below is defined how the higher-level *ecommerce-service* will orchestrate the use of the aggregated lower-level microservices:

- User account domain

  - Delegates CRUD operations to *user-account-service*
  - Delegates to *sales-item-service* to fetch information about user's sales items
  - Delegates to *order-service* to fetch information about user's orders

- Sales item domain

  - Delegates CRUD operations to *sales-item-service*

- Shopping cart domain

  - Delegates read/add/remove/empty operations to *shopping-cart-service*
  - Delegates to *sales-item-service* to fetch information about the sales items in the shopping cart

- Order domain

  - Ensures that the payment gateway confirms payment
  - Delegates CRUD operations to *order-service*
  - Delegates to *shopping-cart-service* to remove bought items from the shopping cart
  - Delegates to *sales-item-service* for marking sales items bought
  - Delegates to *email-notification-service* for sending order confirmation email
  - Delegates to *sales-item-service* to fetch information about order's sales items

The *ecommerce-service* is meant to be used by frontend clients, like a web clients. Backend for Frontend[14] (BFF) term describes a microservice designed to provide an API for frontend clients. Service aggregation is a generic term compared to the BFF term, and there need not be a frontend involved. You can use service aggregation to create an aggregated microservice used by another microservice or microservices. There can even be multiple levels of service aggregation if you have a large and complex software system. Service aggregation can be used to create segregated interfaces for specific clients. Using service aggregation, you

---

[14]https://learn.microsoft.com/en-us/azure/architecture/patterns/backends-for-frontends

can construct an API where clients depend only on what they need. This is called the *interface segregation principle* and is one of the principles of IDEALS[15] microservices.

Clients can have different needs regarding what information they want from an API. For example, a mobile client might be limited to exposing only a subset of all information available from the API. In contrast, a web client can fetch all information.

All of the above requirements are something that a GraphQL-based API can fulfill. For that reason, it would be wise to implement the *ecommerce-service* using GraphQL. I have chosen JavaScript, Node.js, and Express as technologies to implement a single GraphQL query in the *ecommerce-service*. Below is the implementation of a user query, which fetches data from three microservices. It fetches user account information from the *user-account-service*, the user's sales items from the *sales-item-service*, and finally, the user's orders from the *order-service*.

> Source code for the below example is available here[16].

Figure 3.12. server_real.js

```
const express = require('express');
const { createHandler } = require('graphql-http/lib/use/express');
const { buildSchema, GraphQLError } = require('graphql');
const axios = require('axios').default;
var { ruruHTML } = require('ruru/server');

const schema = buildSchema(`
  type UserAccount {
    id: ID!,
    userName: String!
    # Define additional properties...
  }

  type SalesItem {
    id: ID!,
    name: String!
    # Define additional properties...
  }

  type Order {
    id: ID!,
    userId: ID!
    # Define additional properties...
  }

  type User {
    userAccount: UserAccount!
    salesItems: [SalesItem!]!
    orders: [Order!]!
  }

  type Query {
    user(id: ID!): User!
  }
`);

const { ORDER_SERVICE_URL, SALES_ITEM_SERVICE_URL, USER_ACCOUNT_SERVICE_URL } =
```

---

[15]https://www.infoq.com/articles/microservices-design-ideals/

[16]https://github.com/pksilen/clean-code-principles-code/tree/main/chapter1/ecommerceservice

```
  process.env;

const rootValue = {
  user: async ({ id }) => {
    try {
      const [{ data: userAccount }, { data: salesItems }, { data: orders }] =
        await Promise.all([
          axios.get(`${USER_ACCOUNT_SERVICE_URL}/user-accounts/${id}`),
          axios.get(
            `${SALES_ITEM_SERVICE_URL}/sales-items?userAccountId=${id}`,
          ),
          axios.get(`${ORDER_SERVICE_URL}/orders?userAccountId=${id}`),
        ]);

      return {
        userAccount,
        salesItems,
        orders,
      };
    } catch (error) {
      throw new GraphQLError(error.message);
    }
  },
};

var app = express();
app.all('/graphql', createHandler({ schema, rootValue }));

app.get('/', (_req, res) => {
  res.type('html');
  res.end(ruruHTML({ endpoint: '/graphql' }));
});

app.listen(4000);
```

After you have started the above program with the `node server.js` command, you can access the GraphiQL endpoint with a browser at `http://localhost:4000/graphql`.

On the left-hand side pane, you can specify a GraphQL query. For example, to query the user identified with id 2:

```
{
  user(id: 2) {
    userAccount {
      id
      userName
    }
    salesItems {
      id
      name
    }
    orders {
      id
      userId
    }
  }
}
```

Because we haven't implemented the lower-level microservices, let's modify the part of the *server_real.js* where lower-level microservices are accessed to return dummy static results instead of accessing the real lower-level microservices:

Figure 3.13. server_fake.js

```
// ...

const [
        { data: userAccount },
        { data: salesItems },
        { data: orders }
    ] = await Promise.all([
        Promise.resolve({
            data: {
                id,
                userName: 'pksilen'
            }
        }),
        Promise.resolve({
            data: [
                {
                    id: 1,
                    name: 'sales item 1'
                }
            ]
        }),
        Promise.resolve({
            data: [
                {
                    id: 1,
                    userId: id
                }
            ]
        })
    ]);

// ...
```

We should see the result below if we execute the previously specified query. We assume that *sales-item-service* returns a single sales item with id 1.

```
{
  "data": {
    "user": {
      "userAccount": {
        "id": "2",
        "userName": "pksilen"
      },
      "salesItems": [
        {
          "id": "1",
          "name": "Sales item 1"
        }
      ],
      "orders": [
        {
          "id": "1",
          "userId": "2"
        }
      ]
    }
  }
}
```

We can simulate a failure by modifying the *server_fake.js* to contain the following code:

Figure 3.14. server_failure.js

```
// ...

const [
        { data: userAccount },
        { data: salesItems },
        { data: orders }
    ] = await Promise.all([
        axios.get(`http://localhost:3000/user-accounts/${id}`),
        Promise.resolve({
          data: [
            {
              id: 1,
              name: 'sales item 1'
            }
          ]
        }),
        Promise.resolve({
          data: [
            {
              id: 1,
              userId: id
            }
          ]
        })
    ]);

// ...
```

Now, if we execute the query again, we will get the below error response because the GraphQL server cannot connect to a service at localhost:3000 because no service runs at that address.

```
{
  "errors": [
    {
      "message": "connect ECONNREFUSED ::1:3000",
      "locations": [
        {
          "line": 2,
          "column": 3
        }
      ],
      "path": [
        "user"
      ]
    }
  ],
  "data": null
}
```

You can also query a user and specify the query to return only a subset of fields. The query below does not return identifiers and orders. The server-side GraphQL library automatically includes only requested fields in the response. You, as a developer, do not have to do anything. You can optimize your microservice to fetch only the requested fields from the database if you desire.

```
{
  user(id: 2) {
    userAccount {
      userName
    }
    salesItems {
      name
    }
  }
}
```

The result for the above query will be the following:

```
{
  "data": {
    "user": {
      "userAccount": {
        "userName": "pksilen"
      },
      "salesItems": [
        {
          "name": "sales item 1"
        }
      ]
    }
  }
}
```

The above example lacks some features like authorization, which is needed for production. Authorization should ensure users can only execute the user query to fetch their resources. The authorization should fail if a user tries to execute the user query using someone else's id. Security will be discussed more in the coming *security principles* chapter.

The user query in the previous example spanned over multiple lower-level microservices: *user-account-service*, *sales-item-service*, and *order-service*. Because the query is not mutating anything, it can be executed without a distributed transaction. A distributed transaction is similar to a regular (database) transaction, but the difference is that it spans multiple remote services.

The API endpoint for placing an order in the *ecommerce-service* needs to create a new order using the *order-service*, mark purchased sales items as bought using the *sales-item-service*, empty the shopping cart using the *shopping-cart-service*, and finally send order confirmation email using the *email-notification-service*. These actions need to be wrapped inside a distributed transaction because we want to be able to roll back the transaction if any of these operations fail. Guidance on how to implement a distributed transaction is given later in this chapter.

Service aggregation utilizes the facade pattern[17]. The facade pattern allows for hiding individual lower-level microservices behind a facade (the higher-level microservice). The software system clients access the system through the facade. They don't directly contact the individual lower-level microservices behind the facade because it breaks the encapsulation of the lower-level microservices inside the higher-level microservice. A client directly accessing the lower-level microservices creates unwanted coupling between the client and the lower-level microservices, which makes changing the lower-level microservices hard without affecting the client.

Think about a post office counter as an example of a real-world facade. It serves as a facade for the post office and when you need to receive a package, you communicate with that facade (the post office clerk at the counter). You have a simple interface that just requires telling the package code, and the clerk will

---

[17]https://en.wikipedia.org/wiki/Facade_pattern

find the package from the correct shelf and bring it to you. If you hadn't that facade, it would mean that you would have to do lower-level work by yourself. Instead of just telling the package code, you must walk to the shelves and try to find the proper shelf where your package is located, make sure that you pick the correct package, and then carry the package by yourself. In addition to requiring more work, this approach is more error-prone. You can accidentally pick someone else's package if you are not pedantic enough. And think about the case when you go to the post office next time and find out that all the shelves have been rearranged. This wouldn't be a problem if you used the facade.

Service aggregation, where a higher-level microservice delegates to lower-level microservices, also implements the bridge pattern[18]. A higher-level microservice provides only some high-level control and relies on the lower-level microservices to do the actual work.

Service aggregation allows using more design patterns[19] from the object-oriented design world. The most useful design patterns in the context of service aggregation are:

- Decorator pattern[20]
- Proxy pattern[21]
- Adapter pattern[22]

We will discuss design patterns in the next chapter, but I want to give you some examples of the above three design patterns used in conjunction with the *ecommerce-service*.

Decorator pattern can be used to add functionality in a higher-level microservice for lower-level microservices. One example is adding audit logging in a higher-level microservice. For example, you can add audit logging for requests in the *ecommerce-service*. You don't need to implement the audit logging separately in all the lower-level microservices.

Proxy pattern can be used to control the access from a higher-level microservice to lower-level microservices. Typical examples of the proxy pattern are authorization and caching. For example, you can add authorization and caching for requests in the *ecommerce-service*. Only after successful authorization will the requests be delivered to the lower-level microservices. If a request's response is not found in the cache, the request will be forwarded to the appropriate lower-level microservice. You don't need to implement authorization and caching separately in all the lower-level microservices.

Adapter pattern allows a higher-level microservice to adapt to different versions of the lower-level microservices while maintaining the API towards clients unchanged.

3.7: High Cohesion, Low Coupling Principle

A software system should consist of services with high cohesion and low coupling.

Cohesion refers to the degree to which classes inside a service belong together. Coupling refers to how many other services a service is interacting with. When following the *single responsibility principle*, it is possible to implement services as microservices with high cohesion. Service aggregation adds low coupling.

---

[18]https://en.wikipedia.org/wiki/Bridge_pattern
[19]https://en.wikipedia.org/wiki/Software_design_pattern
[20]https://en.wikipedia.org/wiki/Decorator_pattern
[21]https://en.wikipedia.org/wiki/Proxy_pattern
[22]https://en.wikipedia.org/wiki/Adapter_pattern

Microservices and service aggregation together enable high cohesion and low coupling, which is the target of good architecture.

Bad: High coupling, low cohesion

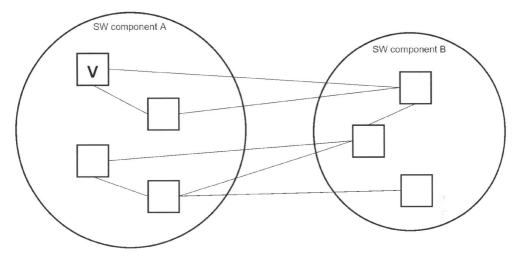

Good: Low coupling, high cohesion

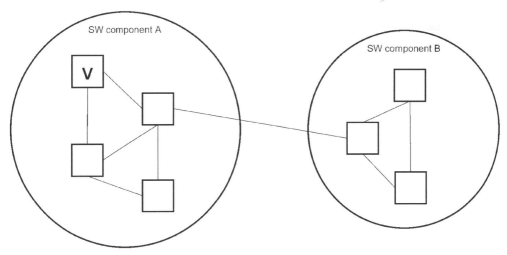

Figure 3.15. Coupling vs. Cohesion

If there were no service aggregation, lower-level microservices would need to communicate with each other, creating high coupling in the architecture. Also, clients would be coupled with the lower-level microservices. For example, in the e-commerce example, the *order-service* would be coupled with almost all the other microservices. And if the *sales-item-service* API changed, in the worst case, a change would be needed in three other microservices. When using service aggregation, lower-level microservices are coupled only to the higher-level microservice.

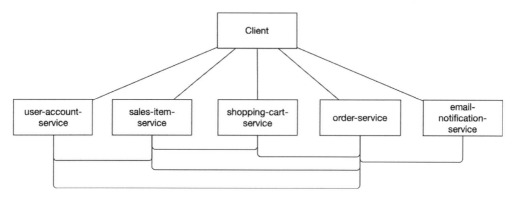

Figure 3.16. E-Commerce Software System With High Coupling

Low coupling means that the development of services can be highly parallelized. In the e-commerce example, the five lower-level microservices don't have coupling with each other. The development of each of those microservices can be isolated and assigned to a single team member or a group of team members. The development of the lower-level microservices can proceed in parallel, and the development of the higher-level microservice can start when the API specifications of the lower-level microservices become stable enough. The target should be to design the lower-level microservices APIs early on to enable the development of the higher-level microservice.

This principle is the same as the *loose-coupling principle* in the IDEALS microservice principles.

The ideal coupling of a microservice is zero, but in practice, a microservice might need to use one or two other microservices. Sometimes, a microservice might need to use 3-4 or even more other microservices. In those cases, the probability of needing to implement distributed transactions becomes higher. Distributed transactions can be challenging to implement correctly and thoroughly test. If you require 100% consistency in all cases, carefully consider if you should use distributed transactions. For example, if you are implementing a banking software system, you need high consistency in many cases. You can be better off not using distributed transactions but grouping closely related microservices into a larger one where you can use ACID[23] transactions instead.

3.8: Library Composition Principle

Higher-level libraries should be composed of lower-level libraries.

---
[23]https://en.wikipedia.org/wiki/ACID

Suppose you need a library for parsing configuration files (in particular syntax) in YAML or JSON format. In that case, you can first create the needed YAML and JSON parsing libraries (or use existing ones). Then, you can create the configuration file parsing library, composed of the YAML and JSON parsing libraries. You would then have three different libraries: one higher-level library and two lower-level libraries. Each library has a single responsibility: one for parsing JSON, one for parsing YAML, and one for parsing configuration files with a specific syntax, either in JSON or YAML. Software components can now use the higher-level library for parsing configuration files, and they need not be aware of the JSON/YAML parsing libraries at all.

3.9: Avoid Duplication Principle

Avoid software duplication at the software system and service level.

Duplication at the software system level happens when two or more software systems use the same services. For example, two different software systems can both have a message broker, API gateway, identity and access management (IAM) application, and log and metrics collection services. You could continue this list even further. The goal of duplication-free architecture is to have only one deployment of these services. Public cloud providers offer these services for your use. If you have a Kubernetes cluster, an alternative solution is to deploy your software systems in different Kubernetes Namespaces[24] and deploy the common services to a shared Kubernetes namespace, which can be called the *platform* or *common-services*, for example.

Duplication at the service level happens when two or more services have common functionality that could be extracted to a separate new microservice. For example, consider a case where both *user-account-service* and *order-service* have the functionality to send notification messages by email to a user. This email-sending functionality is duplicated in both microservices. Duplication can be avoided by extracting the email-sending functionality to a separate new microservice. The single responsibility of the microservices becomes more evident when the email-sending functionality is extracted to its own microservice. Another alternative is extracting the common functionality to a library. This is not the best solution because microservices become dependent on the library. When changes to the library are needed (e.g., security updates), you must change the library version in all the microservices using the library and then test all the affected microservices.

When a company develops multiple software systems in several departments, the software development typically happens in silos. The departments are not necessarily aware of what the other departments are doing. For example, it might be possible that two departments have both developed a microservice for sending emails. There is now software duplication that no one is aware of. This is not an optimal situation. A software development company should do something to enable collaboration between the departments and break the silos. One good way to share software is to establish shared folders or organizations in the source code repository hosting service that the company uses. For example, in GitHub, you could create an organization to share source code repositories for common libraries and another for sharing common services. Each software development department has access to those common organizations and can still develop its software inside its own GitHub organization. In this way, the company can enforce proper access control for the source code of different departments, if needed. When a team needs to develop something new, it can first consult the common source code repositories to find out if something is already available that can be reused as such or extended.

---

[24]https://kubernetes.io/docs/concepts/overview/working-with-objects/namespaces/

3.10: Externalized Service Configuration Principle

The configuration of a service should be externalized. It should be stored in the environment where the service is running, not in the source code. The externalized configuration makes the service adaptable to different environments and needs.

Service configuration means any data that varies between service deployments (different environments, different customers, etc.). The following are typical places where externalized configuration can be stored when software is running in a Kubernetes cluster:

- Environment variables[25]
- Kubernetes ConfigMaps[26]
- Kubernetes Secrets[27]
- External store

---

[25] https://en.wikipedia.org/wiki/Environment_variable
[26] https://kubernetes.io/docs/concepts/configuration/configmap/
[27] https://kubernetes.io/docs/concepts/configuration/secret/

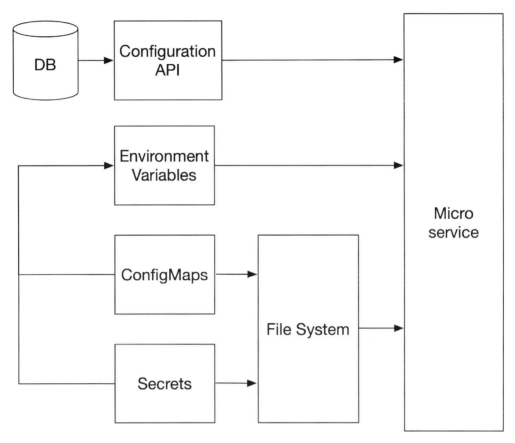

Figure 3.17. Configuration Storage Options

We will discuss these three configuration storage options in the following sections.

3.10.1: Environment Variables

Environment variables can be used to store configuration as simple key-value pairs. They are typically used to store information like connection information (how to connect to dependent services, like a database or message broker) or a microservice's logging level. Environment variables are available for the running process of the microservice, which can access the environment variable values by their names (keys).

You should not hardcode the default values of environment variables in the source code. This is because the default values are typically not for a production but for a development environment. Suppose you deploy a service to a production environment and forget to set all the needed environment variables. In that case, your service will have some environment variables with default values unsuitable for a production environment.

You can supply environment variables for a microservice in environment-specific *.env* files. For example, you can have a *.env.dev* file for storing environment variable values for a development environment and a

.env.ci file for storing environment variable values used in the microservice's *continuous integration* (CI) pipeline. The syntax of *.env* files is straightforward. There is one environment variable defined per line:

Figure 3.18. .env.dev

```
NODE_ENV=development
HTTP_SERVER_PORT=3001
LOG_LEVEL=INFO
MONGODB_HOST=localhost
MONGODB_PORT=27017
MONGODB_USER=
MONGODB_PASSWORD=
```

Figure 3.19. .env.ci

```
NODE_ENV=integration
HTTP_SERVER_PORT=3001
LOG_LEVEL=INFO
MONGODB_HOST=localhost
MONGODB_PORT=27017
MONGODB_USER=
MONGODB_PASSWORD=
```

When a software component is deployed to a Kubernetes cluster using the Kubernetes package manager Helm[28], environment variable values should be defined in the Helm chart's *values.yaml* file:

Figure 3.20. values.yaml

```
nodeEnv: production
httpServer:
  port: 8080
database:
  mongoDb:
    host: my-service-mongodb
    port: 27017
```

The values in the above *values.yaml* file can be used to define environment variables in a Kubernetes Deployment[29] using the following Helm chart template:

Figure 3.21. deployment.yaml

```
apiVersion: apps/v1
kind: Deployment
metadata:
  name: my-service
spec:
  template:
    spec:
      containers:
        - name: my-service
          env:
            - name: NODE_ENV
              value: {{ .Values.nodeEnv }}
            - name: HTTP_SERVER_PORT
              value: "{{ .Values.httpServer.port }}"
            - name: MONGODB_HOST
              value: {{ .Values.database.mongoDb.host }}
            - name: MONGODB_PORT
              value: {{ .Values.database.mongoDb.port }}
```

[28] https://helm.sh/

[29] https://kubernetes.io/docs/concepts/workloads/controllers/deployment/

When Kubernetes starts a microservice Pod[30], the following environment variables will be made available for the running container:

```
NODE_ENV=production
HTTP_SERVER_PORT=8080
MONGODB_HOST=my-service-mongodb
MONGODB_PORT=27017
```

3.10.2: Kubernetes ConfigMaps

A Kubernetes ConfigMap can store a configuration file or files in various formats, like JSON or YAML. These files can be mounted to the filesystem of a microservice's running container. The container can then read the configuration files from the mounted directory in its filesystem.

For example, you can have a ConfigMap for defining the logging level of a *my-service* microservice:

Figure 3.22. configmap.yaml

```
apiVersion: v1
kind: ConfigMap
metadata:
  name: my-service
data:
  LOG_LEVEL: INFO
```

The below Kubernetes Deployment manifest defines that the content of the *my-service* ConfigMap's key LOG_LEVEL will be stored in a volume named config-volume, and the value of the LOG_LEVEL key will be stored in a file named LOG_LEVEL . After mounting the config-volume to the /etc/config directory in a *my-service* container, it is possible to read the contents of the /etc/config/LOG_LEVEL file, which contains the text: INFO.

Figure 3.23. deployment.yaml

```
apiVersion: apps/v1
kind: Deployment
metadata:
  name: my-service
spec:
  template:
    spec:
      containers:
        - name: my-service
          volumeMounts:
            - name: config-volume
              mountPath: "/etc/config"
              readOnly: true
      volumes:
        - name: config-volume
          configMap:
            name: my-service
            items:
              - key: "LOG_LEVEL"
                path: "LOG_LEVEL"
```

In Kubernetes, editing of a ConfigMap is reflected in the respective mounted file. This means you can listen to changes in the /etc/config/LOG_LEVEL file. Below is shown how to do it in Node.js with JavaScript:

---

[30]https://kubernetes.io/docs/concepts/workloads/pods/

```
fs.watchFile('/etc/config/LOG_LEVEL', () => {
  try {
    const newLogLevel = fs.readFileSync(
      '/etc/config/LOG_LEVEL', 'utf-8'
    ).trim();

    // Check here that 'newLogLevel' contains a valid log level

    updateLogLevel(newLogLevel);
  } catch (error) {
    // Handle error
  }
});
```

3.10.3: Kubernetes Secrets

Kubernetes Secrets are similar to ConfigMaps except that they are used to store sensitive information, like passwords and encryption keys.

Below is an example of a *values.yaml* file and a Helm chart template for creating a Kubernetes Secret. The Secret will contain two key-value pairs: the database username and password. The Secret's data needs to be Base64-encoded. In the below example, the Base64 encoding is done using the Helm template function b64enc.

Figure 3.24. values.yaml

```
database:
  mongoDb:
    host: my-service-mongodb
    port: 27017
    user: my-service-user
    password: Ak9(1Kt41uF==%1LO&21mA#gL0!"Dps2
```

Figure 3.25. secret.yaml

```
apiVersion: v1
kind: Secret
metadata:
  name: my-service
type: Opaque
data:
  mongoDbUser: {{ .Values.database.mongoDb.user | b64enc }}
  mongoDbPassword: {{ .Values.database.mongoDb.password | b64enc }}
```

After being created, secrets can be mapped to environment variables in a Deployment manifest for a microservice. In the below example, we map the value of the secret key mongoDbUser from the my-service secret to an environment variable named MONGODB_USER and the value of the secret key mongoDbPassword to an environment variable named MONGODB_PASSWORD.

Figure 3.26. deployment.yaml

```
apiVersion: apps/v1
kind: Deployment
metadata:
  name: my-service
spec:
  template:
    spec:
      containers:
        - name: my-service
          env:
            - name: MONGODB_USER
              valueFrom:
                secretKeyRef:
                  name: my-service
                  key: mongoDbUser

            - name: MONGODB_PASSWORD
              valueFrom:
                secretKeyRef:
                  name: my-service
                  key: mongoDbPassword
```

When a *my-service* pod is started, the following environment variables are made available for the running container:

```
MONGODB_USER=my-service-user
MONGODB_PASSWORD=Ak9(1Kt41uF==%1LO&21mA#gL0!"Dps2
```

3.10.4: External Store

When using an external store, configuration information is removed from the application deployment package (e.g., Helm chart) and put in a centralized location. The external store can be implemented with a configuration API and a persistent data store, like a database. The external store provides opportunities for easier management and control of configuration data and for sharing configuration data across microservices. Configuration management can be made easier for administrators by building user interfaces.

3.11: Service Substitution Principle

Make substituting a service's dependency for another service easy by making the dependencies transparent. A transparent service is exposed to other services by defining a host and port. Use externalized service configuration principle (e.g., environment variables) in your microservice to define the host and port (and possibly other needed parameters like a database username/password) for a dependent service.

Let's have an example where a microservice depends on a MongoDB service. The MongoDB service should expose itself by defining a host and port combination. For the microservice, you can specify the following environment variables for connecting to a *localhost* MongoDB service:

```
MONGODB_HOST=localhost
MONGODB_PORT=27017
```

Suppose that in a Kubernetes-based production environment, you have a MongoDB service in the cluster accessible via a Kubernetes Service[31] named *my-service-mongodb*. In that case, you should have the environment variables for the MongoDB service defined as follows:

```
MONGODB_HOST=my-service-mongodb.default.svc.cluster.local
MONGODB_PORT=8080
```

Alternatively, a MongoDB service can run in the MongoDB Atlas cloud. In that case, the MongoDB service could be connected to using the following kind of environment variable values:

```
MONGODB_HOST=my-service.tjdze.mongodb.net
MONGODB_PORT=27017
```

As shown with the above examples, you can easily substitute a different MongoDB service depending on your microservice's environment. If you want to use a different MongoDB service, you don't need to modify the microservice's source code. You only need to change the *externalized configuration*.

3.12: Inter-Service Communication Methods

Services communicate with each other using the following communication methods: synchronous, asynchronous, and shared data.

3.12.1: Synchronous Communication Method

A synchronous communication method should be used when a service communicates with another service and wants an immediate response. Synchronous communication can be implemented using protocols like HTTP or gRPC (which uses HTTP under the hood).

---

[31]https://kubernetes.io/docs/concepts/services-networking/service/

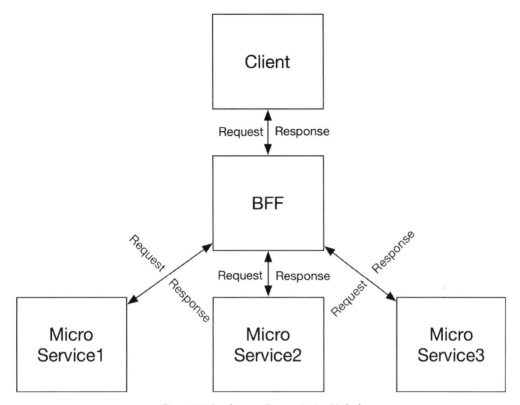

Figure 3.27. Synchronous Communication Method

In case of a failure when processing a request, the request processing microservice sends an error response to the requestor microservice. The requestor microservice can cascade the error up in the synchronous request stack until the initial request maker is reached. That initial request maker is often a client, like a web UI or mobile app. The initial request maker can then decide what to do. Usually, it will attempt to send the request again after a while (we are assuming here that the error is a transient server error, not a client error, like a bad request, for example)

3.12.2: Asynchronous Communication Method

When a service wants to deliver a request to another service but does not expect a response or at least not an immediate response, an asynchronous communication method should be used. Some communication between services is asynchronous by nature. For example, a service might want to instruct an email notification service to email an end-user or to send an audit log entry to an audit logging service. Both examples can be implemented using an asynchronous communication method because no response for the operations is expected.

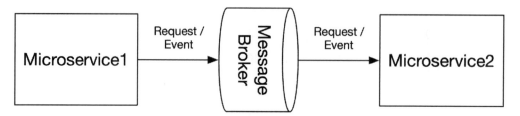

Figure 3.28. Request-Only Asynchronous Communication Method

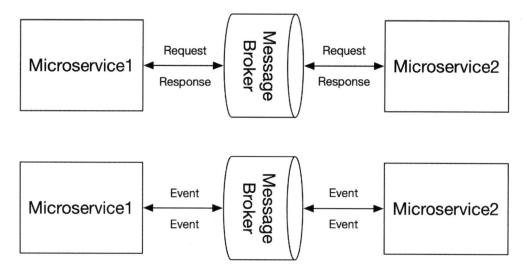

Figure 3.29. Request-Response Asynchronous Communication Method / Event Driven Architecture

Asynchronous communication can be implemented using a message broker. Services can produce messages to the message broker and consume messages from it. Several message broker implementations are available, like Apache Kafka, RabbitMQ, Apache ActiveMQ, and Redis. When a microservice produces a request to a message broker's topic, the producing microservice must wait for an acknowledgment from the message broker indicating that the request was successfully stored to multiple, or preferably all, replicas of the topic. Otherwise, there is no 100% guarantee that the request was successfully delivered in some message broker failure scenarios.

When an asynchronous request is of type fire-and-forget (i.e., no response is expected), the request processing microservice must ensure that the request will eventually get processed. If the request processing fails, the request processing microservice must reattempt the processing after a while. If a process termination signal is received, the request processing microservice instance must produce the request back to the message broker and allow some other microservice instance to fulfill the request. The rare possibility exists that the production of the request back to the message broker fails. Then, you could try to save the request to a persistent volume, for instance, but also that can fail. However, the likelihood of such a situation is very low.

The *API design principles* chapter describes designing APIs for inter-service communication in more detail.

Event-driven architecture (EDA) may offer benefits over traditional synchronous point-to-point architecture. This is because, in EDA, microservices can be loosely coupled. They are not necessarily aware of each other but can communicate via a message broker using a set of events. Microservices in EDA can also process events in parallel. The *event-driven principle* is one of the IDEALS microservice principles.

3.12.3: Shared Data Communication Method

Service communication can also happen via shared data (e.g., a shared database). This method is useful with data-oriented services when storing the same data twice is not meaningful. Typically, one or more microservices produce the shared data, and other microservice(s) consume that data. The interface between these microservices is defined by the schema of the shared data, i.e., by the schemas of database tables. To secure the shared data, only the producing microservice(s) should have write access to the shared data, and the consuming microservice(s) should only have read access to the shared data.

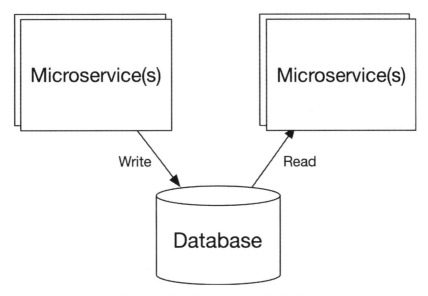

Figure 3.30. Shared Data Communication Method

3.13: Strategical Domain-Driven Design Principle

Design software system architecture by conducting domain-driven design (DDD) starting from the top of the software hierarchy (software system) and ending at the bounded context level.

Strategical DDD aims to divide a large business domain into several bounded contexts with their basic interfacing mechanisms or communication/coordination patterns defined. A single team is responsible for a bounded context. In a microservice architecture, a bounded context can be a microservice, for example.

I often compare software system architectural design to the architectural design of a house. The house represents a software system. The entrances in the house's facade represent the software system's external interfaces. The rooms in the house are the microservices of the software system. Like a microservice, a single room usually has a dedicated purpose. The architectural design of a software system encompasses the definition of external interfaces, microservices, and their interfaces to other services.

The architectural design phase results in a ground plan for the software system. After the architectural design, the facade is designed, and all the rooms are specified: the purpose of each room and how rooms interface with other rooms.

Designing an individual microservice is no longer architectural design, but it can be compared to the interior design of a single room. The microservice design is handled using object-oriented design principles, presented in the next chapter.

Domain-driven design[32] (DDD) is a software design approach where software is modeled to match a problem/business domain according to input from the domain experts. Usually, these experts come from the business and specifically from product management. The idea of DDD is to transfer the domain knowledge from the domain experts to individual software developers so that everyone participating in software development can share a common language that describes the domain. The idea of the common language is that people can understand each other, and no multiple terms are used to describe a single thing. If you have a banking-related domain with an *account* entity, everyone should speak about *accounts*, not *money repositories*. This common language is also called the *ubiquitous language*.

The domain knowledge is transferred from product managers and architects to lead developers and product owners (POs) in development teams. The team's lead developer and PO share the domain knowledge with the rest of the team. This usually happens when the team processes backlog epics and features and splits them into user stories in planning sessions. A software development team can also have a dedicated domain expert or experts.

Strategical DDD starts from the top business/problem domain. The top domain is split into multiple *subdomains*, each on a lower abstraction level than the top domain. A domain should be divided into subdomains so there is minimal overlap between subdomains. Subdomains will be interfacing with other subdomains when needed using well-defined interfaces. Subdomains can be grouped into *bounded contexts*. The ideal mapping is one subdomain per bounded context, but a bounded context can also encompass multiple subdomains. A bounded context is a boundary created to define a shared vocabulary, i.e., a ubiquitous language. The implementation of a bounded context is one or more microservices. If a bounded context consists of multiple subdomains, those subdomains are manifested as software code placed in separate source code directories—more about that in the following chapters. For example, a *purchase-service* bounded context (a part of an e-commerce software system) can have a subdomain for managing shopping carts and another subdomain that handles orders.

Subdomains can be divided into three types: core subdomains, supporting subdomains, and generic subdomains. A core subdomain is core to your business. If you have an e-commerce business, things related to e-commerce are core subdomains. In core subdomains, you must excel and try to beat the competition. The core subdomains are the company's focus areas, and the best talent should be targeted to implement those subdomains. An example of a generic domain is the identity and access management (IAM) subdomain. It is an area where you don't have to excel, but you should use a 3rd party solution because IAM is some other company's core domain, and they know how to do it best!

For example, a banking software system can have a bounded context for loan applications and another for making payments. The ubiquitous languages in bounded contexts can differ. For example, consider an airline software system with the following bounded contexts: customers, ticketing, cargo, and airplane

---

[32]https://en.wikipedia.org/wiki/Domain-driven_design

maintenance. The four bounded contexts can use the term *flight*, but the flights in the different bounded contexts differ. They are entities with the same name but with different attributes. Those bounded contexts can interface with each other by referencing each other's representation of a flight using a flight id that is a common attribute in all the bounded contexts.

Various strategies exist on how bounded contexts interface with each other. This is called *context mapping*. The interface between them can be jointly designed by two teams (a context mapping strategy called *partnership*) or one bounded context defines the interface for others to consume. The interface provider can be sovereign (other bounded contexts must conform to the interface; this context mapping strategy is called *conformist*), or the interface provider can listen to the interface consumer needs (a context mapping strategy called *supplier-consumer*). Perhaps the most modern and useful way to create an interface between two (or more) bounded contexts is for the interface provider to create an *open host service* with a *published language* that can serve all interface consumers. Basically, this means creating a microservice API using a specific API technology like REST. The bounded context acting as the interface provider does not have to expose its model (entities and ubiquitous language) as such to other bounded contexts. It can use DTOs to map entities to clients' expected format and map the client format back to entities. Using DTOs enables smoother interfacing between different ubiquitous languages. A bounded context can create a so-called *anticorruption layer* for talking to another bounded context to translate the other bounded context's ubiquitous language into its own ubiquitous language. This is an excellent example of using the *adapter pattern*. Another example of the *published language* context mapping is when a microservice has a configuration in JSON format, and another team builds a configuration store and UI for defining and storing the configuration. The context mapping between the microservice and the configuration store is *conformist* and *published language*. The configuration store and UI components will conform to the specific configuration format specified by the microservice.

Strategical DDD fits well together with the microservice architecture. In both, something big is split into smaller, more manageable parts. DDD says that a single team should own a bounded context, and each bounded context should have its own source code repository or repositories (this will be automatically true if a bounded context consists of one or more microservices). A bounded context or a microservice can become hard to manage and change if the responsibility is shared between multiple teams.

When the splitting of a software system into subdomains and bounded context is not straightforward, you can use *big-picture event storming* workshop to help you identify your software system's subdomains and bounded context. Event storming is particularly useful when the software system is extensive, and its requirements are unclear. Event storming workshop gathers people with diverse responsibilities, including product management, architects, lead and senior developers, domain experts, and UX designers. The basic idea of the event-storming process is to model your software system's domain events on a timeline and then group a set of domain events to form a subdomain or a bounded context. Domain events can be triggered by various parties like users, admins, external systems, or on schedule. Initially, event storming can be a chaotic exploration, but it does not matter because the main idea is to register everything that can happen in the software system to be built. The structure of the events is emergent. You should be able to move events on the whiteboard and add events to any positions to organize the initial chaos into something more systematic. When you have a large and diverse group of people participating in the event storming session, you get a better and more complete representation of the software system to be built. The likelihood of forgetting major domain events is smaller.

The abstraction level of domain events should not be too high or too low. Events should describe a feature or use case a bounded context implements but not the implementation details. Event *order placed* might be on a too high abstraction level because it is masking the following lower-level events: payment processed, shopping cart emptied, sales item inventory updated, order created, for example. On the other hand, events like *button in order form pressed* and *order entity persisted in the database* are too low-level events. These events describe implementation details and are not part of big-picture event storming but are part of *software design-level event storming* which is part of tactical DDD described in the next chapter. The most experienced and technically oriented participants should guide the domain events' abstraction level.

Below is an example of an event storming workshop result where *domain events* are listed as solid-line boxes along the time axis. The domain events on the timeline usually do not form a single line of events but multiple lines, meaning that many events can happen at the same time. Different lines of events can be used to represent, e.g., failure scenarios and edge cases of a feature. A sticky note can be added before different lines of events to describe whether the event lines are parallel or represent different scenarios. After listing all the domain events, they are grouped into subdomains/bounded contexts, as shown with dotted lines. In addition to the domain events, opportunities and problems related to them should listed so that they can be addressed later in the workshop or afterward, depending on the time reserved for the workshop. At the end of the event storming session, take several photos of the designs and stitch the photos together to form a document for future reference. If you want to read more about strategical DDD, I suggest you consult the following books: *Architecture Modernization* by *Nick Tune* and *Jean-Georges Perrin* and *Strategic Monoliths and Microservices* by *Vaughn Vernon* and *Jaskula Tomasz*.

You should continue the event-storming process with *software design-level event storming* for each bounded context to figure out additional DDD concepts related to the domain events. The *software design-level event-storming* workshop is described in the next chapter.

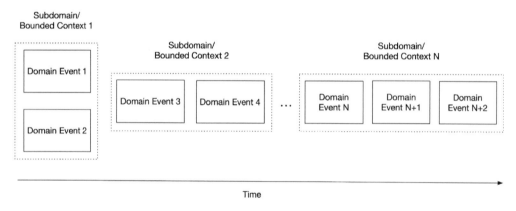

Figure 3.31. Event storming

3.13.1: Strategical DDD Example 1: Mobile Telecom Network Analytics Software System

Suppose an architecture team is assigned to design a mobile telecom network analytics software system. The team starts by defining the problem domain of the software system in more detail. When thinking about the system in more detail, they end up figuring out at least the following domain events:

1) Radio network raw data is ingested
2) Core network raw data is ingested
3) Ingested raw data transformed into meaningful insights
4) Insights are presented to software system users

Each of the high-level domain events can be considered as a subdomain. Let's pick up some keywords from the above definitions and formulate short names for the subdomains:

1) Radio network data ingester
2) Core network data ingester
3) Data aggregator
4) Insights visualizer

The above four subdomains will also be our bounded contexts (a different team is responsible for developing each). The four bounded contexts have different vocabularies, i.e., ubiquitous languages. The first bounded context speaks in radio network terms, the second speaks in core network terms, the third speaks about counters and KPIs, and the last bounded context speaks about data visualization like dashboards and charts.

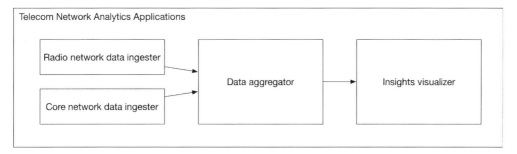

Figure 3.32. Bounded Contexts

Next, we continue architectural design by splitting each subdomain into one or more software components. (microservices, clients, and libraries). When defining the software components, we must remember to follow the *single responsibility principle*, *avoid duplication principle* and *externalized service configuration principle*.

When considering the *Radio network data ingester* and *Core network data ingester* applications, we can notice that we can implement them both using a single microservice, *data-ingester-service*, with different configurations for the radio and core network. This is because the data ingesting protocol is the same for radio and core networks. The two networks differ in the schema of the ingested data. If we have a single configurable microservice, we can avoid code duplication. The microservice and the two sets of configurations are our bounded contexts for the *Ingesting raw data* subdomain.

The *Data aggregator* application can be implemented using a single *data-aggregator-service* microservice that will be one more bounded context. We can use externalized configuration to define what counters and KPIs the microservice should aggregate and calculate from the raw data.

The *Insights visualizer* application consists of three different software components:

- A web client
- A service for fetching aggregated and calculated data (counters and KPIs)
- A service for storing the dynamic configuration of the web client

The dynamic configuration service stores information about what insights to visualize and how in the web client.

Microservices in the *Insights visualizer* application are:

- insights-visualizer-web-client
- insights-visualizer-data-service
- insights-visualizer-configuration-service

Now, we are ready with the microservice-level architectural design for the software system:

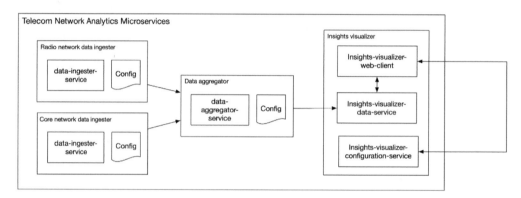

Figure 3.33. Microservices

The last part of architectural design defines inter-service communication methods, i.e., context mapping. The interface between radio and core networks and the *data-ingester-service* could be a *partnership*. The interface is planned together with both sides.

The *data-ingester-service* needs to send raw data to *data-aggregator-service*. The context mapping between them could be *supplier-consumer*, where the *data-ingester-service* is the supplier. Data is sent using asynchronous fire-and-forget requests and is implemented using a message broker.

The *insights-visualizer-data-service* should *conform* to the interface provided by the *data-aggregator-service*. The communication between the *data-aggregator-service* and the *insights-visualizer-data-service* should use the *shared data* communication method because the *data-aggregator-service* generates aggregated data that the *insights-visualizer-data-service* uses.

The context mapping between the *insights-visualizer-web-client* and *insights-visualizer-configuration-service* should be a *partnership* because they are closely related to each other. The best way to achieve a *partnership* is when the same team is responsible for both microservices.

The context mapping between the *insights-visualizer-web-client* and *insights-visualizer-data-service* should be *open host service*. This is because the *insights-visualizer-data-service* is not only used by the *insights-visualizer-web-client* in the future, but it should be made a generic *insights-data-service* that other services can use.

The communication between the *insights-visualizer-web-client* in the frontend and the *insights-visualizer-data-service* and *insights-visualizer-configuration-service* in the backend is synchronous communication that can be implemented using an HTTP-based JSON-RPC, REST, or GraphQL API.

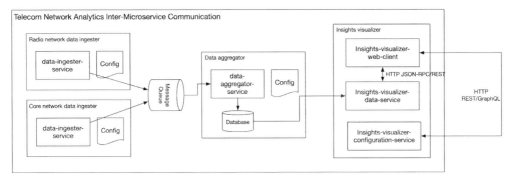

Figure 3.34. Inter-Microservice Communication

Next, design continues in development teams. Teams will specify the APIs between the microservices and conduct *tactical domain-driven design* and object-oriented design for the microservices. API design is covered in a later chapter, and object-oriented design, including tactical domain-driven design, is covered in the next chapter.

3.13.2: Strategical DDD Example 2: Banking Software System

Let's design a partial banking software system. The banking software system should be able to handle customers' loan applications and payments. The banking system problem domain can be divided into two subdomains:

1) Loan applications
2) Making payments

In the loan applications domain, a customer can submit a loan application. The eligibility for the loan will be assessed, and the bank can either accept the loan application and pay the loan or reject the loan application. In the making payments domain, a customer can make payments. Making a payment will withdraw money from the customer's account. It is also a transaction that should be recorded.

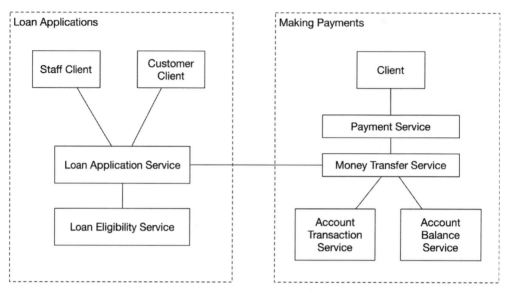

Figure 3.35. Banking Software System Bounded Contexts

Let's add a feature that a payment can be made to a recipient in another bank:

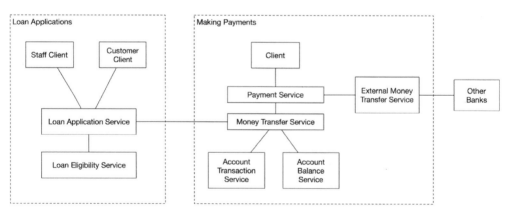

Figure 3.36. Banking Software System Bounded Contexts

Let's add another feature: money can be transferred from external banks to a customer's account.

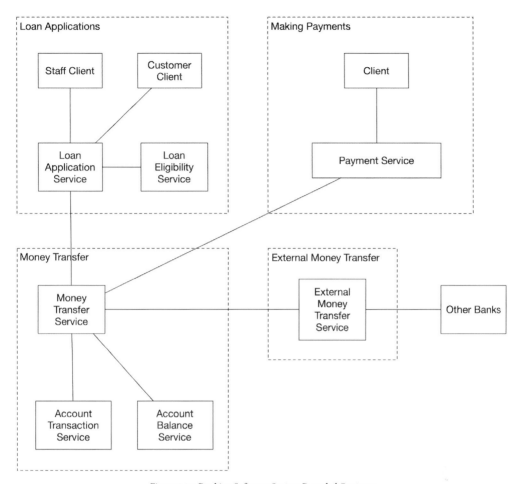

Figure 3.37. Banking Software System Bounded Contexts

As can be noticed from the above pictures, the architecture of the banking software system evolved when new features were introduced. For example, two new bounded contexts were created: money transfer and external money transfer. There was not much change in the microservices themselves, but how they are logically grouped into bounded contexts was altered.

3.14: Autopilot Microservices Principle

Microservices should be architected to run on autopilot in their deployment environment.

An autopilot microservice is a microservice that runs in a deployment environment without human interaction, except in abnormal situations, when it should generate an alert to indicate that human intervention is required.

Autopilot microservices principle requires that the following sub-principles are followed:

- Stateless microservices principle
- Resilient microservices principle
- Horizontally autoscaling microservices principle
- Highly-available microservices principle
- Observable microservices principle

These principles are discussed in more detail next. This principle is basically the same as the *deployability principle* in the IDEALS microservice principles.

3.14.1: Stateless Microservices Principle

Microservices should be stateless to enable resiliency, horizontal scalability, and high availability.

A microservice can be made stateless by storing its state outside itself. The state can be stored in a data store that microservice instances share. Typically, the data store is a database or an in-memory cache (like Redis, for example).

3.14.2: Resilient Microservices Principle

Microservices should be resilient, i.e., quickly recover from failures automatically.

In a Kubernetes cluster, the resiliency of a microservice is handled by the Kubernetes control plane. If the computing node where a microservice instance is located needs to be decommissioned, Kubernetes will create a new instance of the microservice on another computing node and then evict the microservice from the node to be decommissioned.

What needs to be done in the microservice is to make it listen to Linux process termination signals[33], especially the *SIGTERM* signal, which is sent to a microservice instance to indicate that it should terminate. Upon receiving a *SIGTERM* signal, the microservice instance should initiate a graceful shutdown. If the microservice instance does not shut down gracefully, Kubernetes will eventually issue a *SIGKILL* signal to terminate the microservice instance forcefully. The *SIGKILL* signal is sent after a termination grace period has elapsed. This period is, by default, 30 seconds, but it is configurable.

There are other reasons a microservice instance might be evicted from a computing node. One such reason is that Kubernetes must assign (for some reason which can be related to CPU/memory requests, for instance) another microservice to be run on that particular computing node, and your microservice won't fit there anymore and must be moved to another computing node.

If a microservice pod crashes, Kubernetes will notice that and start a new pod so that the desired number of microservice replicas (pods/instances) are always running. The replica count can be defined in the Kubernetes Deployment manifest for the microservice.

But what if a microservice pod enters a deadlock and cannot serve requests? This situation can be remediated with the help of a liveness probe[34]. You should always specify a liveness probe for each microservice Deployment. Below is an example of a microservice Deployment where an HTTP GET type liveness probe is defined:

---

[33]https://en.wikipedia.org/wiki/Signal_(IPC)

[34]https://kubernetes.io/docs/tasks/configure-pod-container/configure-liveness-readiness-startup-probes/

Figure 3.38. deployment.yaml

```
apiVersion: apps/v1
kind: Deployment
metadata:
  name: {{ include "microservice.fullname" . }}
spec:
  replicas: 1
  selector:
    matchLabels:
      {{- include "microservice.selectorLabels" . | nindent 6 }}
  template:
    spec:
      containers:
        - name: {{ .Chart.Name }}
          image: "{{ .Values.imageRegistry }}/{{ .Values.imageRepository }}:{{ .Values.imageTag }}"
          livenessProbe:
            httpGet:
              path: /isAlive
              port: 8080
            initialDelaySeconds: 30
            failureThreshold: 3
            periodSeconds: 3
```

Kubernetes will poll the /isAlive HTTP endpoints of the microservice instances every three seconds (after the initial delay of 30 seconds reserved for the microservice instance startup). The HTTP endpoint should return the HTTP status code 200 *OK*. Suppose requests to that endpoint fail (e.g., due to a deadlock) three times in a row (defined by the failureThreshold property) for a particular microservice instance. In that case, the microservice instance is considered dead, and Kubernetes will terminate the pod and launch a new pod automatically.

The Kubernetes Deployment manifest should be modified when upgrading a microservice to a newer version. A new container image tag should be specified in the image property of the Deployment. This change will trigger an update procedure for the Deployment. By default, Kubernetes performs a rolling update[35], which means your microservice can serve requests during the update procedure with zero downtime.

Suppose you had defined one replica in the microservice Deployment manifest (as shown above with the replicas: 1 property) and performed a Deployment upgrade (change the image to a newer version). In that case, Kubernetes would create a new pod using the new image tag, and only after the new pod is ready to serve requests will Kubernetes delete the pod running the old version. So, there is zero downtime, and the microservice can serve requests during the upgrade procedure.

If your microservice deployment had more replicas, e.g., 10, by default, Kubernetes would terminate a maximum of 25% of the running pods and start a maximum of 25% of the replica count new pods. The *rolling update* means updating pods in chunks, 25% of the pods at a time. The percentage value is configurable.

3.14.3: Horizontally Autoscaling Microservices Principle

Microservices should automatically scale horizontally to be able to serve more requests.

Horizontal scaling means adding new instances or removing instances of a microservice. Horizontal scaling of a microservice requires statelessness. Stateful services are usually implemented using sticky sessions so

[35]https://kubernetes.io/docs/tutorials/kubernetes-basics/update/update-intro/

that requests from a particular client go to the same service instance. The horizontal scaling of stateful services is complicated because a client's state is stored on a single service instance. In the cloud-native world, we want to ensure even load distribution between microservice instances and target a request to any available microservice instance for processing.

Initially, a microservice can have one instance only. When the microservice gets more load, one instance cannot necessarily handle all the work. In that case, the microservice must be scaled horizontally (scaled out) by adding one or more new instances. When several microservice instances are running, the state cannot be stored inside the instances anymore because different client requests can be directed to different microservice instances. A stateless microservice must store its state outside the microservice in an in-memory cache or a database shared by all the microservice instances.

Microservices can be scaled manually, but that is rarely desired. Manual scaling requires someone to constantly monitor the software system and manually perform the needed scaling actions. Microservices should scale horizontally automatically. There are two requirements for a microservice to be horizontally auto-scalable:

- Microservice must be stateless
- There must be one or more metrics that define the scaling behavior

Typical metrics for horizontal autoscaling are CPU utilization and memory consumption. In many cases, using the CPU utilization metric alone can be enough. It is also possible to use a custom or external metric. For example, the Kafka consumer lag metric can indicate if the consumer lag is increasing and if a new microservice instance should be spawned to reduce the consumer lag.

In Kubernetes, you can specify horizontal autoscaling using the HorizontalPodAutoscaler[36] (HPA):

Figure 3.39. hpa.yaml

```yaml
apiVersion: autoscaling/v2beta1
kind: HorizontalPodAutoscaler
metadata:
  name: my-service
spec:
  scaleTargetRef:
    apiVersion: apps/v1
    kind: Deployment
    name: my-service
  minReplicas: 1
  maxReplicas: 99
  metrics:
    - type: Resource
      resource:
        name: cpu
        targetAverageUtilization: 75
    - type: Resource
      resource:
        name: memory
        targetAverageUtilization: 75
```

In the above example, the *my-service* microservice is horizontally auto-scaled so that there is always at least one instance of the microservice running. There can be a maximum of 99 instances of the microservice running. The microservice is scaled out if CPU or memory utilization is over 75%, and it is scaled in (the number of microservice instances is reduced) when both CPU and memory utilization falls below 75%.

---

[36]https://kubernetes.io/docs/tasks/run-application/horizontal-pod-autoscale/

3.14.4: Highly-Available Microservices Principle

Business-critical microservices must be highly available.

If only one microservice instance runs in an environment, it does not make the microservice highly available. If something happens to that one instance, the microservice becomes temporarily unavailable until a new instance has been started and is ready to serve requests. For this reason, you should run at least two or more instances for all business-critical microservices. You should also ensure these two instances don't run on the same computing node. The instances should run in different cloud provider availability zones. Then, a catastrophe in availability zone 1 won't necessarily affect microservices running in availability zone 2.

You can ensure that no two microservice instances run on the same computing node by defining an anti-affinity rule in the microservice's Deployment manifest:

Figure 3.40. deployment.yaml

```
.
.
affinity:
  podAntiAffinity:
    requiredDuringSchedulingIgnoredDuringExecution:
      - labelSelector:
          matchLabels:
            app.kubernetes.io/name: {{ include "microservice.name" . }}
        topologyKey: "kubernetes.io/hostname"
.
.
.
```

You can ensure an even distribution of pods across availability zones of the cloud provider using topology spread constraints:

Figure 3.41. deployment.yaml

```
.
.
topologySpreadConstraints:
  - maxSkew: 1
    topologyKey: failure-domain.beta.kubernetes.io/zone
    whenUnsatisfiable: DoNotSchedule
    labelSelector:
      matchLabels:
        app: my-service
```

For a business-critical microservice, we need to modify the horizontal autoscaling example from the previous section: The `minReplicas` property should be increased to 2:

Figure 3.42. hpa.yaml

```
apiVersion: autoscaling/v2beta1
kind: HorizontalPodAutoscaler
metadata:
  name: my-service
spec:
  scaleTargetRef:
    apiVersion: apps/v1
    kind: Deployment
    name: my-service
  minReplicas: 2
  maxReplicas: 99
  .
  .
  .
```

3.14.5: Observable Microservices Principle

It should be possible to detect any abnormal behavior in deployed microservices immediately. Abnormal behavior should trigger an alert. The deployment environment should offer aids for troubleshooting abnormal behavior.

A modern cloud-native software system consists of multiple microservices running simultaneously. No one can manually check the logs of tens or even hundreds of microservice instances. The key to monitoring microservices is automation. Everything starts with collecting relevant metrics from microservices and their execution environment. These metrics are used to define rules for automatic alerts that trigger when an abnormal condition occurs. Metrics are also used to create monitoring and troubleshooting dashboards, which can be used to analyze the state of the software system and its microservices after an alert is triggered.

In addition to metrics, to enable drill-down to a problem's root cause, distributed tracing should be implemented to log the communication between various microservices to troubleshoot inter-service communication problems. Each microservice must also log at least all errors and warnings. These logs should be fed to a centralized log collection system where querying the logs is made quick and easy.

3.15: Individually Deployable Microservices Principle

Microservices should be individually deployable.

In a software system that consists of possibly hundreds of microservices, you should be able to deploy each of those microservices individually. This means that if you have made a correction to a single microservice, that correction can be deployed individually without affecting any other microservice running in the environment. When you deploy the correction, only the corrected microservice's instances must be restarted. In a Kubernetes environment, you can achieve individual deployment easily by creating a Helm chart for each microservice. The Helm chart should contain everything the microservice needs, e.g., the related configuration and services (like a database), including a Kubernetes Deployment manifest.

When you craft a microservice, don't assume that its dependent services are always and immediately available. For example, if your microservice uses Kafka, the microservice must start and run even if Kafka is deployed after your microservice is deployed.

3.16: Software Versioning Principles

In this section, the following principles related to software versioning will be presented:

- Use semantic versioning
- Avoid using 0.x versions
- Don't increase major versions
- Implement security patches and bug corrections to all major versions
- Avoid using *non*-LTS (Long Term Support) versions in production

3.16.1: Use Semantic Versioning Principle

Use semantic versioning for software components.

Semantic versioning[37] means that given a version number in the format: `<MAJOR>.<MINOR>.<PATCH>`, increment the:

- *MAJOR* value when you make incompatible API changes
- *MINOR* value when you add functionality in a backward-compatible manner
- *PATCH* value when you make backward-compatible bug fixes or security patches

3.16.2: Avoid Using 0.x Versions Principle

If you are using 3rd party components, avoid or at least be thoughtful of using 0.x versioned components.

In semantic versioning, major version zero (0.x.y) is for initial development. Anything can change at any time. The public API should not be considered stable. Typically, software components with a zero major version are still in a proof of concept phase, and anything can change. When you want or need to take a newer version into use, you must be prepared for changes, and sometimes, these changes can be considerable, resulting in a lot of refactoring.

3.16.3: Don't Increase Major Version Principle

In semantic versioning, you must increase the major version when making backward-incompatible public API changes. However, if possible and feasible, I advise against making backward-incompatible changes. Thus, no major version increases need to be made.

If you need to make a backward-incompatible public API change, you should create a totally new software component with a different name. For example, suppose you have a *common-ui-lib* and must make backward-incompatible changes. In that case, I recommend adding the new major version number to the library name and publishing a new library with the name *common-ui-lib-2*. This protects developers from accidentally using a more recent non-compatible version when changing the used library version number.

---

[37]https://semver.org/

Library users don't necessarily know if a library uses semantic versioning properly or not. This information is not usually told in the library documentation, but it is a good practice to communicate it in the library documentation.

If a software component uses the *common-ui-lib*, the latest version of the library can always be safely taken into use because it won't contain any breaking changes, only new features, bug fixes, and security patches.

If you were using Node.js and NPM, this would be safe:

```
npm install --save common-ui-library@latest
```

When you are ready to migrate to the new major version of the library, you can uninstall the old version and install the new major version in the following way:

```
npm uninstall common-ui-library
npm install --save common-ui-library-2
```

Consider when creating a new major version of a library is appropriate. When you created the first library version, you probably did not get everything right in the public API. That is normal. It is challenging to create a perfect API the first time. Before releasing the second major version of the library, I suggest reviewing the new API with a team, collecting user feedback, and waiting long enough to get the API "close to perfect" the second time. No one wants to use a library with frequent backward-incompatible major version changes.

3.16.4: Implement Security Patches and Bug Corrections to All Major Versions Principle

If you have authored a library for others to use, do not force the users to take a new major version of the library into use just because it contains some bug corrections or security patches that are not available for the older major version(s). You should have a comprehensive set of automated tests to ensure that a bug fix or security patch doesn't break anything. Thus, making a security patch or bug fix in multiple branches or source code repositories should be straightforward.

Requiring library users to upgrade to a new major version to get some security patch or a bug correction can create a maintenance hell where the library users must refactor all software components using the library just to get a security patch or bug correction.

3.16.5: Avoid Using Non-LTS Versions in Production Principle

Some software is available as Long Term Support[38] (LTS) and non-LTS versions. Always use only an LTS version in production. You are guaranteed long-term support through bug corrections and security patches. You can use a non-LTS version for proof of concept[39] (PoC) projects where you want to use some new features unavailable in an LTS version. But you must remember that if the PoC succeeds, you can't just throw it into production. You need to productize it first, i.e., replace the non-LTS software with LTS software.

---

[38]https://en.wikipedia.org/wiki/Long-term_support
[39]https://en.wikipedia.org/wiki/Proof_of_concept

3.17: Git Version Control Principle

Use trunk(= main branch) based development and develop software in feature branches merged into the main branch. Use feature toggles (or flags) when needed.

Trunk-based development[40] is suitable for modern software, which has an extensive set of automated functional and non-functional tests and can use feature toggles. There is also an older/legacy branching model called GitFlow[41], which can be used instead of trunk-based development to get better control of releasing software.

When you need to develop a new feature, it can be done using either of the following ways:

1) Using a feature branch
2) Using multiple feature branches and a feature toggle (or flag) if needed

3.17.1: Feature Branch

The feature branch approach is enough for simple features encompassing a single program increment, team, and microservice. A new feature is developed in a feature branch created from the main branch, and when the feature is ready, the feature branch is merged back into the main branch, and the feature branch can be deleted if wanted. The feature branch should be merged using a merge or pull request that triggers a CI pipeline run that must succeed before the merge/pull request can be completed. The merge or pull request should also take care of the code review. There should also be a manual way to trigger a CI/CD pipeline run for the feature branch so developers can test an unfinished feature in a test environment during the development phase. The artifacts produced by a CI/CD pipeline run from a feature branch can be called *in-progress* artifacts, and they should be regularly cleaned (e.g., after 48 hours) from the artifact repository.

Below a sample workflow of creating and using a feature branch is depicted:

```
git clone <repository-url>
git checkout main
git pull --rebase --ff-only

# Create and checkout a feature branch for a feature with id <feature-id>
# The feature id can be a JIRA id, for example
git checkout -b feature/<feature-id>

# Make your changes to code

# First commit
git commit -a -m "Commit message here..."

# Possibly more code changes and commits...

# Fetch the latest commits from remote main branch and
# fast forward your local main branch to match origin/main
git fetch origin main
git update-ref refs/heads/main refs/remotes/origin/main

# Rebase your feature branch on top of main
git rebase origin/main --autostash
```

---

[40] https://trunkbaseddevelopment.com/
[41] https://www.atlassian.com/git/tutorials/comparing-workflows/gitflow-workflow

```
# Push the feature branch to remote
# After successful push, in response to the below git command,
# you should receive a link to create a merge/pull request.
# Create a MR/PR, wait for the CI build to complete and
# perform the merge
git push -u origin feature/<feature-id>

# Other developers can now also use the feature branch
# because it is pushed to origin

# After successfully merging
git checkout main
git pull --rebase

# Now you are ready to create a new feature branch...
```

When the feature is ready, you can create a pull or merge request from the feature branch to the main branch. You can create the pull/merge request in your Git hosting service's web page or use the link in the output of the `git push` command. After creating the pull/merge request, a build pipeline should be started, and colleagues can review the code. The build started after creating the pull/merge request builds *candidate* artifacts, which are stored in the artifact repository but deleted after a certain period. If you need to change the code after making the pull/merge request, just modify the code, then use `git add`, `git commit --amend`, and `git push` commands to push the changes to the merge request. The merge can be completed after the code is reviewed and the build pipeline succeeds. After the merge, a build pipeline from the main branch should be run. This pipeline run should push the final *release* artifacts to the artifact repository.

3.17.2: Feature Toggle

A feature toggle works in a similar way to a feature license. In the case of a feature license, the feature is available only when a user has the respective license activated in their environment. A toggleable feature is available only when the feature toggle is switched on. Feature toggles should be used for complex features spanning multiple program increments, microservices, or teams. Use a feature toggle only if it is needed. Feature toggles are part of the configuration of an environment. For example, feature toggles can be stored in a Kubernetes ConfigMap that any microservice can access. When using a feature toggle, the toggle is initially switched off. Development of the feature happens in multiple feature branches in different teams. Teams merge their part of the feature to the main branch. When all feature branches are merged into the main branch, the feature toggle can be switched on to activate the feature.

People who haven't used feature toggles may have some prejudice and misconceptions:

- Code becomes cluttered with feature toggles

    - Not all features need a toggle. Only those should have a toggle that need it. For example, if a feature is implemented but not yet 100% tested, a feature toggle is needed to keep the feature disabled until it is thoroughly tested

- Code becomes unreadable and cluttered with if-else statements

    - This can be true if the codebase is poorly designed and contains technical debt. (= When you need to apply *shotgun surgery* to *spaghetti code*)
    - Usually, implementing a feature toggle in well-designed code does not need changes in many places but just a single or few places

- Feature toggle causes performance degradation

  - Feature toggles can almost always be implemented with negligible performance degradation, e.g., using one or a few if-statements

- Dismantling feature toggles is extra effort and can cause bugs

  - First of all, do you need to remove them? Many times, feature toggles can be left in the codebase if they don't degenerate the readability or performance of the code
  - When the codebase has the correct design (e.g., *open-closed principle* is used), removing a feature toggle is a lot easier compared to situation where *shotgun surgery* needs to be applied to *spaghetti code*.
  - Comprehensive automated testing should make it relatively safe to remove feature toggles

3.18: Architectural Patterns

3.18.1: Multi-Container Design Patterns

3.18.1.1: Sidecar Pattern

Sidecar means an extra container in your Kubernetes pod to enhance or extend the functionality of the main container.

This is the same as the *decorator pattern* from the OOP world. An example of the sidecar pattern is Istio.

3.18.1.2: Ambassador Pattern

Ambassador means an extra container that proxies the network connection to the main container.

For example, you can use ambassador as a proxy to a Redis caching cluster[42]. This is the same as the *proxy pattern* from the OOP world.

3.18.1.3: Adapter Pattern

An adapter is an extra container that transforms the output of the main container.

3.18.2: Circuit Breaker Pattern

A circuit breaker will handle faults that might take a variable amount of time to recover from when connecting to a remote service.

Applying a circuit breaker improves the stability and resiliency of a microservice. For a Kubernetes microservice, you can add circuit breaking functionality to a pod by configuring circuit breaker in Istio[43].

---

[42]https://www.weave.works/blog/kubernetes-patterns-the-ambassador-pattern
[43]https://istio.io/latest/docs/tasks/traffic-management/circuit-breaking/

3.18.3: Competing Consumers Pattern

Multiple consumers read messages from the same message queue topic in parallel, competing with each other.

New consumers can be added or removed. With Kafka, you define competing consumers by making multiple microservice instances subscribing to the same topic(s) using the same consumer group[44].

3.18.4: API Gateway Offloading Pattern

Offload shared microservice functionality to an API gateway.

Examples of functionality you can offload to the API Gateway are TLS termination, compression, request logging, standard HTTP response headers, and rate limiting. Using the API gateway for these purposes saves you from having to implement them separately in each microservice.

3.18.5: Retry Pattern

Enable a microservice to handle transient failures when it tries to connect to a service by transparently retrying a failed operation.

For a Kubernetes pod, you can configure Istio to perform automatic transparent retries (and timeouts). When using this pattern, you don't have to implement the retry logic in each microservice separately.

3.18.6: Static Content Hosting Pattern

Deploy static content to a cloud object storage that can deliver them directly to clients.

You don't need to spin up compute instances to serve static content to clients. Using this pattern can reduce the need for potentially expensive compute instances.

3.18.7: Event Sourcing Pattern

Use event sourcing to capture state changes as a sequence of events.

Event sourcing ensures that all changes to a service's state are stored as an ordered sequence of events. Event sourcing makes it possible to query state changes. Also, the state change events act as an audit log. It is possible to reconstruct past states and rewind the current state to some earlier state. Unlike CRUD actions on resources, event sourcing utilizes only CR (create and read) actions. It is only possible to create new events and read events. It is not possible to update or delete an existing event.

Let's have an example of using event sourcing to store orders in an e-commerce software system. The *order-service* should be able to store the following events:

---

[44]https://docs.confluent.io/platform/current/clients/consumer.html

- AbstractOrderEvent
  - Abstract base event for other concrete events containing timestamp and order id properties
- OrderCreatedEvent
  - Contains basic information about the order
- OrderPaymentEvent
  - Contains information about the order payment
- OrderModificationEvent
  - Contains information about modifications made by the customer to the order before packaging
- OrderPackagedEvent
  - Contains information about who collected and packaged the order
- OrderCanceledEvent
  - Describes that the customer has canceled the order and the order should not be shipped
- OrderShippedEvent
  - Contains information about the logistics partner and the tracking id of the order shipment
- OrderDeliveredEvent
  - Contains information about the pick-up point of the delivered order
- OrderShipmentReceivedEvent
  - Informs that the customer has received the shipment
- OrderReturnedEvent
  - Contains information about the returned order or order item(s)
- OrderReturnShippedEvent
  - Contains information about the logistics partner and the tracking id of the return shipment
- OrderReturnReceivedEvent
  - Contains information about who handled the order return and the status of returned items
- OrderReimbursedEvent
  - Contains information about the reimbursement for the returned order item(s) to the customer

Event sourcing can be useful when an audit trail of events is wanted or needed. The data store used in event sourcing would then act as an audit logging system. When you use event sourcing, you create events that could also be used in various analytics and machine learning applications. Event sourcing can also help debug a complex system. Debugging events is easier compared to debugging entity modifications. Of course, those entity modifications could be logged, but that would mean a specific low logging level needs to be enabled, and still, not all data should be written to logs due to security reasons. The drawback of event sourcing is recreating the current state of entities from events in the event store. This can be a performance bottleneck if it needs to be done often and the number of events is high. The potential performance bottleneck can be mitigated by creating a snapshot of an entity state, e.g., after a certain number of events created for a specific entity. Then, the current state of an entity can be recreated by finding the latest snapshot and replaying events created after that snapshot. Another alternative is to use partially materialized views and CQRS, as described in the next section.

3.18.8: Command Query Responsibility Segregation (CQRS) Pattern

Use the CQRS pattern if you want to use a different model for create/update (= command) operations than the one you want to use to query information.

Let's consider the previous *order-service* example that used event sourcing. In the *order-service*, all the commands are events. However, we want users to be able to query orders efficiently. We should have an additional representation of an order in addition to events because it is inefficient to always generate the current state of an order by replaying all the related events. For this reason, our architecture should utilize the CQRS pattern and divide the *order-service* into two different services: *order-command-service* and *order-query-service*.

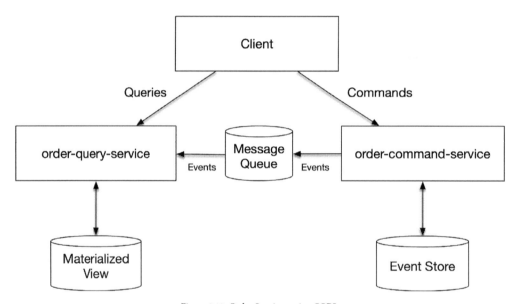

Figure 3.43. Order Services using CQRS

The *order-command-service* is the same as the original *order-service* that uses event sourcing, and the *order-query-service* is a new service. The *order-query-service* has a database with a materialized view of orders. The two services are connected with a message broker. The *order-command-service* sends events to a topic in the message broker. The *order-query-service* reads events from the topic and applies changes to the materialized view. The materialized view is optimized to contain basic information about each order, including its current state, to be consumed by the e-commerce company staff and customers. Because customers query orders, the materialized view should be indexed by the customer's id column to enable fast retrieval. Suppose that, in some particular case, a customer needs more details about an order that is available in the materialized view. In that case, the *order-command-service* can be used to query the events of the order for additional information.

Using event sourcing and CQRS offers availability over consistency, which the system end-users usually prefer, i.e., end users usually prefer to get information fast, even if it is not current but will eventually be up-to-date. *Availability over consistency principle* is one of the IDEALS microservice principles.

It should be noted that using the CQRS pattern does not require the command and query models to use different databases. It is perfectly fine to use the same database. The main idea behind the CQRS pattern is that the models for queries and commands differ, as shown in the below picture.

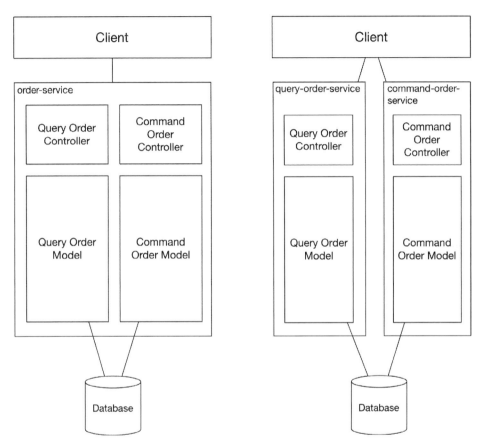

Figure 3.44. CQRS

In the above example, the command model stores entities that are order-related events, and the query model constructs order entities from the stored order-related events. The CQRS pattern is useful in cases where the domain model is relatively complex, and you benefit from separating the command and query models. For a simple API with basic CRUD operations on simple resources, using CQRS is overkill and only makes the code complicated.

3.18.9: Distributed Transaction Patterns

A distributed transaction[45] is a transaction that spans multiple microservices. A distributed transaction consists of one or more remote requests. Distributed transactions can be implemented using the *saga*

---

[45]https://en.wikipedia.org/wiki/Distributed_transaction

pattern. In the saga pattern, each request in a distributed transaction should have a respective compensating action defined. If one request in the distributed transaction fails, compensating requests should be executed for the already executed requests. The idea of executing the compensating requests is to bring the system back to the state where it was before the distributed transaction was started. So, the rollback of a distributed transaction is done via executing the compensating actions.

A failed request in a distributed transaction must be conditionally compensated if we cannot be sure whether the server successfully executed the request. This can happen when a request timeouts and we don't receive a response to indicate the request status.

Also, executing a compensating request can fail. For this reason, a microservice must persist compensating requests so they can be retried later until they all succeed. Persistence is needed because the microservice instance can be terminated before it has completed all the compensating requests successfully. Another microservice instance can continue the work left by the terminated microservice instance.

Some requests in a distributed transaction can be such that they cannot be compensated. One typical example is sending an email. You can't get it unsent once it has been sent. There are at least two approaches to dealing with requests that cannot be compensated. The first one is to delay the execution of the request so that it can be made compensable. For example, instead of immediately sending an email, the email-sending microservice can store the email in a queue for later sending. The email-sending microservice can now accept a compensating request to remove the email from the sending queue.

Another approach is to execute non-compensable requests in the latest possible phase of the distributed transaction. You can, for example, issue the email-sending request as the last request of the distributed transaction. Then, the likelihood of needing to compensate for the email sending is lower than if the email was sent as the first request in the distributed transaction. You can also combine these two approaches. Sometimes, a request can be compensable even if you first think it is not. You should think creatively. Sending an email could be compensated by sending another email where you state that the email you sent earlier should be disregarded (for a specific reason).

3.18.9.1: Saga Orchestration Pattern

Orchestrator or controller microservice orchestrates the execution of a distributed transaction.

Let's have an example of a distributed transaction using the saga orchestration pattern with an online banking system where users can transfer money from their accounts. We have a higher-level microservice called *account-money-transfer-service*, which is used to make money transfers. The banking system also has two lower-level microservices called *account-balance-service* and *account-transaction-service*. The *account-balance-service* holds accounts' balance information while the *account-transaction-service* keeps track of all account transactions. The *account-money-transfer-service* acts as a saga orchestrator and utilizes both lower-level microservices to make a money transfer happen. Do not confuse the distributed transaction with an account transaction. They are two separate things. The distributed transaction spans the whole money transfer process, while an account transaction is a transaction related to a particular account, either a withdrawal or deposit transaction. An account transaction is an entity stored in the *account-transaction-service*'s database.

Let's consider a distributed transaction executed by the *account-money-transfer-service* when a user makes a withdrawal of $25.10:

1) The *account-money-transfer-service* tries to withdraw the amount from the user's account by sending the following request to the *account-balance-service*:

```
POST /account-balance-service/accounts/123456789012/withdraw HTTP/1.1
Content-Type: application/json

{
  "sagaUuid": "e8ab60b5-3053-46e7-b8da-87b1f46edf34",
  "amountInCents": 2510
}
```

The sagaUuid is a universally unique identifier[46] (UUID) generated by the saga orchestrator before the saga begins. If there are not enough funds to withdraw the given amount, the request fails with the HTTP status code 400 *Bad Request*. If the request is successfully executed, the *account-balance-service* should store the saga UUID to a database table temporarily. This table stores information about successful sagas and should be cleaned regularly by deleting old enough saga UUIDs.

2) The *account-money-transfer-service* will create a new account transaction for the user's account by sending the following request to the *account-transaction-service*:

```
POST /account-transaction-service/accounts/123456789012/transactions HTTP/1.1
Content-Type: application/json

{
  "sagaUuid": "e8ab60b5-3053-46e7-b8da-87b1f46edf34",
  // Additional transaction information here...
}
```

The above-described distributed transaction has two requests, each of which can fail. Let's consider the scenario where the first request to the *account-balance-service* fails. If the first request fails due to a request timeout, we don't know if the recipient microservice successfully processed the request. We don't know because we did not get the response and status code. For that reason, we need to perform a conditional compensating action by issuing the following compensating request:

```
POST /account-balance-service/accounts/123456789012/undo-withdraw HTTP/1.1
Content-Type: application/json

{
  "sagaUuid": "e8ab60b5-3053-46e7-b8da-87b1f46edf34",
  "amountInCents": 2510
}
```

The *account-balance-service* will perform the undo-withdraw action only if a withdrawal with the given UUID was made earlier and that withdrawal has not been undone yet. Upon successful undoing, the *account-balance-service* will delete the row for the given saga UUID from the database table where the saga UUID was earlier temporarily stored. Further undo-withdraw requests with the same saga UUID will be no-op actions, making the undo-withdraw action idempotent.

Next, let's consider the scenario where the first request succeeds and the second request fails due to timeout. Now we have to compensate for both requests. First, we compensate for the first request as described earlier. Then, we will compensate for the second request by deleting the account transaction identified with the sagaUuid:

---

[46]https://en.wikipedia.org/wiki/Universally_unique_identifier

```
DELETE /account-transaction-service/accounts/123456789012/transactions?sagaUuid=e8ab60b5-3053-46e7-b8d\
a-87b1f46edf34 HTTP/1.1
```

If a compensating request fails, it must be repeated until it succeeds. Notice that the above compensating requests are both idempotent, i.e., they can be executed multiple times with the same result. Idempotency is a requirement for a compensating request because a compensating request may fail after the compensation has already been performed. That compensation request failure will cause the compensating request to be attempted again. The distributed transaction manager in the *account-money-transfer-service* should ensure that a distributed transaction is successfully completed or roll-backed by the instances of the *account-money-transfer-service*. You should implement a single distributed transaction manager library per programming language or technology stack and use that in all microservices that need to orchestrate distributed transactions. Alternatively, use a 3rd party library.

Let's have another short example with the *ecommerce-service* presented earlier in this chapter. The order-placing endpoint of the *ecommerce-service* should make the following requests in a distributed transaction:

1) Ensure payment
2) Create an order
3) Remove the ordered sales items from the shopping cart
4) Mark the ordered sales items sold
5) Enqueue an order confirmation email for sending

The respective compensating requests are the following:

1) Reimburse the payment
2) Delete the order using the saga UUID
3) Add the ordered sales items back to the shopping cart. (The shopping cart service must ensure that a sales item can be added only once to a shopping cart)
4) Mark the ordered sales items for sale
5) Dequeue the order confirmation email

3.18.9.2: Saga Choreography Pattern

Microservices perform a distributed transaction in a choreography where one microservice initiates the distributed transaction, and the last microservice involved completes the distributed transaction by sending a completion message to the microservice that started the transaction.

The saga choreography pattern utilizes asynchronous communication between microservices. Involved microservices send messages to each other in a choreography to achieve saga completion.

The saga choreography pattern has a couple of drawbacks:

- The execution of a distributed transaction is not centralized like in the saga orchestration pattern, and it can be hard to figure out how a distributed transaction is actually performed.
- It creates coupling between microservices, while microservices should be as loosely coupled as possible.

The saga choreography pattern works best in cases where the number of participating microservices is low. Then the coupling between services is low, and it is easier to reason how a distributed transaction is performed.

Let's have the same money transfer example as earlier, but now using the saga choreography pattern instead of the saga orchestration pattern.

1) The *account-money-transfer-service* initiates the saga by sending the following event to the message broker's *account-balance-service* topic:

```
{
  "event": "WithdrawRequested",
  "data": {
    "sagaUuid": "e8ab60b5-3053-46e7-b8da-87b1f46edf34",
    "amountInCents": 2510
  }
}
```

2) The *account-balance-service* will consume the `WithdrawRequested` event from the message broker, perform a withdrawal, and if successful, send the same event to the message broker's *account-transaction-service* topic.
3) The *account-transaction-service* will consume the `Withdraw` event from the message broker, persist an account transaction, and if successful, send the following event to the message broker's *account-money-transfer-service* topic:

```
{
  "event": "WithdrawCompleted",
  "status": "Complete"
  "data": {
    "sagaUuid": "e8ab60b5-3053-46e7-b8da-87b1f46edf34"
  }
}
```

If either step 2) or 3) fails, the *account-balance-service* or *account-transaction-service* will send the following event to message broker's *account-money-transfer-service* topic:

```
{
  "event": "WithdrawFailed",
  "data": {
    "sagaUuid": "e8ab60b5-3053-46e7-b8da-87b1f46edf34"
  }
}
```

If the *account-money-transfer-service* receives a `WithdrawFailed` event or does not receive a `WithdrawCompleted` event during some timeout period, the *account-money-transfer-service* will initiate a distributed transaction rollback sequence by sending the following event to the message broker's *account-balance-service* topic:

```
{
  "event": "WithdrawRollbackRequested",
  "data": {
    "sagaUuid": "e8ab60b5-3053-46e7-b8da-87b1f46edf34",
    "amountInCents": 2510,
    // Additional transaction information here...
  }
}
```

Once the rollback in the *account-balance-service* is done, the rollback event will be produced to the *account-transaction-service* topic in the message broker. After the *account-transaction-service* successfully performs the rollback, it sends a `WithdrawRollbackCompleted` event to the *account-money-transfer-service* topic. The withdrawal event is successfully rolled back once the *account-money-transfer-service* consumes that message. Suppose the *account-money-transfer-service* does not receive the `WithdrawRollbackCompleted` event during some timeout period. In that case, it will restart the rollback choreography by resending the `WithdrawRollbackRequested` event to the *account-balance-service*.

3.19: Preferred Technology Stacks Principle

Define preferred technology stacks for different purposes.

The microservice architecture enables the use of the most suitable technology stack to develop each microservice. For example, some microservices require high performance and controlled memory allocation, and other microservices don't need such things. You can choose the used technology stack based on the needs of a microservice. For a real-time data processing microservice, you might pick C++ or Rust, and for a simple REST API, you might choose Node.js and Express, Java and Spring Boot, or Python and Django.

Even if the microservice architecture allows different teams and developers to decide what programming languages and technologies to use when implementing a microservice, defining preferred technology stacks for different purposes is still a good practice. Otherwise, you might find yourself in a situation where numerous programming languages and technologies are used in a software system. Some programming languages and technologies like Clojure, Scala, or Haskell can be relatively niche. When software developers in the organization come and go, you might end up in situations where you don't have anyone who knows about some specific niche programming language or technology. In the worst case, a microservice needs to be reimplemented from scratch using some more mainstream technologies. For this reason, you should specify technology stacks that teams should use. These technology stacks should mainly contain mainstream programming languages and technologies.

For example, an architecture team might decide the following:

- Web clients should be developed using TypeScript, React, and Redux
- Non-API backend services should be developed by default in Go or C++ for performance reasons
- APIs should be developed with TypeScript, Node.js, and Nest.js or with Java and Spring Boot
- Integration tests should be implemented with Cucumber using the same language as is used for the implementation or, alternatively, with Python and Behave
- E2E tests should be implemented with Python and Behave
- Scripts should be implemented using Bash for small scripts and Python for larger scripts

The above technology stacks are pretty mainstream. Recruiting talent with needed knowledge and competencies should be effortless.

After you have defined the preferred technology stacks, you should create a utility or utilities that can be used to kick-start a new project using a particular technology stack quickly. This utility or utilities should generate the initial source code repository content for a new microservice, client, or library. The initial source code repository should contain at least the following items for a new microservice:

- Source code folder
- Unit test folder (if separate from source code folder)
- Integration test folder
- Build tools, like Gradle Wrapper for Java, for example
- Initial build definition file(s), like build.gradle for Java, CMakeLists.txt for C++ or package.json for Node.js

  - Initial dependencies defined in the build definition file

- .env file(s) to store environment variables for different environments (dev, CI)
- .gitignore
- Markdown documentation template file(s) (README.MD)
- Linting rules (e.g., .eslintrc.json)
- Code formatting rules (e.g., .prettier.rc)
- Initial code for integration tests, e.g., docker-compose.yml file for spinning up an integration testing environment
- Infrastructure code for the chosen cloud provider, e.g., code to deploy a managed SQL database in the cloud
- Code (e.g., Dockerfile) for building the microservice container image
- Deployment code (e.g., a Helm chart)
- CI/CD pipeline definition code

The utility should ask the following questions from the developer before creating the initial source code repository content for new microservice:

- What is the name of the microservice?
- To what cloud environment will microservice be deployed? (AWS, Azure, Google Cloud, etc.)
- What inter-service communication methods are used? Based on the answer, the utility can add dependencies, e.g., a Kafka client library dependency
- Should microservice have a database, and what database?
- What are the other dependent microservices?

To make things even easier, you could create, e.g., a Jenkins job that asks the questions from the developer in the Jenkins UI and then creates a new source code repository and pushes the content created by the utility to the new source code repository. Developers only need to know the link to the Jenkins job to kickstart a brand-new microservice.

Of course, decisions about the preferred technology stacks are not engraved in stone. They are not static. As time passes, new technologies arise, and new programming languages gain popularity. At some point, a decision could be made that a new technology stack should replace an existing preferred technology stack.

Then, new projects should use the new stack, and old software components will be gradually migrated to use the new technology stack or eventually retired.

Many developers are keen on learning new things on a regular basis. They should be encouraged to work on hobby projects with technologies of their choice, and they should be able to utilize new programming languages and frameworks in selected new projects.

3.20: 8 Fallacies Of Distributed Computing

When you are using a microservice architecture, you have a distributed computing environment and should be aware of the eight fallacies of distributed computing:

1. The network is reliable You don't have to prepare for network unreliability separately in each microservice. You can and should use a service mesh like Istio to handle the main issues related to network unreliability. A service mesh offers automatic retries, timeouts, and circuit breakers, for instance.

2. Latency is zero Latency can vary from time to time. Usually, you deploy your software system to a single cloud region. In that case, latency is small and, for many applications, is on an acceptable level. If you have a real-time application with strict latency requirements, you might need to conduct testing and measure the latency and see if it is acceptable.

3. Bandwidth is infinite. Bandwidth inside a single cloud region is high. If you transfer high amounts of data, with testing, you can measure if the bandwidth is enough.

4. The network is secure. Insider attackers might be able to sniff the network traffic. Use a service mesh to implement mTLS between microservices to secure the network traffic.

5. Network topology does not change Topology can change and produce suboptimal routes that cause bottlenecks.

6. There is one administrator Many admins can cause problems, e.g., if they make conflicting or incompatible configuration changes.

7. Transport cost is zero Even if the transport is not separately charged, its cost is baked in other prices, like the used infrastructure and services. The more data you transfer, the more it can cost you. Remember that when you use microservices, all transferred data must be serialized and deserialized, causing additional CPU consumption compared to a monolith where information can be exchanged in the memory. This is a crucial aspect to consider when deciding between a distributed and monolithic architecture.

8. The network is homogenous The network has many parts. If two communicating virtual machines are in the same rack, the latency and bandwidth are higher compared to connections between VMs in two different availability zones, let alone in two different regions. The network heterogeneity corresponds to varying levels of latency. Microservices on the same node can communicate with minimal latency, but microservices in different availability zones experience higher latency.

4: Object-Oriented Design Principles

This chapter describes principles related to object-oriented design. The following principles are discussed:

- Object-oriented programming concepts
- Programming paradigms
- Why is object-oriented programming hard?
- SOLID principles
- Clean architecture principle
- Vertical slice architecture principle
- Class organization principle
- Package, class, and function sizing principle
- Uniform naming principle
- Encapsulation principle
- Prefer composition over inheritance principle
- Tactical domain-driven design principle
- Use the design patterns principle
- Tell, don't ask principle
- Law of Demeter
- Avoid primitive type obsession principle
- You aren't gonna need it (YAGNI) principle
- Dependency injection principle
- Avoid duplication principle

We start the chapter by defining object-oriented programming (OOP) concepts and discussing different programming paradigms: Object-oriented, imperative, and functional. We also analyze why OOP can be hard to master even though the concepts and fundamental principles are not so difficult to grasp.

4.1: Object-Oriented Programming Concepts

The following are the basic concepts related to OOP:

- Classes/Objects

  - Attributes and methods
  - Composition (= when attributes are other classes)
- Encapsulation
- Abstraction
- Inheritance
- Interfaces

  - Interface evolution
- Polymorphism

  - Dynamic dispatch (late binding)

Let's discuss each of the concepts next.

4.1.1: Classes/Objects

A class is a user-defined data type that acts as the blueprint for individual objects (instances of the class). An object is created using the class's *constructor* method, which sets the object's initial state. A class consists of *attributes* (or *properties*) and *methods*, which can be either *class* or *instance* attributes/methods. Instance attributes define the state of an object. Instance methods act on instance attributes, i.e., they are used to query and modify the state of an object. Class attributes belong to the class, and class methods act on class attributes.

An object can represent either a concrete or abstract entity in the real world. For example, a circle and an employee object represent real-world entities, while an object representing an open file (a file handle) is an abstract entity. Objects can also be hybrid, representing something concrete and abstract.

Attributes of an object can contain other objects to create object hierarchies. This is called *object composition*, and is handled in more detail in the *prefer composition over inheritance principle* section.

In pure object-oriented languages like Java, you must always create a class where you can put functions. Even if you have only class methods and no attributes, you must create a class in Java to host the class methods (static methods). In JavaScript, you don't have to create classes for hosting functions; just put the functions into a single module or create a directory and put each function in a separate module. Putting functions into classes has many benefits (e.g., dependency injection), which is why putting functions into classes is often a good idea.

4.1.2: Encapsulation

Encapsulation makes changing the internal state of an object directly outside of the object impossible. The idea of encapsulation is that the object's state is internal to the object and can be changed externally only by the object's public methods. Encapsulation contributes to better security and avoidance of data corruption. More about that in the *encapsulation principle* section.

4.1.3: Abstraction

Objects only reveal relevant internal mechanisms to other objects, hiding any unnecessary implementation code. Callers of object methods don't need to know the object's internal workings. They adhere only to the object's public API. This makes it possible to change the implementation details without affecting any external code.

4.1.4: Inheritance

Inheritance allows classes to be arranged in a hierarchy representing *is-a* relationships. For example, the Employee class might inherit from the Person class because an employee is also a person. All the attributes and methods in the parent (super) class also appear in the child class (subclass) with the same names. For example, class Person might define attributes name and birthDate. These will also be available in the Employee class. Child class can add methods and attributes. Child class can also override a method in the parent class. For example, the Employee might add attributes employer and salary. This technique allows easy re-use of the same functionality and data definitions, mirroring real-world relationships intuitively.

C++ also supports multiple inheritance, where a child class can have multiple parent classes. The problem with multiple inheritance is that the child class can inherit different versions of a method with the same name. By default, multiple inheritance should be avoided whenever possible. Some languages, like Java, don't support multiple inheritance at all. Inheritance will cram additional functionality into a child class, making the class large and possibly not having a single responsibility. A better way to add functionality to a class is to compose the class of multiple other classes (the mixins). In that way, there is no need to worry about the possibility of clashing method names.

Multiple inheritance is always allowed for interfaces. Interfaces will be discussed in the next section.

4.1.5: Interface

An interface specifies a contract that classes that implement the interface must obey. Interfaces are used to implement polymorphic behavior, which will be described in the next section. An interface consists of one or more methods that classes must implement. You cannot instantiate an interface. It is just a contract specification.

Below are two interfaces and two classes that implement the interfaces:

```
public interface Drawable {
  void draw();
}


public interface Clickable {
  void click();
}


public class Window implements Drawable {
  public void draw() {
    System.out.println("Window drawn");
  }
}


public class Button implements Drawable, Clickable {
  public void draw() {
    System.out.println("Button drawn");
  }

  public void click() {
    System.out.println("Button clicked");
  }
}


final var button = new Button();
button.draw();
button.click();

// Output:
// Button drawn
// Button clicked
```

4.1.5.1: Interface evolution

After an interface has been defined and is used by the implementing classes, and you would like to add method(s) to the interface, you might have to provide a default implementation in your interface because the classes that currently implement your interface don't implement the methods you are about to add to the interface. This is true in cases where the implementing classes are something you cannot or don't want to modify.

Let's imagine you have a `Message` interface with `getData` and `getLengthInBytes` methods, and you have classes implementing the `Message` interface, but you cannot modify the classes. You want to add the `setQueuedAtInstant` and `getQueuedAtInstant` methods to the interface. You can add the methods to the interface but must provide a default implementation, like raising an error indicating the method is not implemented.

```java
import java.time.Instant;

public interface Message {
  byte[] getData();
  int getLengthInBytes();

  default void setQueuedAtInstant(final Instant instant) {
      throw new UnsupportedOperationException();
  }

  default Instant getQueuedAtInstant() {
    throw new UnsupportedOperationException();
  }
}
```

4.1.6: Polymorphism

Polymorphism means that methods are polymorphic when the actual method to be called is decided during the runtime. For this reason, polymorphism is also called *late binding* (to a particular method) or *dynamic dispatch*. Polymorphic behavior is easily implemented using an interface variable. You can assign any object that implements the interface to the interface variable. When you call a method on the interface variable, that actual method to be called is decided based on what type of object is currently assigned to the interface variable. Below is an example of polymorphic behavior:

```java
Drawable drawable = new Button();
drawable.draw();

// Output:
// Button drawn

drawable = new Window();
drawable.draw();

// Output:
// Window drawn
```

Polymorphic behavior is also exhibited when you have a variable of the parent class type and assign a child class object to the variable, like in the below example:

```java
public class IconButton extends Button {
  public void draw() {
    System.out.println("Button with icon drawn");
  }
}
```

```java
var button = new Button();
button.draw();

// Output:
// Button drawn

button = new IconButton();
button.draw();

// Output:
// Button with icon drawn
```

4.2: Programming Paradigms

The most popular programming languages, including C++, Java, and JavaScript, are multi-paradigm. Multi-paradigm languages support the following programming paradigms:

- Imperative programming
- Object-oriented programming
- Functional programming

4.2.1: Imperative Programming

Imperative programming is a programming paradigm that focuses on providing a sequence of explicit instructions or statements for the computer to follow to solve a problem or achieve a desired outcome. The program consists of a series of commands that modify the program state, typically using mutable variables and assignments. Imperative programming emphasizes how to achieve a result step by step, specifying the control flow and state changes explicitly. Typical imperative programming constructs are variable assignments, state mutations, match-case statements, if-statements, and different kinds of loops (for, while). Below is a code sample using imperative programming in JavaScript:

```javascript
const numbers = [1, 2, 3, 4, 5];
const squaredEvenNumbers = [];

for (const number of numbers) {
  if (number % 2 == 0) {
    squaredEvenNumbers.push(number**2)
  }
}

console.log(squaredEvenNumbers)

// Output:
// [4, 16]
```

In the above example, although the squaredEvenNumbers variable is declared as const, it is still a mutable list and we mutate the list inside the for loop.

4.2.2: Functional Programming

Functional programming is a programming paradigm that treats computation as the evaluation of mathematical functions and avoids changing state and mutable data. It emphasizes the use of immutable data and the composition of functions to solve problems. In functional programming, functions are first-class citizens, meaning they can be assigned to variables, passed as arguments to other functions, and returned as results. This enables the creation of higher-order functions and promotes modularity, code re-usability, and concise expression of complex operations in a declarative way. Functional programming avoids side effects, favoring pure functions[1] that consistently produce the same output for a given input without causing side effects, making programs easier to reason about and test.

Unlike in imperative programming, in functional programming, you don't tell the computer *how* to do something but declare *what* you want, e.g., I want to filter even numbers from a sequence and calculate their squares.

In mathematics and computer science, a higher-order function[2] (HOF) is a function that does at least one of the following: 1. Takes one or more functions as arguments 2. Returns a function as its result.

Below is functional code that uses map and filter functions:

```
const numbers = [1, 2, 3, 4, 5];
const isEven = (number: number) => number % 2 == 0;
const squared = (number: number) => number**2;

console.log(numbers.filter(isEven).map(squared));

// Output:
// [4, 16]
```

As you can see, the above code is much safer, shorter, and more straightforward than the earlier imperative code. There are no variable assignments or state modifications. Both the isEven and squared are pure functions because they return the same output for the same input without any side effects.

There is another way to implement the above code, which is by using a composition of functions. We can define reusable functions and compose more specific ones from general-purpose ones. Below is an example of function composition using the compose function from the ramda[3] library. The example also uses the partial function from the same library to create partially applied functions. For example, the filterEven function is a partially applied filter function where the first parameter is bound to the isEven function. Similarly, the mapSquared function is a partially applied map function where the first parameter is bound to the squared function. The compose function composes two or more functions in the following way: compose(f, g)(x) is the same as f(g(x)) and compose(f, g, h)(x) is same as f(g(h(x))) and so on. You can compose as many functions as you need/want.

---

[1]https://en.wikipedia.org/wiki/Pure_function
[2]https://en.wikipedia.org/wiki/Higher-order_function
[3]https://ramdajs.com/

```
import { compose, filter, map, partial } from "ramda";

const numbers = [1, 2, 3, 4, 5];
const isEven = (number: number) => number % 2 == 0;
const squared = (number: number) => number**2;
const filterEven = partial(filter, [isEven]);
const mapSquared = partial(map, [squared]);
const doubledEven = compose(mapSquared, filterEven);
console.log(doubledEven(numbers));

// Output:
// [4, 16]
```

In the above example, all the following functions can be made re-usable and put into a library:

- `isEven`
- `squared`
- `filterEven`
- `mapSquared`

Modern code should favor functional programming over imperative programming when possible. As compared to functional programming, imperative programming comes with the following disadvantages:

1. *Mutable state*: Imperative programming relies heavily on mutable state, where variables can be modified throughout the program's execution. This can lead to subtle bugs and make the program harder to reason about, as the state can change unpredictably. In functional programming, immutability is emphasized, reducing the complexity of state management and making programs more reliable.
2. *Side effects*: Imperative programming often involves side effects, where functions or operations modify the state or interact with the external world. Side effects make the code harder to test, reason about, and debug. On the other hand, functional programming encourages pure functions with no side effects, making the code more modular, reusable, and testable.
3. *Concurrency and parallelism*: Imperative programming can be challenging to parallelize and reason about in concurrent scenarios. Since mutable state can be modified by multiple threads or processes, race conditions and synchronization issues can occur. Functional programming, with its emphasis on immutability and pure functions, simplifies concurrency and parallelism by eliminating shared mutable state.
4. *Lack of referential transparency*: Imperative programming tends to rely on assignments and statements that modify variables in place. This can lead to code that is difficult to reason about due to implicit dependencies and hidden interactions between different parts of the code. In functional programming, referential transparency[4] is a key principle where expressions can be replaced with their values without changing the program's behavior. This property allows for easier understanding, debugging, and optimization.

Pure imperative programming also quickly leads to code duplication, lack of modularity, and abstraction issues. These are issues that can be solved using object-oriented programming.

---

[4]https://en.wikipedia.org/wiki/Referential_transparency

4.3: Multi-Paradigm Programming Principle

You should not use a single programming paradigm only.

To best utilize both object-oriented and functional programming (FP) when developing software, you can leverage the strengths of each paradigm in different parts of your codebase. Use domain-driven design (DDD) and object-oriented design to design the application: interfaces and classes. Implement classes by encapsulating related behavior and (possibly mutable, but aim for immutable) state in the classes. Apply OOP principles like *SOLID principles* and *design patterns*. These principles and patterns make code modular and easily extensible without accidentally breaking existing code. Use FP as much as possible when implementing class and instance methods. Embrace functional composition by creating pure functions that take immutable data as input and always produce the same output for the same input without side effects. Use higher-order functions to compose functions and build complex operations from simpler ones. For example, utilize higher-order functions in OOP by passing functions as arguments to methods or using them as callbacks. This allows for greater flexibility and modularity, enabling functional-style operations within an OOP framework. Also, remember to use functional programming libraries, either the standard or 3rd party libraries. Consider using functional techniques for error handling, such as *Either* or *Maybe/Optional* types. This helps you manage errors without exceptions, promoting more predictable and robust code. This is because function signatures don't tell if they can raise an error. You must remember to consult the documentation and check if a function can raise an error.

Aim for immutability within your codebase, regardless of the paradigm. Immutable data reduces complexity, avoids shared mutable state, and facilitates reasoning about your code. Favor creating new objects or data structures instead of modifying existing ones.

4.4: Why is Object-Oriented Programming Hard?

The basic concepts of OOP are not complex to understand, so why is it hard to master OOP? Below are listed things that can make OOP hard:

- You cannot rush into coding. You must have patience and perform object-oriented design (OOD) first
- You cannot get the OOD right on the first try. You need to have discipline and time reserved for refactoring.
- The difference between object composition and inheritance is not correctly understood, and inheritance is used in place of object composition, making the OOD flawed
- SOLID principles are not understood or followed

    - It can be challenging to create optimal-sized classes and functions with a single responsibility

        * For example, you might have a single-responsibility class, but the class is too big. You must realize that you must split the class into smaller classes the original class is composed of. Each of these smaller classes has a single responsibility on a lower level of abstraction compared to the original class

    - Understanding and following the open-closed principle can be challenging

       * The open-closed principle aims to avoid modifying existing code and thus avoid breaking any existing working code. For example, if you have a collection class and need a thread-safe collection class, don't modify the existing one, e.g., by adding a constructor flag to tell if a collection should be thread-safe. Instead, create a totally new class for thread-safe collections.

    – Liskov's substitution principle is not as simple as it looks

       * Suppose you have a base class `Circle` with a `draw` method. If you derive a `FilledCircle` class from the `Circle` class, you must implement the `draw` function so that it first calls the base class method. In some cases, it is possible to override the base class method with the derived class method

    – Interface segregation is usually left undone if it is not immediately needed. This might hinder the extensibility of the codebase in the future
    – In many texts, the dependency inversion principle is explained in complicated terms. The dependency inversion principle generally means programming against interfaces instead of concrete class types.

- You don't understand the value of dependency injection and are not using it

    – Dependency injection is a requirement for effectively utilizing some other principles, like the open-closed principle
    – Dependency injection makes unit testing a breeze because you can create mock implementations and inject them into the tested code

- You don't know/understand design patterns and don't know when and how to use them

    – Familiarize yourself with the design patterns
    – Some design patterns are more useful than others. You use some patterns basically in every codebase, and some patterns you rarely use
    – Many design patterns help make code more modular and extensible and help avoid modifying existing code. Modifying existing code is always a risk. You can introduce bugs in already working code. These bugs are sometimes very subtle and hard to discover.
    – Learning the design patterns takes time. It can take years to master them, and mastery is only achieved by repeatedly using them in real-life codebases.

Mastering OOD and OOP is a life-long process. You are never 100% ready. The best way to become better in OOD and OOP, as in any other thing in your life, is practicing. I have been practicing OOD and OOP for 29 years and am still improving and learning something new regularly. Start a non-trivial (hobby/work) project and try to make the code 100% clean. Whenever you think you are ready with it, leave the project for some time and later come back to the project, and you might be surprised to notice that there are several things still needing improvement!

4.5: SOLID Principles

All five SOLID principles[5] are covered in this section. The *dependency inversion principle* is generalized as a *program against interfaces principle*. The five SOLID principles are the following:

---

[5] https://en.wikipedia.org/wiki/SOLID

- Single responsibility principle
- Open-closed principle
- Liskov's substitution principle
- Interface segregation principle
- Dependency inversion principle (Generalization: program against interfaces principle)

4.5.1: Single Responsibility Principle

Classes should have one responsibility: representing a thing or providing a single functionality. Functions should do one thing only.

Single responsibility should be at a particular abstraction level. A class or function can become too large if the abstraction level is too high. Then, split the class or function into multiple classes or functions on a lower level of abstraction. The single responsibility principle is akin to the separation of concerns[6] principle. In the *separation of concerns* principle, you divide a software component into distinct "sections". A section can be any size, e.g., a subdomain (package), module, class, or function.

Suppose you need to implement configuration reading and parsing for your software component. Reading and parsing are two different concerns and should be implemented in separate "sections", which in practice means implementing them in different class hierarchies: a ConfigReader interface with various implementation classes, like FileSystemConfigReader, DatabaseConfigReader, RestApiConfigReader, and a ConfigParser interface with various implementation classes like JsonConfigParser, YamlConfigParser, TomlConfigParser, XmlConfigParser, etc.

Single responsibility helps to achieve *high cohesion*, which is the target of good design (another target is *low coupling*, which we will discuss later). If your class or function has multiple distinct responsibilities (and reasons for change), then the class or function does not have high cohesion. Cohesion in a class, for example, means the level to which class methods belong together (i.e., change for the same reason). If you have a class that performs user authentication and configuration parsing, you have a class with two distinct responsibilities at the same abstraction level. That class is against the *single responsibility principle* and has lower cohesion because it has two reasons to change. One great sign of a class possibly having multiple responsibilities is that it can be hard to figure out a good name for the class, or if you could put an *and* word in the class name, like UserAuthenticatorAndConfigParser. *High cohesion* and *low coupling* are both part of the GRASP[7] principles.

Another great example of the separation of concerns principle is the *clean architecture principle* where you separate the microservice's business logic from the microservice's input and output. In this way, it is easy to make the microservice support various inputs and outputs without modifying the business logic "section". The clean architecture principle is discussed later in this chapter.

Let's get back to the single responsibility principle. Each class should have a single dedicated purpose. A class can represent a single thing, like a bank account (Account class) or an employee (Employee class), or provide a single functionality like parsing a configuration file (ConfigFileParser class) or calculating tax (TaxCalculator class).

We should not create a class representing a bank account and an employee. It is simply wrong. Of course, an employee can *have* a bank account. But that is a different thing. It is called object composition. In object

---

[6]https://en.wikipedia.org/wiki/Separation_of_concerns
[7]https://en.wikipedia.org/wiki/GRASP_(object-oriented_design)

composition, an `Employee` class object contains an `Account` class object. The `Employee` class still represents one thing: An employee (who can have a bank account). Object composition is covered in more detail later in this chapter.

At the function level, each function should perform a single task. The function name should describe what task the function performs, meaning each function name should contain a verb. The function name should not contain the word *and* because it can mean that the function is doing more than one thing or you haven't named the function at the correct abstraction level. You should not name a function according to the steps it performs (e.g., `doThisAndThatAndThenSomeThirdThing`) but instead, use wording on a higher level of abstraction.

When a class represents something, it can contain multiple methods. For example, an `Account` class can have methods like `deposit` and `withdraw`. It is still a single responsibility if these methods are simple enough and if there are not too many methods in the class.

Below is a real-life Java code example where the *and* word is used in the function name:

```
void deletePageAndAllReferences(Page page) {
  deletePage(page);
  registry.deleteReference(page.name);
  configKeys.deleteKey(page.name.makeKey());
}
```

In the above example, the function does two things: delete a page and remove all the references to that page. But if we look at the code inside the function, we can realize that it also does a third thing: deleting a page key from configuration keys. So should the function be named `deletePageAndAllReferencesAndConfigKey`? It does not sound reasonable. The problem with the function name is that it is at the same level of abstraction as the function statements. The function name should be at a higher level of abstraction than the statements inside the function.

How should we then name the function? I cannot say for sure because I don't know the context of the function. We could name the function just `delete`. This would tell the function caller that a page will be deleted. The caller does not need to know all the actions related to deleting a page. The caller just wants a page to be deleted. The function implementation should fulfill that request and do the needed housekeeping tasks, like removing all the references to the page being deleted and so on.

Let's consider another example with React Hooks[8]. React Hooks has a function named `useEffect`, which can be used to enqueue functions to be run after component rendering. The `useEffect` function can be used to run some code after the initial render (after the component mount), after every render, or conditionally. This is quite a responsibility for a single function. Also, the function's name does not reveal its purpose; it sounds abstract. The word *effect* comes from the fact that this function is used to enqueue other functions with side effects to be run. The term side effect[9] might be familiar to functional programmers. It indicates that a function is not pure because it causes side effects.

Below is an example of a React functional component:

---

[8] https://react.dev/reference/react/hooks
[9] https://en.wikipedia.org/wiki/Side_effect_(computer_science)

Figure 4.1. MyComponent.jsx

```
import { useEffect } from "react";

export default function MyComponent() {
  useEffect(() => {
    function startFetchData() {
      // ...
    }

    function subscribeToDataUpdates() {
      // ...
    }

    function unsubscribeFromDataUpdates() {
      // ...
    }

    startFetchData();
    subscribeToDataUpdates();
    return function cleanup() { unsubscribeFromDataUpdates() };
  }, []);

  // JSX to render
  return ...;
}
```

In the above example, the useEffect call makes calls to functions startFetchData and subscribeToDataUpdates to happen after the initial render because of the supplied empty array for dependencies (the second parameter to the useEffect function). The cleanup function returned from the function supplied to useEffect will be called before the effect will be rerun or when the component is unmounted and in this case, only on unmount because the effect will only run once after the initial render.

Let's imagine how we could improve the useEffect function. We could split the rather abstract-sounding useEffect method into multiple methods on a lower level of abstraction. The functionality related to mounting and unmounting could be separated into two different functions: afterMount and beforeUnmount. Then, we could change the above example to the following piece of code:

```
export default function MyComponent() {
  function startFetchData() {
    // ...
  }

  function subscribeToDataUpdate() {
    // ...
  }

  function unsubscribeFromDataUpdate() {
    // ...
  }

  afterMount(startFetchData, subscribeToDataUpdates);
  beforeUnmount(unsubscribeFromDataUpdates)

  // JSX to render
  return ...;
}
```

The above example is cleaner and much easier for a reader to understand than the original example. There are no multiple levels of nested functions. You don't have to return a function to be executed on component unmount, and you don't have to supply an array of dependencies.

Let's have another example of a React functional component:

```
import { useEffect, useState } from "react";

export default function ButtonClickCounter() {
  const [clickCount, setClickCount] = useState(0);

  useEffect(() => {
    function updateClickCountInDocumentTitle() {
      document.title = `Click count: ${clickCount}`;
    }

    updateClickCountInDocumentTitle();
  });
}
```

In the above example, the effect is called after every render (because no dependencies array is supplied for the useEffect function). Nothing in the above code clearly states what will be executed and when. We still use the same useEffect function, but now it behaves differently than in the previous example. It seems like the useEffect function is doing multiple things. How to solve this? Let's think hypothetically again. We could extract functionality from the useEffect function and introduce yet another new function called afterEveryRender that can be called when we want something to happen after every render:

```
export default function ButtonClickCounter() {
  const [clickCount, setClickCount] = useState(0);

  afterEveryRender(function updateClickCountInDocumentTitle() {
    document.title = `Click count: ${clickCount}`;
  });
}
```

The intentions of the above React functional component are pretty clear: It will update the click count in the document title after every render.

Let's optimize our example so that the click count update only happens if the click count has changed:

```
import { useEffect, useState } from "react";

export default function ButtonClickCounter() {
  const [clickCount, setClickCount] = useState(0);

  useEffect(() => {
    function updateClickCountInDocumentTitle() {
      document.title = `Click count: ${clickCount}`;
    }

    updateClickCountInDocumentTitle();
  }, [clickCount]);
}
```

Notice how clickCount is now added to the dependencies array of the useEffect function. This means the effect is not executed after every render but only when the click count is changed.

Let's imagine how we could improve the above example. We could once again extract functionality from the useEffect function and introduce a new function that handles dependencies: afterEveryRenderIfChanged. Our hypothetical example would now look like this:

```
export default function ButtonClickCounter() {
  const [clickCount, setClickCount] = useState(0);

  afterEveryRenderIfChanged(
    [clickCount],
    function updateClickCountInDocumentTitle() {
      document.title = `Click count: ${clickCount}`;
  });
}
```

Making functions do a single thing at an appropriate level of abstraction also helped make the code more readable. Regarding the original examples, a reader must look at the end of the useEffect function call to figure out in what circumstances the effect function will be called. Understanding and remembering the difference between a missing and empty dependencies array is cognitively challenging.

> **Good code is such that it does not make the code reader think. At best, the code should read like beautifully written prose.**

In the above example, we can read like prose: *after every render if changed click count, update click count in document title.*

One idea behind the single responsibility principle is that it enables software development using the *open-closed principle* described in the next section. When you follow the single responsibility principle and need to add functionality, you add it to a new class, which means you don't need to modify an existing class. You should avoid modifying existing code but extend it by adding new classes, each with a single responsibility. Modifying existing code always poses a risk of breaking something that works.

4.5.2: Open-Closed Principle

> *Software code should be open for extension and closed for modification. Functionality in existing classes should not be modified, but new classes that implement a new or existing interface or extend an existing class should be introduced.*

Any time you find yourself modifying some method in an existing class, you should consider if this principle could be followed and if the modification could be avoided. Every time you modify an existing class, you can introduce a bug in the working code. The idea of this principle is to leave the working code untouched so it does not get accidentally broken. When applying the *open-closed principle*, you create a kind of plugin architecture where new functionality is introduced as plugins (new implementation classes) that are plugged into existing code using, e.g., factories and dependency injection.

The *open-closed principle* is called *protected variations* in the GRASP principles. The protected variation principle protects existing classes from variations in other classes. For example, if you have a ConfigReader class that needs to parse the configuration, but the configuration format can vary. The ConfigReader class is protected from variations by introducing a ConfigParser interface for which various implementations can be provided. The ConfigReader depends only on the ConfigParser interface and does not need to know what particular parsing implementation is actually used. There could be a JsonConfigParser class for parsing the configuration in JSON format, and later, a YamlConfigParser class could be introduced to parse the configuration in YAML format. The JsonConfigParser class is also protected from variations because possible variations in configuration parsing can be introduced in new classes instead of modifying an existing class.

Let's have an example where this principle is *not* followed. We have the following existing and working Java code:

```
public interface Shape {
}


public class RectangleShape implements Shape {
  private int width;
  private int height;

  public RectangleShape(final int width, final int height) {
    this.width = width;
    this.height = height;
  }

  public int getWidth() {
    return width;
  }

  public int getHeight() {
    return height;
  }

  public void setWidth(final int newWidth) {
    width = newWidth;
  }

  public void setHeight(final int newHeight) {
    height = newHeight;
  }
}
```

Suppose we get an assignment to introduce support for square shapes. Let's try to modify the existing RectangleShape class, because a square is also a rectangle:

```
public class RectangleShape implements Shape {
  private int width;
  private int height;

  // Rectangle constructor
  public RectangleShape(final int width, final int height)  {
    this.width = width;
    this.height = height;
  }

  // Square constructor
  public RectangleShape(final int sideLength) {
    this.width = sideLength;
    this.height = sideLength;
  }

  public int getWidth() {
    return width;
  }

  public int getHeight() {
    return height;
  }

  public void setWidth(final int newWidth) {
    if (height == width) {
      //noinspection SuspiciousNameCombination
      height = newWidth;
    }

    width = newWidth;
  }

  public void setHeight(final int newHeight) {
    if (height == width) {
```

```
      //noinspection SuspiciousNameCombination
      width = newHeight;
    }

    height = newHeight;
  }
}
```

We needed to add a factory method for creating squares and modify two methods in the class. Everything works okay when we run tests. But we have introduced a subtle bug in the code: If we create a rectangle with an equal height and width, the rectangle becomes a square, which is probably not what is wanted. This is a bug that can be hard to find in unit tests. This example showed that modifying an existing class can be problematic. We modified an existing class and accidentally broke it.

A better solution to introduce support for square shapes is to use the *open-closed principle* and create a new class that implements the Shape interface. Then, we don't have to modify any existing class, and there is no risk of accidentally breaking something in the existing code. Below is the new SquareShape class:

```
public class SquareShape implements Shape {
  private int sideLength;

  public SquareShape(final int sideLength) {
    this.sideLength = sideLength;
  }

  public int getSideLength() {
    return sideLength;
  }

  public void setSideLength(final int newSideLength) {
    sideLength = newSideLength;
  }
}
```

An existing class can be safely modified by adding a new method in the following cases:

1) The added method is a pure function, i.e., it always returns the same value for the same arguments and does not have side effects, e.g., it does not modify the object's state.
2) The added method is read-only and tread-safe, i.e., it does not modify the object's state and accesses the object's state in a thread-safe manner in the case of multithreaded code. An example of a read-only method in the Shape class would be a method that calculates a shape's area.
3) Class is immutable, i.e., the added method (or any other method) cannot modify the object's state

There are a couple of cases where the modification of existing code is needed. One example is factories. When you introduce a new class, you need to modify the related factory to be able to create an instance of that new class. For example, if we had a ShapeFactory class, we would need to modify it to support the creation of SquareShape objects. Fortunately, this modification is simple: Just add a new case branch. The probability of introducing a bug is very low. Factories are discussed later in this chapter.

Another case is adding a new enum constant. You typically need to modify existing code to handle the new enum constant. If you forget to add the handling of the new enum constant somewhere in the existing code, a bug will typically arise. For this reason, You should always safeguard switch-case statements with a *default* case that throws an exception and safeguard if/else if structures with an else branch that throws an exception. You can also enable your static code analysis tool to report an issue if a switch statement's *default* case or an else branch is missing from an if/else if structure. Also, some static code analysis tools can report an issue if you miss handling an enum constant in a match-case statement.

Here is an example of safeguarding an if/else if structure in Java:

```
public enum FilterType {
  INCLUDE,
  EXCLUDE
}


public interface Filter {
  boolean isFilteredOut(...);
}


public class FilterImpl implements Filter {
  private final FilterType filterType;

  public FilterImpl(final FilterType filterType, ...) {
    this.filterType = filterType;
    // ...
  }

  public boolean isFilteredOut(...) {
    if (filterType == FilterType.INCLUDE) {
      // ...
    } else if (filterType == FilterType.EXCLUDE) {
      // ..
    } else {
      // Safeguarding
      throw new IllegalArgumentException("Invalid filter type");
    }
  }
}
```

In TypeScript, safeguarding might be needed for union types also:

```
type FilterType = 'include' | 'exclude';

if (filterType === 'include') {
  // ...
} else if (filterType === 'exclude') {
  // ...
} else {
  // Safeguarding
  throw new Error("Invalid filter type");
}
```

In the future, if a new literal is added to the FilterType type and you forget to update the if-statement, you get an exception thrown instead of silently passing through the if-statement without any action.

We can notice from the above examples that if/else if structures could be avoided with a better object-oriented design. For instance, we could create a Filter interface and two separate classes, IncludeFilter and ExcludeFilter. The classes implement the Filter interface. Using object-oriented design allows us to eliminate the FilterType enum and the if/else if structure. This is known as the *replace conditionals with polymorphism* refactoring technique. Refactoring is discussed more in the next chapter. Below is the above example refactored to be more object-oriented:

```
public interface Filter {
  boolean isFilteredOut(...);
}


public class IncludeFilter implements Filter {

  // ...

  public boolean isFilteredOut(...) {
    // ...
  }
}


public class ExcludeFilter implements Filter {

  // ...

  public boolean isFilteredOut(...) {
    // ...
  }
}
```

4.5.3: Liskov's Substitution Principle

Objects of a superclass should be replaceable with objects of its subclasses without breaking the application. I.e., objects of subclasses behave the same way as the objects of the superclass.

Following *Liskov's substitution principle* guarantees semantic interoperability of types in a type hierarchy.

Let's have an example with a Java RectangleShape class and a derived SquareShape class:

```
public interface Shape {
  void draw();
}

public class RectangleShape implements Shape {
  private int width;
  private int height;

  public RectangleShape(final int width, final int height) {
    this.width = width;
    this.height = height;
  }

  public void draw() {
    // ...
  }

  public int getWidth() {
    return this.width;
  }

  public int getHeight() {
    return this.height;
  }

  public void setWidth(final int newWidth) {
    width = newWidth;
  }
```

```
  public void setHeight(final int newHeight) {
    height = newHeight;
  }
}


public class SquareShape extends RectangleShape {
  public SquareShape(final int sideLength) {
    super(sideLength, sideLength);
  }

  public void setWidth(final int newWidth) {
    super.setWidth(newWidth);
    //noinspection SuspiciousNameCombination
    super.setHeight(newWidth);
  }

  public void setHeight(final int newHeight) {
    //noinspection SuspiciousNameCombination
    super.setWidth(newHeight);
    super.setHeight(newHeight);
  }
}
```

The above example does not follow Liskov's substitution principle because you cannot set a square's width and height separately. This means that a square is not a rectangle from an object-oriented point of view. Of course, mathematically, a square is a rectangle. But when considering the above public API of the RectangleShape class, we can conclude that a square is not a rectangle because a square cannot fully implement the API of the RectangleShape class. We cannot substitute a square object for a rectangle object. What we need to do is to implement the SquareShape class without deriving from the RectangleShape class:

```
public class SquareShape implements Shape {
  private int sideLength;

  public SquareShape(final int sideLength) {
    this.sideLength = sideLength;
  }

  public void draw() {
    // ...
  }

  public int getSideLength() {
    return this.sideLength;
  }

  public void setSideLength(final int newSideLength) {
    sideLength = newSideLength;
  }
}
```

Let's have another example where we have the following two Java classes:

```java
public class Dog {
  public void bark() {
    // ...
  }

  public void walk() {
    // ...
  }

  public void eat() {
    // ...
  }

  // ...
}


public class RoboticDog extends Dog {
  public void bark() {
    // Use super class method
    // get_sound()
  }

  public void walk() {
    // Use super class method
    // get_speed()
  }

  public void eat() {
    // Robotic dog cannot eat
    throw new UnsupportedOperationException();
  }
}
```

The above example does not follow *Liskov's substitution principle*, because a RoboticDog object cannot be used in place of a Dog object. The RoboticDog object throws an exception if you call the eat method. There are two solutions to the problem:

1) Abstract away
2) Composition over inheritance

Let's abstract the eat method to something common to both a dog and a robotic dog. We could change the eat method to a recharge method:

```java
public class Dog {
  public void bark() {
    // ...
  }

  public void walk() {
    // ...
  }

  public void recharge() {
    // Eat
  }

  // ...
}


public class RoboticDog extends Dog {
  public void bark() {
    // Use super class method
```

```
    // get_sound()
  }

  public void walk() {
    // Use super class method
    // get_speed()
  }

  public void recharge() {
    // Charge the robot
  }
}
```

The other solution is to use composition over inheritance:

```
public class RoboticDog {
  private final Dog dog;

  public RoboticDog(final Dog dog) {
      this.dog = dog;
  }

  public void bark() {
    // Use dog.get_sound()
  }

  public void walk() {
    // Use dog.get_speed()
  }
}
```

Liskov's substitution principle requires the following:

- A subclass must implement the superclass API and retain (or, in some cases, replace) the functionality of the superclass.
- A superclass should not have protected attributes because it allows subclasses to modify the state of the superclass, which can lead to incorrect behavior in the superclass.

Below is a Java example where a subclass extends the behavior of a superclass in the do_something method. The functionality of the superclass is retained in the subclass making a subclass object substitutable for a superclass object.

```
public class SuperClass {
  // ...

  public void doSomething() {
    // ...
  }
}
public class SubClass extends SuperClass {
  // ...

  public void doSomething() {
    super.doSomething();

    // Some additional behaviour...
  }
}
```

Let's have a concrete example of using the above strategy. We have the following CircleShape class defined:

```
public interface Shape {
  void draw();
}


public class CircleShape implements Shape {
  public void draw() {
    // draw the circle stroke
  }
}
```

Next, we introduce a class for filled circles:

```
public class FilledCircleShape extends CircleShape {
  public void draw() {
    super.draw(); // draws the circle stroke
    // Fill the circle
  }
}
```

The FilledCircleShape class fulfills the requirements of Liskov's substitution principle. We can use an instance of the FilledCircleShape class everywhere where an instance of the CircleShape class is wanted. The FilledCircleShape class does all that the CircleShape class does, plus adds some behavior (= fills the circle).

You can also completely replace the superclass functionality in a subclass:

Figure 4.2. ReverseArrayList.java

```
public class ReverseArrayList<T> extends ArrayList<T>
{
  @Override
  public Iterator<T> iterator() {
    return new ReverseListIterator<>(this);
  }
}
```

The above subclass implements the superclass API and retains its behavior: The iterator method still returns an iterator. It just returns a different iterator compared to the superclass.

4.5.4: Interface Segregation and Multiple Inheritance Principle

No class should depend on other classes' methods it does not use.

When following the *interface segregation principle*, you split larger interfaces into smaller interfaces so that no one should depend on something it does not use. Let's have an example where we have the following classes:

```
public interface InterfaceA {
  void method1();
  void method2();
  void method3();
  void method4();
  void method5();
}


public class ClassB {
  private final InterfaceA someAttribute;

  // Depends on InterfaceA but
  // uses only the following methods:
  // method1, method2, method3
}


public class ClassC {
  private final InterfaceA someAttribute;

  // Depends on InterfaceA and
  // uses all methods from the InterfaceA
}
```

The ClassB depends on method4 and method5 even if it does not use them. We need to apply the *interface segregation principle* and segregate a smaller interface from the InterfaceA:

```
public interface InterfaceA1 {
  void method1();
  void method2();
  void method3();
}


public interface InterfaceA extends InterfaceA1 {
  void method4();
  void method5();
}


public class ClassB() {
  private final InterfaceA1 someAttribute;

  // Depends on InterfaceA1
  // and uses all methods of it
}


public class ClassC() {
  private final InterfaceA someAttribute;

  // Depends on InterfaceA
  // and uses all methods of it
}
```

Interface segregation principle is a way to reduce coupling in your software component. A software component's design is considered the most optimal when it has *low coupling* between classes and *high cohesion* in classes. In the above example, the ClassB only depends on the three methods provided by the InterfaceA1 interface, not all the five methods provided by the InterfaceA interface.

Next, we will have examples of an extreme case of the *interface segregation principle*: Segregating larger interfaces to microinterfaces with a single capability/behavior and constructing larger interfaces by inheriting multiple microinterfaces. Let's have a Java example with several automobile classes:

```
public interface Automobile {
  void drive(final Location start, final Location destination);
  void carryCargo(final double volumeInCubicMeters, final double weightInKgs);
}


public class PassengerCar implements Automobile {
  // Implement drive and carryCargo
}


public class Van implements Automobile {
  // Implement drive and carryCargo
}


public class Truck implements Automobile {
  // Implement drive and carryCargo
}


public interface ExcavatingAutomobile extends Automobile {
  void excavate(...);
}


public class Excavator implements ExcavatingAutomobile {
  // Implement drive, carryCargo and excavate
}
```

Notice how the Automobile interface has two methods declared. This can limit our software if we later want to introduce other vehicles that could be just driven but unable to carry cargo. We should segregate two microinterfaces from the Automobile interface in an early phase. A microinterface defines a single capability or behavior. After segregation, we will have the following two microinterfaces:

```
public interface Drivable {
  void drive(final Location start, final Location destination);
}


public interface CargoCarrying {
  void carryCargo(final double volumeInCubicMeters, final double weightInKgs);
}
```

Now that we have two interfaces, we can use these interfaces separately in our codebase. For example, we can have a list of drivable objects or a list of objects that can carry cargo. We still want to have an interface for automobiles, though. We can use *interface multiple inheritance* to redefine the Automobile interface to extend the two microinterfaces:

```
public interface Automobile extends Drivable, CargoCarrying {
}
```

If we look at the ExcavatingAutomobile interface, we can notice that it extends the Automobile interface and adds excavating behavior. Once again, we have a problem if we want an excavating machine that is not auto-mobile. The excavating behavior should be segregated into its own microinterface:

```
public interface Excavating {
  void excavate(...);
}
```

We can once again use the interface multiple inheritance to redefine the `ExcavatingAutomobile` interface as follows:

```
public interface ExcavatingAutomobile
                     extends Excavating, Automobile {
}
```

The `ExcavatingAutomobile` interface now extends three microinterfaces: `Excavating`, `Drivable`, and `CargoCarrying`. Where-ever you need an excavating, drivable, or cargo-carrying object in your codebase, you can use an instance of the `Excavator` class there.

Let's have another example with a generic collection interface using TypeScript. We should be able to traverse a collection and also be able to compare two collections for equality. First, we define a generic `Iterator` interface for iterators. It has two methods, as described below:

```
interface MyIterator<T> {
  hasNextElement(): boolean;
  getNextElement(): T;
}
```

Next, we can define the collection interface:

```
interface Collection<T> {
  createIterator(): MyIterator<T>;
  equals(anotherCollection: Collection<T>): boolean;
}
```

`Collection` is an interface with two unrelated methods. Let's segregate those methods into two microinterfaces: `Iterable` and `Equatable`. The `Iterable` interface is for objects that you can iterate over. It has one method for creating new iterators. The `Equatable` interface's `equals` method is more generic than the `equals` method in the above `Collection` interface. You can equate an `Equatable[T]` object with another object of type `T`:

```
interface MyIterable<T> {
  createIterator(): MyIterator<T>;
}
```

```
interface Equatable<T> {
  equals(anotherObject: T): boolean;
}
```

We can use interface multiple inheritance to redefine the `Collection` interface as follows:

```
interface Collection<T> extends MyIterable<T>,
                     Equatable<Collection<T>> {
}
```

We can implement the `equals` method by iterating elements in two collections and checking if the elements are equal:

```
abstract class AbstractCollection<T> implements Collection<T> {
  abstract createIterator(): MyIterator<T>;

  equals(anotherCollection: Collection<T>): boolean {
    const iterator = this.createIterator();
    const anotherIterator = anotherCollection.createIterator();
    let collectionsAreEqual = this.areEqual(iterator, anotherIterator);

    if (anotherIterator.hasNextElement()) {
      collectionsAreEqual = false;
    }

    return collectionsAreEqual;
  }

  private areEqual(
    iterator: MyIterator<T>,
    anotherIterator: MyIterator<T>
  ): boolean {
    while (iterator.hasNextElement()) {
      if (anotherIterator.hasNextElement()) {
        if (iterator.getNextElement() !== anotherIterator.getNextElement()) {
         return false;
        }
      } else {
        return false;
      }
    }

    return true;
  }
}
```

Collections can also be compared. Let's introduce support for such collections. First, we define a generic `Comparable` interface for comparing an object with another object:

```
type ComparisonResult = 'isLessThan' | 'areEqual' | 'isGreaterThan' | 'unspecified';

interface Comparable<T> {
  compareTo(anotherObject: T): ComparisonResult;
}
```

Now, we can introduce a comparable collection interface that allows comparing two collections of the same type:

```
interface ComparableCollection<T>
         extends Comparable<Collection<T>>, Collection<T> {
}
```

Let's define a generic sorting algorithm for collections whose elements are comparable:

```
function sort<T, U extends Comparable<T>, V extends Collection<U>>(
  collection: V
): V {
  // ...
}
```

Let's create two interfaces, `Inserting` and `InsertingIterable` for classes whose instances elements can be inserted into:

```
interface Inserting<T> {
  insert(element: T): void;
}


interface InsertingIterable<T> extends Inserting<T>,
                                       MyIterable<T> {
}
```

Let's redefine the `Collection` interface to extend the `InsertingIterable` interface because a collection is iterable, and you can insert elements into a collection.

```
interface Collection<T> extends InsertingIterable<T> {
}
```

Next, we introduce two generic algorithms for collections: `map` and `filter`. We can realize that those algorithms work with more abstract objects than collections. We benefit from interface segregation because instead of the `Collection<T>` interface, we can use the `MyIterable<T>` and `InsertingIterable<T>` interfaces to create generic `map` and `filter` algorithms. Later, it is possible to introduce some additional non-collection iterable objects that can also utilize the algorithms. Below is the implementation of the `map` and `filter` functions:

```
function map<T, U>(
  source: MyIterable<T>,
  mapped: (sourceElement: T) => U,
  destination: InsertingIterable<U>
): InsertingIterable<U> {
  const sourceIterator = source.createIterator();

  while(sourceIterator.hasNextElement()) {
    const sourceElement = sourceIterator.getNextElement();
    destination.insert(mapped(sourceElement));
  }

  return destination;
}


function filter<T>(
  source: MyIterable<T>,
  isIncluded: (sourceElement: T) => boolean,
  destination: InsertingIterable<T>
): InsertingIterable<T> {
  const sourceIterator = source.createIterator();

  while (sourceIterator.hasNextElement()) {
    const sourceElement = sourceIterator.getNextElement();

    if (isIncluded(sourceElement)) {
      destination.insert(sourceElement);
    }
  }

  return destination;
}
```

Let's define the following concrete collection classes:

```
class List<T> implements Collection<T> {
  constructor(...args: T[]) {
    // ...
  }

  // ...
}

class Stack<T> implements Collection<T> {
  // ...
}

class MySet<T> implements Collection<T> {
  // ...
}
```

Now, we can use the `map` and `filter` algorithms with the above-defined collection classes:

```
const numbers = new List<number>(1, 2, 3, 3, 3, 50, 60);
const isLessThan10 = (nbr: number) => nbr < 10;

const uniqueLessThan10Numbers =
  filter(numbers, isLessThan10, new MySet());

const doubled = (nbr: number) => 2 * nbr;
const stackOfDoubledNumbers = map(numbers, doubled, new Stack());
```

Let's create an asynchronous version of the `map` algorithm:

```
interface MaybeCloseable {
  tryClose(): Promise<void>;
}


interface MaybeInserting<T> {
  tryInsert(value: T): Promise<void>;
}


interface MaybeCloseableInserting<T>
            extends MaybeCloseable, MaybeInserting<T> {
}


class MapError extends Error {
  // ...
}


async function tryMap<T, U>(
  source: MyIterable<T>,
  mapped: (sourceElement: T) => U,
  destination: MaybeCloseableInserting<U>
): Promise<void> {
  const sourceIterator = source.createIterator();

  try {
    while (sourceIterator.hasNextElement()) {
      const sourceElement = sourceIterator.getNextElement();
      await destination.tryInsert(mapped(sourceElement));
    }

    await destination.tryClose();
  } catch (error: any) {
    throw new MapError(error.message);
  }
}
```

Let's create a `FileLineInserter` class that implements the `MaybeCloseableInserting` interface:

```
const fs = require('fs');

class FileLineInserter<T extends { toString(): string }>
        implements MaybeCloseableInserting<T> {
  private writeStream: FS.WriteStream;

  constructor(private readonly filePathName: string) {
    this.writeStream =
      fs.createWriteStream(this.filePathName, { flags: 'a' });
  }

  async tryInsert(value: T): Promise<void> {
    try {
      const writePromise = new Promise((resolve, reject) => {
        const line = value.toString() + '\n';

        this.writeStream.write(line, (error: any) => {
          if (error) {
            reject(error);
          } else {
            resolve(undefined);
          }
        });
      });

      await writePromise;
    } catch (error: any) {
      throw new Error(error.message);
    }
  }

  tryClose(): Promise<void> {
    this.writeStream.close();
    return Promise.resolve();
  }
}
```

Let's use the above-defined `try_map` algorithm and the `FileLineInserter` class to write doubled numbers (one number per line) to a file named *file.txt*:

```
const numbers = new List<number>(1, 2, 3, 2, 1, 50, 60);
const doubled = (nbr: number) => 2 * nbr;

try {
  await tryMap(numbers, doubled, new FileLineInserter('file.txt'));
} catch(error: any) { // error will be always MapError type.
  console.log(error.message);
}
```

Python's standard library utilizes interface segregation and multiple interface inheritance in an exemplary way. For example, the Python standard library defines the abstract base classes (or interfaces) listed below that implement a single method only. I.e., they are microinterfaces.

Abstract base class	Method
Container	__contains__
Hashable	__hash__
Iterable	__iter__
Sized	__len__
Callable	__call__
Awaitable	__await__
AsyncIterable	__aiter__

Python standard library also contains the below abstract base classes that inherit from multiple (micro)interfaces:

Abstract base class	Inherits from
Collection	Sized, Iterable, Container
Sequence	Collection, Reversible

4.5.5: Program Against Interfaces Principle (a.k.a. Generalized Dependency Inversion Principle)

Do not write programs where internal dependencies are concrete object types—instead, program against interfaces. Exceptions to this rule are data classes with no behavior (not counting simple getters/setters) and utility classes.

An interface defines an abstract base type. Various implementations of the interface can be introduced. When you want to change the behavior of a program, you create a new class that implements an interface and then use an instance of that class. In this way, you can practice the *open-closed principle*. You can think of this principle as a prerequisite for using the *open-closed principle* effectively.

You should always program against an interface when the implementation can vary. On the other hand, you don't have to program against an interface when the implementation is fixed. This is usually the case with utility classes. For example, you can have a method for parsing an integer from a string. That is a method where implementation is fixed, and the method can be put as a static method in a final utility class:

```
// Utility class is declared final
// You should not be able to extend the utility class,
// because the method implementations are not expected to change
public final class ParseUtils {
  private ParseUtils() {
    // Utility class with static methods only
    // should have a private constructor
    // You should not be able to make instances of
    // the utility class
  }

  static int parseInt(final String string) {
    // ...
  }
```

```
    // Possible other methods ...
}
```

The implementation of the above method is not expected to change in the future. We are not expecting to have different implementations of parsing an integer. But if we have a class for performing application configuration parsing, that functionality *can* change, and the *program against interfaces principle* should be applied. We should create a ConfigParser interface and then provide one or more implementations in various implementation classes, like XyzFormatConfigParser, JsonConfigParser, or YamlConfigParser.

The *program against interfaces principle* was presented by the *Gang of Four* in their book *Design Patterns* and can be seen as a generalization of the *dependency inversion principle* from the SOLID principles:

> The *dependency inversion principle* is a methodology for loosely coupling software classes. When following the principle, the conventional dependency relationships from high-level classes to low-level classes are reversed, making the high-level classes independent of the low-level implementation details.

The *dependency inversion principle* states:

1) High-level classes should not import anything from low-level classes
2) Abstractions (= interfaces) should not depend on concrete implementations (classes)
3) Concrete implementations (classes) should depend on abstractions (= interfaces)

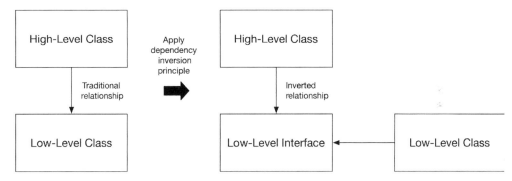

Figure 4.3. Dependency Inversion Principle

Dependency inversion principle is the primary way to reduce coupling in a software component's code (the other way being the *interface segregation principle*). When you use the principle, your classes are not coupled to any concrete implementation but to an interface promising its implementors to offer certain functionality. For example, if your software component needs a collection to store and retrieve items and occasionally get the item count, you should define an interface for the wanted functionality:

```
public interface Collection<T> {
  void add(final T item);
  void remove(final T item);
  long size();
}
```

Being coupled to the above Collection interface is much weaker and less coupling than being coupled to a concrete implementation like a stack or linked list.

An interface is always an abstract type and cannot be instantiated. Below is an example of an interface:

```
public interface Shape {
  void draw();
  double calculateArea();
}
```

The name of an interface describes something abstract, which you cannot create an object of. In the above example, Shape is something abstract. You cannot create an instance of Shape and then draw it or calculate its area because you don't know what shape it is. But when a class implements an interface, a concrete object of the class representing the interface can be created. Below is an example of three different classes that implement the Shape interface:

```
public class CircleShape implements Shape {
  private final int radius;

  public CircleShape(final int radius) {
    this.radius = radius;
  }

  public void draw() {
    // ...
  }

  public double calculateArea() {
    return Math.PI * radius * radius;
  }
}


public class RectangleShape implements Shape {
  private final int width;
  private final int height;

  public RectangleShape(final int width, final int height) {
    this.width = width;
    this.height = height;
  }

  public void draw() {
    // ...
  }

  public double calculateArea() {
    return width * height;
  }
}


public class SquareShape extends RectangleShape {
  public SquareShape(final int sideLength) {
    super(sideLength, sideLength);
  }
}
```

We should program against the Shape interface when using shapes in code. In the below example, we make a high-level class Canvas dependent on the Shape interface, not on any of the low-level classes (CircleShape, RectangleShape or SquareShape). Now, the high-level Canvas class and all the low-level shape classes depend on abstraction only, the Shape interface. We can also notice that the high-level class Canvas does not import anything from the low-level classes. Also, the abstraction Shape does not depend on concrete implementations (classes).

```java
public class Canvas {
  private final List<Shape> shapes = new ArrayList<>(10);

  public void add(final Shape shape) {
    shapes.add(shape);
  }

  public void drawShapes() {
    for(final var shape : shapes) {
      shape.draw();
    }
  }
}
```

A Canvas object can contain any shape and draw any shape. It can handle any of the currently defined concrete shapes and any new ones defined in the future.

If you did not program against interfaces and did not use the dependency inversion principle, your Canvas class would look like the following:

```java
public class Circle {
  public void draw() {
    // ...
  }
}


public class Rectangle {
  public void draw() {
    // ...
  }
}


public class Square {
  public void draw() {
    // ...
  }
}


public class Canvas {
  private final List<Circle> circles = new ArrayList<>(10);
  private final List<Rectangle> rectangles = new ArrayList<>(10);
  private final List<Square> squares = new ArrayList<>(10);

  public void addCircle(final Circle circle) {
    circles.add(circle);
  }

  public void addRectangle(final Rectangle rectangle) {
    rectangles.add(rectangle);
  }

  public void addSquare(final Square square) {
    squares.add(square);
  }
```

```
public void drawShapes() {
  for(final var circle : circles) {
    circle.draw();
  }

  for(final var rectangle : rectangles) {
    rectangle.draw();
  }

  for(final var square : squares) {
    square.draw();
  }
}
}
```

The above high-level `Canvas` class is coupled with all the low-level classes (`Circle`, `Rectangle`, and `Square`). The type annotations in the `Canvas` class must be modified if a new shape type is needed. If something changes in the public API of any low-level class, the `Canvas` class needs to be modified accordingly. In the above example, we implicitly specify the interface for the `draw` method: it does not take arguments and returns nothing. Relying on implicit interfaces is not a good solution, especially in non-trivial applications. It is better to program against interfaces and make interfaces explicit.

Let's have another example. If you have read books or articles about object-oriented design, you may have encountered something similar as is presented in the below example:

```
public class Dog {
  public void walk() {
    // ...
  }

  public void bark() {
    // ...
  }
}


public class Fish {
  public void swim() {
    // ...
  }
}


public class Bird {
  public void fly() {
    // ...
  }

  public void sing() {
    // ...
  }
}
```

Three concrete implementations are defined above, but no interface is defined. Let's say we are making a game that has different animals. The first thing to do when coding the game is to remember to program against interfaces and thus introduce an `Animal` interface that we can use as an abstract base type. Let's try to create the `Animal` interface based on the above concrete implementations:

```
public interface Animal {
  void walk();
  void bark();
  void swim();
  void fly();
  void sing();
}

public class Dog implements Animal {
  public void walk() {
    // ...
  }

  public void bark() {
    // ...
  }

  public void swim() {
    throw new UnsupportedOperationException();
  }

  public void fly() {
    throw new UnsupportedOperationException();
  }

  public void sing() {
    throw new UnsupportedOperationException();
  }
}


// Fish class ...
// Bird class ...
```

The above approach is wrong. We declare that the Dog class implements the Animal interface, but it does not do that. It implements only methods walk and bark while other methods throw an exception. We should be able to supply any concrete animal implementation where an animal is required. But it is impossible because if we have a Dog object, we cannot safely call swim, fly, or sing methods because they will always throw an exception.

The problem is that we defined the concrete classes before defining the interface. That approach is wrong. We should specify the interface first and then the concrete implementations. What we did above was the other way around.

When defining an interface, we should remember that we are defining an abstract base type, so we must think in abstract terms. We must consider what we want the animals to do in the game. If we look at the methods walk, fly, and swim, they are all concrete actions. But what is the abstract action common to these three concrete actions? It is *move*. Walking, flying, and swimming are all ways of moving. Similarly, if we look at the bark and sing methods, they are also concrete actions. What is the abstract action common to these two concrete actions? It is *make sound*. And barking and singing are both ways to make a sound. When we use these abstract actions, our Animal interface becomes the following:

```
public interface Animal {
  void move();
  void makeSound();
}
```

We can now redefine the animal classes to implement the new Animal interface:

```
public class Dog implements Animal {
  public void move() {
    // walk
  }

  public void makeSound() {
    // bark
  }
}


public class Fish implements Animal {
  public void move() {
    // swim
  }

  public void makeSound() {
    // Intentionally no operation
    // (Fishes typically don't make sounds)
  }
}


public class Bird implements Animal {
  public void move() {
    // fly
  }

  public void makeSound() {
    // sing
  }
}
```

Now, we have the correct object-oriented design and can program against the Animal interface. We can call the move method when we want an animal to move and the make_sound method when we want an animal to make a sound.

We can easily enhance our design after realizing that some birds don't fly at all. We can introduce two different implementations:

```
public abstract class AbstractBird implements Animal {
  public abstract void move();

  public void makeSound() {
    // sing
  }
}


public class FlyingBird extends AbstractBird {
  public void move() {
    // fly
  }
}


public class NonFlyingBird extends AbstractBird {
  public void move() {
    // walk
  }
}
```

We might also later realize that not all birds sing but make different sounds. Ducks quack, for example. Instead of using inheritance as was done above, an even better alternative is to use *object composition*. We compose the Bird class of behavioral classes for moving and making sounds. This is called the *strategy pattern*, and is discussed later in this chapter. We can give different moving and sound-making strategies for bird objects upon construction.

```java
public interface Mover {
  void move();
}


public interface SoundMaker {
  void makeSound();
}


public class Bird implements Animal {
  private final Mover mover;
  private final SoundMaker soundMaker;

  public Bird(
    final Mover mover,
    final SoundMaker soundMaker
  ) {
    this.mover = mover;
    this.soundMaker = soundMaker;
  }

  public void move() {
    mover.move();
  }

  public void makeSound() {
    soundMaker.makeSound();
  }
}
```

I don't advocate adding a design pattern name to code entity names, but for demonstration purposes, we could make an exception here, and I can show how the code would look when making the *strategy pattern* explicit:

```java
public interface MovingStrategy {
  void move();
}


public interface SoundMakingStrategy {
  void makeSound();
}


public class Bird implements Animal {
  private final MovingStrategy movingStrategy;
  private final SoundMakingStrategy soundMakingStrategy;

  public Bird(
    final MovingStrategy movingStrategy,
    final SoundMakingStrategy soundMakingStrategy
  ) {
    this.movingStrategy = movingStrategy;
    this.soundMakingStrategy = soundMakingStrategy;
  }

  public void move() {
    movingStrategy.move();
  }

  public void makeSound() {
    soundMakingStrategy.makeSound();
```

```
    }
}
```

As you can see above, adding the design pattern name made many names longer without adding significant value. We should keep names as short as possible to enhance readability.

Now, we can create birds with various behaviors for moving and making sounds. We can use the *factory pattern* to create different birds. The *factory pattern* is described in more detail later in this chapter. Let's introduce three different moving and sound-making behaviors and a factory to make three kinds of birds: goldfinches, ostriches, and domestic ducks.

```java
public class Flyer implements Mover {
  public void move() {
    // fly
  }
}


public class Runner implements Mover {
  public void move() {
    // run
  }
}


public class Walker implements Mover {
  public void move() {
    // walk
  }
}


public class GoldfinchSoundMaker implements SoundMaker {
  public void makeSound() {
    // Sing goldfinch specific songs
  }
}


public class OstrichSoundMaker implements SoundMaker {
  public void makeSound() {
    // Make ostrich specific sounds like whistles,
    // hoots, hisses, growls, and deep booming growls
    // that sound like the roar of a lion
  }
}


public class Quacker implements SoundMaker {
  public void makeSound() {
    // quack
  }
}


public enum BirdType {
  GOLDFINCH,
  OSTRICH,
  DOMESTIC_DUCK
}


public class BirdFactory {
  public Bird createBird(final BirdType birdType) {
    return switch(birdType) {
      case GOLDFINCH ->
```

```
      new Bird(new Flyer(),
             new GoldfinchSoundMaker());

    case OSTRICH ->
      new Bird(new Runner(),
             new OstrichSoundMaker());

    case DOMESTIC_DUCK ->
      new Bird(new Walker(),
             new Quacker());

    default ->
      throw new IllegalArgumentException("Unsupported type");
    };
  }
}
```

4.6: Clean Architecture Principle

*The clean architecture promotes object-oriented design with the separation of con-
cerns achieved by dividing software into layers using the dependency inversion
principle (programming against interfaces).*

Clean architecture focuses on creating a core (or the model) that is devoid of technological concerns, pushing
those to an outer input/output interface adaptation layer that includes, e.g., the persistence mechanism
(an output interface adapter) and controller (an input interface adapter), which can be considered as
technological details that have nothing to do with the core. The benefit of this approach is that you can
modify technological details without affecting the core. Service's input comes from its clients, and output
is anything external the service needs to access to fulfill requests from the input. Input interface adapters
are sometimes called the *presentation layer* that represents the entry point to the service from outside. The
output interface adapters are sometimes called the *infrastructure layer* that represents any external concerns
related to the service.

Clean architecture focuses on designing a single service conducting OOD in a particular fashion.

Clean architecture is a relatively simple concept. If you have used the single responsibility principle, divided
a service into layers, and been programming against interfaces (using the dependency inversion principle),
you may have applied the clean architecture without knowing it. The clean architecture principle also
employs the *adapter pattern* from design patterns discussed later in this chapter. The adapter pattern is used
in input and output interface adapters. We can create separate adapter classes for various input sources and
output destinations. Many resources (books, websites, etc.) explain the clean architecture in rather complex
terms.

If you are interested, there are similar concepts to *clean architecture* called hexagonal architecture[10] (or
ports and adapters architecture) and *onion architecture*. They have the same basic idea of separating
technology-related code from the business logic code, making it easy to change technological aspects
of the software without modifications to the business logic part. They can use different terms, and in

hexagonal architecture, you have co-centric hexagons instead of circles like in clean architecture, but the basic idea in all of them is the same.

Clean architecture comes with the following benefits for the service:

- Not tied to any single framework
- Not tied to any single API technology like REST or GraphQL
- Unit testable
- Not tied to a specific client (works with web, desktop, console, and mobile clients)
- Not tied to a specific database or other storage technology
- Not dependent on any specific external service implementation

A clean architecture for an API service consists of the following layers:

- Input and output interface adapters or the presentation and infrastructure layer (e.g., controllers, repositories, etc.)
- Application services or use cases (i.e., the features the service exposes outside)
- Domain model (a.k.a business logic) that consist of domain services and entities

Use cases and the domain model form the service's *core* or *model*. The outermost use case layer usually contains application service classes implementing the use cases. I use the terms application service(s) and use cases interchangeably. They both mean the client-facing features that a client can access through controller interface(s). For example, one method in an application service class implements one use case. If you are doing CQRS, you can divide the use case layer to commands and queries. The use case layer orchestrates operations on domain entities utilizing domain services and output interfaces, like repositories. The use case layer is devoid of business logic, but contains only procedural orchestration code. The application service classes serve as a facade to the domain model. The application service classes (i.e., the facade) are meant to be used by the *input interface adapters*, i.e., the *controllers*. A controller is a common term used to describe an input interface adapter. The controller should delegate to application service classes. It coordinates and controls the activity but should not do much work itself. *Controller* is a pattern from GRASP principles. Similarly, a repository is a common term for an output interface adapter that stores and retrieves information, usually in/from persistent storage.

---

[10]https://en.wikipedia.org/wiki/Hexagonal_architecture_(software)

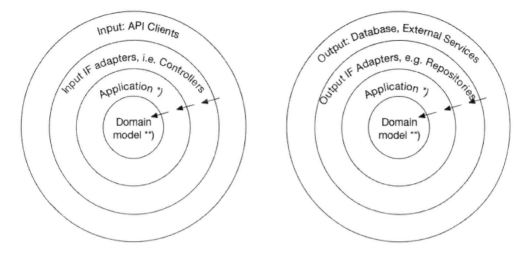

*) Use cases (or application services)

**) Domain objects (entities, value objects
and domain services

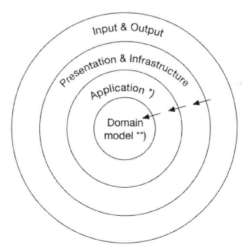

Figure 4.4. Clean Architecture

The direction of dependencies in the above diagrams is shown with arrows. We can see that the service's clients depend on the input interface adapter or *controller* we create. The controller depends on the use cases. The use case layer depends on (business) entities. The purpose of the use case layer is to orchestrate operations on the (business) entities. In the above figure, the parts of software that tend to change most often are located at the outer layers (e.g., controller technology like REST, GraphQL, and database) The most stable part of the software is located at the center (entities).

Let's have an example of an entity: a bank account. We know it is something that doesn't change often. It has a couple of key attributes: owner, account number, interest rate, and balance (and probably some other attributes), but what a bank account is or does has remained the same for tens of years. However, we cannot say the same for API or database technologies. Those are things that change at a much faster pace compared to bank accounts. Because of the direction of dependencies, changes in the outer layers do not affect the inner layers. The clean architecture allows for easy API technology and database change, e.g., from REST to gRPC or SQL to NoSQL database. All these changes can be made without affecting the business logic (use case and entities layers).

Entity classes can depend on other entities to create hierarchical entities (aggregates). For example, the `Order` entity consists of `OrderItem` entities.

Put entity-related business rules into entity classes. A `BankAccount` entity class should have a method for withdrawing money from the account. That method should enforce a business rule: Withdrawal is possible only if the account has enough funds. Don't put the withdrawal functionality into a service class and use `BankAccount`'s `getBalance` and `setBalance` accessors to perform the withdrawal procedure in the service class. That would be against the *tell, don't ask principle* discussed later in this chapter. Also, don't allow service classes to access sub-entities (and their methods) that a `BankAccount` may contain. That would be against DDD principles and the *law of Demeter* (discussed later in this chapter). DDD states that you should access an aggregate (`BankAccount`) by its root only, not directly accessing any sub-entities.

Application services orchestrate operations on one or more entities, e.g., a `BacklogItemService` can have a `setSprint` method that will fetch a `Sprint` entity and pass it to the `BacklogItem` entity's `setSprint` method, which verifies if the sprint for the backlog item can be set (only non-closed sprint can be set, i.e., current or future, not past sprints; a new sprint for a closed backlog item cannot be set. The closed backlog item has to remain in the sprint where it was closed.)

Let's assume that the `BacklogItem` entity class is large and the `setSprint` would contain a lot of validation code, making it even larger. In that case, you should extract a new class for backlog item sprint validation business rules, and the `BacklogItem` class should be composed of that new behavioral class: `BacklogItemSprintValidator`. In the `BacklogItem` class's `setSprint` method, the validation can be done with the following call: `sprintValidator.validate(newSprint, this)`.

4.6.1: Real-Life Example

Let's have a real-life example of creating an API microservice called *order-service*, which handles orders in an e-commerce software system.

Source code for the below example is available here[11].

First, we define a REST API controller using Java and Spring Boot:

---

[11]https://github.com/pksilen/clean-code-principles-code/tree/main/chapter2/orderservice

Figure 4.5. RestOrderController.java

```java
package com.example.orderservice.controllers.rest;

import com.example.orderservice.dtos.InputOrder;
import com.example.orderservice.dtos.OutputOrder;
import com.example.orderservice.services.OrderService;
import jakarta.validation.Valid;
import org.springframework.beans.factory.annotation.Autowired;
import org.springframework.http.HttpStatus;
import org.springframework.web.bind.annotation.*;


@RestController
@RequestMapping("/orders")
public class RestOrderController {
  private final OrderService orderService;

  @Autowired
  public RestOrderController(final OrderService orderService) {
    this.orderService = orderService;
  }

  // Controller methods should not contain any business logic
  // Controller method should delegate to application services (use cases)
  @PostMapping
  @ResponseStatus(HttpStatus.CREATED)
  public final OutputOrder createOrder(
    @Valid @RequestBody final InputOrder inputOrder
  ) {
    return orderService.createOrder(inputOrder);
  }

  @GetMapping("/{id}")
  @ResponseStatus(HttpStatus.OK)
  public final OutputOrder getOrderById(
    @PathVariable("id") final String id
  ) {
    return orderService.getOrderById(id);
  }

  @GetMapping(params = "userAccountId")
  @ResponseStatus(HttpStatus.OK)
  public final Iterable<OutputOrder> getOrdersByUserAccountId(
    @RequestParam("userAccountId") final String userAccountId
  ) {
    return orderService.getOrdersByUserAccountId(userAccountId);
  }

  @PutMapping("/{id}")
  @ResponseStatus(HttpStatus.NO_CONTENT)
  public final void updateOrder(
    @PathVariable final String id,
    @Valid @RequestBody final InputOrder inputOrder
  ) {
    orderService.updateOrder(id, inputOrder);
  }

  @DeleteMapping("/{id}")
  @ResponseStatus(HttpStatus.NO_CONTENT)
  public final void deleteOrder(
    @PathVariable final String id
  ) {
    orderService.deleteOrderById(id);
  }
}
```

The API offered by the microservice depends on the controller, as seen in the earlier diagram. The API is currently a REST API, but we could create and use a GraphQL controller. Then, our API, which depends on the controller, is a GraphQL API. You can create a controller for any client-server technology, like gRPC or WebSocket. You can even create a controller for standard input (stdin) or command line interface (CLI). A CLI controller reads command(s) from the command line arguments supplied to the microservice. Remember that you can have multiple controllers active in the same microservice. Your microservice could be used by frontend clients using a REST controller, or it could be used on the command line using its CLI controller.

Clean architecture also has a concept of a *presenter* which can be used to modify how the service presents its response to a client request. Our example and most modern services are APIs with a predefined way of presenting data to the client (from DDD, remember *open host service* and *published language*). Sometimes, you might want to implement an API where the client can instruct how the returned data should be presented. For example, a client could instruct the service to respond either with JSON or XML depending on the *Accept* HTTP request header value:

```
@RestController
@RequestMapping("/orders")
public class RestOrderController {
  private final OrderService orderService;
  private final OrderPresenterFactory orderPresenterFactory;

  @Autowired
  public RestOrderController(
    final OrderService orderService,
    final OrderPresenterFactory orderPresenterFactory,
  ) {
    this.orderService = orderService;
    this.orderPresenterFactory = orderPresenterFactory;
  }
    @GetMapping("/{id}")
    @ResponseStatus(HttpStatus.OK)
    public final void getOrderById(
      @PathVariable("id") final String id
      @RequestHeader(HttpHeaders.ACCEPT) String accept,
      HttpServletResponse response
    ) {
        final var outputOrder = orderService.getOrderById(id);
        final var orderPresenter = orderPresenterFactory.createPresenter(accept);
        orderPresenter.present(outputOrder, response);
    }
}
```

If the client is a web browser, you might want to return an HTML response. For example, a client will send the wanted HTML view type (list or table) as a query parameter to the service:

```
@RestController
@RequestMapping("/orders")
public class RestOrderController {
  private final OrderService orderService;
  private final OrderPresenterFactory orderPresenterFactory;

  @Autowired
  public RestOrderController(
    final OrderService orderService,
    final OrderPresenterFactory orderPresenterFactory,
  ) {
    this.orderService = orderService;
    this.orderPresenterFactory = orderPresenterFactory;
  }
    @GetMapping("/{id}")
    @ResponseStatus(HttpStatus.OK)
    public final void getOrderById(
      @PathVariable("id") final String id,
```

```
      @RequestParam("viewType") String viewType,
      HttpServletResponse response
    ) {
        final var outputOrder = orderService.getOrderById(id);
        final var orderPresenter = orderPresenterFactory.createPresenter(viewType);
        orderPresenter.present(outputOrder, response);
    }
}
```

Below is an implementation of a GraphQL controller with one mutation and one query:

Figure 4.6. GraphQlOrderController.java

```
package com.example.orderservice.controllers.graphql;

import com.example.orderservice.dtos.InputOrder;
import com.example.orderservice.dtos.OutputOrder;
import com.example.orderservice.repositories.DbOrder;
import com.example.orderservice.services.OrderService;
import jakarta.validation.Valid;
import org.springframework.beans.factory.annotation.Autowired;
import org.springframework.graphql.data.method.annotation.Argument;
import org.springframework.graphql.data.method.annotation.MutationMapping;
import org.springframework.graphql.data.method.annotation.QueryMapping;
import org.springframework.stereotype.Controller;


@Controller
public class GraphQlOrderController {
  private final OrderService orderService;

  @Autowired
  public GraphQlOrderController(final OrderService orderService) {
    this.orderService = orderService;
  }

  @MutationMapping
  public final OutputOrder createOrder(
    @Valid @Argument final InputOrder inputOrder
  ) {
    return orderService.createOrder(inputOrder);
  }

  @QueryMapping
  public final OutputOrder orderById(
    @Argument final String id
  ) {
    return orderService.getOrderById(id);
  }

  // Rest of methods ...
}
```

The RestOrderController and GraphQlOrderController classes depend on the OrderService interface, which is part of the use case layer. Notice that the controllers do not rely on a concrete implementation of the use cases but depend on an interface according to the *dependency inversion principle*. Below is the definition for the OrderService interface:

Figure 4.7. OrderService.java

```
package com.example.orderservice.services;

import com.example.orderservice.dtos.InputOrder;
import com.example.orderservice.dtos.OutputOrder;
import com.example.orderservice.repositories.DbOrder;

public interface OrderService {
  OutputOrder createOrder(final InputOrder inputOrder);
  OutputOrder getOrderById(final String id);
  Iterable<OutputOrder> getOrdersByUserAccountId(final String userAccountId);
  void updateOrder(final String id, final InputOrder inputOrder);
  void deleteOrderById(final String id);
}
```

The below OrderServiceImpl class implements the OrderService interface:

Figure 4.8. OrderServiceImpl.java

```
package com.example.orderservice.services.application;

import com.example.orderservice.Application;
import com.example.orderservice.dtos.InputOrder;
import com.example.orderservice.dtos.OutputOrder;
import com.example.orderservice.entities.Order;
import com.example.orderservice.repositories.DbOrder;
import com.example.orderservice.errors.EntityNotFoundError;
import com.example.orderservice.repositories.OrderRepository;
import org.springframework.beans.factory.annotation.Autowired;
import org.springframework.beans.factory.annotation.Qualifier;
import org.springframework.context.annotation.Primary;
import org.springframework.stereotype.Service;

import java.util.stream.StreamSupport;

@Primary
@Service
public class OrderServiceImpl implements OrderService {
  private static final String ORDER = "Order";
  private final OrderRepository orderRepository;

  @Autowired
  public OrderServiceImpl(
    @Qualifier(Application.DATABASE_TYPE) final OrderRepository orderRepository
  ) {
    this.orderRepository = orderRepository;
  }

  @Override
  public final OutputOrder createOrder(final InputOrder inputOrder) {
    // Input DTO is converted to valid domain entity
    final var order = Order.from(inputOrder);

    // If your model had additional business logic, you
    // could perform it here using domain entity and/or
    // domain service methods
    // Do not inline all the business logic code here, but
    // create separate methods either in domain entity or
    // domain service classes.
    // This example does not have any additional business
    // logic

    // Creates database entity which can be different from domain entity
    final var dbOrder = DbOrder.from(order);

    orderRepository.save(dbOrder);
```

```
  // Returns output DTO which can differ from the domain entity, e.g.
  // domain entity might contain fields not wanted to be delivered to clients
  // Output DTO class contains validations which can be enabled in controllers
  // This can be useful to prevent disclosure of sensitive data upon a successful
  // injection attack
  return order.toOutput();
}

@Override
public final OutputOrder getOrderById(final String id) {
  final var dbOrder = orderRepository.findById(id)
    .orElseThrow(() ->
      new EntityNotFoundError(ORDER, id));

  return dbOrder.toDomainEntity().toOutput();
}

@Override
public Iterable<OutputOrder> getOrdersByUserAccountId(final String userAccountId) {
  final var dbOrders = orderRepository.findByUserAccountId(userAccountId);
  return StreamSupport.stream(dbOrders.spliterator(), false)
    .map(dbOrder -> dbOrder.toDomainEntity().toOutput()).toList();
}

@Override
public void updateOrder(final String id, InputOrder inputOrder) {
  if (orderRepository.existsById(id)) {
    final var order = Order.from(inputOrder);
    final var dbOrder = DbOrder.from(order, id);
    orderRepository.save(dbOrder);
  } else {
    throw new EntityNotFoundError(ORDER, id);
  }
}

@Override
public void deleteOrderById(final String id) {
  if (orderRepository.existsById(id)) {
    orderRepository.deleteById(id);
  }
}
}
```

The `OrderServiceImpl` class has a dependency on an order repository. This dependency is also inverted. The `OrderServiceImpl` class depends only on the `OrderRepository` interface. The order repository is used to orchestrate the persistence of order entities. Note that there is no direct dependency on a database. The term *repository* is abstract. It only means a place where data (entities) are stored. So the repository can be implemented by a relational database, NoSQL database, file system, in-memory cache, message queue, or another microservice, to name a few.

Below is the `OrderRepository` interface:

Figure 4.9. OrderRepository.java

```
package com.example.orderservice.repositories;

import java.util.Optional;

public interface OrderRepository {
  <S extends DbOrder> S save(final S order);
  Optional<DbOrder> findById(final String id);
  boolean existsById(final String id);
  Iterable<DbOrder> findByUserAccountId(final String userAccountId);
  void deleteById(final String id);
}
```

You can introduce an *output interface adapter* class that implements the OrderRepository interface. An output interface adapter adapts a particular concrete output destination (e.g., a database) to the OrderRepository interface. For example, you can define SqlOrderRepository *output interface adapter* class for an SQL database:

Figure 4.10. SqlOrderRepository.java

```
package com.example.orderservice.repositories;

import org.springframework.beans.factory.annotation.Qualifier;
import org.springframework.data.repository.CrudRepository;
import org.springframework.stereotype.Repository;


@Qualifier("sql")
@Repository
public interface SqlOrderRepository extends CrudRepository<DbOrder, String>, OrderRepository {
}
```

Changing the database to MongoDB can be done by creating a new MongoDbOrderRepository output interface adapter class that implements the OrderRepository interface:

Figure 4.11. MongoDbOrderRepository.java

```
package com.example.orderservice.repositories;

import org.springframework.beans.factory.annotation.Qualifier;
import org.springframework.data.mongodb.repository.MongoRepository;
import org.springframework.stereotype.Repository;

@Qualifier("mongodb")
@Repository
public interface MongoDbOrderRepository extends MongoRepository<DbOrder, String>, OrderRepository {
}
```

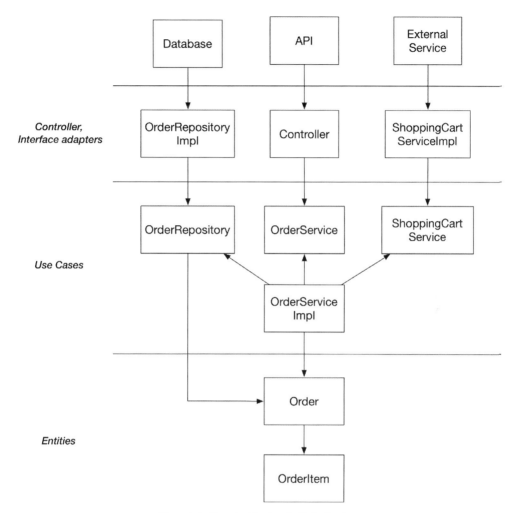

Figure 4.12. Clean Architecture for Order Service

When implementing a clean architecture, everything is wired together using configuration and dependency injection. For example, the Spring framework creates an instance implementing the OrderRepository interface according to configuration and injects it into an OrderServiceImpl instance. In the case of Spring, the dependency injector is configured using a configuration file and annotations. The configuration file or annotations can be used to configure the database used. Additionally, the Spring dependency injector creates an instance of the OrderServiceImpl class and injects it where an OrderService object is wanted.

The dependency injector is the only place in a microservice that contains references to concrete implementations. In many frameworks, the dependency injector is not a visible component, but its usage is configured using a configuration file and annotations. For example, in Spring, the @Autowired annotation tells the dependency injector to inject a concrete implementation into the annotated class field or constructor parameter. The *dependency injection principle* is discussed more in a later section of this chapter. The dependency inversion principle and dependency injection principle usually go hand in hand. Dependency injection is used for wiring interface dependencies so that those become dependencies on concrete implementations, as seen in the figure below.

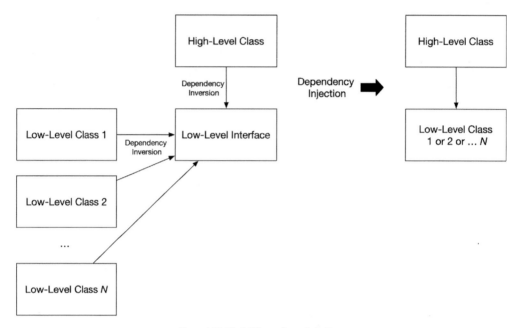

Figure 4.13. Fig 3.4 Dependency Injection

Let's add a feature where the shopping cart is emptied when an order is created:

Figure 4.14. ShoppingCartEmptyingOrderService.java

```
package com.example.orderservice.services.application;

import com.example.orderservice.Application;
import com.example.orderservice.dtos.InputOrder;
import com.example.orderservice.dtos.OutputOrder;
import com.example.orderservice.entities.Order;
import com.example.orderservice.repositories.DbOrder;
import com.example.orderservice.repositories.OrderRepository;
import com.example.orderservice.services.external.ShoppingCartService;
import org.springframework.beans.factory.annotation.Autowired;
import org.springframework.beans.factory.annotation.Qualifier;
import org.springframework.stereotype.Service;


@Service
public class ShoppingCartEmptyingOrderService implements OrderService {
  private final OrderRepository orderRepository;
  private final ShoppingCartService shoppingCartService;

  @Autowired
  public ShoppingCartEmptyingOrderService(
    @Qualifier(Application.DATABASE_TYPE) final OrderRepository orderRepository,
    final ShoppingCartService shoppingCartService
  ) {
```

```
    this.orderRepository = orderRepository;
    this.shoppingCartService = shoppingCartService;
  }

  @Override
  public final OutputOrder createOrder(final InputOrder inputOrder) {
    final var order = Order.from(inputOrder);
    shoppingCartService.emptyCart(order.getUserAccountId());
    final var dbOrder = DbOrder.from(order);
    orderRepository.save(dbOrder);
    return order.toOutput();
  }
}
```

As you can see from the above code, the `ShoppingCartEmptyingOrderService` class does not depend on any concrete implementation of the shopping cart service. We can create an *output interface adapter* class that is a concrete implementation of the `ShoppingCartService` interface. For example, that interface adapter class connects to a particular external shopping cart service via a REST API. Once again, the dependency injector will inject a concrete `ShoppingCartService` implementation to an instance of the `ShoppingCartEmptyingOrderService` class.

Note that the above `createOrder` method is not production quality because it lacks a transaction.

> Only the most relevant source code files were listed above to keep the example short enough. The complete example is available here[12]. The example shows how to use DTOs, domain and database entities, and how to generate UUIDs both on the server and the client side. For ultimate security, consider generating all identifiers only on the server side. These things are covered in detail in later chapters of this book. The given example is not production quality because it lacks detailed error handling, logging, audit logging, authorization, and observability. These aspects are discussed by the end of this book when you should have learned how to craft production-quality software.

Now we have seen examples of the following benefits of clean architecture:

- Not tied to any single API technology like REST or GraphQL
- Not tied to a specific client (works with web, desktop, console, and mobile clients)
- Not tied to a specific database
- Not dependent on any specific external service implementation

The final benefit of clean architecture:

- Not tied to any single framework

This is not always straightforward, and in our case, if we want to change our framework from Spring Boot to, e.g., Jakarta EE or Quarkus, we would have to make changes in places other than the application class and the controller only. This is because we are using Spring-specific dependency injection and Spring-specific repository implementation. Being unable to replace the framework easily is the main drawback

---

[12]https://github.com/pksilen/clean-code-principles-code/tree/main/chapter2/orderservice

of large frameworks like Spring, JakartaEE, Django, or Nest.js. Most of the time, you would be better off with small single-purpose libraries (remember the *microlibraries* from the first chapter) instead of using a massive framework. Switching from one micro library to another is less effort than trying to change a big framework.

In my other book Clean Code Principles And Patterns: Python Edition[13], I give you an example where we easily change a *FastAPI*-based microservice to a *Flask*-based microservice. In that example, we can change the used web framework by introducing two new small modules (application and controller modules). We do not touch any existing modules. Thus, we can be confident that we do not break any existing functionality. We successfully apply the *open-closed principle* to our software.

It should be noted that the clean architecture principle applies to other microservices with input or output, not just API microservices. We will have an example of this later in this chapter. Another benefit of the clean architecture that has not been mentioned yet is that you can write component tests that test the software component's business logic (or the model) using fake input and output adapters instead of the real ones. Let's take a data exporter microservice as an example. It reads data from an input source (e.g., Apache Kafka) and transforms it in various ways before writing to an output destination (e.g., Apache Pulsar). We can test the transformation business logic using a fake input and output adapter injected into the software component. Running the tests will be fast because there is no need to spin up an instance of Kafka and Pulsar. Later, we can augment the component tests with some integration tests that test the integration to real input and output. We will talk more about component and integration tests in a later chapter.

4.7: Vertical Slice Architecture Principle

Vertical slice architecture divides individual features into separate vertical slices. In the source code repository, this means a separate directory for each vertical slice (feature). You can also group these single feature directories under a domain directory. This makes navigating the code-base a breeze and finding a particular feature easy. The main benefit of vertical slice architecture is that it allows you to follow the open-closed principle when adding new features. There is no need to modify existing code and no risk of breaking existing functionality. You can implement a vertical slice (a feature) as you wish, which is a clear benefit when different features have divergent requirements. So, a vertical slice can contain a single class or multiple classes that form a layered design. Vertical slice architecture does not enforce any specific way. However, using some design principles for a vertical slice implementation is good practice. I suggest to use the *clean architecture principle*. You can use vertical slice architecture and clean architecture principles together. They are not mutually exclusive principles.

If your microservice is a small API, e.g., just containing a handful of simple CRUD operations, you don't necessarily get much benefit from vertical slicing. If you are not using the vertical slice architecture, adding a new CRUD operation requires changes to existing classes. These changes include adding new methods to mostly immutable or stateless classes, which can be considered extensions instead of modifications and are according to the open-closed principle. Adding a method to an immutable or stateless class rarely breaks existing functionality in existing methods. This is why I haven't used vertical slicing in the examples in this book.

For example, suppose you have an API providing CRUD operations on a resource and want to use vertical slicing. In that case, you implement each CRUD operation separately in different service/controller/repository classes. Here is an example of the source code directory layout for the *order-service* using vertical slice architecture:

---

[13]https://leanpub.com/cleancodeprinciplesandpatternspythonedition

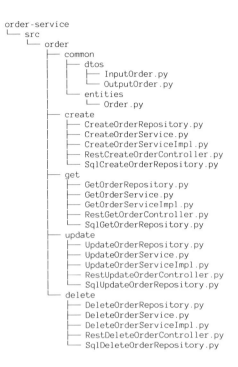

```
order-service
└── src
    └── order
        ├── common
        │   ├── dtos
        │   │   ├── InputOrder.py
        │   │   └── OutputOrder.py
        │   └── entities
        │       └── Order.py
        ├── create
        │   ├── CreateOrderRepository.py
        │   ├── CreateOrderService.py
        │   ├── CreateOrderServiceImpl.py
        │   ├── RestCreateOrderController.py
        │   └── SqlCreateOrderRepository.py
        ├── get
        │   ├── GetOrderRepository.py
        │   ├── GetOrderService.py
        │   ├── GetOrderServiceImpl.py
        │   ├── RestGetOrderController.py
        │   └── SqlGetOrderRepository.py
        ├── update
        │   ├── UpdateOrderRepository.py
        │   ├── UpdateOrderService.py
        │   ├── UpdateOrderServiceImpl.py
        │   ├── RestUpdateOrderController.py
        │   └── SqlUpdateOrderRepository.py
        └── delete
            ├── DeleteOrderRepository.py
            ├── DeleteOrderService.py
            ├── DeleteOrderServiceImpl.py
            ├── RestDeleteOrderController.py
            └── SqlDeleteOrderRepository.py
```

The above example is quite simplistic and *CRUDish*. Let's have a more realistic example where we have also applied *domain-driven design* (DDD). Our example is for a travel booking microservice. After applying the DDD, we should have a ubiquitous language defined for our microservices, and we can define our features using that language. We can end up with the following features:

- Book a trip
- View trips or a trip
- Cancel a trip
- Hotel reservation

  – Add hotel reservation to a trip
  – Replace hotel reservation for a trip
  – Remove hotel reservation from a trip

- Flight reservation

  – Add flight reservation to a trip
  – Replace flight reservation for a trip
  – Remove flight reservation from a trip

- Rental Car Reservation

  – Add rental car reservation to a trip
  – Replace rental car reservation for a trip
  – Remove rental car reservation from a trip

Let's use the *vertical slice architecture principle* and lay out the directory structure for our microservice. As shown below, we can also create vertical slices larger than a single feature, namely vertical slices that can be called *feature sets* or *subdomains*. In the example below, we have grouped related hotel, flight, and rental reservation features to own feature sets or subdomains.

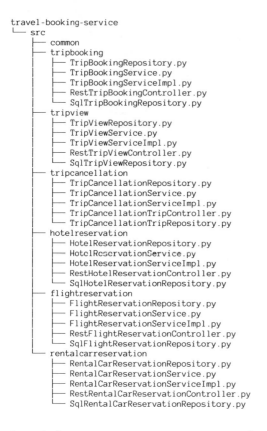

```
travel-booking-service
└── src
    ├── common
    ├── tripbooking
    │   ├── TripBookingRepository.py
    │   ├── TripBookingService.py
    │   ├── TripBookingServiceImpl.py
    │   ├── RestTripBookingController.py
    │   └── SqlTripBookingRepository.py
    ├── tripview
    │   ├── TripViewRepository.py
    │   ├── TripViewService.py
    │   ├── TripViewServiceImpl.py
    │   ├── RestTripViewController.py
    │   └── SqlTripViewRepository.py
    ├── tripcancellation
    │   ├── TripCancellationRepository.py
    │   ├── TripCancellationService.py
    │   ├── TripCancellationServiceImpl.py
    │   ├── TripCancellationTripController.py
    │   └── TripCancellationTripRepository.py
    ├── hotelreservation
    │   ├── HotelReservationRepository.py
    │   ├── HotelReservationService.py
    │   ├── HotelReservationServiceImpl.py
    │   ├── RestHotelReservationController.py
    │   └── SqlHotelReservationRepository.py
    ├── flightreservation
    │   ├── FlightReservationRepository.py
    │   ├── FlightReservationService.py
    │   ├── FlightReservationServiceImpl.py
    │   ├── RestFlightReservationController.py
    │   └── SqlFlightReservationRepository.py
    └── rentalcarreservation
        ├── RentalCarReservationRepository.py
        ├── RentalCarReservationService.py
        ├── RentalCarReservationServiceImpl.py
        ├── RestRentalCarReservationController.py
        └── SqlRentalCarReservationRepository.py
```

Instead of using nouns, we can use sentences and use the term *use case* instead of *service* to denote application services, i.e., use cases:

```
travel-booking-service
└── src
    ├── common
    ├── booktrip
    │   │   ...
    │   └── BookTripUseCase.py
    ├── viewtrips
    │   │   ...
    │   └── ViewTripsUseCase.py
    ├── viewtrip
    │   │   ...
    │   └── ViewTripUseCase.py
    ├── canceltrip
    │   │   ...
    │   └── CancelTripUseCase.py
    ├── addhotelreservation
    │   │   ...
```

```
|       └── AddHotelReservationUseCase.py
├── replacehotelreservation
|       |   ...
|       └── ReplaceHotelReservationUseCase.py
├── removehotelreservation
|       |   ...
|       └── RemoveHotelReservationUseCase.py
├── addflightreservation
|       |   ...
|       └── AddFlightReservationUseCase.py
├── replaceflightreservation
|       |   ...
|       └── ReplaceFlightReservationUseCase.py
├── removeflightreservation
|       |   ...
|       └── RemoveFlightReservationUseCase.py
├── addrentalcarreservation
|       |   ...
|       └── AddRentalCarReservationUseCase.py
├── replacerentalcarreservation
|       |   ...
|       └── ReplaceRentalCarReservationUseCase.py
└── removerentalcarreservation
        |   ...
        └── RemoveRentalCarReservationUseCase.py
```

As can be seen from the above example, *vertical slice architecture* creates a very understandable and easily navigatable directory structure for the microservice source code. The above kind of architecture is also called *screaming architecture* because the directory structure screams about the features the service provides.

4.8: Class Organization Principle

A class should be organized in the following manner:

- Attributes first, methods after them
- Method order: constructor first, then public, then protected, and private last
- Order attributes and public methods by importance or logic, and if there is no logic or importance difference, order alphabetically
- Define public getters/properties/setters after other public methods
- Order private methods in the same order they are used in the public methods

An example of the *logic* is a `Rectangle` class with `width` and `height` attributes. You should give the `width` (x-axis length) before `height` (y-axis length) because coordinates are given x first and then y.

Let's have an example with a `Circle` class. It has the following attributes:

- `origin` (vital because you cannot draw a circle without knowing its origin)
- `radius` (vital because you cannot draw a circle without knowing its radius)
- `strokeColor` (this is a must attribute even though a default value could be used)
- `fillColor` (this is an optional attribute; a default value of `None` could be used)

Attributes `origin` and `radius` should be given in that order because you need to know the *origin* before you can start drawing the circle.

The `Circle` class has the following methods:

- draw (most used method, should be the first)
- calculateArea (calculateXXX methods should be in alphabetical order because there is no logic or importance difference between methods)
- calculatePerimeter
- getters (in the same order as respective attributes)
- setters (in the same order as respective attributes)

Our `Circle` class written in TypeScript would like the following:

```typescript
import Point from 'Point';

class Circle {
  constructor(
    private origin: Point,
    private radius: number,
    private strokeColor: string,
    private fillColor: string | null = null
  ) {
  }

  draw(): void {
    // ...
  }

  calculateArea(): number {
    // ...
  }

  calculatePerimeter(): number {
    // ..
  }

  getOrigin(): Point {
    return this.origin;
  }

  getRadius(): number {
    return this.radius;
  }

  getStrokeColor(): string {
    return this.strokeColor;
  }

  getFillColor(): string | null {
    return this.fillColor;
  }

  setOrigin(origin: Point): void {
    this.origin = origin;
  }

  setRadius(radius: number): void {
    this.radius = radius;
  }

  setStrokeColor(strokeColor: string): void {
    this.strokeColor = strokeColor;
  }

  setFillColor(fillColor: string | null): void {
    this.fillColor = fillColor;
  }
}
```

4.9: Package/Directory, Class and Function Sizing Principle

Use the maximum number of items (5-9) that can be stored in the short-term memory as the maximum size for a package/directory, class, or function.

A package (or directory) should have a maximum of 5-9 modules. This allows you to quickly find a specific module (file) in the package. If you have a package with many modules, it can be hard to find a specific module because they are listed in alphabetical order, and you cannot apply any logical order to them. I usually create packages that may only contain 2 or 3 modules. For example, I could have a *config* directory that has a *Config.java* module, and under the *config* directory, I could have a *parser* subdirectory that has the following modules: *ConfigParser.java*, *JsonConfigParser.java* and *YamlConfigParser.java*.

A class should have a maximum of 5-9 attributes and 5-9 methods. If your class has more than 5-9 attributes, extract attributes to a new class. Let's say you have the following class:

```java
public class User {
  private String id;
  private String firstName;
  private String lastName;
  private String streetAddress;
  private String zipCode;
  private String city;
  private String country;
  private String phoneNumber;
  private String emailAddress;
  private Gender gender;
  private String username;
  private String password;
}
```

The above class can be refactored to use *value objects* to reduce the number of attributes:

```java
public class Name {
  private String firstName;
  private String lastName;
}


public class Address {
  private String streetAddress;
  private String zipCode;
  private String city;
  private String country;
}


public class ContactInfo {
  private String phoneNumber;
  private String emailAddress;
}


public class Credentials {
  private String username;
  private String password;
}

public class User {
  private String id;
  private Name name;
  private Address address;
```

```
    private ContactInfo contactInfo;
    private Gender gender;
    private Credentials credentials;
}
```

If you have too many methods, use the *extract class* refactoring technique explained in the next chapter. As a rule of thumb, consider refactoring the class smaller if your class has more than 100-150 lines of code (not counting the import statements). Here is an example. If you have a software component with 10,000 lines of code, you should have a new class for at least every approx. 200 lines of code, meaning that the total number of classes in the software component should be at least 50, in practice, even more.

A function should have a maximum of 5-9 statements. If you have a longer function, extract a function or functions that the original function calls. If you have a public method that calls several private methods, keep the number of those private methods small, preferably only one or two. This is because when you write a unit test for the public method, testing becomes more complex if many private methods also need to be tested indirectly. More about this topic also in the coming *testing principles* chapter.

A function should have a maximum of 5-9 parameters. You should prefer limiting the maximum number of parameters closer to 5 instead of 9. You can reduce the number of parameters by using the *introduce parameter object* refactoring technique explained in the next chapter.

4.10: Uniform Naming Principle

Use a uniform way to name interfaces, classes, and functions..

This section presents conventions for uniformly naming interfaces, classes, and functions.

4.10.1: Naming Interfaces and Classes

A class represents a thing or an actor. Classes should be named consistently so the class name ends with a noun. An interface represents an abstract thing, actor, or capability. Interfaces representing a thing or an actor should be named like classes but using an abstract noun. Interfaces representing a capability should be named according to the capability.

When an interface represents an abstract thing, name it according to that abstract thing. For example, if you have a drawing application with various geometrical objects, name the geometrical object interface Shape. It is a simple abstract noun. Names should always be the shortest, most descriptive ones. There is no reason to name the geometrical object interface as GeometricalObject or GeometricalShape, if we can use simply Shape.

When an interface represents an abstract actor, name it according to that abstract actor. The name of an interface should be derived from the functionality it provides. For example, suppose there is a parseConfig method in the interface. In that case, the interface should be named ConfigParser, and if an interface has a validateObject method, the interface should be named ObjectValidator. Don't use mismatching name combinations like a ConfigReader interface with a parseConfig method or an ObjectValidator interface with a validateData method.

When an interface represents a capability, name it according to that capability. Capability is something that a concrete class is capable of doing. For example, a class could be sortable, iterable, comparable, equitable, etc. Name the respective interfaces according to the capability: Sortable, Iterable, Comparable, and Equitable. The name of an interface representing a capability usually ends with *able* or *ing*.

Don't name interfaces starting with the *I* prefix (or any other prefix or postfix). Instead, use an *Impl* postfix for class names to distinguish a class from an interface, but only when needed. For example, if you have an interface named ConfigParser and you have a concrete class implementing the interface and parsing configuration in JSON format, name the class JsonConfigParser, not JsonConfigParserImpl, because the Impl prefix is not needed to distinguish between the interface and implementing class. Remember that you should be programming against interfaces, and if every interface has its name prefixed with an *I*, it just adds unnecessary noise to the code. You can use the *I* prefix if it is a strong language convention.

Some examples of class names representing a thing are: Account, Order, RectangleShape, and CircleShape. In a class inheritance hierarchy, the names of classes usually refine the interface name or the base class name. For example, if there is an InputMessage interface, then there can be different concrete implementations (= classes) of the InputMessage interface. They can represent an input message from different sources, like KafkaInputMessage and HttpInputMessage. And there could be different subclasses for different data formats: AvroBinaryKafkaInputMessage or JsonHttpInputMessage.

The interface or base class name should be retained in the class or subclass name. Class names should follow the pattern: <class-purpose> + <interface-name> or <sub-class-purpose> + <super-class-name>, e.g., Kafka + InputMessage = KafkaInputMessage and AvroBinary + KafkaInputMessage = AvroBinaryKafkaInputMessage. Name abstract classes with the prefix Abstract. Java follows the above-described naming convention. For example, there exists an Executor interface. The ThreadPoolExecutor class implements the Executor interface and ScheduledThreadPoolExecutor class extends the ThreadPoolExecutor class.

If an interface or class name is over 20-30 characters long, consider abbreviating one or more words in the name. The reason for this is to keep the code readable. Very long names are harder to read and slow a developer down. (Remember that code is more often read than written).

Only use abbreviations that are commonly used and understandable for other developers. If a word does not have a good abbreviation, don't abbreviate. For example, in the class name AvroBinaryKafkaInputMessage, we can only abbreviate the Message to Msg. There are no well-established abbreviations for other words in the class name. Abbreviating Binary to Bin is questionable because Bin could also mean a *bin*. Don't abbreviate a word if you benefit only one or two characters. For example, there is no reason to abbreviate Account to Accnt.

Instead of abbreviating, you can shorten a name by dropping one or more words from it, provided readers can still easily understand it. For example, if you have classes InternalMessage, InternalMessageSchema and InternalMessageField, you could shorten the last two class names to InternalSchema and InternalField. This is because these two classes are mainly used in conjunction with the InternalMessage class: An InternalMessage object has a schema and one or more fields. You can also use nested classes: InternalMessage.Schema and InternalMessage.Field. The problem with nested classes is that they can make the module too large.

If you have related classes and one or more class names require shortening, you should shorten all related class names to keep the naming uniform. For example, if you have two classes, ConfigurationParser and JsonConfigurationParser, you should shorten the names of both classes, not only the ones longer than 19 characters. The new class names would be ConfigParser and JsonConfigParser.

If an interface or class name is less than 20 characters long, there is usually no need to shorten it.

Don't add a design pattern name to a class name if it does not bring any real benefit. For example, suppose we have a DataStore interface, a DataStoreImpl class, and a class wrapping a DataStore instance using the *proxy pattern* to add caching functionality to the wrapped data store. We should not name the caching class `CachingProxyDataStore` or `CachingDataStoreProxy`. The word *proxy* does not add significant value, so the class should be named simply `CachingDataStore`. That name clearly tells it is a question about a data store with caching functionality. A seasoned developer notices from the `CachingDataStore` name that the class uses the *proxy pattern*. And if not, looking at the class implementation will finally reveal it.

4.10.2: Naming Functions

Functions should do one thing, and the name of a function should describe what the function does. The function name usually contains a verb that indicates what the function does. The function name often starts with a verb, but exceptions exist. If a function returns a value, try to name the function so that the function name describes what it returns.

The general rule is to name a function so that the purpose of the function is clear. A good function name should not make you think. If a function name is *20 or more characters long*, consider abbreviating one or more words in the name. The reason for this is to keep the code readable. The maximum length of function names should be lower than the maximum length of interface/class names because function names are used more often, and if the functions are methods, they are used in conjunction with an object name. Very long names are harder to read and slow a developer down. (Remember that code is more often read than written). Only use abbreviations that are widely used and understandable for other developers. If a word does not have a good abbreviation, don't abbreviate.

Below is an example of an interface containing two methods named with simple verbs only. It is not necessary to name the methods as `startThread` and `stopThread` because the methods are already part of the `Thread` interface, and it is self-evident what the `start` method starts and what the `stop` method ends. You don't need to repeat the class name in the method name.

```
public interface Thread {
  void start();
  void stop();
}
```

Let's have another Java example:

```
grpcChannel.shutdown().awaitTermination(30, TimeUnit.SECONDS);
```

The above example has two issues with the `shutdown` function. Most people probably assume that calling the `shutdown` function will shut down the channel and return after the channel is shut down without any return value. But now the `shutdown` function is returning something. It is not necessarily self-evident what it returns. However, we noticed that the `shutdown` function does not wait for the channel termination.

It would be better to rename the `shutdown` function as `requestShutdown` because it better describes what the function does. Also, we should name the `awaitTermination` to `awaitShutdown` because we should not use two different terms *shutdown* and *termination* to denote a single thing.

```
final var shutdownPromise = grpcChannel.requestShutdown();
shutdownPromise.awaitShutdown(30, TimeUnit.SECONDS);
```

Let's have an example in JavaScript:

```
fetch(url).then(response => response.json()).then(...);
```

In the above example, we have the following issue: the `fetch` function does not properly describe what it does. According to the documentation, it fetches a resource, but it does not return a resource. Instead, it returns a response object. Whenever possible, the function name should indicate what the function returns. The `fetch` performs an action on a resource and does not always return a resource. The action is specified by giving an HTTP verb as a parameter to the function (GET is the default HTTP verb). The most common actions are `GET`, `POST`, `PUT`, and `DELETE`. If you issue a `PUT` request for a REST API, you don't usually get the resource back. Of course, the same is valid for a `DELETE` request. You cannot get the resource back because it was just deleted.

We could name the function `performActionOnResource`, but that is a pretty long name and does not communicate the return value type. We should name the `fetch` function `makeHttpRequest` (or `sendHttpRequest`) to indicate that it is making an HTTP request. The new function name also communicates that it returns an HTTP response. Another possibility is introducing an actor class with static methods for different HTTP methods, for example: `HttpClient.makeGetRequest(url)`.

In the above example, the `json` function name is missing a verb. It should contain the verb *parse* because that is what it is doing. The function name should also tell what it parses: the response body. We should also add a *try* prefix to indicate that the function can throw (more about the *try* prefix and error handling in general in the next chapter). Below is the example with renamed functions:

```
makeHttpRequest(url).then(response =>
  response.tryParseBodyJson()).then(...);
```

Many languages offer streams that can be written to, like the standard output stream. Streams are usually buffered, and the actual writing to the stream does not happen immediately. For example, the below statement does not necessarily write to the standard output stream immediately. It buffers the text to be written later when the buffer is flushed to the stream. This can happen when the buffer is full, some time has elapsed since the last flush, or when the stream is closed.

```
stdOutStream.write(...);
```

The above statement is misleading and could be corrected by renaming the function to describe what it actually does:

```
stdOutStream.writeOnFlush(...);
```

The above function name immediately tells a developer that writing happens only on flush. The developer can consult the function documentation to determine when the flushing happens.

You can introduce a convenience method to perform a write with an immediate flush:

```
// Instead of this:
stdOutStream.writeOnFlush(...);
stdOutStream.flush();

// User can do this:
stdOutStream.writeWithFlush(...);
```

Many times, a function's action is associated with a target, for example:

```
public interface ConfigParser {
  Configuration tryParseConfig(...);
}
```

When a function's action has a target, it is useful to name the function using the following pattern: ‹action-verb› + ‹action-target›, for example, parse + config = parseConfig.

We can drop the action target from the function name if the function's first parameter describes the action target. However, keeping the action target in the function name is not wrong. But if it can be dropped, it usually makes the function call statements read better. In the example below, the word "config" appears to be repeated: tryParseConfig(configJson), making the function call statement read slightly clumsy.

```
final var configuration = configParser.tryParseConfig(configJson);
```

We can drop the action target from the function name:

```
public interface ConfigParser {
  Configuration tryParse(final String configJson);
}
```

As shown below, this change makes the code read better, presuming we use a descriptive variable name. And we should, of course, always use a descriptive variable name.

```
final var configuration = configParser.tryParse(configJson);
```

Here is another example:

```
public class Vector<T> {
  void pushBack(final T value); // OK
  void pushBackValue(final T value); // Not ideal,
                                     // word "value" repeated
}
```

```
public class KafkaAdminClient {
  void create(final String topic);
}
```

The above function name should be used only when a topic is the only thing a Kafka admin client can create. We cannot call the above function in the following way:

```
kafkaAdminClient.create("xyz");
```

We need to introduce a properly named variable:

```
final var topic = "xyz";
kafkaAdminClient.create(topic);
```

In languages where you can use named function parameters, the following is possible:

```
// Python
kafkaAdminClient.create(topic = "xyz");

// Swift
kafkaAdminClient.create(topic: "xyz");
```

4.10.2.1: Preposition in Function Name

Use a preposition in a function name when needed to clarify the function's purpose.

You don't need to add a preposition to a function name if the preposition can be assumed (i.e., the preposition is implicit). In many cases, only one preposition can be assumed. If you have a function named wait, the preposition for can be assumed, and if you have a function named subscribe, the preposition to can be assumed. We don't need to use function names waitFor and subscribeTo.

Suppose a function is named laugh(person: Person). Now, we have to add a preposition because none can be assumed. We should name the function either laughWith(person: Person) or laughAt(person: Person).

The following sections present examples of better naming some existing functions in programming languages.

4.10.2.2: Example 1: Renaming JavaScript Array Methods

Adding elements to a JavaScript array is done with the push method. Where does it push the elements? The method name does not say anything. There are three possibilities:

1) At the beginning
2) Somewhere in the middle
3) At the end

Most definitely, it is not the second one, but it still leaves two possibilities. Most people correctly guess that it pushes elements to the end. To make it 100% clear where the elements are pushed, this function should be named pushBack. Then, it does not make anybody think where the elements are pushed. Remember that a good function name does not make you think.

Popping an element from an array is done with the pop method. But where does it pop from? If you read the method description, it tells that the element is popped at the back. To make it 100% clear, this method should be named popBack.

The Array class also contains methods shift and unshift. They are like push and pop but operate at the beginning of an array. Those method names are extremely non-descriptive and should be named popFront and pushFront.

There are several methods in the JavaScript Array class for finding elements in an array. Here is the list of those methods:

- `find` (finds the first element where the given predicate is true)
- `findIndex` (find the index of the first element where the given predicate is true)
- `includes` (returns true or false based on if the given element is found in the array)
- `indexOf` (returns the first index where the given element is found)
- `lastIndexOf` (returns the last index where the given element is found)

Here are the suggested new names for the above functions:

- `find ==> findFirst`
- `findIndex ==> findFirstIndex`
- `includes ==> include`
- `indexOf ==> findFirstIndexOf`
- `lastIndexOf ==> findLastIndexOf`

Below are examples of these new function names in use:

```
const numbers = [1, 2, 3, 4, 5, 5];
const isEven = nbr => (nbr % 2) === 0;
const firstEvenNumber = numbers.findFirst(isEven);
const firstEvenNumberIndex = numbers.findFirstIndex(isEven);
const numbersIncludeFour = numbers.include(4);
const firstIndexOfFive = numbers.findFirstIndexOf(5);
const lastIndexOfFive = numbers.findLastIndexOf(5);
```

4.10.2.3: Naming Method Pairs

Methods in a class can come in pairs. A typical example is a pair of getter and setter methods. When you define a method pair in a class, name the methods logically. The methods in a method pair often do two opposite things, like getting or setting a value. If you are unsure how to name one of the methods, try to find an antonym for a word. For example, if you have a method whose name starts with "create" and are unsure how to name the method for the opposite action, try a Google search: "create antonym".

Here is a non-comprehensive list of some method names that come in pairs:

- get/set (getters and setters)

  - Name a boolean getter with the same name as the respective field, e.g., `boolean isDone()`
  - Name a boolean setter with `set` + boolean field name, e.g., `void setIsDone(boolean isDone)`

- get/put (especially when accessing a collection)
- read/write
- add/remove
- store/retrieve
- open/close
- load/save
- initialize/destroy
- create/destroy
- insert/delete

- start/stop
- pause/resume
- start/finish
- increase/decrease
- increment/decrement
- construct/destruct
- encrypt/decrypt
- encode/decode
- obtain/relinquish
- acquire/release
- reserve/release
- startup/shutdown
- login/logout
- begin/end
- launch/terminate
- publish/subscribe
- join/detach
- <something>/un<something>, e.g., assign/unassign, install/uninstall, subscribe/unsubscribe, follow/unfollow
- <something>/de<something>, e.g., serialize/deserialize, allocate/deallocate
- <something>/dis<something>, e.g., connect/disconnect

The `apt` tool in Debian/Ubuntu-based Linux has an `install` command to install a package, but the command for uninstalling a package is `remove`. It should be `uninstall`. The Kubernetes package manager Helm has this correct. It has an `install` command to install a Helm release and an `uninstall` command to uninstall it.

4.10.2.4: Naming Boolean Functions (Predicates)

The naming of boolean functions (predicates) should be such that when reading the function call statement, it reads as a boolean statement that can be true or false.

In this section, we consider naming functions that are predicates and return a boolean value. Here, I don't mean functions that return true or false based on the success of the executed action, but cases where the function call is used to evaluate a statement as true or false. The naming of boolean functions should be such that when reading the function call statement, it makes a statement that can be true or false. Below are some Java examples:

```java
public class Response {
  public boolean hasError() {
    // ...
  }
}


public class String {
  public boolean isEmpty() {
    //...
  }

  public boolean startsWith(final String anotherString) {
```

```java
    //...
  }

  public boolean endsWith(final String anotherString) {
    // ...
  }

  public boolean contains(final String anotherString) {
    // ...
  }
}


// Here we have a statement: response has error? true or false?
if (response.hasError()) {
  // ...
}


// Here we have a statement: line is empty? true or false?
final String line = fileReader.readLine();
if (line.isEmpty()) {
  // ...
}


// Here we have statement: line starts with a space character?
// true or false?
if (line.startsWith(" ")) {
    // ...
}


// Here we have statement: line ends with a semicolon?
// true or false?
if (line.endsWith(";")) {
    // ...
}


public class Thread {
  public boolean shouldTerminate() {
    // ...
  }

  public boolean isPaused() {
    // ...
  }

  public boolean canResumeExecution() {
    // ...
  }

  public void run() {
    // ...

    // Here we have statement: [this] should terminate?
    // true or false?
    if (shouldTerminate()) {
      return;
    }

    // Here we have statement: [this] is paused and
    // [this] can resume execution? true or false?
    if (isPaused() && canResumeExecution()) {
      // ...
    }

    // ...
  }
```

```
}
```

A boolean returning function is correctly named when you call the function in code and can read that function call statement in plain English. Below is an example of incorrect and correct naming:

```
public class Thread {
  public boolean stopped() { // Incorrect naming
    // ...
  }

  public boolean isStopped() { // Correct naming
    // ...
  }
}

if (thread.stopped()) {
  // Here we have: if thread stopped
  // This is not a statement with a true or false answer
  // It is a second conditional form,
  // asking what would happen if thread stopped.
  // ...
}

// Here we have statement: if thread is stopped
// true or false?
if (thread.isStopped()) {
  // ...
}
```

From the above examples, we can notice that many names of boolean-returning functions start with either *is* or *has* and follows the below pattern:

- is + <adjective>, e.g. isOpen, isRunning or isPaused
- has + <noun>

Also, these two forms can be relatively common:

- should + <verb>
- can + <verb>

But as we saw with the `startsWith`, `endsWith`, and `contains` functions, a boolean returning function name can start with any verb in third-person singular form (i.e., ending with an *s*). If you have a collection class, its boolean method names should have a verb in the plural form, for example: `numbers.include(...)` instead of `numbers.includes(...)`. Name your collection variables always in plural form (e.g., `numbers` instead of `numberList`). We will discuss the uniform naming principles for variables in the next chapter.

Do not include the *does* word in a function name, like *doesStartWith*, *doesEndWith*, or *doesContain*. Adding the *does* word doesn't add any real value to the name, and such function names are awkward to read when used in code, for example:

```
final String line = textFileReader.readLine();

// "If line does start with" sound awkward
if (!line.doesStartWith(" ")) {
  // ...
}
```

When you want to use the past tense in a function name, use a *did* prefix in the function name, for example:

```
public class DatabaseOperation {
  public void execute() {
    // ...
  }

  // Method name not OK. This is a second conditional form
  // if (dbOperation.startedTransaction())...
  public boolean startedTransaction() {
    // ...
  }

  // Method name OK, no confusion possible
  public boolean didStartTransaction() {
    // ...
  }
}
```

4.10.2.5: Naming Builder Methods

A builder class is used to create builder objects that build a new object of a particular type. If you want to construct a URL, you can introduce a *UrlBuilder* class for that purpose. Builder class methods add properties to the built object. For this reason, it is recommended to name builder class methods starting with the verb *add*. The method that finally builds the wanted object should be named simply *build* or *build + <build-target>*, for example, *buildUrl*. I prefer the longer form to remind the reader what is being built. Below is a Java example of naming the methods in a builder class:

```
public class UrlBuilder {
  public UrlBuilder() {
    // ...
  }

  public UrlBuilder addScheme(final String scheme) {
    // ...
    return this;
  }

  public UrlBuilder addHost(final String host) {
    // ...
    return this;
  }

  public UrlBuilder addPort(final int port) {
    // ...
    return this;
  }

  public UrlBuilder addPath(final String path) {
    // ...
    return this;
  }

  public UrlBuilder addQuery(final String query) {
    // ...
```

```
    return this;
  }

  public Url buildUrl() {
    // ...
  }
};


final var url = new UrlBuilder()
  .addScheme("https://")
  .addHost("google.com")
  .buildUrl();
```

4.10.2.6: Naming Methods with Implicit Verbs

Factory method names usually start with the verb *create*. Factory methods can be named so that the *create* verb is implicit, for example, in Java:

```
Optional.of(final T value)
Optional.empty() // Not optimal, 'empty' can be confused as a verb
Either.withLeft(final L value)
Either.withRight(final R value)
SalesItem.from(final SalesItemArg salesItemArg)
```

The explicit versions of the above method names would be:

```
Optional.createOf(final T value)
Optional.createEmpty()
Either.createWithLeft(final L value)
Either.createWithRight(final L value)
SalesItem.createFrom(final SalesItemArg salesItemArg)
```

Similarly, conversion methods can be named so that the *convert* verb is implicit. Conversion methods without a verb usually start with the *to* preposition, for example:

```
value.toString();
object.toJson();
```

The explicitly named versions of the above methods would be:

```
value.convertToString();
object.convertToJson();
```

Java has some factory methods that could be shortened:

```
final var value = Integer.parseInt(string);
final var value = Long.parseLong(string);
```

Shorter method names would be:

```
final var value = Integer.from(intString);
final var value = Long.from(longString);
```

You can access a collection element in some languages using the method at(index). Here, the implicit verb is get. I recommend using method names with implicit verbs sparingly and only in circumstances where the implicit verb is self-evident and does not force a developer to think.

4.10.2.7: Naming Property Getter Functions

Property getter functions are usually named get + <property-name>. It is also possible to name a property getter without a respective setter using just the property name. This is acceptable in cases where the property name cannot be confused with a verb. Below is a Java example of property getters:

```
final var list = new MyList();

list.size(); // OK
list.length(); // OK
list.empty(); // NOT OK, empty can be a verb.
list.isEmpty(); // OK
```

4.10.2.8: Naming Lifecycle Methods

Lifecycle methods are called on certain occasions only. Lifecycle method names should answer the question: When or "on what occasion" will this method be called? Examples of good names for lifecycle methods are: onInit, onError, onSuccess, afterMount, beforeUnmount. In React, there are lifecycle methods in class components called componentDidMount, componentDidUpdate and componentWillUnmount. There is no reason to repeat the class name in the lifecycle method names. Better names would have been: afterMount, afterUpdate, and beforeUnmount.

4.10.2.9: Naming Generic Type Parameters

Generic type parameters are usually named with a single character only. If there is one generic type parameter, a T is often used, e.g., List<T>. If there are multiple generic type parameters, the letters following T in the alphabet are used, e.g., T and U. If the generic type parameter has a special meaning, use the first letter from that meaning; for example, in Map<K, V>, the K means key and the V means value, or in AbstractAction<S>, the S means state. The problem with single-letter generic type parameters can be lousy readability. For example, in the AbstractAction<S>, can we assume everybody understands what the S means? It is often better to name generic type parameters with the convention T<purpose>, e.g., TKey, TValue, or TState. The initial T is needed to distinguish generic type parameters from similar class names, like Key, Value, or State.

4.10.2.10: Naming Function Parameters

Naming rules for function parameters are mostly the same as for variables. *Uniform naming principle* for variables is described in more detail in the next chapter.

There are some exceptions, like naming object parameters. When a function parameter is an object, the name of the object class can be left out from the parameter name when the parameter name and the function name implicitly describe the class of the parameter. This exception is acceptable because the function parameter type can always be easily checked by looking at the function signature. This should be easily done at a glance because a function should be short (a maximum of 5-7 statements). Below is a TypeScript example of naming object type parameters:

```
// Word 'Location' repeated, not optimal, but allowed
drive(startLocation: Location, destinationLocation: Location): void

// Better way
// When we think about 'drive' and 'start' or 'destination',
// we can assume that 'start' and 'destination' mean locations
drive(start: Location, destination: Location): void
```

Some programming languages like Swift allow the addition of so-called *external names* to function parameters. Using external names can make a function call statement read better, as shown below:

```
func drive(from start: Location, to destination: Location) {
  // ...
}

func send(
  message: String,
  from sender: Person,
  to recipient: Person
) {
  // ...
}


let startLocation = new Location(...);
let destLocation = new Location(...);
drive(from: startLocation, to: destLocation);

let message = "Some message";
let person = new Person(...);
let anotherPerson = new Person(...);
send(message, from: person, to: anotherPerson);
```

Always make the function call expression such that it has maximum readability: e.g., `copy(source, target)` not `copy(target, source)` or `write(line, file)` not `write(file, line)` or `decode(inputMessage, internalMessage)` and `encode(field, outputMessage)`. The examples contain implicit articles and prepositions. You can easily imagine the missing articles and prepositions, e.g., *copy from a source to a target, write a line to a file* or *encode a field to an output message.*

How would you name a UI function that closes a collapsible panel after a timeout if the panel is open? Inside the collapsible panel component, we could specify

```
function closeAfterTimeout(closeTimeoutInMs: number, isOpen: boolean): void {
  // ...
}
```

The above is not the best because `close` and `timeout` are repeated twice. Let's modify the function definition by dropping one `close` and one `timeout` to avoid repetition:

```
function closeAfter(timeoutInMs: number, isOpen: boolean): void {
  // ...
}
```

We could improve the function name a bit more by specifying what the `isOpen` parameter is used for using an `if` word:

```
function closeAfterIf(timeoutInMs: number, isOpen: boolean): void {
  // ...
}
```

Now we read the function definition in plain English: *close [this] after [a] timeout in milliseconds if [this] is open*. And the *[this]*, of course, means the current collapsible panel object so that we could read: *close [the panel] after a timeout in milliseconds if [the panel] is open*.

We could write the above function definition in a very readable manner in Swift:

```
func close(after timeoutInMs: Int, if isOpen: Bool): void {
  // ...
}

// Call it
close(after: timeoutInMs, if: isOpen);
```

4.11: Encapsulation Principle

A class should encapsulate its state so that access to the state happens only via public methods.

Encapsulation is achieved by declaring class attributes private. You can create getter and setter methods if you need the state to be modifiable outside the class. However, encapsulation is best ensured if you don't need to create getter and setter methods for the class attributes. Do not automatically implement or generate getter and setter methods for every class. Only create those accessor methods if needed, like when the class represents a modifiable data structure. An automatically generated getter can break the encapsulation of a class if the getter returns modifiable internal state, like a list. Only generate setter methods for attributes that need to be modified outside the class. If you have a class with many getters, you might be guilty of *feature envy* code smell, where other objects query your object for its internal state and perform operations based on that state. You should follow the *tell, don't ask principle* (discussed later in this chapter) by removing the getters from your class and implementing the operation in your class.

4.11.1: Immutable Objects

The best way to ensure the encapsulation of an object's state is to make the object immutable. This means that once the object is created, its state cannot be modified afterward. Immutability ensures you cannot accidentally or intentionally modify the object's state. Modifying the object's state outside the object can be a source of bugs.

When creating an immutable object, you give the needed parameters for the object in the constructor, and after that, those properties cannot be modified (You don't create any setters for the class). If you need to modify an immutable object, the only way is to create a new object with different values given in the constructor. The drawback of this approach is that a performance penalty is introduced when creating new objects as compared to modifying existing objects' attributes only. But in many cases, this penalty is negligible compared to the benefits of immutability. For example, strings are immutable in Java and JavaScript. Once you create a string, you cannot modify it. You can only create new strings.

Immutability also requires that getters and other methods returning a value may not return a modifiable attribute, like a list. If you return a list from a method, that list could be modified by adding or removing elements without the "owning" object being aware of that.

4.11.2: Don't Leak Modifiable Internal State Outside an Object Principle

Beware when you return values from methods. It is possible that a method accidentally returns some internal state of the object that can be modified later by the method caller. Returning modifiable state from a method breaks the encapsulation.

You can safely return an object's internal state when it has a primitive or so-called value type. Those include bool, int, and float. You can also safely return an immutable object, like a string. But you cannot safely return a mutable collection, for example.

There are two ways to protect against leaking internal state outside an object:

1) Return a copy of the modifiable internal state
2) Return an unmodifiable version of the modifiable internal state

Regarding the first approach, when a copy is returned, the caller can use it as they like. Changes made to the copied object don't affect the original object. I am primarily talking about making a shallow copy. In many cases, a shallow copy is enough. For example, a list of primitive values, immutable strings, or immutable objects does not require a deep copy of the list. But you should make a deep copy when needed.

The copying approach can cause a performance penalty, but in many cases, that penalty is insignificant. In JavaScript, you can easily create a copy of an array:

```
const values = [1, 2, 3, 4, 5];
const copyOfValues = [...values];
```

And in Java:

```
final var values = new ArrayList<Integer>();
// ...
final var copyOfValues = List.copyOf(values);
```

The second approach requires you to create an unmodifiable version of a modifiable object and return that unmodifiable object. Some languages offer an easy way to create unmodifiable versions of certain objects. In Java, you can create an unmodifiable version of a List, Map, or Set using Collections.unmodifiableList, Collections.unmodifiableMap or Collections.unmodifiableSet factory method, respectively.

You can also create an unmodifiable version of a class by yourself. Below is an example in Java:

```
public interface MyList<T> {
  void addToEnd(T item);
  Optional<T> getItem(int index);
}
public class UnmodifiableMyList<T> implements MyList<T> {
  private final MyList<T> list;

  public UnmodifiableMyList(final MyList<T> list) {
    this.list = list;
  }

  public void addToEnd(final T item) {
    throw new UnsupportedOperationException(...);
  }

  public Optional<T> getItem(final int index) {
    return list.getItem(index);
  }
}
```

In the above example, the unmodifiable list class takes another list (a modifiable list) as a constructor argument. It only implements the MyList interface methods that don't attempt to modify the wrapped list. In this case, it implements only the getItem method that delegates to the respective method in the MyList class. The UnmodifiableMyList class methods that attempt to modify the wrapped list should throw an error. The UnmodifiableMyList class utilizes the *proxy pattern* by wrapping an object of the MyList class and partially allowing access to the MyList class methods.

In C++, you can return an unmodifiable version by declaring the return type as *const*, for example:

```
std::shared_ptr<const std::vector<std::string>>
getStringValues() const;
```

Now, callers of the getStringValues method cannot modify the returned vector of strings because it is declared const.

Unmodifiable and immutable objects are slightly different. No one can modify an immutable object, but when you return an unmodifiable object from a class method, that object can still be modified by the owning class, and modifications are visible to everyone who has received an unmodifiable version of the object. If this is something undesirable, you should use a copy instead.

4.11.3: Don't Assign From a Method Parameter to a Modifiable Attribute

If a class receives modifiable objects as a constructor or method arguments, it is typically best practice not to directly assign those arguments to the internal state. If they are assigned directly, the class can purposely or accidentally modify those argument objects, which is probably not what the constructor or method caller expects.

There are two ways to handle this situation:

1) Store a copy of the modifiable argument object to the class's internal state
2) Store an unmodifiable version of the modifiable argument object to the class's internal state

Below is a Java example of the second approach:

```
public class MyClass {
  private final List<Integer> values;

  public MyClass(final List<Integer> values) {
    this.values = Collections.unmodifiableList(values);
  }
}
```

4.12: Prefer Composition Over Inheritance Principle

In object-oriented design, like in real life, objects are constructed by constructing larger objects from smaller objects. This is called object composition. Prefer object composition over inheritance.

This principle is presented in the *Design Patterns* book by the *Gang of Four*. An example of composition is a car object composed of an engine and transmission object (to name a few). Objects are rarely "composed" by deriving from another object, i.e., using inheritance. But first, let's try to specify classes that implement the below Java Car interface using inheritance and see where it leads us:

```
public interface Car {
  void drive(
    Location start,
    Location destination
  );
}


public class CombustionEngineCar implements Car {
  public void drive(
    final Location start,
    final Location destination
  ) {
    // ...
  }
}


public class ElectricEngineCar implements Car {
  public void drive(
    final Location start,
    final Location destination
  ) {
    // ...
  }
}


public class ManualTransmissionCombustionEngineCar
        extends CombustionEngineCar {
  public void drive(
    final Location start,
    final Location destination
  ) {
    // ...
  }
}


public class AutomaticTransmissionCombustionEngineCar
        extends CombustionEngineCar {
  public void drive(
    final Location start,
    final Location destination
  ) {
    // ...
  }
}
```

If we wanted to add other components to a car, like a two or four-wheel drive, the number of classes needed would increase by three. If we wanted to add a design property (sedan, hatchback, wagon, or SUV) to a car, the number of needed classes would explode, and the class names would become ridiculously long, like HatchbackFourWheelDriveAutomaticTransmissionCombustionEngineCar. We can notice that inheritance is not the correct way to build more complex classes here.

Class inheritance creates an *is-a* relationship between a superclass and its subclasses. Object composition creates a *has-a* relationship. We can claim that ManualTransmissionCombustionEngineCar *is a* kind of CombustionEngineCar, so basically, we are not doing anything wrong here, one might think. But when designing classes, you should first determine if object composition could be used: is there a *has-a* relationship? Can you declare a class as an attribute of another class? If the answer is yes, then composition should be used instead of inheritance.

All the above things related to a car are actually properties of a car. A car *has an* engine. A car *has a* transmission. It *has a* two or four-wheel drive and design. We can turn the inheritance-based solution into a composition-based solution:

```
public interface Drivable {
  void drive(
    Location start,
    Location destination
  );
}


public interface Engine {
  // Methods like start, stop ...
}


public class CombustionEngine implements Engine {
  // Methods like start, stop ...
}


public class ElectricEngine implements Engine {
  // Methods like start, stop ...
}


public interface Transmission {
  // Methods like changeGear ...
}


public class AutomaticTransmission implements Transmission {
  // Methods like changeGear ...
}


public class ManualTransmission implements Transmission {
  // Methods like changeGear ...
}


// Define DriveType here...
// Define Design here...


public class Car implements Drivable {
  private final Engine engine;
  private final Transmission transmission;
  private final DriveType driveType;
  private final Design design;

  public Car(
    final Engine engine,
    final Transmission transmission,
    final DriveType driveType,
    final Design design
  ) {
    this.engine = engine;
    this.transmission = transmission;
    this.driveType = driveType;
    this.design = design;
  }

  public void drive(
    final Location start,
    final Location destination
  ) {
    // To implement functionality, delegate to
    // component classes, for example:

    // engine.start();
    // transmission.shiftGear(...);
    // ...
```

```
    // engine.stop();
  }
}
```

Let's have a more realistic example in TypeScript with different chart types. At first, this sounds like a case where inheritance could be used: We have some abstract base charts that different concrete charts extend:

```
interface Chart {
  renderView(): JSX.Element;
  updateData(...): void;
}


abstract class AbstractChart implements Chart {
  abstract renderView(): JSX.Element;
  abstract updateData(...): void;

  // Implement some common functionality
  // shared by all chart types
}


abstract class XAxisChart extends AbstractChart {
  abstract renderView(): JSX.Element;

  updateData(...): void {
    // This is common for all x-axis charts,
    // like ColumnChart, LineChart and AreaChart
  }
}


class ColumnChart extends XAxisChart {
  renderView(): JSX.Element {
    // ...

    return (
      <XYZChart
        type="column"
        data={data}
        options={options}...
      />;
    );
  }
}


// LineChart class definition here...
// AreaChart class definition here...


abstract class NonAxisChart extends AbstractChart {
  abstract renderView(): JSX.Element;

  updateData(...): void {
    // This is common for all non-x-axis charts,
    // like PieChart and DonutChart
  }
}


class PieChart extends NonAxisChart {
  renderView(): JSX.Element {
    // ...

    return (
      <XYZChart
        type="pie"
```

```
      data={data}
      options={options}...
    />;
  );
  }
}


class DonutChart extends PieChart {
  renderView(): JSX.Element {
    // ...

    return (
      <XYZChart
        type="donut"
        data={data}
        options={options}...
      />;
    );
  }
}
```

The above class hierarchy looks manageable: there should not be too many subclasses that need to be defined. We can, of course, think of new chart types, like a geographical map or data table for which we could add subclasses. One problem with a deep class hierarchy arises when you need to change or correct something related to a particular chart type. Let's say you want to change or correct some behavior related to a pie chart. You will first check the PieChart class to see if the behavior is defined there. If you can't find what you are looking for, you need to navigate to the base class of the PieChart class (NonAxisChart) and look there. You need to continue this navigation until you reach the base class where the behavior you want to change or correct is located. Of course, if you are incredibly familiar with the codebase, you might be able to locate the correct subclass on the first try. But in general, this is not a straightforward task.

Using class inheritance can introduce class hierarchies where some classes have significantly more methods than other classes. For example, in the chart inheritance chain, the AbstractChart class probably has significantly more methods than classes at the end of the inheritance chain. This class size difference creates an imbalance between classes, making it hard to reason about the functionality each class provides.

Even if the above class hierarchy might look okay at first sight, there currently lies one problem. We have hardcoded the kind of chart view we are rendering. We use the *XYZ* chart library and render XYZChart views. Let's say we would like to introduce another chart library called *ABC*. We want to use both chart libraries in parallel so that the open-source version of our data visualization application uses the *XYZ* chart library, which is open source. The paid version of our application uses the commercial *ABC* chart library. When using class inheritance, we must create new classes for each concrete chart type for the *ABC* chart library. So, we would have two classes for each concrete chart type, like here for the pie chart:

```
class XYZPieChart extends XyzNonAxisChart {
  renderView(): JSX.Element {
    // ...

    return (
      <XYZChart
        type="pie"
        data={data}
        options={options}...
      />;
    );
  }
}


class ABCPieChart extends AbcNonAxisChart {
```

```
  renderView(): JSX.Element {
    // ...

    return (
      <ABCPieChart
        dataSeries={dataSeries}
        chartOptions={chartOptions}...
      />;
    );
  }
}
```

Implementing the above functionality using composition instead of inheritance has several benefits:

- It is more apparent what behavior each class contains
- There is no significant size imbalance between classes, where some classes are huge and others relatively small
- You can split chart behaviors into classes as you find fit, and is in accordance with the *single responsibility principle*

In the below example, we have split some chart behavior into two types of classes: chart view renderers and chart data factories:

```
interface Chart {
  renderView(): JSX.Element;
  updateData(...): void;
}


interface ChartViewRenderer {
  renderView(data: ChartData, options: ChartOptions): JSX.Element;
}


interface ChartDataFactory {
  createData(...): ChartData
}


// ChartData...
// ChartOptions...


class ChartImpl implements Chart {
  private data: ChartData;
  private options: ChartOptions;

  constructor(
    private readonly viewRenderer: ChartViewRenderer,
    private readonly dataFactory: ChartDataFactory
  ) {
    // ...
  }

  renderView(): JSX.Element {
    return this.viewRenderer.renderView(this.data, this.options);
  }

  updateData(...): void {
    this.data = this.dataFactory.createData(...);
  }
}
```

```
class XYZPieChartViewRenderer implements ChartViewRenderer {
  renderView(data: ChartData, options: ChartOptions): JSX.Element {
    // ...

    return (
      <XYZPieChart
        data={dataInXyzChartLibFormat}
        options={optionsInXyzChartLibFormat}...
      />;
    );
  }
}


class ABCPieChartViewRenderer implements ChartViewRenderer {
    renderView(data: ChartData, options: ChartOptions): JSX.Element {
      // ...

      return (
        <ABCPieChart
          dataSeries={dataInAbcChartLibFormat}
          chartOptions={optionsInAbcChartLibFormat}...
        />;
      );
    }
}


// ABCColumnChartViewRenderer...
// XYZColumnChartViewRenderer...


type ChartType = 'column' | 'pie';

interface ChartFactory {
  createChart(chartType: ChartType): Chart;
}


class ABCChartFactory implements ChartFactory {
  createChart(chartType: ChartType): Chart {
    switch(chartType) {
      case 'column':
        return new ChartImpl(new ABCColumnChartViewRenderer(),
                             new XAxisChartDataFactory());
      case 'pie':
        return new ChartImpl(new ABCPieChartViewRenderer(),
                             new NonAxisChartDataFactory());

      default:
        throw new Error('Invalid chart type');
    }
  }
}


class XYZChartFactory implements ChartFactory {
  createChart(chartType: ChartType): Chart {
    switch(chartType) {
      case 'column':
        return new ChartImpl(new XYZColumnChartViewRenderer(),
                             new XAxisChartDataFactory());
      case 'pie':
        return new ChartImpl(new XYZPieChartViewRenderer(),
                             new NonAxisChartDataFactory());

      default:
        throw new Error('Invalid chart type');
    }
```

```
    }
}
```

The XYZPieChartViewRenderer and ABCPieChartViewRenderer classes use the *adapter pattern* to convert the supplied data and options to an implementation (ABC or XYZ chart library) specific interface.

We can easily add more functionality by composing the ChartImpl class of more classes. There could be, for example, a title formatter, tooltip formatter class, y/x-axis label formatter, and event handler classes.

```
class ChartImpl implements Chart {
  private data: ChartData;
  private options: ChartOptions;

  constructor(
    private readonly viewRenderer: ChartViewRenderer,
    private readonly dataFactory: ChartDataFactory,
    private readonly titleFormatter: ChartTitleFormatter,
    private readonly tooltipFormatter: ChartTooltipFormatter,
    private readonly xAxisLabelFormatter: ChartXAxisLabelFormatter,
    private readonly eventHandler: ChartEventHandler
  ) {
    // ...
  }

  renderView(): JSX.Element {
    return this.viewRenderer.renderView(this.data, this.options);
  }

  updateData(...): void {
    this.data = this.dataFactory.createData(...);
  }
}


class ABCChartFactory implements ChartFactory {
  createChart(chartType: ChartType): Chart {
    switch(chartType) {
      case 'column':
        return new ChartImpl(new ABCColumnChartViewRenderer(),
                             new XAxisChartDataFactory(),
                             new ChartTitleFormatterImpl(),
                             new XAxisChartTooltipFormatter(),
                             new ChartXAxisLabelFormatterImpl(),
                             new ColumnChartEventHandler());

      case 'pie':
        return new ChartImpl(new ABCColumnChartViewRenderer(),
                             new NonAxisChartDataFactory(),
                             new ChartTitleFormatterImpl(),
                             new NonAxisChartTooltipFormatter(),
                             new NullXAxisLabelFormatter(),
                             new NonAxisChartEventHandler());

      default:
        throw new Error('Invalid chart type');
    }
  }
}
```

4.13: Tactical Domain-Driven Design Principle

In Tactical DDD, you define your domain models in more detail. Tactical DDD is applied within a single bounded context.

We continue here where we left off with strategic DDD in the last chapter. Strategic DDD was about dividing a software system into subdomains and bounded contexts (microservices). Tactical DDD is about implementing a single bounded context. Tactical DDD means that the structure of a bounded context and the names appearing in the code (interface, class, function, and variable names) should match the domain's vocabulary and the ubiquitous language. For example, names like *Account, withdraw, deposit, makeMayment* should be used in a *payment-service* bounded context.

4.13.1: Tactical DDD Concepts

Tactical domain-driven design recognizes multiple concepts:

- Entities
- Value Objects
- Aggregates
- Aggregate Roots
- Factories
- Repositories
- Services
- Events

4.13.1.1: Entities

An entity is a domain object that has an identity. Usually, this is indicated by the entity class having some *id* attribute. Examples of entities are an *employee* and a *bank account*. An employee object has an employee id, and a bank account has a number that identifies the bank account. Entities can contain methods that operate on the attributes of the entity. For example, a bank account entity can have methods *withdraw* and *deposit* that operate on the *balance* attribute of the entity.

4.13.1.2: Value Objects

Value objects are domain objects that don't have an identity. Examples of value objects are an address or a price object. The price object can have two attributes: *amount* and *currency*, but it does not have an identity. Similarly, an address object can have the following attributes: *street address, postal code, city* and *country*. Value objects can and many times should have behavior in them. For example, a *price* value object can have a validation rule for accepted currencies. You can also put behavior, like converting a price object to another price object with a different currency, into the Price value object class. So, it should be remembered that value objects are not just holders of a set of primitive values.

4.13.1.3: Aggregates

Aggregates are entities composed of other entities and value objects. For example, an *order* entity can have one or more *order item* entities. Regarding object-oriented design, this is the same as object composition. Each aggregate has a root (entity). The figure below shows a SalesItem aggregate. A SalesItem entity is an aggregate and aggregate root. It can contain one or more images of the sales item, and it consists of a Price value object, which has two attributes: price and currency.

Aggregate

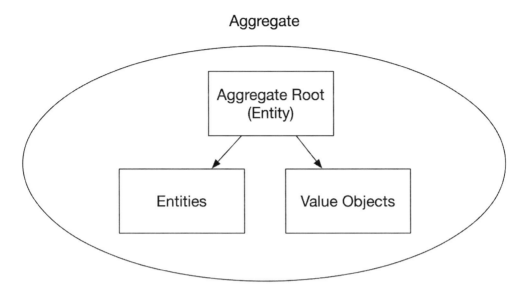

SalesItem

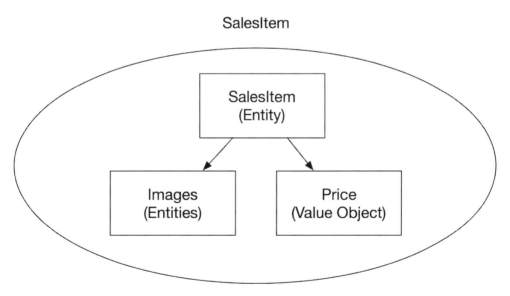

Figure 4.15. Aggregate Example

4.13.1.4: Aggregate Roots

Aggregate roots are domain objects that don't have any parent objects. An *order* entity is an aggregate root when it does not have a parent entity. But an *order item* entity is not an aggregate root when it belongs to an *order*. Aggregate roots serve as facade objects. Operations should be performed on the aggregate root objects, not directly accessing the objects behind the facade (e.g., not directly accessing the individual order items, but performing operations on order objects). For example, if you have an aggregate car object containing wheels, you don't operate the wheels outside of the car object. The car object provides a facade like a *turn* method, and the car object internally operates the wheels, making the car object an aggregate root. The *facade pattern* will be discussed later in this chapter.

Let's have an example of aggregate roots in a microservice architecture. Suppose we have a bank account, an aggregate root containing transaction entities. The bank account and transaction entities can be handled in different microservices (*account-service* and *account-transaction-service*), but only the *account-service* can directly access and modify the transaction entities using the *account-transaction-service*. Our bounded context is the *account-service*. The role and benefit of an aggregate root are the following:

- The aggregate root protects against invariant violation. For example, no other service should directly remove or add transactions using the *account-transaction-service*. That would break the invariant that the sum of transactions should be the same as the balance of the account maintained by the *account-service*.
- The aggregate root simplifies (database/distributed) transactions. Your microservice can access the *account-service* and let it manage the distributed transactions between the *account-service* and *account-transaction-service*. It's not something that your microservice needs to do.

You can easily split an aggregate root into more entities. For example, the bank account aggregate root could contain balance and transaction entities. The balance entity could be handled by a separate *account-balance-service*. Still, all bank account operations must be made to the *account-service*, which will orchestrate, e.g., *withdraw* and *deposit* operations using the *account-balance-service* and *account-transaction-service*. We can even split the *account-service* to two separate microservices: *account-service* for account CRUD operations (excluding updates related to balance) and *account-money-transfer-service* that will handle *withdraw* and *deposit* operations using the two lower-level microservices: *account-balance-service* and *account-transaction-service*. In the previous chapter, we had an example of the latter case when we discussed distributed transactions.

4.13.1.5: Actors

Actors perform commands. End-users are actors in the strategic DDD, but services can be actors in tactical DDD. For example, in a data exporter microservice, there can be an input message consumer service that has a command to consume a message from a data source.

4.13.1.6: Factories

In domain-driven design, the creation of domain objects can be separated from the domain object classes to factories. Factories are objects that are dedicated to creating objects of a particular type. If the factory is not too large, instead of creating a separate factory class, you can create a static factory method in the domain entity class.

4.13.1.7: Repositories

A repository is an object with methods for persisting domain objects and retrieving them from a data store (e.g., a database). Typically, there is one repository for each aggregate root, e.g., an *order repository* for order entities.

4.13.1.8: Services

Services can be divided into *domain* and *application* services. Application services are used to implement business use cases. External clients connect to the application services via input interface adapters. Domain services contain functionality that is not directly part of any specific domain object. For this reason, domain services should be stateless. A domain service is a class that does not represent a concept in the problem domain. It is also called *pure fabrication* according to GRASP[14] principles. Application services orchestrate operations on aggregate roots. For example, an `OrderService` orchestrates operations on order entities. Application services do not contain business logic themselves but only procedural orchestration code to fulfill the wanted use case using other classes (domain services, domain entities and output interfaces) to achieve that An application service typically uses a related repository to perform persistence-related operations. A service can also be seen as an actor with specific command(s). For example, in a data exporter microservice, there can be an input message consumer service that has a command to consume a message from a data source.

Whenever possible, aim for a side-effect-free, functional, and immutable domain model (domain services and objects) and put side effects on the outer application service layer. The application service layer can have several variations. A single application service (or service class method) implements a use case or a feature. In the simplest form, an application service is a *transaction script* when no domain services are involved. This is usually the case for simple CRUD-based APIs where the application service class performs simple CRUD operations like creating a new sales item. Let's have an example of a transaction script with a backlog item service. The service has an update backlog item use case (or feature) where the application service method first fetches the sprint the backlog item is assigned from a repository and then calls the backlog item factory to create a new backlog item with the specific sprint object also given as a parameter in addition to the updated backlog item DTO. The factory should validate if the sprint is valid (a current or a future sprint, not a past one). The factory can be implemented in various ways, using one of the *factory patterns*, e.g., a separate factory class or a static factory method in the entity class. Factory can create different variants of backlog item entities if needed. For example, the factory can create various objects based on the backlog item type, like a `TeamBacklogItem` or `ProductBacklogItem` object. After the backlog item is created using the factory, it can be persisted using a repository's update method. In this simple example, domain services are not needed. In more complex cases, the model usually has domain services.

In your microservice, you can have three kinds of services: domain, application, and external. If you name all the classes implementing the services with `Service` postfix, it can be challenging to distinguish between different service types. For that reason, you can use a directory structure where you separate different types of services into different subdirectories:

---

[14]https://en.wikipedia.org/wiki/GRASP_(object-oriented_design)

```
- ifadapters
  - controllers
  - repositories
  - services
    - SomeRemoteOrderPaymentService.java
    - SomeRemoteShoppingCartService.java
- model (or core)
  - domain
    - entities
      - Order.java
      - OrderItem.java
    - services
      - OrderPaymentService.java
      - ShoppingCartService.java
  - application
    - repositories
    - services
      - OrderService.java
      - OrderServiceImpl.java
```

Alternatively, you can call your application services as use cases and name the use case classes so that they have a `UseCases` postfix.

```
- ifadapters
  - controllers
  - repositories
  - services
    - SomeRemoteOrderPaymentService.java
    - SomeRemoteShoppingCartService.java
- model (or core)
  - domain
    - entities
      - Order.java
      - OrderItem.java
    - services
      - OrderPaymentService.java
      - ShoppingCartService.java
  - application
    - repositories
    - usecases
      - OrderUseCases.java
      - OrderUseCasesImpl.java
```

4.13.1.9: Events

Events are operations on entities and form the business use cases. Services usually handle events. For example, there could be the following events related to order entities: create, update, and cancel an order. These events can be implemented by having an `OrderService` with the following methods: `createOrder`, `updateOrder`, and `cancelOrder`.

4.13.1.10: Design-Level Event Storming

Design-level event storming is a lightweight method (a workshop) that a team can use to discover DDD-related concepts in a bounded context. The event storming process typically follows the below steps:

1) Figure out *domain events* (events are usually written in past tense)
2) Figure out *commands* that caused the *domain events*
3) Add *actors*/*services* that execute the *commands*

4) Figure out related *entities*

In the event storming workshop, the different DDD concepts, such as events, commands, actors, and entities, are represented with sticky notes in different colors. These sticky notes are put on a wall, and related sticky notes are grouped together, like the actor, the command, and entity/entities related to a specific domain event. If you are interested in details of the event storming process, there is a book named *Introducing EventStorming* by *Alberto Brandolini*.

4.13.2: Tactical DDD Example 1: Data Exporter Microservice

Let's have a DDD example with a microservice for exporting data. Data exporting will be our top-level domain. The development team should participate in the DDD and object-oriented design (OOD) process. An expert-level software developer, e.g., the team tech lead, could do the DDD and OOD alone, but it is not how it should be done. Other team members, especially the junior ones, should be involved to learn and develop their skills further.

The DDD process is started by first defining the big picture (top-level domain) based on requirements from the product management and the architecture team:

> Data exporter handles data that consists of messages that contain multiple fields. Data exporting should happen from an input system to an output system. During the export, various transformations to the data can be made, and the data formats in the input and output systems can differ.

Let's start the event-storming process by figuring out the domain events:

1) A message is consumed from the input system
2) The input message is decoded into an internal representation (i.e., an internal message)
3) The internal message is transformed
4) The transformed message is encoded to the wanted output format
5) The transformed message is produced in the output system
6) Configuration is read and parsed

From the above events, we can figure out four subdomains:

- Input (Events 1, 2 and 6)
- Internal Message (Events 2 and 3)
- Transform (Events 3 and 6)
- Output (Events 4, 5 and 6)

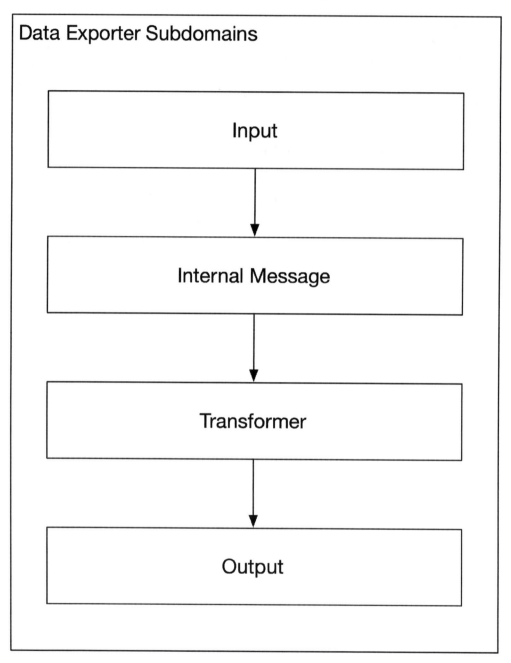

Figure 4.16. Data Exporter Subdomains

Let's take the first domain event, "Messages are consumed from the input system," and figure out what caused the event and who was the actor. Because no end-user is involved, we can conclude that the event was caused by an "input message consumer" *service* executing a "consume message" *command*. This operation creates an "input message" *entity*. The picture below shows how this would look with sticky notes on the wall.

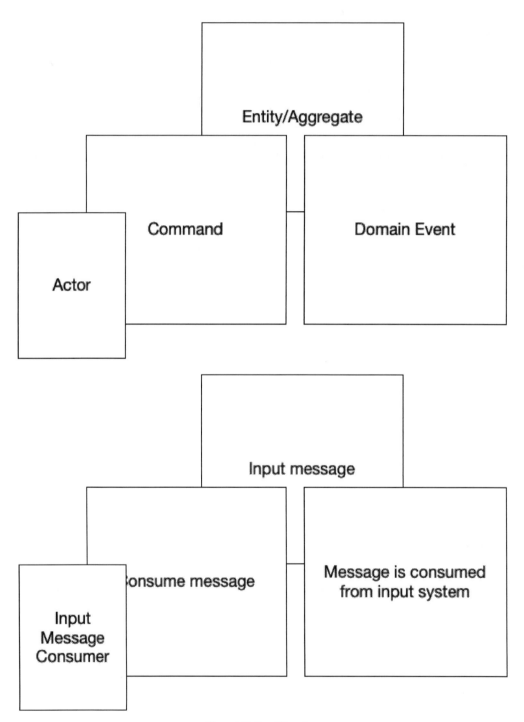

Figure 4.17. Event Storming

When continuing the event storming process further for the *Input* domain, we can figure out that it consists of the following additional DDD concepts:

- Commands

  - Read input configuration
  - Parse input configuration
  - Consume input message
  - Decode input message

- Actors/Services

  - Input configuration reader
  - Input configuration parser
  - Input message consumer
  - Input message decoder

- Entities

  - Input message

- Value Objects

  - Input configuration

The event-storming process that resulted in the above list of DDD concepts is actually object-oriented analysis[15] (OOA). We got an initial set of objects that our use case needs when implemented. We got all of them only by looking at the domain events that consist of a verb and an object. We just have to figure out the actor that causes the domain event to happen. Many times, it can also be directly inferred from the domain event.

The actors/services are often singleton objects. Entities and value objects are objects. Commands are the main methods in the actor/service classes. The OOA phase should result in an initial class diagram[16] showing the main classes and their relationships with other classes.

Below is the list of sub-domains, interfaces, and classes in the *Input* domain:

- Input message

  - Contains the message consumed from the input data source
  - `InputMessage` is an interface that can have several concrete implementations, like `KafkaInputMessage` representing an input message consumed from a Kafka data source

- Input message consumer

  - Consumes messages from the input data source and creates `InputMessage` instances
  - `InputMessageConsumer` is an interface that can have several concrete implementations, like `KafkaInputMessageConsumer` for consuming messages from a Kafka data source

---

[15] https://en.wikipedia.org/wiki/Object-oriented_analysis_and_design#Object-oriented_analysis
[16] https://en.wikipedia.org/wiki/Class_diagram

- Input Message decoder

  - Decodes input messages into internal messages
  - `InputMessageDecoder` is an interface with several concrete implementations, like `AvroBinaryInputMessageDecoder`, which decodes input messages encoded in Avro binary format. (If you provide multiple implementations for the `InputMessageDecoder` interface, you must also create a factory class to create different kinds of input message decoders).

- Input configuration

  - Input configuration reader

    * Reads the domain's configuration
    * `InputConfigReader` is an interface that can have several concrete implementations, like `LocalFileSystemInputConfigReader` or `HttpRemoteInputConfigReader`

  - Input configuration parser

    * Parses the read configuration to produce an `InputConfig` instance
    * `InputConfigParser` is an interface that can have several concrete implementations, like `JsonInputConfigParser` or `YamlInputConfigParser`

  - `InputConfig` instance contains parsed configuration for the domain, lsuch asthe input data source type, host, port, and input data format.

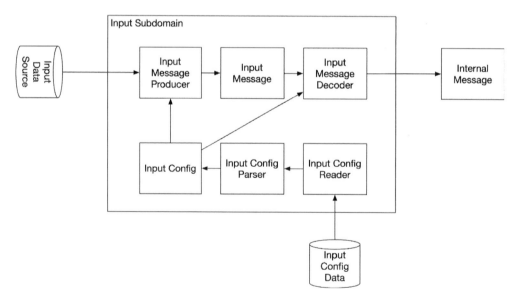

Figure 4.18. Input Subdomain

Next, we should perform object-oriented design[17] (OOD) and design objects in a more detailed way, using various design principles and patterns. As shown in the below class diagram, we have applied the *dependency inversion / program against interfaces principle* to the result of the earlier OOA phase:

---

[17]https://en.wikipedia.org/wiki/Object-oriented_analysis_and_design#Object-oriented_design

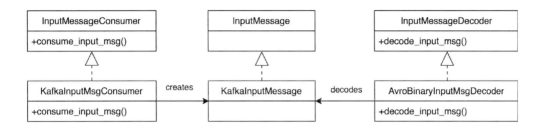

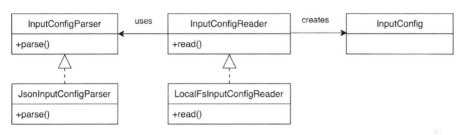

Figure 4.19. Input Subdomain Class Diagram

When applying the event storming process to the *Internal Message* domain, we can figure out that it consists of the following DDD concepts:

- Entities

  - Internal message
  - Internal field

- Aggregate

  - Internal message (consists of fields)

- Aggregate root

  - Internal message

Below is the list of sub-domains, interfaces, and classes in the *Internal Message* domain:

- Internal Message

  - Internal message consists of one or more internal fields
  - `InternalMessage` is an interface for a class that provides an internal representation of an input message

- Internal Field

  - `InternalField` is an interface for classes representing a single field of an internal message

When applying the event storming process to the *Transform* domain, we can figure out that it consists of the following DDD concepts:

- Commands

  - Read transformer configuration
  - Parse transformer configuration
  - Transform message
  - Transform field

- Actors/Services

  - Transformer configuration reader
  - Transformer configuration parser
  - Message transformer
  - Field transformer

- Value objects

  - Transformer configuration

Below is the list of sub-domains, interfaces, and classes in the *Transform* domain:

- Field transformer

  - `FieldTransformers` is a collection of `FieldTransformer` objects
  - A Field transformer transforms the value of an internal field into the value of an output message field
  - `FieldTransformer` is an interface that can have several concrete implementations, like `FilterFieldTransformer`, `CopyFieldTransformer`, `TypeConversionFieldTransformer` and `ExpressionTransformer`

- Message Transformer

  - `MessageTransformer` takes an internal message and transforms it using field transformers

- Transformer configuration

  - Transformer configuration reader

    * Reads the domain's configuration
    * `TransformerConfigReader` is an interface that can have several concrete implementations, like `LocalFileSystemTransformerConfigReader`

  - Transformer configuration parser

    * Parses read configuration to produce a `TransformerConfig` instance
    * `TransformerConfigParser` is an interface that can have several concrete implementations, like `JsonTransformerConfigParser`

  - `TransformerConfig` instance contains parsed configuration for the *Transformer* domain

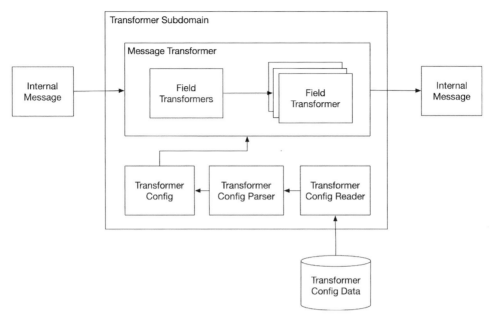

Figure 4.20. Transform Subdomain

Below is the class diagram for the Transform subdomain. I have left the configuration part out of the diagram because it is pretty much the same as the configuration part in the Input domain.

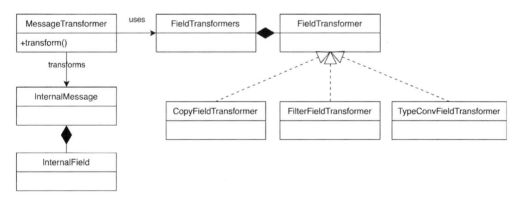

Figure 4.21. Transform Subdomain Class Diagram

When applying the event storming process to the *Output* domain, we can figure out that it consists of the following DDD concepts:

- Commands

  - Read output configuration

- Parse output configuration
- Encode output message
- Produce output message

- Actors/Services

  - Output configuration reader
  - Output configuration parser
  - Output message encoder
  - Output message producer

- Entities

  - Output message

- Value objects

  - Output configuration

Below is the list of sub-domains, interfaces, and classes in the *Output* domain:

- Output Message encoder

  - Encodes transformed message to an output message with a specific data format
  - `OutputMessageEncoder` is an interface that can have several concrete implementations, like `CsvOutputMessageEncoder, JsonOutputMessageEncoder, AvroBinaryOutputMessageEncoder`

- Output message

  - `OutputMessage` is a container for an output byte sequence

- Output message producer

  - Produces output messages to the output destination
  - `OutputMessageProducer` is an interface that can have several concrete implementations, like `KafkaOutputMessageProducer`

- Output configuration

  - Output configuration reader

    * Reads the domain's configuration
    * `OutputConfigReader` is an interface that can have several concrete implementations, like `LocalFileSystemOutputConfigReader`

  - Output configuration parser

    * Parse the read configuration to an `OutputConfig` instance
    * `OutputConfigParser` is an interface that can have several concrete implementations, like `JsonOutputConfigParser`

– `OutputConfig` instance contains parsed configuration for the domain, like output destination type, host, port, and the output data format

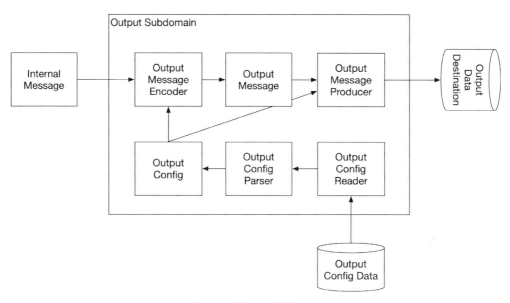

Figure 4.22. Output Subdomain

Below is the class diagram for the Output subdomain. I have left the configuration part out of the diagram because it is pretty much the same as the configuration part in the Input domain.

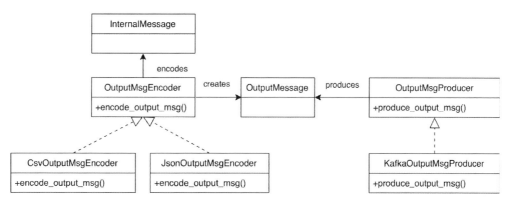

Figure 4.23. Output Subdomain Class Diagram

The above design also follows the *clean architecture principle.* Note that this principle applies to all kinds of microservices with input or output, not just APIs. From the above design, we can discover the following interface adapters that are not part of the business logic of the microservice:

- `InputMessageConsumer` interface implementations
- `InputMessageDecoder` interface implementations
- `OutputMessageEncoder` interface implementations
- `OutputMessageProducer` interface implementations
- `InputConfigReader` interface implementations
- `InputConfigParser` interface implementations
- `TransformerConfigReader` interface implementations
- `TransformerConfigParser` interface implementations
- `OutputConfigReader` interface implementations
- `OutputConfigParser` interface implementations

We should be able to modify the implementations mentioned above or add a new implementation without modifying other parts of the code (the core or business logic). This means that we can easily adapt our microservice to consume data from different data sources in different data formats and output the transformed data to different data sources in various data formats. Additionally, the configuration of our microservice can be read from various sources in different formats. For example, if we now read some configuration from a local file in JSON format, in the future, we could introduce new classes for reading the configuration from an API using some other data format.

After defining the interfaces between the above-defined subdomains, the four subdomains can be developed very much in parallel. This can speed up the microservice development significantly. The code of each subdomain should be put into separate source code folders. We will discuss source code organization more in the next chapter.

Based on the above design, the following data processing pipeline can be implemented (C++):

```
void DataExporterApp::run()
{
  while(m_isRunning)
  {
    const auto inputMessage =
      m_inputMessageConsumer.consumeInputMessage();

    const auto internalMessage =
      m_inputMessageDecoder.decodeToInternalMessage(inputMessage);

    const auto transformedMessage =
      m_messageTransformer.transform(*internalMessage);

    const auto outputMessage =
      m_outputMessageEncoder.encode(transformedMessage);

    m_outputMessageProducer.produce(outputMessage);
  }
}
```

And the `MessageTransformer::transform` method can be implemented in the following way:

```
std::unique_ptr<InternalMessage> MessageTransformer::transform(
  const InternalMessage& internalMessage
)
{
  const auto transformedMessage =
    std::make_unique<InternalMessageImpl>();

  std::ranges::for_each(m_fieldTransformers,
                        [&internalMessage, &transformedMessage]
                        (const auto& fieldTransformer) {
    fieldTransformer.transform(internalMessage,
                               transformedMessage);
  });

  return transformedMessage;
}
```

4.13.3: Tactical DDD Example 2: Anomaly Detection Microservice

Let's have another DDD example with an anomaly detection microservice. The purpose of the microservice is to detect anomalies in measurement data. This concise description of the microservice's purpose reveals the two subdomains of the microservice:

- Anomaly
- Measurement

Let's first analyze the *Measurement* subdomain in more detail and define domain events for it:

- Measurement data source definitions are loaded
- Measurement data source definitions are parsed
- Measurement definitions are loaded
- Measurement definitions are parsed
- Measurement data is fetched from data sources
- Measurement data is scaled (for further AI processing)

Let's continue using the event storming and define additional DDD concepts:

- Commands

    - Load measurement data source definitions
    - Parse measurement data source definitions
    - Load measurement definitions
    - Parse measurement definitions
    - Fetch measurement data from data sources
    - Scale measurement data -Actors/Services
    - Measurement data source definitions loader
    - Measurement data source definitions parser
    - Measurement definitions loader
    - Measurement definitions parser
    - Measurement data fetcher
    - Measurement data scaler

- Entities

  - Measurement data source
  - Measurement data
  - Measurement

- Aggregates

  - Measurement

    * Measurement data source
    * Measurement query
    * Measurement data

- Aggregate root

  - Measurement

- Value Objects

  - Measurement query

Let's define domain events for the *Anomaly* subdomain:

- Anomaly detection configuration is parsed
- Anomaly detection configuration is created
- Anomaly detection rule is parsed
- Anomaly detection rule is created
- Anomalies are detected in a measurement according to the anomaly detection rule using a trained anomaly model
- Anomaly detection is triggered at regular intervals
- Anomaly model is trained for a measurement
- Anomaly model is created
- Anomaly model training is triggered at regular intervals
- A detected anomaly (i.e., an anomaly indicator) is created
- A detected anomaly (i.e., an anomaly indicator) is serialized to a wanted format, e.g., JSON
- The detected anomaly (i.e., an anomaly indicator) is published to a specific destination using a specific protocol

Let's continue with the event storming and define additional DDD concepts:

- Commands

  - Parse anomaly detection configuration
  - Create anomaly detection configuration
  - Parse anomaly detection rule definition
  - Create anomaly detection rule
  - Detect anomalies in a measurement according to the anomaly detection rule using a trained anomaly model

- Trigger anomaly detection at regular intervals
- Train anomaly model for a measurement using a specific AI technique, like self-organizing maps (SOM)
- Create an anomaly model
- Trigger anomaly model training at regular intervals
- Create anomaly indicator
- Serialize anomaly indicator
- Publish anomaly indicator

- Actors/Services

  - Anomaly detection configuration parser
  - Anomaly detection rule parser
  - Anomaly detector
  - Anomaly detection engine
  - Anomaly model trainer (e.g. SOM)
  - Anomaly training engine
  - Anomaly indicator serializer (e.g. JSON)
  - Anomaly indicator publisher (e.g., REST or Kafka)

- Factories

  - Anomaly detection configuration factory
  - Anomaly detection rule factory
  - Anomaly model factory
  - Anomaly indicator factory

- Entities

  - Anomaly detection rule
  - Anomaly model
  - Anomaly indicator

The two domains, anomaly and measurement, can be developed in parallel. The anomaly domain interfaces with the measurement domain to fetch data for a particular measurement from a particular data source. The development effort of both the anomaly and measurement domains can be further split to achieve even more development parallelization. For example, one developer could work with anomaly detection, another with anomaly model training, and the third with anomaly indicators.

If you want to know more about DDD, I suggest you read the *Implementing Domain-Driven Design* book by Vaughn Vernon.

4.14: Design Patterns

The following sections present 25 design patterns, most of which are made famous by the *Gang of Four* and their book Design Patterns[18]. Design patterns are divided into creational, structural, and behavioral patterns.

---

[18]https://en.wikipedia.org/wiki/Design_Patterns

4.14.1: Design Patterns for Creating Objects

This section describes design patterns for creating objects. The following design patterns will be presented:

- Factory pattern
- Abstract factory pattern
- Static factory method pattern
- Builder pattern
- Singleton pattern
- Prototype pattern
- Object pool pattern

4.14.1.1: Factory Pattern

Factory pattern allows deferring what kind of object will be created to the point of calling the create-*method of the factory.*

A factory allows a dynamic way of creating objects instead of a static way by directly calling a concrete class constructor. A factory typically consists of precisely one or multiple methods for creating objects of a particular base type. This base type is usually an interface type. The factory decides what concrete type of object will be created. A factory separates the logic of creating objects from the objects themselves, which is in accordance with the *single responsibility principle*.

Below is an example `ConfigParserFactory` class written in Java that has a single `create` method for creating different kinds of `ConfigParser` objects. In the case of a single create method, the method usually contains a switch-case statement or an if/else-if structure. Factories are the only place where extensive switch-case statements or if/else-if structures are allowed in object-oriented programming. If you have a lengthy switch-case statement or long if/else-if structure somewhere else in code, that is typically a sign of a non-object-oriented design.

```
public interface ConfigParser {
  // ...
}


public class JsonConfigParser implements ConfigParser {
  // ...
}


public class YamlConfigParser implements ConfigParser {
  // ...
}


public enum ConfigFormat {
  JSON,
  YAML
}


public final class ConfigParserFactory {
  public static ConfigParser createConfigParser(
    final ConfigFormat configFormat
  ) {
```

```
    return switch(configFormat) {
      case JSON -> new JsonConfigParser();
      case YAML -> new YamlConfigParser();
      default ->
        throw new IllegalArgumentException(
          "Unsupported config format"
        );
    };
  }
}
```

Below is an example of a factory with multiple *create* methods:

```
public final class ShapeFactory {
  public static Shape createCircleShape(final int radius) {
    return new CircleShape(radius);
  }

  public static Shape createRectangleShape(
    final int width,
    final int height
  ) {
    return new RectangleShape(width, height);
  }

  public static Shape createSquareShape(final int sideLength) {
    return new SquareShape(sideLength);
  }
}
```

4.14.1.2: Abstract Factory Pattern

In the abstract factory pattern, there is an abstract factory (interface) and one or more concrete factories (classes that implement the factory interface).

The abstract factory pattern extends the earlier described *factory pattern*. Usually, the abstract factory pattern should be used instead of the plain factory pattern. Below is a Java example of an abstract ConfigParserFactory with one concrete implementation:

```
public interface ConfigParserFactory {
  ConfigParser createConfigParser(ConfigFormat configFormat);
}

public class ConfigParserFactoryImpl implements
              ConfigParserFactory {
  public final ConfigParser createConfigParser(
    final ConfigFormat configFormat
  ) {
    return switch(configFormat) {
      case JSON -> new JsonConfigParser();
      case YAML -> new YamlConfigParser();
      default ->
        throw new IllegalArgumentException(
          "Unsupported config format"
        );
    };
  }
}
```

You should follow the *program against interfaces principle* and use the abstract `ConfigParserFactory` in your code instead of a concrete factory. Then, using the *dependency injection principle*, you can inject the wanted factory implementation, like `ConfigParserFactoryImpl`.

When unit testing code, you should create mock objects instead of real ones with a factory. The abstract factory pattern comes to your help because you can inject a mock instance of the `ConfigParserFactory` class in the tested code. Then, you can expect the mocked `createConfigParser` method to be called and return a mock instance of the `ConfigParser` interface. Then, you can expect the `parse` method to be called on the `ConfigParser` mock and return a mocked configuration. Below is an example unit test using JUnit5 and JMockit[19] library. We test the `initialize` method in an `Application` class containing a `ConfigParserFactory` field. The `Application` class uses the `ConfigParserFactory` instance to create a `ConfigParser` to parse the application configuration. In the below test, we inject a `ConfigParserFactory` mock to an `Application` instance using the `@Injectable` annotation from JMockit. Unit testing and mocking are better described later in the *testing principles* chapter.

```
public class Application {
  private ConfigParserFactory configParserFactory;
  private Config config;

  public Application(final ConfigParserFactory configParserFactory) {
    this.configParserFactory = configParserFactory;
  }

  public void initialize() {
    // ...

    final var configParser = configParserFactory.createConfigParser(...);
    config = configParser.parse(...);

    // ...
  }

  public Config getConfig() {
    return config;
  }
}

public class ApplicationTests {
  @Tested
  Application application;

  @Injectable
  ConfigParserFactory configParserFactoryMock;

  @Mocked
  ConfigParser configParserMock;

  @Mocked
  Config configMock;

  @Test
  public void testInitialize() {
    // GIVEN
    new Expectations() {{
      configParserFactoryMock.createConfigParser(...);
      result = configParserMock;

      configParserMock.parse(...);
      result = configMock;
    }};
```

[19]https://jmockit.github.io/index.html

```
    // WHEN
    application.initialize();

    // THEN
    assertEquals(application.getConfig(), configMock);
  }
}
```

4.14.1.3: Static Factory Method Pattern

In the static factory method pattern, objects are created using one or more static factory methods in a class, and the class constructor is made private.

If you want to validate the parameters supplied to a constructor, the constructor may throw an error. You cannot return an error value from a constructor. Creating constructors that cannot throw an error is recommended because it is relatively easy to forget to catch errors thrown in a constructor if nothing in the constructor signature tells it can throw an error. See the next chapter for a discussion about the *error/exception handling principle.*

Below is a TypeScript example of a constructor that can throw:

```
class Url {
  constructor(
    scheme: string,
    port; number,
    host: string,
    path: string,
    query: string
  ) {
    // Validate the arguments and throw if invalid
  }
}
```

You can use the static factory method pattern to overcome the problem of throwing an error in a constructor. You can make a factory method to return an optional value (if you don't need to return an error cause) or make the factory method throw an error. You should add a *try* prefix to the factory method name to signify that it can raise an error. Then, the function signature (function name) communicates to readers that the function may raise an error.

Below is an example class with two factory methods and a private constructor:

Figure 4.24. Url.ts

```
class Url {
  private constructor(
    scheme: string,
    port: number,
    host: string,
    path: string,
    query: string
  ) {
    // ...
  }

  static createUrl(
    scheme: string,
    port: number,
    host: string,
    path: string,
```

```
    query: string
  ): Url | null {
    // Validate the arguments and return 'null' if invalid
  }

  static tryCreateUrl(
    scheme: string,
    port: number,
    host: string,
    path: string,
    query: string
  ): Url {
    // Validate the arguments and throw if invalid
  }
}
```

Returning an optional value from a factory method allows functional programming techniques to be utilized. Here is an example in Java:

```java
public class Url {
  private Url(
    final String scheme,
    final String host,
    final int port,
    final String path,
    final String query
  ) {
    // ...
  }

  public static Optional<Url> createUrl(
    final String scheme,
    final String host,
    final int port,
    final String path,
    final String query
  ) {
    // ...
  }
}

final var maybeUrl = Url.createUrl(...);

maybeUrl.ifPresent(url -> {
  // Do something with the validated and correct 'url'
});
```

Java's Optional class utilizes the static factory method pattern in an exemplary way. It has a private constructor and three factory methods: empty, of, and ofNullable to create different kinds of Optional objects. The additional benefit of using the static factory method pattern is that you can name the factory methods descriptively, which you can't do with constructors. The name of the factory method tells what kind of object will be created.

4.14.1.4: Builder Pattern

Builder pattern allows you to construct objects piece by piece.

In the builder pattern, you add properties to the built object with *addXXX* methods of the builder class. After adding all the needed properties, you can build the final object using the *build* or *buildXXX* method of the builder class.

For example, you can construct a URL from parts of the URL. Below is a Java example of using a `UrlBuilder` class:

```
final Optional<Url> url = new UrlBuilder()
  .addScheme("https")
  .addHost("www.google.com")
  .buildUrl();
```

The builder pattern has the benefit that properties given for the builder can be validated in the build method. You can make the builder's build method return an optional indicating whether the building was successful. Or, you can make the build method throw if you need to return an error. Then you should name the build method using a *try* prefix, for example, `tryBuildUrl`. The builder pattern also has the benefit of not needing to add default properties to the builder. For example, *https* could be the default scheme, and if you are building an HTTPS URL, the `addScheme` does not need to be called. The only problem is that you must consult the builder documentation to determine the default values.

One drawback with the builder pattern is that you can give the parameters logically in the wrong order like this:

```
final Optional<Url> url = new UrlBuilder()
  .addHost("www.google.com")
  .addScheme("https")
  .buildUrl();
```

It works but does not look so nice. So, if you are using a builder, always try to give the parameters for the builder in a logically correct order if such an order exists. The builder pattern works well when there isn't any inherent order among the parameters. Below is an example of such a case: A house built with a `HouseBuilder` class.

```
final House house = new HouseBuilder()
  .addKitchen()
  .addLivingRoom()
  .addBedrooms(3)
  .addBathRooms(2)
  .addGarage()
  .buildHouse();
```

You can achieve functionality similar to a builder with a factory method with default parameters:

Figure 4.25. Url.ts

```
class Url {
  private constructor(
    host: string,
    path?: string,
    query?: string,
    scheme = 'https',
    port = 443
  ) {
    // ...
  }

  static createUrl(
    host: string,
    path?: string,
    query?: string,
    scheme = 'https',
    port = 443
  ): Url | null {
    // Validate the arguments and return 'null' if invalid
  }
}
```

In the factory method above, the default values are clearly visible. Of course, you cannot now give the parameters in a logical order. There is also a greater possibility that you accidentally provide some parameters in the wrong order because many of them are of the same type (string). This won't be a potential issue with a builder where you use a method with a specific name to give a specific parameter. In modern development environments, giving parameters in the wrong order is less probable because IDEs offer inlay hints[20] for parameters. It is easy to see if you provide a particular parameter in the wrong position. As shown below, giving parameters in the wrong order can also be avoided using semantically validated function parameter types. Semantically validated function parameters will be discussed later in this chapter.

Figure 4.26. Url.ts

```
class Url {
  static createUrl(
    host: Host,
    path?: Path,
    query?: Query,
    scheme = Scheme.createScheme('https'),
    port = Port.createPort(443)
  ): Url | null {
    // ...
  }
}
```

You can also use factory method overloading in languages like Java, where default parameters are not supported. But that solution, for example, in the Url class case, can not be easily implemented and requires quite many overloaded methods to be introduced, which can be overwhelming for a developer.

You can always use a parameter object, not only in Java but in many other languages, too. Below is an example in Java:

```
import lombok.Getter;
import lombok.Setter;


@Getter
@Setter
public class UrlParams {
  private String scheme = "https";
  private String host;
  private int port = 443;
  private String path = "";
  private String query = "";

  UrlParams(final String host) {
    this.host = host;
  }
}


public class Url {
  private Url(final UrlParams urlParams) {
    // ...
  }

  public static Optional<Url> createUrl(
    final UrlParams urlParams
  ) {
    // ...
  }
}
```

---

[20]https://www.jetbrains.com/help/idea/inlay-hints.html

```
final var urlParams = new UrlParams("www.google.com");
urlParams.setQuery("query=design+patterns");
final var maybeUrl = Url.createUrl(urlParams);
```

4.14.1.5: Singleton Pattern

Singleton pattern defines that a class can have only one instance.

Singletons are very common in pure object-oriented languages like Java. In many cases, a singleton class can be identified as not having any state. This is why only one instance of the class is needed. There is no point in creating multiple instances that are the same. In some non-pure object-oriented languages, singletons are not as common as in pure object-oriented languages and can often be replaced by just defining functions.

In JavaScript/TypeScript, a singleton instance can be created in a module and exported. When you import the instance from the module in other modules, the other modules will always get the same exported instance, not a new instance every time. Below is an example of such a singleton:

Figure 4.27. myClassSingleton.ts

```
class MyClass {
  // ...
}

export const myClassSingleton = new MyClass();
```

Figure 4.28. otherModule.ts

```
import { myClassSingleton } from 'myClassSingleton';

// ...
```

The singleton pattern can be implemented using a static class because it cannot be instantiated. The problem with a static class is that the singleton class is then hardcoded, and static classes can be hard or impossible to mock in unit testing. We should remember to *program against interfaces*. The best way to implement the singleton pattern is by using the *dependency inversion principle* and the *dependency injection principle*. Below is an example in Java using the Google Guice[21] library for handling dependency injection. The constructor of the FileConfigReader class expects a ConfigParser. We annotate the constructor with the @Inject annotation to inject an instance implementing the ConfigParser interface:

---

[21]https://github.com/google/guice

```
import com.google.inject.Inject;


public interface ConfigReader {
  Configuration tryRead(...);
}


public class FileConfigReader
          implements ConfigReader {
  private ConfigParser configParser;

  @Inject
  public FileConfigReader(
    final ConfigParser configParser
  ) {
    this.configParser = configParser;
  }

  public Configuration tryRead(
    final String configFilePathName
  ) {
    final String configFileContents = // Read configuration file

    final var configuration =
      configParser.tryParse(configFileContents);

    return configuration;
  }
}
```

In the DI module below, we configure a singleton with lazy binding. In the lazy binding, the JsonConfigParser class is only created when needed to be used.

```
import com.google.inject.AbstractModule;


public class DiModule extends AbstractModule {
  @Override
  protected void configure() {
    bind(ConfigParser.class)
      .to(JsonConfigParser.class)
      .in(Scopes.SINGLETON);
  }
}
```

Alternatively, we can define an eager singleton:

```
import com.google.inject.AbstractModule;


public class DiModule extends AbstractModule {
  @Override
  protected void configure() {
    bind(ConfigParser.class)
      .to(JsonConfigParser.class)
      .asEagerSingleton();
  }
}
```

The best way to ensure that only one singleton instance is created is to ensure the DI container is created at the beginning of the application initialization (before starting threads) and singletons are created eagerly, not lazily. Eagerly means the singleton is created immediately, and lazily means it is created only when somebody needs it. Of course, lazy instantiation is possible, but it can cause problems in a multi-threaded environment if synchronization is not used when the singleton instance is actually created.

4.14.1.6: Prototype Pattern

The prototype pattern lets you create a new object using an existing object as a prototype.

Let's have a Java example with a `DrawnShape` class:

```java
public interface Shape {
  // ...
}


// Implement concrete shapes...

public interface Position {
  int getX();
  int getY();
}


public class DrawnShape {
  private final Position position;
  private final Shape shape;

  public DrawnShape(
    final Position position,
    final Shape shape
  ) {
    this.position = position;
    this.shape = shape;
  }
  public DrawnShape(
    final Position position,
    final DrawnShape drawnShape
  ) {
    this.position = position;
    shape = drawnShape.getShape();
  }
  public DrawnShape cloneTo(
    final Position position
  ) {
    return new DrawnShape(position, this);
  }
  public Shape getShape() {
    return this.shape;
  }
}
```

In the second constructor, we are using the prototype pattern. A new `DrawnShape` object is created from an existing `DrawnShape` object. An alternative way to use the prototype pattern is to call the `cloneTo` method on a prototype object and give the position parameter to specify where the new shape should be positioned.

The prototype pattern is also used in JavaScript to implement prototypal inheritance. Since EcmaScript version 6, class-based inheritance has been available, and prototypal inheritance does not need to be used.

The idea of prototypal inheritance is that the common parts for the same class objects are stored in a prototype instance. These common parts typically mean the shared methods. There is no sense in storing the methods multiple times in each object. That would be a waste of resources because Javascript functions are objects themselves.

When you create a new object with the `Object.create` method, you give the prototype as a parameter. After that, you can set properties for the newly created object. When you call a method on the created object, and if that method is not found in the object's properties, the prototype object will be looked up for the method. Prototypes can be chained so that a prototype object contains another prototype object. This chaining is used to implement an inheritance chain. Below is a simple example of prototypal inheritance:

```
const pet = {
  name: '',
  getName: function() { return this.name; }
};

// Creates a new object with 'pet' object as a prototype
const petNamedBella = Object.create(pet);

petNamedBella.name = 'Bella';
console.log(petNamedBella.getName()); // Prints 'Bella'

// Prototype of a dog which contains 'pet' as nested prototype
const dog = {
  bark: function() { console.log('bark'); },
  __proto__: pet
}

// Creates a new object with 'dog' object as prototype
const dogNamedLuna = Object.create(dog);

dogNamedLuna.name = 'Luna';
console.log(dogNamedLuna.getName()); // Prints 'Luna'
dogNamedLuna.bark(); // Prints 'bark'
```

4.14.1.7: Object Pool Pattern

In the object pool pattern, created objects are stored in a pool where objects can be acquired from and returned for reuse. The object pool pattern is an optimization pattern because it allows the reuse of once-created objects.

If you need to create many short-lived objects, you should utilize an object pool and reduce the need for memory allocation and de-allocation, which takes time. Frequent object creation and deletion in garbage-collected languages cause extra work for the garbage collector, which consumes CPU time.

Below is an example of an object pool implementation in C++. The below `LimitedSizeObjectPool` class implementation uses a spin lock in its methods to achieve thread safety. More about thread safety in the coming *concurrent programming principles* chapter.

Figure 4.29. ObjectPool.h

```
#include <memory>


template <typename T>
class ObjectPool
{
public:
  virtual ~ObjectPool() = default;

  virtual std::shared_ptr<T> acquireObject() = 0;
  virtual void returnObject(std::shared_ptr<T> object) = 0;
};
```

Figure 4.30. LimitedSizeObjectPool.h

```cpp
#include <deque>
#include "ScopedSpinlock.h"
#include "Spinlock.h"
#include "ObjectPool.h"


template <typename T>
class LimitedSizeObjectPool : public ObjectPool<T>
{
public:
  explicit LimitedSizeObjectPool(const size_t maxPoolSize):
    m_maxPoolSize(maxPoolSize)
  {}

  std::shared_ptr<T> acquireObject()
  {
    std::shared_ptr<T> object;
    const ScopedSpinlock scopedLock{m_lock};

    if (m_pooledObjects.empty())
    {
      object = std::make_shared<T>();
    }
    else
    {
      object = m_pooledObjects.front();
      m_pooledObjects.pop_front();
    }

    return object;
  }

  void returnObject(std::shared_ptr<T> object)
  {
    const ScopedSpinlock scopedLock{m_lock};

    const bool poolIsFull =
      m_pooledObjects.size() >= m_maxPoolSize;

    if (poolIsFull)
    {
      object.reset();
    }
    else
    {
      m_pooledObjects.push_back(object);
    }
  }

private:
  Spinlock m_lock;
  size_t m_maxPoolSize;
  std::deque<std::shared_ptr<T>> m_pooledObjects;
};
```

Below is a slightly different implementation of an object pool. The below implementation accepts clearable objects, meaning objects returned to the pool are cleared before reusing. The below implementation allows you to define whether the allocated objects are wrapped inside a shared or unique pointer. You can also supply parameters used when constructing an object.

Figure 4.31. ObjectPool.h

```
#include <concepts>
#include <deque>
#include <memory>


template<typename T>
concept ClearableObject =
requires(T object)
{
  { object.clear() } -> std::convertible_to<void>;
};

template<typename T, typename U>
concept Pointer = std::derived_from<T, std::shared_ptr<U>> ||
                  std::derived_from<T, std::unique_ptr<U>>;

template<
  ClearableObject O,
  typename ObjectInterface,
  Pointer<ObjectInterface> OP,
  typename ...Args
>
class ObjectPool
{
public:
  virtual ~ObjectPool() = default;

  virtual OP acquireObject(Args&& ...args) = 0;

  virtual void acquireObjects(
    std::deque<OP>& objects,
    size_t objectCount,
    Args&& ...args
  ) = 0;

  virtual void returnObject(OP object) = 0;
  virtual void returnObjects(std::deque<OP>& objects) = 0;
};
```

Figure 4.32. LimitedSizeObjectPool.h

```
#include "ScopedLock.h"
#include "Spinlock.h"
#include "ObjectPool.h"


template<
  ClearableObject O,
  typename ObjectInterface,
  Pointer<ObjectInterface> OP,
  typename ...Args
>
class LimitedSizeObjectPool :
    public ObjectPool<O, ObjectInterface, OP, Args...>
{
public:
  explicit LimitedSizeObjectPool(const size_t maxPoolSize) :
    m_maxPoolSize(maxPoolSize)
  {}

  OP acquireObject(Args&& ...args) override
  {
    const ScopedLock scopedLock(m_lock);
    OP acquiredObject;

    if (const bool poolIsEmpty = m_pooledObjects.empty();
```

```
                      poolIsEmpty)
    {
      acquiredObject = OP{new O{std::forward<Args>(args)...}};
    }
    else
    {
      acquiredObject = m_pooledObjects.front();
      m_pooledObjects.pop_front();
    }

    return acquiredObject;
  }

  void acquireObjects(
    std::deque<OP>& objects,
    const size_t objectCount,
    Args&& ...args
  ) override
  {
    for (size_t n{1U}; n <= objectCount; ++n)
    {
      objects.push_back(acquireObject(std::forward<Args>(args)...));
    }
  }

  void returnObject(OP object) override
  {
    const ScopedLock scopedLock(m_lock);

    if (const bool poolIsFull = m_pooledObjects.size() >=
                                m_maxPoolSize;
             poolIsFull)
    {
      object.reset();
    }
    else
    {
      object->clear();
      m_pooledObjects.push_back(object);
    }
  }

  void returnObjects(std::deque<OP>& objects) override
  {
    while (!objects.empty())
    {
      returnObject(objects.front());
      objects.pop_front();
    }
  }

private:
  size_t m_maxPoolSize;
  Spinlock m_lock;
  std::deque<OP> m_pooledObjects;
};
```

In the below example, we create a message pool for a maximum of 5000 output messages. We get a shared pointer to an output message from the pool. The pool's concrete class for creating new objects is OutputMessageImpl. When we acquire an output message from the pool, we provide a size_t type value (= output message length) to the constructor of the OutputMessageImpl class. The OutputMessageImpl class must be clearable, i.e., it must have a clear method returning void.

```
LimitedSizeObjectPool<
  OutputMessageImpl,
  OutputMessage,
  std::shared_ptr<OutputMessage>,
  size_t
> outputMessagePool{5000U};

// Acquire an output message of 1024 bytes from the pool.
const auto outputMessage = outputMessagePool.acquireObject(1024U);
```

4.14.2: Structural Design Patterns

This section describes structural design patterns. Most patterns use object composition as the primary method to achieve a particular design. The following design patterns are presented:

- Composite pattern
- Facade pattern
- Bridge pattern
- Strategy pattern
- Adapter pattern
- Proxy pattern
- Decorator pattern
- Flyweight pattern

4.14.2.1: Composite Pattern

In the composite pattern, a class can be composed of itself, i.e., the composition is recursive.

Recursive object composition can be depicted by how a user interface can be composed of different widgets. In the Java example below, we have a Pane class that is a Widget. A Pane object can contain several other Widget objects, meaning a Pane object can contain other Pane objects.

```
public interface Widget {
  void render();
}

public class Pane implements Widget {
  private final List<Widget> widgets;

  public void render() {
    // Render each widget inside pane
  }
}

public class StaticText implements Widget {
  public void render() {
    // Render static text widget
  }

  // ...
}
```

```
public class TextInput implements Widget {
  public void render() {
    // Render text input widget
  }
}


public class Button implements Widget {
  public void render() {
    // Render button widget
  }
}


public class UIWindow {
  private final List<Widget> widgets = new ArrayList<>(10);

  public void render() {
    widgets.forEach(Widget::render);
  }
}
```

Objects that form a tree structure are composed of themselves recursively. Below is an Avro[22] record field schema with a nested record field:

```
{
  "type": "record",
  "name": "sampleMessage",
  "namespace": "",
  "fields": [
    {
      "name": "field1",
      "type": "string"
    },
    {
      "name": "nestedRecordField",
      "namespace": "nestedRecordField",
      "type": "record",
      "fields": [
        {
          "name": "nestedField1",
          "type": "int"
        }
      ]
    }
  ]
}
```

To parse an Avro schema, we could define classes for different sub-schemas by the field type. When analyzing the example below, we can notice that the RecordAvroFieldSchema class can contain any AvroFieldSchema object, also other RecordAvroFieldSchema objects, making a RecordAvroFieldSchema object a composite object.

---

[22]https://avro.apache.org/

```
public interface AvroFieldSchema {
  // ...
}

public class RecordAvroFieldSchema implements AvroFieldSchema {
  private final List<AvroFieldSchema> subFieldSchemas;

  // ...
}

public class StringAvroFieldSchema implements AvroFieldSchema {
  // ...
}

public class IntAvroFieldSchema implements AvroFieldSchema {
  // ...
}
```

4.14.2.2: Facade Pattern

In the facade pattern, an object on a higher level of abstraction is composed of objects on a lower level of abstraction. The higher-level object acts as a facade in front of the lower-level objects. Lower-level objects behind the facade are either only or mainly only accessible by the facade.

Let's use the data exporter microservice as an example. For that microservice, we could create a Config interface that can be used to obtain configuration for the different parts (input, transform, and output) of the data exporter microservice. The Config interface acts as a facade. Users of the facade need not see behind the facade. They don't know what happens behind the facade. And they shouldn't care because they are just using the interface provided by the facade.

There can be various classes doing the actual work behind the facade. In the below example, there is a ConfigReader class that reads configuration from possibly different sources (from a local file or a remote service, for example) and there are configuration parsers that can parse a specific part of the configuration, possibly in different data formats like JSON or YAML. None of these implementations and details are visible to the facade user. Any of these implementations behind the facade can change at any time without affecting the users of the facade because facade users are not coupled to the lower-level implementations.

Below is the implementation of the Configuration facade in Java:

```
import com.google.inject.Inject;


public interface Configuration {
  InputConfig tryGetInputConfig();
  TransformerConfig tryGetTransformerConfig();
  OutputConfig tryGetOutputConfig();
}


public class ConfigurationImpl implements Configuration {
  private final ConfigReader configReader;
  private final InputConfigParser inputConfigParser;
  private final TransformerConfigParser transformerConfigParser;
  private final OutputConfigParser outputConfigParser;
  private String configString = "";
  private Optional<InputConfig> inputConfig = Optional.empty();
  private Optional<OutputConfig> outputConfig = Optional.empty();
```

```java
private Optional<TransformerConfig> transformerConfig =
  Optional.empty();

@Inject
public ConfigurationImpl(
  final ConfigReader configReader,
  final InputConfigParser inputConfigParser,
  final TransformerConfigParser transformerConfigParser,
  final OutputConfigParser outputConfigParser
) {
  // ...
}

public InputConfig tryGetInputConfig() {
  return inputConfig.orElseGet(() -> {
    tryReadConfigIfNeeded();
    inputConfig = inputConfigParser.tryParseInputConfig(configString);
    return inputConfig;
  });
}

public TransformerConfig tryGetTransformerConfig() {
  // ...
}

public OutputConfig tryGetOutputConfig() {
  // ...
}

private void tryReadConfigIfNeeded() {
  if (configString.isEmpty()) {
    configString = configReader.tryRead(...);
  }
}
}
```

4.14.2.3: Bridge Pattern

In the bridge pattern, the implementation of a class is delegated to another class. The original class is "abstract" in the sense that it does not have any behavior except the delegation to another class, or it can have some higher level control logic on how it delegates to another class.

Don't confuse the word "abstract" here with an abstract class. In an abstract class, some behavior is not implemented at all, but the implementation is deferred to subclasses of the abstract class. Here, instead of "abstract class", we could use the term *delegating class* instead.

Bridge

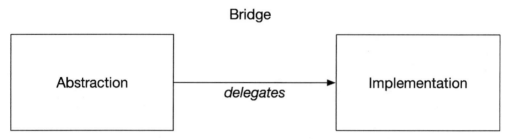

Figure 4.33. Bridge Pattern

Let's have a Java example with shapes and drawings capable of drawing different shapes:

```java
public interface Shape {
  void render(final ShapeRenderer renderer);
}

public class RectangleShape implements Shape {
  private final Point upperLeftCorner;
  private final int width;
  private final int height;

  public RectangleShape(
    final Point upperLeftCorner,
    final int width,
    final int height
    ) {
    this.upperLeftCorner = upperLeftCorner;
    this.width = width;
    this.height = height;
  }

  public void render(final ShapeRenderer renderer) {
    renderer.renderRectangleShape(upperLeftCorner, width, height);
  }
}

public class CircleShape implements Shape {
  private final Point center;
  private final int radius;

  public CircleShape(final Point center, final int radius) {
    this.center = center;
    this.radius = radius;
  }

  public void render(final ShapeRenderer renderer) {
    renderer.renderCircleShape(center, radius);
  }
}
```

The above `RectangleShape` and `CircleShape` classes are abstractions (or delegating classes) because they delegate their functionality (rendering) to an external class (implementation class) of the `ShapeRenderer` type. We can provide different rendering implementations for the shape classes. Let's define two shape renderers, one for rendering raster shapes and another for rendering vector shapes:

```java
public interface ShapeRenderer {
  void renderCircleShape(final Point center, final int radius);

  void renderRectangleShape(
    final Point upperLeftCorner,
    final int width,
    final int height
  );

  // Methods for rendering other shapes...
}


public class RasterShapeRenderer implements ShapeRenderer {
  private final Canvas canvas;

  public RasterShapeRenderer(final Canvas canvas) {
    this.canvas = canvas;
  }

  public void renderCircleShape(
    final Point center,
    final int radius
  ) {
    // Renders circle to canvas
  }

  public void renderRectangleShape(
    final Point upperLeftCorner,
    final int width,
    final int height
  ) {
    // Renders a rectangle to canvas
  }

  // Methods for rendering other shapes to the canvas
}


public class VectorShapeRenderer implements ShapeRenderer {
  private final SvgElement svgRoot;

  public VectorShapeRenderer(final SvgElement svgRoot) {
    this.svgRoot = svgRoot;
  }

  public void renderCircleShape(
    final Point center,
    final int radius
  ) {
    // Render circle as SVG element and attach as child to SVG root
  }

  public void renderRectangleShape(
    final Point upperLeftCorner,
    final int width,
    final int height
  ) {
    // Render rectangle as SVG element
    // and attach as child to SVG root
  }

  // Methods for rendering other shapes
}
```

Let's implement two different drawings, a raster and a vector drawing:

```java
public interface Drawing {

  void draw();
  void save();
}


public abstract class AbstractDrawing implements Drawing {
  private final String name;

  public AbstractDrawing(final String name) {
    this.name = name;
  }

  public final void save() {
    final var fileName = name + getFileExtension();
    final var data = getData();

    // Save the 'data' to 'fileName'
  }

  public final void draw(final List<Shape> shapes) {
    for (final var shape: shapes) {
      shape.render(getShapeRenderer());
    }
  }

  protected abstract ShapeRenderer getShapeRenderer();
  protected abstract String getFileExtension();
  protected abstract byte[] getData();
}


public class RasterDrawing extends AbstractDrawing {
  private final Canvas canvas = new Canvas();

  private final RasterShapeRenderer shapeRenderer =
    new RasterShapeRenderer(canvas);

  public RasterDrawing(final String name) {
    super(name);
  }

  protected ShapeRenderer getShapeRenderer() {
    return shapeRenderer;
  }

  protected String getFileExtension() {
    return ".png";
  }

  protected byte[] getData() {
    // get data from the 'canvas' object
  }
}


public class VectorDrawing extends AbstractDrawing {
  private final SvgElement svgRoot = new SvgElement();

  private final VectorShapeRenderer shapeRenderer =
    new VectorShapeRenderer(svgRoot);

  public VectorDrawing(final String name) {
    super(name);
  }

  protected ShapeRenderer getShapeRenderer() {
    return shapeRenderer;
  }
```

```
  protected String getFileExtension() {
    return ".svg";
  }

  protected byte[] getData() {
    // get data from the 'svgRoot' object
  }
}
```

In the above example, we have delegated the rendering behavior of the shape classes to concrete classes implementing the ShapeRenderer interface. The Shape classes only represent a shape but don't render the shape. They have a single responsibility of representing a shape. Regarding rendering, the shape classes are "abstractions" because they delegate the rendering to another class responsible for rendering different shapes.

Now, we can have a list of shapes and render them differently. We can do this as shown below because we did not couple the shape classes with any specific rendering behavior.

```
final List<Shape> shapes = new ArrayList<>(50);
// Add various shapes to 'shapes' list here...

final var rasterDrawing = new RasterDrawing("raster-drawing-1");
rasterDrawing.draw(shapes);
rasterDrawing.save();

final var vectorDrawing = new VectorDrawing("vector-drawing-1");
vectorDrawing.draw(shapes);
vectorDrawing.save();
```

4.14.2.4: Strategy Pattern

In the strategy pattern, the functionality of an object can be changed by changing an instance of a composed type to a different instance of that type.

Below is a Java example where the behavior of a ConfigReader class can be changed by changing the value of the config_parser attribute to an instance of a different class. The default behavior is to parse the configuration in JSON format, which can be achieved by calling the constructor without a parameter.

```
public class ConfigReader {
  private final ConfigParser configParser;

  public ConfigReader() {
    configParser = new JsonConfigParser();
  }

  public ConfigReader(final ConfigParser configParser) {
    this.configParser = configParser;
  }

  public Configuration tryRead(final String configFilePathName) {
    // Try read the configuration file contents to a string
    // variable named 'configFileContents'

    final Configuration configuration =
      configParser.tryParse(configFileContents);

    return configuration;
  }
}
```

Using the strategy pattern, we can change the functionality of a `ConfigReader` instance by changing the `config_parser` attribute value. For example, there could be the following classes available that implement the `ConfigParser` interface:

- JsonConfigParser
- YamlConfigParser
- TomlConfigParser
- XmlConfigParser

We can dynamically change the behavior of a `ConfigReader` instance to use the YAML parsing strategy by giving an instance of the `YamlConfigParser` class as a parameter for the `ConfigReader` constructor.

4.14.2.5: Adapter Pattern

The adapter pattern changes one interface to another interface. It allows you to adapt different interfaces to a single interface.

In the below C++ example, we have defined a `Message` interface for messages that can be consumed from a data source using a `MessageConsumer`.

Figure 4.34. Message.h

```
#include <cstdint>


class Message
{
public:
  Message() = default;
  virtual ~Message() = default;

  virtual uint8_t* getData() const = 0;
  virtual std::size_t getDataLengthInBytes() const = 0;
};
```

Figure 4.35. MessageConsumer.h

```
#include <memory>
#include "Message.h"


class MessageConsumer
{
public:
  MessageConsumer() = default;
  virtual ~MessageConsumer() = default;

  virtual std::shared_ptr<Message> consumeMessage() = 0;
};
```

Next, we can define the message and message consumer adapter classes for Apache Kafka and Apache Pulsar:

Figure 4.36. KafkaMessageConsumer.h

```
#include "MessageConsumer.h"


class KafkaMessageConsumer : public MessageConsumer
{
public:
  KafkaMessageConsumer(...);
  ~KafkaMessageConsumer() override;

  std::shared_ptr<Message> consumeMessage() override {
    // Consume a message from Kafka using a 3rd party
    // Kafka library, e.g. LibRdKafka
    // Wrap the consumed LibRdKafka message inside an instance
    // of KafkaMessage class
    // Return the KafkaMessage instance
  }
};
```

Figure 4.37. KafkaMessage.h

```
#include <bit>
#include <librdkafka/rdkafkacpp.h>
#include "Message.h"


class KafkaMessage : public Message
{
public:
  explicit KafkaMessage(RdKafka::Message* const message):
    m_message(message)
  {}

  ~KafkaMessage() override
  {
    delete m_message;
  }

  uint8_t* getData() const override
  {
    return std::bit_cast<uint8_t*>(m_message->payload());
  }

  std::size_t getDataLengthInBytes() const override
  {
    return m_message->len();
  }

private:
  RdKafka::Message* m_message;
};
```

Figure 4.38. PulsarMessageConsumer.h

```
#include "MessageConsumer.h"


class PulsarMessageConsumer : public MessageConsumer
{
public:
  PulsarMessageConsumer(...);
  ~PulsarMessageConsumer() override;

  std::shared_ptr<Message> consumeMessage() override {
    // Consume a message from Pulsar using the Pulsar C++ client
    // Wrap the consumed Pulsar message inside an instance
    // of PulsarMessage
    // Return the PulsarMessage instance
  }
};
```

Figure 4.39. PulsarMessage.h

```
#include "Message.h"


class PulsarMessage : public Message
{
public:
  // ...
};
```

Now, we can use Kafka or Pulsar data sources with identical consumer and message interfaces. In the future, it will be easy to integrate a new data source into the system. We only need to implement appropriate adapter classes (message and consumer classes) for the new data source. No other code changes are required. Thus, we would be following the *open-closed principle* correctly.

Let's imagine that the API of the Kafka library that was used changed. We don't need to make changes in many places in the code. We need to create new adapter classes (message and consumer classes) for the new API and use those new adapter classes in place of the old adapter classes. All of this work is again following the *open-closed principle*.

Consider using the adapter pattern even if there is nothing to adapt to, especially when working with 3rd party libraries. Because then you will be prepared for the future when changes can come. It might be possible that a 3rd party library interface changes or there is a need to take a different library into use. If you have not used the adapter pattern, taking a new library or library version into use could mean that you must make many small changes in several places in the codebase, which is error-prone and against the *open-closed principle*.

Let's have an example of using a 3rd party logging library. Initially, our adapter AbcLogger for a fictive *abc-logging-library* is just a wrapper around the abc_logger instance from the library. There is not any actual adapting done.

Figure 4.40. Logger.ts

```
import { LogLevel } from 'LogLevel';


export interface Logger {
  log(logLevel: LogLevel, logMessage: string): void;
}
```

Figure 4.41. AbcLogger.ts

```
import abcLogger from 'abc-logging-library';
import Logger from 'Logger';
import LogLevel   from 'LogLevel';


class AbcLogger implements Logger {
  log(logLevel: LogLevel, logMessage: string): void {
    abcLogger.log(logLevel, logMessage);
  }
}

export default AbcLogger;
```

When you use the logger in your application, you can utilize the *singleton pattern* and create a singleton instance of the AbcLogger in the DI container and let the DI framework inject the logger to all parts of the software component where a logger is needed. Here is how the DI module could look:

Figure 4.42. DiModule.ts

```
import { Module } from 'noicejs';
import AbcLogger from 'AbcLogger';


class DiModule extends Module {
  public async configure(options) {
    await super.configure(options);

    this.bind('logger').toConstructor(AbcLogger);
  }
}
```

When you need the logger in any other class of the application, you can get it:

```
import { Container, Inject } from 'noicejs';


@Inject('logger')
class SomeClass {
  private readonly Logger logger;

  constructor(args) {
    this.logger = args.logger;
  }
}
```

Suppose that in the future, a better logging library called *xyz-logging-library* is available, and we would like to use that, but it has a slightly different interface. Its logging instance is called xyz_log_writer, the logging method is named differently, and the parameters are given in different order compared to the *abc-logging-library*. We can create a XyzLogger adapter class for the new logging library and update the DiContainer. No other code changes are required elsewhere in the codebase to take the new logging library into use.

Figure 4.43. XyzLogger.ts

```
import xyzLogWriter from 'xyz-logging-library';
import Logger from 'Logger';
import LogLevel from 'LogLevel';

class XyzLogger implements Logger {
  log(logLevel: LogLevel, logMessage: string): void {
    xyzLogWriter.writeLogEntry(logMessage, logLevel);
  }
}

export default XyzLogger;
```

Figure 4.44. DiModule.ts

```
import { Module } from 'noicejs';
import XyzLogger from 'XyzLogger';

class DiModule extends Module {
  public async configure(options) {
    await super.configure(options);

    this.bind('logger').toConstructor(XyzLogger);
  }
}
```

We didn't have to modify all the places where logging is used in the codebase (and we can be sure that logging is used in many places!). We have saved ourselves from a lot of error-prone and unnecessary work, and once again, we have successfully followed the *open-closed principle*.

In some languages where mocking of concrete classes is not possible, wrapping a third-party library in an adapter class enables you to unit test against the adapter class interface instead of the concrete classes of the third-party library.

4.14.2.6: Proxy Pattern

The proxy pattern enables conditionally modifying or augmenting the behavior of an object.

When using the proxy pattern, you define a proxy class that wraps another class (the proxied class). The proxy class conditionally delegates to the wrapped class. The proxy class implements the interface of the wrapped class and is used in place of the wrapped class in the code.

Below is an example of a TypeScript proxy class, CachingEntityStore, that caches the results of entity store operations:

```typescript
class MemoryCache<K, V> {
  // ...

  retrieveBy(key: K): V {
    // ...
  }

  store(key: K, value: V, timeToLiveInSecs?: number): void {
    // ...
  }
}


interface EntityStore<T> {
  getEntityById(id: number): Promise<T>;
}


class DbEntityStore<T> implements EntityStore<T> {
  getEntityById(id: number): Promise<T> {
    // Try get entity from database
  }
}


class CachingEntityStore<T> implements EntityStore<T> {
  private readonly entityCache = new MemoryCache<number, T>();

  constructor(private readonly entityStore: EntityStore<T>)
  {}

  async getEntityById(id: number): Promise<T> {
    let entity = this.entityCache.retrieveBy(id);

    if (entity === undefined) {
      entity = await this.entityStore.getEntityById(id);
      const timeToLiveInSecs = 60;
      this.entityCache.store(id, entity, timeToLiveInSecs);
    }

    return entity;
  }
}
```

In the above example, the CachingEntityStore class is the proxy class wrapping an EntityStore. The proxy class modifies the wrapped class behavior by conditionally delegating it to the wrapped class. It delegates to the wrapped class only if an entity is not found in the cache.

Below is another TypeScript example of a proxy class that authorizes a user before performing a service operation:

```typescript
interface UserService {
  getUserById(id: number): Promise<User>;
}


class UserServiceImpl implements UserService {
  getUserById(id: number): Promise<User> {
    // Try get user by id
  }
}


class AuthorizingUserService implements UserService {
  constructor(
    private readonly userService: UserService,
    private readonly userAuthorizer: UserAuthorizer
```

```
  ) {}

  async getUserById(id: number): Promise<User> {
    try {
      await this.userAuthorizer.tryAuthorizeUser(id);
    } catch (error: any) {
      throw new UserServiceError(error.message);
    }

    return this.userService.getUserById(id);
  }
}
```

In the above example, the AuthorizingUserService class is a proxy class that wraps a UserService. The proxy class modifies the wrapped class behavior by conditionally delegating to the wrapped class. It will delegate to the wrapped class only if authorization is successful.

As the last example, we could define a RateLimitedXyzService proxy class that wraps a XyzService class. The rate-limited service class delegates to the wrapped class only if the service calling rate limit is not exceeded. It should raise an error if the rate is exceeded.

4.14.2.7: Decorator Pattern

The decorator pattern enables augmenting the functionality of a class method(s) without the need to modify the class method(s).

A decorator class wraps another class whose functionality will be augmented. The decorator class implements the interface of the wrapped class and is used in place of the wrapped class in the code. The decorator pattern is useful when you cannot modify an existing class, e.g., the existing class is in a 3rd party library. The decorator pattern also helps to follow the *open-closed principle* because you don't have to modify an existing method to augment its functionality. Instead, you can create a decorator class that contains the new functionality.

Below is a TypeScript example of the decorator pattern. There is a standard SQL statement executor implementation and two decorated SQL statement executor implementations: one that adds logging functionality and one that adds SQL statement execution timing functionality. Finally, a double-decorated SQL statement executor is created that logs an SQL statement and times its execution.

```
import logger from 'logger';
import LogLevel from 'LogLevel';


interface SqlStatementExecutor {
  tryExecute(
    sqlStatement: string,
    parameterValues?: any[]
  ): Promise<any>;
}


class SqlStatementExecutorImpl implements SqlStatementExecutor {
  // Implement getConnection()

  tryExecute(
    sqlStatement: string,
    parameterValues?: any[]
  ): Promise<any> {
    return this.getConnection().execute(sqlStatement,
                                        parameterValues);
```

```
      }
}


class LoggingSqlStatementExecutor
        implements SqlStatementExecutor {
  constructor(
    private readonly sqlStatementExecutor: SqlStatementExecutor
  ) {}

  tryExecute(
    sqlStatement: string,
    parameterValues?: any[]
  ): Promise<any> {
    logger.log(LogLevel.Debug,
            `Executing SQL statement: ${sqlStatement}`);

    return this.sqlStatementExecutor
      .tryExecute(sqlStatement, parameterValues);
  }
}


class TimingSqlStatementExecutor
        implements SqlStatementExecutor {
  constructor(
    private readonly sqlStatementExecutor: SqlStatementExecutor
  ) {}

  async tryExecute(
    sqlStatement: string,
    parameterValues?: any[]
  ): Promise<any> {
    const startTimeInMs = Date.now();

    const result =
      await this.sqlStatementExecutor
        .tryExecute(sqlStatement, parameterValues);

    const endTimeInMs = Date.now();
    const durationInMs = endTimeInMs - startTimeInMs;

    logger.log(LogLevel.Debug,
    `SQL statement execution duration: ${durationInMs} ms`);

    return result;
  }
}


const timingAndLoggingSqlStatementExecutor =
  new LoggingSqlStatementExecutor(
    new TimingSqlStatementExecutor(
      new SqlStatementExecutorImpl()));
```

You can also use the decorator pattern with functions and methods in TypeScript. Decorators allow us to wrap a function to extend its behavior. Decorators are functions that take a function as a parameter and return another function used in place of the decorated function. Let's have an elementary example of a function decorator:

```
// Decorator
function printHello(func: any, context: ClassMethodDecoratorContext) {
  function wrappedFunc(this: any, ...args: any[]) {
    console.log('Hello');
    return func.call(this, ...args);
  }

  return wrappedFunc;
}


class Adder {
  @printHello
  add(a: number, b: number): number {
    return a + b;
  }
}


// Prints: Hello 3
const result = new Adder().add(1, 2);
console.log(result);
```

Decorators can accept parameters:

```
function printText(text: string) {
  function decorate(func: any, context: ClassMethodDecoratorContext) {
    function wrappedFunc(this: any, ...args: any[]) {
      console.log(text);
      return func.call(this, ...args);
    }

    return wrappedFunc;
  }

  return decorate;
}

class Adder {
  @printText('Hello World!')
  add(a: number, b: number): number {
    return a + b;
  }
}


// Prints: Hello World! 3
const result = new Adder().add(1, 2);
console.log(result);
```

Let's have another example with a decorator that times the execution of a function and prints it to the console:

```
// Decorator
function timed(func: any, context: ClassMethodDecoratorContext) {
  function wrapped_func(this: any, ...args: any[]) {
    const start_time_in_ns = process.hrtime.bigint();
    const result = func.call(this, ...args);
    const end_time_in_ns = process.hrtime.bigint();
    const duration_in_ns = end_time_in_ns - start_time_in_ns;

    console.log(
      `Exec of func "${String(context.name)}" took ${duration_in_ns} ns`
    );

    return result;
  }

  return wrapped_func;
}


class Adder {
  @timed
  add(a: number, b: number): number {
    return a + b;
  }
}


// Prints, for example: Exec of func "add" took 7500 ns
const result = new Adder().add(1, 2);
```

You can combine multiple decorators, for example:

```
function logged(func: any, context: ClassMethodDecoratorContext) {
  function wrapped_func(this: any, ...args: any[]) {
    const result = func.call(this, ...args);
    console.log(
      `Func "${String(context.name)}" executed`
    );

    return result;
  }

  return wrapped_func;
}

function timed(func: any, context: ClassMethodDecoratorContext) {
  function wrapped_func(this: any, ...args: any[]) {
    const start_time_in_ns = process.hrtime.bigint();
    const result = func.call(this, ...args);
    const end_time_in_ns = process.hrtime.bigint();
    const duration_in_ns = end_time_in_ns - start_time_in_ns;

    console.log(
      `Exec of func "${String(context.name)}" took ${duration_in_ns} ns`
    );

    return result;
  }

  return wrapped_func;
}


class Adder {
  @logged
  @timed
  add(a: number, b: number): number {
    return a + b;
```

```
  }
}

// Prints, e.g.:
// Exec of func "add" took 7200 ns
// Func "add" executed
const result = new Adder().add(1, 2);

// NOTE! Decorators are applied
// in reverse order compared to order
// they are listed above the decorated
// function
```

4.14.2.8: Flyweight Pattern

The flyweight pattern is a memory-saving optimization pattern where flyweight objects reuse objects.

Let's have a simple example with a game where different shapes are drawn at different positions. Let's assume that the game draws a lot of similar shapes but in different positions so that we can notice the difference in memory consumption after applying this pattern.

Shapes that the game draws have the following properties: size, form, fill color, stroke color, stroke width, and stroke style.

```
public interface Shape {
  // ...
}


// Color...
// StrokeStyle...


public class AbstractShape implements Shape {
  private final Color fillColor;
  private final Color strokeColor;
  private final int strokeWidth;
  private final StrokeStyle strokeStyle;

  // ...
}


public class CircleShape extends AbstractShape {
  private final int radius;

  // ...
}


// LineSegment...


public class PolygonShape extends AbstractShape {
  private final List<LineSegment> lineSegments;

  // ...
}
```

When analyzing the PolygonShape class, we notice that it contains many properties that consume memory. A polygon with many line segments can consume a noticeable amount of memory. If the game draws many identical polygons in different screen positions and always creates a new PolygonShape object, there would be a lot of identical PolygonShape objects in the memory. To remediate this, we can introduce a flyweight class, DrawnShapeImpl, which contains the position of a shape and a reference to the actual shape. In this way, we can draw a lot of DrawnShapeImpl objects that all contain a reference to the same PolygonShape object:

```java
public interface DrawnShape {
  // ...
}


public class DrawnShapeImpl implements DrawnShape {
  private final Shape shape;
  private Position screenPosition;

  public DrawnShapeImpl(
    final Shape shape,
    final Position screenPosition
  ) {
    this.shape = shape;
    this.screenPosition = screenPosition;
  }

  // ...
}


final Shape polygon = new PolygonShape(...);
final List<Position> positions = generateLotsOfPositions();

final var drawnPolygons = positions.stream().map(position ->
  new DrawnShapeImpl(polygon, position)
);
```

4.14.3: Behavioral Design Patterns

Behavioral design patterns describe ways to implement new behavior using object-oriented design. The following behavioral design patterns will be presented in the following sections:

- Chain of responsibility pattern
- Observer pattern
- Command/Action pattern
- Iterator pattern
- Interpreter pattern
- State pattern
- Mediator pattern
- Template method pattern
- Memento pattern
- Visitor pattern
- Null object pattern

4.14.3.1: Chain of Responsibility Pattern

The chain of responsibility pattern lets you pass requests along a chain of handlers.

The chain of responsibility pattern allows you to add pluggable behavior to handling requests. That pluggable behavior is something that can be executed always or conditionally. This pattern allows you to follow the open-closed principle because you don't modify the request-handling process directly but only extend it with plug-ins. This pattern allows you to follow the single responsibility principle by putting specific behavior into a plug-in.

When receiving a request, each handler can decide what to do:

- Process the request and then pass it to the next handler in the chain
- Process the request without passing it to the subsequent handlers (terminating the chain)
- Leave the request unprocessed and pass it to the next handler

One of the most famous implementations of this pattern is Java servlet filters. A servlet filter processes incoming HTTP requests before passing them to the actual servlet for handling. Servlet filters can be used to implement various functionality like logging, compression, encryption/decryption, input validation, etc.

Let's have an example of a servlet filter that adds logging before and after each HTTP request is processed:

Figure 4.45. LoggingFilter.java

```java
import java.io.IOException;

import javax.servlet.*;
import javax.servlet.annotation.WebFilter;

@WebFilter(urlPatterns = {"/*"})
public class LoggingFilter implements Filter {
  // No initialization needed, thus empty method
  public void init(final FilterConfig filterConfig)
    throws ServletException
  {}

  // No cleanup needed, thus empty method
  public void destroy()
  {}

  public void doFilter(
    final ServletRequest request,
    final ServletResponse response,
    final FilterChain filterChain
  ) throws IOException, ServletException
  {
    final var responseWriter = response.getWriter();
    responseWriter.print("Before response\n");

    // Sends request to the next filter
    // or when no more filters to the servlet
    filterChain.doFilter(request, response);

    responseWriter.print("\nAfter response");
  }
}
```

Figure 4.46. HelloWorldServlet.java

```
import java.io.IOException;

import javax.servlet.ServletException;
import javax.servlet.annotation.WebServlet;
import javax.servlet.http.*;


@WebServlet("/helloworld")
public class HelloWorldServlet extends HttpServlet {
  public void doGet(
    HttpServletRequest request,
    HttpServletResponse response
  ) throws ServletException, IOException {
    response.setContentType("text/plain");
    final var responseWriter = response.getWriter();
    responseWriter.print("Hello, world!");
  }
}
```

When we send an HTTP GET request to the /helloworld endpoint, we should get the following response:

```
Before response
Hello, world!
After response
```

Let's implement a JWT authorization filter:

Figure 4.47. JwtAuthorizationFilter.java

```
import java.io.IOException;

import javax.servlet.*;
import javax.servlet.annotation.WebFilter;
import javax.servlet.http.HttpServletResponse;


@WebFilter(urlPatterns = {"/*"})
public class AuthorizationFilter implements Filter {
  public void init(final FilterConfig filterConfig)
    throws ServletException
  {}

  public void destroy()
  {}

  public void doFilter(
    final ServletRequest request,
    final ServletResponse response,
    final FilterChain filterChain
  ) throws IOException, ServletException {

    // From request's 'Authorization' header,
    // extract the bearer JWT
    // Set 'tokenIsPresent' variable value
    // to true or false
    // Verify the validity of JWT and assign result
    // to 'tokenIsValid' variable

    HttpServletResponse httpResponse =
      (HttpServletResponse) response;

    if (tokenIsValid) {
      filterChain.doFilter(request, response);
    } else if (tokenIsPresent) {
```

```
    // NOTE! filterChain is not invoked,
    // this will terminate the request
    httpResponse.setStatus(403);
    final var responseWriter = response.getWriter();
    responseWriter.print("Unauthorized");
    responseWriter.close();
  } else {
    // NOTE! filterChain is not invoked,
    // this will terminate the request
    httpResponse.setStatus(401);
    final var responseWriter = response.getWriter();
    responseWriter.print("Unauthenticated");
    responseWriter.close();
    }
  }
}
```

The Express[23] framework for Node.js utilizes the chain of responsibility pattern for handling requests. In the Express framework, you can write pluggable behavior using *middlewares*, a concept similar to servlet filters in Java. Below is the same logging and authorization example as above, but written using JavaScript and the Express framework:

```
const express = require('express')

const app = express()

// Authorization middleware
function authorize(request, response, next) {
  // From request's 'Authorization' header,
  // extract the bearer JWT, if present
  // Set 'tokenIsPresent' variable value
  // Verify the validity of JWT and assign result
  // to 'tokenIsValid' variable

  if (tokenIsValid) {
    next();
  } else if (tokenIsPresent) {
    // NOTE! next is not invoked,
    // this will terminate the request
    response.writeHead(403);
    response.end('Unauthorized');
  } else {
    // NOTE! next is not invoked,
    // this will terminate the request
    response.writeHead(401);
    response.end('Unauthenticated');
  }
}

// Logging before middleware
function logBefore(request, response, next) {
  response.write('Before response\n');
  next();
}

// Use authorization and logging middlewares
app.use(authorize, logBefore);

app.get('/helloworld', (request, response, next) => {
  response.write('Hello World!\n');
  next();
});

// Logging after middleware
```

---

[23]https://expressjs.com/

```
function logAfter(request, response, next) {
  response.write('After response\n');
  response.end();
  next();
}

app.use(logAfter);

app.listen(4000);
```

We cannot use Express middlewares as described below:

```
// Logging middleware
async function log(request, response, next) {
  response.write('Before response\n');
  await next();
  response.write('After response\n');

  // You cannot use response.end('After response\n')
  // because that would close the response stream
  // before Hello World! is written and the output
  // would be just:
  // Before response
  // After response
}

// Use authorization and logging middlewares
app.use(authorize, log);

app.get('/helloworld', (request, response) => {
  setTimeout(() => response.end('Hello World!\n'), 1000);
});
```

The reason is that the next function does not return a promise we could await. For this reason, the output from the /helloworld endpoint would be in the wrong order:

```
Before response
After response
Hello World!
```

ESLint plugins utilize the chain of responsibility pattern, too. Below is code for defining one rule in an ESLint plugin:

```
create(context) {
  return {
    NewExpression(newExpr) {
      if (
        newExpr.callee.name === "SqlFilter" &&
        newExpr.arguments &&
        newExpr.arguments[0] &&
        newExpr.arguments[0].type !== "Literal"
      ) {
        context.report(
          newExpr,
          `SqlFilter constructor's 1st parameter must be a string literal`
        );
      }
    }
  };
}
```

ESLint plugin framework will call the create function and supply the context parameter. The create function should return an object of functions to analyze different *abstract syntax tree* (AST) nodes. In the above example, we are only interested in NewExpression nodes and analyze the creation of a new SqlFilter object. The first parameter supplied for the SqlFilter constructor should be a literal. If not, we report an issue using the context.report method.

When running ESLint with the above plugin and rule enabled, whenever ESLint encounters a *new* expression in a code file, the above-supplied NewExpression handler function will be called to check if the *new* expression in the code is valid.

The following code will pass the above ESLint rule:

```
const sqlFilter = new SqlFilter('field1 > 0');
```

And the following code won't:

```
const sqlExpression = 'field1 > 0';
const sqlFilter = new SqlFilter(sqlExpression);
```

4.14.3.2: Observer Pattern

The observer pattern lets you define an observe-notify (or publish subscribe) mechanism to notify one or more objects about events that happen to the observed object.

One typical example of using the observer pattern is a UI view observing a model. The UI view will be notified whenever the model changes and can redraw itself. Let's have an example with Java:

```java
public interface Observer {
  void notifyAboutChange();
}

public interface Observable {
  void observeBy(Observer observer);
}

public class ObservableImpl {
  private final List<Observer> observers = new ArrayList<>();

  public void observeBy(final Observer observer) {
    observers.add(observer);
  }

  protected void notifyObservers() {
    observers.forEach(Observer::notifyAboutChange);
  }
}

public class TodosModel extends ObservableImpl {
  private List<Todo> todos = new ArrayList<>(25);

  // ...

  public void addTodo(final Todo todo) {
    todos.add(todo);
    notifyObservers();
```

```
  }
  public void removeTodo(final Todo todo) {
    todos.remove(todo);
    notifyObservers();
  }
}


public class TodosView implements Observer {
  private final TodosModel todosModel;

  public TodosView(final TodosModel todosModel) {
    this.todosModel = todosModel;
    todosModel.observeBy(this);
  }

  public void notifyAboutChange() {
    // Will be called when todos model change
    render();
  }

  public void render() {
    // Renders todos...
  }
}
```

Let's look at another example that utilizes the publish-subscribe pattern. Below, we define a `MessageBroker` class that contains the following methods: `publish`, `subscribe`, and `unsubscribe`.

```
public interface MessagePublisher<T> {
  void publish(String topic, T message);
}


@FunctionalInterface
public interface MessageHandler<T> {
  void handle(T message);
}


public interface MessageSubscriber<T> {
  void subscribe(String topic,
                 MessageHandler<T> messageHandler);
}


public class MessageBroker<T> implements
               MessagePublisher<T>, MessageSubscriber<T> {
  private final Map<String, List<MessageHandler<T>>>
    topicToMessageHandlers = new HashMap<>();

  public void publish(
    final String topic,
    final T message
  ) {
    final var messageHandlers =
      topicToMessageHandlers.get(topic);

    if (messageHandlers != null) {
      messageHandlers.forEach(messageHandler ->
        messageHandler.handle(message));
    }
  }

  public void subscribe(
    final String topic,
    final MessageHandler<T> messageHandler
```

```
  ) {
    final var messageHandlers =
      topicToMessageHandlers.get(topic);

    if (messageHandlers == null) {
      topicToMessageHandlers.put(topic, List.of(messageHandler));
    } else {
      messageHandlers.add(messageHandler);
    }
  }

  public void unsubscribe(
    final String topic,
    final MessageHandler<T> messageHandlerToRemove
  ) {
    final var messageHandlers = topicToMessageHandlers.get(topic);

    messageHandlers.removeIf(messageHandler ->
      messageHandler == messageHandlerToRemove);
  }
}
```

In the above example, we could have used the built-in Java Consumer<T> interface instead of the custom
MessageHandler<T> interface.

4.14.3.3: Command/Action Pattern

*Command or action pattern defines commands or actions as objects that can be given
as parameters to other functions for later execution.*

The command/action pattern is one way to follow the open-closed principle, i.e., extending code by creating
new command/action classes for additional functionality instead of modifying existing code.

Let's create a simple action and command interface:

```
public interface Action {
  void perform();
}

public interface Command {
  void execute();
}
```

Let's create a simple concrete action/command that prints a message:

```
public class PrintAction implements Action {
  private final String message;

  public PrintAction(final String message) {
    this.message = message;
  }

  public void perform() {
    System.out.print(message);
  }
}


public class PrintCommand implements Command {
  private final String message;
```

```
  public PrintCommand(final String message) {
    this.message = message;
  }

  public void execute() {
    System.out.print(message);
  }
}
```

As can be seen, the above PrintAction and PrintCommand instances encapsulate the state that is used when the action/command is performed (usually at a later stage compared to action/command instance creation).

Now we can use our print action/command:

```
final var actions = List.of(new PrintAction("Hello"), new PrintAction("World"));

for (final var action : actions) {
  action.perform();
}

final var commands = List.of(new PrintCommand("Hello"), new PrintCommand("World"));

for (final var command : commands) {
  command.execute();
}
```

Using actions or commands makes it possible to follow the open-closed principle because when introducing a new action or command existing code is not modified.

Actions and commands can be made undoable, provided that the action/command is undoable. The above print action/command is not undoable because you cannot undo print to the console. Let's introduce an undoable action: add an item to a list. It is an action that can be undone by removing the item from the list.

```
interface UndoableAction extends Action {
  void undo();
}


class AddToSetAction<T> implements UndoableAction {
    private final T item;
    private final Set<T> items;

    public AddToSetAction(final T item, final Set<T> items) {
        this.item = item;
        this.items = items;
    }

    public void perform() {
        items.add(item);
    }

    public void undo() {
        items.remove(item);
    }
}


final var values = new HashSet<>(Set.of(1, 2));
final var add3ToValuesAction = new AddToSetAction<>(3, values);
add3ToValuesAction.perform();
System.out.println(values);  // Prints [1, 2, 3]
add3ToValuesAction.undo();
System.out.println(values);  // Prints [1, 2]
```

Let's have an example using the Redux[24] library's *legacy syntax*, well-known by many React developers. We are not using the newer syntax offered by the *@reduxjs/toolkit* package.

Below is a Redux reducer:

Figure 4.48. todoReducer.js

```
function todoReducer(state = initialState, action) {
  switch (action.type) {
    case 'ADD_TODO':
      return {
        ...state,
        todos: [...state.todos, {
          id: action.payload.id,
          name: action.payload.name,
          isDone: false
        }]
      };
    case 'MARK_TODO_DONE':
      const newTodos = state.todos.map(todo => {
        if (todo.id !== action.payload.id) {
          return todo;
        }

        return {
          ...todo,
          isDone: true
        };
      });

      return {
        ...state,
        todos: newTodos
      };
    default:
      return state;
  }
}
```

In the above example, we define a todoReducer which can handle two different actions: ADD_TODO and MARK_-TODO_DONE. The implementation of the actions is inlined inside the switch statement, which makes the code somewhat hard to read. We can refactor the above code so that we introduce two classes for action objects:

Figure 4.49. AddTodoAction.ts

```
export default class AddTodoAction {
  constructor(
    private readonly id: number,
    private readonly name: string
  ) {}

  perform(state: TodoState): TodoState {
    return {
      ...state,
      todos: [...state.todos, {
        id: this.id,
        name: this.name,
        isDone: false
      }]
    };
  }
}
```

---

[24]https://redux.js.org/

Figure 4.50. MarkDoneTodoAction.ts

```
export default class MarkDoneTodoAction {
  constructor(private readonly id: number) {}

  perform(state: TodoState): TodoState {
    const newTodos = state.todos.map(todo => {
      if (todo.id !== this.id) {
        return todo;
      }

      return {
        ...todo,
        isDone: true
      };
    });

    return {
      ...state,
      todos: newTodos
    };
  }
}
```

Now, we can redesign the todoReducer to look like the following:

Figure 4.51. todoReducer.ts

```
import AddTodoAction from './AddTodoAction';
import MarkDoneTodoAction from './MarkDoneTodoAction';

function todoReducer(
  state: TodoState = initialState,
  { payload: { id, name }, type }: any
) {
  switch (type) {
    case 'ADD_TODO':
      return new AddTodoAction(id, name).perform(state);
    case 'MARK_TODO_DONE':
      return new MarkDoneTodoAction(id).perform(state);
    default:
      return state;
  }
}
```

We have separated actions into classes, and the todoReducer function becomes simpler. However, we should make the code object-oriented by replacing the conditionals (switch-case) with polymorphism. Let's do the following modifications: introduce a generic base class for actions and a base class for todo-related actions:

Figure 4.52. AbstractAction.ts

```
export default abstract class AbstractAction<S> {
  abstract perform(state: S): S;
}
```

Figure 4.53. AbstractTodoAction.ts

```
import AbstractAction from './AbstractAction';

export default abstract class AbstractTodoAction extends
  AbstractAction<TodoState> {}
```

The todo action classes must be modified to extend the `AbstractTodoAction` class:

Figure 4.54. AddTodoAction.ts

```
import AbstractTodoAction from './AbstractTodoAction';

export default class AddTodoAction extends AbstractTodoAction {
  // ...
}
```

Figure 4.55. MarkDoneTodoAction.ts

```
import AbstractTodoAction from './AbstractTodoAction';

export default class MarkDoneTodoAction extends AbstractTodoAction {
  // ...
}
```

Then, we can introduce a generic function to create a reducer. This function will create a reducer function that perform actions for a given action base class:

Figure 4.56. createReducer.ts

```
import AbstractAction from './AbstractAction';

export default function createReducer<S>(
  initialState: S,
  ActionBaseClass:
    abstract new (...args: any[]) => AbstractAction<S>
) {
  return function(
    state: S = initialState,
    action: { type: AbstractAction<S> }
  ) {
    return action.type instanceof ActionBaseClass
      ? action.type.perform(state)
      : state;
  };
}
```

Let's create the initial state for todos:

Figure 4.57. Todo.ts

```
export type Todo = {
  id: number,
  name: string,
  isDone: boolean
}
```

Figure 4.58. initialTodoState.ts

```
import { Todo } from './Todo';

export type TodoState = {
  todos: Todo[];
}

const initialTodoState = {
  todos: []
} as TodoState

export default initialTodoState;
```

Next, we can create a Redux store using the createReducer function, the initial todo state, and the base action class for todo-related actions:

Figure 4.59. store.ts

```
import { combineReducers, createStore } from "redux";
import createReducer from "./createReducer";
import initialTodoState from "./initialTodoState";
import AbstractTodoAction from "./AbstractTodoAction";

const rootReducer = combineReducers({
  todoState: createReducer(initialTodoState, AbstractTodoAction)
});

export default createStore(rootReducer);
```

Now, we have an object-oriented solution for dispatching actions in the following way:

```
dispatch({ type: new AddTodoAction(id, name) });
dispatch({ type: new MarkTodoDoneAction(id) });
```

Let's modify the AbstractAction class to support undoable actions. By default, an action is not undoable:

Figure 4.60. AbstractAction.ts

```
export default abstract class AbstractAction<S> {
  abstract perform(state: S): S;

  getName(): string {
    return this.constructor.name;
  }

  isUndoable(): boolean {
    return false;
  }
}
```

Let's also create a new class to serve as a base class for undoable actions:

Figure 4.61. AbstractUndoableAction.ts

```ts
import AbstractAction from "./AbstractAction";

export default abstract class AbstractUndoableAction<S> extends
        AbstractAction<S> {
  override isUndoable(): boolean {
    return true;
  }
}
```

Let's define a class for undo-actions. An undo-action sets the state as it was before performing the actual action.

Figure 4.62. UndoAction.ts

```ts
import AbstractAction from "./AbstractAction";

export default class UndoAction<S> extends AbstractAction<S> {
  constructor(
    private readonly actionName: string,
    private readonly ActionBaseClass:
      abstract new (...args: any[]) => AbstractAction<S>,
    private readonly state: S
  ) {
    super();
  }

  override getName(): string {
    return this.actionName;
  }

  override perform(state: S): S {
    return this.state;
  }

  getActionBaseClass():
    abstract new (...args: any[]) => AbstractAction<S>
  {
    return this.ActionBaseClass;
  }
}
```

Let's modify the createReducer function to create undo-actions for undoable actions and store them in a stack named undoActions. When a user wants to perform an undo of the last action, the topmost element from the undoActions stack can be popped and executed.

Figure 4.63. undoActions.ts

```ts
import UndoAction from "./UndoAction";

const undoActions = [] as UndoAction<any>[];
export default undoActions;
```

Figure 4.64. createReducer.ts

```
// ...
import undoActions from './undoActions';
import AbstractAction from "./AbstractAction";
import UndoAction from "./UndoAction";

function createReducer<S>(
  initialState: S,
  ActionBaseClass:
    abstract new (...args : any[]) => AbstractAction<S>
) {
  return function(
    state: S = initialState,
    action: { type: AbstractAction<S> }
  ) {
    let newState;

    if (action.type instanceof UndoAction &&
        action.type.getActionBaseClass() === ActionBaseClass) {
      newState = action.type.perform(state);
    } else if (action.type instanceof ActionBaseClass) {
      if (action.type.isUndoable()) {
        undoActions.unshift(new UndoAction(
          action.type.getName(),
          ActionBaseClass,
          state));
      }

      newState = action.type.perform(state);
    } else {
      newState = state;
    }

    return newState;
  };
}
```

The above demonstrated way of handling Redux actions is presented in an example found here[25].

Commands/Actions can also be defined without an object-oriented approach using a newly created function with a closure. In the below example, the function () => toggleTodoDone(id) is redefined for each todo. The function redefinition will always create a new closure that stores the current id variable value. We can treat the () => toggleTodoDone(id) as an action or command because it "encapsulates" the id value in the closure.

[25]https://github.com/pksilen/clean-code-principles-code/tree/main/chapter2/mvvm

Figure 4.65. TodosTableView.tsx

```tsx
// type Props = ...

export default function TodosTableView(
  { toggleTodoDone, todos }: Props
) {
  const todoElements = todos.map(({ id, name }) => (
    <tr>
      <td>{id}</td>
      <td>{name}</td>
      <td>
        <input
          type="checkbox"
          onChange={() => toggleTodoDone(id)}
        />
      </td>
    </tr>
  ));

  return <table><tbody>{todoElements}</tbody></table>;
}
```

4.14.3.4: Iterator Pattern

The iterator pattern can be used to add iteration capabilities to a class.

Let's create a reverse iterator for Java's List class. We implement the Iterator interface by supplying implementations for the hasNext and the next methods:

Figure 4.66. ReverseListIterator.java

```java
public class ReverseListIterator<T> implements Iterator<T> {
  private final List<T> values;
  private int iteratorPosition;

  public ReverseListIterator(final List<T> values) {
    this.values = Collections.unmodifiableList(values);
    iteratorPosition = values.size() - 1;
  }

  @Override
  public boolean hasNext() {
    return iteratorPosition >= 0;
  }

  @Override
  public T next() {
    // Note! We don't check the iteratorPosition
    // validity here, it is checked in hasNext() method,
    // which must be called before calling next() method
    // and only call next() method if hasNext() method
    // returned true
    final var nextValue = values.get(iteratorPosition);
    iteratorPosition--;
    return nextValue;
  }
}
```

We can put the ReverseListIterator class into use in a ReverseArrayList class defined below:

Figure 4.67. ReverseArrayList.java

```
public class ReverseArrayList<T> extends ArrayList<T>
{
  @Override
  public Iterator<T> iterator() {
    return new ReverseListIterator<>(this);
  }
}
```

Now, we can use the new iterator to iterate over a list in reverse order:

```
final var reversedNumbers = new ReverseArrayList<Integer>();
reversedNumbers.addAll(List.of(1,2,3,4,5));

for (final var number : reversedNumbers) {
  System.out.println(number);
}

// Prints:
// 5
// 4
// 3
// 2
// 1
```

4.14.3.5: Interpreter Pattern

The interpreter pattern evaluates an expression in a specialized computer language using an abstract syntax tree (AST).

The abstract syntax tree[26] (AST) is represented by expression objects using the *composite pattern* to create a tree structure of the expressions. The expressions are divided into two main types: a leaf and a non-leaf expression:

```
public interface Expression {
  void evaluate();
}
```

```
public class LeafExpression implements Expression {
  public void evaluate() {
    // ...
  }
}
```

```
public class NonLeafExpression implements Expression {
  public void evaluate() {
    // ...
  }
}
```

Let's have an example with a simple specialized language where we can write addition operations, like 1 + 2 + 3. We need to define the expression classes. Our implementation will have one non-leaf type expression class called AddExpression that represents an addition operation and another leaf type expression class named LiteralExpression that represents a literal (integer) value.

---

[26]https://en.wikipedia.org/wiki/Abstract_syntax_tree

```
public interface Expression {
  int evaluate();
}


public class AddExpression implements Expression {
  private final Expression left;
  private final Expression right;

  public AddExpression(final Expression left, final Expression right) {
    this.left = left;
    this.right = right;
  }

  public int evaluate() {
    return left.evaluate() + right.evaluate();
  }
}


public class LiteralExpression implements Expression {
  private final int value;

  public LiteralExpression(final int value) {
    this.value = value;
  }

  public int evaluate() {
    return value;
  }
}
```

What we need is a parser for the AST. A parser goes through a "sentence" in the specialized language and produces an AST ready for evaluation. The parser implementation is not part of this design pattern, but I will present the parser implementation below using the *test-driven development* (TDD) process. The TDD process is better described in the coming *testing principles* chapter.

First, we will list the things we need to test.

- Parse a literal, e.g., 5
- Parse another literal, e.g., 7
- Parse an invalid literal, e.g., XX
- Parse empty sentence
- Parse single addition, e.g,. 2+5
- Parse single addition with white space, e.g., ' 2 + 5 '
- Parse invalid operator, e.g., 2 * 5
- Parse addition with invalid left literal, e.g., XX + 5
- Parse addition with invalid right literal, e.g., 2 + YY
- Parse two additions, e.g., 1 + 2 + 3
- Parse two additions with invalid operator, e.g., 1 + 2 ++ 3
- Parse two additions with invalid literal, e.g., 1 + 2 + XX
- Parse three additions, e.g., 1 + 2 + 3 + 4
- Parse nine additions, e.g., '1+ 2 +3 + 4 +5+ 6 +7 +8 +9+10 '
- We can stop adding tests because we have generalized the implementation enough to support any number of additions.

Let's start with the first test:

```
import org.junit.jupiter.api.Test;

import static org.junit.jupiter.api.Assertions.assertEquals;

class ParserTests {
  private final Parser parser = new Parser();

  @Test
  void testParseWithLiteral() {
    // WHEN
    final var ast = parser.parse("5");

    // THEN
    assertEquals(5, ast.evaluate());
  }
}
```

Let's create an implementation that makes the above test pass. We should write the simplest possible code and only enough code to make the test pass.

```
public class Parser {
  Expression parse(final String sentence) {
    return new LiteralExpression(5);
  }
}
```

Let's add a test:

```
class ParserTests {
  private final Parser parser = new Parser();

  @Test
  void testParseWithLiteral() {
    // WHEN
    final var ast = parser.parse("5");
    final var ast2 = parser.parse("7");

    // THEN
    assertEquals(5, ast.evaluate());
    assertEquals(7, ast2.evaluate());
  }
}
```

Let's generalize the implementation:

```
public class Parser {
  Expression parse(final String sentence) {
    final var literal = Integer.parseInt(sentence);
    return new LiteralExpression(literal);
  }
}
```

Let's add a test:

```
class ParserTests {
  // ...

  @Test
  void testParseWithInvalidLiteral() {
    // WHEN + THEN
    assertThrows(Parser.ParseError.class, () -> parser.parse("XX"));
  }
}
```

Let's modify the implementation to make the above test pass:

```
public class Parser {
  public static class ParseError extends Exception {
  }

  Expression parse(final String sentence) throws ParseError {
    try {
      final var literal = Integer.parseInt(sentence);
      return new LiteralExpression(literal);
    } catch(final NumberFormatException error) {
      throw new ParseError();
    }
  }
}
```

Let's add a test:

```
class ParserTests {
  // ...

  @Test
  void testParseWithInvalidLiteral() {
    // WHEN + THEN
    assertThrows(Parser.ParseError.class, () -> parser.parse("XX"));
    assertThrows(Parser.ParseError.class, () -> parser.parse(""));
  }
}
```

The above test passes without implementation code modification. Let's add a test:

```
class ParserTests {
  // ...

  @Test
  void testParseWithAddition() throws Parser.ParseError {
    // WHEN
    final var ast = parser.parse("2+5");

    // THEN
    assertEquals(7, ast.evaluate());
  }
}
```

Let's modify the implementation to make the above test pass. We will split the input sentence and also extract the literal parsing into a separate private method:

```java
public class Parser {
  public static class ParseError extends Exception {
  }

  Expression parse(final String sentence) throws ParseError {
    final var tokens = sentence.split("\\+");
    final var leftLiteral = parseLiteral(tokens[0].trim());

    if (tokens.length == 1) {
      return leftLiteral;
    } else {
      final var rightLiteral = parseLiteral(tokens[1].trim());
      return new AddExpression(leftLiteral, rightLiteral);
    }
  }

  Expression parseLiteral(final String string) throws ParseError {
    try {
      final var literal = Integer.parseInt(string);
      return new LiteralExpression(literal);
    } catch (final NumberFormatException error) {
      throw new ParseError();
    }
  }
}
```

Let's add a test:

```java
class ParserTests {
  // ...

  @Test
  void testParseWithAddition() throws Parser.ParseError {
    // WHEN
    final var ast = parser.parse("2+5");
    final var ast2 = parser.parse(" 3  +   5 ");

    // THEN
    assertEquals(7, ast.evaluate());
    assertEquals(8, ast2.evaluate());
  }
}
```

We notice that the above test passes. Let's add another test, then:

```java
class ParserTests {
  // ...

  @Test
  void testParseWithInvalidAddition() {
    // WHEN + THEN
    assertThrows(Parser.ParseError.class, () -> parser.parse("2 * 5"));
    assertThrows(Parser.ParseError.class, () -> parser.parse("XX + 5"));
    assertThrows(Parser.ParseError.class, () -> parser.parse("2 + YY"));
  }
}
```

These tests pass. Let's add a test with more than one addition:

```
class ParserTests {
  // ...

  @Test
  void testParseWithAddition() throws Parser.ParseError {
    // WHEN
    final var ast = parser.parse("2+5");
    final var ast2 = parser.parse(" 3  +   5 ");
    final var ast3 = parser.parse("1 + 2 + 3");

    // THEN
    assertEquals(7, ast.evaluate());
    assertEquals(8, ast2.evaluate());
    assertEquals(6, ast3.evaluate());
  }
}
```

Let's make the test pass:

```
class Parser {
  // ...

  Expression parse(final String sentence) throws ParseError {
    final var tokens = sentence.split("\\+");
    final var leftLiteral = parseLiteral(tokens[0].trim());

    if (tokens.length == 1) {
      return leftLiteral;
    } else if (tokens.length == 2){
      final var rightLiteral = parseLiteral(tokens[1].trim());
      return new AddExpression(leftLiteral, rightLiteral);
    } else {
      final var restOfSentence = Arrays
          .stream(tokens, 1, tokens.length)
          .collect(Collectors.joining("+"));

      return new AddExpression(leftLiteral, parse(restOfSentence));
    }
  }

  // ...
}
```

We can refactor:

```
class Parser {
  // ...

  Expression parse(final String sentence) throws ParseError {
    final var tokens = sentence.split("\\+");
    return parse(tokens);
  }

  private Expression parse(final String[] tokens) throws ParseError {
    final var leftLiteral = parseLiteral(tokens[0].trim());

    if (tokens.length == 1) {
      return leftLiteral;
    } else if (tokens.length == 2){
      final var rightLiteral = parseLiteral(tokens[1].trim());
      return new AddExpression(leftLiteral, rightLiteral);
    } else {
      final var restOfTokens = Arrays.copyOfRange(tokens, 1, tokens.length)
      return new AddExpression(leftLiteral, parse(restOfTokens));
    }
  }
```

```
  // ...
}
```

The final four tests also pass:

```
class ParserTests {
  // ...

  @Test
  void testParseWithInvalidAddition() {
    // WHEN + THEN
    assertThrows(Parser.ParseError.class, () -> parser.parse("2 * 5"));
    assertThrows(Parser.ParseError.class, () -> parser.parse("XX + 5"));
    assertThrows(Parser.ParseError.class, () -> parser.parse("2 + YY"));

    // Added tests
    assertThrows(
      Parser.ParseError.class, () -> parser.parse("1 + 2 ++ 3")
    );

    assertThrows(
      Parser.ParseError.class, () -> parser.parse("1 + 2 + XX")
    );
  }
}
```

```
class ParserTests {
  // ...

  @Test
  void testParseWithAddition() throws Parser.ParseError {
    // WHEN
    final var ast = parser.parse("2+5");
    final var ast2 = parser.parse(" 3  +   5 ");
    final var ast3 = parser.parse("1 + 2 + 3");
    final var ast4 = parser.parse("1 + 2 + 3 + 4");
    final var ast5 = parser.parse("1+  2 +3 +   4 +5+ 6 +7 +8 +9+10 ");

    // THEN
    assertEquals(7, ast.evaluate());
    assertEquals(8, ast2.evaluate());
    assertEquals(6, ast3.evaluate());
    assertEquals(10, ast4.evaluate());
    assertEquals(55, ast5.evaluate());
  }
}
```

In the above example, I added new tests to existing methods. You can also put each test into a separate test method. I didn't do that because most test methods would have been only 1-2 statements long. We can refactor the above two tests to parameterized tests:

```
class ParserTests {
  // ...

  @ParameterizedTest
  @ValueSource(strings = {"2 * 5", "XX + 5", "2 + YY", "1 + 2 ++ 3", "1 + 2 + XX"})
  void testParseWithInvalidAddition(final String sentence) {
    // WHEN + THEN
    assertThrows(Parser.ParseError.class, () -> parser.parse(sentence));
  }
}
```

class ParserTests { // ...

@ParameterizedTest @CsvSource({ "2+5, 7", " 3 + 5 , 8", "1 + 2 + 3, 6", "1 + 2 + 3 + 4, 10", "1+ 2 +3 + 4 +5+ 6 +7 +8 +9+10 , 55" }) void testParseWithAddition(final String sentence, final int evalResult) throws Parser.ParseError { // WHEN final var ast = parser.parse(sentence);

```
// THEN
assertEquals(ast.evaluate(), evalResult);
```

}}

If you are interested in creating a parser, read about Recursive descent parser[27].

For the expression 1 + 2 + 3, the parser should produce the following kind of AST:

```
// Parser should return 'ast' of below kind
final var ast = new AddExpression(
  new LiteralExpression(1),
  new AddExpression(
    new LiteralExpression(2),
    new LiteralExpression(3)
  )
);

// Prints 6
System.out.print(ast.evaluate());
```

4.14.3.6: State Pattern

The state pattern lets an object change its behavior depending on its current state.

Developers don't often treat an object's state as an object but as an enumerated value (enum), for example. Below is a Java example where we have defined a UserStory class representing a user story that can be rendered on screen. An enum value represents the state of a UserStory object.

---

[27] https://en.wikipedia.org/wiki/Recursive_descent_parser

```
public enum UserStoryState {
  TODO, IN_DEVELOPMENT, IN_VERIFICATION, READY_FOR_REVIEW, DONE
}


public class UserStory {
  private String name;
  private UserStoryState state = UserStoryState.TODO;
  // Other properties...

  public UserStory(final String name, ...) {
    this.name = name;
    // ...
  }

  public void setState(
    final UserStoryState newState
  ) {
    state = newState;
  }

  public void render() {
    final var icon = switch(state) {
      case TODO -> new TodoIcon();
      case IN_DEVELOPMENT -> new InDevelopmentIcon();
      case IN_VERIFICATION -> new InVerificationIcon();
      case READY_FOR_REVIEW -> new ReadyForReviewIcon();
      case DONE -> new DoneIcon();
      default -> throw new IllegalArgumentException(...);
    };

    // Draw a UI elements on screen representing the user story
    // using the given 'icon'
  }
}
```

The above solution is not an object-oriented one. We should replace the conditionals (switch-case statement) with a polymorphic design. This can be done by introducing state objects. In the state pattern, an object's state is represented with an object instead of an enum value. Below is the above code modified to use the state pattern:

```
public interface UserStoryState {
  Icon getIcon();
}


public class TodoUserStoryState implements UserStoryState {
  public Icon getIcon() {
    return new TodoIcon();
  }
}


public class InDevelopmentUserStoryState
         implements UserStoryState {
  public Icon getIcon() {
    return new InDevelopmentIcon();
  }
}


public class InVerificationUserStoryState
         implements UserStoryState {
  public Icon getIcon() {
    return new InVerificationIcon();
  }
}
```

```
public class ReadyForReviewUserStoryState
        implements UserStoryState {
  public Icon getIcon() {
    return new ReadyForReviewIcon();
  }
}


public class DoneUserStoryState
        implements UserStoryState {
  public Icon getIcon() {
    return new DoneIcon();
  }
}


public class UserStory {
  private String name;
  private UserStoryState state = new TodoUserStoryState();
  // Other properties...

  public UserStory(final String name, ...) {
    this.name = name;
    // ...
  }

  public void setState(
    final UserStoryState newState
  ) {
    state = newState;
  }

  public void render() {
    final Icon icon = state.getIcon();
    // Draw a UI element on screen representing
    // the user story using the given 'icon'
  }
}
```

Let's have another example with an `Order` class. An order can have a state, like paid, packaged, delivered, etc. Below, we implement the order states as classes:

```
public interface OrderState {
  String getMessage(String orderId);
}


public class PaidOrderState implements OrderState {
  public String getMessage(final String orderId) {
    return "Order " + orderId + " is successfully paid";
  }
}


public class DeliveredOrderState implements OrderState {
  public String getMessage(final String orderId) {
    return "Order " + orderId + " is delivered";
  }
}


// Implement the rest of possible order states here...


public class Order {
  private String id;
```

```
  private OrderState state;
  private Customer customer;

  // ...

  public String getCustomerEmailAddress() {
    return customer.getEmailAddress();
  }

  public String getStateMessage() {
    return state.getMessage(id);
  }
}


emailService.sendEmail(order.getCustomerEmailAddress(),
                       order.getStateMessage());
```

4.14.3.7: Mediator Pattern

The mediator pattern lets you reduce dependencies between objects. It restricts direct communication between two different layers of objects and forces them to collaborate only via a mediator object or objects.

The mediator pattern eliminates the coupling of two different layers of objects. So, changes to one layer of objects can be made without the need to change the objects in the other layer. This pattern is called *indirection* in GRASP principles.

A typical example of the mediator pattern is the Model-View-Controller (MVC) pattern. In the MVC pattern, model and view objects do not communicate directly but only via mediator objects (controllers). Next, several ways to use the MVC pattern in frontend clients are presented. Traditionally, the MVC pattern was used in the backend when the backend also generated the view to be shown in the client device (web browser). With the advent of single-page web clients[28], a modern backend is a simple API containing only a model and controller (MC).

Figure 4.68. Model-View-Controller

In the picture below, you can see how dependency inversion is used. None of the implementation classes depend on concrete implementations. You can easily change any implementation class to a different one without the need to modify any other implementation class. Notice how the `ControllerImpl` class uses the *bridge pattern* and implements two bridges, one towards the model and the other towards the view.

We should be able to replace a view implementation or create a new one without changes to other layers (model and controller). For example, we could have a view implementation that is a GUI, and we could have a "view" implementation where input and output are voice. This is called *orthogonality*, a concept from the *Pragmatic Programmer* book. Orthogonality means that a change in one place should not require

---

[28]https://en.wikipedia.org/wiki/Single-page_application

a change in another place. The orthogonality principle is related to the *single responsibility principle* and the *separation of concerns principle*. When you implement software using the two latter principles, the software becomes orthogonal.

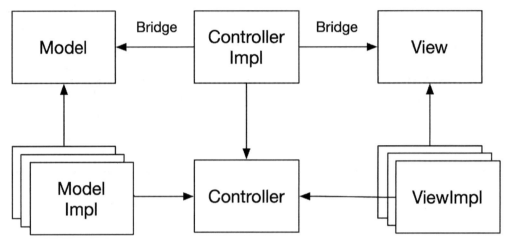

Figure 4.69. Dependencies in MVC pattern

The picture below shows that the controller can also be used as a bridge adapter. The controller can be modified to adapt to changes in the view layer (View2 instead of View) without changing the model layer. The modified modules are shown in the picture with a gray background. Similarly, the controller can be modified to adapt to changes in the model layer without changing the view layer (not shown in the picture).

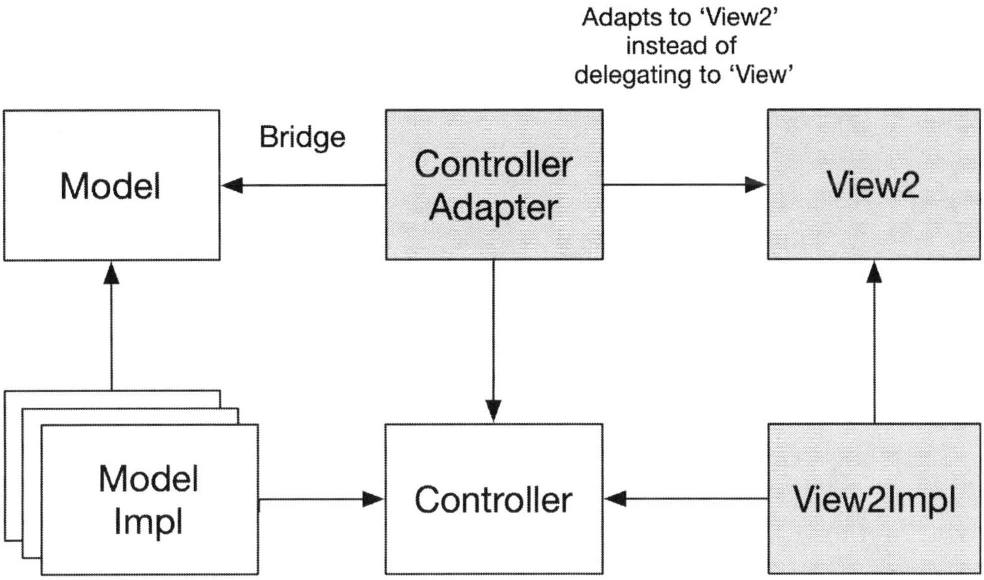

Figure 4.70. Adapting to Changes in MVC pattern

The following examples use a specialization of the MVC pattern called Model-View-Presenter (MVP). In the MVP pattern, the controller is called the presenter. I use the more generic term *controller* in all examples, though. A presenter acts as a middle-man between a view and a model. A presenter-type controller object has a reference to a view object and a model object. A view object commands the presenter to perform actions on the model. The model object asks the presenter to update the view object.

In the past, making desktop UI applications using Java Swing as the UI layer was popular. Let's have a simple todo application as an example:

First, we implement the Todo class, which is part of the model.

Figure 4.71. Todo.java

```java
public class Todo {
  private int id;
  private String name;
  private boolean isDone;

  // Constructor...

  public int getId() {
    return id;
  }

  public void setId(final int id) {
    this.id = id;
  }

  public String getName() {
    return name;
  }

  public void setName(final String name) {
    this.name = name;
```

```
  }

  public boolean isDone() {
    return isDone;
  }

  public void setIsDone(final boolean isDone) {
    this.isDone = isDone;
  }
}
```

Next, we implement the view layer:

Figure 4.72. TodoView.java

```
public interface TodoView {
  void show(List<Todo> todos);
  void show(String message);
}
```

Figure 4.73. TodoViewImpl.java

```
public class TodoViewImpl implements TodoView {
  private final TodoController controller;

  public TodoViewImpl(final TodoController controller) {
    this.controller = controller;
    controller.setView(this);
    controller.startFetchTodos();
  }

  public void show(final List<Todo> todos) {
    // Update the view to show the given todos
    // Add listener for each todo checkbox.
    // Listener should call: controller.toggleTodoDone(todo.id)
  }

  public void show(final String errorMessage) {
    // Update the view to show error message
  }
}
```

Then, we implement a generic `Controller` class that acts as a base class for concrete controllers:

Figure 4.74. Controller.java

```
public class Controller<M, V> {
  private M model;
  private V view;

  public M getModel() {
    return model;
  }

  public void setModel(final M model) {
    this.model = model;
  }

  public V getView() {
    return view;
  }

  public void setView(final V view) {
    this.view = view;
  }
}
```

The below `TodoControllerImpl` class implements two actions, `startFetchTodos` and `toggleTodoDone`, which delegate to the model layer. It also implements two actions, `updateViewWith(todos)` and `updateViewWith(errorMessage)`, that delegate to the view layer. The latter two actions are executed in the Swing UI thread using `SwingUtilities.invokeLater`.

Figure 4.75. **TodoController.java**

```
public interface TodoController {
  void startFetchTodos();
  void toggleTodoDone(final int id);
  void updateViewWith(final List<Todo> todos);
  void updateViewWith(final String errorMessage);
}
```

Figure 4.76. **TodoControllerImpl.java**

```
public class TodoControllerImpl
        extends Controller<TodoModel, TodoView>
        implements TodoController {

  public void startFetchTodos() {
    getModel().fetchTodos();
  }

  public void toggleTodoDone(final int id) {
    getModel().toggleTodoDone(id);
  }

  public void updateViewWith(final List<Todo> todos) {
    SwingUtilities.invokeLater(() ->
      getView().show(todos));
  }

  public void updateViewWith(final String errorMessage) {
    SwingUtilities.invokeLater(() ->
      getView().show(errorMessage));
  }
}
```

The below `TodoModelImpl` class implements the fetching of todos (`fetchTodos`) using the supplied `todoService`. The `todoService` accesses the backend to read todos from a database, for example. When todos are successfully fetched, the controller is told to update the view. If fetching of the todos fails, the view is updated to show an error. Toggling a todo done is implemented using the `todoService` and its `updateTodo` method.

Figure 4.77. **TodoService.java**

```
public interface TodoService {
  public List<Todo> getTodos();
  public void updateTodo(Todo todo);
}
```

Figure 4.78. **TodoModel.java**

```
public interface TodoModel {
  public void fetchTodos();
  public void toggleTodoDone(int id);
}
```

Figure 4.79. TodoModelImpl.java

```java
public class TodoModelImpl implements TodoModel {
  private final TodoController controller;
  private final TodoService todoService;
  private List<Todo> todos = new ArrayList<>();

  public TodoModelImpl(
    final TodoController controller,
    final TodoService todoService
  ) {
    this.controller = controller;
    controller.setModel(this);
    this.todoService = todoService;
  }

  public void fetchTodos() {
    CompletableFuture
      .supplyAsync(todoService::getTodos)
      .thenAccept(todos -> {
        this.todos = todos;
        controller.updateViewWith(todos);
      })
      .exceptionally((error) -> {
        controller.updateViewWith(error.getMessage());
        return null;
      });
  }

  public void toggleTodoDone(final int id) {
    todos.stream()
      .filter(todo -> todo.getId() == id)
      .findAny()
      .ifPresent(todo -> {
        todo.setIsDone(!todo.isDone());

        CompletableFuture
          .runAsync(() ->
            todoService.updateTodo(todo))
          .exceptionally((error) -> {
            controller.updateViewWith(error.getMessage());
            return null;
          });
      });
  }
}
```

Let's have the same example using Web Components[29]. The web component view should extend the HTMLElement class. The connectedCallback method of the view will be called on the component mount. It starts fetching todos. The showTodos method renders the given todos as HTML elements. It also adds event listeners for the *Mark done* buttons. The showError method updates the inner HTML of the view to show an error message.

Figure 4.80. Todo.ts

```typescript
export type Todo = {
  id: number;
  name: string;
  isDone: boolean;
};
```

---

[29]https://developer.mozilla.org/en-US/docs/Web/API/Web_components

Figure 4.81. TodoView.ts

```
interface TodoView {
  showTodos(todos: Todo[]): void;
  showError(errorMessage: string): void;
}
```

Figure 4.82. TodoViewImpl.ts

```
import controller from './todoController';
import { Todo } from './Todo';

export default class TodoViewImpl
        extends HTMLElement implements TodoView {
  constructor() {
    super();
    controller.setView(this);
  }

  connectedCallback() {
    controller.startFetchTodos();
    this.innerHTML = '<div>Loading todos...</div>';
  }

  showTodos(todos: Todo[]) {
    const todoElements = todos.map(({ id, name, isDone }) => `
      <li id="todo-${id}">
        ${id} ${name} 
        ${isDone ? '' : '<button>Mark done</button>'}
      </li>
    `);

    this.innerHTML = `<ul>${todoElements}</ul>`;

    todos.map(({ id }) => this
      .querySelector(`#todo-${id} button`)?
      .addEventListener('click',
                        () => controller.toggleTodoDone(id)));
  }

  showError(errorMessage: string) {
    this.innerHTML = `
      <div>
        Failure: ${errorMessage}
      </div>
    `;
  }
}
```

We can use the same controller and model APIs for this web component example as in the Java Swing example. We just need to convert the Java code to TypeScript code:

Figure 4.83. Controller.ts

```
export default class Controller<M, V> {
  private model: M | undefined;
  private view: V | undefined;

  getModel(): M | undefined {
    return this.model;
  }

  setModel(model: M): void {
    this.model = model;
  }

  getView(): V | undefined {
    return this.view;
  }

  setView(view: V): void {
    this.view = view;
  }
}
```

Figure 4.84. TodoController.ts

```
import { Todo } from "./Todo";

export interface TodoController {
  startFetchTodos(): void;
  toggleTodoDone(id: number): void;
  updateViewWithTodos(todos: Todo[]): void;
  updateViewWithError(message: string): void;
}
```

Figure 4.85. todoController.ts

```
import TodoView from './TodoView';
import Controller from "./Controller";
import { TodoController } from './TodoController';
import { Todo } from "./Todo";
import TodoModel from './TodoModel';

class TodoControllerImpl
        extends Controller<TodoModel, TodoView>
        implements TodoController {

  startFetchTodos(): void {
    this.getModel()?.fetchTodos();
  }

  toggleTodoDone(id: number): void {
    this.getModel()?.toggleTodoDone(id);
  }

  updateViewWithTodos(todos: Todo[]): void {
    this.getView()?.showTodos(todos);
  }

  updateViewWithError(message: string): void {
    this.getView()?.showError(message);
  }
}

const controller = new TodoControllerImpl();
export default controller;
```

243

Figure 4.86. TodoService.ts

```
export interface TodoService {
  getTodos(): Promise<Todo[]>;
  updateTodo(todo: Todo): Promise<void>;
}
```

Figure 4.87. TodoModel.ts

```
export interface TodoModel {
  fetchTodos(): void;
  toggleTodoDone(id: number): void;
}
```

Figure 4.88. TodoModelImpl.ts

```
import controller, { TodoController } from './todoController';
import { TodoModel } from './TodoModel';
import { Todo } from "./Todo";

export default class TodoModelImpl implements TodoModel {
  private todos: Todo[] = [];

  constructor(
    private readonly controller: TodoController,
    private readonly todoService: TodoService
  ) {
    controller.setModel(this);
  }

  fetchTodos(): void {
    this.todoService.getTodos()
      .then((todos) => {
        this.todos = todos;
        controller.updateViewWithTodos(todos);
      })
      .catch((error) =>
        controller.updateViewWithError(error.message));
  }

  toggleTodoDone(id: number): void {
    const foundTodo = this.todos.find(todo => todo.id === id);

    if (foundTodo) {
      foundTodo.isDone = !foundTodo.isDone;
      this.todoService
        .updateTodo(foundTodo)
        .catch((error: any) =>
          controller.updateViewWithError(error.message));
    }
  }
}
```

We could use the above-defined controller and model as such with a React view component:

Figure 4.89. ReactTodoView.tsx

```
// ...
import controller from './todoController';

// ...

export default class ReactTodoView
        extends Component<Props, State>
        implements TodoView {

  constructor(props: Props) {
    super(props);
    controller.setView(this);

    this.state = {
      todos: []
    }
  }

  componentDidMount() {
    controller.startFetchTodos();
  }

  showTodos(todos: Todo[]) {
    this.setState({ ...this.state, todos });
  }

  showError(errorMessage: string) {
    this.setState({ ...this.state, errorMessage });
  }

  render() {
    // Render todos from 'this.state.todos' here
    // Or show 'this.state.errorMessage' here
  }
}
```

If you have multiple views using the same controller, you can derive your controller from the below-defined MultiViewController class:

Figure 4.90. MultiViewController.ts

```
export default class MultiViewController<M, V> {
  private model: M | undefined;
  private views: V[] = [];

  getModel(): M | undefined {
    return this.model;
  }

  setModel(model: M): void {
    this.model = model;
  }

  getViews(): V[]  {
    return this.views;
  }

  addView(view: V): void {
    this.views.push(view);
  }
}
```

Let's say we want to have two views for todos, one for the actual todos and one viewing the todo count. We need to modify the controller slightly to support multiple views:

Figure 4.91. todoController.ts

```ts
import TodoView from './TodoView';
import MultiViewController from './MultiViewController';
import { Todo } from "./Todo";
import { TodoController } from './TodoController';
import TodoModel from './TodoModel';

class TodoControllerImpl
        extends MultiViewController<TodoModel, TodoView>
        implement TodoController {
  startFetchTodos(): void {
    this.getModel()?.fetchTodos();
  }

  toggleTodoDone(id: number): void {
    this.getModel()?.toggleTodoDone(id);
  }

  updateViewsWithTodos(todos: Todo[]): void {
    this.getViews().forEach(view => view.showTodos(todos));
  }

  updateViewWithError(message: string): void {
    this.getViews().forEach(view => view.showError(message));
  }
}

const controller = new TodoController();
export default controller;
```

Many modern UI frameworks and state management libraries implement a specialization of the MVC pattern called, Model-View-ViewModel (MVVM). In the MVVM pattern, the controller is called the view model. I use the more generic term *controller* in the below example, though. The main difference between the view model and the presenter in the MVP pattern is that in the MVP pattern, the presenter has a reference to the view, but the view model does not.

MVVM is an application of *clean architecture*. As seen in the picture below, the dependencies go from views to view models to the model (actions and entities). Similarly, the model does not depend on particular services but on service interfaces that concrete services implement. For example, if you have a weather forecast web application, the model of the application should define a weather forecast API service interface for fetching weather information. The model should not depend on any particular weather forecast API. If you want to integrate your application with a new weather forecast API, you should be able to do it by defining a new service class that implements the weather forecast API service interface. Next, in the dependency injection container, you can define that you want to use the new service implementation instead of some old implementation. Now, you have successfully modified your web application using the *open-closed principle*. You can apply the *open-closed principle* as you introduce various views that use existing view models. For example, in a todo application, you could introduce todo list, todo table, and todo grid views that all use the same todo view model.

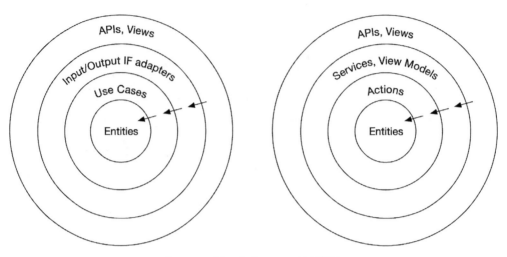

Figure 4.92. Clean Architecture with MVVM

The view model provides bindings between the view's events and actions in the model. This can happen so that the view model adds action dispatcher functions as properties of the view. In the other direction, the view model maps the model's state to the properties of the view. When using React and Redux, for example, you can connect the view to the model using the `mapDispatchToProps` function and connect the model to the view using the `mapStateToProps` function. These two mapping functions form the view model (or the controller) that binds the view and model together.

Let's first implement the todo example with React and Redux and later show how the React view can be replaced with an Angular view without modifying the controller or the model layer. Note that the code for some classes is not listed below. You can assume those classes are the same as defined in *command/action pattern* examples.

Source code for the below example is available here[30].

Let's implement a list view for todos:

Figure 4.93. TodoListView.tsx

```
import { connect } from 'react-redux';
import { useEffect } from 'react';
import { controller, ActionDispatchers, State } from '../../todoController';


type Props = ActionDispatchers & State;

function TodoListView({ toggleTodoDone, startFetchTodos, todos }: Props) {
  useEffect(() => {
    startFetchTodos();
  }, [startFetchTodos]);

  const todoElements = todos.map(({ id, name, isDone }) => (
    <li key={id}>
      {id} 
      {name} 
      {isDone || <button onClick={() => toggleTodoDone(id)}>Mark done</button>}
    </li>
  ));

  return <ul>{todoElements}</ul>;
}

// Here we connect the view to the model using the controller
export default connect(controller.getState, () =>
  controller.getActionDispatchers()
)(TodoListView);
```

Below is the base class for controllers:

Figure 4.94. Controller.ts

```
import AbstractAction from './AbstractAction';


export type ReduxDispatch =
 (reduxActionObject: { type: AbstractAction<any> }) => void;

export default class Controller {
  protected readonly dispatch:
    (action: AbstractAction<any>) => void;

  constructor(reduxDispatch: ReduxDispatch) {
    this.dispatch = (action: AbstractAction<any>) =>
      reduxDispatch({ type: action });
  }
}
```

Below is the controller for todos:

Figure 4.95. todoController.ts

```
import store from '../common/model/state/store';
import { AppState } from '../common/model/state/AppState';
import ToggleDoneTodoAction from './model/actions/ToggleDoneTodoAction';
import StartFetchTodosAction from './model/actions/StartFetchTodosAction';
import Controller from '../common/Controller';


class TodoController extends Controller {
  getState(appState: AppState) {
    return {
      todos: appState.todosState.todos,
```

```
    };
  }

  getActionDispatchers() {
    return {
      toggleTodoDone: (id: number) =>
        this.dispatch(new ToggleDoneTodoAction(id)),

      startFetchTodos: () => {
        this.dispatch(new StartFetchTodosAction());
      }
    };
  }
}

export const controller = new TodoController(store.dispatch);
export type State = ReturnType<typeof controller.getState>;

export type ActionDispatchers = ReturnType<
  typeof controller.getActionDispatchers
>;
```

In the development phase, we can use the following temporary implementation of the StartFetchTodosAction class:

Figure 4.96. StartFetchTodosAction.ts

```
import { TodoState } from '../state/TodoState';
import AbstractTodoAction from './AbstractTodoAction';


export default class StartFetchTodosAction extends AbstractTodoAction {
  // We return a static response for demonstration purposes
  // In real-life, you would call a method of a class implementing
  // TodoService interface to fetch todos from remote API
  // You should use dependency injection to inject an instance
  // implementing TodoService interface here.
  // In that way, you can switch to a new todo service API implementation
  // without modifying any existing code (open-closed principle)
  perform(state: TodoState): TodoState {
    return {
      todos: [
        {
          id: 1,
          name: 'Todo 1',
          isDone: false,
        },
        {
          id: 2,
          name: 'Todo 2',
          isDone: false,
        },
      ],
    };
  }
}
```

Now we can introduce a new view for todos, a TodoTableView, which can utilize the same controller as the TodosListView.

Figure 4.97. TodoTableView.tsx

```
import { connect } from 'react-redux';
import { useEffect } from 'react';
import { controller, ActionDispatchers, State } from '../../todoController';


type Props = ActionDispatchers & State;

function TodosListView({ toggleTodoDone, startFetchTodos, todos }: Props) {
  useEffect(() => {
    startFetchTodos();
  }, [startFetchTodos]);

  const todoElements = todos.map(({ id, isDone, name }) => (
    <tr key={id}>
      <td>{id}</td>
      <td>{name}</td>
      <td>
        <input type="checkbox" checked={isDone} onChange={() => toggleTodoDone(id)} />
      </td>
    </tr>
  ));

  return (
    <table>
      <tbody>{todoElements}</tbody>
    </table>
  );
}

export default connect(controller.getState, () =>
  controller.getActionDispatchers()
)(TodosListView);
```

We can notice some duplication in the TodoListView and TodoTableView components. For example, both are using the same effect. We can create a TodosView for which we can give as parameter the type of a single todo view, either a list item or a table row view:

Figure 4.98. TodosView.tsx

```
import { useEffect } from 'react';
import { connect } from 'react-redux';
import ListItemTodoView from './list/ListItemTodoView';
import TableRowTodoView from './table/TableRowTodoView';
import { controller, ActionDispatchers, State } from '../todoController';


type Props = ActionDispatchers &
  State & {
    TodoView: typeof ListItemTodoView | typeof TableRowTodoView;
  };

function TodosView({
  toggleTodoDone,
  startFetchTodos,
  todos,
  TodoView
}: Props) {
  useEffect(() => {
    startFetchTodos();
  }, [startFetchTodos]);

  const todoViews = todos.map((todo) => (
    <TodoView key={todo.id} todo={todo} toggleTodoDone={toggleTodoDone} />
  ));
```

```
  return TodoView === ListItemTodoView
    ? <ul>{todoViews}</ul>
    : <table><tbody>{todoViews}</tbody></table>;
}

export default connect(controller.getState, () =>
  controller.getActionDispatchers()
)(TodosView);
```

Below is the view for showing a single todo as a list item:

Figure 4.99. TodosViewProps.ts

```
import { Todo } from '../model/state/Todo';


export type TodosViewProps = {
  toggleTodoDone: (id: number) => void;
  todo: Todo;
};
```

Figure 4.100. ListItemTodoView.tsx

```
import { TodosViewProps } from '../TodosViewProps';


export default function ListItemTodoView({
  toggleTodoDone,
  todo: { id, name, isDone },
}: TodosViewProps) {
  return (
    <li>
      {id} 
      {name} 
      {isDone || <button onClick={() => toggleTodoDone(id)}>Mark done</button>}
    </li>
  );
}
```

Below is the view for showing a single todo as a table row:

Figure 4.101. TableRowTodoView.tsx

```
import { TodosViewProps } from '../TodosViewProps';


export default function TableRowTodoView({
  toggleTodoDone,
  todo: { id, name, isDone },
}: TodosViewProps) {
  return (
    <tr>
      <td>{id}</td>
      <td>{name}</td>
      <td>
        <input type="checkbox" checked={isDone} onChange={() => toggleTodoDone(id)} />
      </td>
    </tr>
  );
}
```

In the above `TodosView.tsx`, we used a conditional statement to render the component. As said earlier, we should limit this kind of code primarily to factories only. Let's create a view factory method and make the `TodosView.tsx` to use it:

Figure 4.102. createTodosView.tsx

```
import ListItemTodoView from "./list/ListItemTodoView";
import TableRowTodoView from "./table/TableRowTodoView";

export default function createTodosView(
    TodoView: typeof ListItemTodoView | typeof TableRowTodoView,
    todoViews: JSX.Element[]
): JSX.Element {
    if (TodoView === ListItemTodoView) {
        return <ul>{todoViews}</ul>;
    } else {
        return <table><tbody>{todoViews}</tbody></table>;
    }
}
```

Figure 4.103. TodosView.tsx

```
import { useEffect } from "react";
import { connect } from "react-redux";
import ListItemTodoView from "./list/ListItemTodoView";
import TableRowTodoView from "./table/TableRowTodoView";
import { controller, ActionDispatchers, State } from "../todoController";
import createTodosView from "./createTodosView";

type Props = ActionDispatchers &
  State & {
    TodoView: typeof ListItemTodoView | typeof TableRowTodoView;
  };

function TodosView({
  toggleTodoDone,
  startFetchTodos,
  todos,
  TodoView,
}: Props) {
  useEffect(() => {
    startFetchTodos();
  }, [startFetchTodos]);

  const todoViews = todos.map((todo) => (
    <TodoView key={todo.id} todo={todo} toggleTodoDone={toggleTodoDone} />
  ));

  return createTodosView(TodoView, todoViews);
}

export default connect(controller.getState, () =>
  controller.getActionDispatchers()
)(TodosView);
```

We should improve the part where we call the useEffect hook to make the code more readable. Let's introduce a custom hook:

Figure 4.104. afterMount.ts

```
import { useEffect } from "react";

export default function afterMount(func: () => void) {
  useEffect(() => func(), [func]);
}
```

Note that you will get a React Hooks linter error from the above code because the hook function name does not begin with "use". Disable that rule or rename the function to useAfterMount. I prefer the first alternative.

Figure 4.105. TodosView.tsx

```
import { useEffect } from "react";
import { connect } from "react-redux";
import ListItemTodoView from "./list/ListItemTodoView";
import TableRowTodoView from "./table/TableRowTodoView";
import { controller, ActionDispatchers, State } from "../todoController";
import createTodosView from "./createTodosView";

type Props = ActionDispatchers &
  State & {
    TodoView: typeof ListItemTodoView | typeof TableRowTodoView;
  };

function TodosView({
  toggleTodoDone,
  startFetchTodos,
  todos,
  TodoView,
}: Props) {
  afterMount(startFetchTodos);

  const todoViews = todos.map((todo) => (
    <TodoView key={todo.id} todo={todo} toggleTodoDone={toggleTodoDone} />
  ));

  return createTodosView(TodoView, todoViews);
}

export default connect(controller.getState, () =>
  controller.getActionDispatchers()
)(TodosView);
```

In the AppView component, we can decide how to render todos:

Figure 4.106. AppView.tsx

```
import React from 'react';
import {Provider} from 'react-redux';
import store from '../common/model/store';
import TodosView from '../todo/view/TodosView';
import ListItemTodoView from '../todo/view/list/ListItemTodoView';

function AppView() {
  return (
    <div>
      <Provider store={store}>
        { /*You can change the TodoView to TableRowTodoView */ }
        <TodosView TodoView={ListItemTodoView} />
      </Provider>
    </div>
  );
}

export default AppView;
```

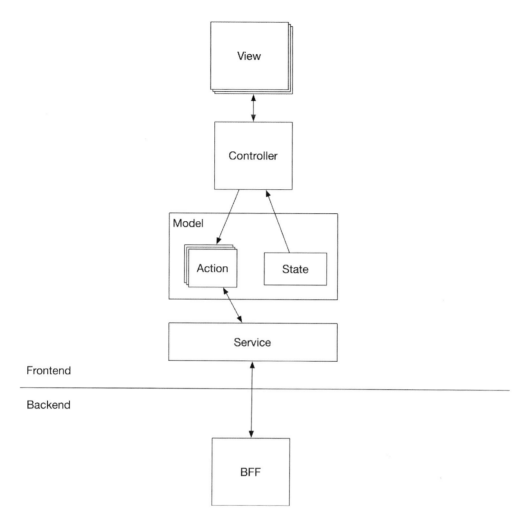

Figure 4.107. Figure 3.9 Frontend MVC Architecture with Redux

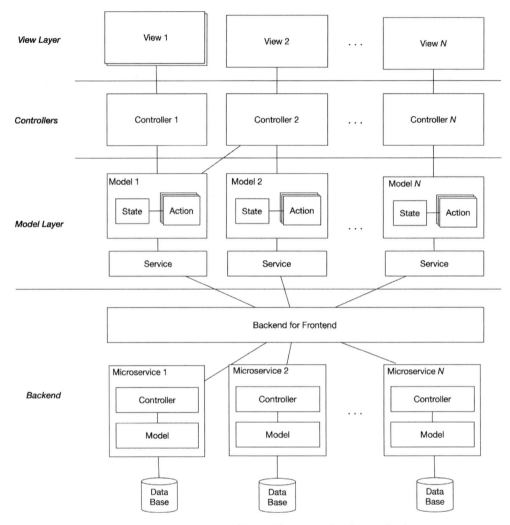

Figure 4.108. Figure 3.10 Frontend MVC Architecture with Redux + Backend

In most non-trivial projects, you should not store the state in a view, even if the state is for that particular view only. Instead, when you store it in the model, it brings the following benefits:

- Possibility to easily persist state either in the browser or in the backend
- Possibility to easily implement undo-actions
- State can be easily shared with another view(s) later if needed
- Migrating views to use a different view technology is more straightforward
- Easier debugging of state-related problems, e.g., using the Redux DevTools browser extension

We can also change the view implementation from React to Angular without modifying the controller or model layer. This can be done, for example, using the @angular-redux2/store[31] library. Let's have an example of that next.

Source code for the below example is available here[32].

Below is a todos table view implemented as an Angular component:

Figure 4.109. todos-table-view.component.ts

```
import { Component, OnInit } from "@angular/core";
import { NgRedux, Select } from '@angular-redux2/store';
import { Observable } from "rxjs";
import { controller } from '../todoController';
import { TodoState } from "../model/state/TodoState";
import { AppState } from "../../common/model/state/AppState";

const { startFetchTodos,
  toggleTodoDone } = controller.getActionDispatchers();

@Component({
  selector: 'todos-table-view',
  template: `
    <table>
      <tr *ngFor="let todo of (todoState | async)?.todos">
        <td>{{ todo.id }}</td>
        <td>{{ todo.name }}</td>
        <td>
          <input
            type="checkbox"
            [checked]="todo.isDone"
            (change)="toggleTodoDone(todo.id)"
          />
        </td>
      </tr>
    </table>
  `
})
export class TodosTableView implements OnInit {
  // @ts-ignore
  @Select(controller.getState) todoState: Observable<TodoState>;

  constructor(private ngRedux: NgRedux<AppState>) {}

  ngOnInit(): void {
    startFetchTodos();
  }

  toggleTodoDone(id: number) {
    toggleTodoDone(id);
  }
}
```

---

[31]https://www.npmjs.com/package/@angular-redux2/store
[32]https://github.com/pksilen/clean-code-principles-code/tree/main/chapter2/mvvm_angular

Figure 4.110. app.component.ts

```
import { Component } from '@angular/core';

@Component({
  selector: 'app-root',
  template: `
  <div>
    <todos-table-view></todos-table-view>
  </div>`,
  styleUrls: ['./app.component.css']
})
export class AppComponent {
  title = 'angular-test';
}
```

Figure 4.111. app.module.ts

```
import { NgModule } from '@angular/core';
import { BrowserModule } from '@angular/platform-browser';
import { NgReduxModule, NgRedux } from '@angular-redux2/store';
import { AppComponent } from './app.component';
import store from '../common/model/state/store';
import { AppState } from "../common/model/state/AppState";
import { TodosTableView } from "../todo/view/todos-table-view.component";

@NgModule({
  declarations: [
    AppComponent, TodosTableView
  ],
  imports: [
    BrowserModule,
    NgReduxModule
  ],
  providers: [],
  bootstrap: [AppComponent]
})
export class AppModule {
  constructor(ngRedux: NgRedux<AppState>) {
    ngRedux.provideStore(store);
  }
}
```

4.14.3.8: Template Method Pattern

Template method pattern allows you to define a template method in a base class, and subclasses define the final implementation of that method. The template method contains one or more calls to abstract methods implemented in the subclasses.

In the example below, the AbstractDrawing class contains a template method called draw. This method includes a call to the getShapeRenderer method, an abstract method implemented in the subclasses of the AbstractDrawing class. The draw method is a template method, and a subclass defines how to draw a single shape.

```
public interface Drawing {
  ShapeRenderer getShapeRenderer();
  void draw();
}


public abstract class AbstractDrawing implements Drawing {
  private final List<Shape> shapes;

  public AbstractDrawing(final List<Shape> shapes) {
    this.shapes = shapes;
  }

  public final void draw() {
    for (final Shape shape: shapes) {
      shape.render(getShapeRenderer());
    }
  }

  protected abstract ShapeRenderer getShapeRenderer();
}
```

We can now implement two subclasses of the AbstractDrawing class, which define the final behavior of the templated draw method. We mark the template method draw as final because subclasses should not override it. It is best practice to declare a template method as final. They should only provide an implementation for the abstract getShapeRenderer method.

```
public class RasterDrawing extends AbstractDrawing {
  public RasterDrawing(final List<Shape> shapes) {
    super(shapes);
  }

  protected ShapeRenderer getShapeRenderer() {
    return new RasterShapeRenderer(new Canvas());
  }
}


public class VectorDrawing extends AbstractDrawing {
  public VectorDrawing(final List<Shape> shapes) {
    super(shapes);
  }

  protected ShapeRenderer getShapeRenderer() {
    return new VectorShapeRenderer(new SvgElement());
  }
}
```

Template method pattern is useful to avoid code duplication in case two subclasses have methods with almost identical behavior. In that case, make that common functionality a template method in a common superclass and refine that template method behavior in the two subclasses.

4.14.3.9: Memento Pattern

The memento pattern can be used to save the internal state of an object to another object called the memento object.

Let's have a Java example with a TextEditor class. First, we define a TextEditorState interface and its implementation. Then, we define a TextEditorStateMemento class for storing a memento of the text editor's state.

```
public interface TextEditorState {
  TextEditorState clone();
}


public class TextEditorStateImpl implements TextEditorState {
  // Implement text editor state here
}


public class TextEditorStateMemento {
  private final TextEditorState state;

  public TextEditorStateMemento(final TextEditorState state) {
    this.state = state.clone();
  }

  public TextEditorState getState() {
    return state;
  }
}
```

The TextEditor class stores mementos of the text editor's state. It provides methods to save a state, restore a state, or restore the previous state:

Figure 4.112. TextEditor.java

```
class TextEditor {
  private final List<TextEditorStateMemento> stateMementos =
    new ArrayList<>(20);

  private TextEditorState currentState;
  private int currentVersion = 1;

  public void saveState() {
    stateMementos.add(new TextEditorStateMemento(currentState));
    currentVersion += 1;
  }

  public void restoreState(final int version) {
    if (version >= 1 && version <= stateMementos.size()) {
      currentState = stateMementos.get(version - 1).getState();
      currentVersion += 1;
    }
  }

  public void restorePreviousState() {
    if (currentVersion > 1) {
      restoreState(currentVersion - 1);
    }
  }
}
```

In the above example, we can add a memento for the text editor's state by calling the saveState method. We can recall the previous version of the text editor's state with the restorePreviousState method, and we can recall any version of the text editor's state using the restoreState method.

4.14.3.10: Visitor Pattern

Visitor pattern allows adding functionality to a class (like adding new methods) without modifying the class. This is useful, for example, with library classes that you cannot modify.

First, let's have a Java example with classes that we can modify:

```
public interface Shape {
  void draw();
}


public class CircleShape implements Shape {
  private final int radius;

  // ...

  public void draw() {
    // ...
  }

  public int getRadius() {
    return radius;
  }
}


public class RectangleShape implements Shape {
  private final int width;
  private final int height;

  // ...

  public void draw() {
    // ...
  }

  public int getWidth() {
    return width;
  }

  public int getHeight() {
    return height;
  }
}
```

Let's assume we need to calculate the total area of shapes in a drawing. Currently, we are in a situation where we can modify the shape classes, so let's add calculateArea methods to the classes:

```
public interface Shape {
  // ...

  double calculateArea();
}


public class CircleShape implements Shape {
  // ...

  public double calculateArea() {
    return Math.PI * radius * radius;
  }
}


class RectangleShape implements Shape {
  // ...

  public double calculateArea() {
    return width * height;
  }
}
```

Adding a new method to an existing class may be against the *open-closed principle*. In the above case, adding the calculateArea methods is safe because the shape classes are immutable. And even if they were not, adding the `calculateArea` methods would be safe because they are read-only methods, i.e., they don't modify the object's state, and we don't have to worry about thread safety because we can agree that our example application is not multithreaded.

Now we have the area calculation methods added, and we can use a common algorithm to calculate the total area of shapes in a drawing:

```
final var totalAreaOfShapes = drawing
  .getShapes()
  .stream()
  .reduce(0.0, (subTotalArea, shape) ->
    subTotalArea + shape.calculateArea(), Double::sum);
```

But what if the shape classes, without the area calculation capability, were in a 3rd party library that we cannot modify? We would have to do something like this:

```
final var totalAreaOfShapes = drawing
  .getShapes()
  .stream()
  .reduce(0.0, (subTotalArea, shape) -> {
    double shapeArea;

    if (shape instanceof CircleShape) {
      shapeArea = Math.PI *
              Math.pow(((CircleShape)shape).getRadius(), 2);
    } else if (shape instanceof RectangleShape){
      shapeArea = ((RectangleShape)shape).getWidth() *
              ((RectangleShape)shape).getHeight();
    }
    else {
      throw new IllegalArgumentException("Invalid shape");
    }

    return subTotalArea + shapeArea;
  }, Double::sum);
```

The above solution is complicated and needs updating every time a new type of shape is introduced. The above example does not follow object-oriented design principles: it contains an if/else-if structure with `instanceof` checks.

We can use the visitor pattern to replace the above conditionals with polymorphism. First, we introduce a visitor interface that can be used to provide additional behavior to the shape classes. Then, we introduce an `execute` method in the `Shape` interface. In the shape classes, we implement the `execute` methods so that additional behavior provided by a concrete visitor can be executed:

```
// This is our visitor interface that
// provides additional behaviour to the shape classes
public interface ShapeBehavior {
  Object executeForCircle(final CircleShape circle);
  Object executeForRectangle(final RectangleShape rectangle);

  // Add methods for possible other shape classes here...
}


public interface Shape {
  // ...

  Object execute(final ShapeBehavior behavior);
}
```

```
public class CircleShape implements Shape {
  public Object execute(final ShapeBehavior behavior) {
    return behavior.executeForCircle(this);
  }
}


public class RectangleShape implements Shape {
  public Object execute(final ShapeBehavior behavior) {
    return behavior.executeForRectangle(this);
  }
}
```

Suppose that the shape classes were mutable and made thread-safe. We would have to define the execute methods with appropriate synchronization to make them also thread-safe:

```
public class CircleShape implements Shape {
  public synchronized Object execute(
    final ShapeBehavior behavior
  ) {
    return behavior.executeForCircle(this);
  }
}


public class RectangleShape implements Shape {
  public synchronized Object execute(
    final ShapeBehavior behavior
  ) {
    return behavior.executeForRectangle(this);
  }
}
```

Let's implement a concrete visitor for calculating areas of different shapes:

```
public class AreaCalculationShapeBehavior implements
              ShapeBehavior {
  public Object executeForCircle(final CircleShape circle) {
    return (Double)(Math.PI * Math.pow(circle.getRadius(), 2));
  }

  public Object executeForRectangle(
    final RectangleShape rectangle
  ) {
    return (Double)(double)(rectangle.getWidth() * rectangle.getHeight());
  }
}
```

Now we can implement the calculation of shapes' total area using a common algorithm, and we get rid of the conditionals. We execute the areaCalculation behavior for each shape and convert the result of behavior execution to Double. Methods in a visitor usually return some common type like Object. This enables various operations to be performed. After executing a visitor, the return value should be cast to the right type.

```
final var areaCalculation = new AreaCalculationShapeBehavior();

final var totalAreaOfShapes = drawing
  .getShapes()
  .stream()
  .reduce(0.0, (subTotalArea, shape) ->
    subTotalArea + (Double)shape.execute(areaCalculation),
      Double::sum);
```

You can add more behavior to the shape classes by defining a new visitor. Let's define a PerimeterCalculationShapeBehaviour class:

```
public class PerimeterCalculationShapeBehavior
            implements ShapeBehavior {
  public Object executeForCircle(final CircleShape circle) {
    return (Double)(2 * Math.PI * circle.getRadius());
  }

  public Object executeForRectangle(
    final RectangleShape rectangle
  ) {
    return (Double)(double)(2 * rectangle.getWidth() +
                           2 * rectangle.getHeight());
  }
}
```

Notice that we did not need to use the *visitor* term in our code examples. Adding the design pattern name to the names of software entities (class/function names, etc.) often does not bring any real benefit but makes the names longer. However, there are some design patterns, like the *factory pattern* and *builder pattern* where you always use the design pattern name in a class name.

If you develop a third-party library and want the behavior of its classes to be extended by its users, you should make your library classes accept visitors who can perform additional behavior. Using the visitor pattern allows for adding behavior to existing classes without modifying them, i.e., in accordance with the open-closed principle. However, there is one drawback to using the visitor pattern. You must create getters and setters for class attributes to allow visitors to add behavior. Adding getters and setters breaks the class encapsulation, as was discussed earlier in this chapter.

4.14.3.11: Null Object Pattern

A null object is an object that does nothing.

Use the null object pattern to implement a class for null objects that don't do anything. A null object can be used in place of a real object that does something.

Let's have an example with a Shape interface:

Figure 4.113. Shape.java

```
public interface Shape {
  void draw();
}
```

We can easily define a class for null shape objects:

Figure 4.114. NullShape.java

```
public class NullShape implements Shape {
  void draw() {
    // Intentionally no operation
  }
}
```

We can use an instance of the NullShape class everywhere where a concrete implementation of the Shape interface is wanted.

4.15: Don't Ask, Tell Principle

Don't ask, tell principle states that you should tell *another object what to do, and not ask about the other object's state and then do the work by yourself in your object.*

If your object asks many things from another object using, e.g., multiple getters, you might be guilty of the *feature envy* design smell. Your object is envious of a feature that the other object should have.

Let's have an example and define a cube shape class:

```
public interface ThreeDShape {
  // ...
}

public class Cube3DShape implements ThreeDShape {
  private final int width;
  private final int height;
  private final int depth;

  // Constructor...

  public int getWidth() {
    return width;
  }

  public int getHeight() {
    return height;
  }

  public int getDepth() {
    return depth;
  }
}
```

Next, we define another class, CubeUtils, that contains a method for calculating the total volume of cubes:

```
public class CubeUtils {
  public int calculateTotalVolume(
    final List<Cube3DShape> cubes
  ) {
    int totalVolume = 0;

    for (final Cube3DShape cube : cubes) {
      final var width = cube.getWidth();
      final var height = cube.getHeight();
      final var depth = cube.getDepth();
      totalVolume += width * height * depth;
    }

    return totalVolume;
  }
}
```

In the `calculateTotalVolume` method, we ask three times about a cube object's state. This is against the *tell, don't ask principle*. Our method is envious of the volume calculation feature and wants to do it by itself rather than telling a `Cube3DShape` object to calculate its volume.

Let's correct the above code so that it follows the *tell, don't ask principle*:

```
public interface ThreeDShape {
  int calculateVolume();
}

public class Cube3DShape implements ThreeDShape {
  private final int width;
  private final int height;
  private final int depth;

  // Constructor

  public int calculateVolume() {
    return height * width * depth;
  }
}

public class ThreeDShapeUtils {
  public int calculateTotalVolume(
    final List<ThreeDShape> threeDShapes
  ) {
    int totalVolume = 0;

    for (final var threeDShape : threeDShapes) {
      totalVolume += threeDShape.calculateVolume();
    }

    return totalVolume;
  }
}
```

Now, our `calculateTotalVolume` method does not ask anything about a cube object. It just tells a cube object to calculate its volume. We also removed the *asking* methods (getters) from the `Cube3DShape` class because they are no longer needed.

Below is a C++ example of asking instead of telling:

```cpp
using namespace std::chrono_literals;
using std::chrono::system_clock;

void AnomalyDetectionEngine::runEngine()
{
  while (m_isRunning)
  {
    const auto now = system_clock::now();

    if (m_anomalyDetector->shouldDetectAnomalies(now))
    {
      const auto anomalies = m_anomalyDetector->detectAnomalies();
      // Do something with the detected anomalies
    }

    std::this_thread::sleep_for(1s);
  }
}
```

In the above example, we ask the anomaly detector if we should detect anomalies now. Then, depending on the result, we call another method on the anomaly detector to detect anomalies. This could be simplified by making the detectAnomalies method to check if anomalies should be detected using the shouldDetectAnomalies method. Then, the shouldDetectAnomalies method can be made private, and we can simplify the above code as follows:

```cpp
using namespace std::chrono_literals;

void AnomalyDetectionEngine::runEngine()
{
  while (m_isRunning)
  {
    const auto anomalies = m_anomalyDetector->detectAnomalies();
    // Do something with the detected anomalies
    std::this_thread::sleep_for(1s);
  }
}
```

Following the *tell, don't ask principle* is a great way to reduce coupling in your software component. In the above example, we reduced the number of methods the calculateTotalVolume method depends on from three to one. Following the principle also contributed to higher cohesion in the software component because operations related to a cube are now inside the Cube class and are not scattered around in the code base. The *tell, don't ask principle* is the same as the *information expert* from the GRASP principles. The information expert principle says to put behavior in a class with the most information required to implement the behavior. In the above example, the Cube class clearly has the most information needed (width, height, and depth) to calculate a cube's area.

4.16: Law of Demeter

A method on an object received from another object's method call should not be called.

The below statements are considered to break the law:

```
user.getAccount().getBalance();
user.getAccount().withdraw(...);
```

The above statements can be corrected either by moving functionality to a different class or by making the second object to act as a facade between the first and the third object.

Below is an example of the latter solution, where we introduce two new methods in the User class and remove the getAccount method:

```
user.getAccountBalance();
user.withdrawFromAccount(...);
```

In the above example, the User class is a facade in front of the Account class that we should not access directly from our object.

However, you should always check if the first solution alternative could be used instead. It makes the code more object-oriented and does not require the introduction of additional methods.

Below is a Java example that uses User and SalesItem entities and does not obey the law of Demeter:

```java
void purchase(final User user, final SalesItem salesItem) {
  final var account = user.getAccount();

  // Breaks the law
  final var accountBalance = account.getBalance();

  final var salesItemPrice = salesItem.getPrice();

  if (accountBalance >= salesItemPrice) {
    account.withdraw(salesItemPrice); // Breaks the law
  }

  // ...
}
```

We can resolve the problem in the above example by moving the purchase method to the correct class, in this case, the User class:

```java
class User {
  private Account account;

  // ...

  void purchase(final SalesItem salesItem) {
    final var accountBalance = account.getBalance();
    final var salesItemPrice = salesItem.getPrice();

    if (accountBalance >= salesItemPrice) {
      account.withdraw(salesItemPrice);
    }

    // ...
  }
}
```

Following the *law of Demeter* is a great way to reduce coupling in your software component. When you follow the *law of Demeter* you are not depending on the objects behind another object, but that other object provides a facade to the objects behind it.

4.17: Avoid Primitive Obsession Principle

Avoid primitive obsession by defining semantic types for function parameters and function return value.

Some of us have experienced situations where we have supplied arguments to a function in the wrong order. This is easy if the function, for example, takes two integer parameters, but you accidentally give those two integer parameters in the wrong order. You don't get a compilation error.

Another problem with primitive types as function arguments is that the argument values are not necessarily validated. You have to implement the validation logic in your function.

Suppose you accept an integer parameter for a port number in a function. In that case, you might get any integer value as the parameter value, even though the valid port numbers are from 1 to 65535. Suppose you also had other functions in the same codebase accepting a port number as a parameter. In that case, you could end up using the same validation logic code in multiple places and thus have duplicate code in your codebase.

Let's have a simple Java example of using this principle:

Figure 4.115. RectangleShape.java

```java
public class RectangleShape implements Shape {
  private int width;
  private int height;

  public RectangleShape(final int width, final int height) {
    this.width = width;
    this.height = height;
  }
}
```

In the above example, the constructor has two parameters with the same primitive type (int). It is possible to give width and height in the wrong order. But if we refactor the code to use objects instead of primitive values, we can make the likelihood of giving the arguments in the wrong order much smaller:

```java
public class Value<T> {
  private final T value;

  public Value(final T value) {
    this.value = checkNotNull(value);
  }

  T get() {
    return value;
  }
}


public class Width extends Value<Integer> {
  public Width(final int width) {
    super(width);
  }
}


public class Height extends Value<Integer> {
  public Height(final int height) {
    super(height);
  }
```

```
}

public class RectangleShape implements Shape {
  private final int width;
  private final int height;

  public RectangleShape(final Width width, final Height height) {
    this.width = width.get();
    this.height = height.get();
  }
}

final var width = new Width(20);
final var height = new Height(50);

// OK
final Shape rectangle = new RectangleShape(width, height);

// Does not compile, parameters are in wrong order
final Shape rectangle2 = new RectangleShape(height, width);

// Does not compile, first parameter is not a width
final Shape rectangle3 = new RectangleShape(height, height);

// Does not compile, second parameter is not a height
final Shape rectangle4 = new RectangleShape(width, width);

// Does not compile, Width and Height objects must be used
// instead of primitive types
final Shape rectangle5 = new RectangleShape(20, 50);
```

In the above example, Width and Height are simple data classes. They don't contain any behavior. You can use concrete data classes as function parameter types. There is no need to create an interface for a data class. So, the *program against interfaces* principle does not apply here.

Let's have another simple example where we have the following function signature:

```
public void doSomething(final String namespacedName, ...) {
  // ...
}
```

The above function signature allows function callers to accidentally supply a non-namespaced name. By using a custom type for the namespaced name, we can formulate the above function signature to the following:

```
public class NamespacedName {
  private final String namespacedName;

  public NamespacedName(
    final String namespace,
    final String name
  ) {
    this.namespacedName = namespace.isEmpty()
                              ? name
                              : (namespace + '.' + name);
  }

  public String get() {
    return this.namespacedName;
  }
}
```

```
public void doSomething(final NamespacedName namespacedName, ...) {
  // ...
}
```

Let's have a more comprehensive example with an `HttpUrl` class. The class constructor has several parameters that should be validated upon creating an HTTP URL:

Figure 4.116. HttpUrl.java

```
public class HttpUrl {
  private final String httpUrl;

  public HttpUrl(
    final String scheme,
    final String host,
    final int port,
    final String path,
    final String query
  ) {
    httpUrl = scheme +
              "://" +
              host +
              ":" +
              port +
              path +
              "?" +
              query;
  }
}
```

Let's introduce an abstract class for validated values:

Figure 4.117. AbstractValidatedValue.java

```
public abstract class AbstractValidatedValue<T> {
  protected final T value;

  public AbstractValidatedValue(final T value) {
    this.value = checkNotNull(value);
  }

  abstract boolean valueIsValid();

  Optional<T> get() {
    return valueIsValid()
            ? Optional.of(value)
            : Optional.empty();
  }

  T tryGet() {
    if (valueIsValid()) {
      return value;
    } else {
      throw new ValidatedValueGetError(...);
    }
  }
}
```

Let's create a class for validated HTTP scheme objects:

Figure 4.118. HttpScheme.java

```
public class HttpScheme extends AbstractValidatedValue<String> {
  public HttpScheme(final String value) {
    super(value);
  }

  public boolean valueIsValid() {
    // Because the AbstractValidatedValue<String> is immutable,
    // if you had complex validation logic, you could cache
    // the validation result and store it to a class attribute.

    return "https".equalsIgnoreCase(value) ||
           "http".equalsIgnoreCase(value);
  }
}
```

Let's create a Port class (and similar classes for the host, path, and query should be created):

```
public class Port extends AbstractValidatedValue<Integer> {
  public Port(final Integer value) {
    super(value);
  }

  public boolean valueIsValid() {
    return value >= 1 && value <= 65535;
  }
}

// public class Host ...
// public class Path ...
// public class Query ...
```

Let's create a utility class, OptionalUtils, with a method for mapping a result for five optional values:

```
@FunctionalInterface
public interface Mapper<T, U, V, X, Y, R> {
  R map(T value,
        U value2,
        V value3,
        X value4,
        Y value5);
}


public final class OptionalUtils {
  public static <T, U, V, X, Y, R> Optional<R>
    mapAll(
      final Optional<T> opt1,
      final Optional<U> opt2,
      final Optional<V> opt3,
      final Optional<X> opt4,
      final Optional<Y> opt5,
      final Mapper<T, U, V, X, Y, R> mapper
  ) {
    if (opt1.isPresent() &&
        opt2.isPresent() &&
        opt3.isPresent() &&
        opt4.isPresent() &&
        opt5.isPresent()
    ) {
      return Optional.of(mapper.map(opt1.get(),
                                    opt2.get(),
                                    opt3.get(),
                                    opt4.get(),
```

```
                                        opt5.get()));
    } else {
      return Optional.empty();
    }
  }
}
```

Next, we can reimplement the `HttpUrl` class to contain two alternative factory methods for creating an HTTP URL:

Figure 4.119. HttpUrl.java

```
public class HttpUrl {
  private final String httpUrl;

  // Constructor is private because factory methods
  // should be used to create instances of this class
  private HttpUrl(final String httpUrl) {
    this.httpUrl = httpUrl;
  }

  // Factory method that returns an optional HttpUrl
  public static Optional<HttpUrl> create(
    final HttpScheme scheme,
    final Host host,
    final Port port,
    final Path path,
    final Query query
  ) {
    return OptionalUtils.mapAll(scheme.get(),
                                host.get(),
                                port.get(),
                                path.get(),
                                query.get(),
            (schemeValue,
             hostValue,
             portValue,
             pathValue,
             queryValue) ->
                    new HttpUrl(schemeValue +
                                "://" +
                                hostValue +
                                ":" +
                                portValue +
                                pathValue +
                                "?" +
                                queryValue));
  }

  // Factory method that returns a valid HttpUrl or
  // throws an error
  public static HttpUrl tryCreate(
    final HttpScheme scheme,
    final Host host,
    final Port port,
    final Path path,
    final Query query
  ) {
    try {
      return new HttpUrl(scheme.tryGet() +
                         "://" +
                         host.tryGet() +
                         ":" +
                         port.tryGet() +
                         path.tryGet() +
                         "?" +
                         query.tryGet());
    } catch (final ValidatedValueGetError error) {
```

```
    throw new HttpUrlCreateError(error);
    }
  }
}
```

Notice how we did not hardcode the URL validation inside the HttpUrl class, but we created small validated value classes: HttpScheme, Host, Port, Path, and Query. These classes can be further utilized in other parts of the codebase if needed and can even be put into a common validation library for broader usage.

For TypeScript, I have created a library called *validated-types* for easily creating and using semantically validated types. The library is available at https://github.com/pksilen/validated-types. The library's idea is to validate data when the data is received from the input. You can then pass already validated, strongly typed data to the rest of the functions in your software component.

An application typically receives unvalidated input data from external sources in the following ways:

- Reading command line arguments
- Reading environment variables
- Reading standard input
- Reading files from the file system
- Reading data from a socket (network input)
- Receiving input from a user interface (UI)

Make sure that you validate any data received from the sources mentioned above. Use a ready-made validation library or create your own validation logic if needed. Validate the input immediately after receiving it from an untrustworthy source and only pass valid values to other functions in the codebase. In this way, other functions in the codebase can trust the input they receive, and they don't have to validate it again. If you pass unvalidated data freely around in your application, you may need to implement validation logic in every function, which is unreasonable.

Below is an example of using the validated-types[33] library to create a validated integer type that allows values between 1 and 10. The VInt generic type takes a type argument of string type, which defines the allowed value range in the following format: <min-value>,<max-value>

```
import { VInt } from 'validated-types';

function useInt(int: VInt<'1,10'>) {
  // The wrapped integer value can be accessed
  // through the 'value' property
  console.log(int.value);
}

const int: VInt<'1,10'> = VInt.tryCreate('1,10', 5);
useInt(int); // prints to console: 5

// Returns null, because 12 is not between 1 and 10
const maybeInt: VInt<'1,10'> | null = VInt.create('1,10', 12);

// Prints to console: 10
useInt(maybeInt ?? VInt.tryCreate('1,10', 10));

// Throws, because 500 is not between 1 and 10
const int2: VInt<'1,10'> = VInt.tryCreate('1,10', 500);
```

---
[33]https://www.npmjs.com/package/validate-types

The below example defines an `Url` type that contains six validations that validate a string matching the following criteria:

- is at least one character long
- is at most 1024 characters long
- is a lowercase string
- is a valid URL
- URL starts with 'https'
- URL ends with '.html'

```
import { SpecOf, VString } from 'validated-types';

// First element in the VString type parameter array validates
// a lowercase string between 1-1024 characters long

// Second element in the VString type parameter array validates
// an URL

// Third element in the VString type parameter array validates
// a string that starts with "https"

// Fourth element in the VString type parameter array validates
// a string that ends with ".html"

type Url = VString<['1,1024,lowercase',
                    'url',
                    'startsWith,https',
                    'endsWith,.html']>;

const urlVSpec: VSpecOf<Url> = ['1,1024,lowercase',
                                'url',
                                'startsWith,https',
                                'endsWith,.html'];

function useUrl(url: Url) {
  console.log(url.value);
}

const url: Url = VString.tryCreate(
  urlVSpec,
  'https://server.domain.com:8080/index.html'
);

// Prints to console: https://server.domain.com:8080/index.html
useUrl(url);

// 'maybeUrl' will be null
const maybeUrl: Url | null = VString.create(urlVSpec,
                                            'invalid URL');

const defaultUrl: Url = VString.tryCreate(
  urlVSpec,
  'https://default.domain.com:8080/index.html'
);

// Prints to console: https://default.domain.com:8080/index.html
useUrl(maybeUrl ?? defaultUrl);
```

If you don't need validation but would like to create a semantic type, you can use the `SemType` class from the *validated-types* library:

```
import { SemType } from 'validated-types';

// Defines a semantic boolean type with name 'isRecursiveCall'
type IsRecursiveCall = SemType<boolean, 'isRecursiveCall'>

// Defines a semantic boolean type with name 'isInternalCall'
type IsInternalCall = SemType<boolean, 'isInternalCall'>;

function myFunc(isRecursiveCall: IsRecursiveCall,
               isInternalCall: IsInternalCall) {
  // The value of a semantic type variable
  // can be obtained from the 'value' property
  console.log(isRecursiveCall.value);
  console.log(isInternalCall.value);
}

const isRecursiveCall = false;
const isInternalCall = true;

// This will succeed
myFunc(new SemType({ isRecursiveCall }),
       new SemType({ isInternalCall }));

// All the below myFunc calls will fail during
// the compilation
myFunc(new SemType({ isInternalCall }),
       new SemType({ isRecursiveCall }));

myFunc(true, true);

myFunc(new SemType('isSomethingElse', true),
       new SemType('isInternalCall', true));

myFunc(new SemType('isRecursiveCall', false),
       new SemType('isSomethingElse', true));

myFunc(new SemType('isSomethingElse', true),
       new SemType('isSomethingElse', true));
```

4.18: You Aren't Gonna Need It (YAGNI) Principle

A programmer should not add functionality until deemed necessary.

The above is the definition from Wikipedia. This principle is also interpreted as "do the simplest thing that could work". This interpretation is questionable because it can justify sloppy design and avoidance of future planning, possibly causing a massive amount of future refactoring that could have been avoided with some upfront design. The YAGNI principle applies to functionality but not necessarily to architecture and main design, which should be considered future-proof from the beginning. Exceptions are trivial software components where you don't see future changes coming. For example, you might need to build a simple web client and don't want to use a state management library because you can survive with component-specific state and using e.g., React Context. But for non-trivial, e.g., enterprise software, you should consider architectural design from the beginning, e.g., using clean architecture, because changing large existing software to use clean architecture later can lead to massive refactoring down the line. What matters the most is the lifetime total cost of development.

4.19: Dependency Injection (DI) Principle

Dependency injection (DI) allows changing the behavior of an application based on static or dynamic configuration.

When using dependency injection, the dependencies are injected only after the application startup. The application can first read its configuration and then decide what objects are created for the application. In many languages, dependency injection is crucial for unit tests, too. When executing a unit test using DI, you can inject mock dependencies into the tested code instead of using the application's standard dependencies.

Below is a C++ example of using the singleton pattern without dependency injection:

Figure 4.120. main.cpp

```
int main()
{
  Logger::initialize();

  Logger::writeLogEntry(LogLevel::Info,
                        std::source_location::current(),
                        "Starting application");

  // ...
}
```

A developer must remember to call the `initialize` method before calling any other method on the `Logger` class. This kind of coupling between methods should be avoided. Also, it is hard to unit test the static methods of the `Logger` class.

We should refactor the above code to use dependency injection:

Figure 4.121. main.cpp

```
int main()
{
  DependencyInjectorFactory::createDependencyInjector(...)
    ->injectDependencies();

  Logger::getInstance()->writeLogEntry(
    LogLevel::Info,
    std::source_location::current(),
    "Starting application"
  );

  // ...
}
```

Figure 4.122. Singleton.h

```
template<typename T>
class Singleton
{
public:
  Singleton() = default;

  virtual ~Singleton()
  {
    m_instance.reset();
  };

  static inline std::shared_ptr<T>& getInstance()
  {
    return m_instance;
  }

  static void setInstance(const std::shared_ptr<T>& instance)
  {
    m_instance = instance;
  }

private:
  static inline std::shared_ptr<T> m_instance;
};
```

Figure 4.123. Logger.h

```
class Logger : public Singleton<Logger>
{
public:
  virtual void writeLogEntry(...) = 0;
};
```

Figure 4.124. StdOutLogger.h

```
class StdOutLogger : public Logger
{
public:
  void writeLogEntry(...) override
  {
    // Write the log entry
    // to the standard output
  }
};
```

Figure 4.125. DependencyInjectorFactory.h

```
class DependencyInjectorFactory {
public:
  static std::shared_ptr<DependencyInjector>
  createDependencyInjector(...)
  {
    // You can use a switch-case here to create
    // different kinds of dependency injectors
    // that inject different kinds of dependencies
    return std::make_shared<DefaultDependencyInjector>();
  }
}
```

Figure 4.126. DependencyInjector.h

```
class DependencyInjector {
public:
  virtual ~DependencyInjector = default;
  virtual void injectDependencies() = 0;
}
```

Figure 4.127. DefaultDependencyInjector.h

```
class DefaultDependencyInjector : public DependencyInjector {
public:
  void injectDependencies() override;
}
```

Figure 4.128. DefaultDependencyInjector.cpp

```
void DefaultDependencyInjector::injectDependencies()
{
  // Inject other dependencies...

  Logger::setInstance(
    std::make_shared<StdOutLogger>()
  );
}
```

Let's introduce a new kind of logger:

Figure 4.129. FileLogger.h

```
class FileLogger : public Logger
{
public:
  void writeLogEntry(...) override
  {
    // Write the log entry
    // to a file
  }
};
```

We could modify the default dependency injector to choose a logger implementation dynamically based on an environment variable value:

Figure 4.130. DefaultDependencyInjector.cpp

```
void DefaultDependencyInjector::injectDependencies()
{
  // Inject other dependencies...

  const auto maybeLogDestination = std::getenv("LOG_DESTINATION");
  const auto logDestination =
    maybeLogDestination == null ? std::string{} : std::string{maybeLogDestination};

  if (logDestination == "file")
  {
    Logger::setInstance(std::make_shared<FileLogger>());
  }
  else
  {
    Logger::setInstance(std::make_shared<StdOutLogger>());
  }
}
```

If you have a very simple microservice with few dependencies, you might think dependency injection is an overkill. One thing that is sure in software development is change. Change is inevitable, and you cannot predict the future. For example, your microservice may start growing larger. Introducing DI in a late phase of a project might require substantial refactoring. Therefore, consider using DI in all non-trivial applications from the beginning.

Below is a TypeScript example of a *data-visualization-web-client* where the noicejs[34] NPM library is used for dependency injection. This library resembles the famous Google Guice[35] library. Below is a FakeServicesModule class that configures dependencies for different backend services that the web client uses. As you can notice, all the services are configured to use fake implementations because this DI module is used when the backend services are not yet available. A RealServicesModule class can be implemented and used when the backend services become available. In the RealServicesModule class, the services are bound to their actual implementation classes instead of fake implementations.

```
import { Module } from 'noicejs';
import FakeDataSourceService from ...;
import FakeMeasureService from ...;
import FakeDimensionService from ...;
import FakeChartDataService from ...;

export default class FakeServicesModule extends Module {
  override async configure(): Promise<void> {
    this.bind('dataSourceService')
      .toInstance(new FakeDataSourceService());

    this.bind('measureService')
      .toInstance(new FakeMeasureService());

    this.bind('dimensionService')
      .toInstance(new FakeDimensionService());

    this.bind('chartDataService')
      .toInstance(new FakeChartDataService());
    );
  }
}
```

With the *noicejs* library, you can configure several DI modules and create a DI container from the wanted modules. The module approach lets you divide dependencies into multiple modules, so you don't have a single big module and lets you instantiate a different module or modules based on the application configuration.

In the below example, the DI container is created from a single module, an instance of the FakeServicesModule class:

Figure 4.131. diContainer.ts

```
import { Container } from 'noicejs';
import FakeServicesModule from './FakeServicesModule';

const diContainer = Container.from(new FakeServicesModule());

export default diContainer;
```

In the development phase, we could create two separate modules, one for fake services and another one for real services, and control the application behavior based on the web page's URL query parameter:

---

[34] https://github.com/ssube/noicejs
[35] https://github.com/google/guice

Figure 4.132. diContainer.ts

```
import { Container } from 'noicejs';
import FakeServicesModule from './FakeServicesModule';
import RealServicesModule from './RealServicesModule';

const diContainer = (() => {
  if (location.href.includes('useFakeServices=true')) {
    // Use fake services if web page URL
    // contains 'useFakeServices=true'
    return Container.from(new FakeServiceModule());
  } else {
    // Otherwise use real services
    return Container.from(new RealServicesModule());
  }
})();

export default diContainer;
```

Then, you must configure the diContainer before the dependency injection can be used. In the below example, the diContainer is configured before a React application is rendered:

Figure 4.133. index.ts

```
import React from 'react';
import ReactDOM from 'react-dom';
import diContainer from './diContainer';
import AppView from './app/view/AppView';

diContainer.configure().then(() => {
  ReactDOM.render(<AppView />, document.getElementById('root'));
});
```

Then, in Redux actions, where you need a service, you can inject the required service with the @Inject decorator. You specify the name of the service you want to inject. The service will be injected as the class constructor argument's property (with the same name).

Figure 4.134. StartFetchChartDataAction.ts

```
// Imports ...

type Args = {
  chartDataService: ChartDataService,
  chart: Chart,
  dispatch: Dispatch;
};

export default
@Inject('chartDataService')
class StartFetchChartDataAction extends AbstractChartAreaAction {
  constructor(private readonly args: Args) {
    super();
  }

  perform(currentState: ChartAreaState): ChartAreaState {
    const { chartDataService, chart, dispatch } = this.args;

    chartDataService
      .fetchChartData(
        chart.dataSource,
        chart.getColumns(),
        chart.getFilters(),
        chart.getSortBys()
      )
```

```
        .then((columnNameToValuesMap: ColumnNameToValuesMap) => {
          dispatch(
            new FinishFetchChartDataAction(columnNameToValuesMap,
                                           chart.id)
          );
        })
        .catch((error) => {
          // Handle error
        });

    chart.isFetchingChartData = true;

    return ChartAreaStateUpdater
            .getNewStateForChangedChart(currentState, chart);
  }
}
```

To be able to dispatch the above action, a controller should be implemented:

```
import diContainer from './diContainer';
import StartFetchChartDataAction from './StartFetchChartDataAction';
import Controller from './Controller';
import store from './store';

class ChartAreaController extends Controller {
  readonly actionDispatchers = {
    startFetchChartData: (chart: Chart) =>
      // the 'chart' is given as a property to
      // StartFetchChartDataAction class constructor
      this.dispatchWithDi(diContainer,
                          StartFetchChartDataAction,
                          { chart });
  }
}

export const controller = new ChartAreaController(store.dispatch);
export type ActionDispatchers = typeof controller.actionDispatchers;
```

The following base classes are also defined:

Figure 4.135. AbstractAction.ts

```
export default abstract class AbstractAction<S> {
  abstract perform(state: S): S;
}
```

Figure 4.136. AbstractChartAreaAction.ts

```
// Imports...

export default abstract class AbstractChartAreaAction
        extends AbstractAction<ChartAreaState> {
}
```

Figure 4.137. Controller.ts

```
export type Dispatch = (action: AbstractAction<any>) => void;

export type ReduxDispatch =
  (reduxActionObject: { type: AbstractAction<any> }) => void;

export default class Controller {
  protected readonly dispatch: Dispatch;

  constructor(reduxDispatch: ReduxDispatch) {
    this.dispatch = (action: AbstractAction<any>) =>
      reduxDispatch({ type: action });
  }

  dispatchWithDi(
    diContainer: { create: (...args: any[]) => Promise<any> },
    ActionClass:
      abstract new (...args: any[]) => AbstractAction<any>,
    otherArgs?: {}
  ) {
    // diContainer.create will create a new object of
    // class ActionClass.
    // The second parameter of the create function defines
    // additional properties supplied to ActionClass constructor.
    // The create method is asynchronous. When it succeeds,
    // the created action object is available in the 'then'
    // function and it can be now dispatched

    diContainer
      .create(ActionClass, {
        dispatch: this.dispatch,
        ...(otherArgs ?? {})
      })
      .then((action: any) => this.dispatch(action));
  }
}
```

An example of using dependency injection with *noicejs* library is available here[36].

4.20: Avoid Code Duplication Principle

At the class level, when you spot duplicated code in two different classes imple-
menting the same interface, you should create a new base class to accommodate the
common functionality and let the classes extend the new base class.

Below is an AvroBinaryKafkaInputMessage class that implements the InputMessage interface:

---

[36]https://github.com/pksilen/clean-code-principles-code/tree/main/chapter2/mvvm_di

Figure 4.138. InputMessage.h

```cpp
class InputMessage
{
public:
  virtual ~InputMessage() = default;

  virtual uint32_t tryDecodeSchemaId() const = 0;

  virtual std::shared_ptr<DecodedMessage>
  tryDecodeMessage(const std::shared_ptr<Schema>& schema)
  const = 0;
};
```

Figure 4.139. AvroBinaryKafkaInputMessage.h

```cpp
class AvroBinaryKafkaInputMessage : public InputMessage
{
public:
  AvroBinaryKafkaInputMessage(
    std::unique_ptr<RdKafka::Message> kafkaMessage
  ) : m_kafkaMessage(std::move(kafkaMessage))
  {}

  uint32_t tryDecodeSchemaId() const override;

  std::shared_ptr<DecodedMessage>
  tryDecodeMessage(const std::shared_ptr<Schema>& schema)
  const override;

private:
  std::unique_ptr<RdKafka::Message> m_kafkaMessage;
};

uint32_t AvroBinaryKafkaInputMessage::tryDecodeSchemaId() const
{
  // Try decode schema id from the beginning of
  // the Avro binary Kafka message
}

std::shared_ptr<DecodedMessage>
AvroBinaryKafkaInputMessage::tryDecodeMessage(
  const std::shared_ptr<Schema>& schema
) const
{
  return schema->tryDecodeMessage(m_kafkaMessage->payload(),
                                  m_kafkaMessage->len());
}
```

If we wanted to introduce a new Kafka input message class for JSON, CSV, or XML format, we could create a class like the `AvroBinaryKafkaInputMessage` class. But then we can notice the duplication of code in the `tryDecodeMessage` method. We can notice that the `tryDecodeMessage` method is the same regardless of the input message source and format. According to this principle, we should move the duplicate code to a common base class, `BaseInputMessage`. We could make the `tryDecodeMessage` method a template method according to the *template method pattern* and create abstract methods for getting the message data and its length:

Figure 4.140. BaseInputMessage.h

```
class BaseInputMessage : public InputMessage
{
public:
  std::shared_ptr<DecodedMessage>
  tryDecodeMessage(const std::shared_ptr<Schema>& schema)
  const final;

protected:
  // Abstract methods
  virtual uint8_t* getData() const = 0;
  virtual size_t getLengthInBytes() const = 0;
};

// This is a template method
// 'getData' and 'getLengthInBytes' will be
// implemented in subclasses
std::shared_ptr<DecodedMessage>
BaseInputMessage::tryDecodeMessage(
  const std::shared_ptr<Schema>& schema
) const
{
  return schema->tryDecodeMessage(getData(), getLengthInBytes());
}
```

Next, we should refactor the AvroBinaryKafkaInputMessage class to extend the new BaseInputMessage class and implement the getData and getLengthInBytes methods. But we can realize these two methods are the same for all Kafka input message data formats. We should not implement those two methods in the AvroBinaryKafkaInputMessage class because we would need to implement them as duplicates if we needed to add a Kafka input message class for another data format. Once again, we can utilize this principle and create a new base class for Kafka input messages:

Figure 4.141. KafkaInputMessage.h

```
class KafkaInputMessage : public BaseInputMessage
{
public:
  KafkaInputMessage(
    std::unique_ptr<RdKafka::Message> kafkaMessage
  ) : m_kafkaMessage(std::move(kafkaMessage))
  {}

protected:
  uint8_t* getData() const final;
  size_t getLengthInBytes() const final;

private:
  std::unique_ptr<RdKafka::Message> m_kafkaMessage;
};

uint8_t* KafkaInputMessage::getData() const
{
  return std::bit_cast<uint8_t*>(m_kafkaMessage->payload());
}

size_t KafkaInputMessage::getLengthInBytes() const
{
  return m_kafkaMessage->len();
}
```

Finally, we can refactor the AvroBinaryKafkaInputMessage class to contain no duplicated code:

Figure 4.142. AvroBinaryKafkaInputMessage.h

```
class AvroBinaryKafkaInputMessage : public KafkaInputMessage
{
public:
  uint32_t tryDecodeSchemaId() const final;
};

uint32_t AvroBinaryKafkaInputMessage::tryDecodeSchemaId() const
{
  // Try decode the schema id from the beginning of
  // the Avro binary Kafka message
  // Use base class getData() and getDataLengthInBytes()
  // methods to achieve that
}
```

4.21: Inheritance in Cascading Style Sheets (CSS)

This last section of this chapter is for developers interested in how inheritance works in CSS. In HTML, you can define classes (class names) for HTML elements in the following way:

```
<span class="icon pie-chart-icon">...</span>
```

In a CSS file, you define CSS properties for CSS classes, for example:

```
.icon {
  background-repeat: no-repeat;
  background-size: 1.9rem 1.9rem;
  display: inline-block;
  height: 2rem;
  margin-bottom: 0.2rem;
  margin-right: 0.2rem;
  width: 2rem;
}

.pie-chart-icon {
  background-image: url('pie_chart_icon.svg');
}
```

The problem with the above approach is that it is not correctly object-oriented. In the HTML code, you must list all the class names to combine all the needed CSS properties. It is easy to forget to add a class name. For example, you could specify pie-chart-icon only and forget to specify the icon.

It is also difficult to change the inheritance hierarchy afterward. Suppose you wanted to add a new class chart-icon for all the chart icons:

```
.chart-icon {
  // Define properties here...
}
```

You would have to remember to add the chart-icon class name to all places in the HTML code where you are rendering chart icons:

```
<span class="icon chart-icon pie-chart-icon">...</span>
```

The above-described approach is very error-prone. You should introduce proper object-oriented design. You need a CSS preprocessor that makes extending CSS classes possible. In the below example, I am using SCSS[37]:

```
<span class="pieChartIcon">...</span>
```

```
.icon {
  background-repeat: no-repeat;
  background-size: 1.9rem 1.9rem;
  display: inline-block;
  height: 2rem;
  margin-bottom: 0.2rem;
  margin-right: 0.2rem;
  width: 2rem;
}

.chartIcon {
  @extend .icon;

  // Other chart icon related properties...
}

.pieChartIcon {
  @extend .chartIcon;

  background-image: url('../../../../../assets/images/icons/chart/pie_chart_icon.svg');
}
```

In the above example, we define only one class for the HTML element. The inheritance hierarchy is defined in the SCSS file using the @extend directive. We are now free to change the inheritance hierarchy in the future without any modification needed in the HTML code.

---

[37]https://sass-lang.com/guide/

5: Coding Principles

This chapter presents principles for coding. The following principles are presented:

- Uniform variable naming principle
- Uniform source code repository structure principle
- Domain-based source code structure principle
- Avoid comments principle
- Function single return statement principle
- Prefer statically typed language principle
- Refactoring principle
- Static code analysis principle
- Error/Exception handling principle
- Avoid off-by-one errors principle
- Be critical when googling principle
- Make one change at a time principle
- Choosing right 3rd party component principle
- Use appropriate data structure principle
- Optimization principle

5.1: Uniform Variable Naming Principle

A good variable name should describe the variable's purpose and its type.

Writing your code with great names, at best, makes it read like prose. And remember that code is more often read than written, so code must be easy to read and understand.

Naming variables with names that convey information about the variable's type is crucial in untyped languages and beneficial in typed languages because modern typed languages use automatic type deduction, and you won't always see the actual variable type. But when the variable's name tells its type, it does not matter if the type name is not visible.

If a variable name is 20 or more characters long, consider making it shorter. Try to abbreviate one or more words in the variable name, but only use meaningful and well-known abbreviations. If such abbreviations don't exist, then don't abbreviate at all. For example, if you have a variable named `environmentVariableName`, you should try to shorten it because it is over 20 characters long. You can abbreviate *environment* to *environ* and *variable* to *var*, resulting in a variable name `environVarName` that is short enough. Both abbreviations `environ` and `var` are commonly used and well understood. Let's have another example with a variable named `loyaltyBonusPercentage`. You cannot abbreviate *loyalty*. You cannot abbreviate *bonus*. But you can abbreviate *percentage* to *percent* or even *pct*. I would rather use *percent* instead of *pct*. Using *percent* makes the variable name shorter than 20 characters. The maximum length of a variable name should be less than the maximum length for a class/interface name because variables are used in code more often and often in combination with a method name.

If a variable name is less than 20 characters long, you don't need to shorten it. If you have several variables named in similar wording and one or more need abbreviating, you can use that abbreviation for consistency in all the variable names. For example, if you have variables `configurationFile` and `configurationFilePparser`, you can abbreviate both to `configFile` and `configFileParser`.

In the following sections, naming conventions for different types of variables are proposed.

5.1.1: Naming Integer Variables

Some variables are intrinsically integers, like *age* or *year*. Everybody immediately understands that the type of an *age* or *year* variable is a number and, more specifically, an integer. So, you don't have to add anything to the variable's name to indicate its type. It already tells you its type.

One of the most used categories of integer variables is a count or number of something. You see those kinds of variables in every piece of code. I recommend using the following convention for naming those variables: *numberOf<something>* or alternatively *<something>Count*. For example, *numberOfFailures* or *failureCount*. You should not use a variable named *failures* to designate a failure count. The problem with that variable name is that it does not specify the variable type, which can confuse. This is because a variable named *failures* can be misunderstood as a collection variable (e.g., a list of failures).

If the unit of a variable is not self-evident, always add information about the unit to the end of the variable name. For example, instead of naming a variable *tooltipShowDelay*, you should name it *tooltipShowDelayInMillis* or *tooltipShowDelayInMs*. If you have a variable whose unit is self evident, unit information is not needed. So, there is no need to name an *age* variable as *ageInYears*. But if you are measuring age in months, you must name the respective variable as *ageInMonths* so that people don't assume that age is measured in years.

5.1.2: Naming Floating-Point Number Variables

Floating-point numbers are not as common as integers, but sometimes you need them too. Some values are intrinsically floating-point numbers, like most un-rounded measures (e.g., price, height, width, or weight). A floating-point variable would be a safe bet if you need to store a measured value.

If you need to store an amount of something that is not an integer, use a variable named *<something>Amount*, like *rainfallAmount*. When you see the "amount of something" in code, you can automatically think it is a floating-point number. If you need to use a number in arithmetic, depending on the application, you might want to use either floating-point or integer arithmetic. In the case of money, you should use integer arithmetic to avoid rounding errors. Instead of a floating-point *moneyAmount* variable, you should have an integer variable, like *moneyInCents*.

If the unit of a variable is not self-evident, add information about the unit to the end of the variable name, like *rainfallAmountInMm*, *widthInInches*, *angleInDegrees* (values 0-360), *failurePercent* (values 0-100), or *failureRatio* (values 0-1).

5.1.3: Naming Boolean Variables

Boolean variables can have only one of two values: true or false. The name of a boolean variable should form a statement where the answer is true or false, or yes or no. Typical boolean variable naming patterns are: *is<something>*, *has<something>*, *did<something>*, *should<something>*, *can<something>*, or *will<something>*. Some examples of variable names following the above patterns are *isDisabled*, *hasErrors*, *didUpdate*, *shouldUpdate*, and *willUpdate*.

The verb in the boolean variable name does not have to be at the beginning. It can and should be in the middle if it improves the code's readability. Boolean variables are often used in if-statements where changing the word order in the variable name can make the code read better. Remember that, at best, code reads like beautiful prose and is read more often than written.

Below is a C++ code snippet where we have a boolean variable named `isPoolFull`:

```cpp
if (const bool isPoolFull = m_pooledMessages.size() >= 200U;
       isPoolFull)
{
  // ...
}
else
{
  // ...
}
```

We can change the variable name to `poolIsFfull` to make the if-statement read more fluently. In the below example, the if-statement reads "if poolIsFull" instead of "if isPoolFull":

```cpp
if (const bool poolIsFull = m_pooledMessages.size() >= 200U;
       poolIsFull)
{
  // ...
```

Don't use boolean variable names in the form of *<passive-verb>Something*, like *insertedField*, because this can confuse the reader. It is unclear if the variable name is a noun (a field that was inserted) that names an object or a boolean statement. Instead, use either *didInsertField* or *fieldWasInserted*.

Below is a Go language example of the incorrect naming of a variable used to store a function return value. Someone might think `tablesDropped` means a list of dropped table names. So, the name of the variable is obscure and should be changed.

```go
tablesDropped := dropRedundantTables(prefix,
                                vmsdata,
                                cfg.HiveDatabase,
                                hiveClient,
                                logger)
if tablesDropped {
  // ...
}
```

Below is the above example modified so that the variable name is changed to indicate a boolean statement:

```
tablesWereDropped := dropRedundantTables(prefix,
                                         vmsdata,
                                         cfg.HiveDatabase,
                                         hiveClient,
                                         logger)
if tablesWereDropped {
  // ...
}
```

You could have used a variable named didDropTables, but the tablesWereDropped makes the if-statement more readable. If the return value of the dropRedundantTables function were a list of dropped table names, I would name the return value receiving variable as droppedTableNames.

When you read code containing a negated boolean variable, it usually reads terrible, for example:

```
final var appWasStarted = app.start();

// Reads: if not app was started
if (!appWasStarted) {
  // ...
}
```

To improve the readability, you can mentally move the not word to the correct place to make the sentence read like proper English. For example: *if appWas not Started*

The other option is to negate the variable. That is done by negating both sides of the assignment by adding not on both sides of the assignment operator. Here is an example:

```
final var appWasNotStarted = !app.start();

if (appWasNotStarted) {
  // ...
}
```

Below is a real-life example where a boolean property is named wrong:

```
sonar.buildBreaker.skip = true
```

The skip is not a correctly named boolean property. From the above statement, it is difficult to understand when a build is broken because no boolean statement that evaluates either true or false is made. Let's refactor the statement:

```
sonar.shouldBreakBuildOnQualityGateFailure = true
```

5.1.4: Naming String Variables

String variables are prevalent, and many things are intrinsically strings, like *name, title, city, country,* or *topic*. When you need to store numerical data in a string variable, tell the code reader clearly that it is a question about a number in string format, and use a variable name in the following format: *<someValue>String* or *<someValue>AsString*. It makes the code more prominent and easier to understand. Here is an example in JavaScript:

```
const year = parseInt(yearAsString, 10);
```

If you have a string variable that could be confused with an object variable, like schema (could be confused with an instance of Schema class), but it is a string, add *string* to the end of the variable name, e.g., schemaString. Here is an example:

```
final var schema = schemaParser.parse(schemaString);
```

5.1.5: Naming Enum Variables

Name enum variables using the same name as the enum type. E.g., a CarType enum variable should be named carType. If the name of an enum type is very generic, like Result, you might benefit from declaring an enum variable with some detail added to the variable name. Below is an example of a very generic enum type name:

Figure 5.1. PulsarProducer.cpp

```
// Returns enum type 'Result'
const auto result = pulsar::createProducer(...);

if (result == Result.Ok) {
  // ...
}
```

Let's add some detail and context to the result variable name:

Figure 5.2. PulsarProducer.cpp

```
const auto producerCreationResult = pulsar::createProducer(...);

if (producerCreationResult == Result.Ok) {
  // ...
}
```

5.1.6: Naming Collection (List and Set) Variables

When naming lists and sets, you should use the plural form of a noun, like *customers*, *errors*, or *tasks*. These kinds of names work well in the code, for example:

```
function handle(customers: Customer[]): Customer[] {
  // ...
}

const customers = [new Customer()];

for (const customer of customers) {
  // ...
}

const processedCustomers = handle(customers);

function isEven(integer: number): boolean {
  return integer % 2 === 0;
}

const integers = [1, 2, 3, 4, 5];
const evenIntegers = integers.filter(isEven);
```

This plural noun naming convention is usually enough because you don't necessarily need to know the underlying collection implementation. Using this naming convention allows you to change the type of a collection variable without changing the variable name. If you are iterating over a collection, it does not matter if it is a list or set. Thus, it does not bring any benefit if you add the collection type name to the variable name, for example, *customerList* or *taskSet*. Those names are just longer. You might want to specify the collection type in some special cases. Then, you can use the following kinds of variable names: *queueOfTasks*, *stackOfCards*, or *setOfTimestamps*.

Below is an example in Go language, where the function is named correctly to return a collection (of categories), but the variable receiving the return value is not named according to the collection variable naming convention:

```
vmsdata, error = vmsClient.GetCategories(vmsUrl, logger)
```

Correct naming would be:

```
vmsCategories, error = vmsClient.GetCategories(vmsUrl, logger)
```

5.1.7: Naming Map Variables

Maps are accessed by requesting a *value* for a certain *key*. I recommend naming maps using the pattern *keyToValue* or keyToValueMap_. Let's say we have a map containing order counts for customer ids. This map should be named customerIdToOrderCount or customerIdToOrderCountMap. Or if we have a list of suppliers for product names, the map variable should be named productNameToSuppliers or productNameToSuppliersMap. I prefer the shorter version because it is enough to tell that a variable is a map because of the to word in the middle. Below is an example of accessing maps in Java:

```
final var orderCount = customerIdToOrderCount.get(customerId);
final var suppliers = productNameToSuppliers.get(productName);
```

Below is an example of iterating over a map in JavaScript:

```
Object.entries(customerIdToOrderCount)
    .map(([customerId, orderCount]) => ...);
```

5.1.8: Naming Pair and Tuple Variables

A variable containing a pair should be named using the pattern *variable1AndVariable2*. For example: heightAndWidth. And for tuples, the recommended naming pattern is *variable1Variable2...andVariableN*. For instance: heightWidthAndDepth.

Below is an example of using pairs and tuples in JavaScript:

```
const heightAndWidth = [100, 200];
const heightWidthAndDepth = [100, 200, 40];
const [height, , depth] = heightWidthAndDepth;
```

5.1.9: Naming Object Variables

Object variables refer to an instance of a class. Class names are nouns written in CapWords, like *Person*, *CheckingAccount*, or *Task*. Object variable names should contain the related class name: a *person* object of the *Person* class, an *account* object of the *Account* class, etc. You can freely decorate the object's name, for example, with an adjective: *completedTask*. Including the class name or at least a significant part of it at the end of the variable name is useful because looking at the end of the variable name tells what kind of object is in question.

Do not add an article a or an to an object variable's name. This is redundant because you usually know if it is a question about an object variable when you follow all the naming conventions presented in this book.

```
// Not so good, explicit articles and prepositions and wrong order of arguments
writeTo(aBuffer, aMessage)

// Better, implicit articles and prepositions and correct order of arguments
write(message, buffer)
```

Sometimes, you might want to name an object variable so that the name of its class is implicit, for example:

```
// The class of the function parameters, 'Location', is implicit
drive(home, destination);
```

In the above example, the classes of home and destination objects are not explicit. In most cases, it is preferable to make the class name explicit in the variable name when it does not make the variable name too long. This is because of the variable type deduction. The types of variables are not necessarily visible in the code, so the variable name should communicate the type of a variable. Below is an example where the types of function parameters are explicit.

```
// The class of the function parameters, 'Location', is now explicit
drive(homeLocation, destLocation);
```

5.1.10: Naming Optional Variables

How to name optional variables depends on the programming language and how the optional types are implemented. An optional variable name should be prefixed with *maybe* in languages where you must unwrap the possible value from an optional object.

In Java, when using Optional<T>, name variables of this type using the following pattern: *maybe<Something>*:

```
maybeLoggedInUser.ifPresent(loggedInUser -> loggedInUser.logout());
final User currentUser = maybeLoggedInUser.orElse(guestUser);
```

In TypeScript and other languages where optional types are created using type unions, you don't need prefixes in optional variable names. In the below example, the discount parameter is optional, and its type is number | undefined:

```
function addTax(
  price: number,
  discount?: number
): number {
  return 1.2 * (price - (discount ?? 0));
}

const priceWithTax = addTax(priceWithoutTax);
```

5.1.11: Naming Function Variables (Callbacks)

Callback functions are functions supplied to other functions to be called at some point. If a callback function returns a value, it can be named according to the returned value, but it should still contain a verb. If the callback function does not return a value, you should name the callback function like any other function, indicating what the function does. Suppose you have a variable storing a function object, like a Java Function instance. In that case, you need to name the variable according to the rules for an object variable, i.e., the variable name should be a noun. For example, if you have a Java Function object currently named map, you should correct the name as a noun, like mapper.

```
const doubled = value => 2 * value;
const squared = value => value * value;
const isEven = nbr => (nbr % 2) === 0;
const values = [1, 2, 3, 4, 5]

// You can imagine an implicit "to" preposition after the map function name
const doubledValues = values.map(doubled);
const squaredValues = values.map(squared);

const evenValues = values.filter(isEven);

const strings = [" string1", "string2 "];
const trimmed = str => str.trim();
const trimmedStrings = strings.map(trimmed);

const sumOfValues = (sum, value) => sum + value;
// You can imagine an implicit "to" preposition after the reduce function name
values.reduce(sumOfValues, 0);
```

Let's have a quick detour with an example written in Clojure:

```
(defn print-first-n-doubled-integers [n]
  (println (take n (map (fn [x] (* 2 x)) (range)))))
```

To understand what happens in the above code, you should start reading from the innermost function call and proceed toward the outermost function call. A function call is inside parenthesis. When traversing the function call hierarchy, the difficulty lies in storing and retaining information about all the nested function calls in short-term memory.

We could simplify reading the above example by naming the anonymous function and introducing variables (constants) for intermediate function call results. Of course, our code becomes more prolonged, but coding is not a competition to write the shortest possible code but to write the shortest, most readable, and understandable code for other people and your future self. It is a compiler's job to compile the longer code below into code that is as efficient as the shorter code above.

Below is the above code refactored:

```
(defn print-first-n-doubled-integers [n]
  (let [doubled (fn [x] (* 2 x))
        doubled-integers (map doubled (range))
        first-n-doubled-integers (take n doubled-integers)]
    (println first-n-doubled-integers)))
```

Let's think hypothetically: if Clojure's `map` function took parameters in a different order and the `range` function was named `integers` and the `take` function was named `take-first` (like there is the `take-last` function), we would have an even more explicit version of the original code:

```
(defn print-first-n-doubled-integers [n]
  (let [doubled (fn [x] (* 2 x))
        doubled-integers (map (integers) doubled)
        first-n-doubled-integers (take-first n doubled-integers)]
    (println first-n-doubled-integers)))
```

There is a reason why the `map` function takes the parameters in that order. It is to make function partial application possible.

5.1.12: Naming Class Properties

Class properties (i.e., class attributes, fields, or member variables) should be named so that the class name is not repeated in the property names. Below is a Java example of incorrect naming:

```
public class Order {
  private long orderId;
  private OrderState orderState;
}
```

Below is the above code with corrected names:

```
public class Order {
  private long id;
  private OrderState state;
}
```

If you have a class property to store a callback function (e.g., event handler or lifecycle callback), you should name it so that it tells on what occasion the stored callback function is called. You should name properties storing event handlers using the following pattern: on + <event-type>, e.g., `onClick` or `onSubmit`. Name properties storing lifecycle callbacks in a similar way you would name a lifecycle method, for example: `onInit`, `afterMount`, or `beforeMount`.

5.1.13: General Naming Rules

5.1.13.1: Use Short, Common Names

When picking a name for something, use the most common shortest name. If you have a function named *relinquishSomething*, consider a shorter and more common name for the function. You could rename the function to *releaseSomething*, for example. The word "release" is shorter and more common than the "relinquish" word. Use Google to search for word synonyms, e.g., "relinquish synonym", to find the shortest and most common similar term.

5.1.13.2: Pick One Term And Use It Consistently

Let's assume that you are building a data exporter microservice and you are currently using the following terms in the code: *message, report, record* and *data*. Instead of using four different terms to describe the same thing, you should pick just one term, like *message*, for example, and use it consistently throughout the microservice code.

Suppose you need to figure out a term to indicate a property of a class. You should pick just one term, like *property*, and use it consistently everywhere. You should not use multiple terms like *attribute, field*, and *member* to describe a class property.

If you have person objects, do not add them to a peopleList; add them to a persons list. Do not use the terms person and people interchangeably.

5.1.13.3: Avoid Obscure Abbreviations

Many abbreviations are commonly used, like *str* for a string, *num/nbr* for a number, *prop* for a property, or *val* for a value. Most programmers use these, and I use them to make long names shorter. If a variable name is short, the full name should be used, like *numberOfItems* instead of *nbrOfItems*. Use abbreviations when the variable name becomes too long (20 or more characters). You should especially avoid using uncommon abbreviations. For example, do not abbreviate *amount* to *amnt* or *discount* to *dscnt* because those abbreviations are not used.

5.1.13.4: Avoid Too Short Or Meaningless Names

Names that are too short do not communicate what the variable is about. Variable names like *tmp, temp, ret*, or *retval* are all meaningless. You should figure out a name that describes the value a variable holds. This is not always an easy task, and naming things is hard and one of the hardest things in software engineering. The good news is that you get better at it with more practice. As loop counters, use a variable name like *index* or *<something>Index* if the loop variable is used to index something, like an array, for example. An indexing variable should start from zero. If the loop variable is counting the number of things, use *number* or *<something>Number* as the variable name, and start the loop counter from value one instead of zero. For example, a loop to start five threads should be written in C++ in the following way:

```
for (size_t threadNumber{1U}; threadNumber <= 5U; ++threadNumber)
{
  startThread(threadNumber);
}
```

If you don't need to use the loop counter value inside the loop, you can use a loop variable named *count*:

```
for (size_t count{1U}; count <= objectCount; ++count)
{
  objects.push_back(acquireObject(std::forward<Args>(args)...));
}
```

Let's have another example. Suppose you have a class named ImageGetter with a method getImage. Both of the names are too abstract and can mean several things in practice, like the image could be gotten from a local disk, local cache, database, or remote location. If the ImageGetter is always getting images from a remote location, it is better to name the class with a descriptive name, like ImageDownloader, and have a method downloadImage in it. You should not use abstract names with concrete classes, but you can create an interface named `ImageGetter` with a method `getImage`. This is because, by nature, interfaces are abstract, and you cannot create an instance of them. You can then create concrete implementations of the `ImageGetter` interface, like `LocalDiskImageGetter`, `LocalCacheImageGetter`, `MySqlDbImageGetter`, or `RemoteUrlImageGetter`.

Even if you don't agree with all naming conventions presented here and in the previous chapter, I recommend you create rules for naming code entities, like classes, functions, and variables. That would make your code look consistent and professional. It makes the code look pretty bad if no naming conventions are used, and naming inside a single module or even a function varies dramatically. For example, a 'customers' variable is used somewhere, while a `customer_list` variable is used elsewhere, and the `customers` variable is used to store a list of customers in some place and the number of customers in another place. It is preferable if a whole development team or, even better, all development teams could share a common set of naming conventions.

5.2: Uniform Source Code Repository Structure Principle

Structuring a source code repository systematically in a certain way makes it easy for other developers to discover wanted information quickly.

Below are examples of ways to structure source code repositories for Java, C++, and JavaScript/TypeScript microservices. In the below examples, a containerized (Docker) microservice deployed to a Kubernetes cluster is assumed. Your CI tool might require that the CI/CD pipeline code reside in a specific directory. If not, place it in a *ci-cd* directory.

Top-level source code repository directory names can contain dashes, but package/directory names inside the *src* directory should not contain separator characters. This is not mandatory in all languages, but it is in Java.

5.2.1: Java Source Code Repository Structure

Below is the proposed source code repository structure for a Java microservice (Gradle build tool is used):

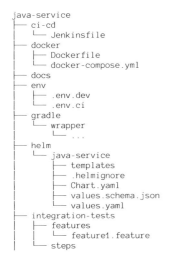

```
java-service
├── ci-cd
│   └── Jenkinsfile
├── docker
│   ├── Dockerfile
│   └── docker-compose.yml
├── docs
├── env
│   ├── .env.dev
│   └── .env.ci
├── gradle
│   └── wrapper
│       └── ...
├── helm
│   └── java-service
│       ├── templates
│       ├── .helmignore
│       ├── Chart.yaml
│       ├── values.schema.json
│       └── values.yaml
├── integration-tests
│   ├── features
│   │   └── feature1.feature
│   └── steps
```

```
├── scripts
│   └── // Bash scripts here...
├── src
│   ├── main
│   │   ├── java
│   │   │   └── com.domain.java-service
│   │   │       └── // source code
│   │   └── resources
│   └── test
│       ├── java
│       │   └── com.domain.java-service
│       │       └── // unit test code
│       └── resources
├── .gitignore
├── build.gradle
├── gradlew
├── gradlew.bat
├── README.MD
└── settings.gradle
```

5.2.2: C++ Source Code Repository Structure

Below is the proposed source code repository structure for a C++ microservice (CMake build tool is used):

```
cpp-service
├── ci-cd
│   └── Jenkinsfile
├── docker
│   ├── Dockerfile
│   └── docker-compose.yml
├── docs
├── env
│   ├── .env.dev
│   └── .env.ci
├── helm
│   └── cpp-service
│       ├── templates
│       ├── .helmignore
│       ├── Chart.yaml
│       ├── values.schema.json
│       └── values.yaml
├── integration-tests
│   ├── features
│   │   └── feature1.feature
│   └── steps
├── scripts
│   └── // Bash scripts here...
├── src
│   ├── // source code here
│   │   main.cpp
│   └── CMakeLists.txt
├── test
│   ├── // unit test code
│   │   main.cpp
│   └── CMakeLists.txt
├── .gitignore
├── CMakeLists.txt
└── README.MD
```

5.2.3: JavaScript/TypeScript Source Code Repository Structure

Below is the proposed source code repository structure for a JavaScript/TypeScript microservice:

```
ts-service
├── ci-cd
│   └── Jenkinsfile
├── docker
│   ├── Dockerfile
│   └── docker-compose.yml
├── docs
├── env
│   ├── .env.dev
│   └── .env.ci
├── helm
│   └── ts-service
│       ├── templates
│       ├── .helmignore
│       ├── Chart.yaml
│       ├── values.schema.json
│       └── values.yaml
├── integration-tests
│   ├── features
│   │   └── feature1.feature
│   └── steps
├── scripts
│   └── // Bash scripts here...
├── src
│   └── // source code here
├── test
│   └── // unit test code here
├── .gitignore
├── .eslintrc.json
├── .prettier.rc
├── package.json
├── package-lock.json
├── README.MD
└── tsconfig.json
```

Unit test modules should be in the same directory as source code modules, but you can also put them in a specific *test* directory.

5.3: Domain-Based Source Code Structure Principle

Structure the source code tree primarily by domains (or feature sets), not by technical details. Each source code directory should have a single responsibility at its abstraction level.

Below is an example of a Spring Boot microservice's *src* directory that is not organized by domains (or feature sets) but is incorrectly organized according to technical details:

```
spring-example-service/
└── src/
    └── main/java/
        └── com.silensoft.springexampleservice/
            ├── controllers/
            │   ├── AController.java
            │   └── BController.java
            ├── entities/
            │   ├── AEntity.java
            │   └── BEntity.java
            ├── errors/
            │   ├── AError.java
            │   └── BError.java
            ├── dtos/
```

```
    │   ├── ADto.java
    │   └── BDto.java
    ├── repositories/
    │   ├── DbAEntity.java
    │   ├── DbBEntity.java
    │   ├── ARepository.java
    │   └── BRepository.java
    └── services/
        ├── AService.java
        └── BService.java
```

Below is the above example modified so that directories are organized by domains (or feature sets):

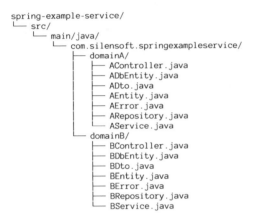

```
spring-example-service/
└── src/
    └── main/java/
        └── com.silensoft.springexampleservice/
            ├── domainA/
            │   ├── AController.java
            │   ├── ADbEntity.java
            │   ├── ADto.java
            │   ├── AEntity.java
            │   ├── AError.java
            │   ├── ARepository.java
            │   └── AService.java
            └── domainB/
                ├── BController.java
                ├── BDbEntity.java
                ├── BDto.java
                ├── BEntity.java
                ├── BError.java
                ├── BRepository.java
                └── BService.java
```

You can have several levels of nested domains:

```
spring-example-service/
└── src/
    └── main/java/
        └── com.silensoft.springexampleservice/
            ├── domainA/
            │   ├── domainA-1/
            │   │   ├── A1Controller.java
            │   │   └── ...
            │   └── domainA-2/
            │       ├── A2Controller.java
            │       └── ...
            └── domainB/
                └── BController.java
```

If you want, you can create subdirectories for technical details inside a domain directory. This is the recommended approach if, otherwise, the domain directory would contain more than 5 to 7 files. Below is an example of the *salesitem* domain:

```
sales-item-service
└── src
    └── main/java
        └── com.silensoft.salesitemservice
            └── salesitem
                ├── dtos
                │   ├── InputSalesItem.java
                │   └── OutputSalesItem.java
                ├── entities
                │   └── SalesItem.java
                ├── errors
                │   ├── SalesItemRelatedError.java
                │   └── SalesItemRelatedError2.java
                ├── repository
                │   ├── DbSalesItem.java
                │   └── SalesItemRepository.java
                ├── service
                │   ├── SalesItemService.java
                │   └── SalesItemServiceImpl.java
                └── SalesItemController.java
```

To highlight the *clean architecture principle*, we could also use the following kind of directory layout:

```
sales-item-service
└── src
    └── main/java
        └── com.silensoft.salesitemservice
            └── salesitem
                ├── ifadapters
                │   ├── controllers
                │   │   ├── GraphQlSalesItemController.java
                │   │   └── RestSalesItemController.java
                │   └── repositories
                │       ├── MongoDbalesItemRepository.java
                │       └── SqlSalesItemRepository.java
                └── model (or core)
                    ├── domain
                    │   ├── entities
                    │   │   └── SalesItem.java
                    │   └── errors
                    │       ├── SalesItemServiceError.java
                    │       └── SalesItemServiceError2.java
                    └── application
                        ├── dtos
                        │   ├── InputSalesItem.java
                        │   └── OutputSalesItem.java
                        ├── repositories
                        │   └── SalesItemRepository.java
                        └── services (or usecases)
                            ├── SalesItemService.java
                            └── SalesItemServiceImpl.java
```

If you follow the *clean architecture principle* and add or change an interface adapter (e.g., a controller or a repository), you should not need to make any code changes to the application or business logic part of the service (the *model* directory).

Below is the source code directory structure for the data exporter microservice designed in the previous chapter. There are subdirectories for the four subdomains: input, internal message, transformer, and output. A subdirectory is created for each common nominator in the class names. It is effortless to navigate the directory tree when locating a particular file. Also, the number of source code files in each directory is low. You can grasp the contents of a directory with a glance. The problem with directories containing many files is that it is not easy to find the wanted file. For this reason, a single directory should ideally have 2-4 files. The absolute maximum is 5-7 files.

Note that a couple of directories are left unexpanded below to shorten the example. It should be easy for the reader to infer the contents of the unexpanded directories.

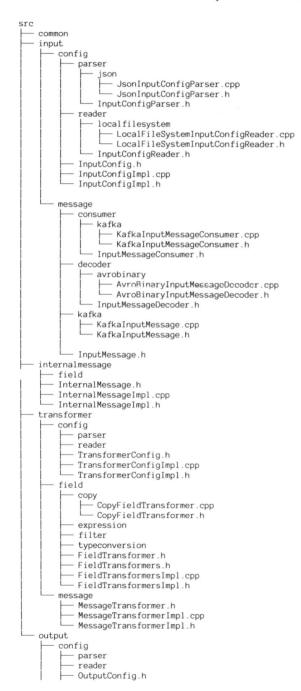

```
src
├── common
├── input
│   ├── config
│   │   ├── parser
│   │   │   ├── json
│   │   │   │   ├── JsonInputConfigParser.cpp
│   │   │   │   └── JsonInputConfigParser.h
│   │   │   └── InputConfigParser.h
│   │   ├── reader
│   │   │   ├── localfilesystem
│   │   │   │   ├── LocalFileSystemInputConfigReader.cpp
│   │   │   │   └── LocalFileSystemInputConfigReader.h
│   │   │   └── InputConfigReader.h
│   │   ├── InputConfig.h
│   │   ├── InputConfigImpl.cpp
│   │   └── InputConfigImpl.h
│   │
│   └── message
│       ├── consumer
│       │   ├── kafka
│       │   │   ├── KafkaInputMessageConsumer.cpp
│       │   │   └── KafkaInputMessageConsumer.h
│       │   └── InputMessageConsumer.h
│       ├── decoder
│       │   ├── avrobinary
│       │   │   ├── AvroBinaryInputMessageDecoder.cpp
│       │   │   └── AvroBinaryInputMessageDecoder.h
│       │   └── InputMessageDecoder.h
│       ├── kafka
│       │   ├── KafkaInputMessage.cpp
│       │   └── KafkaInputMessage.h
│       │
│       └── InputMessage.h
├── internalmessage
│   ├── field
│   ├── InternalMessage.h
│   ├── InternalMessageImpl.cpp
│   └── InternalMessageImpl.h
├── transformer
│   ├── config
│   │   ├── parser
│   │   ├── reader
│   │   ├── TransformerConfig.h
│   │   ├── TransformerConfigImpl.cpp
│   │   └── TransformerConfigImpl.h
│   ├── field
│   │   ├── copy
│   │   │   ├── CopyFieldTransformer.cpp
│   │   │   └── CopyFieldTransformer.h
│   │   ├── expression
│   │   ├── filter
│   │   ├── typeconversion
│   │   ├── FieldTransformer.h
│   │   ├── FieldTransformers.h
│   │   ├── FieldTransformersImpl.cpp
│   │   └── FieldTransformersImpl.h
│   └── message
│       ├── MessageTransformer.h
│       ├── MessageTransformerImpl.cpp
│       └── MessageTransformerImpl.h
└── output
    ├── config
    │   ├── parser
    │   ├── reader
    │   ├── OutputConfig.h
```

```
│   │   ├── OutputConfigImpl.cpp
│   │   └── OutputConfigImpl.h
│   └── message
│       ├── encoder
│       │   ├── avrobinary
│       │   └── OutputMessageEncoder.h
│       ├── producer
│       │   ├── pulsar
│       │   └── OutputMessageProducer.h
│       ├── OutputMessage.h
│       ├── OutputMessageImpl.cpp
│       └── OutputMessageImpl.h
```

Below is the Java version of the above directory structure:

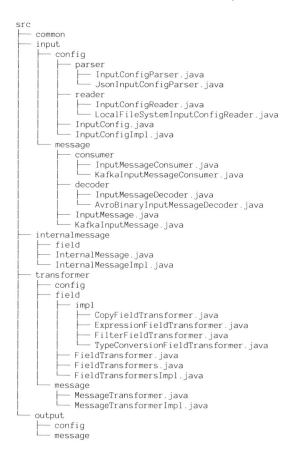

```
src
├── common
├── input
│   ├── config
│   │   ├── parser
│   │   │   ├── InputConfigParser.java
│   │   │   └── JsonInputConfigParser.java
│   │   ├── reader
│   │   │   ├── InputConfigReader.java
│   │   │   └── LocalFileSystemInputConfigReader.java
│   │   ├── InputConfig.java
│   │   └── InputConfigImpl.java
│   └── message
│       ├── consumer
│       │   ├── InputMessageConsumer.java
│       │   └── KafkaInputMessageConsumer.java
│       ├── decoder
│       │   ├── InputMessageDecoder.java
│       │   └── AvroBinaryInputMessageDecoder.java
│       ├── InputMessage.java
│       └── KafkaInputMessage.java
├── internalmessage
│   ├── field
│   ├── InternalMessage.java
│   └── InternalMessageImpl.java
├── transformer
│   ├── config
│   ├── field
│   │   ├── impl
│   │   │   ├── CopyFieldTransformer.java
│   │   │   ├── ExpressionFieldTransformer.java
│   │   │   ├── FilterFieldTransformer.java
│   │   │   └── TypeConversionFieldTransformer.java
│   │   ├── FieldTransformer.java
│   │   ├── FieldTransformers.java
│   │   └── FieldTransformersImpl.java
│   └── message
│       ├── MessageTransformer.java
│       └── MessageTransformerImpl.java
└── output
    ├── config
    └── message
```

We could also structure the code according to the *clean architecture* in the following way:

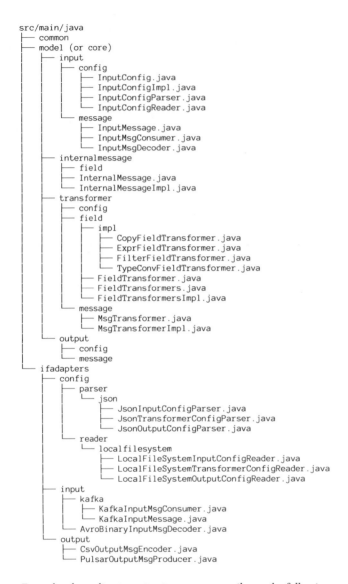

```
src/main/java
├── common
├── model (or core)
│   ├── input
│   │   ├── config
│   │   │   ├── InputConfig.java
│   │   │   ├── InputConfigImpl.java
│   │   │   ├── InputConfigParser.java
│   │   │   └── InputConfigReader.java
│   │   └── message
│   │       ├── InputMessage.java
│   │       ├── InputMsgConsumer.java
│   │       └── InputMsgDecoder.java
│   ├── internalmessage
│   │   ├── field
│   │   ├── InternalMessage.java
│   │   └── InternalMessageImpl.java
│   ├── transformer
│   │   ├── config
│   │   ├── field
│   │   │   ├── impl
│   │   │   │   ├── CopyFieldTransformer.java
│   │   │   │   ├── ExprFieldTransformer.java
│   │   │   │   ├── FilterFieldTransformer.java
│   │   │   │   └── TypeConvFieldTransformer.java
│   │   │   ├── FieldTransformer.java
│   │   │   ├── FieldTransformers.java
│   │   │   └── FieldTransformersImpl.java
│   │   └── message
│   │       ├── MsgTransformer.java
│   │       └── MsgTransformerImpl.java
│   └── output
│       ├── config
│       └── message
└── ifadapters
    ├── config
    │   ├── parser
    │   │   └── json
    │   │       ├── JsonInputConfigParser.java
    │   │       ├── JsonTransformerConfigParser.java
    │   │       └── JsonOutputConfigParser.java
    │   └── reader
    │       └── localfilesystem
    │           ├── LocalFileSystemInputConfigReader.java
    │           ├── LocalFileSystemTransformerConfigReader.java
    │           └── LocalFileSystemOutputConfigReader.java
    ├── input
    │   ├── kafka
    │   │   ├── KafkaInputMsgConsumer.java
    │   │   └── KafkaInputMessage.java
    │   └── AvroBinaryInputMsgDecoder.java
    └── output
        ├── CsvOutputMsgEncoder.java
        └── PulsarOutputMsgProducer.java
```

From the above directory structure, we can easily see the following:

- Configurations are in JSON format and read from the local file system
- For the input, Avro binary messages are read from Apache Kafka
- For the output, CSV records are produced to Apache Pulsar

Any change we want or need to make in the *ifadapters* directory should not affect the business logic part in the *model* directory.

Below is the source code directory structure for the anomaly detection microservice designed in the previous chapter. The *anomaly* directory is expanded. Our implementation uses JSON for various parsing activities and self-organizing maps (SOM) is used for anomaly detection. JSON and Kafka are used to publish anomaly indicators outside the microservice. Adding new concrete implementations to the below directory structure is straightforward. For example, if we wanted to add YAML support for configuration files, we could create *yaml* subdirectories to place YAML-specific implementation classes.

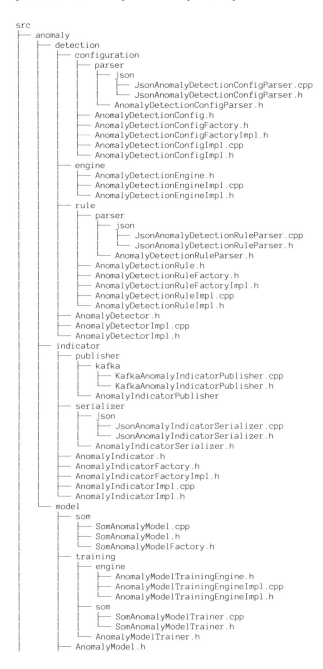

```
src
├── anomaly
│   ├── detection
│   │   ├── configuration
│   │   │   ├── parser
│   │   │   │   ├── json
│   │   │   │   │   ├── JsonAnomalyDetectionConfigParser.cpp
│   │   │   │   │   └── JsonAnomalyDetectionConfigParser.h
│   │   │   │   └── AnomalyDetectionConfigParser.h
│   │   │   ├── AnomalyDetectionConfig.h
│   │   │   ├── AnomalyDetectionConfigFactory.h
│   │   │   ├── AnomalyDetectionConfigFactoryImpl.h
│   │   │   ├── AnomalyDetectionConfigImpl.cpp
│   │   │   └── AnomalyDetectionConfigImpl.h
│   │   ├── engine
│   │   │   ├── AnomalyDetectionEngine.h
│   │   │   ├── AnomalyDetectionEngineImpl.cpp
│   │   │   └── AnomalyDetectionEngineImpl.h
│   │   ├── rule
│   │   │   ├── parser
│   │   │   │   ├── json
│   │   │   │   │   ├── JsonAnomalyDetectionRuleParser.cpp
│   │   │   │   │   └── JsonAnomalyDetectionRuleParser.h
│   │   │   │   └── AnomalyDetectionRuleParser.h
│   │   │   ├── AnomalyDetectionRule.h
│   │   │   ├── AnomalyDetectionRuleFactory.h
│   │   │   ├── AnomalyDetectionRuleFactoryImpl.h
│   │   │   ├── AnomalyDetectionRuleImpl.cpp
│   │   │   └── AnomalyDetectionRuleImpl.h
│   │   ├── AnomalyDetector.h
│   │   ├── AnomalyDetectorImpl.cpp
│   │   └── AnomalyDetectorImpl.h
│   ├── indicator
│   │   ├── publisher
│   │   │   ├── kafka
│   │   │   │   ├── KafkaAnomalyIndicatorPublisher.cpp
│   │   │   │   └── KafkaAnomalyIndicatorPublisher.h
│   │   │   └── AnomalyIndicatorPublisher
│   │   ├── serializer
│   │   │   ├── json
│   │   │   │   ├── JsonAnomalyIndicatorSerializer.cpp
│   │   │   │   └── JsonAnomalyIndicatorSerializer.h
│   │   │   └── AnomalyIndicatorSerializer.h
│   │   ├── AnomalyIndicator.h
│   │   ├── AnomalyIndicatorFactory.h
│   │   ├── AnomalyIndicatorFactoryImpl.h
│   │   ├── AnomalyIndicatorImpl.cpp
│   │   └── AnomalyIndicatorImpl.h
│   └── model
│       ├── som
│       │   ├── SomAnomalyModel.cpp
│       │   ├── SomAnomalyModel.h
│       │   └── SomAnomalyModelFactory.h
│       ├── training
│       │   ├── engine
│       │   │   ├── AnomalyModelTrainingEngine.h
│       │   │   ├── AnomalyModelTrainingEngineImpl.cpp
│       │   │   └── AnomalyModelTrainingEngineImpl.h
│       │   ├── som
│       │   │   ├── SomAnomalyModelTrainer.cpp
│       │   │   └── SomAnomalyModelTrainer.h
│       │   └── AnomalyModelTrainer.h
│       ├── AnomalyModel.h
```

```
|         └── AnomalyModelFactory.h
├── common
├── measurement
├── Application.h
├── Application.cpp
├── DependencyInjector.h
└── main.cpp
```

Let's have one more example with a *data-visualization-web-client.*

This web client's UI consists of the following pages, which all include a common header:

- Dashboards
- Data Explorer
- Alerts

The *Dashboards* page contains a dashboard group selector, dashboard selector, and chart area to display the selected dashboard's charts. You can select the shown dashboard by first selecting a dashboard group and then a dashboard from that group.

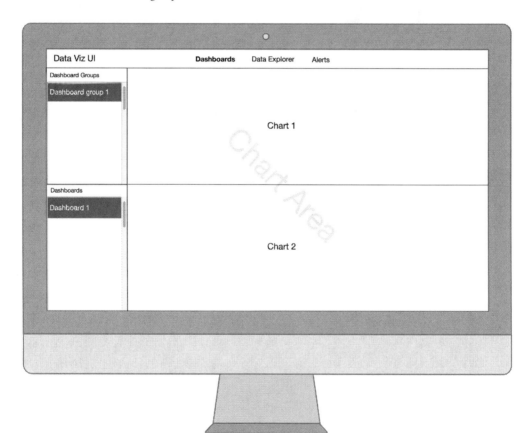

Figure 5.3. Dashboards Page

The *Data Explorer* page contains selectors for choosing a data source, measure(s), and dimension(s). The page also contains a chart area to display charts. Using the selectors, a user can change the shown measure(s) and dimension(s) for the currently selected chart in the chart area.

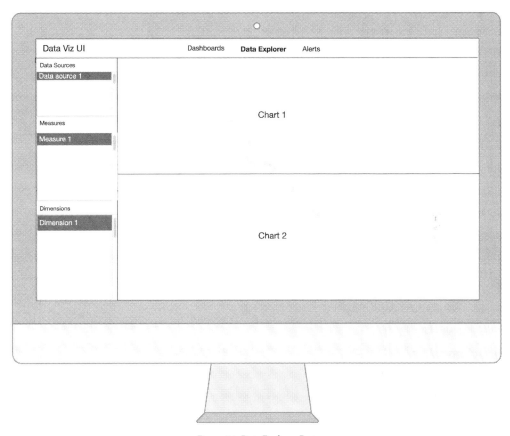

Figure 5.4. Data Explorer Page

Based on the above design, the web client can be divided into the following subdomains:

- Common UI components
    - Chart Area
        * Chart
- Header
- Pages
    - Alerts
    - Dashboards
    - Data Explorer

The source code tree should look like the following:

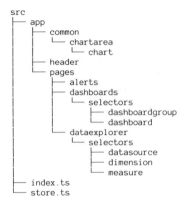

```
src
├── app
│   ├── common
│   │   └── chartarea
│   │       └── chart
│   ├── header
│   └── pages
│       ├── alerts
│       ├── dashboards
│       │   └── selectors
│       │       ├── dashboardgroup
│       │       └── dashboard
│       └── dataexplorer
│           └── selectors
│               ├── datasource
│               ├── dimension
│               └── measure
├── index.ts
└── store.ts
```

Below is an example of what a single subdomain directory would look like when using React, Redux, and SCSS modules:

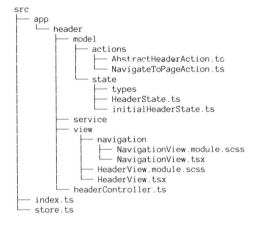

```
src
├── app
│   └── header
│       ├── model
│       │   ├── actions
│       │   │   ├── AbstractHeaderAction.ts
│       │   │   └── NavigateToPageAction.ts
│       │   └── state
│       │       ├── types
│       │       ├── HeaderState.ts
│       │       └── initialHeaderState.ts
│       ├── service
│       ├── view
│       │   ├── navigation
│       │   │   ├── NavigationView.module.scss
│       │   │   └── NavigationView.tsx
│       │   ├── HeaderView.module.scss
│       │   └── HeaderView.tsx
│       └── headerController.ts
├── index.ts
└── store.ts
```

In the above example, we have created two directories for the technical details of the *header* domain: model, service, and view directories. The model directory contains actions and the state, and the view directory contains the view component, its possible subcomponents, and CSS definitions. The model's state directory can contain a subdirectory for types used in the subdomain state. The state directory should always contain the type definition for the subdomain's state and the initial state. The service directory contains one or more services that use the respective backend services to control the backend model.

5.4: Avoid Comments Principle

Avoid code comments. The only exception is when documenting the public API of a library.

Comments can be problematic. You cannot trust them 100% because they can be misleading, outdated, or downright wrong. You can only trust the source code itself. Comments are often entirely unnecessary and only make the code more verbose. Allowing comments can produce unreadable code containing bad names explained by comments. The code typically also contains long functions where functionality blocks are described with attached comments instead of refactoring the code by extracting well-named functions. The idea behind this principle is that when writing comments is disallowed, you are forced to communicate better with the code only. The following sections describe several ways to avoid writing comments while keeping your code understandable. The following things can be done to avoid writing comments:

- Name things like classes, functions, and variables properly

    - For example, if you are using a particular algorithm, don't document that algorithm in a comment, but name the respective class/function so that it contains the algorithm name. Readers can then google the algorithm by name if unfamiliar with it

- You should not add comments about variable/function types. Use type annotations everywhere
- You don't need to comment that a function can raise an error. Use the function name *try* prefix convention described later in this chapter
- Don't add a comment to a piece of code, but extract a new well-named function
- Keep your functions small. They are easier to understand because they cannot contain too complex logic that could justify a comment
- Don't add as a comment information that can be obtained from the version control system
- Don't comment out the code. Just remove the unused code. The removed code will be available in the version control system forever
- You don't have to comment on a function's logic. Code readers should be able to infer that information from the code itself and the related unit tests. Complex code logic and behavior do not usually need comments if you have practiced *test-driven development* and a complete set of well-named unit tests is available. You should not comment on what value a function should return with certain input. Create a test case for that.

Code comments often duplicate information already available in the code itself or related tests. This is called information duplication, which should be avoided according to the *don't repeat yourself* (DRY) principle. This principle was introduced in the *Pragmatic Programmer* book by *David Thomas* and *Andrew Hunt*.

Comments for a public API in a library are needed because the library needs API documentation that can be automatically generated from the comments to avoid situations where API comments and docs are out of sync. API documentation is usually unnecessary in non-library software components because you can access the API interface, implementation, and unit tests. The unit tests, for example, specify what the function does in different scenarios. The unit test name tells the scenario, and the expectations and assertions in the unit test code tell the expected behavior in the particular situation. API implementation and unit tests are not typically available for library users, and even if they are, a user should not adhere to them because they are internal details subject to change.

5.4.1: Name Things Properly

When you name things like a function poorly, you might end up attaching a comment to the function. To avoid writing comments, it is imperative to focus on naming things correctly. When following the *single responsibility principle* and the *uniform naming principle*, it should be easier to name things correctly and avoid comments. Below is a C++ example of a function with a comment:

Figure 5.5. MessageBuffer.h

```
class MessageBuffer
{
public:
  // Return false if buffer full,
  // true if message written to buffer
  bool write(const std::shared_ptr<Message>& message);
}
```

If we drop the comment, we will have the following code:

Figure 5.6. MessageBuffer.h

```
class MessageBuffer
{
public:
  bool write(const std::shared_ptr<Message>& message);
}
```

Dropping the comment alone is not the best solution because some crucial information is now missing. What does that boolean return value mean? It is not 100% clear. We can assume that returning `true` means the message was successfully written, but nothing is communicated about returning `false`. We can only assume it is some error, but we are not sure what error.

In addition to removing the comment, we should give a better name for the function and rename it as follows:

Figure 5.7. MessageBuffer.h

```
class MessageBuffer
{
public:
  bool writeIfBufferNotFull(
    const std::shared_ptr<Message>& message
  );
}
```

Now, the purpose of the function is clear, and we can be sure of what the boolean return value means. It means whether the message was written to the buffer. Now we also know why the writing of a message can fail: the buffer is full. This will give the function caller sufficient information about what to do next. It should probably wait a while so that the buffer reader has enough time to read messages from the buffer and free up some space.

Below is a real-life example of C++ code where the comment and the function name do not match.

```
/**
 * @brief Add new counter or get existing, if same labels used already.
 * @param counterName Name of the counter
 * @param help Help text added for counter, if new countername
 * @param labels Specific labels for counter.
 * @return counter pointer used when increasing counter, or nullptr
 *         if metrics not initialized or invalid name or labels
 */
static prometheus::Counter* addCounter(
  std::string counterName,
  std::string help,
  const std::map<std::string, std::string>& labels
);
```

In the above example, the function name says that it adds a counter, but the comment says it adds or gets an existing counter. The real problem is that once someone first reads the function name addCounter, they do not necessarily read the 'brief' in the comments because they immediately understand what the function does after reading its name: it should add a counter. We could improve the function's name and rename it to addOrGetExistingCounter as a solution.

Below is a real-life Java example from a book that I once read:

```java
public interface Mediator {
  // To register an employee
  void register(Person person);

  // To send a message from one employee to another employee
  void connectEmployees(
    Person fromPerson,
    Person toPerson,
    String msg
  );

  // To display currently registered members
  void displayDetail();
}
```

There are three functions in the above example, each of which has a problem. The first function is registering a person, but the comment says it is registering an employee. So, there is a mismatch between the comment and the code. In this case, I trust the code over the comment. The correction is to remove the comment because it does not bring any value. It only causes confusion.

The second function says in the comment that it sends a message from one employee to another. The function name tells about connecting employees, but the parameters are persons. I assume that a part of the comment is correct: to send a message from someone to someone else. But once again, I trust the code more over the comment and assume the message is sent from one person to another. We should remove the comment and rename the function.

In the third function, the comment adds information missing from the function name. The comment also discusses members, as other parts of the code speak about employees and persons. There are three different terms used: employee, person, and member. Just one term should be picked. Let's choose the term *person* and use it systematically.

Below is the refactored version without the comments:

```java
public interface Mediator {
  void register(Person person);

  void send(
    String message,
    Person sender,
    Person recipient
  );

  void displayDetailsOfRegisteredPersons();
}
```

5.4.2: Single Return Of Named Value At The End Of Function

A function should have a single return statement and return a named value at the end. This allows the code reader to infer the meaning of the return value by looking at the end of the function.

This principle is relevant for return types that do not convey enough semantic meaning, such as numbers or strings. Boolean and object type return values often convey semantic meaning.

Consider the following C++ example:

Figure 5.8. Metrics.h

```
class Metrics
{
public:
  // ...

  static uint32_t addCounter(
    CounterFamily counterFamily,
    const std::map<std::string, std::string>& labels
  );

  static void incrementCounter(
    uint32_t counterIndex,
    size_t incrementAmount
  );

  // addGauge...
  // setGaugeValue...
}
```

What is the return value of the `addCounter` function? Someone might think a comment is needed to describe the return value because it is unclear what `uint32_t` means. Instead of writing a comment, we can introduce a named value (= variable/constant) to be returned from the function. The idea behind the named return value is that it communicates the semantics of the return value without the need for a comment. In C++, you jump from the function declaration to the function definition to see what the function returns. Below is the implementation for the `addCounter` function:

Figure 5.9. Metrics.cpp

```
uint32_t Metrics::addCounter(
  const CounterFamily counterFamily,
  const std::map<std::string, std::string>& labels)
{
  uint32_t counterIndex;

  // Perform adding a counter here and
  // set value for the 'counterIndex'

  return counterIndex;
}
```

In the above implementation, we have a single return of a named value at the end of the function. All we have to do is look at the end of the function and spot the return statement, which should tell us the meaning of the mysterious `uint32_t` typed return value: It is a counter index. We can spot that the `increaseCounter` function requires a `counterIndex` argument, and this establishes a connection between calling the `addCounter` function first, storing the returned counter index, and later using that stored counter index in calls to the `increaseCounter` function.

5.4.3: Return Type Aliasing

In the previous example, there was the mysterious return value of type `uint32_t` in the `addCounter` function. We learned how introducing a named value returned at the end of the function helped to communicate the semantics of the return value. But there is an even better way to communicate the semantics of a return value. Many languages like C++ and TypeScript offer type aliasing that can be used to communicate the return value semantics. Below is a C++ example where we introduce a `CounterIndex` type alias for the `uint32_t` type:

Figure 5.10. Metrics.h_

```cpp
class Metrics
{
public:
  using CounterIndex = uint32_t;

  // ...

  static CounterIndex addCounter(
    CounterFamily counterFamily,
    const std::map<std::string, std::string>& labels
  );

  static void incrementCounter(
    CounterIndex counterIndex,
    size_t incrementAmount
  );
}
```

Here is the same example in TypeScript:

Figure 5.11. Metrics.ts

```typescript
export type CounterIndex = number;

export default class Metrics {
  // ...

 static addCounter(
    counterFamily: CounterFamily,
    labels: Record<string, string>
  ): CounterIndex;

  static incrementCounter(
    counterIndex: CounterIndex,
    incrementAmount: number
  ): void;
}
```

Some languages, like Java, don't have type aliases. In that case, you can introduce a wrapper class for the returned value. Here is the same example in Java:

Figure 5.12. CounterIndex.java

```java
public class CounterIndex {
  private final int value;

  public CounterIndex(final int value) {
    this.value = value;
  }

  public int get() {
    return value;
  }
}
```

Figure 5.13. Metrics.java

```
public final class Metrics {
  // ...

  public static CounterIndex addCounter(
    final CounterFamily counterFamily,
    final Map<String, String> labels
  ) {
    // ...
  }

  public static void incrementCounter(
    CounterIndex counterIndex,
    double incrementAmount
  ) {
    // ...
  }
}
```

We can improve the above example. The CounterIndex class could be derived from a generic Value class:

```
public class Value<T> {
  private final T value;

  public Value(final T value) {
    this.value = value;
  }

  public T get() {
    return value;
  }
}

public class CounterIndex extends Value<Integer> {
  // ...
}
```

We can improve the above metrics example a lot. First, we should avoid the primitive type obsession. We should not be returning an index from the addCounter method, but we should rename the method as createCounter and return an instance of a Counter class from the method. Then we should make the example more object-oriented by moving the incrementCounter method to the Counter class and naming it just increment. Also, the name of the Metrics class should be changed to MetricFactory. Finally, we should make the MetricFactory class a singleton instead of containing static methods.

5.4.4: Extract Constant for Boolean Expression

By extracting a constant for a boolean expression, we can eliminate comments. Below is an example where a comment is written after an if-statement and its boolean expression:

Figure 5.14. MessageBuffer.cpp

```cpp
bool MessageBuffer::writeIfBufferNotFull(
  const std::shared_ptr<Message>& message
) {
  bool messageWasWritten{false};

  if (m_messages.size() < m_maxBufferSize)
  {
    // Buffer is not full
    m_messages.push_back(message);
    messageWasWritten = true;
  }

  return messageWasWritten;
}
```

By introducing a constant to be used in the "buffer is full" check, we can get rid of the "Buffer is not full" comment:

Figure 5.15. MessageBuffer.cpp

```cpp
bool MessageBuffer::writeIfBufferNotFull(
  const std::shared_ptr<Message> message
) {
  bool messageWasWritten{false};

  const bool bufferIsNotFull =
    m_messages.size() < m_maxBufferSize;

  if (bufferIsNotFull)
  {
    m_messages.push_back(message);
    messageWasWritten = true;
  }

  return messageWasWritten;
}
```

When writing comparison expressions, remember to write the comparison so that it is fluent to read:

```
// Wrong, not fluent to read
if ('John' === customerName) {
  // ...
}

// Correct
if (customerName === 'John') {
  // ...
}

// Wrong
bufferIsNotFull = maxLength > messages.length;

// Correct
bufferIsNotFull = messages.length < maxLength;
```

You should also have matching names for the variables being compared:

```
// Correct
bufferIsNotFull = messages.length < maxLength;

// Incorrect
// Left side of comparison speaks about length and
// right side speaks about size
bufferIsNotFull = messages.length < maxSize;
```

5.4.5: Extract Named Constant or Enumerated Type

If you encounter a magic number[1] in your code, you should introduce either a named constant or an enumerated type (enum) for that value. In the below example, we are returning two magic numbers, 0 and 1:

Figure 5.16. main.cpp

```
int main()
{
  Application application;

  if (application.run())
  {
    // Application was run successfully
    return 0;
  }

  // Exit code: failure
  return 1;
}
```

Let's introduce an enumerated type, ExitCode, and use it instead of magic numbers:

Figure 5.17. main.cpp

```
enum class ExitCode
{
  Success = 0,
  Failure = 1
};

int main()
{
  Application application;
  const bool appWasRun = application.run();

  return static_cast<int>(
    appWasRun ? ExitCode::Success : ExitCode::Failure
  );
}
```

It is now easy to add more exit codes with descriptive names later if needed.

5.4.6: Extract Function

If you are planning to write a comment above a piece of code, you should extract that piece of code to a new function. When you extract a well-named function, you don't need to write that comment. The name of the newly extracted function serves as documentation. Below is an example with some commented code:

---

[1]https://en.wikipedia.org/wiki/Magic_number_(programming)

Figure 5.18. MessageBuffer.cpp

```
void MessageBuffer::writeFitting(
  std::deque<std::shared_ptr<Message>>& messages
) {
  if (m_messages.size() + messages.size() <= m_maxBufferSize)
  {
    // All messages fit in buffer
    m_messages.insert(m_messages.end(),
                      messages.begin(),
                      messages.end());

    messages.clear();
  }
  else
  {
    // All messages do not fit, write only messages that fit
    const auto messagesEnd = messages.begin() +
                             m_maxBufferSize -
                             m_messages.size();

    m_messages.insert(m_messages.end(),
                      messages.begin(),
                      messagesEnd);

    messages.erase(messages.begin(), messagesEnd);
  }
}
```

Here is the same code with comments refactored out by extracting two new methods:

Figure 5.19. MessageBuffer.cpp

```
void MessageBuffer::writeFitting(
  std::deque<std::shared_ptr<Message>>& messages
) { const bool allMessagesFit = m_messages.size() +
                                messages.size() <= m_maxBufferSize;

  if (allMessagesFit)
  {
    writeAll(messages)
  }
  else
  {
    writeOnlyFitting(messages);
  }
}

void MessageBuffer::writeAll(
  std::deque<std::shared_ptr<Message>>& messages
) {
  m_messages.insert(m_messages.end(),
                    messages.begin(),
                    messages.end());

  messages.clear();
}

void MessageBuffer::writeOnlyFitting(
  std::deque<std::shared_ptr<Message>>& messages
) {
  const auto messageCountThatFit = m_maxBufferSize -
                                   m_messages.size();

  const auto messagesEnd = messages.begin() +
                           messageCountThatFit;
```

```
m_messages.insert(m_messages.end(),
                  messages.begin(),
                  messagesEnd);

messages.erase(messages.begin(), messagesEnd);
}
```

5.4.7: Avoid Comments for Regular Expression

When you have a complex regular expression, you might be tempted to attach a comment to it to explain the meaning of it. But there is an alternative way. You can split the complex regular expression into well-named parts and construct the final regular expression from those well-named parts. For example, suppose you must create a regular expression to validate phone numbers in the international format. In that case, you can split the regular expression into the following parts: plus sign, country code, area code, and the rest of the phone number (local number). You can define the regular expression using the parts: `intlPhoneNbrRegExpr = plusSign + countryCode + areaCode + localNumber`.

5.4.8: Name Anonymous Function

Anonymous functions are common in functional programming, e.g., when using algorithms like *forEach*, *map, filter*, and *reduce*. When an anonymous function is long or complex, you should give it a descriptive name and split it into multiple functions if it is too long. This way, you can eliminate comments.

In the below TypeScript example, we have an anonymous function with a comment:

```
// ...
fs.watchFile('/etc/config/LOG_LEVEL', () => {
  // Update new log level
  try {
    const newLogLevel = fs.readFileSync('/etc/config/LOG_LEVEL',
                                        'utf-8'}).trim();
    tryValidateLogLevel(newLogLevel);
    process.env.LOG_LEVEL = newLogLevel;
  } catch (error) {
    // ...
  }
});
```

We can refactor the above example so that the comment is removed and the anonymous function is given a name:

```
function updateNewLogLevel() {
  try {
    const newLogLevel = fs.readFileSync('/etc/config/LOG_LEVEL',
                                        'utf-8'}).trim();
    tryValidateLogLevel(newLogLevel);
    process.env.LOG_LEVEL = newLogLevel;
  } catch (error) {
    // ...
  }
}

fs.watchFile('/etc/config/LOG_LEVEL', updateNewLogLevel);
```

5.4.9: Avoiding Comments in Bash Shell Scripts

Many programmers, myself included, don't enjoy the mysterious syntax of Linux shell commands and scripts. Even the syntax of the simplest expressions can be hard to understand and remember if you don't regularly work with scripts and commands. Of course, the best thing is to avoid writing complex Linux shell scripts and use a proper programming language like Python instead. But sometimes, performing some actions using a shell script is easier. Because the syntax and commands in shell scripts can be hard to understand, many developers tend to solve the problem by adding comments to scripts.

Next, alternative ways to make scripts more understandable without comments are presented. Let's consider the below example from one real-life script I have bumped into:

```
create_network() {
  #create only if not existing yet
  if [[ -z "$(docker network ls | grep $DOCKER_NETWORK_NAME )" ]];
  then
    echo Creating $DOCKER_NETWORK_NAME
    docker network create $DOCKER_NETWORK_NAME
  else
    echo Network $DOCKER_NETWORK_NAME already exists
  fi
}
```

Below is the same example with the following changes:

- The comment was removed, and the earlier commented expression was moved to a well-named function
- The negation in the expression was removed, and the contents of the *then* and *else* branches were swapped
- Variable names were made camel case to enhance readability. All-caps names are harder to read.

```
dockerNetworkExists() { [[ -n "$(docker network ls | grep $1 )" ]]; }

createDockerNetwork() {
  if dockerNetworkExists $networkName; then
    echo Docker network $networkName already exists
  else
    echo Creating Docker network $networkName
    docker network create $networkName
  fi
}
```

If your script accepts arguments, give the arguments proper names, for example:

```
dataFilePathName=$1
schemaFilePathName=$2
```

The script reader does not have to remember what $1 or $2 means, and you don't have to insert any comments to clarify the meaning of the arguments.

If you have a complex command in a Bash shell script, you should not attach a comment to it but extract a function with a proper name to describe the command.

The below example contains a comment:

```
# Update version in Helm Chart.yaml file
sed -i "s/^version:.*/version: $VERSION/g" helm/service/Chart.yaml
```

Here is the above example refactored to contain a function and a call to it:

```
updateHelmChartVersionInChartYamlFile() {
  sed -i "s/^version:.*/version: $1/g" helm/service/Chart.yaml
}

updateHelmChartVersionInChartYamlFile $version
```

Here is another example:

```
getFileLongestLineLength() {
  echo $(awk '{ if (length($0) > max) max = length($0) } END { print max }' $1)
}

configFileLongestLineLength = $(getFileLongestLineLength $configFilePathName)
```

5.5: Function Single Return Principle

Prefer a single return statement at the end of a function to clearly communicate the return value's meaning and make refactoring the function easier.

A single return statement with a named value at the end of a function clearly communicates the return value semantics if the return value type does not directly communicate it. For example, if you return a value of a primitive type like an integer or string from a function, it is not necessarily 100% clear what the return value means. But when you return a named value at the end of the function, the name of the returned variable communicates the semantics.

You might think that being unable to return a value in the middle of a function would make the function less readable because of lots of nested if-statements. This is possible, but one should remember that a function should be small. Aim to have a maximum of 5-9 lines of statements in a single function. Following that rule, you never have *a hell of nested if-statements* inside a single function.

Having a single return statement at the end of a function makes refactoring the function easier. You can use automated refactoring tools provided by your IDE. It is always harder to extract a new function from code containing a return statement. The same applies to loops with a *break* or *continue* statement. It is easier to refactor code inside a loop that does not contain a break or continue statement.

In some cases, returning a single value at the end of a function makes the code more straightforward and requires fewer lines of code.

Below is an example of a function with two return locations:

Figure 5.20. TransformThread.cpp

```cpp
bool TransformThread::transform(
  const std::shared_ptr<InputMessage>& inputMessage
) {
  auto outputMessage = m_outputMessagePool->acquireMessage();
  bool messageIsFilteredIn;

  const bool messageWasTransformed =
    m_messageTransformer->transform(inputMessage,
                                    outputMessage,
                                    messageIsFilteredIn);

  if (messageWasTransformed && messageIsFilteredIn)
  {
    m_outputMessages.push_back(outputMessage);
  }
  else
  {
    m_outputMessagePool->returnMessage(outputMessage);

    if (!messageWasTransformed)
    {
      return false;
    }
  }

  return true;
}
```

When analyzing the above function, we notice that it transforms an input message into an output message. We can conclude that the function returns *true* on successful message transformation. We can shorten the function by refactoring it to contain only one return statement. After refactoring, it is 100% clear what the function return value means.

Figure 5.21. TransformThread.cpp

```cpp
bool TransformThread::transform(
  const std::shared_ptr<InputMessage>& inputMessage
) {
  auto outputMessage = m_outputMessagePool->acquireMessage();
  bool messageIsFilteredIn;

  const bool messageWasTransformed =
      m_messageTransformer->transform(inputMessage,
                                      outputMessage,
                                      messageIsFilteredIn);

  if (messageWasTransformed && messageIsFilteredIn)
  {
    m_outputMessages.push_back(outputMessage);
  }
  else
  {
    m_outputMessagePool->return(outputMessage);
  }

  return messageWasTransformed;
}
```

As an exception to this rule, you can have multiple return statements in a function when the function has optimal length and would become too long if it is refactored to contain a single return statement. Additionally, it is required that the semantic meaning of the return value is evident from the function name or the return type of the function. This is usually true if the return value is a boolean value or an object. You can use so-called guard clauses[2] at the beginning of the function. These guard clauses are if-statements that can return early from the function if a certain condition is met. You can have multiple guard clauses. Here is a Java example of a guard clause:

```java
public Optional<Session> getSession(final String userName){
    if (userName.isEmpty()) {
        return Optional.empty();
    }

    // Rest of the method code follows here...
}
```

Below is an example of a function with multiple return statements. It is also clear from the function \ name what the return value means. Also, the length of the function is optimal: seven statements.

```ts
private areEqual(
  iterator: MyIterator<T>,
  anotherIterator: MyIterator<T>
): boolean {
  while (iterator.hasNextElement()) {
    if (anotherIterator.hasNextElement()) {
      if (iterator.getNextElement() !==
          anotherIterator.getNextElement()) {
       return false;
      }
    } else {
      return false;
    }
  }

  return true;
}
```

If we refactored the above code to contain a single return statement, the code would become too long (10 statements) to fit in one function, as shown below. In this case, we would prefer the above code over the code below.

```
private areEqual(
  iterator: MyIterator<T>,
  anotherIterator: MyIterator<T>
): boolean {
  let areEqual = true;

  while (iterator.hasNextElement()) {
    if (anotherIterator.hasNextElement()) {
      if (iterator.getNextElement() !==
          anotherIterator.getNextElement()) {
       areEqual = false;
       break;
      }
    } else {
      areEqual = false;
      break;
    }
  }

  return areEqual;
}
```

---

[2]https://en.wikipedia.org/wiki/Guard_(computer_science)

As the second exception to this rule, you can use multiple return locations in a factory because you know from the factory name what type of objects it creates. Below is an example factory with multiple return statements:

```cpp
enum class CarType
{
  Audi,
  Bmw,
  MercedesBenz
};

class Car
{
  // ...
};

class Audi : public Car
{
  // ...
};

class Bmw : public Car
{
  // ...
};

class MercedesBenz : public Car
{
  // ...
};

class CarFactory
{
public:
  std::shared_ptr<Car> createCar(const CarType carType)
  {
    switch(carType)
    {
      case CarType::Audi:
        return std::make_shared<Audi>();
      case CarType::Bmw:
        return std::make_shared<Bmw>();
      case CarType::MercedesBenz:
        return std::make_shared<MercedesBenz>();
      default:
        throw std::invalid_argument("Unknown car type");
    }
  }
};
```

5.6: Prefer a Statically Typed Language for Production Code Principle

Prefer a statically typed language when implementing production software. You can use an untyped language like Python for non-production code like integration, end-to-end and automated non-functional tests. And you can use Bash shell scripting for small scripts.

You can manage with a trivial software component without types, but when it grows bigger and more people are involved, the benefits of static typing become evident.

Let's analyze what potential problems using an untyped language might incur:

- Function arguments might be given in the wrong order
- Function argument might be given with the wrong type
- Function return value type might be misunderstood
- Refactoring code is more difficult
- Forced to write public API comments to describe function signatures
- Type errors are not necessarily found in testing

5.6.1: Function Arguments Might Be Given in Wrong Order

When not using type annotations for functions, you can accidentally give function arguments in the wrong order. When you use type annotations, this kind of error is less common. Modern IDEs can display inlay hints for parameters in a function call. This is a feature you should consider enabling in your IDE. Those parameter hints might reveal cases where arguments for a function are not given in the correct order.

5.6.2: Function Argument Might Be Given with Wrong Type

You can give a function argument with the wrong type when type annotations are not used. For example, a function requires a string representation of a number, but you provide a number. Correctly naming function arguments can help. Instead of naming a string argument, *amount*, the argument should be named as *amountString* or *amountAsString*.

5.6.3: Function Return Value Type Might Be Misunderstood

Determining the function return value type can be difficult. It is not necessarily 100% clear from the name of the function. For example, if you have a function named `getValue`, the return value type is not 100% clear. It might be apparent only if you know the context of the function well. As an improvement, the function should be appropriately named, for example: `getValueAsString()`, if the returned value is always a string. If the return value type is unclear when looking at the function name, you must analyze the function's source code to determine the return value type. That is unnecessary and error-prone manual work that can be avoided using function return type annotations.

5.6.4: Refactoring Code Is More Difficult

Refactoring code is usually more difficult if you don't have type annotations. But when you have type annotations and make a change to, e.g., a function argument type, you will get type check errors in parts of code where this function is called. Then, it is easy to refactor those parts. But if you didn't have type annotations and made this same change, you would have to manually find all the places where a change is needed, which is clearly more error-prone.

5.6.5: Forced to Write Public API Comments

You might be forced to document a public API using comments when not using type annotations. That is additional work that could be avoided by using type annotations. Writing API documentation with comments is error-prone. You can accidentally write wrong information in the API documentation or forget to update the documentation when you make changes to the API code itself. Similarly, the API documentation readers can make mistakes. They might not read the API documentation at all. Or they have read it earlier but later misremembered it.

5.6.6: Type Errors Are Not Found in Testing

This is the biggest problem. You might think that if you have mistakes in your code related to having correct function arguments with the correct types, testing will reveal those mistakes. This is typically a wrong assumption. Unit tests won't find the issues because you mock other classes and their methods. You can only find the issues in integration testing when you integrate the software component (i.e., test functions calling other real functions instead of mocks). According to the testing pyramid, integration tests only cover a subset of the codebase, less than unit tests. Depending on the code coverage of the integration tests, some function argument order or argument/return value type correctness issues may be left untested and escape to production.

5.7: Refactoring Principle

You cannot write the perfect code on the first try, so you should always reserve some time for future refactoring.

You must refactor even if you write code for a new software component. Refactoring is not related to legacy codebases only. If you don't refactor, you let technical debt grow in the software. The main idea behind refactoring is that no one can write the perfect code on the first try. Refactoring means that you change code without changing the actual functionality. After refactoring, most tests should still pass, the code is organized differently, and you have a better object-oriented design and improved naming of things. Refactoring does not usually affect integration tests but can affect unit tests depending on the type and scale of refactoring. Keep this in mind when estimating refactoring effort. When you practice test-driven development (TDD), you are bound to refactor. Refactoring is a practice built into the TDD process. In TDD, the final function implementation results from a series of refactorings. This is one of the biggest benefits of TDD. We will discuss TDD more in the next chapter.

Software developers don't necessarily reserve any or enough time for refactoring when they plan things. When we provide work estimates for epics, features, and user stories, we should be conscious of the need to refactor and add some extra time to our initial work estimates (which don't include refactoring). When you use TDD, you start automatically reserving some time for refactoring because refactoring is an integral part of the TDD process. Refactoring is work that is not necessarily understood clearly by the management. The management should support the need to refactor even if it does not bring clear added value to an end user. But it brings value by not letting the codebase rot and removing technical debt. If you have software with lots of accumulated technical debt, developing new features and maintaining the software is costly. Also, the quality of the software is lower, which can manifest in several bugs and lowered customer satisfaction.

Below is a list of the most common code smells[3] and refactoring techniques to resolve them:

---

[3] https://en.wikipedia.org/wiki/Code_smell

Code Smell	Refactoring Solution
Non-descriptive name	Rename
Long method	Extract method
Large class	Extract class
Complex expression	Extract constant
Long switch-case or if/elif/else statement	Replace conditionals with polymorphism
Long parameter list	Introduce parameter object
Shotgun surgery	Replace conditionals with polymorphism
Negated boolean condition	Invert if-statement
Anemic object	Creating rich object

There are other refactoring techniques, but the ones explained here are the most relevant and valuable. You can find other refactoring techniques in *Martin Fowler*'s book *Refactoring*. Some of the refactorings presented in that book are pretty self-evident for experienced OOP practitioners; others are also handled in this book but scattered around and described as part of different principles and patterns, and some refactorings are primarily for legacy code only. You don't need them when writing new code with appropriate linter settings active. One example of such a refactoring is "Remove Assignments to Parameters". You don't need that when writing new code because you should have a linting rule that disallows assignments to parameters.

5.7.1: Rename

This is probably the single most used refactoring technique. You often don't get the names right on the first try and need to do renaming. Modern IDEs offer tools that help rename things in the code: interfaces, classes, functions, and variables. The IDE's renaming functionality is always better than the plain old search-and-replace method. When using the search-and-replace method, you can accidentally rename something you do not want to be renamed or don't rename something that should have been renamed.

5.7.2: Extract Method

This is probably the second most used refactoring technique. When you implement a public method of a class, the method quickly grows in the number of code lines. A function should contain a maximum of 5-9 statements to keep it readable and understandable. When a public method is too long, you should extract one or more private methods and call these private methods from the public method. Every modern IDE has an *extract method* refactoring tool that allows you to extract private methods easily. Select the code lines you want to extract to a new method and press the IDE's shortcut key for the *extract method* functionality. Then, give a descriptive name for the extracted method, and you are done. (An additional thing you can do is organize the arguments for the extracted method in better order before completing the extraction in the IDE). In some cases, the refactoring is not automatic. For example, if the code to be extracted contains a *return*, *break*, or *continue* statement, that affects the execution flow of the function (causing multiple return points). To keep your code refactorable, avoid using *break* and *continue* statements and have only a single return statement at the end of the function.

5.7.3: Extract Class

This refactoring technique is used to make a large class smaller. A large class contains several hundreds of lines of code or tens of methods. To make a class smaller, you need to extract one or more behavioral classes from it and use them in the original class. This refactoring technique allows you to use the *strategy pattern* described in the previous chapter. Let's have a simple example with a Bird class, which we assume to be large:

```
public class Bird {
  public void move() {
    // This method uses the below helper methods
  }

  public void makeSound() {
    // This method uses the below helper methods
  }

  // Possibly some other public methods ...

  private void moveHelper1() {
    // ...
  }

  // ...

  private void moveHelper4() {
    // ...
  }


  private void makeSoundHelper1() {
    // ...
  }

  // ...

  private void makeSoundHelper4() {
    // ...
  }
}
```

To make the above class smaller, we can extract two behavioral classes: BirdMover and BirdSoundMaker. After refactoring, we have the following classes:

```
public interface BirdMover {
  void move();
}


public class BirdMoverImpl implements BirdMover {
  public void move() {
    // Use the below helper methods ...
  }

  private void moveHelper1() {
    // ...
  }

  // ...

  private void moveHelper4() {
    // ...
  }
}
```

```
public interface BirdSoundMaker {
  void makeSound();
}


public class BirdSoundMakerImpl implements BirdSoundMaker {
  public void makeSound() {
    // Use the below helper methods ...
  }

  private void makeSoundHelper1() {
    // ...
  }

  // ...

  private void makeSoundHelper4() {
    // ...
  }
}


public class Bird {
  private final BirdMover mover;
  private final BirdSoundMaker soundMaker;

  public Bird(final BirdMover mover, final BirdSoundMaker soundMaker) {
    this.mover = mover;
    this.soundMaker = soundMaker;
  }

  public void move() {
    // Call mover.move()
  }

  public void makeSound() {
    // Call soundMaker.makeSound()
  }

  // Possibly some other public methods ...
}
```

The above solution allows us to use the *strategy pattern*. We can introduce new classes that implement the BirdMover and BirdSoundMaker interfaces and supply them to the Bird class constructor. We can now modify the behavior of the Bird class using the *open-closed principle*.

5.7.4: Extract Constant

If you have a complex expression (boolean or numeric), assign the value of the expression to a constant. The name of the constant conveys information about the expression. Below is a JavaScript example where we make the if-statements read better by extracting expressions to constants:

```
// ...

if (dataSourceSelectorIsOpen &&
    measureSelectorIsOpen &&
    dimensionSelectorIsOpen
) {
  dataSourceSelectorContentElem.style.height =
    `${0.2 * availableHeight}px`;

  measureSelectorContentElem.style.height =
    `${0.4 * availableHeight}px`;

  dimensionSelectorContentElem.style.height =
    `${0.4 * availableHeight}px`;
} else if (!dataSourceSelectorIsOpen &&
           !measureSelectorIsOpen &&
           dimensionSelectorIsOpen
) {
    dimensionSelectorContentElem.style.height
      = `${availableHeight}px`;
}
```

Let's extract constants:

```
// ...

const allSelectorsAreOpen = dataSourceSelectorIsOpen &&
                            measureSelectorIsOpen &&
                            dimensionSelectorIsOpen;

const onlyDimensionSelectorIsOpen =
    !dataSourceSelectorIsOpen &&
    !measureSelectorIsOpen &&
    dimensionSelectorIsOpen;

if (allSelectorsAreOpen) {
  dataSourceSelectorContentElem.style.height =
    `${0.2 * availableHeight}px`;

  measureSelectorContentElem.style.height =
    `${0.4 * availableHeight}px`;

  dimensionSelectorContentElem.style.height =
    `${0.4 * availableHeight}px`;
} else if (onlyDimensionSelectorIsOpen) {
  dimensionSelectorContentElem.style.height =
    `${availableHeight}px`;
}
```

Below is an example in C++ where we return a boolean expression:

```
bool AvroFieldSchema::equals(
  const std::shared_ptr<AvroFieldSchema>& otherFieldSchema
) const
{
  return m_type == otherFieldSchema->getType() &&
         m_name.substr(m_name.find_first_of('.') + 1U) ==
         otherFieldSchema->getName().substr(
          otherFieldSchema->getName().find_first_of('.') + 1U);
}
```

It can be challenging to understand what the boolean expression means. We could improve the function by adding a comment: (We assume that each field name has a root namespace that cannot contain a dot character)

```
bool AvroFieldSchema::equals(
    const std::shared_ptr<AvroFieldSchema>& otherFieldSchema
) const
{
  // Field schemas are equal if field types are equal and
  // field names without the root namespace are equal
  return m_type == otherFieldSchema->getType() &&
         m_name.substr(m_name.find_first_of('.') + 1U) ==
         otherFieldSchema->getName().substr(
           otherFieldSchema->getName().find_first_of('.') + 1U);
}
```

However, we should not write comments because comments are never 100% trustworthy. It is possible that a comment and the related code are not in synchrony: someone has changed the function without updating the comment or modified only the comment but did not change the function. Let's refactor the above example by removing the comment and extracting multiple constants. The below function is longer than the original, but it is, of course, more readable. If you look at the last two statements of the method, you can understand in what case two field schemas are equal. It should be the compiler's job to make the below longer version of the function as performant as the original function.

```
bool AvroFieldSchema::equals(
    const std::shared_ptr<AvroFieldSchema>& otherFieldSchema
) const
{
  const auto fieldNameWithoutRootNamespace =
    m_name.substr(m_name.find_first_of('.') + 1U);

  const auto otherFieldName = otherFieldSchema->getName();

  const auto otherFieldNameWithoutRootNamespace =
    otherFieldName.substr(otherFieldName.find_first_of('.') + 1U);

  const bool fieldTypesAndNamesWithoutRootNsAreEqual =
    m_type == otherFieldSchema->getType() &&
    fieldNameWithoutRootNamespace == otherFieldNameWithoutRootNamespace;

  return fieldTypesAndNamesWithoutRootNsAreEqual;
}
```

5.7.5: Replace Conditionals with Polymorphism

Suppose you encounter a sizeable match-case statement or if/else-structure in your code (not considering code in factories). This means that your software component does not have a proper object-oriented design. You should replace the conditionals with polymorphism. When you introduce proper OOD in your software component, you move the functionality from a match statement's case branches to different classes that implement a particular interface. And similarly, you move the code from if and elif-statements to different classes that implement a specific interface. This way, you can eliminate the switch-case and if/else-statements and replace them with polymorphic method calls. Crafting proper OOD helps in creating a software component with classes that have high cohesion. The functionality of the classes is no longer scattered around in the codebase.

Below is a TypeScript example of non-object-oriented design:

```
function doSomethingWith(chart: Chart) {
  if (chart.getType() === 'column') {
    // do this
  } else if (chart.getType() === 'pie') {
    // do that
  } else if (chart.getType() === 'geographic-map') {
    // do a third thing
  }
}
```

Let's replace the above conditionals with polymorphism:

```
interface Chart {
  doSomething(...): void;
}

class ColumnChart implements Chart {
  doSomething(...): void {
    // do this
  }
}

class PieChart implements Chart {
  doSomething(...): void {
    // do that
  }
}

class GeographicMapChart implements Chart {
  doSomething(...): void {
    // do a third thing
  }
}

function doSomethingWith(chart: Chart) {
  chart.doSomething();
}
```

Suppose you are implementing a data visualization application and have many places in your code where you check the chart type and need to introduce a new chart type. It could mean you must add a new *case* or *elif* statement in many places in the code. This approach is very error-prone. It is called *shotgun surgery* because you need to find all the places in the codebase where the code needs to be modified. What you should do is conduct proper object-oriented design and introduce a new chart class containing the new functionality instead of introducing that new functionality by modifying code in multiple places.

5.7.6: Introduce Parameter Object

If you have more than 5-7 parameters for a function, you should introduce a parameter object to reduce the number of parameters to keep the function signature more readable. Below is an example constructor with too many parameters:

Figure 5.22. KafkaConsumer.java

```
public class KafkaConsumer {
  public KafkaConsumer(
    final List<String> brokers,
    final List<String> topics,
    final List<String> extraConfigEntries,
    final boolean tlsIsUsed,
    final boolean certShouldBeVerified,
    final String caFilePathName,
    final String certFilePathName,
    final String keyFilePathName)
  {
    // ...
  }
}
```

Let's group the Transport Layer Security (TLS) related parameters to a parameter class named TlsOptions:

Figure 5.23. TlsOptions.java

```
public class TlsOptions {
  public TlsOptions(
    final boolean tlsIsUsed,
    final boolean certShouldBeVerified,
    final String caFilePathName,
    final String certFilePathName,
    final String keyFilePathName
  ) {
    // ...
  }
}
```

Now we can modify the KafkaConsumer constructor to utilize the TlsOptions parameter class:

Figure 5.24. KafkaConsumer.java

```
public class KafkaConsumer {
  public KafkaConsumer(
    final List<String> brokers,
    final List<String> topics,
    final List<String> extraConfigEntries,
    final TlsOptions tlsOptions
  ) {
    // ...
  }
}
```

5.7.7: Invert If-Statement

This is a refactoring that a modern IDE can do for you.

Below is a Python example with a negated boolean expression in the if-statement condition. Notice how difficult the boolean expression reads: host_mount_folder is not None. It is a double-negative statement and thus can be difficult to read.

```
import os

def get_behave_test_folder(relative_test_folder = ""):
  host_mount_folder = os.environ.get("HOST_MOUNT_FOLDER")

  if host_mount_folder is not None:
    final_host_mount_folder = host_mount_folder
    if host_mount_folder.startswith("/mnt/c/"):
      final_host_mount_folder = host_mount_folder.replace("/mnt/c/", \
                                                          "/c/", 1)

    behave_test_folder = final_host_mount_folder + "/" + \
                         relative_test_folder
  else:
    behave_test_folder = os.getcwd()

  return behave_test_folder
```

Let's refactor the above code so that the if and else statements are inverted:

```
def get_behave_test_folder(relative_test_folder = ""):
  host_mount_folder = os.environ.get("HOST_MOUNT_FOLDER")

  if host_mount_folder is None:
    behave_test_folder = os.getcwd()
  else:
    final_host_mount_folder = host_mount_folder
    if host_mount_folder.startswith("/mnt/c/"):
      final_host_mount_folder = host_mount_folder.replace("/mnt/c/", \
                                                          "/c/", 1)
    behave_test_folder = final_host_mount_folder + "/" + \
                         relative_test_folder

  return behave_test_folder
```

Below is another example in C++:

```
if (somePointer != nullptr)
{
  // Do thing 1
}
else
{
  // Do thing 2
}
```

We should not have a negation in the if-statement's condition. Let's refactor the above example:

```
if (somePointer == nullptr)
{
  // Do thing 2
}
else
{
  // Do thing 1
}
```

5.7.8: Creating Rich Object

An object can be a so-called anemic object[4] with little or no behavior. The object class might only contain attributes and getters and setters for them, making it a kind of data class only. Sometimes, this is okay if there is no business logic related to the object, but many times, there exists some business logic, but that logic is not implemented in the anemic object class itself but in other places in the code. This kind of software "design" (a better term is lack of design) is deemed to be problematic when you need to change the anemic object class. You might need to make changes to various unrelated places in the code. Making all these changes is manual and error-prone work. Making those changes is called shotgun surgery[5]. What you should do is make an anemic object a rich object. This is done by moving behavior from other classes to the anemic class, making it a rich class. A rich class typically has attributes and behavior but it lacks getters and setters to enforce proper encapsulation of the object state.

Let's have an example of a anemic class:

```
public class Rectangle {
  private float width;
  private float height;

  public Rectangle(final float width, final float height) {
    this.width = width;
    this.height = height;
  }

  public float getWidth() {
    return width;
  }

  public float getHeight() {
    return height;
  }

  public void setWidth(final float width) {
    this.width = width;
  }

  public void setHeight(final float height) {
    this.height = height;
  }
}

public class Drawer {
  // Possible other methods ...

  public void drawRectangle(final Rectangle rectangle) {
    // ...
  }
}

public class Calculator {
  // Possible other methods

  public float calcRectArea(final Rectangle rectangle) {
    // ...
  }

  public float calcRectPerimeter(final Rectangle rectangle) {
    // ...
```

---

[4]https://en.wikipedia.org/wiki/Anemic_domain_model
[5]https://en.wikipedia.org/wiki/Shotgun_surgery

```
  }
}

public class Sizer {
  // Possible other methods

  public void increaseRectWidth(
    final Rectangle rectangle,
    final float percentage
  ) {
    // ...
  }


  public void increaseRectHeight(
    final Rectangle rectangle,
    final float percentage
  ) {
    // ...
  }
}
```

What we should do is to make the `Rectangle` objects rich objects by moving functionality from various classes into the `Rectangle` class and removing the getters and setters:

```
public class Rectangle {
  private float width;
  private float height;

  public Rectangle(final float width, final float height) {
    this.width = width;
    this.height = height;
  }

  public void draw() {
    // Implement drawing here ...
  }

  public float calculateArea() {
    // Calculate area here ...
  }

  public float calculatePerimeter() {
    // Calculate perimeter here ...
  }

  public void increaseWidth(final float percentage) {
    // Increase width here ...
  }

  public void increaseHeight(final float percentage) {
    // Increase height here ...
  }
}
```

Let's imagine that the methods added to the `Rectangle` class are large, and the whole class becomes too large. In that case, we can use the *bridge pattern* and refactor the classes as shown below. We still have a rich `Rectangle` class with attached behavior, and we do not need any getters or setters because we are not passing the `this` to any outside object of the `Rectangle` class.

```
public interface Drawer {
  void drawRectangle(final float width, final float height);

  // Possible other methods ...
}


public interface Calculator {
  float calcRectArea(final float width, final float height);
  float calcRectPerimeter(final float width, final float height);

  // Possible other methods ...
}


public interface Sizer {
  float increase(final float length, final float percentage);

  // Possible other methods ...
}


public class Rectangle {
  private float width;
  private float height;
  private final Drawer drawer;
  private final Calculator calculator;
  private final Sizer sizer;

  public Rectangle(
    final float width,
    final float height,
    final Drawer drawer,
    final Calculator calculator,
    final Sizer sizer
  ) {
    this.width = width;
    this.height = height;
    this.drawer = drawer;
    this.calculator = calculator;
    this.sizer = sizer;
  }

  public void draw() {
    drawer.drawRectangle(width, height);
  }

  public float calculateArea() {
    return calculator.calcRectArea(width, height);
  }

  public float calculatePerimeter() {
    return calculator.calcRectPerimeter(width, height);
  }

  public void increaseWidth(final float percentage) {
    width = sizer.increase(width, percentage);
  }

  public void increaseHeight(final float percentage) {
    height = sizer.increase(height, percentage);
  }
}
```

You can see from the above code that we no longer need to perform *shotgun surgery* if we need to change the Rectangle class. For example, let's say that our rectangles should always have a height double the width. We can refactor the Rectangle class to the following:

```
public class Rectangle {
  private float width;
  private float height;
  private final Drawer drawer;
  private final Calculator calculator;
  private final Sizer sizer;

  public Rectangle(
    final float width,
    final Drawer drawer,
    final Calculator calculator,
    final Sizer sizer
  ) {
    this.width = width;
    this.height = 2 * width;
    this.drawer = drawer;
    this.calculator = calculator;
    this.sizer = sizer;
  }

  public void draw() {
    drawer.drawRectangle(width, height);
  }

  public float calculateArea() {
    return calculator.calcRectArea(width, height);
  }

  public float calculatePerimeter() {
    return calculator.calcRectPerimeter(width, height);
  }

  public void increaseWidth(final float percentage) {
    width = sizer.increase(width, percentage);
    height = 2 * width;
  }

  public void increaseHeight(final float percentage) {
    height = sizer.increase(height, percentage);
    width = height / 2;
  }
}
```

5.8: Static Code Analysis Principle

Let the computer find bugs and issues in the code for you.

Static code analysis tools find bugs and design-related issues on your behalf. Use multiple static code analysis tools to get the full benefit. Different tools might detect different issues. Using static code analysis tools frees people's time in code reviews to focus on things that automation cannot tackle.

Below is a list of some common static code analysis tools for different languages:

- Java

  - Jetbrains IntelliJ IDEA IDE inspections
  - SonarLint
  - SonarQube/SonarCloud

- C++

     – Jetbrains CLion IDE inspections
     – Clang-Tidy
     – MISRA C++ 2008 guidelines
     – CppCheck
     – SonarLint
     – SonarQube/SonarCloud

- TypeScript

     – Jetbrains WebStorm IDE inspections
     – ESLint (+ various plugins, like TypeScript plugin)
     – SonarLint
     – SonarQube/SonarCloud

Infrastructure and deployment code should be treated the same way as source code. Remember to run static code analysis tools on your infrastructure and deployment code, too. Several tools are available for analyzing infrastructure and deployment code, like *Checkcov*, which can be used for analyzing Terraform, Kubernetes, and Helm code. Helm tool contains a linting command to analyze Helm chart files, and *Hadolint* is a tool for analyzing *Dockerfiles* statically.

5.8.1: Common Static Code Analysis Issues

Issue	Description/Solution
Chain of instance of checks	This issue indicates a chain of conditionals in favor of object-oriented design. Use the *replace conditionals with polymorphism* refactoring technique to solve this issue.
Feature envy	Use the *don't ask, tell principle* from the previous chapter to solve this issue.
Use of concrete classes	Use the *program against interfaces* principle from the previous chapter to solve this issue.
Assignment to a function argument	Don't modify function arguments but introduce a new variable. You can avoid this issue in Java by declaring function parameters as *final*.
Commented-out code	Remove the commented-out code. If you need that piece of code in the future, it is available in the version control system forever.
Const correctness	Make variables and parameters const or final whenever possible to achieve immutability and avoid accidental modifications
Nested switch statement	Use switch statements mainly only in factories. Do not nest them.

Issue	Description/Solution
Nested conditional expression	Conditional expression (?:) should not be nested because it greatly hinders the code readability.
Overly complex boolean expression	Split the boolean expression into parts and introduce constants to store the parts and the final expression
Expression can be simplified	This can be refactored automatically by the IDE.
Switch statement without default branch	Always introduce a default branch and throw an exception from there. Otherwise, when you are using a switch statement with an enum, you might encounter strange problems after adding a new enum value that is not handled by the switch statement.
Law of Demeter	The object knows too much. It is coupled to the dependencies of another object, which creates additional coupling and makes code harder to change.
Reuse of local variable	Instead of reusing a variable for a different purpose, introduce a new variable. That new variable can be named appropriately to describe its purpose.
Scope of variable is too broad	Introduce a variable only just before it is needed.
Protected field	Subclasses can modify the protected state of the superclass without the superclass being able to control that. This is an indication of breaking the encapsulation and should be avoided.
Breaking the encapsulation: Return of modifiable/mutable field	Use the *don't leak modifiable internal state outside an object principle* from the previous chapter to solve this issue.
Breaking the encapsulation: Assignment from a method parameter to a modifiable/mutable field	Use the *don't assign from a method parameter to a modifiable field principle* from the previous chapter to solve this issue.
Non-constant public field	Anyone can modify a public field. This breaks the encapsulation and should be avoided.
Overly broad catch-block	This can indicate a wrong design. Don't catch the language's base exception class if you should only catch your application's base error class, for example. Read more about handling exceptions in the next section.

5.9: Error/Exception Handling Principle

Many languages like C++, Java, and JavaScript/TypeScript have an exception-handling mechanism that can handle errors and exceptional situations. First of all, I want to make a clear distinction between these two words:

> **An error can happen, and one should be prepared for it. An exception is something that should never happen.**

You define errors in your code and throw them in your functions. For example, if you try to write to a file, you must be prepared for the error that the disk is full, or if you are reading a file, you must be prepared for the error that the file does not exist (anymore).

Some errors are recoverable. You can delete files from the disk to free up some space to write to a file. Or, in case a file is not found, you can give a "file not found" error to the user, who can then retry the operation using a different file name, for example.

You usually don't need to define your own exceptions in your application, but the system throws built-in exceptions in *exceptional situations*, like when a programming error is encountered. An exception can be thrown, for example, when memory is low, and memory allocation cannot be performed, or when a programming error results in an array index out of bounds or a null pointer access. When an exception is thrown, the program cannot continue executing normally and might need to terminate. This is why many exceptions can be categorized as unrecoverable errors. In some cases, it is possible to recover from exceptions. Suppose a web service encounters an exception while handling an HTTP request. In that case, you can terminate the handling of the current request, return an error response to the client, and continue handling further requests normally. It depends on the software component how it should handle exceptional situations. This is important to consider when designing a new software component. You should define (and document) how the software component should handle exceptions. Should it terminate the process or perhaps do something else?

Errors define situations where the execution of a function fails for some reason. Typical examples of errors are a file not found error, an error in sending an HTTP request to a remote service, or a failure to parse a configuration file. Suppose a function can throw an error. The function caller can decide how to handle the error depending on the error. With transient errors, like a failing network request, the function caller can wait a while and call the function again. Or, the function caller can use a default value. For example, if a function tries to load a configuration file that does not exist, it can use some default configuration instead. In some cases, the function caller cannot do anything but leave the error unhandled or catch the error but throw another error at a higher level of abstraction. Suppose a function tries to load a configuration file, but the loading fails, and no default configuration exists. In that case, the function cannot do anything but pass the error to its caller. Eventually, this error bubbles up in the call stack, and the whole process is terminated due to the inability to load the configuration. This is because the configuration is needed to run the application. Without configuration, the application cannot do anything but exit.

When defining error classes, define a base error class for your software component. You can name the base error class according to the name of the software component. For example, for the data exporter microservice, you can define a `DataExporterError` (or `DataExporterServiceError`) base error class. For *common-utils-lib*, you can define `CommonUtilsError` (or `CommonUtilsLibError`), and for *sales-item-service*, you can define `SalesItemServiceError`. The popular Python requests[6] library implements this convention. It

---

[6]https://requests.readthedocs.io/en/latest/

defines a requests.RequestException, which is the base class for all other errors the library methods can raise. Many other Python libraries also define a common base error class.

For each function that can throw an error, define a base error class at the same abstraction level as the function. That error class should extend the software component's base error class. For example, if you have a parse(configStr) method in the ConfigParser class, define a base error class for the function inside the class with the name ParseError, i.e., ConfigParser.ParseError. If you have a readFile method in the FileReader class, define a base error class in the FileReader class with the name ReadFileError, i.e., FileReader.ReadFileError. If all the methods in a class can throw the same error, it is enough to define only one error at the class level. For example, if you have a HttpClient class where all methods like get, post, put etc., can throw an error, you can only define a single Error error class in the HttpClient class. The idea behind defining error classes next to the methods that can throw them is to make the method signatures clearer and better. By looking above the method definition, you can see the errors it can throw. This is a bit similar to Java's checked exceptions (which we will discuss a bit later) where you define thrown exceptions in the throws clause.

Below is a Java example of errors defined for the data exporter microservice:

```java
// Base error class for the software component
public class DataExporterError extends RuntimeException {
  public DataExporterError(final Exception error) {
    super(error);
  }
}


public class FileReader {
  // Base error class for the 'readFile' method
  // Extends the base error class of the software component
  public static class ReadFileError extends DataExporterError {
    public ReadFileError(final Exception error) {
      super(error);
    }
  }

  void readFile(final String pathName) {
    // ...
    // throw new ReadFileError(...);
  }
}


public class ConfigParser {
  // Base error class for the 'parse' method
  // Extends the base error class of the software component
  public static class ParseError extends DataExporterError {
      public ParseError(final Exception error) {
        super(error);
      }
    }

  void parse(final String configStr) {
  // ...
  // throw new ParseError(...)
  }
}
```

Following the previous rules makes catching errors in the code easy because you can infer the error class name from the called method name. In the below example, we can infer the ReadFileError error class name from the readFile method name:

```
try {
  final var fileContents = fileReader.readFile(...);
} catch (final FileReader.ReadFileError error) {
  // Handle error
}
```

You can also catch all user-defined errors using the software component's base error class in the catch clause. The below two examples have the same effect.

```
try {
  final var configFileContents = fileReader.readFile(...);
  return configParser.parse(configFileContents);
} catch (final FileReader.ReadFileError | ConfigParser.ParseError error) {
  // Handle error situation
}
```

```
try {
  final var configFileContents = fileReader.readFile(...);
  return configParser.parse(configFileContents);
} catch (final DataExporterError error) {
  // Handle error situation
}
```

Don't catch the language's base exception class or some other too-generic exception class because that will catch, in addition to all user-defined errors, exceptions, like null pointer exceptions, which is probably not what you want. So, do not catch a too-generic exception class like this:

```
try {
  final var configFileContents = fileReader.readFile(...);
  return configParser.parse(configFileContents);
} catch (final Exception exception) {
  // Do not use! Catches all exceptions
}
```

Also, do not catch the Throwable class in Java because it will also catch any fatal errors that are not meant to be caught:

```
try {
  final var configFileContents = fileReader.readFile(...);
  return configParser.parse(configFileContents);
} catch (final Throwable throwable) {
  // Do not use! Catches everything including
  // all exceptions and fatal errors
}
```

Catch all exceptions only in special places in your code, like in the main function or the main loop, like the loop in a web service processing HTTP requests or the main loop of a thread. Below is an example of correctly catching the language's base exception class in the main function. When you catch an unrecoverable exception in the main function, log it and exit the process with an appropriate error code. When you catch an unrecoverable error in a main loop, log it and continue the loop if possible.

```java
public static void main(final String[] args) {
  // ...

  try {
    application.run(...);
  } catch (final Exception exception) {
    logger.log(exception);
    System.exit(1);
  }
}
```

Using the above-described rules, you can make your code future-proof or forward-compatible so that adding new errors to be thrown from a function in the future is possible. Let's say that you are using a fetchConfig function like this:

```java
try {
  final var config = configFetcher.fetchConfig(url);
} catch(final ConfigFetcher.FetchConfigError error) {
  // Handle error ...
}
```

Your code should still work if a new type of error is raised in the fetchConfig function. Let's say that the following new errors could be thrown from the fetchConfig function:

- Malformed URL error
- Server not found error
- Connection timeout error

When classes for these new errors are implemented, they must extend the function's base error class, in this case, the FetchConfigError class. Below are the error classes defined:

```java
public class ConfigFetcher {
  // Base error class for 'fetchConfig' method
  // Extends the base error class of the software component
  public static class FetchConfigError extends DataExporterError {
    public FetchConfigError(final Exception error) {
      super(error);
    }
  }

  // An additional error for 'fetchConfig' method
  // Extends the base error class of the method
  public static class MalformedUrlError extends FetchConfigError {
    public MalformedUrlError(final Exception error) {
      super(error);
    }
  }

  // An additional error for 'fetchConfig' method
  // Extends the base error class of the method
  public static class ServerNotFoundError extends FetchConfigError {
    public ServerNotFoundError(final Exception error) {
      super(error);
    }
  }

  // An additional error for 'fetchConfig' method
  // Extends the base error class of the method
  public static class ConnectionTimeoutError extends FetchConfigError {
    public ConnectionTimeoutError(final Exception error) {
```

```
      super(error);
    }
  }

  public Config fetchConfig(final String url) {
    // ...
    // throw new MalformedUrlError(...)
    // throw new ServerNotFoundError(...)
    // throw new ConnectionTimeoutError(...)
  }
}
```

You can enhance your code at any time to handle different errors thrown from the `fetchConfig` method differently. For example, you might want to handle a `ConnectionTimeoutError` so that the function will wait a while and then retry the operation because the error is usually transient:

```
try {
  final var config = configFetcher.fetchConfig(url);
} catch (final ConfigFetcher.ConnectionTimeoutError error) {
  // Retry after a while
} catch (final ConfigFetcher.MalformedUrlError error) {
  // Inform caller that URL should be checked
} catch (final ConfigFetcher.ServerNotFoundError error) {
  // Inform caller that URL host/port cannot be reached
} catch (final ConfigFetcher.FetchConfigError error) {
  // Handle possible other error situations
  // This will catch any error that could be raised
  // in 'fetchConfig' method now and in the future
}
```

In the above examples, we handled thrown errors correctly, but you can easily forget to handle a thrown error. This is because nothing in the function signature tells you whether the function can throw an error. The only way to find out is to check the documentation (if available) or investigate the source code (if available). This is one of the biggest problems regarding exception handling because you must know and remember that a function can throw an error, and you must remember to catch and handle errors. You don't always want to handle an error immediately, but still, you must be aware that the error will bubble up in the call stack and should be dealt with eventually somewhere in the code.

Below is an example extracted from the documentation of the popular Python *requests* library:

```
import requests

r = requests.get('https://api.github.com/events')
r.json()
# [{'repository': {'open_issues': 0, 'url': 'https://github.com/...
```

Did you know that both `requests.get` and `r.json` can raise an error? Unfortunately, the above documentation extract does not include error handling at all. If you copy-paste the above code sample directly into your production code, you forget to handle errors. If you go to the API reference documentation of the *requests* library, you can find the documentation for the `get` method. That documentation (when writing this book) does not tell that the method can raise an error. The documentation only speaks about the method parameters, return value, and its type. Scrolling down the documentation page, you will find a section about exceptions. But what if you don't scroll down? You might think that the method does not raise an error. The `get` method documentation should be corrected to tell that the method can raise an error and contain a link to the section where possible errors are described.

The above-described problems can be mitigated, at least on some level, when practicing *test-driven development* (TDD). TDD will be described in the next chapter, which covers testing-related principles.

In TDD, you define the tests before the implementation, forcing you to think about error scenarios and make tests for them. When you have tests for error scenarios, leaving those scenarios unhandled in the actual implementation code is impossible.

One great solution to the problem that error handling might be forgotten is to make throwing errors more explicit:

> ### Use a 'try' prefix in a function name if the function can throw an error.

This is a straightforward rule. If a function can throw an error, name the function so that its name starts with try. This makes it clear to every caller that the function can throw an error, and the caller should be prepared for that. For the caller of the function, there are three alternatives to deal with a thrown error:

1) Catch the base error class of the called function (or software component) and handle the error, e.g., catch `DataFetcher.FetchDataError` if you are calling a method named `tryFetchData` in a class named `DataFetcher`.
2) Catch the base error class of the called function (or software component) and throw a new error on a higher level of abstraction. You must also name the calling function with a try prefix.
3) Don't catch errors. Let them propagate upwards in the call stack. You must also name the calling function with a try prefix.

Here is an example of alternative 1:

```
public class ConfigFetcher {
  public Configuration fetchConfig(final String configUrl) {
    try {
      final var configString = dataFetcher.tryFetchData(configUrl);
      return configParser.tryParse(configString);
    } catch (final DataFetcher.FetchDataError | ConfigParser.ParseError error) {
      // You could also catch DataFetchError and
      // ConfigParseError in different catch clauses
      // if their handling differs
      // You could also catch the base error class DataExporterError
      // of the software component
    }
  }
}
```

Here is an example of alternative 2:

```
public class ConfigFetcher {
  public static class FetchConfigError extends DataExporterError {
    public FetchConfigError(final Exception error) {
      super(error);
    }
  }

  public Configuration tryFetchConfig(final String configUrl) {
    try {
      final var configString = dataFetcher.tryFetchData(configUrl);
      return configParser.tryParse(configString);
    } catch (final DataFetcher.FetchDataError | ConfigParser.ParseError error) {
      // Error on higher level of abstraction is thrown
      // This function must be named with the 'try' prefix
      // to indicate that it can throw
      throw new FetchConfigError(...);
    }
  }
}
```

Here is an example of alternative 3:

```
public class ConfigFetcher {
  public Configuration tryFetchConfig(final String configUrl) {
    // No try-except, all raised errors from both tryFetchData
    // and try_parse method calls propagate
    // to the caller and
    // this function must be named with the 'try' prefix
    // to indicate that it can raise an error
    final var configString = dataFetcher.tryFetchData(configUrl);
    return configParser.tryParse(configString);
  }
}
```

```
public class DataExporter {
  public void initialize() {
    try {
      final var config = configFetcher.tryFetchConfig(url);
    } catch (final DataExporterError error) {
      // In this case you must catch the base error class of
      // the software component (DataExporterError), because
      // you don't know what errors tryFetchConfig can
      // raise, because no FetchConfigError class
      // has been defined in the ConfigFetcher class
    }
  }
}
```

If we go back to the *requests* library usage example, the error-raising methods `requests.get` and `Response.json` could be renamed to `requests.try_get` and `Response.try_parse_body_json`. That would make the earlier example look like the following:

```
import requests

response = requests.try_get('https://api.github.com/events')
response.try_parse_body_json()
# [{'repository': {'open_issues': 0, 'url': 'https://github.com/...
```

Now, we can see that the two methods can raise an error. It is easier to remember to put them inside a try/except-block:

```
import requests

try:
    response = requests.try_get('https://api.github.com/events')
    response.try_parse_body_json()
    # [{'repository': {'open_issues': 0, 'url': 'https://github.com/...
except ...
    # ...
```

To make the try-prefix convention even better, a linting rule that enforces the correct naming of error-throwing functions could be developed. The rule should force the function name to have a *try* prefix if the function throws or propagates errors. A function propagates errors when it calls an error-raising (try-prefixed) method outside a try-except block.

You can also create a library that has try-prefixed functions that wrap error-throwing functions that don't follow the try-prefix rule:

Figure 5.25. JsonParser.js

```javascript
export default class JsonParser {
  static ParseError = class extends Error {
  }

 static tryParse(json, reviver) {
  try {
    return JSON.parse(json, reviver);
  } catch(error) {
    throw new JsonParser.ParseError(error);
  }
 }
}
```

Now, if you use the JsonParser's tryParse method, you can easily infer the class name of the possibly raised errors without the need to consult any documentation.

A web framework usually provides an error-handling mechanism. The framework catches all possible errors and exceptions when processing a request and maps them to HTTP responses with HTTP status codes indicating a failure. Typically, the default status code is 500 *Internal Server Error*. When you utilize the web framework's error-handling mechanism, there is no significant benefit in naming error-raising functions with the try-prefix because it won't be problematic if you forget to catch an error. So, you can opt out of the try-prefix rule. Many times, this is what you want to do: pass the error to the web framework's error handler. Usually, you provide your own error handler instead of using the default one, so you get responses in the format you want. Also, you don't have to declare your error classes inside the respective class that can throw the errors. If you want, of course, you can still do that. We will discuss API error handling again in the *API design principles* chapter.

It is usually a good practice to document the error handling mechanism used in the software component's documentation.

The best way to avoid forgetting to handle errors is to practice rigorous *test-driven development* (TDD) described in the next chapter. Another great way to avoid forgetting to handle errors is to walk through the final code line by line and check if the particular line can produce an error. If it can produce an error, what kind of error, and are there multiple errors the line can produce? Let's have an example with the following code (we focus only on possible errors, not what the function does):

```python
from typing import Any

import requests
from jwt import PyJWKClient, decode

class JwtAuthorizer:
    # ...

    def __try_get_jwt_claims(
            self, auth_header: str | None
        ) -> dict[str, Any]:
            if not self.__jwks_client:
                oidc_config_response = requests.get(self.__oidc_config_url)
                oidc_config = oidc_config_response.json()
                self.__jwks_client = PyJWKClient(oidc_config['jwks_uri'])

            jwt = auth_header.split('Bearer ')[1] if auth_header else ''
            signing_key = self.__jwks_client.get_signing_key_from_jwt(jwt)
            jwt_claims = decode(jwt, signing_key.key, algorithms=['RS256'])
            return jwt_claims
```

The code on the first line cannot produce an error. On the second line, the requests.get method can raise an error on connection failure, for example. Can it produce other errors? It can produce the following errors:

- Malformed URL (requests.URLRequired)
- Connection error (requests.ConnectionError)
- Connection timeout (requests.ConnectTimeout)
- Read timeout (requests.ReadTimeout)

It can also produce an error response, e.g., an internal server error. Our code does not handle that currently, which is why we should add the following line after the requests.get method call: oidc_config_-response.raise_for_status(). That call will raise an HttpError if the response status code is >= 400. The third line can raise a JSONDecodeError if the response is not valid JSON. The fourth line can raise a KeyError because it is possible that the key jwks_uri does not exist in the response JSON. The fifth line can raise an IndexError because the list returned by the split does not necessarily have an element at index one. Also, the sixth line can raise an error when the JWKS client cannot connect to the IAM system, or the JWT is invalid. The second last line can raise an InvalidTokenError when the JWT is invalid. In summary, all the lines in the above code can produce at least one kind of error except the first and last lines.

Let's modify the code to implement error handling instead of passing all possible errors and exceptions to the caller:

```python
from typing import Any

import requests
from jwt import PyJWKClient, PyJWKClientError, decode
from jwt.exceptions import InvalidTokenError


class JwtAuthorizer:
    class GetJwtClaimsError(Exception):
        pass

    def __try_get_jwt_claims(
        self, auth_header: str | None
    ) -> dict[str, Any]:
        try:
            if not self.__jwks_client:
                oidc_config_response = requests.get(self.__oidc_config_url)
                oidc_config_response.raise_for_status()
                oidc_config = oidc_config_response.json()
                self.__jwks_client = PyJWKClient(oidc_config['jwks_uri'])

            jwt = auth_header.split('Bearer ')[1] if auth_header else ''
            signing_key = self.__jwks_client.get_signing_key_from_jwt(jwt)
            jwt_claims = decode(jwt, signing_key.key, algorithms=['RS256'])
            return jwt_claims
        except (
            # RequestException is the base error for all errors
            # in the 'requests' library
            requests.RequestException,
            KeyError,
            IndexError,
            PyJWKClientError,
            # Base error when decode() fails on a token
            InvalidTokenError,
        ) as error:
            raise self.GetJwtClaimsError(error)
```

Make yourself a habit of walking through the code of a function line by line once you think it is ready to find out if you have accidentally missed handling some error.

5.9.1: Handling Checked Exceptions in Java

You can use checked exceptions in Java when defining your software component's errors. Using checked exceptions helps you to remember to handle errors or let them propagate upwards in the call stack.

When using Java's checked exceptions, define the software component's base error class to extend the `Exception` class instead of the `RuntimeException` class. When a function throws a checked exception, prefixing the function name with the *try* prefix becomes unnecessary. You can also declare your error classes as top-level classes. You don't need to put them inside the class whose methods can throw them. Below is an example of defining checked exceptions:

```java
public class DataExporterError extends Exception {
  public DataExporterError(final Exception error) {
    super(error);
  }
}

public class DataFetcher {
  public class FetchDataError extends DataExporterError {
    public FetchDataError(final Exception error) {
      super(error);
    }
  }

  public String fetchData(...) throws FetchDataError {
    // ...
  }
}

public class ConfigParser {
  public class ParseError extends DataExporterError {
    public ParseError(final Exception error) {
      super(error);
    }
  }

  public Configuration parse(...) throws ParseError {
    // ...
  }
}

public class DataExporter {
  public class InitializeError extends DataExporterError {
    public InitializeError(final Exception error) {
      super(error);
    }
  }

  public void initialize(...) throws InitializeError {
    try {
      final var configString = dataFetcher.fetchData(configUrl);
      final var config = configParser.parse(configString);

      // ...
    } catch (
      final DataFetcher.FetchDataError | ConfigParser.ParseError error
    ) {
      throw new InitializeError(error);
    }
  }
}
```

Later, it is possible to modify the implementation of the `parse` function to throw other errors that derive from the `ParseError` class. This kind of change does not require modifications to other parts of the codebase.

On higher levels of the software component code, you can also use the base error class of the software component in the `throws` clause to propagate errors upwards in the call stack:

```
public class DataExporter {
  public void initialize(...) throws DataExporterError {
    final var configString = dataFetcher.fetchData(configUrl);
    final var config = configParser.parse(configDataString);

    // ...
  }
}
```

5.9.2: Returning Errors

As an alternative to throwing errors, it is possible to communicate erroneous behavior to the function caller using a return value. Using an exception-handling mechanism provides some advantages over returning errors. When a function can return an error, you must always check for the error right after the function call. This can cause the code to contain nested if-statements, which hinders code readability. The exception-handling mechanism allows you to propagate an error to a higher level in the call stack. You can also execute multiple function calls that can fail inside a single `try` block and provide a single error handler in the `catch` block. Some languages do not provide an exception-handling mechanism, meaning you must return errors from functions. In languages like C++, you can optimize mission-critical code by returning error values or indicators instead of throwing exceptions.

5.9.2.1: Returning Failure Indicator

You can return a failure indicator from a failable function when the function does not need to return any additional value. It is enough to return a failure indicator from the function when there is no need to return any specific error code or message. This can be because there is only one reason the function can fail, or function callers are not interested in error details. To return a failure indicator, return a boolean value from the function: *true* means a successful operation and *false* indicates a failure:

```
bool performTask(...)
{
  bool taskWasPerformed;

  // Perform the task and set the value of 'taskWasPerformed'

  return taskWasPerformed;
}
```

5.9.2.2: Returning an Optional Value

Suppose a function should return a value, but the function call can fail, and there is precisely one cause why the function call can fail. In this case, return an optional value from the function. In the below example, getting a value from the cache can only fail when no value for a specific key is stored in the cache. We don't need to return any error code or message.

Figure 5.26. Cache.java

```
public interface Cache<TKey, TValue> {
  void add(final TKey key, final TValue value);
  Optional<TValue> get(final TKey key);
}
```

In TypeScript, you can return an optional value using a type union:

Figure 5.27. Cache.ts

```
interface MyCache<TKey, TValue> {
  add(key: TKey, value: TValue): void;
  get(key: TKey): TValue | null;
}
```

5.9.2.3: Returning an Error Object

When you need to provide details about an error to a function caller, you can return an error object from the function:

Figure 5.28. BackendError.ts

```
export type BackendError = {
  statusCode: number;
  errorCode: number;
  message: string;
};
```

If a function does not return any value but can produce an error, you can return either an error object or *null* in languages that have *null* defined as a distinct type and the language supports type unions (e.g., TypeScript):

Figure 5.29. DataStore.ts

```
export interface DataStore {
  updateEntity<T extends Entity>(...):
    Promise<BackendError | null>;
}
```

Alternatively, return an optional error. Below is an example in Java:

```
import lombok.experimental.Value;


@Value
public class BackendError {
  int statusCode;
  int errorCode;
  String message;
}


public interface DataStore {
  <T extends Entity> Optional<BackendError> updateEntity(...);
}
```

Suppose a function needs to return a value or an error. In that case, you can use a 2-tuple (i.e., a pair) type, where the first value in the tuple is the actual value or *null* in case of an error and the second value in the tuple is an error object or *null* value in case of a successful operation. Below are examples in TypeScript and Java. In the Java example, you, of course, need to return optionals instead of nulls.

Figure 5.30. DataStore.ts

```
export class DataStore {
  createEntity<T extends Entity>(...):
    Promise<[T, null] | [null, BackendError]>;
}
```

Figure 5.31. DataStore.java

```
import org.javatuples.Pair;

public interface DataStore {
  <T extends Entity> Pair<Optional<T>, Optional<BackendError>>
  createEntity(...);
}
```

The above Java code is cumbersome to use, and the type definition looks long. We should use an `Either` type here, but Java does not have that. Either type contains one of two values, either a left value or a right value. The function returns the left value when the operation is successful, and the right value is an error.

Source code for the below example is available here[7].

The `Either` type can be defined as follows:

Figure 5.32. Either.java

```
public class Either<L, R> {
  private final Optional<L> maybeLeftValue;
  private final Optional<R> maybeRightValue;

  private Either(
    final Optional<L> maybeLeftValue,
    final Optional<R> maybeRightValue
  ) {
    this.maybeLeftValue = maybeLeftValue;
    this.maybeRightValue = maybeRightValue;
  }

  public static <L, R> Either<L, R> withLeft(
    final L value
  ) {
    return new Either<>(Optional.of(value), Optional.empty());
  }

  public static <L, R> Either<L, R> withRight(
    final R value
  ) {
    return new Either<>(Optional.empty(), Optional.of(value));
  }

  public boolean hasLeftValue() {
    return maybeLeftValue.isPresent();
  }
```

---

[7]https://github.com/pksilen/clean-code-principles-code/tree/main/chapter3/either

```
  public boolean hasRightValue() {
    return maybeRightValue.isPresent();
  }

  public <T> Either<T, R> mapLeft(
    Function<? super L, ? extends T> mapper
  ) {
    return new Either<>(maybeLeftValue.map(mapper),
                        maybeRightValue);
  }

  public <T> Either<L, T> mapRight(
    Function<? super R, ? extends T> mapper)
  {
      return new Either<>(maybeLeftValue,
                          maybeRightValue.map(mapper));
  }

  public <T> T map(
    Function<? super L, ? extends T> leftValueMapper,
    Function<? super R, ? extends T> rightValueMapper)
  {
    return maybeLeftValue.<T>map(leftValueMapper)
      .orElseGet(() ->
        maybeRightValue.map(rightValueMapper).get());
  }

  public void apply(
    Consumer<? super L> leftValueConsumer,
    Consumer<? super R> rightValueConsumer
  ) {
    maybeLeftValue.ifPresent(leftValueConsumer);
    maybeRightValue.ifPresent(rightValueConsumer);
  }
}
```

Below are some examples of how to use the Either class:

```
class Error extends RuntimeException {
}

final Either<Integer, Error> intOrError = Either.withLeft(3);
final Either<Integer, Error> intOrError2 = Either.withRight(new Error());

System.out.println(intOrError.hasLeftValue()); // Prints true
System.out.println(intOrError2.hasRightValue()); // Prints true

// Prints true
System.out.println(
  intOrError.mapLeft(number -> number * 2).hasLeftValue()
);

// Prints 6
System.out.println(
  intOrError.<Integer>map(number -> number * 2, error -> 0)
);

// Prints 0
System.out.println(
  intOrError2.<Integer>map(number -> number * 2, error -> 0)
);
```

Now, we can use the new Either type and rewrite the example as follows:

Figure 5.33. DataStore.java

```
public interface DataStore {
  <T extends Entity> Either<T, BackendError> createEntity(...);
}
```

5.9.2.4: Adapt to Wanted Error Handling Mechanism

You can adapt to a desired error-handling mechanism by creating an adapter method. For example, if a library has a throwing method, you can create an adapter method returning an optional value or error object. Below is a tryCreate factory method in a VInt class that can throw:

Figure 5.34. VInt.ts

```
class VInt {
  // ...

  private constructor(...) {
    // ...
  }

  // this will throw if invalid 'value' is given
  // that doesn't match the 'validationSpec'
  static tryCreate<VSpec extends string>(
    validationSpec: IntValidationSpec<VSpec>,
    value: number
  ): VInt<VSpec> | never {
    // constructor can throw
    return new VInt(validationSpec, value);
  }

  // ...
}
```

We can create a VIntFactory class with an adapter method for the tryCreate factory method in the VInt class. The VIntFactory class offers a non-throwing create method:

Figure 5.35. VIntFactory.ts

```
class VIntFactory {
  static create<VSpec extends string>(
    validationSpec: IntValidationSpec<VSpec>,
    value: number
  ): VInt<VSpec> | null {
    try {
      return VInt.tryCreate(validationSpec, value);
    } catch {
      return null;
    }
  }
}
```

We can also create a method that does not throw but returns either a value or an error:

Figure 5.36. VIntFactory.ts

```
class VIntFactory {
  static createOrError<VSpec extends string>(
    validationSpec: IntValidationSpec<VSpec>,
    value: number
  ): [VInt<VSpec>, null] | [null, Error] {
    try {
      return [VInt.tryCreate(validationSpec, value), null];
    } catch (error) {
      return [null, error as Error];
    }
  }
}
```

We can also introduce a simplified version of the Either type for TypeScript:

Figure 5.37. Either.ts

```
export type Either<L, R> = [L, null] | [null, R];
```

Now, we can rewrite the above example like this:

Figure 5.38. VIntFactory.ts

```
class VIntFactory {
  static createOrError<VSpec extends string>(
    validationSpec: IntValidationSpec<VSpec>,
    value: number
  ): Either<VInt<VSpec>, Error> {
    try {
      return [VInt.tryCreate(validationSpec, value), null];
    } catch (error) {
      return [null, error as Error];
    }
  }
}
```

5.9.2.5: Asynchronous Function Error Handling

Asynchronous functions are functions that usually can fail. They often execute I/O operations like file or network I/O. For a failable asynchronous operation, you must remember to handle the failure case. For this reason, it is suggested to name a failable asynchronous operation using the same *try* prefix used in function names that can throw. Below are two examples of handling an asynchronous operation failure in JavaScript/TypeScript:

```
tryMakeHttpRequest(url).then((value) => {
  // success
}, (error) => {
  // Handle error
});
```

```
tryMakeHttpRequest(url).then((value) => {
  // success
}).error((error) => {
  // Handle error
});
```

As you can see from the above examples, it is easy to forget to add the error handling. It would be better if there was a thenOrCatch method in the Promise class that accepted the following kind of callback:

```
tryMakeHttpRequest(url).thenOrCatch(([value, error]) => {
  // Now it is harder to forget to handle an error
  // Check 'error' before using the 'value'
});
```

You can make asynchronous function calls synchronous. In JavaScript/TypeScript, this can be done using the async and await keywords. A failable asynchronous operation made synchronous can throw. Below is the same example as above made synchronous:

```
async function fetchData() {
  try {
    await tryMakeHttpRequest(url);
  } catch {
    // Handle error
  }
}
```

5.9.2.6: Functional Exception Handling

Source code for the below example is available here[8].

The below Failable<T> class can be used in functional error handling. A Failable<T> object represents either a value of type T or an instance of the RuntimeException class.

Figure 5.39. Failable.java

```
public class Failable<T> {
  private final Either<T, RuntimeException> valueOrError;

  private Failable(
    final Either<T, RuntimeException> valueOrError
  ) {
    this.valueOrError = valueOrError;
  }

  public static <T> Failable<T> withValue(
    final T value
  ) {
    return new Failable<>(Either.withLeft(value));
  }

  public static <T> Failable<T> withError(
    final RuntimeException error
```

---

[8]https://github.com/pksilen/clean-code-principles-code/tree/main/chapter3/failable

```
) {
  return new Failable<>(Either.withRight(error));
}

public T orThrow(
  final Class<? extends RuntimeException> ErrorClass
) {
  return valueOrError.map(
    (value) -> value,
    (error) -> {
      try {
        throw (RuntimeException)ErrorClass
          .getConstructor(String.class)
          .newInstance(error.getMessage());
      } catch (InvocationTargetException |
               InstantiationException |
               IllegalAccessException |
               IllegalArgumentException |
               NoSuchMethodException exception) {
        throw new RuntimeException(exception);
      }
    });
}

public T orElse(final T otherValue) {
  return valueOrError.map(value -> value,
                          error -> otherValue);
}

public <U> Failable<U> mapValue(
  final Function<? super T, ? extends U> mapper
) {
  return new Failable<>(valueOrError.mapLeft(mapper));
}

public Failable<T> mapError(
  final Function<? super RuntimeException,
                 ? extends RuntimeException> mapper
) {
  if (valueOrError.hasLeftValue()) {
    final var error =
      new RuntimeException(mapper
        .apply(new RuntimeException(""))
        .getMessage());

    return Failable.withError(error);
  } else {
    return new Failable<>(valueOrError.mapRight(mapper));
  }
}
}
```

In the below example, the `readConfig` method returns a `Failable<Configuration>`. The `tryInitialize` function either obtains an instance of `Configuration` or throws an error of type `InitializeError`.

```
public void tryInitialize() {
  final var configuration = configReader
    .readConfig(...)
    .orThrow(InitializeError.class);
}
```

The benefit of the above functional approach is that it is shorter than an entire try-catch block. The above functional approach is also as understandable as a try-catch block. Remember that you should write the shortest, most understandable code. When a method returns a failable, you don't have to name the method with the *try* prefix because the method does not throw.

You can also use other methods of the `Failable` class. For example, a default value can be returned with the `orElse` method:

```
public void initialize() {
  final var configuration = configReader
    .readConfig(...)
    .orElse(new DefaultConfiguration());
}
```

You can also transform multiple imperative failable statements into functional failable statements. For example, instead of writing:

```
public void tryInitialize() {
  try {
    final var configDataStr = dataFetcher.tryFetchData(configUrl);
    final var configuration = configParser.tryParse(configDataStr);
  } catch (final DataExporterError error) {
    throw new InitializeError(error.getMessage());
  }
}
```

You can write:

```
public void tryInitialize() {
  try {
    final var configuration = dataFetcher
      .fetchData(configUrl)
      .mapValue(configParser::parse)
      .orThrow(InitializeError.class);
}
```

It is error-prone to use failable imperative code together with functional programming constructs. Let's assume we have the below TypeScript code that reads and parses multiple configuration files to a single configuration object:

```
configFilePathNames
  .reduce((accumulatedConfig, configFilePathName) => {
    const configJson = fs.readFileSync(configFilePathName, 'utf-8');
    const configuration = JSON.parse(configJson);
    return { ...accumulatedConfig, ...configuration };
}, {});
```

In the above example, it is easy to forget to handle errors because the throwability of the `reduce` function depends on the supplied callback function. We cannot use the try-prefix anywhere in the above example. What we can do is the following:

```
function tryReadConfig(
  accumulatedConfig: Record<string, unknown>,
  configFilePathName: string
) {
  const configJson = fs.readFileSync(configFilePathName, 'utf-8');
  const configuration = JSON.parse(configJson);
  return { ...accumulatedConfig, ...configuration };
}

export function getConfig(
  configFilePathNames: string[]
): Record<string, unknown> {
  try {
    return configFilePathNames.reduce(tryReadConfig, {});
  } catch (error) {
    // ...
  }
}
```

We have now added the try-prefix, but the code could read better. A better alternative is to use a functional programming construct, `Failable<T>`, to return a failable configuration. The `Failable<T>` class implementation in TypeScript is not presented here, but it can be implemented similarly to Java. Below is an example of using the `Failable<T>` class:

```
function accumulatedConfigOrError(
  accumulatedConfigOrError: Failable<Record<string, unknown>>,
  configFilePathName: string
): Failable<Record<string, unknown>> {
  try {
    const configJson = fs.readFileSync(configFilePathName, 'utf-8');
    const config = JSON.parse(configJson);

    return accumulatedConfigOrError.mapValue(accumulatedConfig =>
      ({ ...accumulatedConfig, ...config }));
  } catch (error: any) {
    return accumulatedConfigOrError.mapError(accumulatedError =>
      new Error(`${accumulatedError.message}\n${error.message}`)
    );
  }
}

export function getConfig(
  configFilePathNames: string[]
): Failable<Record<string, unknown>> {
  return configFilePathNames.reduce(
    accumulatedConfigOrError,
    Failable.withValue({})
  );
}
```

If we have a *config1.json* file with the following contents:

```
{
    "foo": 1,
    "bar": 2
}
```

and we have a *config2.json* file with the following contents:

```
{
    "xyz": 3
}
```

Then, we can run the following code:

```
const configFilePathNames = ['config1.json', 'config2.json'];
const maybeConfig = getConfig(configFilePathNames);
console.log(maybeConfig.orThrow(Error));
// Prints {'foo': 1, 'bar': 2, 'xyz': 3}
```

Let's introduce an error (a missing comma after the first property) in the *config1.json* file:

```
{
    "foo": 1
    "bar": 2
}
```

Let's also try to provide a non-existing configuration file *config3.json*:

```
const configFilePathNames = ['config1.json', 'config3.json'];
constmaybeConfig = getConfig(configFilePathNames);
console.log(maybeConfig.orThrow(Error));
// Throws an error with a two-line message saying config1.json content
// cannot be parsed due to invalid JSON and config3.json file cannot
// be read because it does not exists.
```

5.9.2.7: Stream Error Handling

Handling errors for a stream is also something that can be easily forgotten. Streams are usually used for I/O operations that can fail. You should be prepared to handle errors when using a stream. In JavaScript/TypeScript, an error handler for a stream can be registered using the stream's on method in the following way: `stream.on('error', () => { ... })`.

Below is an example of using a stream:

```
// ...

const writeStream = fs.createWriteStream(filePathName);

this.writeStream.on('error', (error) => {
    // Handle errors
});

writeStream.write(...);
// More writes...

writeStream.close();
```

How could we improve developer experience with streams so that error handling is not forgotten? Adding an error handler callback parameter to the stream factory method is one solution. This callback will be called upon an error. If no error handling is needed, a *null* value could be given for the callback. This way, a developer creating a stream can't forget to supply an error handler function.

5.10: Don't Pass or Return Null Principle

This principle is for languages like Java and C++ that don't implement null values as separate types. TypeScript implements nulls as distinct types when the *strictNullChecks* configuration parameter is set to true (in tsconfig.json), and you should always set it to true. So, this principle does not apply to TypeScript.

The null value is the misguided invention of British computer scientist *Tony Hoare* who coined his invention of null references as a *billion-dollar mistake*. The reason is quite evident because we all have done it: forgetting to handle a null value. And when we don't handle a null value, we pass it to other functions that never expect to be called with a null value. Eventually, this will lead to a null value exception thrown somewhere in the code.

When you return a value from a function, never return a null value. You should return an optional value instead. In the example below, we return an optional value for a key in a map because there can be no value associated with a particular key in the map.

```
// BAD!
public class Map<K, V> {
  public V get(final K key) {
    if (...) {
      // ...
    } else {
      return null;
    }
  }
}


// GOOD!
public class Map<K, V> {
  public Optional<V> get(final K key) {
    // ...
  }
}
```

When you pass arguments to a function, never pass a null value. The called function usually never expects to be called with null arguments. Suppose a function expects an argument that can be missing. In that case, the function can define a default value for that argument (possible in C++ and JavaScript/TypeScript, but not in Java), or an overloaded function can be defined where the optional argument is not present. A function can also be defined so that an argument has an optional type, but you should prefer an optional parameter or an overloaded version of the function.

5.11: Avoid Off-By-One Errors Principle

Off-by-one errors usually result from the fact that collections in programming languages are indexed with zero-based indexes. Zero-based indexing is unnatural for human beings but excellent for computers. However, programming languages should be designed with humans in mind. People never speak about getting the zeroth value of an array. We speak of getting the first value in the array. As the null value was called a billion-dollar mistake, I would call the zero-based indexing another billion-dollar mistake. Let's hope that someday we get a programming language with one-based indexing! But then we must unlearn the zero-based indexing habit...and that's another problem.

Below are two examples of programming errors in JavaScript that are easy to make if you are not careful enough:

```
for (let index = 0; index <= array.length; index++) {
  // ...
}

for (let index = 0; index < array.length - 1; index++) {
  // ...
}
```

In the first example, there should be '<' instead of '<=', and in the latter example, there should be '<=' instead of '<'. Fortunately, the above mistakes can be avoided using modern programming language constructs like Java's enhanced for-loop or C++'s range-based for-loop or functional programming.

Below are two examples of avoiding off-by-one errors in Java:

```
for (final var value : values) {
  // ...
}

values.stream().forEach(value -> ...);
```

Some languages, like JavaScript, offer a nice way to access an array's last element(s). Instead of writing `array[array.length - 1]`, you can write `array.at(-1)`. Similarly, `array[array.length - 2]` is the same as `array.at(-2)`. You can think that a negative index is a one-based index starting from the end of an array.

Let's consider the description of JavaScript's `slice` method:

> The slice() method returns a shallow copy of a portion of an array into a new array object selected from start index to end index (end not included).

The problem here is the 'end not included' part. Many people, by default, think that if given a range, it is inclusive, but in the case of the `slice` method, it is inclusive at the beginning and exclusive at the end: `[start, end[`. This kind of function definition that is against first assumptions can easily cause off-by-one errors. It would be better if the `slice` method by default works with an inclusive range `[start, end]`.

Additionally, unit tests are your friend when trying to spot off-by-one errors. So remember to write unit tests for the edge cases, too.

5.12: Be Critical When Googling or Using Generative AI Principle

You should always analyze code taken from the web to ensure it meets the criteria for production code. Don't let the AI be the master, but an apprentice.

We all have done it, and we have done it hundreds of times: googled for answers. Usually, you find good resources by googling, but the problem often is that examples in the Google results are not necessarily production quality. One specific thing missing in them is error handling. If you copy and paste code from a website, it is possible that errors in that copy-pasted code are not handled appropriately. You should always analyze the copy-pasted code to see if error handling needs to be added.

When you provide answers for other people, try to make the code as production-like as possible. In Stack Overflow[9], you find the most up-voted answer right below the question. If the answer is missing error

---

[9]https://stackoverflow.com/

handling, you can comment on that and let the author improve their answer. You can also up-vote an answer that seems the most production-ready. The most up-voted answers tend to be pretty old. For this reason, it is useful to scroll down to see if a more modern solution fits your needs better. You can also up-vote that more modern solution to make it eventually rank higher in the list of answers.

Regarding open-source libraries, the first examples in their documentation can describe only the "happy path" usage scenario, and error handling is described only in later parts of the documentation. This can cause problems if you copy-paste code from the "happy path" example and forget to add error handling. For this reason, open-source library authors should give production-quality examples early in the documentation.

Regarding generative AI, e.g., ChatGPT, I have a couple of experiences. I asked ChatGPT to generate simple Python Django code. The generated code was about 95% correct, but it did not work. The problem was that ChatGPT forgot to provide code for generating the database tables (makemigrations, migrate). If you are inexperienced with the Django framework, that problem might be challenging to solve. In that case, continue the discussion with ChatGPT and ask it to solve the problem for you.

My other experiment with ChatGPT was to generate GraphQL server code using the Python *Ariadne* library. The ChatGPT-generated code was for an old version of Ariadne and did not work correctly with a newer version of the Ariadne library. (Notice that the data used to train ChatGPT contains more older than newer data. ChatGPT could not prioritize the less and newer data over the older and more data.) It also generated some lines of code in the wrong order, which prevented the GraphQL API from working at all. It took quite a lot of debugging for such a small program to find out what was wrong: The executable schema was created before the query resolver. It should have been created only after defining the resolver.

You should familiarize yourself with the AI-generated code when using ChatGPT or other generative AI tools. Otherwise, you don't know what your program is doing, and if the AI-generated code contains bug(s), those will be hard to find because you don't clearly understand what the code is actually doing. Don't let the AI be the master, but an apprentice.

The best way to prevent bugs related to code taken from the web is to practice *test-driven development* (TDD). TDD is better described in the next chapter. The idea behind TDD is to specify the function first and write unit test cases for different scenarios: edge/corner cases, error scenarios, and security scenarios. For example, let's say you are new to Python and google for a code snippet to perform an HTTP request to an API endpoint. You copy-paste the code into your function. Now, error scenarios are not handled. What you should do is practice TDD and write unit test cases for different scenarios, like, what if the remote server cannot be contacted or the contact results in timeout, or what if the remote server responds with an error (an HTTP response with a status code greater than or equal to 400). What if you need to parse the result from the API (e.g., parse JSON), and it fails? Once you have written a unit test case for all those scenarios, you can be sure that error handling in the function implementation is not forgotten.

5.13: Make One Change At A Time Principle

Don't try to make multiple distinct changes at the same time.

If you try to make multiple unrelated changes simultaneously, you are focusing on too many things and are more likely to introduce a bug or bugs. Don't try to implement two distinct features at the same time. Don't try to make two distinct refactorings at the same time. Don't try to implement a new feature and do refactoring simultaneously. Try to make a single change as small and isolated as possible. I have violated this principle so many times. I thought, okay, this is a small change I can make together with this other change. But later, I realized that the changes were not so small after all and that I had created some bugs.

I didn't know which of the many changes caused the bug. That made the bug hunting more difficult than it should have been. So, resist the urge to make multiple distinct changes simultaneously. Have all changes that need to be made as separate user stories in the team backlog or list small changes to be done in a TODO.MD file so that they are not forgotten.

If you need to implement a new feature, analyze if you should refactor the code first to make the feature implementation easier. If the refactoring is not necessary for the feature and the feature is important, you can implement the feature first and refactor the code later. If you gain benefit by refactoring first and the feature is not time-critical, refactor first and only after that, implement the feature.

5.14: Choosing Right 3rd Party Component Principle

When choosing the suitable 3rd party component, you should take the following into account:

- It provides the needed functionality
- If you are looking for an open-source component, check that the license is appropriate, e.g., without a viral effect (GPL)
- Prefer a well-established component over a brand new component because the brand new component may have bugs, and a smaller community can offer you support. You shouldn't determine a well-established component solely by its number of GitHub stars. Instead, check the component download statistics from the package manager.
- Prefer a component that has a higher number of contributors because you can have your reported bugs corrected faster and also new features implemented faster.
- Ensure that dependencies are up-to-date. It is a red flag if the component has its dependencies updated like several years ago

5.15: Use Appropriate Data Structure Principle

Next, the main built-in data structures with their use cases will be presented.

Use a list when you need an ordered collection or should be able to store the same item multiple times.

To implement lists, JavaScript has arrays, C++ has the `std::vector` class, and Java has the `ArrayList` class. Java also has a `Vector` class, but it is advised to use `ArrayList` unless you need synchronization (vectors are synchronized). Lists are mutable and can contain duplicate elements. Each element can be accessed by its index in a performant way. If you need to add or remove elements at the beginning of the list, that is not a cheap operation because all existing elements in the list must be moved by one index to the right or left. Similarly, if you add an element to the end of a list and the allocated space for the list is full, new space must be allocated, and the list elements must be copied to the newly allocated space.

5.15.1: Map

Use a map when you need quick access to a value by a key.

To implement maps, you can use a plain object or the `Map` class in JavaScript, `HashMap` in Java, and `std::ordered_map` or `std::unordered_map` in C++. Accessing a value by its key is always a cheap operation. In Java, you can use an `EnumMap` when the map keys are of an enumerated type. For a synchronized map in Java, you can use `ConcurrentHashMap`. You can iterate over a JavaScript object using one of the following methods: `keys()`, `values()`, or `entries()`. You can iterate over a Java `Map` using one of the following methods: `keySet()`, `values()`, or `entrySet()`.

5.15.2: Tuple

Use a tuple for a fixed size ordered collection.

In a tuple, each element can be accessed by its index in a performant way. In TypeScript, you don't have tuples separately, but you can use fixed-size arrays. In C++, you can use `std::pair` and `std::tuple`. In Java, you must use a library like javatuples[10].

5.15.3: Set

Use a set when you don't need an ordered collection, and duplicate elements are not allowed.

Accessing a set by a value is cheap when the set is implemented as a hash table. On the contrary, if you have a list, the whole list may need to be gone through to find a specific value. If you have a list and want to remove duplicates from it, you can convert the list into a set. You can do that with the `HashSet` constructor in Java or the `Set` constructor in JavaScript. The `unordered_set` and `ordered_set` classes provide set functionality in C++.

5.15.4: String

Use a string to store an immutable ordered collection of characters.

In JavaScript and Java, strings are immutable. In C++, you can mutate a `std::string`. Accessing a character by its index is always a cheap operation O(1).

5.15.5: Deque (Double Ended Queue)

Use a deque when you need cheap insertion and removal of elements at either or both ends of the collection.

Adding and removing elements at the ends of a deque are cheap (O(1)) operations because the deque is implemented as a doubly linked list. The drawback of the deque is that randomly accessing an element at a specific index is slow (O(n)). To implement deques, you can use the `std::deque` class in C++ and the `ArrayDeque` class in Java.

---

[10]https://www.javatuples.org/index.html

5.15.6: Stack (LIFO Queue)

A stack can be implemented using a deque.

You can push an element into the stack with the deque's push-back method and pop an element out of the stack with the deque's pop-back method. You can also implement a stack using a list, but operations can be slower sometimes, especially if the stack is large. C++ has a `std::stack` class that, by default, utilizes the `std::deque` class to implement a stack. Java also has a `Stack` class, which should not be used, but you should use the `ArrayDeque` class to implement a stack in Java.

5.15.7: Queue (FIFO Queue)

A queue can be implemented using a deque.

You can add an element to a queue with the deque's push-back method and pop an element from the queue with the deque's pop-front method. You can also implement a queue using a list, but operations can be slower sometimes, especially if the queue is large. C++ has a `std::queue` class that, by default, utilizes the `std::deque` class to implement a queue. In Java, you can use `ArrayDeque` or a `LinkedList` to implement a queue. Java also provides concurrent blocking queues, like `ArrayBlockingQueue`, useful for implementing multithreaded applications with one or more producer and consumer threads.

5.15.8: Priority Queue

Use a priority queue to retrieve elements based on their priority.

In C++, you can use the `std::priority_queue` class. In Java, you can use `PriorityQueue` or `PriorityBlockingQueue`.

5.16: Optimization Principle

Code optimization makes code run faster and/or consume less memory. Faster code improves the end-user experience, and optimization reduces the need for computing resources (CPU/memory), making operating the software cheaper.

> *Avoid premature optimization. Premature optimization may hinder crafting a proper object-oriented design for a software component.*

Measure unoptimized performance first. Then, decide if optimization is needed. Implement optimizations individually and measure the performance after each optimization to determine if the particular optimization matters. You can then utilize the knowledge you gained in future projects only to make optimizations that boost performance significantly enough. Sometimes, you can make performance optimization in the early phase of a project if you know that a particular optimization is needed (e.g., from previous experience), and the optimization can be implemented without negatively affecting the object-oriented design.

5.16.1: Optimization Patterns

The following optimization patterns are described in this section:

- Optimize busy loops only pattern
- Remove unnecessary functionality pattern
- Object pool pattern
- Algorithm complexity reduction pattern
- Cache function results pattern
- Buffer file I/O pattern
- Share identical objects, a.k.a flyweight pattern
- Copy memory in chunks pattern (C++)
- Replace virtual methods with non-virtual methods pattern (C++)
- Inline methods pattern (C++)
- Use unique pointer pattern (C++)

5.16.1.1: Optimize Busy Loops Only Pattern

Optimizations should primarily target only the busy loop or loops in a software component. Busy loops are the loops in threads that execute over and over again, possibly thousands or more iterations in a second. Performance optimization should not target functionality that executes only once or a couple of times during the software component's lifetime, and running that functionality does not take a long time. For example, an application can execute configuration reading and parsing functionality when it starts. This functionality takes a short time to execute. It is not reasonable to optimize that functionality because it runs only once. It does not matter if you can read and parse the configuration in 200 or 300 milliseconds, even if there is a 50% difference in performance.

Let's use the data exporter microservice as an example. Our data exporter microservice consists of input, transformer, and output parts. The input part reads messages from a data source. We cannot affect the message reading part if we use a 3rd party library for that purpose. Of course, if multiple 3rd party libraries are available, it is possible to craft performance tests and evaluate which library offers the best performance. If several 3rd party libraries are available for the same functionality, we tend to use the most popular library or a library we know beforehand. If performance is an issue, we should evaluate different libraries and compare their performances.

The data exporter microservice has the following functionality in its busy loop: decode an input message to an internal message, perform transformations, and encode an output message. Decoding an input message requires decoding each field in the message. Let's say there are 10000 messages handled per second, each with 100 fields. During one second, 100,000 fields must be decoded. This reveals that the optimization of the decoding functionality is crucial. The same applies to output message encoding. We at Nokia have implemented the decoding and encoding of Avro binary fields ourselves. We were able to make them faster than what was provided by a 3rd party library.

5.16.1.2: Remove Unnecessary Functionality Pattern

Removing unnecessary functionality is something that will boost performance. Every now and then, you should stop and think critically about your software component: Is my software component doing only the necessary things considering all circumstances?

Let's consider the data exporter's functionality in a special case. It is currently decoding an input message to an internal message. This internal message is used when making various transformations to the data. Transformed data is encoded in a desired output format. The contents of the final output message can be a small subset of the original input message. This means that only a tiny part of the decoded message is used. In that case, it is unnecessary to decode all the fields of an input message if, for example, only 10% of the fields are used in the transformations and output messages. By removing unnecessary decoding, we can improve the performance of the data exporter microservice.

5.16.1.3: Object Pool Pattern

In garbage-collected languages like Python, the benefit of using an object pool is evident from the garbage-collection point of view. Objects are created only once in the object pool pattern and then reused. This will take pressure away from garbage collection. If we didn't use an object pool, new objects could be created in a busy loop repeatedly, and soon after they were created, they could be discarded. This would cause many objects to be made available for garbage collection in a short time. Garbage collection takes processor time, and if the garbage collector has a lot of garbage to collect, it can slow the application down for an unknown duration at unknown intervals.

5.16.1.4: Algorithm Complexity Reduction Pattern

Choose an algorithm with reduced complexity as measured using the Big-O notation[11]. This usually boosts the performance. In the below Python example, we are using the find algorithm with a list:

```
values = [1, 2, 3, 4, 5, ..., 2000]
if 2000 in values:
    print("Value 2000 found")
```

The above algorithm must traverse the list, which makes it slower ($O(n)$) compared to the find algorithm with a set ($O(1)$):

```
values = {1, 2, 3, 4, 5, ..., 2000}
if 2000 in values:
    print("Value 2000 found")
```

The below algorithm (list comprehension) will generate a list of 20,000 values:

```
values = [value for value in range(20_000)]
```

If we don't need all the 20,000 values in the memory at the same time, we could use a different algorithm (generator expression) which consumes much less memory because not all the 20,000 values are in the memory:

```
values = (value for value in range(20_000))
```

The type of the values object in the above example is Generator, which inherits from Iterator. You can use the values anywhere an iterator is expected.

---

[11]https://en.wikipedia.org/wiki/Big_O_notation

5.16.1.5: Cache Function Results Pattern

You can benefit from caching the function results if you have an expensive pure function that always returns the same result for the same input without any side effects. In Python, you can cache function results using the @cache or @lru_cache decorator. Here is an example:

```
from functools import lru_cache

# Results of 500 most recent calls to the function
# will be cached
@lru_cache(maxsize=500)
def make_expensive_calc(value: int):
    # ...

print(make_expensive_calc(1))
# After the first call,
# the function result for the input value 1
# will be cached

print(make_expensive_calc(1))
# The result of function call is fetched from the cache
```

@cache is the same as @lru_cache(maxsize=None), i.e., the cache does not have a maximum size limit. With relative ease, you can implement a caching decorator in JavaScript/TypeScript.

5.16.1.6: Buffer File I/O Pattern

You can benefit from setting custom buffer sizes if you are reading/writing large files. The below Pyton examples set buffer sizes to 1MB:

```
with open('data.json', 'r', buffering=1_048_576) as data_file:
    data = data_file.read()

with open('data.json', 'w', buffering=1_048_576) as data_file:
    data_file.write(data)
```

5.16.1.7: Share Identical Objects a.k.a Flyweight Pattern

If your application has many objects with some identical properties, those parts of the objects with identical properties are wasting memory. You should extract the common properties to a new class and make the original objects reference a shared object of that new class. Now, your objects share a single common object, and possibly significantly less memory is consumed. This design pattern is called the *flyweight pattern* and was described in more detail in the earlier chapter.

5.16.1.8: Copy Memory in Chunks Pattern (C++)

If you have a contiguous memory chunk, copy it using memcpy. Don't copy memory byte by byte in a for-loop. The implementation of the memcpy function is optimized by a C++ compiler to produce machine code that optimally copies various sizes of memory chunks. Instead of copying a memory chunk byte by byte, it can, for example, copy memory as 64-bit values in a 64-bit operating system.

In the data exporter microservice, there is the possibility that the input message format and output message format are the same, e.g., Avro binary. We can have a situation where an Avro record field can be copied as such from an input message to an output message without any transformation. In that case, decoding that record field is unnecessary functionality, and we can skip that. What we will do instead is copy a chunk of memory. An Avro record field can be relatively large, even 200 bytes consisting of 40 subfields. We can now skip the decoding and encoding of those 40 subfields. We simply copy 200 bytes from the input message to the output message.

5.16.1.9: Replace Virtual Methods with Non-Virtual Methods Pattern (C++)

If you are using a lot of calls to virtual functions in a busy loop, there will be some overhead in checking which virtual method to call due to dynamic dispatch. In C++, this is done using virtual tables (*vtables*) which are used to check which actual method will be called. The additional vtable check can negatively affect performance in busy loops if virtual methods are called frequently. For example, the data exporter microservice's busy can call an Avro binary decoding and encoding function 50000 times a second. We could optimize these calls by implementing Avro binary decoding functions as non-virtual (if previously declared as virtual functions). Non-virtual functions don't need to check the *vtable*, so the call to the function is direct.

5.16.1.10: Inline Methods Pattern (C++)

Suppose you have made the optimization of making a virtual method non-virtual. One more optimization could still be made if the method is small: inline the method. Inlining a method means that calls to the method are eliminated, and the code of the method is placed at the sites where the calls to the method are made. So, the method does not need to be called at all when it has been inlined. In the data exporter microservice, we made the Avro binary encoding and decoding functions non-virtual, and now we can make them also inlined to speed up the microservice. However, a C++ compiler can decide whether an inline function is really inlined or not. We cannot be 100% sure if the function is inlined. It's up to the compiler. When we define a function as an inline function with the C++'s `inline` keyword, we are just giving a hint to the compiler that the function should be inlined. Only non-virtual methods can be inlined. Virtual methods cannot be inlined because they require checking the *vtable* to decide which method should be called.

5.16.1.11: Use Unique Pointer Pattern (C++)

If you are using shared pointers, they need to keep the reference count to the shared pointer up to date. In a busy loop, if you use a shared pointer, say a hundred thousand times a second, it starts to show a difference whether you use a shared pointer or a unique pointer (`std::unique_ptr`). A unique pointer has little to no overhead compared to a raw pointer. For this reason, there is no need to use a raw pointer in modern C++. It would not bring much to the table performance-wise. If you use a raw pointer, you must remember to release the allocated memory associated with the raw pointer by yourself. If you don't need a pointed object to be shared by multiple other objects, you can optimize your code in busy loops by changing shared pointers to unique pointers. Unique pointers always have only one owner, and multiple objects cannot share them.

6: Testing Principles

Testing is traditionally divided into two categories: functional and non-functional testing. This chapter will first describe the functional testing principles and then the non-functional testing principles.

6.1: Functional Testing Principles

Functional testing is divided into three phases:

- Unit testing
- Integration testing
- End-to-end (E2E) testing

Functional test phases can be described with the testing pyramid[1]:

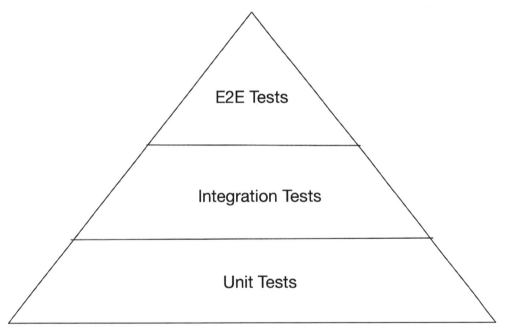

Figure 6.1. Testing Pyramid

The testing pyramid depicts the relative number of tests in each phase. Most tests are unit tests. The second most tests are integration tests; the fewest are E2E tests. Unit tests should cover the whole codebase

---

[1]https://martinfowler.com/articles/practical-test-pyramid.html

of a software component. Unit testing focuses on testing individual public functions as units (of code). Software component integration tests cover the integration of the unit-tested functions to a complete working software component, including testing the interfaces to external services. External services include a database, a message broker, and other microservices. E2E testing focuses on testing the end-to-end functionality of a complete software system.

There are various other terms used to describe different testing phases:

- Module testing (an older term for unit testing)
- (Software) Component testing (same as integration testing)
- System (Integration) testing (same as E2E testing)

The term *component testing* is also used to denote only the integration of the unit-tested modules in a software component without testing the external interfaces. In connection with the *component testing* term, there is the term *integration testing* used to denote the testing of external interfaces of a software component. Here, I use the term *integration testing* to denote both the integration of unit-tested modules and external interfaces.

6.1.1: Unit Testing Principle

Unit tests should test the functionality of public functions as isolated units with as high coverage as possible. The isolation means that dependencies (other classes/-modules/services) are mocked.

Complete isolation is not a mandatory requirement, but you should mock at least all external dependencies, such as external services and databases. This is required to keep the execution time of the unit tests as short as possible. In your unit tests, you can use other dependencies, like other classes, if they are already implemented and available. If not available, you can use mocks or implement the dependencies on the go to be able to use them.

6.1.1.1: TDD Schools: London vs. Detroit/Chicago

Two schools of thought exist regarding unit testing and test-driven development (TDD): *London* and *Detroit/Chicago.* In the London school of TDD, unit tests are created from top to bottom (from higher to lower-level classes) or from outside to inside (considering clean architecture). In practice, this means that you must create mocks for lower-level classes when you implement unit tests for the high-level classes because the low-level classes do not exist yet. London school of TDD is also called *Mockist.* It focuses on interactions between objects and ensuring correct messages are sent between them.

On the other hand, in the Detroit or Chicago school of TDD, unit tests are created from bottom to top (from lower-level classes to higher-level classes) or from inside to outside when considering clean architecture. This TDD style is also called *Classic.* Using the Detroit/Chicago school of TDD means you don't necessarily need to create so many mocks. When you test a higher-level class, you have already implemented the needed lower-level classes, and you can use their implementation in your higher-level class tests. This will make the higher-level class tests partial integration tests.

There are benefits and drawbacks in both TDD schools. These styles are not mutually exclusive. The drawback of the London school of TDD is that mocks create tight coupling to lower-level interfaces, and changing them requires changes to tests. The benefit is that you can follow the natural path of creating higher-level classes first and lower-level classes later as needed. The drawback of the Detroit/Chicago school of TDD is that you need to figure out and implement the lower-level classes first, which might be slow and feel unnatural. In theory, the Detroit/Chicago school tests can be slower if they test dependencies, especially in cases where a high-level class depends on many levels of lower-level classes. Also, a bug in a single unit can cause many tests to fail. The benefit of the Detroit/Chicago school of TDD is that code refactoring is easier, and tests don't break easily because they do not heavily rely on mocks.

Which of the TDD schools is better? It is hard to say. London school of TDD (or unit testing in general) is probably more popular, but it does not make it necessarily better. Many TDD veterans favor the classic approach, i.e., Detroit/Chicago school. Hybrid approaches, where elements from both schools are taken, are also popular. Many developers don't even know these two schools exist. Later in this chapter, I will show you how both schools are used.

Unit tests should be written for public functions only. Do not try to test private functions separately. They should be indirectly tested when testing public functions. Unit tests should test the function specification, i.e., what the function is expected to do in various scenarios, not how the function is implemented. When you unit test only public functions, you can easily refactor the function implementation, e.g., rewrite the private functions that the public function uses without modifying the related unit tests (or with minimal changes).

Below is a JavaScript example:

Figure 6.2. parseConfig.js

```
import { doSomething } from 'other-module';

function readFile(...) {
  // ...
}

export default function parseConfig(...) {
  // ...
  // readFile(...)
  // doSomething(...)
  // ...
}
```

The above module has one public function, parseConfig, and one private function, readFile. In unit testing, you should test the public parseConfig function in isolation and mock the doSomething function, which is imported from another module. You indirectly test the private readFile function when testing the public parseConfig function.

Below is the above example written in Java. You test the Java version in a similar way as the JavaScript version. You write unit tests for the public parseConfig method only. Those tests will test the private readFile function indirectly. You can supply a mock instance of the OtherInterface interface for the ConfigParser constructor when you don't want to test dependencies of the ConfigParser class in the unit tests of the ConfigParser class.

```
public interface OtherInterface {
  void doSomething(...);
}


public class OtherClass implements OtherInterface {
 // ...

 public void doSomething(...) {
    // ...
 }
}


public class ConfigParser {
   private OtherInterface otherObject;

   public ConfigParser(final OtherInterface otherObject) {
      this.otherObject = otherObject;
   }

   // ...

   public Configuration parseConfig(...) {
      // ...
      // readFile(...)
      // otherClass.doSomething(...)
      // ...
   }

   private String readFile(...) {
      // ...
   }
}
```

If you have a public function using many private methods, testing the public method can become complicated, and the test method becomes long, possibly with many expectations on mocks. It can be challenging to remember to test every scenario that exists in the public and related private methods. What you should do is refactor all or some private methods into public methods of one or more new classes (This is the *extract class* refactoring technique explained in the previous chapter). Then, the test method in the original class becomes shorter and more straightforward, with less expectation of mocks. This is an essential refactoring step that should not be forgotten. It helps keep both the source code and unit tests readable and well-organized. The unit test code must be the same high quality as the source. Unit test code should use type annotations and the same linter rules as the source code itself. The unit test code should not contain duplicate code. A unit test method should be a maximum of 5-9 statements long. Aim for a single assertion or put assertions in one well-named private method. If you have more than 5-6 expectations on mocks, you need to refactor the source code the way described above to reduce the number of expectations and shorten the test method.

Unit tests should test all the functionality of a public function: happy path(s), possible failure situations, security issues, and edge/corner cases so that each code line of the function is covered by at least one unit test. If a single line of code contains, e.g., a complex boolean statement, you might need several unit tests to cover all the sub-conditions in the boolean statement. For example:

```
if (isEmpty() || !isInitialized()) {
  // ...
}
```

To fully cover the functionality of the above unit, you need to write three tests: one for the `isEmpty()` condition to be true, one for the `!isInitialized()` to be true, and a test where the if-statement's condition is evaluated to false. If you use a test coverage tool, it will report about untested sub-conditions of boolean expressions. You should always use a test coverage tool.

Security issues in functions are mostly related to the input the function gets. You should ask yourself if the input is secure. If your function receives unvalidated input data from an end-user, that data must be validated against a possible attack by a malicious end-user.

Below are some examples of edge/corner test cases listed:

- Is the last loop counter value correct? This test should detect possible off-by-one errors
- Test with an empty array
- Test with the smallest allowed value
- Test with the biggest allowed value
- Test with a negative value
- Test with a zero value
- Test with a very long string
- Test with an empty string
- Test with floating-point values having different precisions
- Test with floating-point values that are rounded differently
- Test with an extremely small floating-point value
- Test with an extremely large floating-point value

Unit tests should not test the functionality of external dependencies. That is something to be tested with integration tests. A unit test should test a function in isolation from external dependencies. If a function depends on another module that performs database operations, that dependency should be mocked. A *mock* is something that mimics the behavior of a real object or function. Mocking will be described in more detail later in this section.

Testing functions in isolation from external dependencies has two benefits. It makes tests faster. This is a real benefit because you can have a lot of unit tests, and you run them often, so the execution time of the unit tests must be as short as possible. Another benefit is that you don't need to set up external dependencies, like a database, a message broker, and other microservices because you are mocking the functionality of the dependencies.

Unit tests protect you against introducing accidental bugs when refactoring code. Unit tests ensure that the implementation code meets the function specification. It should be remembered that it is hard to write the perfect code on the first try. You are bound to practice refactoring to keep your code base clean and free of technical debt. And when you refactor, the unit tests are on your side to prevent accidentally introducing bugs.

6.1.1.2: Test-Driven Development (TDD)

Test-driven development (TDD) is a software development process in which software requirements are formulated as (unit and integration) test cases before the software is implemented. This is as opposed to the practice where software is implemented first, and test cases are written only after that.

The benefits of TDD are many:

- Lesser likelihood of forgetting to implement some failure scenarios or edge cases
- No big upfront design, but emergent (and usually better) design because of constant refactoring

- Existing tests make the developer feel confident when refactoring
- Less cognitive load for the developer because only one scenario is implemented at a time
- You automatically write testable code
- You don't write unnecessary code because you only write code that makes the tests pass (you can follow the YAGNI principle[2])
- Less need for debugging

TDD's main benefit is not finding bugs early but improving design due to constant refactoring. TDD is both an effective design tool and a testing tool. TDD aims to maximize the software's external and internal quality. External quality is the quality the users see, e.g., a minimal number of bugs and correct features. Internal quality is what the developers see: good design and lack of technical debt. If internal quality is low, it is more likely that a developer can introduce bugs (i.e., cause low external quality) to the software. High internal quality can be achieved with TDD. You have a comprehensive set of tests and a good design with low technical debt. It will be easy for any developer to maintain and develop such software further. I have been in the industry for almost 30 years, and when I began coding, there were no automated tests or test-driven development. Only since around 2010 have I been writing automated unit tests. Due to this background, TDD has been quite difficult for me because there is something I have grown accustomed to: Implement the software first and then do the testing. I assume many of you have also learned it like that, which can make switching to TDD rather difficult. Little material exists that teaches topics using TDD. The Internet is full of books, courses, videos, blogs, and other posts that don't teach you the proper way of development: TDD. The same applies to this book, also. I present code samples in the book but don't always use TDD because it would make everything complicated and more verbose. We are constantly taught to program test-last! When asking people who have conducted TDD, they say the main benefit is that it reduces stress because you don't have to achieve multiple goals simultaneously, like designing the function, thinking of and implementing (and remembering to implement) all possible execution paths.

TDD can feel unnatural at the beginning. It can slow you down at first. You just have to keep practicing it systematically. In that way, you can start gradually seeing the benefits and build a habit of always using TDD. Later, you will notice that it begins to feel natural, and it does not slow you down anymore but brings you the many benefits depicted above. It can actually speed you up because less complex thinking (no big upfront design, safe refactoring) and debugging are needed.

The complete TDD cycle, as instructed by *Kent Beck* in his book *Test-Driven Development by Example* consists of the following steps:

1) Add a test for a specified functionality
2) Run all the tests (The just added test should fail if the functionality it is testing is not implemented yet)
3) Write the simplest possible code that makes the tests pass
4) Run all the tests. (They should pass now)
5) Refactor as needed (Existing tests should ensure that anything won't break)
6) Start again from the first step until all functionality is implemented, refactored, and tested

Instead of TDD, you should actually use low-level behavior-driven development (BDD). We discuss BDD later in this chapter when addressing integration testing. Low-level BDD extends TDD by more formally defining the low-level (function/unit-level) behavior. To use BDD, ensure the following in your unit tests:

---

[2]https://en.wikipedia.org/wiki/You_aren%27t_gonna_need_it

- Test method name tells the tested public function name (feature name) and the scenario that is tested in that particular test method
- The test method body is organized into three sections: Given, When, and Then steps. This is basically the same thing as Arrange-Act-Assert, which is the suggested way to structure unit tests. In the Given/Arrange phase, you prepare everything for the test. In the Act/When phase, you perform an operation; in the Assert/Then phase, you make assertions about the operation result. Try to keep the assertion phase as simple as possible. The best is to have only a single assertion, but that is not always possible. You can also extract multiple assertions into a well-named private method and call that method from the test method in the assertion phase.

Some TDD practitioners suggest naming a test method after the feature it tests, including a description of the scenario and expected outcome. That approach can easily make the test method names too long and hard to read. You can always see the expected result by looking at the end of the test method, which should preferably contain only a single assertion. I also like to put test methods in a test class in the same order I have in the tested class. Also, the scenarios can be ordered from a more specialized scenario to a more generalized scenario (or vice versa). This makes navigating between test methods a breeze. Also, there is not much difference between a class's features and its public methods. Each public method should implement a single feature only (remember the *single responsibility principle*). A single feature (method) consists of one or more scenarios. For example, a Stack class has four features: You can push an item to the stack and pop an item from the stack. You can also ask if the stack isEmpty or ask its size. These features have multiple scenarios: for example, how they behave if the stack is empty versus the stack with items in it. When you add features to a class, you should either put them into new methods or, preferably, use the *open-closed principle* and introduce a totally new class.

Below are two Java examples of test method names in a StackTests class. The first one contains the method name that is tested, and the second one is named after the feature:

```
class StackTests {
  @Test
  void testPop_whenStackIsEmpty() {
    // WHEN + THEN
    assertThrows(...);
  }

  // You can also use method name prefixed with 'it':
  // itShouldRaiseErrorWhenPoppingItemFromEmptyStack
  // The 'it' means what is tested: a stack
  @Test
  void shouldRaiseErrorWhenPoppingItemFromEmptyStack() {
    // WHEN + THEN
    assertThrows(...);
  }
}
```

Here is another Java example:

```
class CarTests {
  @Test
  void testAccelerate() {
    // GIVEN
    final var initialSpeed = ...
    final var car = new Car(initialSpeed);

    // WHEN
    car.accelerate();

    // THEN
    assertTrue(car.getSpeed() > initialSpeed);
  }

  @Test
  void testDecelerate() {
    // GIVEN
    final var initialSpeed = ...
    final var car = new Car(initialSpeed);

    // WHEN
    car.decelerate();

    // THEN
    assertTrue(car.getSpeed() < initialSpeed);
  }

  @Test
  void shouldIncreaseSpeedWhenAccelerates() {
    // GIVEN
    final var initialSpeed = ...
    final var car = new Car(initialSpeed);

    // WHEN
    car.accelerate();

    // THEN
    assertTrue(car.getSpeed() > initialSpeed);
  }

  @Test
  void shouldDecreaseSpeedWhenDecelerates() {
    // GIVEN
    final var initialSpeed = ...
    final var car = new Car(initialSpeed);

    // WHEN
    car.decelerate();

    // THEN
    assertTrue(car.getSpeed() < initialSpeed);
  }
}
```

You could make the assertion even more readable by extracting a well-named method, for example:

```
class CarTests {
  private final int INITIAL_SPEED = ...
  private Car car;

  @BeforeEach
  void setUp() {
    car = new Car(INITIAL_SPEED);
  }

  @Test
  void testAccelerate() {
    // WHEN
    car.accelerate();

    // THEN
    assertSpeedIsIncreased();
  }

  private void assertSpeedIsIncreased() {
    assertTrue(car.getSpeed() > INITIAL_SPEED);
  }
}
```

Notice how well the testAccelerate test method now reads:

> When car accelerate[s], then assert speed is increased

You can use the feature-based naming instead of the method-based naming convention if you want. I use the method-based naming convention in all unit tests in this book.

Let's continue with an example. Suppose there is the following user story in the backlog waiting to be implemented:

> *Parse configuration properties from a configuration string to a configuration object. Config-uration properties can be accessed from the configuration object. If parsing the configuration fails, an error should be produced.*

Let's first write a test for the simplest 'happy path' scenario of the specified functionality: parsing a single property only.

```
class ConfigParserTests {
  private final ConfigParser configParser = new ConfigParserImpl();

  @Test
  void testParse_whenSuccessful() {
    // GIVEN
    final var configString = "propName1=value1";

    // WHEN
    final var config = configParser.parse(configString);

    // THEN
    assertEquals('value1', config.getPropertyValue('propName1'));
  }
}
```

If we run the test, we get a compilation error, meaning the test case we wrote won't pass. Next, we shall write the simplest possible code to make the test case both compile and pass. We can make shortcuts like using a fixed value (constant) instead of a more generalized solution. That is called *faking it*. We can fake it until we make it. We "make it" when we add a new test that forces us to eliminate the constant value and write more generalized code. The part of TDD where you add more tests to drive for a more generalized solution is called *triangulation*.

```
public interface Config {
  String getPropertyValue(final String propertyName);
}


public class ConfigImpl implements Config {
  public String getPropertyValue(final String propertyName) {
    return "value1";
  }
}


public interface ConfigParser {
  Config parse(final String configString);
}


public class ConfigParserImpl implements ConfigParser {
  public Config parse(final String configString) {
    return new ConfigImpl();
  }
}
```

Let's write a test for a 'happy path' scenario where we have two properties. This forces us to make the implementation more generalized. We cannot use a constant anymore, and we should not use two constants with an if/else statement because if we want to parse more than two properties, the approach using constants does not scale.

```
class ConfigParserTests {
  private final ConfigParser configParser = new ConfigParserImpl();

  @Test
  void testParse_whenSuccessful() {
    // GIVEN
    final var configString = "propName1=value1\npropName2=value2";

    // WHEN
    final var config = configParser.parse(configString);

    // THEN
    assertEquals('value1', config.getPropertyValue('propName1'));
    assertEquals('value2', config.getPropertyValue('propName2'));
  }
}
```

If we run all the tests, the new test will fail in the second assertion. Next, we shall write code to make the test cases pass:

```
public class ConfigImpl implements Config {
  private final Map<String, String> propNameToValue;

  public ConfigImpl(final Map<String, String> propNameToValue) {
    this.propNameToValue = propNameToValue;
  }

  public String getPropertyValue(final String propertyName) {
    return propNameToValue.get(propertyName);
  }
}


public class ConfigParserImpl implements ConfigParser {
  Config parse(final String configString) {
    // Parse configString and assign properties to
```

```
    // 'propNameToValue' variable

    return new ConfigImpl(propNameToValue);
  }
}
```

Now, the tests pass, and we can add new functionality. Let's add a test for the case when parsing fails. We can now repeat the TDD cycle from the beginning by creating a failing test first:

```
class ConfigParserTests {
  // ...

  @Test
  void testParse_whenParsingFails() {
    // GIVEN
    final var configString = "invalid";

    try {
      // WHEN
      configParser.parse(configString);

      // THEN
      fail("ConfigParser.ParseError should have been raised");
    } catch(final ConfigParser.ParseError error) {
      // THEN error was successfully raised
    }
  }
}
```

Next, we should refactor the implementation to make the second test pass:

```
public interface ConfigParser {
  // We assume here that this code is part of Data exporter app
  public static class ParseError extends DataExporterError {
    // ...
  }

  Config parse(final String configString) throws ParseError;
}
```

```
public class ConfigParserImpl extends ConfigParser {
  Config parse(final String configString) throws ParseError {
    // Try parse configString and if successful
    // assign config properties to 'maybePropNameToValue'
    // variable

    return maybePropNameToValue
      .map(propNameToValue -> ConfigImpl::new)
      .orElseThrow(ParseError::new);
  }
}
```

We could continue the TDD cycle by adding new test cases for additional functionality if such existed.

Before starting the TDD process, list all the requirements (scenarios) with bullet points so you don't forget any. The scenarios should cover all happy paths, edge cases, and failure/security scenarios. For example, for a single method, you might identify the following six scenarios:

- Edge case scenarios

  - Scenario A

    – Scenario B

- Failure scenarios

    – Scenario C
    – Scenario D

- Security scenarios

    – Scenario E

- Success scenarios

    – Scenario F

Listing all scenarios is an important step in order not to forget to test something because if you don't write a test for something, it's highly likely you won't implement it either. During the TDD process, you often come up with additional scenarios and should add any missing scenarios to the list. Always immediately add a new scenario to the list so you don't forget it. Order the list so that the most specialized scenarios are listed first. Then, start the TDD process by following the ordered list. The most specialized scenarios are typically the easiest to implement, and this is why you should start with them. Specialized scenarios typically include edge cases and failure scenarios.

In the simplest case, a specialized scenario can be implemented, for example, by returning a constant from a function. An example of a specialized scenario with a `List` class's `isEmpty` method is when the list is empty after creating a new `List` object. Test that first, and only after that test a scenario in which something is added to the list, and it is no longer empty.

The generalized scenarios that should make the function work with any input are at the end of the scenario list. To summarize, during the TDD process, you work from a specialized implementation towards a more generalized implementation.

The drawback of TDD is that you cannot always be 100% sure if you have a generalized enough implementation. You can only be 100% sure that your implementation works with the input used in the tests, but you cannot be sure if any input works correctly. To ensure that, you would have to test all possible input values (like all integer values), which is typically unreasonable.

Let's have another TDD example with a function that has edge cases. We should implement a `contains` method for a Java string class. (we assume here that the Java String class's `contains` method does not exist). The method should do the following:

> *The method takes a string argument, and if that string is found in the string the string object represents, then* `true` *is returned. Otherwise,* `false` *is returned.*

There are several scenarios we might want to test to make sure that the function works correctly in every case:

- Edge cases

    1) Strings are equal
    2) Both strings are empty

3) The argument string is empty
4) The string under test is empty
5) The argument string is found at the beginning of the other string
6) The argument string is found at the end of the other string
7) The argument string is longer than the other string

- Happy paths 8) The argument string is found in the middle of the other string 9) The argument string is not found in the other string

Let's start with the first scenario:

```
class MyStringTests {
  @Test
  void testContains_whenStringsAreEqual() {
    // GIVEN
    final var string = new MyString("String");
    final var anotherString = "String";

    // WHEN
    final var strContainsAnotherStr =
      string.contains(anotherString);

    // THEN
    assertTrue(strContainsAnotherStr);
  }
}
```

Next, we implement as much as needed to make the above test pass. The simplest thing to do is to return a constant:

```
public class MyString {
  private final String value;

  public MyString(final String value) {
    this.value = value;
  }

  boolean contains(final String anotherString) {
    return true;
  }
}
```

Let's add a failing test for the second scenario:

```
class MyStringTests {
  // ...

  @Test
  void testContains_whenBothStringsAreEmpty() {
    // GIVEN
    final var string = new MyString("");
    final var anotherString = "";

    // WHEN
    final var strContainsAnotherStr =
      string.contains(anotherString);

    // THEN
    assertTrue(strContainsAnotherStr);
  }
}
```

We don't have to modify the implementation to make the above test pass. Let's add a test for the third scenario:

```
class MyStringTests {
  // ...

  @Test
  void testContains_whenArgumentStringsIsEmpty() {
    // GIVEN
    final var string = new MyString("String");
    final var anotherString = "";

    // WHEN
    final var strContainsAnotherStr =
      string.contains(anotherString);

    // THEN
    assertTrue(strContainsAnotherStr);
  }
}
```

We don't have to modify the implementation to make the above test pass. Let's add a test for the fourth scenario:

```
class MyStringTests {
  // ...

  @Test
  void testContains_whenStringsIsEmpty() {
    // GIVEN
    final var string = new MyString("");
    final var anotherString = "String";

    // WHEN
    final var strContainsAnotherStr =
      string.contains(anotherString);

    // THEN
    assertFalse(strContainsAnotherStr);
  }
}
```

Let's modify the implementation to make the above (and earlier tests) pass:

```
public class MyString {
  private final String value;

  public MyString(final String value) {
    this.value = value;
  }

  boolean contains(final String anotherString) {
    return !value.isEmpty() || anotherString.isEmpty();
  }
}
```

Let's add a test for the fifth scenario:

```
class MyStringTests {
  // ...

  @Test
  void testContains_whenArgStringIsFoundAtBegin() {
    // GIVEN
    final var string = new MyString("String");
    final var anotherString = "Str";

    // WHEN
    final var strContainsAnotherStr =
      string.contains(anotherString);

    // THEN
    assertTrue(strContainsAnotherStr);
  }
}
```

We don't have to modify the implementation to make the above test pass. Let's add a test for the sixth scenario:

```
class MyStringTests {
  // ...

  @Test
  void testContains_whenArgStringIsFoundAtEnd() {
    // GIVEN
    final var string = new MyString("String");
    final var anotherString = "ng";

    // WHEN
    final var strContainsAnotherStr =
      string.contains(anotherString);

    // THEN
    assertTrue(strContainsAnotherStr);
  }
}
```

Let's add a test for the seventh scenario:

```
class MyStringTests {
  // ...

  @Test
  void testContains_whenArgStringIsLongerThanOtherString() {
    // GIVEN
    final var string = new MyString("String");
    final var anotherString = "String111";

    // WHEN
    final var strContainsAnotherStr =
      string.contains(anotherString);

    // THEN
    assertFalse(strContainsAnotherStr);
  }
}
```

Let's modify the implementation:

```
public class MyString {
  private final String value;

  public MyString(final String value) {
    this.value = value;
  }

  boolean contains(final String anotherString) {
   return (!value.isEmpty() || anotherString.isEmpty()) &&
           anotherString.length() <= value.length();
  }
}
```

Let's add a test for the eighth scenario:

```
class MyStringTests {
  // ...

  @Test
  void testContains_whenArgStringIsFoundInMiddle() {
    // GIVEN
    final var string = new MyString("String");
    final var anotherString = "ri";

    // WHEN
    final var strContainsAnotherStr =
      string.contains(anotherString);

    // THEN
    assertTrue(strContainsAnotherStr);
  }
}
```

We don't have to modify the implementation to make the above test pass. Let's add the final test:

```
class MyStringTests {
  // ...

  @Test
  void testContains_whenArgStringIsNotFound() {
    // GIVEN
    final var string = new MyString("String");
    final var anotherString = "aa";

    // WHEN
    final var strContainsAnotherStr =
      string.contains(anotherString);

    // THEN
    assertFalse(strContainsAnotherStr);

  }
}
```

Let's modify the implementation to make the above (and, of course, earlier tests) pass:

```
public class MyString {
  private final String value;

  public MyString(final String value) {
    this.value = value;
  }

  boolean contains(final String anotherString) {
    return (!value.isEmpty() || anotherString.isEmpty()) &&
                    anotherString.length() <= value.length() &&
                    value.indexOf(anotherString) != -1;
  }
}
```

Next, we should refactor. We can notice that the if-statement condition can be simplified to the following:

```
public class MyString {
  private final String value;

  public MyString(final String value) {
    this.value = value;
  }

  boolean contains(final String anotherString) {
    return value.indexOf(anotherString) != -1;
  }
}
```

You may have noticed that some refactoring was needed until we came up with the final solution. This is what happens with TDD. You only consider implementation one scenario at a time, which can result in writing code that will be removed/replaced when making a test for the next scenario pass. This is called *emergent design*.

The above example is a bit contrived because we finally used the indexOf method, which we could have done already in the first test case, but we didn't because we were supposed to write the simplest implementation to make the test pass. Consider the same example when no indexOf method is available, and we must implement the indexOf method functionality (looping through the characters, etc.) in the contains method ourselves. Then, all the tests start to make sense. Many of them are testing edge/corner cases that are important to test. If you are still in doubt, think about implementing the contains method in a language that does not have a range-based for-loop, but you must use character indexes. Then, you would finally understand the importance of testing the edge cases: reveal possible off-by-one errors, for example.

When you encounter a bug, it is usually due to a missing scenario: An edge case is not considered, or implementation for a failure scenario or happy path is missing. To remedy the bug, you should practice TDD by adding a failing test for the missing scenario and then make the bug correction in the code to make the added test (and other tests) pass.

There will be one more TDD example later in this chapter when we have an example using BDD, DDD, OOD, and TDD. If you are not yet fully convinced about TDD, the following section presents an alternative to TDD that is still better than doing tests last.

6.1.1.3: Unit Specification-Driven Development (USDD)

For some of you, the above-described TDD cycle may sound cumbersome, or you may not be fully convinced of its benefits. For this reason, I am presenting an alternative to TDD that you can use until you are ready to try it. The approach I am presenting is inferior to TDD but superior to the traditional "test-last" approach because it reduces the number of bugs by concentrating on the unit (function) specification before the implementation. Specifying the function behavior beforehand has clear benefits. I call this approach *unit specification-driven development* (USDD). When function behavior is defined first, one is usually less likely to forget to test or implement something. The USDD approach forces you to consider the function specification: happy path(s), possible security issues, edge, and failure cases.

If you don't practice USDD and always do the implementation first, it is more likely you will forget an edge case or a particular failure/security scenario. When you don't practice USDD, you go straight to the implementation, and you tend to think only about the happy path(s) and strive to get them working. When focusing 100% on getting the happy path(s) working, you don't consider the edge cases and failure/security scenarios. You might forget to implement them or some of them. If you forget to implement an edge case or failure scenario, you don't also test it. You can have 100% unit test coverage for a function, but a particular edge case or failure/security scenario is left unimplemented and untested. This is what has happened to me, also. And it has happened more than once. After realizing that the USDD approach could save me from those bugs, I started to take it seriously.

You can conduct USDD as an alternative to TDD/BDD. In USDD, you first specify the unit (i.e., function). You extract all the needed tests from the function specification, including the "happy path" or "happy paths", edge cases, and failure/security scenarios. Then, you put a `fail` call in all the tests so as not to forget to implement them later. Additionally, you can add a comment on the expected result of a test. For example, in failure scenarios, you can write a comment that tells what kind of error is expected to be raised, and in an edge case, you can put a comment that tells with the input of x, the output of y is expected. (Later, when the tests are implemented, the comments can be removed.)

Let's say that we have the following function specification:

> *Configuration parser's* `parse` *method parses configuration in JSON format into a configuration object. The method should produce an error if the configuration JSON cannot be parsed. Configuration JSON consists of optional and mandatory properties (name and value of specific type). A missing mandatory property should produce an error, and a missing optional property should use a default value. Extra properties should be discarded. A property with an invalid type of value should produce an error. Two property types are supported: integer and string. Integers must have value in a specified range, and strings have a maximum length. The mandatory configuration properties are the following:* `name` (`type`) *... The optional configuration properties are the following:* `name` (`type`) *...*

Let's first write a failing test case for the "happy path" scenario:

```
class ConfigParserTests {
  @Test
  void testParse_whenSuccessful() {
    // Happy path scenario, returns a 'Config' object
    fail();
}
```

Next, let's write a failing test case for the other scenarios extracted from the above function specification:

```
class ConfigParserTests {
  // ...

  @Test
  void testParse_whenParsingFails() {
    // Failure scenario, should produce an error
    fail();
  }

  @Test
  void testParse_whenMandatoryPropIsMissing() {
    // Failure scenario, should produce an error
    fail();
  }

  @Test
  void testParse_whenOptionalPropIsMissing() {
    // Should use default value
    fail();
  }

  @Test
  void testParse_withExtraProps() {
    // Extra props should be discarded
    fail();
  }

  @Test
  void testParse_whenPropHasInvalidType() {
    // Failure scenario, should produce an error
    fail();
  }

  @Test
  void testParse_whenIntegerPropOutOfRange() {
    // Input validation security scenario, should produce an error
    fail();
  }

  @Test
  void testParse_whenStringPropTooLong() {
    // Input validation security scenario, should produce an error
    fail();
  }
}
```

Now, you have a high-level specification of the function in the form of scenarios. Next, you can continue with the function implementation. After you have completed the function implementation, implement the tests one by one and remove the `fail` calls from them.

Compared to TDD, the benefit of this approach is that you don't have to switch continuously between the implementation source code file and the test source code file. In each phase, you can focus on one thing:

1) Function specification

   - What does the function do? (The happy path scenario(s))
   - What failures are possible? (The failure scenario(s))

     - For example, if a function makes a REST API call, all scenarios related to the failure of the call should be considered: connection failure, timeout, response status code not being 2xx, any response data parsing failures

   - Are there security issues? (The security scenarios)

- For example, if the function gets input from the user, it must be validated, and in case of invalid input, a proper action is taken , like raising an error. Input from the user can be obtained via environment variables, reading files, reading a network socket , and reading standard input.

- Are there edge cases? (The edge case scenario(s))
- When you specify the function, it is not mandatory to write the specification down. You can do it in your head if the function is simple. With a more complex function, you might benefit from writing the specification down to fully understand what the function should do

2) Define different scenarios as failing unit tests
3) Function implementation
4) Implementation of unit tests

In real life, the initial function specification is not always 100% correct or complete. During the function implementation, you might discover, e.g., a new failure scenario that was not in the initial function specification. You should immediately add a new failing unit test for that new scenario so you don't forget to implement it later. Once you think your function implementation is complete, go through the function code line-by-line and check if any line can produce an error that has not yet been considered. Having this habit will reduce the possibility of accidentally leaving some error unhandled in the function code.

Sometimes, you need to modify an existing function because you are not always able to follow the *open-closed principle* for various reasons, such as not possible or feasible. When you need to modify an existing function, follow the below steps:

1) Specification of changes to the function

- What changes in function happy path scenarios?
- What changes in failure scenarios?
- What changes in security scenarios?
- What changes in edge cases?

2) Add/Remove/Modify tests

- Add new scenarios as failing tests
- Remove tests for removed scenarios
- Modify existing tests

3) Implementation changes to the function
4) Implement added unit tests

Let's have an example where we change the configuration parser so that it should produce an error if the configuration contains extra properties. Now we have the specification of the change defined. Next, we need to modify the tests. We need to modify the testParseWithExtraProps method as follows:

```
class ConfigParserTests {
  // ...

  @Test
  void testParse_withExtraProps() {
    // Change this scenario so that an error
    // is expected
  }
}
```

Next, we implement the wanted change and check that all tests pass.

Let's have another example where we change the configuration parser so that the configuration can be given in YAML in addition to JSON. We need to add the following failing unit tests:

```
class ConfigParserTests {
  // ...

  @Test
  void testParse_whenYamlParsingSucceeds() {
    fail();
  }

  @Test
  void testParse_whenYamlParsingFails() {
    // Should produce an error
    fail();
  }
}
```

We should also rename the following test methods: `testParse_whenSuccessful` and `testParse_-whenParsingFails` to `testParse_whenJsonParsingSucceeds` and `testParse_whenJsonParsingFails`. Next, we implement the changes to the function, and lastly, we implement the two new tests. (Depending on the actual test implementation, you may or may not need to make small changes to JSON parsing-related tests to make them pass.)

As the final example, let's make the following change: Configuration has no optional properties, but all properties are mandatory. This means that we can remove the following test: `testParse_whenOptionalPropIsMissing`. We also need to change the `testParse_whenMandatoryPropIsMissing` test:

```
class ConfigParserTests {
  // ...

  @Test
  void testParse_whenMandatoryPropIsMissing() {
    // Change this scenario so that an error
    // is expected
  }
}
```

Once we have implemented the change, we can run all the tests and ensure they pass.

I have presented two alternative methods for writing unit tests: TDD and USDD. As a professional developer, you should use either of them. TDD brings more benefits because it is also a design tool, but USDD is much better than *test-last*, i.e., writing unit tests only after implementation is ready. If you think you are not ready for TDD yet, try USDD first and reconsider TDD at some point in the future.

6.1.1.4: Naming Conventions

When functions to be tested are in a class, a respective class for unit tests should be created. For example, if there is a ConfigParser class, the respective class for unit tests should be ConfigParserTests. This makes locating the file containing unit tests for a particular implementation class easy.

If you are naming your test methods according to the method they test, use the following naming convention. For example, if the tested method is tryParse, the test method name should be testParse. There are usually several tests for a single function. All test method names should begin with *test<function-name>*, but the test method name should also describe the specific scenario the test method tests, for example: testParse_whenParsingFails. The method name and the scenario should be separated by a single underscore to enhance readability.

When using the BDD-style Jest testing library with JavaScript or TypeScript, unit tests are organized and named in the following manner:

```
describe('<class-name>', () => {
  describe('<public-method-name>', () => {
    it('should do this...', () => {
      // ...
    });

    it('should do other thing when...', () => {
      // ...
    });

    // Other scenarios...
  });
});

// Example:
describe('ConfigParser', () => {
  describe('parse', () => {
    it('should parse config string successfully', () => {
      // ...
    });

    it('should throw an error if parsing fails', () => {
      // ...
    });

    // Other scenarios...
  });
});
```

6.1.1.5: Mocking

Mocks are one form of *test doubles*. Test doubles are any kind of pretend objects used in place of real objects for testing purposes. The following kinds of test doubles can be identified:

- *Fakes* are objects that have working implementations but are usually simplified versions (suitable for testing) of the real implementations.
- *Stubs* are objects providing fixed responses to calls made to them.
- *Spies* are stubs that record information based on how they were called.
- *Mocks* are the most versatile test doubles. They are objects pre-programmed with expectations (e.g., what a method should return when it is called), and like spies, they record information based on how they were called, and those calls can be verified in the test. Mocks are probably the ones you use on a daily basis.

Let's have a small Spring Boot example of mocking dependencies in unit tests. We have a service class that contains public functions for which we want to write unit tests:

Figure 6.3. SalesItemServiceImpl.java

```java
@Service
public class SalesItemServiceImpl implements SalesItemService {
  @Autowired
  private SalesItemRepository salesItemRepository;

  @AutoWired
  private SalesItemFactory salesItemFactory;

  @Override
  public final SalesItem createSalesItem(
    final InputSalesItem inputSalesItem
  ) {
    return salesItemRepository.save(
      salesItemFactory.createFrom(inputSalesItem));
  }

  @Override
  public final Iterable<SalesItem> getSalesItems() {
    return salesItemRepository.findAll();
  }
}
```

In the Spring Boot project, we need to define the following dependency in the build.gradle file:

```
dependencies {
  // Other dependencies ...
  testImplementation 'org.springframework.boot:spring-boot-starter-test'
}
```

Now, we can create unit tests using JUnit and use the Mockito[3] library for mocking. The above code shows that the SalesItemServiceImpl service depends on a SalesItemRepository. According to the unit testing principle, we should mock that dependency. Similarly, we should also mock the SalesItemFactory dependency:

Figure 6.4. SalesItemServiceTests.java

```java
import org.junit.jupiter.api.Test;
import org.mockito.InjectMocks;
import org.mockito.Mock;
import org.mockito.Mockito;
import org.springframework.boot.test.context.SpringBootTest;

import java.util.List;

import static org.junit.jupiter.api.Assertions.assertEquals;
import static org.mockito.ArgumentMatchers.any;
import static org.mockito.ArgumentMatchers.refEq;


@SpringBootTest
class SalesItemServiceTests {
  private static final String SALES_ITEMS_NOT_EQUAL = "Sales items not equal";

  // Create sales item mock
  @Mock
  private SalesItem mockSalesItem;
```

[3]https://site.mockito.org/

```
// Create input sales item mock
@Mock
private InputSalesItem mockInputSalesItem;

// Create mock implementation of
// SalesItemRepository interface
@Mock
private SalesItemRepository mockSalesItemRepository;

// Create mock implementation of
// SalesItemFactory interface
@Mock
private SalesItemFactory mockSalesItemFactory;

// Injects 'mockSalesItemRepository' and 'mockSalesItemFactory'
// mocks to 'salesItemService'
@InjectMocks
private SalesItemService salesItemService = new SalesItemServiceImpl();

@Test
final void testCreateSalesItem() {
  // GIVEN
  // Instructs to return 'mockSalesItem' when
  // salesItemFactoryMock's createFrom
  // method is called with an argument that reference
  // equals 'mockInputSalesItem'
  Mockito
    .when(salesItemFactoryMock.createFrom(refEq(mockInputSalesItem)))
    .thenReturn(mockSalesItem);

  // Instructs to return 'mockSalesItem' when
  // salesItemRepositoryMock's 'save' method is called
  // with an argument that reference equals 'mockSalesItem'
  Mockito
    .when(salesItemRepositoryMock.save(refEq(mockSalesItem)))
    .thenReturn(mockSalesItem);

  // WHEN
  final var salesItem = salesItemService.createSalesItem(mockInputSalesItem);

  // THEN
  assertEquals(mockSalesItem, salesItem, SALES_ITEMS_NOT_EQUAL);
}

@Test
final void testGetSalesItems() {
  // GIVEN
  // Instructs to return a list of containing one sales item
  // 'mockSalesItem' when salesItemRepository's 'findAll'
  // method is called
  Mockito
    .when(salesItemRepositoryMock.findAll())
    .thenReturn(List.of(mockSalesItem));

  // WHEN
  final var salesItems = salesItemService.getSalesItems();

  // THEN
  final var iterator = salesItems.iterator();

  assertEquals(iterator.next(), mockSalesItem, SALES_ITEMS_NOT_EQUAL);
  assertFalse(iterator.hasNext());
}
}
```

Java has many testing frameworks and mocking libraries. Below is a small example from a JakartaEE microservice that uses TestNG[4] and JMockit[5] libraries for unit testing and mocking, respectively. In the below example, we are testing a couple of methods from a `ChartStore` class, which is responsible for handling the persistence of chart entities using Java Persistence API (JPA).

Figure 6.5. ChartStoreTests.java

```
import com.silensoft.conflated...DuplicateEntityError;
import mockit.Expectations;
import mockit.Injectable;
import mockit.Mocked;
import mockit.Tested;
import mockit.Verifications;
import org.testng.annotations.Test;

import javax.persistence.EntityExistsException;
import javax.persistence.EntityManager;

import java.util.Collections;
import java.util.List;

import static org.testng.Assert.assertEquals;
import static org.testng.Assert.fail;


public class ChartRepositoryTests {
  // chartRepository will contain an instance
  // of ChartRepositoryImpl after @Tested
  // annotation is processed
  @Tested
  private ChartRepositoryImpl chartRepository;

  // @Injectable annotation creates a mock instance
  // of EntityManager interface and then injects
  // it to tested object, in this case 'chartRepository'
  // ChartRepositoryImpl class has an attribute of
  // type EntityManager which is annotated with an
  // @Inject annotation from JakartaEE
  @Injectable
  private EntityManager mockEntityManager;

  // Create a mock instance of Chart
  // (does not inject anywhere)
  @Mocked
  private Chart mockChart;

  @Test
  void testCreate() {
    // WHEN
    chartRepository.create(mockChart);

    // THEN
    // JMockit's verification block checks
    // that below mock functions are called
    new Verifications() {{
      mockEntityManager.persist(mockChart);
      mockEntityManager.flush();
    }};
  }

  @Test
  void testCreate_whenChartAlreadyExists() {
    // GIVEN
    // JMockit's expectations block will define what mock methods
    // calls are expected and also can specify
    // the return value or result of the mock method call.
```

[4]https://testng.org/

[5]https://jmockit.github.io/

```
    // Below the 'persist' mock method call will throw
    // EntityExistsException
    new Expectations() {{
      mockEntityManager.persist(mockChart);
      result = new EntityExistsException();
    }};

    // WHEN + THEN
    assertThrows(
      DuplicateEntityError.class,
      () -> chartRepository.create(mockChart)
    );
  }

  @Test
  void testGetById() {
    // GIVEN
    new Expectations() {{
      mockEntityManager.find(Chart.class, 1L);
      result = mockChart;
    }};

    // WHEN
    final var chart = chartRepository.getById(1L);

    // THEN
    assertEquals(mockChart, chart);
  }
}
```

Let's have a unit testing example with JavaScript/TypeScript. We will write a unit test for the following function using the Jest library:

Figure 6.6. fetchTodos.ts

```
import store from '../../store/store';
import todoService from '../services/todoService';

export default async function fetchTodos(): Promise<void> {
  const { todoState } = store.getState();
  todoState.isFetching = true;

  try {
    todoState.todos = await todoService.tryFetchTodos();
    todoState.fetchingHasFailed = false;
  } catch(error) {
    todoState.fetchingHasFailed = true;
  }

  todoState.isFetching = false;
}
```

Below is the unit test case for the happy path scenario:

Figure 6.7. fetchTodos.test.ts

```
import store from '../../store/store';
import todoService from '../services/todoService';
import fetchTodos from 'fetchTodos';
// ...

// Mock both 'store' and 'todoService' objects
jest.mock('../../store/store');
jest.mock('../services/todoService');

describe('fetchTodos', async () => {
  it('should fetch todos from todo service', async () => {
    // GIVEN
    const todoState = { todos: [] } as TodoState;
    store.getState.mockReturnValue({ todoState });

    const todos = [{
      id: 1,
      name: 'todo',
      isDone: false
    }];

    todoService.tryFetchTodos.mockResolvedValue(todos);

    // WHEN
    await fetchTodos();

    // THEN
    expect(todoState.isFetching).toBe(false);
    expect(todoState.fetchingHasFailed).toBe(false);
    expect(todoState.todos).toBe(todos);
  });
});
```

In the above example, we used the jest.mock function to create mocked versions of the store and todoService modules. Another way to handle mocking with Jest is using jest.fn(), which creates a mocked function. Let's assume that the fetchTodos function is changed so that it takes a store and todoService as its arguments:

Figure 6.8. fetchTodos.ts

```
// ...

export default async function fetchTodos(
  store: Store,
  todoService: TodoService
): Promise<void> {
  // Same code here as in above example...
}
```

Now, the mocking would look like the following:

Figure 6.9. fetchTodos.test.ts

```
import fetchTodos from 'fetchTodos';
// ...

const store = {
  getState: jest.fn()
};

const todoService = {
  tryFetchTodos: jest.fn();
}

describe('fetchTodos', async () => {
  it('should fetch todos from todo service', async () => {
    // GIVEN
    // Same code as in earlier example...

    // WHEN
    await fetchTodos(store as any, todoService as any);

    // THEN
    // Same code as in earlier example...
  });
});
```

Let's have an example using C++ and Google Test unit testing framework. In C++, you can define a mock class by extending a pure virtual base class ("interface") and using Google Mock macros to define mocked methods.

Source code for below two C++ examples can be found here[6].

Below is the definition of a detectedAnomalies method that we want to unit test:

Figure 6.10. AnomalyDetectionEngine.h

```
class AnomalyDetectionEngine
{
public:
  virtual ~AnomalyDetectionEngine() = default;

  virtual void detectAnomalies() = 0;
};
```

[6]https://github.com/pksilen/clean-code-principles-code/tree/main/chapter4/cpptests

Figure 6.11. AnomalyDetectionEngineImpl.h

```
#include <memory>
#include "AnomalyDetectionEngine.h"
#include "Configuration.h"


class AnomalyDetectionEngineImpl : public AnomalyDetectionEngine
{
public:
  explicit AnomalyDetectionEngineImpl(
    std::shared_ptr<Configuration> configuration
  );

  void detectAnomalies() override;

private:
  void detectAnomalies(
    const std::shared_ptr<AnomalyDetectionRule>& anomalyDetectionRule
  );

  std::shared_ptr<Configuration> m_configuration;
};
```

Figure 6.12. AnomalyDetectionEngineImpl.cpp

```
#include <algorithm>
#include <execution>
#include "AnomalyDetectionEngineImpl.h"


AnomalyDetectionEngineImpl::AnomalyDetectionEngineImpl(
  std::shared_ptr<Configuration> configuration
) : m_configuration(std::move(configuration))
{}

void AnomalyDetectionEngineImpl::detectAnomalies()
{
  const auto anomalyDetectionRules =
    m_configuration->getAnomalyDetectionRules();

  std::for_each(std::execution::par,
                anomalyDetectionRules->cbegin(),
                anomalyDetectionRules->cend(),
                [this](const auto& anomalyDetectionRule)
                {
                  detectAnomalies(anomalyDetectionRule);
                });
}
void AnomalyDetectionEngineImpl::detectAnomalies(
  const std::shared_ptr<AnomalyDetectionRule>& anomalyDetectionRule
)
{
  const auto anomalyIndicators = anomalyDetectionRule->detectAnomalies();

  std::ranges::for_each(*anomalyIndicators,
                        [](const auto& anomalyIndicator)
                        {
                          anomalyIndicator->publish();
                        });
}
```

Let's create a Configuration class and a ConfigurationMock class for mocks:

Figure 6.13. Configuration.h

```
#include <memory>
#include <vector>
#include "AnomalyDetectionRule.h"


class Configuration
{
public:
  virtual ~Configuration() = default;

  virtual std::shared_ptr<AnomalyDetectionRules>
  getAnomalyDetectionRules() const = 0;
};
```

Figure 6.14. ConfigurationMock.h

```
#include <gmock/gmock.h>
#include "Configuration.h"


class ConfigurationMock : public Configuration
{
public:
  MOCK_METHOD(std::shared_ptr<AnomalyDetectionRules>,
              getAnomalyDetectionRules, (), (const)
  );
};
```

Let's create an `AnomalyDetectionRule` class and a respective mock class, `AnomalyDetectionRuleMock`:

Figure 6.15. AnomalyDetectionRule.h

```
#include "AnomalyIndicator.h"


class AnomalyDetectionRule
{
public:
  virtual ~AnomalyDetectionRule() = default;

  virtual std::shared_ptr<AnomalyIndicators>
  detectAnomalies() = 0;
};

using AnomalyDetectionRules =
  std::vector<std::shared_ptr<AnomalyDetectionRule>>;
```

Figure 6.16. AnomalyDetectionRuleMock.h

```
#include <gmock/gmock.h>
#include "AnomalyDetectionRule.h"


class AnomalyDetectionRuleMock : public AnomalyDetectionRule
{
  public:
    MOCK_METHOD(std::shared_ptr<AnomalyIndicators>,
                detectAnomalies, ());
};
```

Let's create an `AnomalyIndicator` class and a mock class, `AnomalyIndicatorMock`:

Figure 6.17. AnomalyIndicator.h

```
#include <memory>
#include <vector>


class AnomalyIndicator
{
public:
  virtual ~AnomalyIndicator() = default;

  virtual void publish() = 0;
};

using AnomalyIndicators =
  std::vector<std::shared_ptr<AnomalyIndicator>>;
```

Figure 6.18. AnomalyIndicatorMock.h

```
#include <gmock/gmock.h>
#include "AnomalyIndicator.h"


class AnomalyIndicatorMock : public AnomalyIndicator
{
public:
  MOCK_METHOD(void, publish, ());
};
```

Let's create a unit test for the detectAnomalies method in the AnomalyDetectionEngineImpl class:

Figure 6.19. AnomalyDetectionEngineImplTests.h

```
#include <gtest/gtest.h>
#include "ConfigurationMock.h"
#include "AnomalyDetectionRuleMock.h"
#include "AnomalyIndicatorMock.h"


class AnomalyDetectionEngineImplTests : public testing::Test
{
protected:
  void SetUp() override {
    m_anomalyDetectionRules->push_back(m_anomalyDetectionRuleMock);
    m_anomalyIndicators->push_back(m_anomalyIndicatorMock);
  }

  std::shared_ptr<ConfigurationMock> m_configurationMock{
    std::make_shared<ConfigurationMock>()
  };

  std::shared_ptr<AnomalyDetectionRuleMock> m_anomalyDetectionRuleMock{
    std::make_shared<AnomalyDetectionRuleMock>()
  };

  std::shared_ptr<AnomalyDetectionRules> m_anomalyDetectionRules{
    std::make_shared<AnomalyDetectionRules>()
  };

  std::shared_ptr<AnomalyIndicatorMock> m_anomalyIndicatorMock{
    std::make_shared<AnomalyIndicatorMock>()
  };

  std::shared_ptr<AnomalyIndicators> m_anomalyIndicators{
    std::make_shared<AnomalyIndicators>()
  }
};
```

Figure 6.20. AnomalyDetectionEngineImplTests.cpp

```cpp
#include "../src/AnomalyDetectionEngineImpl.h"
#include "AnomalyDetectionEngineImplTests.h"

using testing::Return;

TEST_F(AnomalyDetectionEngineImplTests, testDetectAnomalies)
{
  // GIVEN
  AnomalyDetectionEngineImpl anomalyDetectionEngine{m_configurationMock};

  // EXPECTATIONS
  EXPECT_CALL(*m_configurationMock, getAnomalyDetectionRules)
    .Times(1)
    .WillOnce(Return(m_anomalyDetectionRules));

  EXPECT_CALL(*m_anomalyDetectionRuleMock, detectAnomalies)
    .Times(1)
    .WillOnce(Return(m_anomalyIndicators));

  EXPECT_CALL(*m_anomalyIndicatorMock, publish).Times(1);

  // WHEN
  anomalyDetectionEngine.detectAnomalies();
}
```

The above example did not contain dependency injection, so let's have another example in C++ where dependency injection is used. First, we define a generic base class for singletons:

Figure 6.21. Singleton.h

```cpp
#include <memory>

template<typename T>
class Singleton
{
public:
  Singleton() = default;

  virtual ~Singleton()
  {
    m_instance.reset();
  };

  static inline std::shared_ptr<T>& getInstance()
  {
    return m_instance;
  }

  static void setInstance(const std::shared_ptr<T>& instance)
  {
    m_instance = instance;
  }
private:
  static inline std::shared_ptr<T> m_instance;
};
```

Next, we implement a configuration parser that we will later unit test:

Figure 6.22. ConfigParserImpl.h

```
#include <memory>
#include "Configuration.h"


class ConfigParserImpl {
public:
  std::shared_ptr<Configuration> parse();
};
```

Figure 6.23. ConfigParserImpl.cpp

```
#include "AnomalyDetectionRulesParser.h"
#include "Configuration.h"
#include "ConfigFactory.h"
#include "ConfigParserImpl.h"
#include "MeasurementDataSourcesParser.h"


std::shared_ptr<Configuration>
ConfigParserImpl::parse(...)
{
  const auto measurementDataSources =
    MeasurementDataSourcesParser::getInstance()->parse(...);

  const auto anomalyDetectionRules =
    AnomalyDetectionRulesParser::getInstance()->parse(...);

  return ConfigFactory::getInstance()
    ->createConfig(anomalyDetectionRules);
}
```

Next, we define MeasurementDataSource, MeasurementDataSourcesParser, and MeasurementDataSourcesParserImpl classes:

Figure 6.24. MeasurementDataSource.h

```
#include <memory>
#include <vector>


class MeasurementDataSource {
  // ...
};

using MeasurementDataSources =
  std::vector<std::shared_ptr<MeasurementDataSource>>;
```

Figure 6.25. MeasurementDataSourcesParser.h

```
#include "Singleton.h"
#include "MeasurementDataSource.h"


class MeasurementDataSourcesParser :
  public Singleton<MeasurementDataSourcesParser>
{
public:
  virtual std::shared_ptr<MeasurementDataSources> parse(...) = 0;
};
```

Figure 6.26. MeasurementDataSourcesParserImpl.h

```
#include "MeasurementDataSourcesParser.h"


class MeasurementDataSourcesParserImpl :
  public MeasurementDataSourcesParser
{
public:
  std::shared_ptr<MeasurementDataSources> parse(...) override {
    // ...
  }
};
```

Next, we define `AnomalyDetectionRulesParser` and `AnomalyDetectionRulesParserImpl` classes:

Figure 6.27. AnomalyDetectionRulesParser.h

```
#include "Singleton.h"
#include "AnomalyDetectionRule.h"


class AnomalyDetectionRulesParser :
  public Singleton<AnomalyDetectionRulesParser>
{
public:
  virtual std::shared_ptr<AnomalyDetectionRules> parse(...) = 0;
};
```

Figure 6.28. AnomalyDetectionRulesParserImpl.h

```
#include "AnomalyDetectionRulesParser.h"


class AnomalyDetectionRulesParserImpl :
  public AnomalyDetectionRulesParser
{
public:
  std::shared_ptr<AnomalyDetectionRules> parse(...) override {
    // ...
  }
};
```

Next, we define the `ConfigFactory` and `ConfigFactoryImpl` classes:

{title: "ConfigFactory.h"

```
#include "Singleton.h"
#include "Configuration.h"


class ConfigFactory :
  public Singleton<ConfigFactory>
{
public:
  virtual std::shared_ptr<Configuration>
  createConfig(
    const std::shared_ptr<AnomalyDetectionRules>& rules
  ) = 0;
};
```

Figure 6.29. ConfigFactoryImpl.h

```
#include "ConfigFactory.h"


class ConfigFactoryImpl : public ConfigFactory
{
public:
  std::shared_ptr<Configuration>
  createConfig(
    const std::shared_ptr<AnomalyDetectionRules>& rules
  ) override {
    // ...
  }
};
```

Then, we define a dependency injector class:

Figure 6.30. DependencyInjector.h

```
#include "AnomalyDetectionRulesParserImpl.h"
#include "ConfigFactoryImpl.h"
#include "MeasurementDataSourcesParserImpl.h"


class DependencyInjector final
{
public:
  static void injectDependencies()
  {
    AnomalyDetectionRulesParser::setInstance(
      std::make_shared<AnomalyDetectionRulesParserImpl>()
    );

    ConfigFactory::setInstance(
      std::make_shared<ConfigFactoryImpl>()
    );

    MeasurementDataSourcesParser::setInstance(
      std::make_shared<MeasurementDataSourcesParserImpl>()
    );
  }

private:
  DependencyInjector() = default;
};
```

We inject dependencies upon application startup using the dependency injector:

Figure 6.31. main.cpp

```
#include "DependencyInjector.h"


int main()
{
  DependencyInjector::injectDependencies();

  // Initialize and start application...
}
```

Let's define a unit test class for the ConfigParserImpl class:

Figure 6.32. ConfigParserImplTests.h

```
#include "MockDependenciesInjectedTest.h"

class ConfigParserImplTests :
  public MockDependenciesInjectedTest
{};
```

All unit test classes should inherit from a base class that injects mock dependencies. When tests are completed, the mock dependencies will be removed. The Google Test framework requires this removal because it only validates expectations on a mock upon the mock object destruction.

Figure 6.33. MockDependenciesInjectedTest.h

```
#include <gtest/gtest.h>
#include "MockDependencyInjector.h"

class MockDependenciesInjectedTest :
  public testing::Test
{
protected:
  void SetUp() override
  {
    m_mockDependencyInjector.injectMockDependencies();
  }

  void TearDown() override
  {
    m_mockDependencyInjector.removeMockDependencies();
  }

  MockDependencyInjector m_mockDependencyInjector;
};
```

Below are all the mock classes defined:

Figure 6.34. AnomalyDetectionRulesParserMock.h

```
#include <gmock/gmock.h>
#include "AnomalyDetectionRulesParser.h"

class AnomalyDetectionRulesParserMock :
  public AnomalyDetectionRulesParser
{
public:
  MOCK_METHOD(std::shared_ptr<AnomalyDetectionRules>, parse, (...));
};
```

Figure 6.35. ConfigFactoryMock.h

```
#include <gmock/gmock.h>
#include "ConfigFactory.h"


class ConfigFactoryMock : public ConfigFactory
{
public:
  MOCK_METHOD(
    std::shared_ptr<Configuration>,
    createConfig,
    (const std::shared_ptr<AnomalyDetectionRules>& rules)
  );
};
```

Figure 6.36. MeasurementDataSourcesParserMock.h

```
#include <gmock/gmock.h>
#include "MeasurementDataSourcesParser.h"


class MeasurementDataSourcesParserMock :
  public MeasurementDataSourcesParser
{
public:
  MOCK_METHOD(std::shared_ptr<MeasurementDataSources>, parse, (...));
};
```

Below is the MockDependencyInjector class defined:

Figure 6.37. MockDependencyInjector.h

```
#include "AnomalyDetectionRulesParserMock.h"
#include "ConfigFactoryMock.h"
#include "MeasurementDataSourcesParserMock.h"


class MockDependencyInjector final
{
public:
  std::shared_ptr<AnomalyDetectionRulesParserMock>
  m_anomalyDetectionRulesParserMock{
    std::make_shared<AnomalyDetectionRulesParserMock>()
  };

  std::shared_ptr<ConfigFactoryMock> m_configFactoryMock{
    std::make_shared<ConfigFactoryMock>()
  };

  std::shared_ptr<MeasurementDataSourcesParserMock>
  m_measurementDataSourcesParserMock{
    std::make_shared<MeasurementDataSourcesParserMock>()
  };

  void injectMockDependencies() const
  {
    AnomalyDetectionRulesParser::setInstance(
      m_anomalyDetectionRulesParserMock
    );

    ConfigFactory::setInstance(
      m_configFactoryMock
    );

    MeasurementDataSourcesParser::setInstance(
```

```
      m_measurementDataSourcesParserMock
    );
  }

  void removeMockDependencies() const {
    AnomalyDetectionRulesParser::setInstance({nullptr});
    ConfigFactory::setInstance({nullptr});
    MeasurementDataSourcesParser::setInstance({nullptr});
  }
};
```

Below is the unit test implementation that uses the mocks:

Figure 6.38. ConfigParserImplTests.cpp

```cpp
#include "ConfigParserImplTests.h"
#include "ConfigParserImpl.h"


using testing::Eq;
using testing::Return;

TEST_F(ConfigParserImplTests, testParseConfig)
{
  // GIVEN
  ConfigParserImpl configParser;

  // EXPECTATIONS
  EXPECT_CALL(
    *m_mockDependencyInjector.m_anomalyDetectionRulesParserMock,
    parse
  ).Times(1)
   .WillOnce(Return(m_anomalyDetectionRules));

  EXPECT_CALL(
    *m_mockDependencyInjector.m_measurementDataSourcesParserMock,
    parse
  ).Times(1)
   .WillOnce(Return(m_measurementDataSources));

  EXPECT_CALL(
    *m_mockDependencyInjector.m_configFactoryMock,
    createConfig(Eq(m_anomalyDetectionRules))
  ).Times(1)
   .WillOnce(Return(m_configMock));

  // WHEN
  const auto configuration = configParser.parse();

  // THEN
  ASSERT_EQ(configuration, m_configMock);
}
```

You can also make sure that implementation class instances can be created only in the `DependencyInjector` class by declaring implementation class constructors private and making the `DependencyInjector` class a friend of the implementation classes. In this way, no one can accidentally create an instance of an implementation class. Instances of implementation classes should be created by the dependency injector only. Below is an implementation class where the constructor is made private, and the dependency injector is made a friend of the class:

Figure 6.39. AnomalyDetectionRulesParserImpl.h

```
#include "AnomalyDetectionRulesParser.h"

class AnomalyDetectionRulesParserImpl :
  public AnomalyDetectionRulesParser
{
  friend class DependencyInjector;

public:
  std::shared_ptr<AnomalyDetectionRules> parse() override;

private:
  AnomalyDetectionRulesParserImpl() = default;
};
```

6.1.1.6: Web UI Component Testing

UI component testing differs from regular unit testing because you cannot necessarily test the functions of a UI component in isolation if you have, for example, a React functional component. You must conduct UI component testing by mounting the component to the DOM and then perform tests by triggering events, for example. This way, you can test the event handler functions of a UI component. The rendering part should also be tested. It can be tested by producing a snapshot of the rendered component and storing that in version control. Further rendering tests should compare the rendered result to the snapshot stored in the version control.

Below is an example of testing the rendering of a React component, NumberInput:

Figure 6.40. NumberInput.test.jsx

```
import renderer from 'react-test-renderer';
// ...

describe('NumberInput') () => {
  // ...

  describe('render', () => {
    it('renders with buttons on left and right"', () => {
      const numberInputAsJson =
        renderer
          .create(<NumberInput buttonPlacement="leftAndRight"/>)
          .toJSON();

      expect(numberInputAsJson).toMatchSnapshot();
    });

    it('renders with buttons on right', () => {
      const numberInputAsJson =
        renderer
          .create(<NumberInput buttonPlacement="right"/>)
          .toJSON();

      expect(numberInputAsJson).toMatchSnapshot();
    });
  });
});
```

Below is an example unit test for the number input's decrement button's click event handler function, decrementValue:

Figure 6.41. NumberInput.test.jsx

```
import { render, fireEvent, screen } from '@testing-library/react'
// ...

describe('NumberInput') () => {
  // ...

  describe('decrementValue', () => {
    it('should decrement value by given step amount', () => {
      render(<NumberInput value="3" stepAmount={2} />);
      fireEvent.click(screen.getByText('-'));
      const numberInputElement = screen.getByDisplayValue('1');
      expect(numberInputElement).toBeTruthy();
    });
  });
});
```

In the above example, we used the testing-library[7], which has implementations for all the common UI frameworks: React, Vue, and Angular. It means you can use mostly the same testing API regardless of your UI framework. There are tiny differences, basically only in the syntax of the render method. If you have implemented some UI components and unit tests for them with React and would like to reimplement them with Vue, you don't need to reimplement all the unit tests. You only need to modify them slightly (e.g., make changes to the render function calls). Otherwise, the existing unit tests should work because the behavior of the UI component did not change, only its internal implementation technology from React to Vue.

6.1.2: Software Component Integration Testing Principle

Integration testing aims to test that a software component works against actual dependencies and that its public methods correctly understand the purpose and signature of other public methods they are using.

The target of software component integration testing is that all public functions of the software component should be touched by at least one integration test. Not all functionality of the public functions should be tested because that has already been done in the unit testing phase. This is why there are fewer integration tests than unit tests. The term *integration testing* sometimes refers to integrating a complete software system or a product. However, it should only be used to describe software component integration. When testing a product or a software system, instead of *product integration [testing]* or *system integration [testing]*, the term *end-to-end testing* should be preferred to avoid confusion and misunderstandings.

The best way to do the integration testing is using black-box testing[8]. The software component is treated as a black box with inputs and outputs. Test automation developers can use any programming language and testing framework to develop the tests. Integration tests do not depend on the source code. It can be changed or completely rewritten in a different programming language without the need to modify the integration tests. Test automation engineers can also start writing integration tests immediately and don't have to wait for the implementation to be ready.

The best way to define integration tests is by using behavior-driven development[9] (BDD). and acceptance test-driven development[10] ATDD. BDD and ATDD encourage teams to use domain-driven design and

[7]https://testing-library.com/
[8]https://en.wikipedia.org/wiki/Black-box_testing
[9]https://en.wikipedia.org/wiki/Behavior-driven_development
[10]https://en.wikipedia.org/wiki/Acceptance_test-driven_development

concrete examples to formalize a shared understanding of how a software component should behave. In BDD and ATDD, behavioral specifications are the root of the integration tests. A development team should create behavioral specifications for each backlog feature. The specifications are the basis for integration tests that also serve as acceptance tests for the feature. When the team demonstrates a complete feature in a system demo, they should also demonstrate the passing acceptance tests. This practice will shift the integration testing to the left, meaning writing the integration tests can start early and proceed in parallel with the actual implementation. The development team writes a failing integration test and only after that implements enough source code to make that test pass. BDD and ATDD also ensure that it is less likely to forget to test some functionality because the functionality is first formally specified as tests before implementation begins.

When writing behavioral specifications, happy-path scenarios and the main error scenarios should be covered. The idea is not to test every possible error that can occur.

One widely used way to write behavioral specifications is the Gherkin[11] language. However, it is not the only way. So, we cannot say that BDD equals Gherkin. You can even write integration tests using a unit testing framework if you prefer. An example of that approach is available in *Steve Freeman*'s and *Nat Pryce*'s book *Growing Object-Oriented Software, Guided by Tests*. The problem with using a unit testing framework for writing integration tests has been how to test external dependencies, such as a database. Finally, a clean and easy solution to this problem is available. It is called testcontainers[12]. Testcontainers allow you to programmatically start and stop containerized external dependencies, like a database in test cases with only one or two lines of code.

You can also write integration tests in two parts: component tests and external integration tests, where the component tests test internal integration (of unit-tested modules with faked external dependencies) and the external integration tests test integration to external services. The component tests could be written using a unit test framework, and external integration tests could be written by a test automation developer using tools like Behave and Docker Compose. I have also worked with the approach of creating just a handful of fast-executing component tests to act as smoke tests (focusing on the most essential part of business logic). All integration tests are written using Behave and Docker Compose. I can execute those smoke tests together with unit tests to quickly see if something is broken. The Behave + Docker Compose integration tests take longer to start and run, so they are not executed as often. Remember that if you want to be able to execute component tests with fake external dependencies, you need to follow the *clean architecture principle* so that you can create fake input/output interface adapter classes used in the tests.

When using the Gherkin language, the behavior of a software component is described as features. There should be a separate file for each feature. These files have the *.feature* extension. Each feature file describes one feature and one or more scenarios for that feature. The first scenario should be the so-called "happy path" scenario, and other possible scenarios should handle additional happy paths, failures, and edge cases that need to be tested. Remember that you don't have to test every failure and edge case because those were already tested in the unit testing phase.

When the integration tests are black-box tests, the Gherkin features should be end-to-end testable (from software component input to output); otherwise, writing integration tests would be challenging. For example, suppose you have a backlog feature for the data exporter microservice for consuming Avro binary messages from Kafka. In that case, you cannot write an integration test because it is not end-to-end testable. You can't verify that an Avro binary message was successfully read from Kafka because there is no output in the feature to compare the input with. If you cannot write integration tests for a backlog feature, then you cannot prove and demonstrate to relevant stakeholders that the feature is completed by executing the

---

[11]https://cucumber.io/docs/gherkin/

[12]https://testcontainers.com/

integration (i.e., acceptance) tests, e.g., in a SAFe system demo. For this reason, it is recommended to make all backlog features such that they can be demonstrated with an end-to-end integration (=acceptance) test case.

Let's consider the data exporter microservice. If we start implementing it from scratch, we should define features in such an order that we first build capability to test end-to-end, for example:

- Export a message from Apache Kafka to Apache Pulsar
- Export single field Avro binary message from Apache Kafka to Apache Pulsar with copy transformation and field type x

    - Repeat the above feature for all possible Avro field types (primitive and complex)

- Message filtering
- Type conversion transformations from type x to type y
- Expression transformations
- Output field filtering
- Pulsar export with TLS
- Kafka export
- Kafka export with TLS
- CSV export
- JSON export

The first feature in the above list builds the capability for black-box/E2E integration tests (from software component input to output). This process is also called creating a *walking skeleton* of the software component first. After you have a walking skeleton, you can start adding some "flesh" (other features) around the bones.

Below is a simplified example of one feature in a *data-visualization-configuration-service*. We assume that the service is a REST API. The feature is for creating a new chart. (In a real-life scenario, a chart contains more properties like the chart's data source and what measure(s) and dimension(s) are shown in the chart, for example). In our simplified example, a chart contains the following properties: layout id, type, number of x-axis categories shown, and how many rows of chart data should be fetched from the chart's data source.

Figure 6.42. createChart.feature

```
Feature: Create chart
  Creates a new chart

  Scenario: Creates a new chart successfully
    Given chart layout id is "1"
    And chart type is "line"
    And X-axis categories shown count is 10
    And fetchedRowCount is 1000

    When I create a new chart

    Then I should get the chart given above
         with response code 201 "Created"
```

The above example shows how the feature's name is given after the Feature keyword. You can add free-form text below the feature's name to describe the feature in more detail. Next, a scenario is defined after the Scenario keyword. First, the name of the scenario is given. Then comes the steps of the scenario. Each step is defined using one of the following keywords: Given, When, Then, And, and But. A scenario should follow this pattern:

- Steps to describe initial context/setup (Given/And steps)
- Steps to describe an event (When step)
- Steps to describe the expected outcome for the event (Then/And steps)

We can add another scenario to the above example:

Figure 6.43. createChart.feature

```
Feature: Create chart
  Creates a new chart

  Scenario: Creates a new chart successfully
    Given chart layout id is "1"
    And chart type is "line"
    And X-axis categories shown count is 10
    And fetchedRowCount is 1000

    When I create a new chart

    Then I should get the chart given above
        with status code 201 "Created"

  Scenario: Chart creation fails due to missing mandatory parameter
    When I create a new chart

    Then I should get a response with status code 400 "Bad Request"
    And response body should contain "is mandatory field" entry
        for following fields
      | layoutId                 |
      | fetchedRowCount          |
      | xAxisCategoriesShownCount |
      | type                     |
```

Now, we have one feature with two scenarios specified. Next, we shall implement the scenarios. Our *data-visualization-configuration-service* is implemented in Java, and we also want to implement the integration tests in Java. Cucumber[13] has BDD tools for various programming languages. We will be using the Cucumber-JVM[14] library.

We place integration test code into the source code repository's *src/test* directory. The feature files are in the *src/test/resources/features* directory. Feature directories should be organized into subdirectories in the same way source code is organized into subdirectories: using domain-driven design and creating subdirectories for subdomains. We can put the above *createChart.feature* file to the *src/test/resources/features/chart* directory.

Next, we need to provide an implementation for each step in the scenarios. Let's start with the first scenario. We shall create a file *TestContext.java* for the test context and a *CreateChartStepDefs.java* file for the step definitions:

Figure 6.44. TestContext.java

```
public class TestContext {
  public io.restassured.response.Response response;
}
```

[13]https://cucumber.io/docs/installation/
[14]https://cucumber.io/docs/installation/java/

Figure 6.45. CreateChartStepDefs.java

```java
import integrationtests.TestContext;
import com.silensoft.dataviz.configuration.service.chart.Chart;
import io.cucumber.java.en.Given;
import io.cucumber.java.en.Then;
import io.cucumber.java.en.When;
import io.restassured.http.ContentType;
import io.restassured.mapper.ObjectMapperType;

import static io.restassured.RestAssured.given;
import static org.hamcrest.Matchers.equalTo;
import static org.hamcrest.Matchers.greaterThan;


public class CreateChartStepDefs {
  private static final String BASE_URL =
    "http://localhost:8080/data-visualization-configuration-service/";

  private final TestContext testContext;
  private final Chart chart = new Chart();

  public CreateChartStepDefs(final TestContext testContext) {
    this.testContext = testContext;
  }

  @Given("chart layout id is {string}")
  public void setChartLayoutId(final String layoutId) {
    chart.setLayoutId(layoutId);
  }

  @Given("chart type is {string}")
  public void setChartType(final String chartType) {
    chart.setType(chartType);
  }

  @Given("X-axis categories shown count is {int}")
  public void setXAxisCategoriesShownCount(
    final Integer xAxisCategoriesShownCount
  ) {
    chart
      .setxAxisCategoriesShownCount(xAxisCategoriesShownCount);
  }

  @Given("fetchedRowCount is {int}")
  public void setFetchedRowCount(final Integer fetchedRowCount) {
    chart.setFetchedRowCount(fetchedRowCount);
  }

  @When("I create a new chart")
  public void createNewChart() {
    testContext.response = given()
      .contentType("application/json")
      .body(chart, ObjectMapperType.GSON)
      .when()
      .post(Constants.BASE_URL + "charts");
  }

   @Then("I should get the chart given above with status code {int} {string}")
   public void iShouldGetTheChartGivenAbove(
     final int statusCode,
     final String statusCodeName
   ) {
     testContext.response.then()
       .assertThat()
       .statusCode(statusCode)
       .body("id", greaterThan(0))
       .body("layoutId", equalTo(chart.getLayoutId()))
       .body("type", equalTo(chart.getType()))
       .body("xAxisCategoriesShownCount",
```

```
            equalTo(chart.getXAxisCategoriesShownCount())))
        .body("fetchedRowCount",
              equalTo(chart.getFetchedRowCount())));
  }
}
```

The above implementation contains a function for each step. Each function is annotated with an annotation for a specific Gherkin keyword: @Given, @When, and @Then. Note that a step in a scenario can be templated. For example, the step Given chart layout id is "1" is templated and defined in the function @Given("chart layout id is {string}") public void setChartLayoutId(final String layoutId) where the actual layout id is given as a parameter for the function. You can use this templated step in different scenarios that can give a different value for the layout id, for example: Given chart layout id is "8".

The createNewChart method uses REST-assured[15] to submit an HTTP POST request to the *data-visualization-configuration-service*. The iShouldGetTheChartGivenAbove function takes the HTTP POST response and validates the status code and the properties in the response body.

The second scenario is a common failure scenario where you create something with missing parameters. Because this scenario is common (i.e., we can use the same steps in other features), we put the step definitions in a file named *CommonStepDefs.java* in the *common* subdirectory of the *src/test/java/integrationtests* directory.

Here are the step definitions:

Figure 6.46. CommonStepDefs.java

```
import integrationtests.TestContext;
import io.cucumber.java.en.And;
import io.cucumber.java.en.Then;

import java.util.List;

import static org.hamcrest.Matchers.hasItems;

public class CommonStepDefs {
  private final TestContext testContext;

  public CommonStepDefs(final TestContext testContext) {
    this.testContext = testContext;
  }

  @Then("I should get a response with status code {int} {string}")
  public void iShouldGetAResponseWithResponseCode(
    final int statusCode,
    final String statusCodeName
  ) {
      testContext.response.then()
        .assertThat()
        .statusCode(statusCode);
  }

  @And("response body should contain {string} entry for following fields")
  public void responseBodyShouldContainEntryForFollowingFields(
    final String entry,
    final List<String> fields
  ) {
    testContext.response.then()
      .assertThat()
      .body("", hasItems(fields
                        .stream()
                        .map(field -> field + ' ' + entry)
```

---

[15]https://rest-assured.io/

```
                              .toArray()));
    }
}
```

Cucumber is available in many other languages in addition to Java. It is available for JavaScript with the (Cucumber.js[16]) library and for Python with the (Behave[17]) library. Integration tests can be written in a language different from the language used for implementation and unit test code. For example, I am currently developing a microservice in C++. Our team has a test automation developer working with integration tests using the Gherkin language for feature definitions and Python and Behave to implement the steps.

Some frameworks offer their way of creating integration tests. For example, the Python Django and Spring Boot web frameworks offer their own ways of doing integration tests. There are two reasons why I don't recommend using framework-specific testing tools. The first reason is that your integration tests are coupled to the framework, and if you decide to reimplement your microservice using a different language or framework, you also need to reimplement the integration tests. When you use a generic BDD tool like Behave, your integration tests are not coupled to any microservice implementation programming language or framework. The second reason is that there is less learning and information burden for QA/test engineers when they don't have to master multiple framework-specific integration testing tools. If you use a single tool like Behave in all the microservices in a software system, it will be easier for QA/test engineers to work with different microservices.

Even though I don't recommend framework-specific integration testing tools, I will give you one example with Spring Boot and the MockMVC[18] to test a simple *sales-item-service* REST API with some CRUD operations:

Figure 6.47. SalesItemControllerTests.java

```
import com.fasterxml.jackson.databind.ObjectMapper;
import org.junit.jupiter.api.MethodOrderer;
import org.junit.jupiter.api.Order;
import org.junit.jupiter.api.Test;
import org.junit.jupiter.api.TestMethodOrder;
import org.junit.jupiter.api.extension.ExtendWith;
import org.springframework.beans.factory.annotation.Autowired;
import org.springframework.boot.test.autoconfigure.web.servlet.AutoConfigureMockMvc;
import org.springframework.boot.test.context.SpringBootTest;
import org.springframework.http.MediaType;
import org.springframework.test.context.junit.jupiter.SpringExtension;
import org.springframework.test.web.servlet.MockMvc;

import static org.springframework.test.web.servlet.request.MockMvcRequestBuilders.delete;
import static org.springframework.test.web.servlet.request.MockMvcRequestBuilders.get;
import static org.springframework.test.web.servlet.request.MockMvcRequestBuilders.post;
import static org.springframework.test.web.servlet.request.MockMvcRequestBuilders.put;
import static org.springframework.test.web.servlet.result.MockMvcResultHandlers.print;
import static org.springframework.test.web.servlet.result.MockMvcResultMatchers.jsonPath;
import static org.springframework.test.web.servlet.result.MockMvcResultMatchers.status;


@SpringBootTest
@AutoConfigureMockMvc
@ExtendWith(SpringExtension.class)
@TestMethodOrder(MethodOrderer.OrderAnnotation.class)
class SalesItemControllerTests {
  private static final long SALES_ITEM_USER_ACCOUNT_ID = 1L;
```

[16]https://cucumber.io/docs/installation/javascript/
[17]https://behave.readthedocs.io/en/stable/
[18]https://docs.spring.io/spring-framework/reference/testing/spring-mvc-test-framework.html

```
private static final String SALES_ITEM_NAME = "Test sales item";
private static final int SALES_ITEM_PRICE = 10;
private static final int UPDATED_SALES_ITEM_PRICE = 20;

private static final String UPDATED_SALES_ITEM_NAME =
  "Updated test sales item";

@Autowired
private MockMvc mockMvc;

@Test
@Order(1)
final void testCreateSalesItem() throws Exception {
  // GIVEN
  final var salesItemArg =
    new SalesItemArg(SALES_ITEM_USER_ACCOUNT_ID,
                     SALES_ITEM_NAME,
                     SALES_ITEM_PRICE);

  final var salesItemArgJson =
    new ObjectMapper().writeValueAsString(salesItemArg);

  // WHEN
  mockMvc
    .perform(post(SalesItemController.API_ENDPOINT)
             .contentType(MediaType.APPLICATION_JSON)
             .content(salesItemArgJson))
    .andDo(print())
    // THEN
    .andExpect(jsonPath("$.id").value(1))
    .andExpect(jsonPath("$.name").value(SALES_ITEM_NAME))
    .andExpect(jsonPath("$.price").value(SALES_ITEM_PRICE))
    .andExpect(status().isCreated());
}

@Test
@Order(2)
final void testGetSalesItems() throws Exception {
  // WHEN
  mockMvc
    .perform(get(SalesItemController.API_ENDPOINT))
    .andDo(print())
    // THEN
    .andExpect(jsonPath("$[0].id").value(1))
    .andExpect(jsonPath("$[0].name").value(SALES_ITEM_NAME))
    .andExpect(status().isOk());
}

@Test
@Order(3)
final void testGetSalesItemById() throws Exception {
  // WHEN
  mockMvc
    .perform(get(SalesItemController.API_ENDPOINT + "/1"))
    .andDo(print())
    // THEN
    .andExpect(jsonPath("$.name").value(SALES_ITEM_NAME))
    .andExpect(status().isOk());
}

@Test
@Order(4)
final void testGetSalesItemsByUserAccountId() throws Exception {
  // GIVEN
  final var url = SalesItemController.API_ENDPOINT +
                  "?userAccountId=" + SALES_ITEM_USER_ACCOUNT_ID;

  // WHEN
  mockMvc
    .perform(get(url))
```

```
      .andDo(print())
      // THEN
      .andExpect(jsonPath("$[0].name").value(SALES_ITEM_NAME))
      .andExpect(status().isOk());
  }

  @Test
  @Order(5)
  final void testUpdateSalesItem() throws Exception {
    // GIVEN
    final var salesItemArg =
      new SalesItemArg(SALES_ITEM_USER_ACCOUNT_ID,
                       UPDATED_SALES_ITEM_NAME,
                       UPDATED_SALES_ITEM_PRICE);

    final var salesItemArgJson =
      new ObjectMapper().writeValueAsString(salesItemArg);

    // WHEN
    mockMvc
      .perform(put(SalesItemController.API_ENDPOINT + "/1")
                .contentType(MediaType.APPLICATION_JSON)
                .content(salesItemArgJson))
      .andDo(print());

    // THEN
    mockMvc
      .perform(get(SalesItemController.API_ENDPOINT + "/1"))
      .andDo(print())
      .andExpect(jsonPath("$.name").value(UPDATED_SALES_ITEM_NAME))
      .andExpect(jsonPath("$.price").value(UPDATED_SALES_ITEM_PRICE))
      .andExpect(status().isOk());
  }

  @Test
  @Order(6)
  final void testDeleteSalesItemById() throws Exception {
    // WHEN
    mockMvc
      .perform(delete(SalesItemController.API_ENDPOINT + "/1"))
      .andDo(print());

    // THEN
    mockMvc
      .perform(get(SalesItemController.API_ENDPOINT + "/1"))
      .andDo(print())
      .andExpect(status().isNotFound());
  }

  @Test
  @Order(7)
  final void testDeleteSalesItems() throws Exception {
    // GIVEN
    final var salesItemArg =
      new SalesItemArg(SALES_ITEM_USER_ACCOUNT_ID,
                       SALES_ITEM_NAME,
                       SALES_ITEM_PRICE);

    final var salesItemArgJson =
      new ObjectMapper().writeValueAsString(salesItemArg);

    mockMvc
      .perform(post(SalesItemController.API_ENDPOINT)
                .contentType(MediaType.APPLICATION_JSON)
                .content(salesItemArgJson))
      .andDo(print());

    // WHEN
    mockMvc
      .perform(delete(SalesItemController.API_ENDPOINT))
```

```
      .andDo(print());

    // THEN
    mockMvc
      .perform(get(SalesItemController.API_ENDPOINT))
      .andDo(print())
      .andExpect(jsonPath("$").isEmpty())
      .andExpect(status().isOk());
  }
}
```

For API microservices, one more alternative to implement integration tests is an API development platform like Postman[19]. Postman can be used to write integration tests using JavaScript.

Suppose we have an API microservice called *sales-item-service* that offers CRUD operations on sales items. Below is an example API request for creating a new sales item. You can define this in Postman as a new request:

```
POST http://localhost:3000/sales-item-service/sales-items HTTP/1.1
Content-Type: application/json

{
  "name": "Test sales item",
  "price": 10,
}
```

Here is a Postman test case to validate the response to the above request:

```
pm.test("Status code is 201 Created", function () {
  pm.response.to.have.status(201);
});

const salesItem = pm.response.json();
pm.collectionVariables.set("salesItemId", salesItem.id)

pm.test("Sales item name", function () {
  return pm.expect(salesItem.name).to.eql("Test sales item");
})

pm.test("Sales item price", function () {
  return pm.expect(salesItem.price).to.eql(10);
})
```

In the above test case, the response status code is verified first, and then the salesItem object is parsed from the response body. Value for the variable salesItemId is set. This variable will be used in subsequent test cases. Finally, the values of the name and price properties are checked.

Next, a new API request could be created in Postman to retrieve the just created sales item:

```
GET http://localhost:3000/sales-item-service/sales-items/{{salesItemId}} HTTP/1.1
```

We used the value stored earlier in the salesItemId variable in the request URL. Variables can be used in the URL and request body using the following notation: {{<variable-name>}}. Let's create a test case for the above request:

---

[19]https://www.postman.com/

```
pm.test("Status code is 200 OK", function () {
  pm.response.to.have.status(200);
});

const salesItem = pm.response.json();

pm.test("Sales item name", function () {
  return pm.expect(salesItem.name).to.eql("Test sales item");
})

pm.test("Sales item price", function () {
  return pm.expect(salesItem.price).to.eql(10);
})
```

API integration tests written in Postman can be utilized in a CI pipeline. An easy way to do that is to export a Postman collection to a file that contains all the API requests and related tests. A Postman collection file is a JSON file. Postman offers a Node.js command-line utility called Newman[20]. It can run API requests and related tests from an exported Postman collection file.

You can run integration tests stored in an exported Postman collection file with the below command in a CI pipeline:

```
newman run integrationtests/integrationTestsPostmanCollection.json
```

In the above example, we assume that a file named *integrationTestsPostmanCollection.json* has been exported from the Postman to the *integrationtests* directory in the source code repository.

6.1.2.1: Web UI Integration Testing

You can also use the Gherkin language to specify UI features. For example, the TestCafe[21] UI testing tool can be used with the gherkin-testcafe[22] tool to make TestCafe support the Gherkin syntax. Let's create a simple UI feature:

```
Feature: Greet user
  Entering user name and clicking submit button
  displays a greeting for the user

  Scenario: Greet user successfully
    Given there is "John Doe" entered in the input field
    When I press the submit button
    Then I am greeted with text "Hello, John Doe"
```

Next, we can implement the above steps in JavaScript using the TestCafe testing API:

---

[20]https://learning.postman.com/docs/running-collections/using-newman-cli/installing-running-newman/
[21]https://testcafe.io/
[22]https://www.npmjs.com/package/gherkin-testcafe

```
// Imports...

// 'Before' hook runs before the first step of each scenario.
// 't' is the TestCafe test controller object
Before('Navigate to application URL', async (t) => {
  // Navigate browser to application URL
  await t.navigateTo('...');
});

Given('there is {string} entered in the input field',
      async (t, [userName]) => {
  // Finds an HTML element with CSS id selector and
  // enters text to it
  await t.typeText('#user-name', userName);
});

When('I press the submit button', async (t) => {
  // Finds an HTML element with CSS id selector and clicks it
  await t.click('#submit-button');
});

When('I am greeted with text {string}', async (t, [greeting]) => {
  // Finds an HTML element with CSS id selector
  // and compares its inner text
  await t.expect(Selector('#greeting').innerText).eql(greeting);
});
```

Another tool similar to TestCafe is Cypress[23]. You can also use Gherkin with Cypress with the cypress-cucumber-preprocessor[24] library. Then, you can write your UI integration tests like this:

```
Feature: Visit duckduckgo.com website

  Scenario: Visit duckduckgo.com website successfully
    When I visit duckduckgo.com
    Then I should see the search bar
```

```
import { When, Then } from
  '@badeball/cypress-cucumber-preprocessor';

When("I visit duckduckgo.com", () => {
  cy.visit("https://www.duckduckgo.com");
});

Then("I should see the search bar", () => {
  cy.get("input").should(
    "have.attr",
    "placeholder",
    "Search the web without being tracked"
  );
});
```

6.1.2.2: Setting Up Integration Testing Environment

If you have implemented integration tests as black-box tests outside the microservice, an integration testing environment must be set up before integration tests can be run. An integration testing environment is where the tested microservice and all its dependencies are running. The easiest way to set up an integration testing

---

[23]https://www.cypress.io/

[24]https://github.com/badeball/cypress-cucumber-preprocessor

environment for a containerized microservice is to use Docker Compose[25], a simple container orchestration tool for a single host. Docker Compose offers a clean, declarative way of defining the external services on which your microservice depends.

If you have implemented integration tests using a unit testing framework, i.e., inside the microservice, you don't need to set up a testing environment (so this section does not apply). You can set up the needed environment (external dependencies) in each integration test separately by using testcontainers, for example.

When a developer needs to debug a failing test in integration tests using Docker Compose, they must attach the debugger to the software component's running container. This is more work compared to typically debugging source code. Another possibility is to introduce temporary debug-level logging in the microservice source code. That logging can be removed after the bug is found and corrected. However, if you cannot debug the microservice in a customer's production environment, it is good practice to have some debug-level logging in the source code to enable troubleshooting of a customer's problems that cannot be reproduced in a local environment. For viewing logs, the integration tests should write logs to the console in case of a test execution failure. This can be done, e.g., by running the docker logs command for the application container. It should be noted that when the application development has been done using low-level (unit/function-level) BDD (or TDD), the debugging need at the integration testing level is significantly reduced.

Let's create a *docker-compose.yml* file for the *sales-item-service* microservice, which has a MySQL database as a dependency. The microservice uses the database to store sales items.

Figure 6.48. docker-compose.yaml

```
version: "3.8"

services:
  wait-for-services-ready:
    image: dokku/wait
  sales-item-service:
    restart: always
    build:
      context: .
    env_file: .env.ci
    ports:
      - "3000:3000"
    depends_on:
      - mysql
  mysql:
    image: mysql:8.0.22
    command: --default-authentication-plugin=mysql_native_password
    restart: always
    cap_add:
      - SYS_NICE
    environment:
      MYSQL_ROOT_PASSWORD: ${MYSQL_PASSWORD}
    ports:
      - "3306:3306"
```

In the above example, we first define a service *wait-for-services-ready*, which we will use later. Next, we define our microservice, *sales-item-service*. We ask Docker Compose to build a container image for the *sales-item-service* using the *Dockerfile* in the current directory. Then, we define the environment for the microservice to be read from an *.env.ci* file. We expose port 3000 and tell that our microservice depends on the *mysql* service.

---

[25]https://docs.docker.com/compose/

Next, we define the `mysql` service. We tell what image to use, give a command-line parameter, and define the environment and expose a port.

Before we can run the integration tests, we must spin the integration testing environment up using the `docker-compose up` command:

```
docker-compose up --env-file .env.ci --build -d
```

We tell the `docker-compose` command to read environment variables from an *.env.ci* file that should contain an environment variable named `MYSQL_PASSWORD`. We ask Docker Compose to always build the *sales-item-service* by specifying the `--build` flag. The `-d` flag tells the `docker-compose` command to run in the background.

Before we can run the integration tests, we must wait until all services defined in the *docker-compose.yml* are up and running. We use the *wait-for-services-ready* service provided by the dokku/wait[26] image. We can wait for the services to be ready by issuing the following command:

```
docker-compose
  --env-file .env.ci
  run wait-for-services-ready
  -c mysql:3306,sales-item-service:3000
  -t 600
```

The above command will finish after *mysql* service's port 3306 and *sales-item-service's* port 3000 can be connected (as specified with the `-c` flag, the `-t` flag specifies a timeout for waiting). After the above command is finished, you can run the integration tests. In the below example, we run the integration tests using the *newman* CLI tool:

```
newman run integrationtests/integrationTestsPostmanCollection.json
```

If your integration tests are implemented using Behave, you can run them in the *integrationtests* directory with the `behave` command. Instead of using the *dokku/wait* image for waiting services to be ready, you can do the waiting in Behave's `before_all` function. Just make a loop that tries to make a TCP connection to `mysql:3306` and `sales-item-service:3000`. When both connections succeed, break the loop to start the tests.

> With the advent of *testcontainers*, you can use testcontainers instead of the Docker Compose setup provided there are testcontainers available for all needed services. With testcontainers, you must also ensure they are up and running and ready to serve requests before executing the tests.

After integration tests are completed, you can shut down the integration testing environment:

```
docker-compose down
```

---

[26]https://hub.docker.com/r/dokku/wait

If you need other dependencies in your integration testing environment, you can add them to the *docker-compose.yml* file. If you need to add other microservices with dependencies, you must also add transitive dependencies. For example, if you needed to add another microservice that uses a PostgreSQL database, you would have to add the other microservice and PostgreSQL database to the *docker-compose.yml* file as new services.

Let's say the *sales-item-service* depends on Apache Kafka 2.x that depends on a Zookeeper service. The *sales-item-service's docker-compose.yml* looks like the below after adding Kafka and Zookeeper:

Figure 6.49. docker-compose.yaml

```
version: "3.8"

services:
  wait-for-services-ready:
    image: dokku/wait
  sales-item-service:
    restart: always
    build:
      context: .
    env_file: .env.ci
    ports:
      - 3000:3000
    depends_on:
      - mysql
      - kafka
  mysql:
    image: mysql:8.0.22
    command: --default-authentication-plugin=mysql_native_password
    restart: always
    cap_add:
      - SYS_NICE
    environment:
      MYSQL_ROOT_PASSWORD: ${MYSQL_PASSWORD}
    ports:
      - "3306:3306"
  zookeeper:
    image: bitnami/zookeeper:3.7
    volumes:
      - "zookeeper_data:/bitnami"
    ports:
      - 2181:2181"
    environment:
      - ALLOW_ANONYMOUS_LOGIN=yes
  kafka:
    image: bitnami/kafka:2.8.1
    volumes:
      - "kafka_data:/bitnami"
    ports:
      - "9092:9092"
    environment:
      - KAFKA_CFG_ZOOKEEPER_CONNECT=zookeeper:2181
      - ALLOW_PLAINTEXT_LISTENER=yes
    depends_on:
      - zookeeper

volumes:
  zookeeper_data:
    driver: local
  kafka_data:
    driver: local
```

6.1.3: Complete Example with BDD, ATDD, DDD, OOD and TDD

Let's have a complete example using the following design principles: BDD, ATDD, DDD, OOD, and TDD. We will implement a *gossiping bus drivers* application, which some of you might be familiar with. Product management gives us the following user story:

> *Each bus driver drives a bus along a specified circular route. A route consists of one or more bus stops. Bus drivers drive the route and stop at each bus stop. Bus drivers have a set of rumors. At the bus stop, drivers gossip (share rumors) with other drivers stopped at the same bus stop. The application stops when all rumors are shared or bus drivers have driven for a maximum number of bus stops. Upon exit, the application should inform the user whether all rumors were successfully shared.*

We start with BDD and ATDD and write a formal behavioral specification for the above informal description:

```
Feature: Gossiping bus drivers

  Scenario: Bus drivers successfully share all rumors
    Given maximum number of bus stops driven is 100
    Given bus drivers with the following routes and rumors
      | Route                            | Rumors                  |
      | stop-a, stop-b, stop-c           | rumor1, rumor2          |
      | stop-d, stop-b, stop-e           | rumor1, rumor3, rumor4  |
      | stop-f, stop-g, stop-h, stop-i, stop-e  | rumor1, rumor5, rumor6  |

    When bus drivers have completed driving
    Then all rumors are successfully shared

  Scenario: Bus drivers fails to share all rumors due to driving maximum number of stops
    Given maximum number of bus stops driven is 5
    Given bus drivers with the following routes and rumors
      | Route                            | Rumors                  |
      | stop-a, stop-b, stop-c           | rumor1, rumor2          |
      | stop-d, stop-b, stop-e           | rumor1, rumor3, rumor4  |
      | stop-f, stop-g, stop-h, stop-i, stop-e  | rumor1, rumor5, rumor6  |

    When bus drivers have completed driving
    Then all rumors are not shared

  Scenario: Bus drivers fail to share all rumors because bus routes never cross
    Given maximum number of bus stops driven is 100
    Given bus drivers with the following bus routes and rumors
      | Route                  | Rumors                  |
      | stop-a, stop-b, stop-c | rumor1, rumor2          |
      | stop-d, stop-e, stop-f | rumor1, rumor3, rumor4  |

    When bus drivers have completed driving
    Then all rumors are not shared
```

Next, we add a task to the team's backlog for write integration (acceptance) tests for the above scenarios. The implementation of the integration tests can start parallel to the actual implementation of the user story. The user story description provided by product management does not specify exactly how the following things should be implemented:

- Upon application exit, inform the user whether all rumors were successfully shared or not

- How bus drivers are supplied to the application

The team should discuss the above two topics and consult the product manager for specific requirements. If there is no feedback from the product manager, the team can decide how to implement the above things. For example, the team could specify the following:

- If all rumors were successfully shared, the application should exit with an exit code zero; otherwise, exit with a non-zero exit code.
- Application gets the maximum number of driven bus stops as the first command line parameter
- Application gets drivers as subsequent command line parameters
- Each driver is specified with a string in the following format: , e.g., `bus-stop-a,bus-stop-b;rumor-1,rumor-2`

We will use Python and Behave to implement the integration tests. Below are the step implementations for the above Gherkin feature specification:

```python
import subprocess

from behave import given, then, when
from behave.runner import Context


@given('maximum number of bus stops driven is {max_driven_bus_stop_count:d}')
def step_impl(context: Context, max_driven_bus_stop_count: int):
    context.max_driven_bus_stop_count = max_driven_bus_stop_count


@given('bus drivers with the following routes and rumors')
def step_impl2(context: Context):
    context.drivers = []

    for driver in context.table:
        bus_route = ','.join(
            bus_stop.strip() for bus_stop in driver['Route'].split(',')
        )

        rumors = ','.join(
            rumor.strip() for rumor in driver['Rumors'].split(',')
        )

        context.drivers.append(f'{bus_route};{rumors}')


@when('bus drivers have completed driving')
def step_impl3(context: Context):
    context.exit_code = subprocess.run(
        [
            'java',
            '-jar',
            'build/libs/gbd_detroitchicago-1.0.jar',
            str(context.max_driven_bus_stop_count),
            *context.drivers,
        ],
    ).returncode


@then('all rumors are successfully shared')
def step_impl4(context: Context):
    assert context.exit_code == 0


@then('all rumors are not shared')
def step_impl5(context: Context):
    assert context.exit_code != 0
```

In the @given steps, we store information in the context. We store driver definitions as strings to the drivers attribute of the context. In the @when step, the application is launched with command line arguments, and in the @then steps, the exit code of the sub-process is examined to be either 0 (successful sharing of all rumors) or non-zero (sharing of all rumors failed).

Before starting the implementation using TDD, we must first design our application using DDD and then OOD. Let's continue with the DDD phase. We can start with event storming and define the *domain events* first:

- The maximum number of driven bus stops is parsed from the command line
- Bus drivers are parsed from the command line
- The bus driver has driven to the next bus stop according to the bus route
- Rumors are shared with the drivers at the bus stop
- Bus drivers have driven until all rumors have been shared

Let's introduce the *actors*, *commands* and *entities* related to the above domain events:

- The maximum number of driven bus stops is parsed from the command line

    - Actor: MaxDrivenStopCountParser, Command: parse

- Bus drivers are parsed from the command line

    - Actor: BusDriversParser, Command: parse, Entities: BusDriver

- Bus drivers have driven until all rumors have been shared

    - Actor: GossipingBusDrivers, Command: drive_until_all_rumors_shared, Entities: Rumor, BusDriver

- The bus driver has driven to the next bus stop according to the bus route

    - Actor: BusDriver, Command: drive_to_next_bus_stop, Entities: BusStop
    - Actor: BusRoute, Command: get_next_bus_stop, Entities: BusStop

- Rumors are shared with the drivers at the bus stop

    - Actor: BusStop, Command: share_rumors_with_drivers, Entities BusDriver, Rumor

Based on the above output of the DDD phase, we can design our classes using OOD. We design actor classes and put public behavior to them and design the Rumor entity class with no behavior. Below is the class diagram:

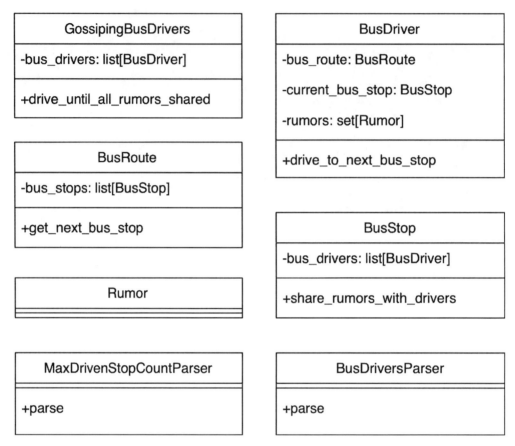

Figure 6.50. Class diagram

We should not forget the *program against interfaces principle* (dependency inversion principle). So, let's add interfaces to the class diagram:

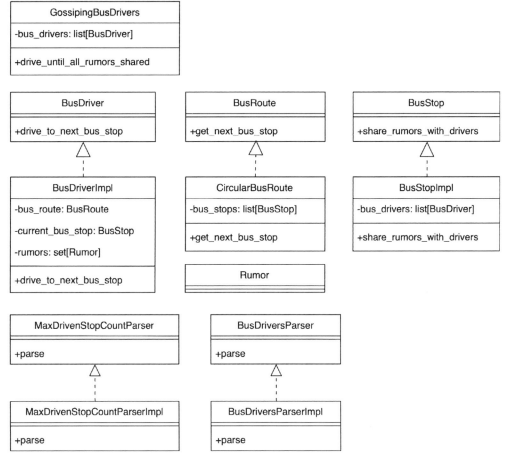

Figure 6.51. Class diagram with interfaces

Now that we have our design done, we can add the following tasks to the team's backlog:

- GossipingBusDrivers class implementation
- BusDriverImpl class implementation
- CircularBusRoute class implementation
- BusStopImpl class implementation
- Rumor class implementation
- MaxDrivenStopCountParser class implementation
- BusDriversParser class implementation

We already had the integration tests implementation task added to the backlog earlier. There are eight tasks in the backlog, and each can be implemented (either entirely or at least partially) in parallel. If the team has eight members, they can pick a task and proceed in parallel to complete the user story as quickly as possible.

> You can find source code for the below example here[27]. If you are interested in this same example done using the London school of TDD, you can find the source code here[28].

We can start implementing classes one public method at a time. Let's start with the most straightforward class, Rumor, which does not have any behavior. Our implementation will be in Java.

```
public class Rumor {
}
```

Next, we can implement the CircularBusRoute class using TDD. Let's start with the simplest case, which is also a failure scenario: If the bus route has no bus stops, an IllegalArgumentException with an informative message should be raised. Let's implement a unit test for that scenario:

```
class CircularBusRouteTests {

  @Test
  void testConstructor_whenNoBusStops() {
    // GIVEN
    final List<BusStop> noBusStops = List.of();

    // WHEN + THEN
    assertThrows(IllegalArgumentException.class, () -> {
      new CircularBusRoute(noBusStops);
    }, "Bus route must have at least one bus stop");
  }
}
```

Let's implement the constructor of the CircularBusRoute class to make the above test pass:

```
public interface BusStop {
}
```

```
public interface BusRoute {
}
```

```
public class CircularBusRoute implements BusRoute {
  private final List<BusStop> busStops;

  public CircularBusRoute(final List<BusStop> busStops) {
    if (busStops == null || busStops.isEmpty()) {
      throw new IllegalArgumentException("Bus route must have at least one bus stop");
    }

    this.busStops = List.copyOf(busStops);
  }
}
```

The unit test for the next scenario is the following: if there is only one stop in the bus route, the getNextBusStop method should always return that bus stop (because the bus route is circular).

---

[27]https://github.com/pksilen/clean-code-principles--code/tree/main/chapter4/gbd_detroitchicago

[28]https://github.com/pksilen/clean-code-principles-code/tree/main/chapter4/gbd_london

```
class CircularBusRouteTests {
  // ...

  @Test
  void testGetNextBusStop_whenOneBusStop() {
    // GIVEN
    BusStop busStop = new BusStopImpl();
    CircularBusRoute busRoute = new CircularBusRoute(List.of(busStop));

    // WHEN
    BusStop nextBusStop = busRoute.getNextBusStop(busStop);

    // THEN
    assertEquals(nextBusStop, busStop);
  }
}
```

Let's implement the getNextBusStop method to make the above test pass:

```
public interface BusRoute {
  BusStop getNextBusStop(final BusStop currentBusStop);
}
```

```
public class CircularBusRoute implements BusRoute {
  // ...

  @Override
  public BusStop getNextBusStop(final BusStop currentBusStop) {
    return busStops.get(0);
  }
}
```

Let's implement a unit test for the following scenario: If the getNextBusStop method's argument is a bus stop not belonging to the bus route, an IllegalArgumentException with an informative message should be raised.

```
class CircularBusRouteTests {
  // ...

  @Test
  void testGetNextBusStop_whenBusStopDoesNotBelongToRoute() {
    // GIVEN
    BusStop busStopA = new BusStopImpl();
    BusStop busStopB = new BusStopImpl();
    CircularBusRoute busRoute = new CircularBusRoute(List.of(busStopA));

    // WHEN + THEN
    assertThrows(IllegalArgumentException.class, () -> {
      busRoute.getNextBusStop(busStopB);
    }, "Bus stop does not belong to bus route");
  }
}
```

Let's modify the getNextBusStop method implementation:

```
public class CircularBusRoute implements BusRoute {
  // ...

  @Override
  public BusStop getNextBusStop(final BusStop currentBusStop) {
    if (!busStops.contains(currentBusStop)) {
      throw new IllegalArgumentException("Bus stop does not belong to bus route");
    }

    return busStops.get(0);
  }
}
```

Next, we specify two scenarios of how the getNextBusSstop method should behave when there is more than one stop in the bus route:

> When a current bus stop is given, the getNextBusStop method should return the next bus stop in a list of bus stops for the route.

Let's write a failing unit test for the above scenario:

```
class CircularBusRouteTests {
  // ...

  @Test
  void testGetNextBusStop_whenNextBusStopInListExists() {
    // GIVEN
    BusStop busStopA = new BusStopImpl();
    BusStop busStopB = new BusStopImpl();
    CircularBusRoute busRoute = new CircularBusRoute(List.of(busStopA, busStopB));

    // WHEN
    BusStop nextBusStop = busRoute.getNextBusStop(busStopA);

    // THEN
    assertEquals(nextBusStop, busStopB);
  }
}
```

Let's modify the source code to make the above test pass:

```
public class CircularBusRoute implements BusRoute {
  // ...

  @Override
  public BusStop getNextBusStop(final BusStop currentBusStop) {
    if (!busStops.contains(currentBusStop)) {
      throw new IllegalArgumentException("Bus stop does not belong to bus route");
    }

    if (busStops.size() == 1) {
      return busStops.get(0);
    }

    final int currBusStopIndex = busStops.indexOf(currentBusStop);
    return busStops.get(currBusStopIndex + 1);
  }
}
```

Let's add a test for the following scenario:

> If there is no next bus stop in the list of the route's bus stops, the getNextBusStop method should return the first bus stop (due to the route being circular).

```
class CircularBusRouteTests {
  // ...

  @Test
  void testGetNextBusStop_whenNoNextBusStopInList() {
    // GIVEN
    BusStop busStopA = new BusStopImpl();
    BusStop busStopB = new BusStopImpl();
    CircularBusRoute busRoute = new CircularBusRoute(List.of(busStopA, busStopB));

    // WHEN
    BusStop nextBusStop = busRoute.getNextBusStop(busStopB);

    // THEN
    assertEquals(nextBusStop, busStopA);
  }
}
```

Let's make the above test pass:

```
public class CircularBusRoute implements BusRoute {
  private final List<BusStop> busStops;
  private final int busStopCount;

  public CircularBusRoute(final List<BusStop> busStops) {
    if (busStops == null || busStops.isEmpty()) {
      throw new IllegalArgumentException("Bus route must have at least one bus stop");
    }

    this.busStops = List.copyOf(busStops);
    this.busStopCount = busStops.size();
  }

  @Override
  public BusStop getNextBusStop(final BusStop currentBusStop) {
    if (!busStops.contains(currentBusStop)) {
      throw new IllegalArgumentException("Bus stop does not belong to bus route");
    }

    final int currBusStopIndex = busStops.indexOf(currentBusStop);
    final int nextBusStopIndex = (currBusStopIndex + 1) % busStopCount;
    return busStops.get(nextBusStopIndex);
  }
}
```

Next, we shall implement the BusStopImpl class and the shareRumorsWithDdrivers method. Let's start by specifying what that method should do: After the execution of the method is completed, all the drivers at the bus stop should have the same set of rumors that is a union of all the rumors that the drivers at the bus stop have.

Let's create a test for the above specification. We will have three bus drivers at a bus stop. Because bus drivers are implemented in a separate class, we will use mocks for the drivers.

```
class BusStopImplTests {
  @Test
  void testShareRumorsWithDrivers() {
    // GIVEN
    final var rumor1 = new Rumor();
    final var rumor2 = new Rumor();
    final var rumor3 = new Rumor();
    final var allRumors = Set.of(rumor1, rumor2, rumor3);

    final var busRoute = new CircularBusRoute(List.of(new BusStopImpl()));
    final var busDriver1 = new BusDriverImpl(busRoute, Set.of(rumor1, rumor2));
    final var busDriver2 = new BusDriverImpl(busRoute, Set.of(rumor2));
    final var busDriver3 = new BusDriverImpl(busRoute, Set.of(rumor2, rumor3));

    final var busStop = new BusStopImpl();
    busStop.add(busDriver1);
    busStop.add(busDriver2);
    busStop.add(busDriver3);

    // WHEN
    busStop.shareRumorsWithDrivers();

    // THEN
    for (final BusDriver busDriver : List.of(busDriver1, busDriver2, busDriver3)) {
      assertEquals(busDriver.getRumors(), allRumors);
    }
  }
}
```

We need to add getRrumors method to the BusDriver interface. Let's make a unit test for the getRrumors method, which returns the rumors given for the driver in the constructor:

```
class BusDriverImplTests {
  final Rumor rumor1 = new Rumor();
  final Rumor rumor2 = new Rumor();

  @Test
  void testGetRumors() {
    // GIVEN
    final var busDriver = new BusDriverImpl(
      new CircularBusRoute(List.of(new BusStopImpl())), Set.of(rumor1, rumor2)
    );

    // WHEN
    final var rumors = busDriver.getRumors();

    // THEN
    assertEquals(rumors, Set.of(rumor1, rumor2));
  }
}
```

Now we can implement the getRrumors method to make the above test pass:

```
public interface BusDriver {
  Set<Rumor> getRumors();
}


public class BusDriverImpl implements BusDriver {
  private Set<Rumor> rumors;

  public BusDriverImpl(final BusRoute busRoute, final Set<Rumor> rumors) {
    this.rumors = Set.copyOf(rumors);
  }

  @Override
  public Set<Rumor> getRumors() {
    return rumors;
  }
}
```

We must also add the setRumors method to the BusDriver interface. Let's make a unit test for the setRumors method, which should override the rumors given in the constructor:

```
class BusDriverImplTests {
  // ...

  @Test
  void testSetRumors() {
    // GIVEN
    final var rumor3 = new Rumor();
    final var rumor4 = new Rumor();

    final var busDriver = new BusDriverImpl(
      new CircularBusRoute(List.of(new BusStopImpl())), Set.of(rumor1, rumor2)
    );

    // WHEN
    busDriver.setRumors(Set.of(rumor3, rumor4));

    // THEN
    assertEquals(busDriver.getRumors(), Set.of(rumor3, rumor4));
  }
}
```

Here is the implementation for the setRumors method:

```
public interface BusDriver {
  // ...

  void setRumors(Set<Rumor> rumors);
}


public class BusDriverImpl implements BusDriver {
  // ...

  @Override
  public void setRumors(final Set<Rumor> rumors) {
    this.rumors = Set.copyOf(rumors);
  }
}
```

Let's implement the BusStopImpl class to make the above test pass:

```
public interface BusStop {
  void shareRumorsWithDrivers();

  void add(final BusDriver busDriver);
}


public class BusStopImpl implements BusStop {
  private final Set<BusDriver> busDrivers = new HashSet<>();

  @Override
  public void shareRumorsWithDrivers() {
    final Set<Rumor> allRumors = new HashSet<>();

    for (final BusDriver busDriver : busDrivers) {
      allRumors.addAll(busDriver.getRumors());
    }

    for (final BusDriver busDriver : busDrivers) {
      busDriver.setRumors(allRumors);
    }
  }

  @Override
  public void add(final BusDriver busDriver) {
    busDrivers.add(busDriver);
  }
}
```

Let's finalize the BusDriverImpl class next. We need to implement the driveToNextBusSstop method in the BusDriverImpl class: A bus driver has a current bus stop that is initially the first bus stop of the route. The driver drives to the next bus stop according to its route. When the driver arrives at the next bus stop, the driver is added to the bus stop. The driver is removed from the current bus stop, which is changed to the next bus stop.

```
class BusDriverImplTests {
  final Rumor rumor1 = new Rumor();
  final Rumor rumor2 = new Rumor();

  @Test
  void testDriveToNextBusStop() {
    // GIVEN
    final var busStopA = new BusStopImpl();
    final var busStopB = new BusStopImpl();
    final var busRoute = new CircularBusRoute(List.of(busStopA, busStopB));
    final var busDriver = new BusDriverImpl(busRoute, Set.of());

    // WHEN
    busDriver.driveToNextBusStop();

    // THEN
    assertSame(busDriver.getCurrentBusStop(), busStopB);
  }
}
```

Let's implement the BusDriverImpl class to make the above test pass. Before that, we must add a test for the new getFirstBusStop method in the BusRouteImpl class.

```
class CircularBusRouteTests {
  @Test
  void testGetFirstBusStop() {
    // GIVEN
    final var busStopA = new BusStopImpl();
    final varbusStopB = new BusStopImpl();
    final var busRoute = new CircularBusRoute(List.of(busStopA, busStopB));

    // WHEN
    final var firstBusStop = busRoute.getFirstBusStop();

    / THEN
    assertSame(firstBusStop, busStopA);
  }
}
```

Let's modify the `CircularBusRoute` class to make the above test pass:

```
public interface BusRoute {
  BusStop getFirstBusStop();

  // ...
}
```

```
public class CircularBusRoute implements BusRoute {
  // ...

  public BusStop getFirstBusStop() {
    return busStops.get(0);
  }

  // ...
}
```

Here is the implementation of the `driveToNextBusStop` method in the `BusDriverImpl` class:

```
public class BusDriverImpl implements BusDriver {
  private final BusRoute busRoute;
  private BusStop currentBusStop;
  private Set<Rumor> rumors;

  public BusDriverImpl(BusRoute busRoute, Set<Rumor> rumors) {
    this.busRoute = busRoute;
    this.currentBusStop = busRoute.getFirstBusStop();
    this.currentBusStop.add(this);
    this.rumors = Set.copyOf(rumors);
  }

  public BusStop driveToNextBusStop() {
    this.currentBusStop.remove(this);
    this.currentBusStop = busRoute.getNextBusStop(this.currentBusStop);
    this.currentBusStop.add(this);
    return this.currentBusStop;
  }

  public BusStop getCurrentBusStop() {
    return this.currentBusStop;
  }

  public Set<Rumor> getRumors() {
    return rumors;
  }

  public void setRumors(Set<Rumor> rumors) {
    this.rumors = Set.copyOf(rumors);
  }
}
```

Finally, we should implement the `GossipingBusDrivers` class and its `driveUntilAllRumorsShared`. Let's write a unit test for the first scenario, in which all rumors are shared after driving from one bus stop to the next. The `driveUntilAllRumorsShared` method makes drivers drive to the next bus stop (the same for both drivers) and share rumors there.

```java
class GossipingBusDriversTests {
  final Rumor rumor1 = new Rumor();
  final Rumor rumor2 = new Rumor();
  final Set<Rumor> allRumors = Set.of(rumor1, rumor2);

  @Test
  void testDriveUntilAllRumorsShared_afterOneStop() {
    // GIVEN
    final var busStop = new BusStopImpl();
    final var busRoute = new CircularBusRoute(List.of(busStop));
    final var busDriver1 = new BusDriverImpl(busRoute, Set.of(rumor1));
    final var busDriver2 = new BusDriverImpl(busRoute, Set.of(rumor2));

    final var gossipingBusDrivers = new GossipingBusDrivers(List.of(busDriver1, busDriver2));

    // WHEN
    boolean allRumorsWereShared = gossipingBusDrivers.driveUntilAllRumorsShared();

    // THEN
    assertTrue(allRumorsWereShared);
    assertEquals(busDriver1.getRumors(), allRumors);
    assertEquals(busDriver2.getRumors(), allRumors);
  }
}
```

Let's make the above test pass with the below code.

```java
public class GossipingBusDrivers {
  private final List<BusDriver> busDrivers;
  private final Set<Rumor> allRumors;

  public GossipingBusDrivers(final List<BusDriver> busDrivers) {
    this.busDrivers = List.copyOf(busDrivers);
    this.allRumors = getAllRumors();
  }

  public boolean driveUntilAllRumorsShared() {
    while (true) {
      for (final var busDriver : busDrivers) {
        final var busStop = busDriver.driveToNextBusStop();
        busStop.shareRumorsWithDrivers();
      }

      if (allRumorsAreShared()) {
        return true;
      }
    }
  }

  private Set<Rumor> getAllRumors() {
    return busDrivers.stream()
      .flatMap(driver -> driver.getRumors().stream())
      .collect(Collectors.toSet());
  }

  private boolean allRumorsAreShared() {
    return busDrivers.stream()
      .allMatch(driver -> driver.getRumors().equals(allRumors));
  }
}
```

Let's add a test for a scenario where two bus drivers drive from their starting bus stops to two different bus stops and must continue driving because all rumors were not shared at the first bus stop. Rumors are shared when drivers continue driving to their next bus stop, which is the same for both drivers.

```
class GossipingBusDriversTests {
  // ...

  @Test
  void testDriveUntilAllRumorsShared_afterTwoStops() {
    // GIVEN
    final var busStopA = new BusStopImpl();
    final var busStopB = new BusStopImpl();
    final var busStopC = new BusStopImpl();
    final var busRoute1 = new CircularBusRoute(List.of(busStopA, busStopC));
    final var busRoute2 = new CircularBusRoute(List.of(busStopB, busStopC));
    final var busDriver1 = new BusDriverImpl(busRoute1, Set.of(rumor1));
    final var busDriver2 = new BusDriverImpl(busRoute2, Set.of(rumor2));

    final var gossipingBusDrivers = new GossipingBusDrivers(List.of(busDriver1, busDriver2));

    // WHEN
    boolean allRumorsWereShared = gossipingBusDrivers.driveUntilAllRumorsShared();

    // THEN
    assertTrue(allRumorsWereShared);
    assertEquals(busDriver1.getRumors(), allRumors);
    assertEquals(busDriver2.getRumors(), allRumors);
  }
}
```

Let's modify the implementation:

```
public class GossipingBusDrivers {
  // ...

  public boolean driveUntilAllRumorsShared() {
    while (true) {
      Set<BusStop> busStops = busDrivers.stream()
        .map(BusDriver::driveToNextBusStop)
        .collect(Collectors.toSet());

      for (final var busStop : busStops) {
        busStop.shareRumorsWithDrivers();
      }

      if (allRumorsAreShared()) {
        return true;
      }
    }
  }

  // ...
}
```

Next, we should implement a test where drivers don't have common bus stops, and they have driven the maximum number of bus stops:

```java
class GossipingBusDriversTests {
  // ...

  @Test
  void testDriveUntilAllRumorsShared_whenRumorsAreNotShared() {
    // GIVEN
    final var busStopA = new BusStopImpl();
    final var busStopB = new BusStopImpl();
    final var busRoute1 = new CircularBusRoute(List.of(busStopA));
    final var busRoute2 = new CircularBusRoute(List.of(busStopB));
    final var busDriver1 = new BusDriverImpl(busRoute1, Set.of(rumor1));
    final var busDriver2 = new BusDriverImpl(busRoute2, Set.of(rumor2));
    final var gossipingBusDrivers = new GossipingBusDrivers(List.of(busDriver1, busDriver2));
    final int maxDrivenStopCount = 2;

    // WHEN
    boolean allRumorsWereShared = gossipingBusDrivers.driveUntilAllRumorsShared(maxDrivenStopCount);

    // THEN
    assertFalse(allRumorsWereShared);
    assertEquals(busDriver1.getRumors(), Set.of(rumor1));
    assertEquals(busDriver2.getRumors(), Set.of(rumor2));
  }
}
```

Let's modify the implementation to make the above test pass:

```java
public class GossipingBusDrivers {
  private final List<BusDriver> busDrivers;
  private final Set<Rumor> allRumors;
  private int drivenStopCount = 0;

  public GossipingBusDrivers(List<BusDriver> busDrivers) {
    this.busDrivers = List.copyOf(busDrivers);
    this.allRumors = getAllRumors();
  }

  public boolean driveUntilAllRumorsShared(int maxDrivenStopCount) {
    while (true) {
      Set<BusStop> busStops = busDrivers.stream()
        .map(BusDriver::driveToNextBusStop)
        .collect(Collectors.toSet());

      drivenStopCount++;
      shareRumors(busStops);

      if (allRumorsAreShared()) {
        return true;
      } else if (drivenStopCount == maxDrivenStopCount) {
        return false;
      }
    }
  }

  private static void shareRumors(Set<BusStop> busStops) {
    for (final var busStop : busStops) {
      busStop.shareRumorsWithDrivers();
    }
  }

  // ...
}
```

Next, we shall implement the MaxDrivenStopCountParser class and its 'parse' method. Let's create a failing test:

```
class MaxDrivenStopCountParserTests {
  @Test
  void testParse_whenItSucceeds() {
    // GIVEN
    final var maxDrivenStopCountStr = "2";
    final var parser = new MaxDrivenStopCountParserImpl();

    // WHEN
    final var maxDrivenStopCount = parser.parse(maxDrivenStopCountStr);

    // THEN
    assertEquals(2, maxDrivenStopCount);
  }
}
```

Now we can implement the class to make the above test pass:

```
public interface MaxDrivenStopCountParser {
  int parse(final String maxDrivenStopCountStr);
}


public class MaxDrivenStopCountParserImpl implements MaxDrivenStopCountParser {

  @Override
  public int parse(String maxDrivenStopCountStr) {
    try {
      return Integer.parseInt(maxDrivenStopCountStr);
    } catch (NumberFormatException e) {
      throw new InputMismatchException(
        "Invalid max driven stop count: " + maxDrivenStopCountStr
      );
    }
  }
}
```

Next, we specify that the parse method should throw an InputMismatchException if the parsing fails:

```
class MaxDrivenStopCountParserTests {
  // ...

  @Test
  void testParse_whenItFails() {
    // GIVEN
    final var maxDrivenStopCountStr = "invalid";
    final var parser = new MaxDrivenStopCountParserImpl();

    // WHEN + THEN
    assertThrows(InputMismatchException.class, () -> {
      parser.parse(maxDrivenStopCountStr);
    });
  }
}
```

The above test will pass without modification to the implementation.

Next, we shall implement the BusDriversParser and its 'parse' method. We will skip the failure scenarios, like when a bus driver specification does not contain at least one bus stop and one rumor. Let's first create a failing test for a scenario where we have only one driver with one bus stop and one rumor:

```
class BusDriversParserTests {

  @Test
  void testParse_withOneDriverOneBusStopAndOneRumor() {
    // GIVEN
    final var busDriverSpec = "bus-stop-a;rumor1";
    final var parser = new BusDriversParserImpl();

    // WHEN
    final var busDrivers = parser.parse(List.of(busDriverSpec));

    // THEN
    assertHasCircularBusRouteWithOneStop(busDrivers);
    assertEquals(1, busDrivers.get(0).getRumors().size());
  }

  private void assertHasCircularBusRouteWithOneStop(
    final List<BusDriver> busDrivers
  ) {
    assertEquals(1, busDrivers.size());

    final var busDriver = busDrivers.get(0);
    final var originalBusStop = busDriver.getCurrentBusStop();
    final var nextBusStop = busDriver.driveToNextBusStop();

    assertSame(originalBusStop, nextBusStop);
  }
}
```

Let's implement the parse method to make the above test pass:

```
public interface BusDriversParser {
  List<BusDriver> parse(final List<String> busDriverSpecs);
}
```

```
public class BusDriversParserImpl implements BusDriversParser {

  @Override
  public List<BusDriver> parse(final List<String> busDriverSpecs) {
    return busDriverSpecs.stream().map(this::getBusDriver).toList();
  }

  private BusDriver getBusDriver(final String busDriverSpec) {
    return new BusDriverImpl(
      new CircularBusRoute(List.of(new BusStopImpl())),
      Set.of(new Rumor())
    );
  }
}
```

Let's create a test for a scenario where we have multiple drivers with one bus stop and one rumor each; both bus stops and rumors for drivers are different:

```
class BusDriversParserTests {
  // ...

  @Test
  void testParse_withMultipleDriversDifferentBusStopAndRumor() {
    // GIVEN
    final var busDriverSpec1 = "bus-stop-a;rumor1";
    final var busDriverSpec2 = "bus-stop-b;rumor2";
    final var parser = new BusDriversParserImpl();

    // WHEN
    final var busDrivers = parser.parse(List.of(busDriverSpec1, busDriverSpec2));

    // THEN
    assertBusStopsAreNotSame(busDrivers);
    assertNotEquals(busDrivers.get(0).getRumors(), busDrivers.get(1).getRumors());
  }

  // ...

  private void assertBusStopsAreNotSame(final List<BusDriver> busDrivers) {
    assertEquals(2, busDrivers.size());
    final var driver1Stop1 = busDrivers.get(0).getCurrentBusStop();
    final var driver2Stop1 = busDrivers.get(1).getCurrentBusStop();
    assertNotSame(driver1Stop1, driver2Stop1);
  }
}
```

The above test will pass without modifications to the implementation.

Let's create a test for a scenario where we have multiple drivers with one bus stop and one rumor each; the bus stops are the same, but rumors are different:

```
class BusDriversParserTests {
  // ...

  @Test
  void testParse_withMultipleDriversWithCommonBusStop() {
    // GIVEN
    final var busDriverSpec1 = "bus-stop-a;rumor1";
    final var busDriverSpec2 = "bus-stop-a;rumor2";
    final var parser = new BusDriversParserImpl();

    // WHEN
    final var busDrivers = parser.parse(List.of(busDriverSpec1, busDriverSpec2));

    // THEN
    assertBusStopsAreSame(busDrivers);
  }

  // ...

  private void assertBusStopsAreSame(final List<BusDriver> busDrivers) {
    final var driver1Stop = busDrivers.get(0).getCurrentBusStop();
    final var driver2Stop = busDrivers.get(1).getCurrentBusStop();
    assertSame(driver1Stop, driver2Stop);
  }
}
```

Let's modify the implementation to make the above test pass:

```java
public class BusDriversParserImpl implements BusDriversParser {
  private final Map<String, BusStop> nameToBusStop = new HashMap<>();

  @Override
  public List<BusDriver> parse(final List<String> busDriverSpecs) {
    return busDriverSpecs.stream().map(this::getBusDriver).toList();
  }

  private BusDriver getBusDriver(final String busDriverSpec) {
    final var parts = busDriverSpec.split(";");
    final var busStopName = parts[0];
    nameToBusStop.computeIfAbsent(busStopName, key -> new BusStopImpl());

    return new BusDriverImpl(
      new CircularBusRoute(List.of(nameToBusStop.get(busStopName))),
      Set.of(new Rumor())
    );
  }
}
```

Let's create a test for a scenario where we have multiple drivers with one rumor each, and the rumors are the same:

```java
class BusDriversParserTests {
  // ...

  @Test
  void testParse_withMultipleDriversAndCommonRumor() {
    // GIVEN
    final var busDriverSpec1 = "bus-stop-a;rumor1";
    final var busDriverSpec2 = "bus-stop-b;rumor1";
    final var parser = new BusDriversParserImpl();

    // WHEN
    final var busDrivers = parser.parse(List.of(busDriverSpec1, busDriverSpec2));

    // THEN
    assertEquals(busDrivers.get(0).getRumors(), busDrivers.get(1).getRumors());
  }
}
```

Let's modify the implementation to make the test pass:

```java
public class BusDriversParserImpl implements BusDriversParser {
  private final Map<String, BusStop> nameToBusStop = new HashMap<>();
  private final Map<String, Rumor> nameToRumor = new HashMap<>();

  @Override
  public List<BusDriver> parse(final List<String> busDriverSpecs) {
    return busDriverSpecs.stream().map(this::getBusDriver).toList();
  }

  private BusDriver getBusDriver(final String busDriverSpec) {
    final var parts = busDriverSpec.split(";");
    final var busStopName = parts[0];
    final var rumorName = parts[1];
    nameToBusStop.computeIfAbsent(busStopName, key -> new BusStopImpl());
    nameToRumor.computeIfAbsent(rumorName, key -> new Rumor());

    return new BusDriverImpl(
      new CircularBusRoute(List.of(nameToBusStop.get(busStopName))),
      Set.of(nameToRumor.get(rumorName))
    );
  }
}
```

Let's create a test for a scenario where we have multiple drivers with multiple bus stops (the first bus stop is the same):

```
class BusDriversParserTests {
  // ...

  @Test
  void testParse_withMultipleDriversAndMultipleBusStopsWhereFirstIsCommon() {
    // GIVEN
    final var busDriverSpec1 = "bus-stop-a,bus-stop-b;rumor1";
    final var busDriverSpec2 = "bus-stop-a,bus-stop-c;rumor2";
    final var parser = new BusDriversParserImpl();

    // WHEN
    final var busDrivers = parser.parse(List.of(busDriverSpec1, busDriverSpec2));

    // THEN
    assertOnlyFirstBusStopIsSame(busDrivers);
  }

  // ...

  private void assertOnlyFirstBusStopIsSame(final List<BusDriver> busDrivers) {
    final var driver1Stop1 = busDrivers.get(0).getCurrentBusStop();
    final var driver2Stop1 = busDrivers.get(1).getCurrentBusStop();
    assertSame(driver1Stop1, driver2Stop1);

    final var driver1Stop2 = busDrivers.get(0).driveToNextBusStop();
    final var driver2Stop2 = busDrivers.get(1).driveToNextBusStop();
    assertNotSame(driver1Stop2, driver2Stop2);
  }
}
```

Let's make the above test pass:

```
public class BusDriversParserImpl implements BusDriversParser {
  // ...

  private BusDriver getBusDriver(final String busDriverSpec) {
    final var parts = busDriverSpec.split(";");
    final var busRouteSpec = parts[0];
    final var rumorName = parts[1];

    final var busStops = Arrays.stream(busRouteSpec.split(","))
      .map(busStopName -> {
        nameToBusStop.computeIfAbsent(busStopName, key -> new BusStopImpl());
        return nameToBusStop.get(busStopName);
      })
      .toList();

    nameToRumor.computeIfAbsent(rumorName, key -> new Rumor());

    return new BusDriverImpl(
      new CircularBusRoute(busStops),
      Set.of(nameToRumor.get(rumorName))
    );
  }
}
```

Let's create a test for a scenario where we have multiple drivers with multiple rumors (one of which is the same):

```
class BusDriversParserTests {
  // ...

  @Test
  void testParse_withMultipleDriversAndMultipleRumors() {
    // GIVEN
    final var busDriverSpec1 = "bus-stop-a;rumor1,rumor2,rumor3";
    final var busDriverSpec2 = "bus-stop-b;rumor1,rumor3";
    final var parser = new BusDriversParserImpl();

    // WHEN
    final var busDrivers = parser.parse(List.of(busDriverSpec1, busDriverSpec2));

    // THEN
    assertRumorsDifferByOne(busDrivers);
  }

  // ...

  private void assertRumorsDifferByOne(final List<BusDriver> busDrivers) {
    assertEquals(3, busDrivers.get(0).getRumors().size());
    assertEquals(2, busDrivers.get(1).getRumors().size());
    final var rumorDiff = new HashSet<>(busDrivers.get(0).getRumors());
    rumorDiff.removeAll(busDrivers.get(1).getRumors());
    assertEquals(1, rumorDiff.size());
  }
}
```

Let's modify the implementation to make the above test pass:

```
public class BusDriversParserImpl implements BusDriversParser {
  // ...

  private BusDriver getBusDriver(final String busDriverSpec) {
    final var parts = busDriverSpec.split(";");
    final var busRouteSpec = parts[0];
    final var rumorsSpec = parts[1];
    final var busStops = getBusStops(List.of(busRouteSpec.split(",")));
    final var rumors = getRumors(List.of(rumorsSpec.split(",")));

    return new BusDriverImpl(
      new CircularBusRoute(busStops),
      rumors
    );
  }

  private List<BusStop> getBusStops(final List<String> busStopNames) {
    return busStopNames.stream()
      .map(busStopName -> {
        nameToBusStop.computeIfAbsent(busStopName, key -> new BusStopImpl());
        return nameToBusStop.get(busStopName);
      })
      .toList();
  }

  private Set<Rumor> getRumors(final List<String> rumorNames) {
    return rumorNames.stream()
      .map(rumorName -> {
        nameToRumor.computeIfAbsent(rumorName, key -> new Rumor());
        return nameToRumor.get(rumorName);
      })
      .collect(Collectors.toSet());
  }
}
```

Finally, we need to implement the main class:

```
public class Main {
  public static void main(final String[] args) {
    if (args.length < 3) {
      System.err.println(
        "Usage: Main <maxDrivenStopCount> <busDriverSpec1> <busDriverSpec2> ..."
      );

      System.exit(1);
    }

    try {
      final var maxDrivenStopCount = new MaxDrivenStopCountParserImpl().parse(args[0]);
      final var busDriverSpecs = List.of(args).subList(1, args.length);
      final var busDrivers = new BusDriversParserImpl().parse(busDriverSpecs);

      boolean allRumorsWereShared = new GossipingBusDrivers(busDrivers)
        .driveUntilAllRumorsShared(maxDrivenStopCount);

      System.exit(allRumorsWereShared ? 0 : 1);

    } catch (final NumberFormatException exception) {
      System.err.println("Invalid max driven stop count: " + args[0]);
      System.exit(1);
    } catch (final Exception exception) {
      System.err.println("Exception: " + exception.getMessage());
      System.exit(1);
    }
  }
}
```

Let's say that product management wants a new feature and puts the following user story on the backlog:

- Support a back-and-forth bus route in addition to the circular bus route.

Because we used the *program against interfaces principle* earlier, we can implement this new feature using the *open-closed principle* by implementing a new BackNForthBusRoute class that implements the BusRoute interface. How about integrating that new class with existing code? Can we also follow the *open-closed principle*? For the most part, yes. As I have mentioned earlier, it is challenging and often impossible to 100% follow the *open-closed principle* principle. And that is not the goal. However, we should use it as much as we can. In the above code, the CircularBusRoute class was hardcoded in the BusDriversParserImpl class. We should create a bus route factory that creates circular or back-and-forth bus routes. Here, we again follow the *open-closed principle*. Then, we use that factory in the BusDriversParserImpl class instead of the hard-coded CircularBusRoute constructor. The BusDriversParserImpl class's parse method should get the bus route type as a parameter and forward it to the bus route factory. These last two modifications are not following the *open-closed principle* because we were obliged to modify an existing class.

Similarly, we could later introduce other new features using the *open-closed principle*:

- Quick bus stops where drivers don't have time to share rumors could be implemented in a new QuickBusStop class implementing the BusStop interface
- Forgetful bus drivers that remember others' rumors only, e.g., for a certain number of bus stops, could be implemented with a new ForgetfulBusDriver class that implements the BusDriver interface

As another example, let's consider implementing a simple API containing CRUD operations. Product management has defined the following feature (or epic) in the backlog:

The sales item API creates, reads, updates, and deletes sales items. Sales items are stored in persistent storage and consist of the following attributes: unique ID, name, and price. Sales items can be created, updated, and deleted only by administrators.

First, the architecture team should provide technical guidance on implementing the backlog feature (or epic). The guidance could be the following: API should be a REST API, MySQL database should be used as persistent storage, and Keycloak should be used as the IAM system. Next, the development team should perform threat modeling (facilitated by the product security lead if needed). Threat modelling should result in additional security-related user stories that should be added to the backlog feature (or epic) and implemented by the team.

> Consider implementing the above-specified sales item API in a real-life scenario as two separate APIs for improved security: One public internet-facing API for reading sales items and another private API for administrator-related operations. The private admin API is accessible only from the company intranet and should not be accessible from the public internet directly, but access from the internet should require a company VPN connection (and proper authorization, of course), for example.

The development team should split the backlog feature into user stories in the PI planning[29] (or before it in the IP iteration[30]). The team will come up with the following user stories:

1) As an admin user, I want to create a new sales item in a persistent storage. A sales item contains the following attributes: id, name, and price
2) As a user, I want to read sales items from the persistent storage
3) As an admin user, I want to update a sales item in the persistent storage
4) As an admin user, I want to delete a sales item from the persistent storage

Next, the team should continue by applying BDD to each user story:

User story 1:

Figure 6.52. create_sales_item.feature

```
Feature: Create sales item

  Background: Database is available and a clean table exists
    Given database is available
    And table is empty
    And auto increment is reset

  Scenario: Successfully create sales item as admin user
    When the following sales items are created as admin user
        | name         | price |
        | Sales item 1 | 10    |
        | Sales item 2 | 20    |
        | Sales item 3 | 30    |

    Then a response with status code 201 is received
    And the following sales items are received as response
        | name         | price | Id |
        | Sales item 1 | 10    | 1  |
        | Sales item 2 | 20    | 2  |
        | Sales item 3 | 30    | 3  |
```

[29] https://scaledagileframework.com/pi-planning/
[30] https://scaledagileframework.com/innovation-and-planning-iteration/

```
Scenario: Try to create a sales item with invalid data
  When the following sales items are created as admin user
    | name         | price |
    | Sales item 1 | aa    |

  Then a response with status code 400 is received


Scenario: Try to create new sales when database is unavailable
  Given database is unavailable

  When the following sales items are created as admin user
    | name         | price |
    | Sales item 1 | 10    |

  Then a response with status code 503 is received


Scenario: Try to create a sales item as normal user
  When the following sales items are created as normal user
    | name         | price |
    | Sales item 1 | 10    |

  Then a response with status code 403 is received


Scenario: Try to create a sales item unauthenticated
  When the following sales items are created unauthenticated
    | aame         | price |
    | Sales item 1 | aa    |

  Then a response with status code 401 is received
```

User story 2:

Figure 6.53. read_sales_item.feature

```
Feature: Read sales items

  Background: Database is available and a clean table exists
    Given database is available
    And table is empty
    And auto increment is reset


  Scenario: Successfully read sales items
    Given the following sales items are created
      | name         | price |
      | Sales item 1 | 10    |
      | Sales item 2 | 20    |
      | Sales item 3 | 30    |

    When sales items are read

    Then a response with status code 200 is received
    And the following sales items are received as response
      | name         | price | Id |
      | Sales item 1 | 10    | 1  |
      | Sales item 2 | 20    | 2  |
      | Sales item 3 | 30    | 3  |


  Scenario: Try to read sales items when database is unavailable
    Given database is unavailable
    When sales items are read
    Then a response with status code 503 is received
```

User story 3:

Figure 6.54. update_sales_item.feature

```
Feature: Update sales item

  Background: Database is available and a clean table exists
    Given database is available
    And table is empty
    And auto increment is reset


  Scenario: Successfully update sales item as admin user
    Given the following sales items are created as admin user
      | name         | price |
      | Sales item 1 | 10    |

    When the created sales item is updated to the following as admin user
      | name         | price |
      | Sales item X | 100   |

    Then reading the sales item should provide the following response
      | name         | price |
      | Sales item X | 100   |


  Scenario: Try to update sales item with invalid data
    When sales item with id 1 is updated to the following
      | name         | price |
      | Sales item X | aa    |

    Then a response with status code 400 is received


  Scenario: Sales item update fails because sales item is not found
    When sales item with id 999 is updated to the following
      | name         | price |
      | Sales item X | 100   |

    Then a response with status code 404 is received


  Scenario: Try to update sales item when database is unavailable
    Given database is unavailable

    When sales item with id 1 is updated to the following
      | name         | price |
      | Sales item X | 100   |

    Then a response with status code 503 is received


  Scenario: Try to update sales as normal user
    When sales item with id 1 is updated to the following as normal user
      | name         | price |
      | Sales item X | aa    |

    Then a response with status code 403 is received


  Scenario: Try to update sales unauthenticated
    When sales item with id 1 is updated to the following unauthenticated
      | name         | price |
      | Sales item X | aa    |

    Then a response with status code 401 is received
```

User story 4:

Figure 6.55. delete_sales_item.feature

```
Feature: Delete sales item

  Background: Database is available and clean table exists
    Given database is available
    And table is empty
    And auto increment is reset


  Scenario: Successfully delete sales item as admin user
    Given the following sales items are created as admin user
      | name         | price |
      | Sales item 1 | 10    |

    When the created sales item is deleted as admin user

    Then a response with status code 204 is received
    And reading sales items should provide an empty array as response


  Scenario: Try to delete a non-existent sales with
    When sales item with id 9999 is deleted as admin user
    Then a response with status code 204 is received


  Scenario: Try to delete a sales item when database is unavailable
    Given database is unavailable
    When sales item with id 1 is deleted as admin user
    Then a response with status code 503 is received


  Scenario: Try to delete a sales as normal user
    When sales item with id 1 is deleted as normal user
    Then a response with status code 403 is received


  Scenario: Try to delete a sales unauthenticated
    When sales item with id 1 is deleted unauthenticated
    Then a response with status code 401 is received
```

In the above features, we have considered the main failure scenarios in addition to the happy path scenario. Remember that you should also test the most common failure scenarios as part of integration testing.

The above features include a `Background` section defining steps executed before each scenario. In the `Background` section, we first ensure the database is available. This is needed because some scenarios make the database unavailable on purpose. Then, we clean the sales items table in the database. This can be done by connecting to the database and executing SQL statements like `DELETE FROM sales_items` and `ALTER TABLE sales_items AUTO_INCREMENT=1`. Here, I am assuming a MySQL database is used. The database availability can be toggled by issuing `docker pause` and `docker unpause` commands for the database server container using `subprocess.run` or `subprocess.Popen`. You should put the step implementations for the `Background` section into a common `background_steps.py` file because the same `Background` section is used in all features. Before being able to execute integration tests, a *docker-compose.yml* file must be created. The file should define the microservice itself and its dependencies, the database (MySQL), and the IAM system (Keycloak).

Additionally, we must configure the IAM system before executing the integration tests. This can be done in the *environment.py* file in the `before_all` function. This function is executed by the `behave` command before executing the integration tests. Let's assume we are using Keycloak as the IAM system. To configure Keycloak, we can use the Keycloak's Admin REST API. We need to perform the following (Change the hardcoded version number in the URLs to the newest):

- Create a client (https://www.keycloak.org/docs-api/23.0.2/rest-api/index.html#_clients)

- Create an admin role for the client (https://www.keycloak.org/docs-api/23.0.2/rest-api/index.html#_roles)
- Create an admin user with the admin role (https://www.keycloak.org/docs-api/23.0.2/rest-api/index.html#_users)
- Create a regular user without the admin role

An alternative method to test authorization is to use a configurable mock OAuth2 server instead of a real IAM system.

Let's implement the steps for the first scenario of the first user story (creating a sales item) using Python and Behave:

Figure 6.56. create_sales_item_steps.py

```
import requests
from behave import then, when
from behave.runner import Context
from environment import SALES_ITEM_API_URL


@when('the following sales items are created {user_type}')
def step_impl(context: Context, user_type: str):
    # Obtain an 'access token' for an admin or normal user based on 'user_type'
    # from the IAM system using OAuth2 Resource Owner Password Flow
    # https://auth0.com/docs/get-started/authentication-and-authorization-flow/resource-owner-password\
-flow
    # Using this flow, you exchange client_id, client_secret,
    # username and password for an access token

    auth_header = (
        None
        if user_type == 'unauthenticated'
        else f'Bearer {access_token}'
    )

    context.received_sales_items = []
    context.status_codes = []

    for row in context.table:
        sales_item = {key: row[key] for key in row.keys()}

        response = requests.post(
            SALES_ITEM_API_URL,
            sales_item,
            headers={'Authorization': auth_header},
        )

        context.status_codes.append(response.status_code)
        received_sales_item = response.json()
        context.received_sales_items.append(received_sales_item)


@then('a response with status code {expected_status_code:d} is received')
def step_impl(context: Context, expected_status_code: int):
    for received_status_code in context.status_codes:
        assert received_status_code == expected_status_code


@then('the following sales items are received as response')
def step_impl(context: Context):
    recv_and_expected_sales_items = zip(
        context.received_sales_items,
        context.table,
    )

    for (
```

```
        recv_sales_item,
        expected_sales_item,
    ) in recv_and_expected_sales_items:
        for key in expected_sales_item.keys():
            assert recv_sales_item[key] == expected_sales_item[key]
```

To make the rest of the scenarios for the first feature pass, we need to add the following:

Figure 6.57. common_steps.py

```
@given('database is unavailable')
def step_impl(context: Context):
    # Use subprocess.run or subprocess.Popen to execute
    # 'docker pause' command for the
    # database container
```

We will skip implementing the rest of the steps because they are similar to those we implemented above. The main difference is using different methods of the request library: get for reading, put for updating and delete for deleting.

Next, the development team should perform DDD for the user stories. The first user story is comprised of the following domain events:

- user is authorized
- sales item is validated
- sales item is created
- sales item is persisted

From the above domain events, we can infer the following:

- Actor: UserAuthorizer, Command: authorize
- Actor: InputSalesItemValidator, Command: validate, Entity: InputSalesItem
- Actor: CreateSalesItemService: Command: create_sales_item, Entities: InputSalesItem, OutputSalesItem
- Actor: CreateSalesItemRepository, Command: save, Entity: SalesItem

Let's conduct DDD for the second user story. We will have the following domain events:

- sales items are read from the persistent store
- sales items are converted to output format

From the above domain events, we can infer the following:

- Actor: ReadSalesItemsRepository, Command: read_all, Entity: SalesItem
- Actor: ReadSalesItemsService: Command: read_sales_items, Entities: OutputSalesItem

The team decides to use the *clean architecture principle*. Thus, interfaces and controller classes should be added for both user stories. The source code directory should look like the following:

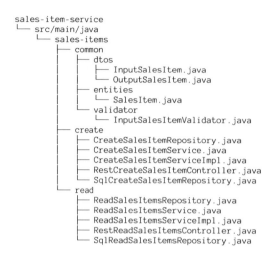

```
sales-item-service
└── src/main/java
    └── sales-items
        ├── common
        │   ├── dtos
        │   │   ├── InputSalesItem.java
        │   │   └── OutputSalesItem.java
        │   ├── entities
        │   │   └── SalesItem.java
        │   └── validator
        │       └── InputSalesItemValidator.java
        ├── create
        │   ├── CreateSalesItemRepository.java
        │   ├── CreateSalesItemService.java
        │   ├── CreateSalesItemServiceImpl.java
        │   ├── RestCreateSalesItemController.java
        │   └── SqlCreateSalesItemRepository.java
        └── read
            ├── ReadSalesItemsRepository.java
            ├── ReadSalesItemsService.java
            ├── ReadSalesItemsServiceImpl.java
            ├── RestReadSalesItemsController.java
            └── SqlReadSalesItemsRepository.java
```

When we continue with DDD for the rest of the user stories, we should eventually have subdirectories for update and delete features like those for create and read features. What we ended up having is called *vertical slice architecture*, which we presented in the second chapter. A different team member can implement each user story, and each team member has their own subdirectory (a vertical slice) to work on to minimize merge conflicts. Things common to all features are put into the common subdirectory. The development continues with each team member conducting TDD for the public methods in the classes. This kind of parallel development provides better agility when the whole team (instead of just one team member) can focus on the same feature (or epic) to complete it as fast as possible, and only after that proceed to the next feature (or epic) on the prioritized backlog. The implementation details of the classes are not shown here, but the coming chapters about API design and databases show details how to create a REST controller, DTOs, a service class, and repositories like ORM, SQL, and MongoDB.

As I mentioned earlier, Gherkin is not the only syntax, and Behave is not the only tool to conduct BDD. I want to give you an example where Robot Framework[31] (RF) is used as an alternative to Gherkin and Behave. You don't have to completely say goodbye to the Gherkin syntax because the Robot framework also supports a Gherkin-style way to define test cases. The below example is for the first user story we defined earlier: creating a sales item. The example shows how to test that user story's first two scenarios (or *test cases* in RF vocabulary). The below *.robot* file resembles the Gherkin *.feature* file. Each test case in the *.robot* file contains a list of steps that are *keywords*, defined in the *.resource* files. Each keyword defines code (a list of functions) to execute. The functions are implemented in the *libraries*.

Figure 6.58. create_sales_item.robot

```
*** Settings ***
Documentation    Create sales item
Resource         database_setup.resource
Resource         create_sales_item.resource
Test Setup       Database is available and a clean table exists


*** Test Cases ***
Successfully create sales item as admin user
    When a sales item is created as admin user          salesitem1   ${10}
    Then a response with status code is received         ${201}
    And the following sales item is received as response  salesitem1   ${10}
```

---

[31]https://robotframework.org/

```
Try to create a sales item with invalid data
    When a sales item is created as admin user         salesitem    aa
    Then a response with status code is received        ${400}
```

Figure 6.59. database_setup.resource

```
*** Settings ***
Documentation
Library          ./DatabaseSetup.py


*** Keywords ***
Database is available and a clean table exists
    Start database if needed
    Clear table
    Reset auto increment
```

Figure 6.60. create_sales_item.resource

```
*** Settings ***
Documentation
Library          ./CreateSalesItem.py


*** Keywords ***
Database is available and a clean table exists
    Start database if needed
    Clear table
    Reset auto increment


A sales item is created as admin user
    [Arguments]    ${name}    ${price}
    Create sales item as admin user    ${name}    ${price}


A response with status code is received
    [Arguments]    ${status_code}
    Verify response    ${status code}


The following sales item is received as response
    [Arguments]    ${name}    ${price}
    Verify received sales item  ${name}       ${price}
```

Figure 6.61. DatabaseSetup.py

```
class DatabaseSetup:
    def __init__(self):
        pass

    def start_database_if_needed(self):
        # ...

    def clear_table(self):
        # ...

    def reset_auto_increment(self):
        # ...
```

Figure 6.62. CreateSalesItem.py

```python
import requests
from environment import SALES_ITEM_API_URL


class CreateSalesItem:
    def __init__(self):
        self.response = None

    def create_sales_item_as_admin_user(self, name: str, price: str | int):
        # Obtain admin user access token from the IAM system
        access_token = ''
        sales_item = {'name': name, 'price': price}

        self.response = requests.post(
            SALES_ITEM_API_URL,
            sales_item,
            headers={'Authorization': f'Bearer {access_token}'},
        )

    def verify_response(self, status_code: int):
        assert self.response.status_code == status_code

    def verify_received_sales_item(self, name: str, price: int):
        sales_item = self.response.json()
        assert sales_item['name'] == name
        assert sales_item['price'] == price
```

6.1.4: End-to-End (E2E) Testing Principle

End-to-end (E2E) testing should test a complete software system (i.e., the integration of microservices) so that each test case is end-to-end (from the software system's south-bound interface to the software system's north-bound interface).

As the name says, in E2E testing, test cases should be end-to-end. They should test that each microservice is deployed correctly to the test environment and connected to its dependent services. The idea of E2E test cases is not to test details of microservices' functionality because that has already been tested in unit and software component integration testing. This is why there should be only a handful of E2E test cases.

Let's consider a telecom network analytics software system that consists of the following applications:

- Data ingestion
- Data correlation
- Data aggregation
- Data exporter
- Data visualization

North-bound Interfaces

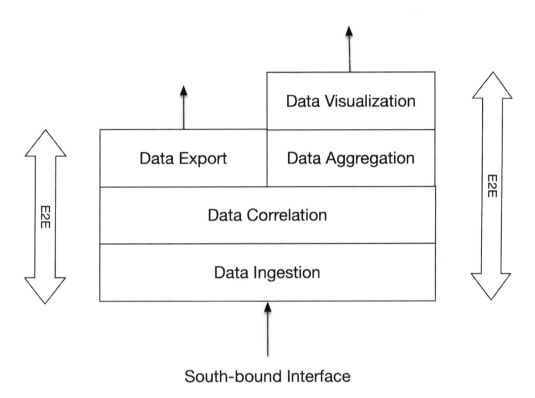

Figure 6.63. Telecom Network Analytics Software System

The southbound interface of the software system is the data ingestion application. The data visualization application provides a web client as a northbound interface. The data exporter application also provides another northbound interface for the software system.

E2E tests are designed and implemented similarly to software component integration tests. We are just integrating different things (microservices instead of functions). E2E testing starts with the specification of E2E features. These features can be specified using, for example, the Gherkin language and put in *feature* files.

You can start specifying and implementing E2E tests right after the architectural design for the software system is completed. This way, you can shift the implementation of the E2E test to the left and speed up the development phase. You should not start specifying and implementing E2E only after the whole software system is implemented.

Our example software system should have at least two happy-path E2E features. One is for testing the data flow from data ingestion to data visualization, and another feature is to test the data flow from data ingestion to data export. Below is the specification of the first E2E feature:

```
Feature: Visualize ingested, correlated and
         aggregated data in web UI's dashboard's charts

  Scenario: Data ingested, correlated and aggregated is visualized
            successfully in web UI's dashboard's charts

    Given southbound interface simulator is configured
          to send input messages that contain data...
    And data ingester is configured to read the input messages
        from the southbound interface
    And data correlator is configured to correlate
        the input messages
    And data aggregator is configured to calculate
        the following counters...
    And data visualization is configured with a dashboard containing
        the following charts viewing the following counters/KPIs...

    When southbound interface simulator sends the input messages
    And data aggregation period is waited
    And data content of each data visualization web UI's dasboard's
        chart is exported to a CSV file

    Then CSV export file of the first chart should
         contain the following values...
    And the CSV export file of the second chart should
        contain the following values...
    .
    .
    .
    And CSV export file of the last chart should
        contain the following values...
```

Then, we can create another feature that tests the E2E path from data ingestion to data export:

```
Feature: Export ingested, correlated and transformed data
         to Apache Pulsar

  Scenario: Data ingested, correlated and transformed is
            successfully exported to Apache Pulsar
    Given southbound interface simulator is configured to send
          input messages that contain data...
    And data ingester is configured to read the input messages
        from the southbound interface
    And data correlator is configured to correlate
        the input messages
    And data exporter is configured to export messages with
        the following transformations to Apache Pulsar...

    When southbound interface simulator sends the input messages
    And messages from Apache Pulsar are consumed

    Then first message from Apache Pulsar should have
         the following fields with following values...
    And second message from Apache Pulsar should have
        the following fields with following values...
    .
    .
    .
    And last message from Apache Pulsar should have
        the following fields with following values...
```

Next, E2E tests can be implemented. Any programming language and tool compatible with the Gherkin syntax, like Behave with Python, can be used. If the QA/test engineers in the development teams already use Behave for integration tests, it would be a natural choice to use Behave also for the E2E tests.

The software system we want to E2E test must reside in a production-like test environment. Usually, E2E testing is done in both the CI and the staging environment(s). Before running the E2E tests, the software needs to be deployed to the test environment.

Considering the first feature above, the E2E test steps can be implemented so that the steps in the Given part of the scenario are implemented using an externalized configuration. If our software system runs in a Kubernetes cluster, we can configure the microservices by creating the needed ConfigMaps. The southbound interface simulator can be controlled by launching a Kubernetes Job or, if it is a microservice with an API, commanding it via its API. After waiting for all the ingested data to be aggregated and visualized, the E2E test can launch a test tool suited for web UI testing (like TestCafe) to export chart data from the web UI to downloaded files. Then, the E2E test compares the content of those files with expected values.

You can run E2E tests in a CI environment after each commit to the main branch (i.e., after the microservice CI pipeline run has finished) to test that the new commit did not break any E2E tests. Alternatively, if the E2E tests are complex and take a long time to execute, you can run the E2E tests in the CI environment on a schedule, like hourly, but at least nightly.

You can run E2E tests in a staging environment using a separate pipeline in your CI/CD tool.

6.2: Non-Functional Testing Principle

In addition to multi-level functional testing, non-functional testing, as automated as possible, should be performed for a software system.

The most important categories of non-functional testing are the following:

- Performance testing
- Data volume testing
- Stability testing
- Reliability testing
- Stress and scalability testing
- Security testing

6.2.1: Performance Testing

The goal of performance testing is to verify the performance of a software system. This verification can be done on different levels and in different ways, for example, by verifying each performance-critical microservice separately.

To measure the performance of a microservice, performance tests can be created to benchmark the busy loop or loops in the microservice. If we take the data exporter microservice as an example, there is a busy loop that performs message decoding, transformation, and encoding. We can create a performance test using a unit testing framework for this busy loop. The performance test should execute the code in the busy loop for a certain number of rounds (like 50,000 times) and verify that the execution duration does not exceed a specified threshold value obtained on the first run of the performance test. The performance test aims to verify that performance remains at the same level as it has been or is better. If the performance has worsened, the test won't pass. In this way, you cannot accidentally introduce changes that negatively affect the performance without noticing it. This same performance test can also be used to measure the effects of optimizations. First, you write code for the busy loop without optimizations, measure the performance, and use that measure as a reference point. After that, you introduce optimizations individually and see if and how they affect the performance.

The performance test's execution time threshold value must be separately specified for each developer's computer. This can be achieved by having a different threshold value for each computer hostname running the test.

You can also run the performance test in a CI pipeline, but you must first measure the performance in that pipeline and set the threshold value accordingly. Also, the computing instances running CI pipelines must be homogeneous. Otherwise, you will get different results on different CI pipeline runs.

The above-described performance test was for a unit (one public function without mocking), but performance testing can also be done on the software component level. This is useful if the software component has external dependencies whose performance needs to be measured. In the telecom network analytics software system, we could introduce a performance test for the *data-ingester-service* to measure how long it takes to process a certain number of messages, like one million. After executing that test, we have a performance measurement available for reference. When we try to optimize the microservice, we can measure the performance of the optimized microservice and compare it to the reference value. If we make a change known to worsen the performance, we have a reference value to which we can compare the deteriorated performance and see if it is acceptable. And, of course, this reference value will prevent a developer from accidentally making a change that negatively impacts the microservice's performance.

You can also measure end-to-end performance. In the telecom network analytics software system, we could measure the performance from data ingestion to data export, for example.

6.2.2: Data Volume Testing

The goal of data volume testing is to measure the performance of a database by comparing an empty database to a database with a sizeable amount of data stored in it. With data volume testing, we can measure the impact of data volume on a software component's performance. Usually, an empty database performs better than a database containing a large amount of data. This depends on the database and how it scales with large amounts of data.

6.2.3: Stability Testing

Stability testing aims to verify that a software system remains stable when running for an extended period of time under load. This testing is also called *load*, *endurance*, or *soak* testing. The term "extended period" can be interpreted differently depending on the software system. But this period should be many hours, preferably several days, even up to one week. Stability testing aims to discover problems like sporadic bugs or memory leaks. A sporadic bug is a bug that occurs only in certain conditions or at irregular intervals. A memory leak can be so small that the software component must run for tens of hours after it becomes clearly visible. It is recommended that when running the software system for a longer period, the induced load to the software system follows a natural pattern (mimicking the production load), meaning that there are peaks and lows in the load.

Stability testing can be partly automated. The load to the system can be generated using tools created for that purpose, like Apache JMeter, for example. Each software component can measure crash count, and those statistics can be analyzed automatically or manually after the stability testing is completed. Analyzing memory leaks can be trickier, but crashes due to out-of-memory and situations where a software component is scaling out due to lack of memory should be registered.

6.2.4: Reliability Testing

Reliability testing aims to verify that a software system runs reliably. The software system is reliable when it is resilient to failures and recovers from failures automatically as fast as possible. Reliability testing is also called availability, *recovery*, or *resilience* testing.

Reliability testing involves chaos engineering to induce various failures in the software system's environment. It should also ensure the software system stays available and can automatically recover from failures.

Suppose you have a software system deployed to a Kubernetes cluster. You can make stateless services highly available by configuring them to run multiple pods. If one node goes down, it will terminate one of the pods (never allow scheduling all the microservice pods on the same node). However, the service remains available and usable because at least one other pod is still running on a different node. Also, after a short while, when Kubernetes notices that one pod is missing, it will create a new pod on a new node, and there will be the original number of pods running, and the recovery from the node down is successful.

Many parts of the reliability testing can be automated. You can use ready-made chaos engineering tools or create and use your tools. Use a tool to induce failures in the environment. Then, based on the service's business criticality, verify that the service remains highly available or swiftly recovers from a failure.

Considering the telecom network analytics software system, we could introduce a test case where the message broker (e.g., Kafka) is shut down. Then, we expect alerts to be triggered after a while by the microservices that try to use the unavailable message broker. After the message broker is restarted, the alerts should cancel automatically, and the microservices should continue normal operation.

6.2.5: Stress and Scalability Testing

Stress testing aims to verify that a software system runs under high load. In stress testing, the software system is exposed to a load higher than the system's usual load. The software system should be designed as scalable, which means that the software system should also run under high load. Thus, stress testing should test the scalability of the software system and see that microservices scale out when needed. At the end of stress testing, the load is returned back to the normal level, and scaling in the microservices can also be verified.

You can specify a HorizontalPodAutoscaler (HPA) for a Kubernetes Deployment. In the HPA manifest, you must specify the minimum number of replicas. This should be at least two if you want to make your microservice highly available. You also need to specify the maximum number of replicas so that your microservice does not consume too many computing resources in some weird failure case. You can make the horizontal scaling (in and out) happen by specifying a target utilization rate for CPU and memory. Below is an example Helm chart template for defining a Kubernetes HPA:

```
{{- if eq .Values.env "production" }}
apiVersion: autoscaling/v2beta1
kind: HorizontalPodAutoscaler
metadata:
  name: {{ include "microservice.fullname" . }}
  labels:
    {{- include "microservice.labels" . | nindent 4 }}
spec:
  scaleTargetRef:
    apiVersion: apps/v1
    kind: Deployment
    name: {{ include "microservice.fullname" . }}
  minReplicas: {{ .Values.hpa.minReplicas }}
  maxReplicas: {{ .Values.hpa.maxReplicas }}
  metrics:
```

```
{{- if .Values.hpa.targetCPUUtilizationPercentage }}
- type: Resource
  resource:
    name: cpu
    targetAverageUtilization: {{ .Values.hpa.targetCPUUtilizationPercentage }}
{{- end }}
{{- if .Values.hpa.targetMemoryUtilizationPercentage }}
- type: Resource
  resource:
    name: memory
    targetAverageUtilization: {{ .Values.hpa.targetMemoryUtilizationPercentage }}
{{- end }}
{{- end }}
```

It is also possible to specify the autoscaling to use an external metric. An external metric could be Kafka consumer lag, for instance. If the Kafka consumer lag grows too high, the HPA can scale the microservice out to provide more processing power for the Kafka consumer group. When the Kafka consumer lag decreases below a defined threshold, HPA can scale in the microservice to reduce the number of pods.

6.2.6: Security Testing

Security testing aims to verify that a software system is secure and does not contain security vulnerabilities. One part of security testing is performing vulnerability scans of the software artifacts. Typically, this means scanning the microservice containers using an automatic vulnerability scanning tool. Another essential part of security testing is penetration testing, which simulates attacks by a malicious party. Penetration testing can be performed using an automated tool like ZAP[32] or Burp Suite[33].

Penetration testing tools try to find security vulnerabilities in the following categories:

- Cross-site scripting
- SQL injection
- Path disclosure
- Denial of service
- Code execution
- Memory corruption
- Cross-site request forgery (CSRF)
- Information disclosure
- Local/remote file inclusion

A complete list of possible security vulnerabilities found by the ZAP tool can be found at ZAP Alert Details[34].

6.2.7: Other Non-Functional Testing

Other non-functional testing is documentation testing and several UI-related non-functional testing, including accessibility (A11Y) testing, visual testing, usability testing, and localization and internationalization (I18N) testing.

---

[32]https://www.zaproxy.org/

[33]https://portswigger.net/

[34]https://www.zaproxy.org/docs/alerts/

6.2.7.1: Visual Testing

I want to bring up visual testing here because it is important. Backstop.js[35] and cypress-plugin-snapshots[36] test web UI's HTML and CSS using snapshot testing. Snapshots are screenshots taken of the web UI. Snapshots are compared to ensure that the visual look of the application stays the same and no bugs are introduced with HTML or CSS changes.

---

[35]https://github.com/garris/BackstopJS
[36]https://github.com/meinaart/cypress-plugin-snapshots

7: Security Principles

This chapter describes security principles and addresses the main security features from a software developer's perspective.

7.1: Shift Security to Left Principle

Shift security implementation to the left. Implement security-related features sooner rather than later.

Security is integral to production-quality software, like the source code and all the tests. Suppose that security-related features are implemented only in a very late project phase. In that case, there is a greater possibility of not finding time to implement them or forgetting to implement them. For that reason, security-related features should be implemented first rather than last. The threat modeling process described in the next section should be used to identify the potential threats and provide a list of security features that need to be implemented as threat countermeasures.

7.2: Have a Product Security Lead Principle

Each product team should have a security lead appointed. The security lead's role is to ensure that the product is secure.

The security lead works tightly with development teams. They educate teams on security-related processes and security features. The security lead facilitates the teams in the below-described threat modeling process, but following the process is the team's responsibility, as is the actual implementation of security features.

7.3: Use Threat Modelling Process Principle

The threat modeling process enables you to identify, quantify, and address security risks associated with a software component or an application. The threat modeling process is composed of three high-level steps:

- Decompose the application
- Determine and rank threats
- Determine countermeasures and mitigation

7.3.1: Decompose Application

The application decomposition step is to gain knowledge of what parts the application is composed of, the external dependencies, and how they are used. This step can be performed after the application architecture is designed. The results of this step are:

- Identify an attacker's entry points to the application
- Identify assets under threat. These assets are something that an attacker is interested in
- Identify trust levels, e.g., what users with different user roles can do

7.3.2: Determine and Rank Threats

A threat categorization methodology should be used to determine possible threats.

7.3.2.1: STRIDE method

The *STRIDE* method categorizes threats into the following categories:

Category	Description
Spoofing	Attacker acting as another user without real authentication or using stolen credentials
Tampering	Attacker maliciously changing data
Repudiation	Attacker being able to perform prohibited operations
Information disclosure	Attacker gaining access to sensitive data
Denial of service	Attacker trying to make the service unusable
Elevation of privilege	Attacker gaining unwanted access rights

7.3.2.2: STRIDE Threat Examples

- Spoofing

    - The attacker can read other users' data using the other user's id when there is proper authorization missing
    - The attacker can steal user credentials on the network because insecure protocol, like HTTP instead of HTTPS, is used
    - The attacker creates a fake website login page to steal user credentials
    - The attacker can intercept network traffic and replay some user's requests as such or modified

- Tampering

    - The attacker gains access to the database using SQL injection and can change existing data
    - The attacker can modify other users' data using the other user's id when there is proper authorization missing

- Repudiation

  - The attacker can perform malicious action without notice when there is audit logging missing

- Information disclosure

  - Sensitive information is accidentally sent in request responses (like error stack traces or business confidential data)
  - Sensitive information is not adequately encrypted
  - Sensitive information is accessible without proper authorization (e.g., role-based)

- Denial of service

  - The attacker can create an unlimited number of requests when proper request rate limiting is missing
  - Attacker can send requests with large amounts of data when data size is not limited at all
  - Attacker can try to make regular expression DoS attacks by sending strings that can cause regular expression evaluation to take a lot of CPU time
  - The attacker can send invalid values in requests to try to crash the service or cause a forever loop if no proper input validation is in place

- Elevation of privilege An attacker who does not have a user account can access the service because of missing authentication/authorization

  - The attacker can act as an administrator because the service does not check that the user has a proper role
  - The attacker can access the operating system with root rights because the process runs with root user rights.

7.3.2.3: Application Security Frame (ASF) method

The *Application Security Frame* (ASF) categorizes application security features into the following categories:

Category	Description
Audit & Logging	Logging user actions to detect, e.g., repudiation attacks
Authentication	Prohibit identity spoofing attacks
Authorization	Prohibit elevation of privilege attacks
Configuration Management	Proper storage of secrets and configuring the system with the least privileges
Data Protection in Transit and Rest	Using secure protocols like TLS, encrypting sensitive information like PII in databases
Data Validation	Validate input data from users to prevent, e.g., injection and ReDoS attacks

Category	Description
Exception Management	Do not reveal implementation details in error messages to end-users

When using the above-described threat categorization methodologies, threats in each category should be listed based on the information about the decomposed application: what are the application entry points and assets that need to be secured? After listing potential threats in each category, the threats should be ranked. There are several ways to rank threats. The simplest way to rank threats is to put them in one of the three categories based on the risk: high, medium, and low. As a basis for the ranking, you can use information about the threat's probability and how big an adverse effect (impact) it has. The idea of ranking is to prioritize security features. Security features for high-risk threats should be implemented first.

7.3.3: Determine Countermeasures and Mitigation

The determining countermeasures step should list user stories for the needed security features. These security features should eliminate or at least mitigate the threats. If you have a threat that cannot be eliminated or mitigated, you can accept the risk if the threat is categorized as a low-risk threat. A low-risk threat has a low impact on the application, and the probability of the threat realization is low. Suppose you have found a threat with a very high risk in your application, and you cannot eliminate or mitigate that threat. In that case, you should eliminate the threat by removing the threat-related features from the application.

7.3.4: Threat Modeling Example using STRIDE

Let's have a simple example of threat modeling in practice. We will perform threat modeling for a REST API microservice called *order-service*. The microservice handles orders (CRUD operations on order entities) in an e-commerce software system. Orders are persisted in a database. The microservice communicates with another microservice(s). The first step in the threat modeling process is to decompose the application.

7.3.4.1: Decompose Application

In this phase, we will decompose the *order-service* to see what parts it is composed of and what its dependencies are.

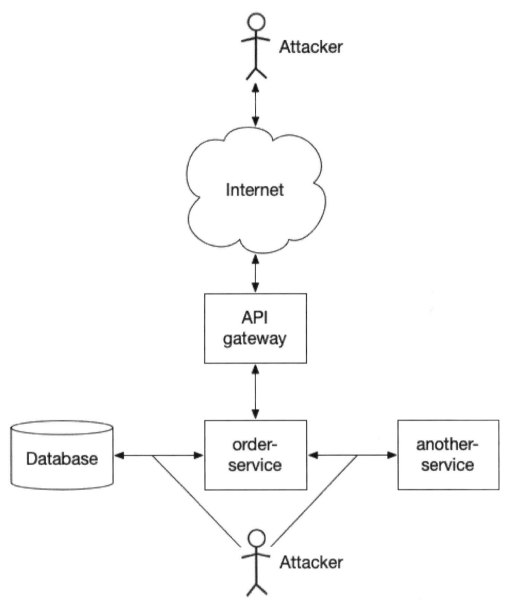

Figure 7.1. Decomposed Order Service

Based on the above view of the *order-service*, we shall next identify the following:

- Identify an attacker's entry points to the application
- Identify assets under threat. These assets are something that an attacker is interested in
- Identify trust levels, e.g., what users with different user roles can do

As drawn in the above picture, the attacker's entry points are from the internet (the *order-service* is exposed to the public internet via API Gateway[1]), and an internal attacker could be able to sniff the network traffic between services.

Assets under threat are the API Gateway, *order-service*, its database, and unencrypted network traffic.

The *order-service* has the following trust levels:

- Users can place orders for themselves (not for other users)
- Users can view their orders (not other users)
- Users can update their order only before it is packaged and shipped
- Administrator can create/read/update/delete any order

7.3.4.2: Determine and Rank Threats

Next, we should list possible threats in each category of the STRIDE method. We also define the risk level for each possible threat.

1. Spoofing

    1. Attacker trying to create an order for someone else (Risk: High)
    2. Attacker trying to read/update someone else's order (Risk: High)
    3. Attacker acting as someone else using stolen credentials (Risk: Medium)

2. Tampering

    1. Attacker trying to tamper with database using SQL injection (Risk: High)
    2. Attacker able to capture and modify unencrypted internet traffic (Risk: High)
    3. Attacker able to capture and modify unencrypted internal network traffic (Risk: Low)

3. Repudiation

    1. Attacker being able to conduct malicious operations without getting caught (Risk: High)

4. Information disclosure

    1. The attacker can access sensitive information because it is not adequately encrypted (Risk: Medium)
    2. The attacker receives sensitive information like detailed stack traces in request responses. (Risk: Medium) The attacker can use that information and exploit possible security holes in the implementation.
    3. Information is disclosed to the attacker because internet traffic is plain text, i.e., not secured (Risk: High)
    4. Information is disclosed to the attacker because internal network traffic is plain text, i.e., not secured (Risk: Low)

5. Denial of service

---

[1]https://en.wikipedia.org/wiki/API_management

1. Attacker trying to make too many requests (Risk: High)
2. Attacker trying to send requests with large amounts of data when data size is not limited at all (Risk: High)
3. Attacker trying to make regular expression DoS (ReDos) attacks by sending strings that can cause regular expression evaluation to take a lot of CPU time (Risk: High)
4. Attacker trying to send invalid values in requests to try to crash the service or cause a forever loop if no proper input validation is in place (Risk: High)

6. Elevation of Privilege

   1. An attacker who does not have a user account can access the service because of missing authentication/authorization (Risk: High)
   2. Attacker can act as an administrator because the service does not check that the user has a proper role (Risk: High)
   3. The attacker can access the operating system with root rights because the process is running with root user rights (Risk: Medium)

7.3.5: Determine Countermeasures and Mitigation

Next, we shall define countermeasure user stories for each threat. The threat numbers a countermeasure is for are listed after the countermeasure.

1. Allow only the user that owns a particular resource to access it (1.1, 1.2)
2. Implement audit logging for operations that create/modify/delete orders (1.3, 3.1)
3. Use parameterized SQL statements or ORM and configure the least permissions for the database user (2.1). The normal database user should not be able to do anything that is only administrator-related, like deleting, creating/dropping tables, etc.
4. Only allow secure internet traffic to the API gateway (TLS is terminated at the API gateway) (1.3, 2.2)
5. Implement mTLS[2] between services using a service mesh like Istio[3] (2.3, 4.4)
6. Encrypt all sensitive information like Personally Identifiable Information[4] (PII) and critical business data in the database (4.1)
7. Do not return error stack traces when the microservice is running in production (4.2)
8. Implement request rate-limiting in the API gateway (5.1.)
9. Validate input data to the microservice and define the maximum allowed string, array, and request lengths (5.2). Additionally, consider audit logging input validation failures
10. Do not use regular expressions in validation or use regular expressions that cannot cause ReDoS (5.3.)
11. Validate input data to the microservice, e.g., correct types, min/max of numeric values, and list of allowed values (5.4). Additionally, consider audit logging input validation failures
12. Implement user authentication and authorization using JWTs (1.1, 1.2, 6.1). Consider audit logging authentication/authorization failures to detect possible attacks
13. Verify that the JWT contains an admin role for administrator-only operations before allowing the operation (1.1, 1.2, 6.2). Additionally, configure the system so that admin operations are inaccessible from the Internet unless needed.

---

[2]https://en.wikipedia.org/wiki/Mutual_authentication
[3]https://istio.io/
[4]https://en.wikipedia.org/wiki/Personal_data

14. For the containerized microservice, define the following:

- Container should not be privileged
- All capabilities are dropped
- Container filesystem is read-only
- Only a non-root user is allowed to run inside the container
- Define the non-root user and group under which the container should run
- Disallow privilege escalation
- Use a distroless or the smallest possible container base image

Next, we should prioritize the above user stories according to related threat risk levels. Let's calculate a priority index for each user story using the following values for threat risk levels:

- High = 3
- Medium = 2
- Low = 1

Here are the prioritized user stories from the highest priority index (PI) to the lowest:

1. Implement user authentication and authorization using JWTs (PI: 9)
2. For administrator-only operations, verify that the JWT contains an admin role before allowing the operation (PI: 9). Additionally, configure the system so that admin operations are not accessible from the internet unless needed
3. Only allow secure internet traffic to the API gateway (TLS is terminated at the API gateway) (PI: 6)
4. Allow only the user that owns a specific resource to access it (PI: 6)
5. Implement audit logging for operations that create/modify/delete orders (PI: 5)
6. Implement request rate-limiting, e.g. in the API gateway (PI: 3)
7. Validate input data to the microservice and define maximum allowed string and array lengths (PI: 3)
8. Use parameterized SQL statements or ORM, and configure the least permissions for the database user (PI: 3). The normal database user should not be able to do anything that is only administrator-related, like deleting, creating/dropping tables, etc.
9. Do not use regular expressions in validation or use regular expressions that cannot cause ReDoS (PI: 3)
10. Validate input data to the microservice, e.g., min/max numeric values, list of allowed values (PI: 3)
11. Encrypt all sensitive information like Personally Identifiable Information (PII) and critical business data in the database (PI: 2)
12. Implement mTLS between services using a service mesh like Istio (PI: 2)
13. Do not return error stack traces when the microservice is running in production (PI: 2)
14. For the containerized microservice, define the following: ... (PI: 2)

The team should review the prioritized list of security user stories with the product security lead. Because security is an integral part of a software system, at least all the above user stories with a priority index greater than two should be implemented before delivering the first production version. The user stories with PI <= 2 could be delivered immediately in the first feature package after the initial delivery. This is just an example. Everything depends on what level of security is wanted and required. The relevant stakeholders should be involved in making decisions about product security.

In the above example, we did not list threats for missing security-related HTTP response headers. This is because they are the same for any REST API. These security-related HTTP response headers are discussed in a later section of this chapter. The sending of these headers should be consolidated to the API gateway so that all API microservices don't have to implement sending security headers themselves.

7.3.6: Threat Modeling Example Using ASF

Threat modeling using ASF goes the same way as in the previous example using the STRIDE method. The only difference is that the threats are categorized differently. We should be able to find all the same threats. Let's try to put the earlier found threats into ASF categories:

- Audit & Logging

  - Attacker being able to conduct malicious operations without getting caught (Risk: High)
  - Attacker acting as someone else using stolen credentials (Risk: Medium)

- Authentication An attacker who does not have a user account can access the service because of missing authentication/authorization (Risk: High)
- Authorization

  - The attacker can act as an administrator because the service does not check that the user has a proper role (Risk: High)
  - Attacker trying to create an order for someone else (Risk: High)
  - Attacker trying to read/update someone else's order (Risk: High)

- Configuration Management

  - The attacker can access the operating system with root rights because the process is running with root user rights (Risk: Medium)

- Data Protection in Transit and Rest

  - Attacker trying to tamper with database using SQL injection (Risk: High)
  - Attacker able to capture and modify unencrypted internet traffic (Risk: High)
  - Attacker able to capture and modify unencrypted internal network traffic (Risk: Low)
  - Attacker able to access sensitive information because it is not adequately encrypted (Risk: Medium)
  - Information is disclosed to the attacker because internet traffic is plain text, i.e., not secured (Risk: High)
  - Information is disclosed to the attacker because internal network traffic is plain text, i.e., not secured (Risk: Low)

- Data Validation

  - Attacker trying to make too many requests (Risk: High)
  - Attacker trying to send requests with large amounts of data when data size is not limited at all (Risk: High)
  - Attacker trying to tamper with database using SQL injection (Risk: High)
  - Attacker trying to make regular expression DoS (ReDos) attacks by sending strings that can cause regular expression evaluation
  - Attacker trying to send invalid values in requests to try to crash the service or cause a forever loop if no proper input validation is in place (Risk: High)

- Exception Management

- The attacker receives sensitive information like detailed stack traces in request responses. (Risk: Medium)

You can even use two different threat categorization methods, like STRIDE and ASF, together because when using multiple methods, it is more likely to discover all the possible threats. Considering the ASF categorization, we can see that the Configuration Management category speaks about the storage of secrets. When we used STRIDE, we did not discover any secrets-related threats. But if we think about it, our *order-service* should have at least three secrets: database user name, database user password, and the encryption key used to encrypt sensitive data in the database. We must store these secrets safely, like using a Secret in a Kubernetes environment. None of these secrets should be hard-coded in the source code.

7.4: Security Features

This section focuses on security features that are relevant for software developers. It lists the most common security features that need to be implemented in typical software systems. It also provides some guidance on how to implement these security features. For example, you should use a secure algorithm and encryption key when implementing encryption.

7.4.1: Authentication and Authorization

When implementing user authentication and authorization for an application, use a 3rd party authorization service. Don't try to build an authorization service by yourself. You can easily make mistakes. Also, it can be a security risk if your application handles plaint-text user credentials. It is better to use a battle-tested solution that has the most significant bugs corrected and can store user credentials securely. In the coming examples, we use Keycloak[5] as an authorization service.

Also, try using established 3rd party libraries as much as possible instead of writing all authorization-related code yourself. It is also helpful to create a single frontend authentication/authorization library and use that same library in multiple projects instead of constantly implementing authentication and authorization-related functionality from scratch in different projects.

7.4.1.1: OpenID Connect Authentication and Authorization in Frontend

Regarding frontend authorization, attention must be paid to the secure storage of authorization-related secrets like *code verifier* and *tokens*. Those must be stored in a secure location in the browser. Below is a list of some insecure storing mechanisms:

- Cookies

    - Sent automatically, a CSRF[6] threat

- Session/Local Storage[7]

---

[5]https://www.keycloak.org/
[6]https://owasp.org/www-community/attacks/csrf
[7]https://developer.mozilla.org/en-US/docs/Web/API/Web_Storage_API

- Easily stolen by malicious code (XSS[8] threat)
- Encrypted session/local storage
  - Easily stolen by malicious code because the encryption key is in plain text
- Global variable
  - Easily stolen by malicious code (XSS threat)

Storing secrets in closure variables is not inherently insecure, but secrets are lost when a page refreshes or a new page is opened.

Below is an example that uses a service worker[9] to store secrets securely. The additional benefit of a service worker is that it does not allow malicious 3rd party code to modify the service worker's fetch method so that it can, for example, steal access tokens.

It is easy for malicious code to change the global fetch function:

```
fetch = () => console.log('hacked');
fetch() // prints 'hacked' to console
```

Below is a more realistic example:

```
originalFetch = fetch;
fetch = (url, options) => {
  // Implement malicious attack here
  // For example: change some data in the request body

  // Then call original fetch implementation
  return originalFetch(url, options);
}
```

Of course, one can ask: why is it possible to modify the built-in method on the global object like that? Of course, it should not be possible, but unfortunately, it is.

Let's create a Vue.js[10] application that performs authentication and authorization using the OpenID Connect[11] protocol, an extension of the OAuth2[12] protocol.

Source code for the below example is available here[13].

In the main module below, we set up the global fetch to always return an error and only allow our tryMakeHttpRequest function to use the original global fetch method. Then, we register a service worker. If the service worker has already been registered, it is not registered again. Finally, we create the application (AppView component), activate the router, activate the Pinia[14] middleware for state management, and mount the application to a DOM node:

[8]https://owasp.org/www-community/attacks/xss/
[9]https://developer.mozilla.org/en-US/docs/Web/API/Service_Worker_API
[10]https://vuejs.org/
[11]https://openid.net/developers/how-connect-works/
[12]https://oauth.net/2/
[13]https://github.com/pksilen/clean-code-principles-code/tree/main/chapter5/auth_frontend
[14]https://pinia.vuejs.org/

Figure 7.2. main.ts

```
import { setupFetch } from "@/tryMakeHttpRequest";
setupFetch();
import { createApp } from "vue";
import { createPinia } from "pinia";
import AppView from "@/views/AppView.vue";
import router from "@/router";

if ("serviceWorker" in navigator) {
  await navigator.serviceWorker.register("/serviceWorker.js");
}

const app = createApp(AppView);
const pinia = createPinia();
app.use(pinia);
app.use(router);
app.mount("#app");
```

Below is the definition of the AppView component. After mounting, it will check whether the user is already authorized.

If the user is authorized, their authorization information will be fetched from the service worker, and the user's first name will be updated in the authorization information store. The user will be forwarded to the *HomeView* page. If the user is not authorized, authorization will be performed.

Figure 7.3. AppView.vue

```
<template>
  <HeaderView />
  <router-view></router-view>
</template>

<script setup>
import { onMounted } from "vue";
import { useRouter, useRoute } from "vue-router";
import authorizationService from "@/authService";
import { useAuthInfoStore } from "@/authInfoStore";
import HeaderView from "@/views/HeaderView.vue";
import tryMakeHttpRequest from "@/tryMakeHttpRequest";

const router = useRouter();
const route = useRoute();

onMounted(async () => {
  const response = await tryMakeHttpRequest("/authorizedUserInfo");
  const responseBody = await response.text();
  if (responseBody !== "") {
    const authorizedUserInfo = JSON.parse(responseBody);
    const { setFirstName } = useAuthInfoStore();
    setFirstName(authorizedUserInfo.firstName);
    router.push({ name: "home" });
  } else if (route.path !== "/auth") {
    authorizationService
      .tryAuthorize()
      .catch(() => router.push({ name: "auth-error" }));
  }
});
</script>
```

Figure 7.4. authInfoStore.ts

```
import { ref } from "vue";
import { defineStore } from "pinia";

export const useAuthInfoStore =
  defineStore("authInfoStore", () => {
    const firstName = ref('');

    function setFirstName(newFirstName: string) {
      firstName.value = newFirstName;
    }

    return { firstName, setFirstName };
  });
```

The header of the application displays the first name of the logged-in user and a button for logging the user out:

Figure 7.5. HeaderView.vue

```
<template>
  <span>{{authInfoStore.firstName}}</span>
   
  <button @click="logout">Logout</button>
</template>

<script setup>
import { useRouter } from "vue-router";
import authorizationService from "@/authService";
import { useAuthInfoStore } from "@/authInfoStore";

const authInfoStore = useAuthInfoStore();
const router = useRouter();

function logout() {
  authorizationService
    .tryLogout()
    .catch(() => router.push({ name: "auth-error" }));
}
</script>
```

The `tryMakeHttpRequest` function is a wrapper around the browser's global `fetch` method. It will start an authorization procedure if an HTTP request returns the HTTP status code 403 *Forbidden*.

Figure 7.6. tryMakeHttpRequest.ts

```
import authorizationService from "@/authService";

let originalFetch: typeof fetch;

export default function tryMakeHttpRequest(
  url: RequestInfo,
  options?: RequestInit
): Promise<Response> {
  return originalFetch(url, options).then(async (response) => {
    if (response.status === 403) {
      try {
        await authorizationService.tryAuthorize();
      } catch {
        // Handle auth error, return response with status 403
      }
    }

    return response;
```

```
  });
}

export function setupFetch() {
  originalFetch = fetch;
  // @ts-ignore
  // eslint-disable-next-line no-global-assign
  fetch = () =>
    Promise.reject(new Error('Global fetch not implemented'));
}
```

Below is the implementation of the service worker:

Figure 7.7. serviceWorker.js

```
const allowedOrigins = [
  "http://localhost:8080", // IAM in dev environment
  "http://localhost:8000", // API in dev environment
  "https://software-system-x.domain.com" // prod environment
];

const apiEndpointRegex = /\/api\//;
const tokenEndpointRegex = /\/openid-connect\/token$/;
const data = {};

// Listen to messages that contain data
// to be stored inside the service worker
addEventListener("message", (event) => {
  if (event.data) {
    data[event.data.key] = event.data.value;
  }
});

function respondWithUserInfo(event) {
  const response =
    new Response(data.authorizedUserInfo
                   ? JSON.stringify(data.authorizedUserInfo)
                   : '');
  event.respondWith(response);
}

function respondWithIdToken(event) {
  const response = new Response(data.idToken
                                  ? data.idToken
                                  : '');
  event.respondWith(response);
}

function respondWithTokenRequest(event) {
  let body = "grant_type=authorization_code";
  body += `&code=${data.code}`;
  body += `&client_id=app-x`;
  body += `&redirect_uri=${data.redirectUri}`;
  body += `&code_verifier=${data.codeVerifier}`;
  const tokenRequest = new Request(event.request, { body });

  // Verify that state received from the authorization
  // server is same as sent by this app earlier
  if (data.state === data.receivedState) {
    event.respondWith(fetch(tokenRequest));
  } else {
    // Handle error
  }
}

function respondWithApiRequest(event) {
  const headers = new Headers(event.request.headers);
```

```
  // Add Authorization header that contains the access token
  if (data.accessToken) {
    headers.append("Authorization",
                   `Bearer ${data.accessToken}`);
  }

  const authorizedRequest = new Request(event.request, {
    headers
  });

  event.respondWith(fetch(authorizedRequest));
}

function fetchHandler(event) {
  const requestUrl = new URL(event.request.url);

  if (event.request.url.endsWith('/authorizedUserInfo') &&
      !apiEndpointRegex.test(requestUrl.pathname)) {
    respondWithUserInfo(event);
  } else if (event.request.url.endsWith('/idToken') &&
             !apiEndpointRegex.test(requestUrl.pathname)) {
    respondWithIdToken(event);
  } else if (allowedOrigins.includes(requestUrl.origin)) {
    if (tokenEndpointRegex.test(requestUrl.pathname)) {
      respondWithTokenRequest(event);
    } else if (apiEndpointRegex.test(requestUrl.pathname)) {
      respondWithApiRequest(event);
    }
  } else {
    event.respondWith(fetch(event.request));
  }
}

// Intercept all fetch requests and handle
// them with 'fetchHandler'
addEventListener("fetch", fetchHandler);
```

Authorization using the OAuth2 Authorization Code Flow[15] is started with a browser redirect to a URL of the following kind:

```
https://authorization-server.com/auth?response_type=code&client_id=CLIENT_ID&redirect_uri=https://exam\
ple-app.com/cb&scope=photos&state=1234zyx...ghvx3&code_challenge=CODE_CHALLENGE&code_challenge_method=
SHA256
```

The query parameters in the above URL are the following:

- *response_type=code* - Indicates that you expect to receive an authorization code
- *client_id* - The client id you used when you created the client on the authorization server (We'll create the client a bit later)
- *redirect_uri* - Indicates the URI to redirect the browser after authorization is completed. You also need to define this URI in the authorization server. (We'll see this a bit later)
- *scope* - One or more scope values indicating which parts of the user's account you wish to access. Scopes should be separated by URL-encoded space characters
- *state* - A random string generated by your application, which you'll verify later
- *code_challenge* - PKCE extension: URL-safe base64-encoded SHA256 hash of the code verifier. A code verifier is a random string secret you generate

---

[15]https://oauth.net/2/grant-types/authorization-code/

- *code_challenge_method=S256* - PKCE extension: indicates which hashing method is used (S256 means SHA256)

We should use the PKCE[16] extension as an additional security measure. PKCE extends the Authorization Code Flow to prevent CSRF and authorization code injection attacks.

If authorization is successful, the authorization server will redirect the browser to the above-given *redirect_uri* with *code* and *state* given as URL query parameters, for example:

```
https://example-app.com/cb?code=AUTH_CODE_HERE&state=1234zyx...ghvx3
```

- *code* - The authorization code returned from the authorization server
- *state* - The same state value that you passed earlier

After the application is successfully authorized, tokens can be requested with the following kind of HTTP POST request:

```
POST https://authorization-server.com/token HTTP/1.1
Content-Type: application/x-www-form-urlencoded

grant_type=authorization_code&
code=AUTH_CODE_HERE&
redirect_uri=REDIRECT_URI&
client_id=CLIENT_ID&
code_verifier=CODE_VERIFIER
```

- *grant_type=authorization_code* - The grant type for this flow is _authorizationcode_
- *code=AUTH_CODE_HERE* - This is the code you received when the browser was redirected back to your application from the authorization server.
- *redirect_uri=REDIRECT_URI* - Must be identical to the redirect URI provided earlier during authorization
- *client_id=CLIENT_ID* - The client id you used when you created the client on the authorization server
- *code_verifier=CODE_VERIFIER* - The random string secret you generated earlier

Below is the implementation of the `AuthorizationService` class. It provides methods for authorization, getting tokens and logout.

Figure 7.8. AuthorizationService.ts

```
import pkceChallenge from "pkce-challenge";
import { jwtDecode } from "jwt-decode";
import tryMakeHttpRequest from "@/tryMakeHttpRequest";
import type { useAuthInfoStore } from "@/authInfoStore";

export default class AuthorizationService {
  constructor(
    private readonly oidcConfigurationEndpoint: string,
    private readonly clientId: string,
    private readonly authRedirectUrl: string,
    private readonly loginPageUrl: string,
  ) {}

  // Try to authorize the user using the OpenID Connect
  // Authorization Code Flow
```

[16]https://oauth.net/2/pkce/

```
async tryAuthorize(): Promise<void> {
  // Store the redirect URI in service worker
  navigator.serviceWorker?.controller?.postMessage({
    key: "redirectUri",
    value: this.authRedirectUrl,
  });

  // Store the state secret in service worker
  const state = crypto.randomUUID();
  navigator.serviceWorker?.controller?.postMessage({
    key: "state",
    value: state,
  });

  // Generate a PKCE challenge and store
  // the code verifier in service worker
  const challenge = await pkceChallenge(128);

  navigator.serviceWorker?.controller?.postMessage({
    key: "codeVerifier",
    value: challenge.code_verifier,
  });

  // Redirect the browser to authorization server's
  // authorization URL
  location.href = await this.tryCreateAuthUrl(state, challenge);
}

// Try to get access, refresh and ID token from
// the authorization server's token endpoint
async tryGetTokens(
  authInfoStore: ReturnType<typeof useAuthInfoStore>,
): Promise<void> {
  const oidcConfiguration = await this.getOidcConfiguration();

  const response = await tryMakeHttpRequest(
    oidcConfiguration.token_endpoint,
    {
      method: "post",
      mode: "cors",
      headers: {
        "Content-Type": "application/x-www-form-urlencoded",
      },
    },
  );

  const tokens = await response.json();
  this.storeTokens(tokens);
  this.storeAuthorizedUserInfo(tokens.id_token, authInfoStore);
}

// Logout and redirect to login page
async tryLogout(): Promise<void> {
  const oidcConfiguration = await this.getOidcConfiguration();

  // Clear authorized user info in service worker
  navigator.serviceWorker?.controller?.postMessage({
    key: "authorizedUserInfo",
    value: undefined,
  });

  // Get ID token from service worker
  const response = await tryMakeHttpRequest("/idToken");
  const idToken = await response.text();

  // Redirect browser to authorization server's
  // logout endpoint
  if (idToken !== "") {
    location.href =
      oidcConfiguration.end_session_endpoint +
```

```
        `?post_logout_redirect_uri=${this.loginPageUrl}` +
        `&id_token_hint=${idToken}`;
    } else {
      location.href = oidcConfiguration.end_session_endpoint;
    }
  }

  private async getOidcConfiguration(): Promise<any> {
    const response = await tryMakeHttpRequest(this.oidcConfigurationEndpoint);

    return response.json();
  }

  private async tryCreateAuthUrl(
    state: string,
    challenge: Awaited<ReturnType<typeof pkceChallenge>>,
  ) {
    const oidcConfiguration = await this.getOidcConfiguration();
    let authUrl = oidcConfiguration.authorization_endpoint;

    authUrl += "?response_type=code";
    authUrl += "&scope=openid+profile+email";
    authUrl += `&client_id=${this.clientId}`;
    authUrl += `&redirect_uri=${this.authRedirectUrl}`;
    authUrl += `&state=${state}`;
    authUrl += `&code_challenge=${challenge.code_challenge}`;
    authUrl += "&code_challenge_method=S256";

    return authUrl;
  }

  private storeTokens(tokens: any) {
    navigator.serviceWorker?.controller?.postMessage({
      key: "accessToken",
      value: tokens.access_token,
    });

    navigator.serviceWorker?.controller?.postMessage({
      key: "refreshToken",
      value: tokens.refresh_token,
    });

    navigator.serviceWorker?.controller?.postMessage({
      key: "idToken",
      value: tokens.id_token,
    });
  }

  private storeAuthorizedUserInfo(
    idToken: any,
    authInfoStore: ReturnType<typeof useAuthInfoStore>,
  ) {
    const idTokenClaims: any = jwtDecode(idToken);

    const authorizedUserInfo = {
      userName: idTokenClaims.preferred_username,
      firstName: idTokenClaims.given_name,
      lastName: idTokenClaims.family_name,
      email: idTokenClaims.email,
    };

    navigator.serviceWorker?.controller?.postMessage({
      key: "authorizedUserInfo",
      value: authorizedUserInfo,
    });

    authInfoStore.setFirstName(idTokenClaims.given_name);
  }
}
```

Below is an example response you get when you execute the `tryMakeHttpRequest` function in the `tryGetTokens` method:

```
{
  "access_token": "eyJz93a...k4laUWw",
  "id_token": "UFn43f...c5vvfGF",
  "refresh_token": "GEbRxBN...edjnXbL",
  "token_type": "Bearer",
  "expires_in": 3600
}
```

The `AuthCallbackView` component is the component that will be rendered when the authorization server redirects the browser back to the application after successful authorization. This component stores the authorization code and the received state in the service worker and initiates a token request. After receiving tokens, it will route the application to the home page. As an additional security measure, the token request will only be performed if the original *state* and *received state* are equal. This check is done using the service worker code.

Figure 7.9. AuthCallbackView.vue

```
<template>
  <div></div>
</template>

<script setup>
import { onMounted } from "vue";
import { useRouter, useRoute } from "vue-router";
import authorizationService from "@/authService";
import { useAuthInfoStore } from "@/authInfoStore";

const { query } = useRoute();
const router = useRouter();
const authInfoStore = useAuthInfoStore();

onMounted(async () => {
  // Store authorization code in service worker
  navigator.serviceWorker?.controller?.postMessage({
    key: "code",
    value: query.code,
  });

  // Store received state in service worker
  navigator.serviceWorker?.controller?.postMessage({
    key: "receivedState",
    value: query.state,
  });

  // Try fetch tokens
  try {
    await authorizationService.tryGetTokens(authInfoStore);
    router.push({ name: "home" });
  } catch (error) {
    router.push({ name: "auth-error" });
  }
});
</script>
```

Other UI components the application uses are defined below:

Figure 7.10. AuthErrorView.vue

```
<template>
  <div>Error</div>
</template>
```

Figure 7.11. LoginView.vue

```
<template>
  <div>Login</div>
</template>
```

Figure 7.12. HomeView.vue

```
<template>
  <div>Home</div>
</template>

<script setup>
import { onMounted } from "vue";
import tryMakeHttpRequest from "@/tryMakeHttpRequest";

onMounted(async () => {
  try {
    const response = await tryMakeHttpRequest(
      "http://localhost:8000/api/messaging-service/messages",
      {
        method: "POST",
      },
    );

    console.log(
      `Message creation response status: ${response.status} ${response.statusText}`,
    );
  } catch (error) {
    console.log("Message creation request failed");
    console.log(error);
  }
});
</script>
```

The application's router is the following:

Figure 7.13. router.ts

```
import { createRouter, createWebHistory } from "vue-router";
import AuthorizationCallback from "@/views/AuthCallbackView.vue";
import AuthorizationError from "@/views/AuthErrorView.vue";
import HomeView from "@/views/HomeView.vue";
import LoginView from "@/views/LoginView.vue";

const routes = [
  {
    path: "/",
    name: "login",
    component: LoginView,
  },
  {
    path: "/auth",
    name: "auth",
    component: AuthCallbackView,
  },
  {
```

```
    path: "/auth-error",
    name: "auth-error",
    component: AuthErrorView,
  },
  {
    path: "/home",
    name: "home",
    component: HomeView,
  },
];

const router = createRouter({
  history: createWebHistory(),
  routes,
});

export default router;
```

The below *authService* module contains definitions of needed constants and creates an instance of the `AuthorizationService` class. The below code contains hard-coded values for a local development environment. In real life, these values should be taken from environment variables. The below values work if you have a Keycloak service running at *localhost:8080* and the Vue app running at *localhost:5173*. You must create a client in the Keycloak named 'app-x'. Additionally, you must define a valid redirect URI and add an allowed web origin. Lastly, you must configure a valid post-logout redirect URI (see the below image). The default access token lifetime in Keycloak is just one minute. You can increase that for testing purposes in the realm settings (the token tab)

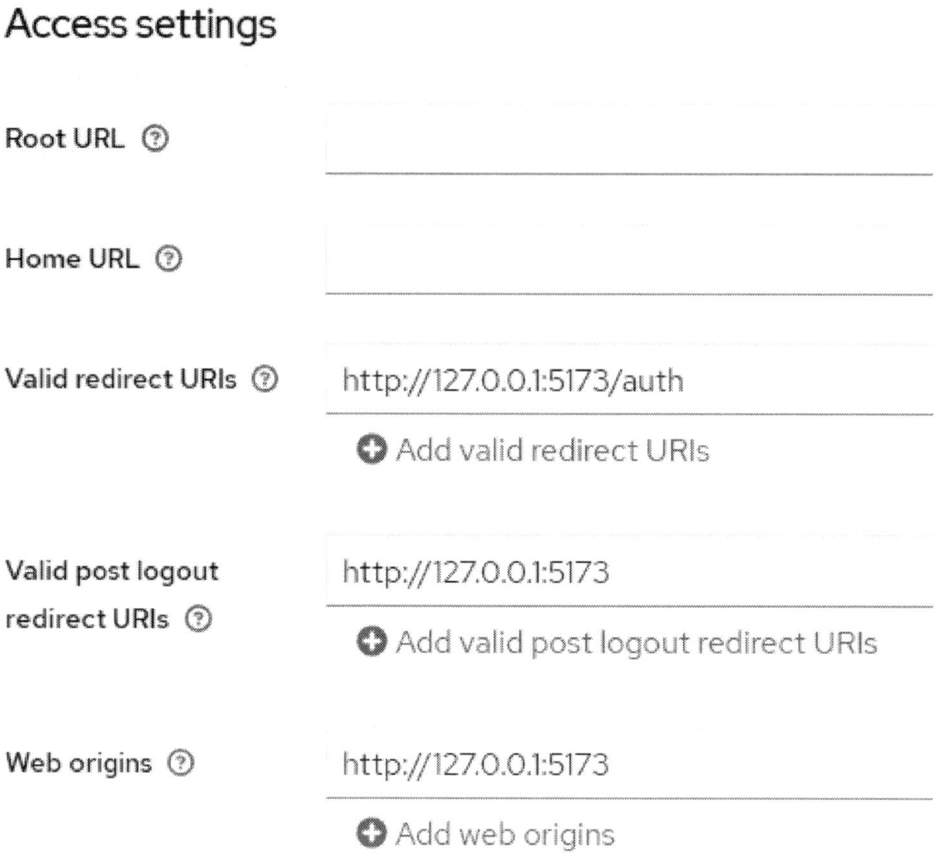

Access settings

Root URL ⑦

Home URL ⑦

Valid redirect URIs ⑦   http://127.0.0.1:5173/auth

➕ Add valid redirect URIs

Valid post logout
redirect URIs ⑦   http://127.0.0.1:5173

➕ Add valid post logout redirect URIs

Web origins ⑦   http://127.0.0.1:5173

➕ Add web origins

Figure 7.14. Keycloak Settings for the Client

Figure 7.15. authService.ts

```
import AuthorizationService from "@/AuthorizationService";

const oidcConfigurationEndpoint =
  "http://localhost:8080/realms/master/.well-known/openid-configuration";

const clientId = "app-x";
const redirectUrl = "http://127.0.0.1:5173/auth";
const loginPageUrl = "http://127.0.0.1:5173";

const authorizationService = new AuthorizationService(
  oidcConfigurationEndpoint,
  clientId,
  redirectUrl,
  loginPageUrl
);

export default authorizationService;
```

7.4.1.2: OAuth2 Authorization in Backend

Only let authorized users access resources. The best way not to forget to implement authorization is to deny access to resources by default. For example, you can require that an authorization decorator is specified for all controller methods. If an API endpoint does not require authorization, a special decorator like @allow_-any_user could be used. An exception should be thrown if a controller method lacks an authorization decorator. This way, you can never forget to add an authorization annotation to a controller method.

Broken access control is number one in the OWASP Top 10 for 2021[17]. Remember to disallow users from creating resources for other users. Also, you must disallow users to view, edit, or delete resources belonging to someone else (also known as Insecure Direct Object Reference (IDOR) prevention[18]). Using universally unique ids (UUIDs) as ids for resources instead of basic integers is not enough. This is because if an attacker can obtain a URL for an object with a UUID, he can access the object behind the URL because there is no access control in place.

Below is a JWT[19]-based authorizer class that can be used in a backend API service implemented with the Express framework. The below example utilizes role-based access control (RBAC), but there are more modern alternatives, including attribute-based access control (ABAC) and relationship-based access control (ReBAC). More information about those is available in OWASP Authorization Cheat Sheet[20]

Source code for the below example is available here[21].

Figure 7.16. Authorizer.ts

```
export default interface Authorizer {
  authorize(authHeader: string | undefined): Promise<void>;

  authorizeForSelf(
    userId: number,
    authHeader: string | undefined
  ): Promise<void>;

  authorizeIfUserHasOneOfRoles(
    allowedRoles: string[],
    authHeader: string | undefined
  ): Promise<void>;

  getUserId(authHeader: string | undefined): Promise<number>;
}
```

[17]https://owasp.org/www-project-top-ten/
[18]https://cheatsheetseries.owasp.org/cheatsheets/Insecure_Direct_Object_Reference_Prevention_Cheat_Sheet.html
[19]https://jwt.io/
[20]https://cheatsheetseries.owasp.org/cheatsheets/Authorization_Cheat_Sheet.html
[21]https://github.com/pksilen/clean-code-principles-code/tree/main/chapter5/auth_backend

Figure 7.17. AbstractAuthorizer.ts

```
export default abstract class AbstractAuthorizer implements Authorizer {
  // An example implementation for 'ApiError' class is given
  // in API principles chapter
  static readonly UnauthenticatedError = class extends ApiError {
  };

  static readonly UnauthorizedError = class extends ApiError {
  };

  static readonly IamError = class extends ApiError {
  };

  abstract authorize(authHeader: string | undefined): Promise<void>;

  abstract authorizeForSelf(
    userId: number,
    authHeader: string | undefined
  ): Promise<void>;

  abstract authorizeIfUserHasOneOfRoles(
    allowedRoles: string[],
    authHeader: string | undefined
  ): Promise<void>;

  abstract getUserId(authHeader: string | undefined): Promise<number>;
}
```

Figure 7.18. jwt_authorizer.ts

```
import _ from 'lodash';
import { decode, verify } from 'jsonwebtoken';
import { fetch } from 'fetch-h2';
import { Request } from 'express';
import jwks from 'jwks-rsa';
import Authorizer from './Authorizer';
import throwError from './throwError';
import throwException from './throwException';

export default class JwtAuthorizer extends AbstractAuthorizer {
  private readonly oidcConfigUrl: string;
  private readonly rolesClaimPath: string;
  private readonly getUsersUrl: string;
  private jwksClient: any;

  constructor() {
    // URL for OpenId Connect configuration endpoint in the IAM system
    this.oidcConfigUrl =
      process.env.OIDC_CONFIG_URL ??
        throwException('OIDC_CONFIG_URL is not defined');

    // With Keycloak you can use e.g., realm_access.roles
    this.rolesClaimPath = process.env.JWT_ROLES_CLAIM_PATH ??
      throwException('JWT_ROLES_CLAIM_PATH is not defined')

    // This is the URL where you can fetch the user id for a
    // specific 'sub' claim value in the access token
    // For example: http://localhost:8082/user-service/users
    this.getUsersUrl =
      process.env.GET_USERS_URL ??
        throwException('GET_USERS_URL is not defined');
  }

  async authorize(authHeader: string | undefined): Promise<void> {
    await this.decodeJwtClaims(authHeader);
  }
```

```
// Authorize a user for him/herself
async authorizeForSelf(
  userId: number,
  authHeader: string | undefined
): Promise<void> {
  const userIdInJwt = await this.getUserId(authHeader);

  if (userId !== userIdInJwt) {
    throw new UnauthorizedError();
  }
}

async authorizeIfUserHasOneOfRoles(
  allowedRoles: string[],
  authHeader: string | undefined
): Promise<void> {
  const claims = await this.decodeJwtClaims(authHeader);
  const roles = _.get(claims, this.rolesClaimPath, []);

  const isAuthorized = allowedRoles.some((allowedRole) =>
      roles.includes(allowedRole));

  if (!isAuthorized) {
    throw new UnauthorizedError();
  }
}

async getUserId(authHeader: string | undefined): Promise<number> {
  const claims = await this.decodeJwtClaims(authHeader);
  const getUsersUrl = this.getUsersUrl + `?sub=${claims?.sub}&fields=id`

  try {
   const usersResponse = await fetch(getUsersUrl);
   const users = await response.json();
  } catch (error) {
    // Log error details
    throw new IamError()
  }

  return users?.[0]?.id ?? throwError(new UnauthorizedError());
}

private async tryGetClaims(authHeader: string | undefined ): Promise<any> {
  if (!authHeader) {
    throw new UnauthenticatedError();
  }

  try {
    const oidcConfigResponse = await fetch(this.oidcConfigUrl);
    const oidcConfig = await oidcConfigResponse.json();
  } catch (error) {
    // Log error details
    throw new IamError();
  }

  if (!this.jwksClient) {
    this.jwksClient = jwks({ jwksUri: oidcConfig?.jwks_uri });
  }

  const jwt = authHeader?.split('Bearer ').pop() ?? '';

  try {
    const decodedJwt = decode(jwt, { complete: true });
    const kid = decodedJwt?.header?.kid;
    const signingKey = await this.jwksClient.getSigningKey(kid);
    return verify(jwt, signingKey.getPublicKey());
  } catch (error) {
    throw new UnauthorizedError();
  }
}
```

```
}

export const authorizer = new JwtAuthorizer();
```

Below is an example API service that utilizes the above-defined JwtAuthorizer class:

Figure 7.19. app.js

```
import express from 'express';
import cors from 'cors';
import { authorizer } from './jwt_authorizer';

const app = express();
app.use(express.json());
app.use(cors());

// @ts-ignore
app.use((error, request, response, next) => {
  // Error handler for converting a thrown error
  // to an error response
  // Example of an error handler implementation
  // is given in API principles chapter
});

app.get('/api/sales-item-service/sales-items', () => {
  // No authorization needed
  // Send sales items
});

app.post('/api/messaging-service/messages', async (request, response) => {
  await authorizer.authorize(request.headers.authorization);
  // Authorized user can create a message
  console.log('Message created');
});

app.get('/api/order-service/orders/:id', async (request, response) => {
  const userIdFromJwt = await authorizer.getUserId(request.headers.authorization);
  const id = request.params.id;

  // Try get order using 'userIdFromJwt' as user id and 'id'
  // as order id, e.g. orderService.getOrder(id, userIdFromJwt)
  // It is important to notice that when trying to retrieve
  // the order from database, both 'id' and 'userIdFromJwt'
  // are used as query filters
  // If the user is not allowed to access the resource
  // 404 Not Found is returned from the service method
  // This approach has the security benefit of not revealing
  // to an attacker whether an order with 'id' exists or not
});

app.post('/api/order-service/orders', async (request, response) => {
  await authorizer.authorizeForSelf(
    request.body.userId,
    request.headers.authorization
  );

  // Create an order for the user
  // User cannot create orders for other users
});

app.delete('/api/sales-item-service/sales-items', async (request, response) => {
  await authorizer.authorizeIfUserHasOneOfRoles(
    ['admin'],
    request.headers.authorization
  );

  // Only admin user can delete all sales items
});
```

```
app.listen(8000);
```

The authorization is separately coded inside each request handler in the above example. We could extract the authorization code from the request handler methods and use decorators to perform authorization. You can then write code that forces each request handler method to have an authorization decorator in order not to forget to add authorization to your backend. Below is a short example of an authorization decorator in one controller method using Nest.js.

Source code for the below example is available here[22].

Figure 7.20. app.controller.ts

```
import { Controller, Post, Req, UseGuards } from '@nestjs/common';
import { AllowForAuthorized } from './AllowForAuthorized';

@Controller()
export class AppController {
  constructor() {
  }

  @UseGuards(AllowForAuthorized)
  @Post('/api/messaging-service/messages')
  createMessage(@Req() request: Request): void {
    console.log('Message created');
  }
}
```

Figure 7.21. AllowForAuthorized.ts

```
import { CanActivate, ExecutionContext, Inject, Injectable } from '@nestjs/common';
import Authorizer from './Authorizer';

@Injectable()
export class AllowForAuthorized implements CanActivate {
  constructor(@Inject('authorizer') private authorizer: Authorizer) {
  }

  async canActivate(context: ExecutionContext): Promise<boolean> {
    const request = context.switchToHttp().getRequest();
    await this.authorizer.authorize(request.headers.authorization);
    console.log('Authorized');
    return true;
  }
}
```

---

[22]https://github.com/pksilen/clean-code-principles-code/tree/main/chapter5/auth_backend_nest

Figure 7.22. app.module.ts

```
import { Module } from '@nestjs/common';
import { AppController } from './app.controller';
import { AllowForAuthorized } from './AllowForAuthorized';
import JwtAuthorizer from './JwtAuthorizer';

@Module({
  imports: [],
  controllers: [AppController],
  providers: [{ provide: 'authorizer', useClass: JwtAuthorizer }, AllowForAuthorized],
})
export class AppModule {
}
```

Below is a simple example of implementing an OAuth2 resource server using Spring Boot. First, you need to add the OAuth2 resource server dependency:

Figure 7.23. build.gradle

```
dependencies {
    implementation 'org.springframework.boot:spring-boot-starter-oauth2-resource-server'
}
```

Next, you need to configure a JWT issuer URL. In the below example, we use a localhost Keycloak service.

Figure 7.24. application.yml

```
spring:
  security:
    oauth2:
      resourceserver:
        jwt:
          issuer-uri: http://localhost:8080/realms/master/
```

Then, you will configure which API endpoints must be authorized with a valid JWT. The example below requires requests to all API endpoints to contain a valid JWT.

Figure 7.25. SecurityConfiguration.java

```
import org.springframework.context.annotation.Configuration;
import org.springframework.security.config.annotation.web.builders.HttpSecurity;
import org.springframework.security.config.annotation.web.configuration.WebSecurityConfigurerAdapter;

@Configuration
public class SecurityConfiguration
                extends WebSecurityConfigurerAdapter {
  @Override
  protected final void configure(
    final HttpSecurity httpSecurity
  ) throws Exception {
    httpSecurity.authorizeRequests()
      .antMatchers("/**")
      .authenticated()
      .and()
      .oauth2ResourceServer()
      .jwt();
  }
}
```

In a REST controller, you can inject the JWT using the `AuthenticationPrincipal` annotation to perform additional authorization in the controller methods:

Figure 7.26. SalesItemController.java

```
@RestController
@RequestMapping(SalesItemController.API_ENDPOINT)
@Slf4j
public class SalesItemController {
  public static final String API_ENDPOINT = "/salesitems";

  @Autowired
  private SalesItemService salesItemService;

  @PostMapping
  @ResponseStatus(HttpStatus.CREATED)
  public final SalesItem createSalesItem(
    @RequestBody final SalesItemArg salesItemArg,
    @AuthenticationPrincipal final Jwt jwt
  ) {
    log.info("Username: {}", jwt.getClaimAsString("preferred_username"));

    // You can now use the "jwt" object to get a claim about
    // user's roles and verify a needed role, for example.
    return salesItemService.createSalesItem(salesItemArg);
  }
}
```

7.4.2: Password Policy

Implement a password policy requiring strong passwords and prefer passphrases over passwords. A passphrase is supposed to contain multiple words. Passphrases are harder for attackers to guess and easier for users to remember than strong passwords. Allow passphrases to contain Unicode characters. This allows users to create passphrases using their mother tongue.

You should require that passwords are strong and match the following criteria:

- At least 12 characters long
- At least one uppercase letter
- At least one lowercase letter
- At least one number
- At least one special character
- May not contain the username
- May not contain too many identical digits or letters, e.g., a password containing "111111", "aaaaaa," or "1a1a1a1a1a" should be denied
- May not contain too many consecutive numbers or letters, e.g., a password containing "12345", "56789", "abcdef", or "klmno" should be denied
- May not contain too many adjacent letters in the keyboard, e.g., a password containing "qwerty" should be denied
- May not contain a black-listed word: black-list all commonly used, easy-to-guess passwords.

Machine-to-machine (non-human-related) passwords (like database passwords) should be automatically generated separately for each production environment during the deployment. These passwords should be random and significantly longer than 12 characters.

7.4.3: Cryptography

The following are the key security features to implement related to cryptography:

- Do not transmit data in clear text

    - You don't need to implement HTTPS in all the microservices because you can set up a service mesh, like Istio, and configure it to implement mTLS between services

- Do not store sensitive information like personally identifiable information (PII) in clear text

    - Encrypt sensitive data before storing it in a database and decrypt it upon fetching from the database
    - Remember to identify which data is classified as sensitive according to privacy laws, regulatory requirements, or business needs
    - Do not use legacy protocols such as FTP and SMTP for transporting sensitive data
    - Discard sensitive data as soon as possible or use tokenization (e.g., PCI DSS compliant) or even truncation
    - Do not cache sensitive data

- Do not use old/weak cryptographic algorithms. Use robust algorithms like SHA-256 or AES-256
- Do not allow the use of default/weak passwords or default encryption keys in a production environment

    - You can implement validation logic for passwords/encryption keys in microservices. This validation logic should be automatically activated when the microservice runs in production. The validation logic should be the following: If passwords/encryption keys supplied to the microservice are not strong enough, the microservice should not run at all but exit with an error

7.4.3.1: Encryption Key Lifetime and Rotation

Encryption keys should be rotated (i.e., changed) when one or more of the following criteria is met:

- The current key is known to be compromised, or there is a suspicion of compromise
- A specified period of time has elapsed (this is known as the cryptoperiod[23])
- The key has been used to encrypt a particular amount of data
- There is a significant change to the security the used encryption algorithm provides (for example, a new attack was announced)

Encryption key rotation should happen so that all existing data is decrypted and encrypted with the new key. This will happen gradually, so each encrypted database table row must contain an id of the used encryption key. When all existing data is encrypted with the new key, meaning all references to it are removed, the old key can be destroyed.

---

[23]https://en.wikipedia.org/wiki/Cryptoperiod

7.4.4: Denial-of-service (DoS) Prevention

DoS prevention should happen at least in the following ways:

- Establish request rate limiting for microservices. This can be done at the API gateway level or by the cloud provider
- Use a Captcha[24] to prevent non-human (robotic) users from performing potentially expensive operations like creating new resources or fetching large resources, like large files, for example

7.4.5: Database Security

- Connection from a microservice to a database must be secured using TLS. In a Kubernetes environment, you can implement this by taking a service mesh (like Istio) into use and configuring mTLS between all services in the environment
- Database credentials (username and password) must be stored in a secure location, like in a Secret in a Kubernetes environment. Never store credentials in source code
- Use a strong password, preferably an automatically generated one for the specific environment. The password must be random and long enough. The password should be at least 32 characters long if the database engine allows it
- Configure different database user accounts for admin and regular usage. Assign minimum privileges to both user accounts. Have separate passwords for each account. The regular database user can usually only execute the following SQL statements: SELECT, INSERT, UPDATE, and DELETE. Only an administrator database user can create/modify/drop tables/indexes, etc.

7.4.6: SQL Injection Prevention

- Use parameterized SQL statements[25]. Do not concatenate user-supplied data directly to an SQL statement string
- Remember that you cannot use parameterization in all parts of an SQL statement. If you must put user-supplied data into an SQL statement without parameterization, sanitize/validate it first. For example, for LIMIT, you must validate that the user-supplied value is an integer and in a given range
- Migrate to use ORM[26] (Object Relational Mapping)
- Use proper limiting on the number of fetched records within queries to prevent mass disclosure of records
- Verify the correct shape of at least the first query result row. Do not send the query result to the client if the shape of the data in the first row is wrong, e.g., it contains the wrong fields.

7.4.7: OS Command Injection Prevention

You should not allow user-supplied data to be used when executing OS commands in a shell. For example, in Python, don't allow the following:

---

[24]https://en.wikipedia.org/wiki/CAPTCHA
[25]https://en.wikipedia.org/wiki/Prepared_statement
[26]https://en.wikipedia.org/wiki/Object%E2%80%93relational_mapping

```
import os

user_supplied_dir = ...
os.system(f'mkdir {user_supplied_dir}')
```

A malicious user can supply, for example, the following kind of directory: `some_dir && rm -rf /`.

Instead, use a specific function provided by the `os` module:

```
import os

user_supplied_dir = ...
os.mkdir(user_supplied_dir)
```

7.4.8: Security Configuration

By default, the security context for containers should be the following:

- Container should not be privileged
- All capabilities are dropped
- Container filesystem is read-only
- Only a non-root user is allowed to run inside the container
- Define the non-root user and group under which the container should run
- Disallow privilege escalation

The *DevSecOps principles* chapter later in the book gives an example of the above Docker container security configuration.

Implement the sending of security-related HTTP response headers in the API gateway:

- `X-Content-Type-Options: nosniff`
- `Strict-Transport-Security: max-age: ; includeSubDomains`
- `X-Frame-Options: DENY`
- `Content-Security-Policy: frame-ancestors 'none'`
- `Content-Type: application/json`
- If caching is not specifically enabled and configured, the following header should be set: `Cache-Control: no-store`
- `Access-Control-Allow-Origin: https://your_domain_here`

If you are returning HTML instead of JSON, you should replace/add the following response headers:

- `Content-Security-Policy: default-src 'none'`
- `Referrer-Policy: no-referrer`

Disable browser features that are not needed/wanted using the `Permissions-Policy` response header. The below example turns off all the listed features:

```
Permissions-Policy: accelerometer=(), ambient-light-sensor=(),
  autoplay=(), battery=(), camera=(), cross-origin-isolated=(),
  display-capture=(), document-domain=(), encrypted-media=(),
  execution-while-not-rendered=(), execution-while-out-of-viewport=(),
  fullscreen=(), geolocation=(), gyroscope=(), keyboard-map=(),
  magnetometer=(), microphone=(), midi=(), navigation-override=(),
  payment=(), picture-in-picture=(), publickey-credentials-get=(),
  screen-wake-lock=(), sync-xhr=(), usb=(), web-share=(), xr-spatial-tracking=()
```

Read more about HTTP response security headers[27].

7.4.9: Automatic Vulnerability Scanning

Implement automatic vulnerability scanning in microservice CI pipelines and/or the container registry at regular intervals. It is vital to configure container vulnerability scanning in the container registry (e.g., Docker or one provided by the cloud vendor). This scanning should preferably happen once a day. All software components of the software system should be scanned. You should correct critical or high-severity vulnerabilities as soon as possible.

7.4.10: Integrity

Use only container images with tags that have an SHA digest. If an attacker succeeds in publishing a malicious container image with the same tag, the SHA digest prevents that malicious image from being taken into use. Ensure you use libraries and dependencies from trusted sources, like PyPi. You can also host internal mirrors of repositories to avoid accidentally using any untrusted repository. Ensure a review process exists for all code (source, deployment, infrastructure) and configuration changes so that no malicious code can be introduced into your software system.

7.4.11: Error Handling

Ensure that error messages in API responses do not contain sensitive information or details of the implementation. Do not add stack traces to error responses transmitted to clients in a production environment.

For example, suppose an API request produces an internal server error related to connectivity to an IAM system. In that case, you should not reveal implementation details in the error response, like talk about *Keycloak 18.06* if that's what you are using, but use an abstract term, like the *IAM system*. Suppose an attacker gets an error response revealing details about a 3rd party software component and its version. In that case, the attacker can exploit possible vulnerabilities of the particular software component.

7.4.12: Logging

When writing log entries, never write any of the below to the log:

- Session ids
- Access tokens
- Personally identifiable information (PII)

---

[27]https://cheatsheetseries.owasp.org/cheatsheets/HTTP_Headers_Cheat_Sheet.html

- Passwords
- Database connection strings
- Encryption keys
- Information that is not legal to collect
- Information that the end-user has opted out of the collection

7.4.13: Audit Logging

Auditable end-user-related events, such as logins, failed logins, unauthorized or invalid requests, and high-value transactions, should be logged and stored in an external audit logging system. The audit logging system should automatically detect suspicious action related to an end-user and alert about it. See also OWASP Logging Vocabulary Cheat Sheet[28]

7.4.14: Input Validation

Always validate input from untrusted sources, like from an end-user. There are many ways to implement validation, and several libraries exist for that purpose. Let's assume you implement entities and data transfer objects (DTOs). The best way to ensure proper validation is to require that each DTO property must have a validation decorator. If a property in a DTO does not require any validation, annotate that property with a special annotation, like @any_value, for example. Don't use entities in data transfer. Always use DTOs in both directions, in data transfer from the client to the server and from the server to the client. This is because the entities usually contain some data that is not expected from clients and can contain sensitive/confidential information that should not be exposed to clients. The input DTOs verify that the client supplies correct data: All needed properties are supplied with correct types and semantics, and no extra properties are supplied. If you need dynamic validation, i.e., enforce a business rule, put that validation code into the entity class. It is essential to filter out extra properties because otherwise, those might end up in the database if a schemaless database table (e.g., a MongoDB collection) is used. Disallowing a schemaless database table in a production system is good practice.

For example, a User entity might have an attribute is_admin. You should not expect a User entity as input from a client, but you should expect a DTO, InputUser, which has the same attributes as the User entity, except specific attributes like id, created_at_timestamp and is_admin. Similarly, if the User entity contains a password attribute, that attribute should not be sent to a client. For this reason, you need to define an OutputUser DTO, which has the same attributes as the User entity except the password attribute. When you use DTOs both in input and output data transfer, you safeguard the service against situations where you add a new sensitive or internal attribute to an entity, and that new sensitive or internal attribute should not be received from or transmitted to clients.

Remember to validate data from all untrusted sources:

- Command line arguments
- Environment variables
- Standard input (stdin)
- Data from the file system
- Data from a socket (network input)

---

[28]https://cheatsheetseries.owasp.org/cheatsheets/Logging_Vocabulary_Cheat_Sheet.html

- Input from the user interface (UI)

You don't need to validate function arguments in all functions, but always validate data from an untrusted source before passing that value to other functions in the software component. For example, don't access environment variables directly (using `os.environ`) all over the code, but create a dedicated class that provides controlled access to environment variables. That class should validate the environment variable values (correct type, allowed values, allowed value range, etc.). If the validation fails, a default value can be returned, or an error will be raised.

7.4.14.1: Validating Numbers

When validating numeric values, always validate that a value is in a specified range. For example, if you use an unvalidated number to check if a loop should end and that number is huge, it can cause a denial of service (DoS).

If a number should be an integer, don't allow floating-point values.

7.4.14.2: Validating Strings

When validating a string, always validate the maximum length of the string first. Only after that should additional validation be performed. Validating a long string using a regular expression can cause a regular expression denial of service (ReDoS). You should avoid crafting your own regular expressions for validation purposes. Instead, use a ready-made library that contains battle-tested code. Consider also using the Google RE2 library[29]. It is safer than regular expression functionality provided by many language runtimes, and your code will be less susceptible to ReDoS attacks.

7.4.14.3: Validating Timestamps

Timestamps (or times or dates) are usually given as an integer or string. Apply needed validation to a timestamp/time/date value. For example, you can validate if a timestamp is in the future or past or if a timestamp is earlier or later than another timestamp.

7.4.14.4: Validating Arrays

When validating an array, you should validate the size of the array. It should not be too small or large. You can validate the uniqueness of values if needed. Also, after validating the size of the array, remember to validate each value separately.

7.4.14.5: Validating Objects

Validate an object by validating each attribute of the object separately. Remember to validate nested objects also.

7.4.14.6: Validating Files Uploaded to Server

- Ensure the file name extension of the uploaded file is one of the allowed extensions

---

[29]https://github.com/google/re2/tree/abseil/python

- Ensure the file is not larger than a defined maximum size
- Check the uploaded file against viruses and malware
- If the uploaded file is compressed (e.g., a zip file) and you are going to unzip it, verify the following before unzipping:

  - Target path is acceptable
  - Estimated decompressed size is not too large

- When storing an uploaded file on the server side, pay attention to the following:

  - Do not use a file name supplied by the user, but use a new filename to store the file on the server
  - Do not let the user choose the path where the uploaded file is stored on the server

7.4.14.7: Validation Library Example

Check *Appendix A* for creating a TypeScript validation library using the *validated-types* NPM library. The validation library can validate JavaScript objects, e.g., parsed JSON/YAML-format configuration, environment variables (process.env object), and input DTOs. The validation library accepts an object schema and validates an object according to the given schema and produces a strongly typed validated object.

8: API Design Principles

This chapter presents design principles for both frontend-facing and inter-microservice APIs. First, frontend-facing API design is discussed, and then inter-microservice API design is covered.

8.1: Frontend Facing API Design Principles

Most frontend-facing APIs should be HTTP-based JSON-based RPC, REST, or GraphQL APIs. Use GraphQL especially when the API handles heavily nested resources or clients want to decide what fields queries should return. For subscription-based APIs, use Server-Sent Events (SSE) or GraphQL subscriptions, and for real-time bidirectional communication, use WebSocket. If you transfer a lot of data or binary data between the frontend and backend, consider implementing the API using gRPC and gRPC Web[1]. gRPC Web is not covered in this book. gRPC uses Protocol Buffers to binary encode data and is thus more efficient than JSON encoding.

8.1.1: JSON-based RPC API Design Principle

Design a JSON-based RPC API to perform a single action (procedure) for an API endpoint.

As the name suggests, JSON-based RPC APIs are for executing remote procedure calls using JSON-encoded payloads. The remote procedure argument is a JSON object in the HTTP request body. The remote procedure return value is a JSON object in the HTTP response body. A client calls a remote procedure by issuing an HTTP POST request where it specifies the procedure's name in the URL path and gives the argument for the remote procedure call in the request body in JSON.

Below is an example request for a translation service's *translate* procedure:

```
POST /translation-service/translate HTTP/1.1
Content-Type: application/json

{
  "text": "Ich liebe dich"
  "fromLanguage": "German",
  "toLanguage": "English"
}
```

The API server shall respond with an HTTP status code and include the procedure's response in the HTTP response body in JSON.

For the above request, you get the following response:

---

[1]https://github.com/grpc/grpc-web

```
HTTP/1.1 200 OK
Content-Type: application/json

{
  "translatedText": "I love you"
}
```

A JSON-RPC specification[2] exists that defines one way to create JSON-based RPC APIs. I do not follow that specification in the examples below because there are many ways to create a JSON-based RPC API. But as an example, the above example rewritten using the *JSON-RPC specification* would look like the following:

```
POST /translation-service HTTP/1.1
Content-Type: application/json

{
  "jsonrpc": "2.0",
  "method": "translate",
  "params": {
    "text": "Ich liebe dich",
    "fromLanguage": "German",
    "toLanguage": "English"
  }
  "id": 1
}
```

And the response would look like as follows:

```
HTTP/1.1 200 OK
Content-Type: application/json

{
  "jsonrpc": "2.0",
  "result": "I love you",
  "id": 1
}
```

Let's have another example with a *web-page-search-service*:

```
POST /web-page-search-service/search-web-pages HTTP/1.1
Content-Type: application/json

{
  "containingText": "Software design patterns"
}
```

The response could look like as follows:

---

[2]https://www.jsonrpc.org/specification

```
HTTP/1.1 200 OK
Content-Type: application/json

[
  {
    "url": "https://...",
    "title": "...",
    "date": "...",
    "contentExcerpt": "..."
  },
  More results here ...
]
```

You can create a complete service using JSON-based RPC instead of REST or GraphQL. Below are five remote procedures defined for a *sales-item-service*. The procedures are for basic CRUD operations. The benefit of using JSON-based RPC instead of REST, GraphQL, or gRPC is that you don't have to learn or use conventions of any specific technology.

```
POST /sales-item-service/create-sales-item HTTP/1.1
Content-Type: application/json

{
  "name": "Sample sales item",
  "price": 20
}
```

```
POST /sales-item-service/get-sales-items HTTP/1.1
```

```
POST /sales-item-service/get-sales-item-by-id HTTP/1.1
Content-Type: application/json

{
  "id": 1
}
```

```
POST /sales-item-service/update-sales-item HTTP/1.1
Content-Type: application/json

{
  "id": 1,
  "name": "Sample sales item name modified",
  "price": 30
}
```

```
POST /sales-item-service/delete-sales-item-by-id HTTP/1.1
Content-Type: application/json

{
  "id": 1
}
```

```
POST /sales-item-service/delete-sales-items HTTP/1.1
```

You can easily create a controller for the above service. Below is an example of such a controller with one remote procedure defined:

Figure 8.1. SalesItemController.java

```java
@RestController
public class SalesItemController {
  @Autowired
  private SalesItemService salesItemService;

  @PostMapping("/create-sales-tem")
  @ResponseStatus(HttpStatus.CREATED)
  public final SalesItem createSalesItem(
    @RequestBody final InputSalesItem inputSalesItem
  ) {
    return salesItemService.createSalesItem(inputSalesItem);
  }

  // Rest of the methods ...
}
```

You can version your API by adding a version number to the URL. In the below example, the new API version 2 allows a new procedure argument `someNewParam` to be supplied for the `search-web-pages` procedure.

```
POST /web-page-search-service/v2/search-web-pages HTTP/1.1
Content-Type: application/json

{
  "containingText": "Software design patterns"
  "someNewParam": "..."
}
```

8.1.2: REST API Design Principle

Design a REST API for interaction with a resource (or resources) using CRUD (create, read, update, delete) operations.

Many APIs fall into the category of performing CRUD operations on resources. Let's create an example REST API called *sales-item-service* for performing CRUD operations on sales items. You can also define non-CRUD endpoints for a REST API. For example, you can define some JSON-based RPC endpoints if needed.

You can also remodel an RPC-style API to support CRUD operations. For example, suppose you need to create an API to start and stop some processes. Instead of creating a JSON-based RPC API with `start-process` and `stop-process` procedures, you can create a CRUD-based REST API where you create a resource to start a process and delete a resource to stop a process, i.e., a process is a resource you can perform CRUD operations on.

8.1.2.1: Creating a Resource

Creating a new resource using a REST API is done by sending an HTTP POST request to the API's resource endpoint. The API's resource endpoint should be named according to the resources it handles. The resource endpoint name should be a noun and always given in the plural form, for example, for the *sales-item-service* handling sales items, the resource endpoint should be *sales-items*, and for an *order-service* handling orders, the resource endpoint should be called *orders*.

You give the resource to be created in the HTTP request body in JSON. To create a new sales item, you can issue the following request:

```
POST /sales-item-service/sales-items HTTP/1.1
Content-Type: application/json

{
  "name": "Sample sales item",
  "price": 20
}
```

The server will respond with the HTTP status code 201 *Created*. The server can add properties to the resource upon creation. Typically, the server will add an id property to the created resource but can also add other properties. The server will respond with the created resource in the HTTP response body in JSON. Below is a response to the sales item creation request. You can notice that the server added the id property to the resource. Other properties that are usually added are the creation timestamp and the version of the resource (the version of a newly created resource should be one).

```
HTTP/1.1 201 Created
Content-Type: application/json

{
  "id": 1,
  "name": "Sample sales item",
  "price": 20
}
```

If the supplied resource to be created is somehow invalid, the server should respond with the HTTP status code 400 *Bad Request* and explain the error in the response body. The response body should be in JSON format containing information about the error, like the error code and message.

To make API error responses consistent, use the same error response format throughout all the APIs in a software system. Below is an example of an error response:

```
{
  "statusCode": 500,
  "statusText": "Internal Server Error",
  "endpoint": "POST /sales-item-service/sales-items",
  "timestamp": "2024-03-10T13:31:40+0000",
  "errorCode": "IAMError",
  "errorMessage": "Unable to connect to the Identity and Access Management service"
  "errorDescription": "Describe the error in more detail here, if relevant/needed..."
  "stackTrace": "Call stack trace here..."
}
```

NOTE! In the above example, the stackTrace property should NOT be included in the production environment by default because it can reveal internal implementation details to possible attackers. Use it only in development and other internal environments, and if needed, enable it in the production environment only for a short time to conduct debugging. The errorCode property is useful for updating error counter metric(s). Use it as a label for the error counter(s). There will be more discussion about metrics in the coming *DevSecOps principles* chapter.

If the created resource is huge, there is no need to return the resource to the caller and waste network bandwidth. You can return the added properties only. For example, if the server only adds the id property, it is possible to return only the id in the response body as follows:

```
HTTP/1.1 201 Created
Content-Type: application/json

{
  "id": 1
}
```

The request sender can construct the created resource by merging the sent resource object with the received resource object.

Ensure that no duplicate resources are created.

When a client tries to create a new resource, the resource creation request may fail so that the resource was created successfully on the server, but the client did not receive a response on time, and the request failed due to timeout. From the server's point of view, the request was successful, but from the client's point of view, the request's status was indeterminate. The client, of course, needs to re-issue the time-outed request, and if it succeeds, the same resource is created twice on the server side (with two distinct IDs), which is probably unwanted in most cases.

Suppose a resource contains a unique property, like a user's email. In that case, it is impossible to create a duplicate resource if the server is correctly implemented (= the unique property is marked as a unique column in the database table definition). In many cases, such a unique field does not exist in the resource. In those cases, the client can supply a universally unique identifier (UUID), like`creationUuid`. The role of the server is to check if a resource with the same `creationUuid` was already created and to fail the creation of a duplicate resource. As an alternative to the UUID approach, the server can ask for verification from the client if the creation of two identical resources is intended in case the server receives two identical resources from the same client in a short period of time.

8.1.2.2: Reading Resources

Reading resources with a REST API is done by sending an HTTP GET request to the API's resource endpoint. To read all sales items, you can issue the following request:

```
GET /sales-item-service/sales-items HTTP/1.1
```

The server will respond with the HTTP status code 200 *OK* and a JSON array of resources in the response body or an empty array if none is found. Below is an example response to a request to get the sales items:

```
HTTP/1.1 200 OK
Content-Type: application/json

[
  {
    "id": 1,
    "name": "Sample sales item",
    "price": 20
  }
]
```

To read a single resource by its id, add the resource's id to the request URL as follows:

```
GET /sales-item-service/sales-items/<id> HTTP/1.1
```

The following request can be issued to read the sales item identified with id 1:

```
GET /sales-item-service/sales-items/1 HTTP/1.1
```

The response to the above request will contain a single resource:

```
HTTP/1.1 200 OK
Content-Type: application/json

{
  "id": 1,
  "name": "Sample sales item",
  "price": 20
}
```

The server responds with the HTTP status code 404 *Not Found* if the requested resource is not found.

You can define parameters in the URL query string[3] to filter what resources to read. A query string is the last part of the URL and is separated from the URL path by a question mark (?) character. A query string can contain one or more parameters separated by ampersand (&) characters. Each query string parameter has the following format: `<query-parameter-name>=<query-parameter-value>`. Below is an example request with two query parameters: *name-contains* and *price-greater-than*.

```
GET /sales-item-service/sales-items?name-contains=Sample&price-greater-than=10 HTTP/1.1
```

The above request gets sales items whose name contains the string *Sample* and whose price is greater than 10.

To define a filter, you can specify a query parameter in the following format: `<fieldName>[-<condition>]=<value>`, for example:

- `price=10`
- `price-not-equal=10`
- `price-less-than=10`
- `price-less-than-equal=10`
- `price-greater-than=10`
- `price-greater-than-equal=10`
- `name-starts-with=Sample`
- `name-ends-with=item`
- `name-contains=Sample`
- `createdAtTimestamp-before=2022-08-02T05:18:00Z`
- `createdAtTimestamp-after=2022-08-02T05:18:00Z`
- `images.url-starts-with=https`

Remember that when implementing the server side and adding the above-given parameters to an SQL query, you must use a parameterized SQL query to prevent SQL injection attacks because an attacker can send malicious data in the query parameters.

Other actions like projection, sorting, and pagination for the queried resources can also be defined with query parameters in the URL:

---

[3]https://en.wikipedia.org/wiki/Query_string

```
GET /sales-item-service/sales-items?fields=id,name&sort-by=price:asc&offset=0&limit=100 HTTP/1.1
```

The above request gets sales items sorted by price (ascending). The number of fetched sales items is limited to 100. Sales items are fetched starting from the offset 0, and the response contains only fields *id* and *name* for each sales item.

The *fields* parameter defines what resource fields (properties) are returned in the response. The wanted fields are defined as a comma-separated list of field names. If you want to define sub-resource fields, those can be defined with the dot notation, for example:

```
fields=id,name,images.url
```

The *sort-by* query parameter defines sorting using the following format:

```
sort-by=<fieldName>:asc|desc,[<fieldName>:asc|desc]
```

For example:

```
sort-by=price:asc,images.rank:asc
```

In the above example, the resources are returned as sorted first by ascending price and secondarily by image rank.

The *limit* and *offset* parameters are used for pagination. The *limit* query parameter defines the maximum number of resources that can be returned. The *offset* query parameter specifies the offset from which resources are returned. You can also paginate sub-resources by giving the *offset* and *limit* in the form of `<sub-resource>:<number>`. Below is an example of using pagination query parameters:

```
offset=0&limit=50,images:5
```

The above query parameters define that the first page of 50 sales items is fetched, and each sales item contains the first five images of the sales item. Instead of *offset* and *limit* parameters, you can use *page* and *page-size* parameters. The *page* parameter defines the page number, and the *page-size* parameter defines the number of resources a page should contain.

Remember to validate user-supplied data to prevent SQL injection attacks when implementing the server side and adding data from URL query parameters to an SQL query. For example, field names in the *fields* query parameter should only contain characters allowed in an SQL column name. Similarly, the value of the *sort-by* parameter should only contain characters allowed in an SQL column name and words *asc* and *desc*. And finally, the values of the *offset* and *limit* (or *page* and *page-size*) parameters must be integers. You should also validate the *limit/page-size* parameter against the maximum allowed value because you should not allow clients to fetch too many resources at a time.

Some HTTP servers log the URL of an HTTP GET request. For this reason, it is not recommended to put sensitive information in the URL. Sensitive information should be included in the request body. Also, browsers can have a limit for the maximum length of a URL. If you have a query string thousands of characters long, you should give parameters in the request body instead. You should not put a request body to an HTTP GET request. What you should do is issue the request using the HTTP POST method instead, for example:

```
POST /sales-item-service/sales-items HTTP/1.1
Content-Type: application/json
X-HTTP-Method-Override: GET

{
  "fields": ["name"],
  "sortBy": "price:asc",
  "limit": 100
}
```

The server can confuse the above request with a sales item creation request because the URL and the HTTP method are identical to a resource creation request. For this reason, a custom HTTP request header *X-HTTP-Method-Override* has been added to the request. The server should read the custom header and treat the above request as a GET request. The *X-HTTP-Method-Override* header tells the server to override the request method with the method supplied in the header.

8.1.2.3: Updating Resources

A resource is updated with a REST API by sending an HTTP PUT or PATCH request to the API's resource endpoint. To update the sales item identified with id 1, you can issue the following request:

```
PUT /sales-item-service/sales-items/1 HTTP/1.1
Content-Type: application/json

{
  "name": "Sample sales item name modified",
  "price": 30
}
```

The server will respond without content:

```
HTTP/1.1 204 No Content
```

Instead of sending no content, the server can return the updated resource in the response. This is needed if the server modifies the resource during the update process. The server will respond with the HTTP status code 404 *Not Found* if the requested resource is not found.

If the supplied resource in the request is invalid, the server should respond with the HTTP status code 400 *Bad Request*. The response body should contain an error object in JSON.

HTTP PUT request will replace the existing resource with the supplied resource. You can also modify an existing resource partially using the HTTP PATCH method:

```
PATCH /sales-item-service/sales-items/1 HTTP/1.1
Content-Type: application/json

{
  "price": 30
}
```

The above request only modifies the price property of the sales item identified with id 1. Other properties remain intact. You can do bulk updates by specifying a filter in the URL, for example:

```
PATCH /sales-item-service/sales-items?price-less-than=10 HTTP/1.1
Content-Type: application/json

{
  "price": 10
}
```

The above example will update the price property of each resource where the price is currently less than ten. On the server side, the API endpoint could use the following parameterized SQL statement to implement the update functionality:

```
UPDATE salesitems SET price = %s WHERE price < %s
```

The above SQL statement will only modify the price column; other columns remain intact.

Use resource versioning when needed.

When you get a resource from the server and try to update it, someone else may have updated it after you got it but before trying to update it. This can be okay if you don't care about other clients' updates. But sometimes, you want to ensure no one else has updated the resource before you update it. In that case, you should use resource versioning. In the resource versioning, there is a version field in the resource, which is incremented by one during each update. If you get a resource with version x and then try to update the resource, giving back the same version x to the server, but someone else has updated the resource to version $x + 1$, your update will fail because of the version mismatch (x != $x + 1$). The server should respond with the HTTP status code 409 *Conflict*. After receiving the conflict response, you can fetch the latest version of the resource from the server and, based on the resource's new state, decide whether your update is still relevant or not, and retry the update.

The server should assign the resource version value to the HTTP response header ETag[4]. A client can use the received ETag value in a conditional HTTP GET request by assigning the received ETag value to the request header If-None-Match[5]. The server will return the requested resource only if it has a newer version. Otherwise, the server returns nothing with the HTTP status code 304 *Not Modified*. This brings the advantage of not re-transferring an unmodified resource from the server to the client, which can be especially beneficial when the resource is large or the connection between the server and the client is slow.

8.1.2.4: Deleting Resources

Deleting a resource with a REST API is done by sending an HTTP DELETE request to the API's resource endpoint. To delete the sales item identified with id 1, you can issue the following request:

```
DELETE /sales-item-service/sales-items/1 HTTP/1.1
```

The server will respond without content:

```
HTTP/1.1 204 No Content
```

If the requested resource has already been deleted, the API should still respond with the HTTP status code 204 *No Content*, meaning a successful operation. It should not respond with the HTTP status code 404 *Not Found*.

To delete all sales items, you can issue the following request:

---

[4]https://en.wikipedia.org/wiki/HTTP_ETag
[5]https://developer.mozilla.org/en-US/docs/Web/HTTP/Headers/If-None-Match

```
DELETE /sales-item-service/sales-items HTTP/1.1
```

To delete sales items using a filter, you can issue the following kind of request:

```
DELETE /sales-item-service/sales-items?price-less-than=10 HTTP/1.1
```

On the server side, the API endpoint handler can use the following parameterized SQL query to implement the deleting functionality:

```
DELETE FROM salesitems WHERE price < %s
```

8.1.2.5: Executing Non-CRUD Actions on Resources

Sometimes, you need to perform non-CRUD actions on resources. In those cases, you can issue an HTTP POST request and put the name of the action (a verb) after the resource name in the URL. The below example will perform a *deposit* action on an account resource:

```
POST /account-balance-service/accounts/12345678912/deposit HTTP/1.1
Content-Type: application/json

{
  "amountInCents": 2510
}
```

Similarly, you can perform a withdrawal action:

```
POST /account-balance-service/accounts/12345678912/withdraw HTTP/1.1
Content-Type: application/json

{
  "amountInCents": 2510
}
```

8.1.2.6: Resource Composition

A resource can be composed of other resources. There are two ways to implement resource composition: Nesting resources or linking resources. Let's have an example of nesting resources first. A sales item resource can contain one or more image resources. We don't want to return all images when a client requests a sales item because images can be large and are not necessarily used by the client. What we could return is a set of small thumbnail images. For a client to get the full images of a sales item, we could implement an API endpoint for image resources. The following API call can be issued to get images for a specific sales item:

```
GET /sales-item-service/sales-items/<id>/images HTTP/1.1
```

You can also add a new image for a sales item:

```
POST /sales-item-service/sales-items/<id>/images HTTP/1.1
```

Also, other CRUD operations could be made available:

```
PUT /sales-item-service/sales-items/<salesItemId>/images/<imageId> HTTP/1.1
```

```
DELETE /sales-item-service/sales-items/<salesItemId>/images/<imageId> HTTP/1.1
```

The problem with this approach is that the *sales-item-service* will grow in size, and if you need to add more nested resources in the future, the size will grow even more, making the microservice too complex and being possibly responsible for too many things.

A better alternative might be to create a separate microservice for the nested resources. This will enable the utilization of the best-suited technologies to implement the microservice. Regarding the sales item images, the *sales-item-image-service* could employ a cloud object storage to store images, and the *sales-item-service* could utilize a standard relational database for storing sales items.

When having a separate microservice for sales item images, you can get the images for a sales item by issuing the following request:

```
GET /sales-item-image-service/sales-item-images?salesItemId=<salesItemId> HTTP/1.1
```

You can notice that the *sales-item-service* and *sales-item-image-service* are now linked by the *salesItemId*.

Note that the *sales-item-image-service* should be a service aggregated by the *sales-item-service*. The higher-level *sales-item-service* calls the lower-level *sales-item-image-service* because a sales item is a root aggregate, and sales item images are child entities that should not be accessed directly but only via the root aggregate, according to DDD. This helps with enforcing business rules. For example, let's hypothesize that a particular type of sales item should have at least x images. This kind of business rule should be enforced by the *sales-item-service*. The *sales-item-image-service* cannot do it because it does not have (and should not have) detailed information about the sales item itself. It only has the sales item's id.

8.1.2.7: HTTP Status Codes

Use the following HTTP status codes:

HTTP Status Code	When to Use
200 OK	Successful API operations with the GET method
201 Created	Successful API operations with the POST method

HTTP Status Code	When to Use
202 Accepted	The request has been accepted for processing. This can be used as the response status code for an asynchronous operation request (Asynchronous request-reply[6]). For example, a POST request can get a response with this status code, an empty body, and a link to the resource that will eventually be created. The link is usually provided in the Location response header. That link will return 404 *Not Found* until the asynchronous creation is complete.
204 No Content	Successful API operations with the PUT, PATCH, or DELETE method
400 Bad Request	Client error in API operations, e.g., invalid data supplied by the client
401 Unauthorized	Client does not provide an authorization header in the request
403 Forbidden	Client provides an authorization header in the request, but the user is not authorized to perform the API operation
404 Not Found	When requesting a non-existent resource with the GET, PUT, or PATCH method
405 Method Not Allowed	When a client tries to use the wrong method for an API endpoint
406 Not Acceptable	When a client requests a response in a format that the server cannot produce, e.g., requests XML, but the server provides only JSON
409 Conflict	When a client is trying to update a resource that has been updated after the client got the resource
413 Payload Too Large	When a client tries to supply a too large payload in a request. To prevent DoS attacks, do not accept arbitrarily large payloads from clients
429 Too Many Requests	Configure rate limiting in your API gateway to send this status code when the request rate is exceeded
500 Internal Server Error	When a server error occurs, for example, an exception is thrown
503 Service Unavailable	Server's connections to dependent services fail. This indicates that clients should retry the request after a while because this issue is usually temporary.

8.1.2.8: HATEOAS and HAL

Hypermedia as the Engine of Application State[7] (HATEOAS) can be used to add hypermedia/metadata to a requested resource. Hypertext Application Language[8] (HAL) is a convention for defining hypermedia (metadata), such as links to external resources. Below is an example response to a request that fetches the sales item with id 1234. The sales item is owned by the user with id 5678. The response provides a link to the fetched resource itself and another link to fetch the user (account) that owns the sales item:

---

[7]https://en.wikipedia.org/wiki/HATEOAS
[8]https://en.wikipedia.org/wiki/Hypertext_Application_Language

```json
{
  "_links": {
    "self": {
      "href": "https://.../sales-item-service/sales-items/1234"
    },
    "userAccount": {
      "href": "https://.../user-account-service/user-accounts/5678"
    }
  },
  "id": 1234,
  "name": "Sales item xyz",
  "userAccountId": 5678
}
```

When fetching a collection of sales items for page 3 using HAL, we can get the following kind of response:

```json
{
  "_links": {
    "self": {
      "href": "https://.../sales-items?page=3"
    },
    "first": {
      "href": "https://...sales-items"
    },
    "prev": {
      "href": "https://.../sales-items?page=2"
    },
    "next": {
      "href": "https://.../sales-items?page=4"
    },
  },
  "count": 25,
  "total": 1500,
  "_embedded": {
    "salesItems": [
      {
        "_links": {
          "self": {
            "href": "https://.../sales-items/123"
          }
        },
        "id": 123,
        "name": "Sales item 123"
      },
      {
        "_links": {
          "self": {
            "href": "https://.../sales-items/124"
          }
        },
        "id": 124,
        "name": "Sales item 124"
      },
      .
      .
      .
    ]
  }
}
```

The above response contains links to fetch sales items' first, current, previous, and last pages. It also states that there are 1500 sales items, and a page lists 25. The _embedded property contains a salesItems property containing the 25 sales items with links to themselves and the sales item data.

8.1.2.9: API Versioning

You can introduce a new version of an API using a versioning URL path segment. Below are example endpoints for API version 2:

```
GET /sales-item-service/v2/sales-items HTTP/1.1
...
```

8.1.2.10: Documentation

If you need to document or provide interactive online documentation for a REST API, there are two ways:

1) Spec-first: create a specification for the API and then generate code from the specification
2) Code-first: implement the API and then generate the API specification from the code

Tools like Swagger[9] and Postman can generate both static and interactive documentation for your API based on the API specification. You should specify APIs using the OpenAPI specification[10].

When using the first alternative, you can specify your API using the OpenAPI specification language. You can use tools like SwaggerHub[11] or Postman to write the API specification. Swagger Codegen[12] offers code-generation tools for multiple languages. Code generators generate code based on the OpenAPI specification. They can generate client-side code in addition to the server-side code.

When using the second alternative, you can use a web framework-specific way to build the API spec from the API implementation. For example, if you are using Spring Boot, you can use the springdoc-openapi-ui[13] library, and with Nest.js, you can use the @nestjs/swagger[14] library.

I prefer to use the second approach of writing the code first. I like it better when I don't have to work with both auto-generated and handwritten code. Many web frameworks offer automatic generation of the OpenAPI schema and interactive documentation from the source code.

8.1.2.11: Implementation Example

Let's implement *sales-item-service* API endpoints for CRUD operations on sales items using TypeScript and Nest.js.

Source code for the below example is available here[15].

We use the *clean architecture principle* introduced earlier and write the API endpoints inside a controller class:

---

[9]https://swagger.io/

[10]https://swagger.io/specification/

[11]https://swagger.io/tools/swaggerhub/

[12]https://swagger.io/tools/swagger-codegen/

[13]https://springdoc.org/

[14]https://docs.nestjs.com/openapi/introduction

[15]https://github.com/pksilen/clean-code-principles-code/tree/main/chapter6/salesitemservice

Figure 8.2. RestSalesItemController.ts

```typescript
import {
  Body,
  Controller,
  Delete,
  Get,
  HttpCode,
  Inject,
  Param,
  Post,
  Put,
  UseGuards,
  UseInterceptors,
} from '@nestjs/common';
import SalesItemService from '../services/SalesItemService';
import InputSalesItem from '../dtos/InputSalesItem';
import OutputSalesItem from '../dtos/OutputSalesItem';
import { AuditLogger } from '../interceptors/AuditLogger';
import { RequestCountIncrementor } from '../interceptors/RequestCounter';
import { RequestTracer } from '../interceptors/RequestTracer';
import { AllowForUserThatHasOneOfRoles } from '../guards/AllowForUserThatHasOneOfRoles';
import { authorizer } from '../common/authorizer/FakeAuthorizer';


@UseInterceptors(RequestCounter, RequestTracer)
@Controller('sales-items')
export default class RestSalesItemController {
  constructor(
    @Inject('salesItemService')
    private readonly salesItemService: SalesItemService,
  ) {}

  @Post()
  createSalesItem(
    @Body() inputSalesItem: InputSalesItem,
  ): Promise<OutputSalesItem> {
    return this.salesItemService.createSalesItem(inputSalesItem);
  }

  @Get()
  getSalesItems() // @Query('userAccountId') userAccountId: string,
  : Promise<OutputSalesItem[]> {
    return this.salesItemService.getSalesItems();
  }

  @Get('/:id')
  getSalesItem(@Param('id') id: string): Promise<OutputSalesItem> {
    return this.salesItemService.getSalesItem(id);
  }

  @Put('/:id')
  @HttpCode(204)
  updateSalesItem(
    @Param('id') id: string,
    @Body() inputSalesItem: InputSalesItem,
  ): Promise<void> {
    return this.salesItemService.updateSalesItem(id, inputSalesItem);
  }

  @UseGuards(new AllowForUserThatHasOneOfRoles(['admin'], authorizer))
  @UseInterceptors(AuditLogger)
  @Delete('/:id')
  @HttpCode(204)
  deleteSalesItem(@Param('id') id: string): Promise<void> {
    return this.salesItemService.deleteSalesItem(id);
  }
}
```

The above controller contains Nest.js interceptors[16] and guards[17] that are needed to implement the below functionality for production quality software:

- Audit logging
- Request tracing
- Observability, e.g., updating metric(s) like request counts
- Authorization

Below are example implementations of the above used interceptors and guards:

Figure 8.3. AllowForUserThatHasOneOfRoles.ts

```
import { CanActivate, ExecutionContext, Injectable } from '@nestjs/common';
import { Observable } from 'rxjs';
import { Authorizer } from '../common/authorizer/Authorizer';


@Injectable()
export class AllowForUserThatHasOneOfRoles implements CanActivate {
  constructor(
    private readonly roles: string[],
    // Authorizer interface is defined in the GitHub repo
    // that contains source code for this example
    private readonly authorizer: Authorizer,
  ) {}

  canActivate(
    context: ExecutionContext,
  ): boolean | Promise<boolean> | Observable<boolean> {
    const request = context.switchToHttp().getRequest();

    this.authorizer.authorizeIfUserHasOneOfRoles(
      this.roles,
      request.headers.authorization,
    );

    return true;
  }
}
```

Figure 8.4. AuditLogger.ts

```
import {
  CallHandler,
  ExecutionContext,
  Inject,
  Injectable,
  NestInterceptor,
} from '@nestjs/common';
import { Observable } from 'rxjs';
import { AuditLoggingService } from '../common/logger/audit/AuditLoggingService';


@Injectable()
export class AuditLogger implements NestInterceptor {
  constructor(
    // AuditLoggingService interface is defined in the GitHub repo
    // that contains source code for this example
    @Inject('auditLoggingService')
```

[16]https://docs.nestjs.com/interceptors
[17]https://docs.nestjs.com/guards

```
    private readonly auditLogger: AuditLoggingService,
  ) {}

  intercept(context: ExecutionContext, next: CallHandler): Observable<any> {
    const httpArgumentsHost = context.switchToHttp();
    const request = httpArgumentsHost.getRequest();

    this.auditLogger.log(
      `Endpoint ${request.method} ${request.url} accessed from ${request.ip}`,
    );

    return next.handle();
  }
}
```

Figure 8.5. RequestCounter.ts

```
import {
  CallHandler,
  ExecutionContext,
  Inject,
  Injectable,
  NestInterceptor,
} from '@nestjs/common';
import { Observable } from 'rxjs';
import { Metrics } from '../common/metrics/Metrics';


@Injectable()
export class RequestCounter implements NestInterceptor {
  constructor(
    // Metrics interface is defined in the GitHub repo
    // that contains source code for this example
    @Inject('metrics') private readonly metrics: Metrics
  ) {}

  intercept(context: ExecutionContext, next: CallHandler): Observable<any> {
    const httpArgumentsHost = context.switchToHttp();
    const request = httpArgumentsHost.getRequest();

    this.metrics.incrementRequestCounter(
      `${request.method} ${request.url.split('/')[1]}`,
    );

    return next.handle();
  }
}
```

Figure 8.6. RequestTracer.ts

```
import {
  CallHandler,
  ExecutionContext,
  Inject,
  Injectable,
  NestInterceptor,
} from '@nestjs/common';
import { Observable } from 'rxjs';
import { Logger } from '../common/logger/Logger';


@Injectable()
export class RequestTracer implements NestInterceptor {
  constructor(
    // Logger interface is defined in the GitHub repo
    // that contains source code for this example
```

```
    @Inject('logger') private readonly logger: Logger
  ) {}

  intercept(context: ExecutionContext, next: CallHandler): Observable<any> {
    const httpArgumentsHost = context.switchToHttp();
    const request = httpArgumentsHost.getRequest();

    // Log at TRACE level
    this.logger.log(
      'TRACE',
      `${request.method} ${request.url} ${JSON.stringify(request.body)}`,
    );

    return next.handle();
  }
}
```

Notice how the above decorators are general purpose and not specific to this *sales-item-service* API. Instead of adding the decorators to the controller class methods, you might be better off creating decorators that can be added to the service class methods. In that case, you need to supply the needed information from the controller methods to the service methods, like the request method, URL and client's host for the audit logging decorator and the JWT for the authorization decorators. You can group these into a `ClientInfo` object passed from the controller to the service class. The service class decorators then operate with that object.

The DTOs (objects that specify what data is transferred (input or output) between clients and the server) are defined as shown below. For validating DTOs, we need to use the class-validator[18] and class-transformer[19] libraries as instructed in Nest.js validation guide[20]. In the below example, the following decorators are only needed for the further Nest.js GraphQL example: `@InputType`, `@ObjectType`, `@Field`. If you are not using Nest.js GraphQL, these decorators can be removed.

Figure 8.7. InputSalesItem.ts

```
import { Type } from 'class-transformer';
import {
  ArrayMaxSize,
  IsInt,
  MaxLength,
  ValidateNested,
} from 'class-validator';
import { Field, InputType, Int } from '@nestjs/graphql';
import InputSalesItemImage from './InputSalesItemImage';


@InputType()
export default class InputSalesItem {
  @Field()
  @MaxLength(256)
  name: string;

  // We accept negative prices for sales items that act
  // as discount items
  @Field(() => Int)
  @IsInt()
  priceInCents: number;

  @Field(() => [InputSalesItemImage])
  @Type(() => InputSalesItemImage)
```

---

[18]https://github.com/typestack/class-validator
[19]https://github.com/typestack/class-transformer
[20]https://docs.nestjs.com/techniques/validation

```
  @ValidateNested()
  @ArrayMaxSize(25)
  images: InputSalesItemImage[];
}
```

Figure 8.8. InputSalesItemImage.ts

```
import { IsInt, IsPositive, IsUrl } from 'class-validator';
import { Field, InputType, Int } from '@nestjs/graphql';


@InputType()
export default class InputSalesItemImage {
  @Field(() => Int)
  @IsInt()
  @IsPositive()
  rank: number;

  @Field()
  @IsUrl()
  url: string;
}
```

Figure 8.9. OutputSalesItem.ts

```
import {
  ArrayMaxSize,
  IsInt,
  MaxLength,
  ValidateNested,
  validateOrReject,
} from 'class-validator';
import { Type } from 'class-transformer';
import { Field, Int, ObjectType } from '@nestjs/graphql';
import SalesItem from '../entities/SalesItem';
import OutputSalesItemImage from './OutputSalesItemImage';


@ObjectType()
export default class OutputSalesItem {
  @Field()
  @MaxLength(36)
  id: string;

  @Field()
  @MaxLength(20)
  createdAtTimestampInMs: string;

  @Field()
  @MaxLength(256)
  name: string;

  // We accept negative prices for sales items that act
  // as discount items
  @Field(() => Int)
  @IsInt()
  priceInCents: number;

  @Field(() => [OutputSalesItemImage])
  @Type(() => OutputSalesItemImage)
  @ValidateNested()
  @ArrayMaxSize(25)
  images: OutputSalesItemImage[];

  // Factory method for constructing output sales item DTOs
  // from sales item domain entities
```

```
  // Here we use one-to-one mapping but that is not always
  // desired because you might have properties in domain entities
  // that should not be exposed to clients, for example. Or you
  // want to perform type conversions, etc...
  static async from(salesItem: SalesItem): Promise<OutputSalesItem> {
    const outputSalesItem = new OutputSalesItem();
    outputSalesItem.id = salesItem.id;
    outputSalesItem.createdAtTimestampInMs = salesItem.createdAtTimestampInMs;
    outputSalesItem.name = salesItem.name;
    outputSalesItem.priceInCents = salesItem.priceInCents;

    outputSalesItem.images = salesItem.images.map((salesItemImage) => {
      const outputSalesItemImage = new OutputSalesItemImage();
      outputSalesItemImage.id = salesItemImage.id;
      outputSalesItemImage.rank = salesItemImage.rank;
      outputSalesItemImage.url = salesItemImage.url;
      return outputSalesItemImage;
    });

    await validateOrReject(outputSalesItem);
    return outputSalesItem;
  }
}
```

Figure 8.10. OutputSalesItemImage.ts

```
import { IsInt, IsPositive, IsUrl, MaxLength } from 'class-validator';
import { Field, Int, ObjectType } from '@nestjs/graphql';

@ObjectType()
export default class OutputSalesItemImage {
  @Field()
  @MaxLength(36)
  id: string;

  @Field(() => Int)
  @IsInt()
  @IsPositive()
  rank: number;

  @Field()
  @IsUrl()
  url: string;
}
```

Notice that we have specified validation for each attribute in all DTO classes. This is important because of security. For example, string and list attributes should have maximum length validators to prevent possible denial of service attacks. Output DTOs should have validation as well. This is important because of security. Output validation can protect against injection attacks that try to return data that has an invalid shape. With Nest.js, the output DTOs are not validated (at the moment of writing this book). You need to implement it by yourself, e.g., using the validateOrReject function from the *class-validator* library as was shown above.

Here are the domain entity classes:

Figure 8.11. SalesItem.ts

```typescript
import { v4 as uuidv4 } from 'uuid';
import InputSalesItem from '../dtos/InputSalesItem';
import SalesItemImage from './SalesItemImage';


type ConstructorArgs = {
  id: string;
  createdAtTimestampInMs: string;
  name: string;
  priceInCents: number;
  images: SalesItemImage[];
};

export default class SalesItem {
  private _id: string;
  private _createdAtTimestampInMs: string;
  private _name: string;
  private _priceInCents: number;
  private _images: SalesItemImage[];

  constructor(args: ConstructorArgs) {
    this._id = args.id;
    this._createdAtTimestampInMs = args.createdAtTimestampInMs;
    this._name = args.name;
    this._priceInCents = args.priceInCents;
    this._images = args.images;
  }

  // Domain entity factory method
  // You could instantiate different types of domain entities here like
  // BusinessSalesItem or ConsumerSalesItem if you had such types
  static from(inputSalesItem: InputSalesItem, id?: string): SalesItem {
    return new SalesItem({
      ...inputSalesItem,
      // Generating entity id on server side is good practice
      // for high security and distributed databases
      // Having all ids as string allows represents ids
      // consistently regardless of database engine and programming
      // languages used
      id: id ?? uuidv4(),
      createdAtTimestampInMs: Date.now().toString(),
      images: (inputSalesItem.images ?? []).map(
        (image: any) => new SalesItemImage(image),
      ),
    });
  }

  get id(): string {
    return this._id;
  }

  get createdAtTimestampInMs(): string {
    return this._createdAtTimestampInMs;
  }

  get name(): string {
    return this._name;
  }

  get priceInCents(): number {
    return this._priceInCents;
  }

  get images(): SalesItemImage[] {
    return this._images;
  }
}
```

Figure 8.12. SalesItemImage.ts

```
import { v4 as uuidv4 } from 'uuid';


type Args = {
  id: string;
  rank: number;
  url: string;
};

export default class SalesItemImage {
  private _id: string;
  private _rank: number;
  private _url: string;

  constructor(args: Args) {
    this._id = args.id ?? uuidv4();
    this._rank = args.rank;
    this._url = args.url;
  }

  get id(): string {
    return this._id;
  }

  get rank(): number {
    return this._rank;
  }

  get url(): string {
    return this._url;
  }
}
```

The SalesItemService interface looks like the following:

Figure 8.13. SalesItemService.ts

```
import InputSalesItem from '../dtos/InputSalesItem';
import OutputSalesItem from '../dtos/OutputSalesItem';


export default interface SalesItemService {
  createSalesItem(inputSalesItem: InputSalesItem): Promise<OutputSalesItem>;
  getSalesItems(): Promise<OutputSalesItem[]>;
  getSalesItem(id: string): Promise<OutputSalesItem>;
  updateSalesItem(id: string, inputSalesItem: InputSalesItem): Promise<void>;
  deleteSalesItem(id: string): Promise<void>;
}
```

Next, we can implement the above interface:

Figure 8.14. SalesItemServiceImpl.ts

```ts
import { Inject, Injectable } from '@nestjs/common';
import SalesItemService from './SalesItemService';
import InputSalesItem from '../dtos/InputSalesItem';
import OutputSalesItem from '../dtos/OutputSalesItem';
import SalesItem from '../entities/SalesItem';
import SalesItemRepository from '../repositories/SalesItemRepository';
import EntityNotFoundError from '../errors/EntityNotFoundError';


@Injectable()
export default class SalesItemServiceImpl implements SalesItemService {
  constructor(
    @Inject('salesItemRepository')
    private readonly salesItemRepository: SalesItemRepository,
  ) {}

  async createSalesItem(
    inputSalesItem: InputSalesItem,
  ): Promise<OutputSalesItem> {
    // Use a factory method to create a domain entity
    // from an input DTO
    const salesItem = SalesItem.from(inputSalesItem);

    // Persist the domain entity
    await this.salesItemRepository.save(salesItem);

    // Use a factory method to create an output DTO
    // from the domain entity
    return OutputSalesItem.from(salesItem);
  }

  async getSalesItems(): Promise<OutputSalesItem[]> {
    const salesItems = await this.salesItemRepository.findAll();

    return await Promise.all(
      salesItems.map(
        async (salesItem) => await OutputSalesItem.from(salesItem),
      ),
    );
  }

  async getSalesItem(id: string): Promise<OutputSalesItem> {
    const salesItem = await this.salesItemRepository.find(id);

    if (!salesItem) {
      throw new EntityNotFoundError('Sales item', id);
    }

    return await OutputSalesItem.from(salesItem);
  }

  async updateSalesItem(
    id: string,
    inputSalesItem: InputSalesItem,
  ): Promise<void> {
    if (!(await this.salesItemRepository.find(id))) {
      throw new EntityNotFoundError('Sales item', id);
    }

    const salesItem = SalesItem.from(inputSalesItem, id);
    return this.salesItemRepository.update(salesItem);
  }

  async deleteSalesItem(id: string): Promise<void> {
    if (await this.salesItemRepository.find(id)) {
      await this.salesItemRepository.delete(id);
    }
  }
}
```

```
}
```

Below is the definition of the `SalesItemRepository` interface:

Figure 8.15. SalesItemRepository.ts

```
import SalesItem from '../entities/SalesItem';
import InputSalesItem from '../dtos/InputSalesItem';

export default interface SalesItemRepository {
  save(salesItem: SalesItem): Promise<void>;
  findAll(): Promise<SalesItem[]>;
  find(id: string): Promise<SalesItem | null>;
  update(inputSalesItem: InputSalesItem): Promise<void>;
  delete(id: string): Promise<void>;
}
```

Various implementations for the `SalesItemRepository` are presented in the next chapter, where we focus on database principles. The next chapter provides three different implementations for the repository: Object-Relational Mapping (ORM), parameterized SQL queries, and MongoDB.

For error handling, we depend on the `catch` block provided by the Nest.js web framework. We could throw errors of the Nest.js `HTTPException` type in our business logic, but then we would be coupling our web framework with business logic, which is not desired. Remember how in the *clean architecture principle*, the dependency goes only from the web framework (controller) towards business logic, not vice versa. If we used web framework-specific error classes in our business and logic, and we would like to migrate the microservice to a different web framework; we would have to refactor the whole business logic concerning raised errors.

What we should do is introduce a base error class for our microservice and provide a custom exception filter for Nest.js. The custom exception filter translates our business logic-specific errors into HTTP responses. The possible errors the microservice can raise should all derive from the base error class. The `ApiError` class below is a general-purpose base error class for any API.

Figure 8.16. ApiError.ts

```
import { getStackTrace } from '../common/utils/utils';

export default class ApiError extends Error {
  constructor(
    private readonly _statusCode: number,
    private readonly statusText: string,
    private readonly errorMessage: string,
    private readonly errorCode: string | undefined,
    private readonly errorDescription?: string,
    private readonly cause?: Error,
  ) {
    super(errorMessage);
  }

  toResponse(requestOrEndpoint: any) {
    const endpoint =
      requestOrEndpoint?.method && requestOrEndpoint?.url
        ? `${requestOrEndpoint.method} ${requestOrEndpoint.url}`
        : requestOrEndpoint;

    return {
      statusCode: this._statusCode,
      statusText: this.statusText,
```

```
      timestamp: new Date().toISOString(),
      endpoint,
      errorCode: this.errorCode,
      errorMessage: this.errorMessage,
      errorDescription: this.errorDescription,
      // getStackTrace returns stack trace only
      // when environment is not production
      // otherwise it returns 'undefined'
      // This method is specified in utils.ts in GitHub repo
      stackTrace: getStackTrace(this.cause),
    };
  }

  get statusCode(): number {
    return this._statusCode;
  }
}
```

The code property could also be named type. The idea behind that property is to tell what kind of an error is in question. This property can be used on the server side as a label for failure metrics, and on the client side, special handling for particular error codes can be implemented. If you want, you can even add one more property to the above class, namely recoveryAction. This optional property contains information about recovery steps for an actionable error. For example, a database connection error might have a recoveryAction property value: *Please retry after a while. If the problem persists, contact the technical support at <email address>*.

Below is the base error class for the *sales-item-service*:

Figure 8.17. SalesItemServiceError.ts

```
export default class SalesItemServiceError extends ApiError {}
```

Let's then define one error class that is used by the API:

Figure 8.18. EntityNotFoundError.ts

```
import SalesItemServiceError from './SalesItemServiceError';

export default class EntityNotFoundError extends SalesItemServiceError {
  constructor(entityName: string, entityId: string) {
    super(
      404,
      'Not Found',
      `${entityName} with id ${entityId} not found`,
      'EntityNotFound',
    );
  }
}
```

Let's implement a custom exception filter for our API. Notice how the exception filter is general purpose and It can be used with any API with its errors derived from the ApiError.

Figure 8.19. SalesItemServiceErrorFilter.ts

```
import { ApolloError } from 'apollo-server-express';
import { ArgumentsHost, Catch, ExceptionFilter } from '@nestjs/common';
import SalesItemServiceError from '../errors/SalesItemServiceError';


@Catch(SalesItemServiceError)
export default class SalesItemServiceErrorFilter implements ExceptionFilter {
  catch(error: SalesItemServiceError, host: ArgumentsHost) {
    const context = host.switchToHttp();
    const response = context.getResponse();
    const request = context.getRequest();

    // Log error.cause at least always
    // when error.status_code >= 500

    // Increment 'request_failures' counter by one
    // with three labels:
    // api_endpoint=`${request.method} ${request.url}`
    // status_code=error.statusCode
    // error_code=error.code
    if (process.env.CONTROLLER_TYPE === 'graphql') {
      return new ApolloError(
        error.message,
        undefined,
        error.toResponse(undefined),
      );
    }

    response.status(error.statusCode).json(error.toResponse(request));
  }
}
```

Now, if the business logic raises the following error:

```
throw new EntityNotFoundError('Sales item', '10')
```

The following API response should be expected in a production environment (Notice how the stackTrace is missing when the service is running in the production environment):

```
HTTP/1.1 404 Not Found
Content-Type: application/json

{
  "statusCode": 404,
  "statusText": "Not Found",
  "endpoint": "GET .../sales-item-service/sales-items/1",
  "timestamp": "2024-02-26T12:32:49+0000",
  "errorCode": "EntityNotFound",
  "errorMessage": "Sales item with id 10 not found"
}
```

You should also add specific exception filter for DTO validation errors and other possible errors:

Figure 8.20. ValidationErrorFilter.ts

```
import { ApolloError } from 'apollo-server-express';
import {
  ArgumentsHost,
  BadRequestException,
  Catch,
  ExceptionFilter,
} from '@nestjs/common';
import { createErrorResponse } from '../common/utils/utils';


@Catch(BadRequestException)
export class ValidationErrorFilter implements ExceptionFilter {
  catch(error: BadRequestException, host: ArgumentsHost) {
    const context = host.switchToHttp();
    const response = context.getResponse();
    const request = context.getRequest();

    // Audit log

    // Increment 'request_failures' counter by one
    // with three labels:
    // api_endpoint=`${request.method} ${request.url}`
    // status_code=400
    // errorCode="RequestValidationError"

    if (process.env.CONTROLLER_TYPE === 'graphql') {
      return new ApolloError(
        error.message,
        undefined,
        // This method is specified in utils.ts in GitHub repo
        createErrorResponse(error, 400, 'RequestValidationError', undefined),
      );
    }

    response
      .status(400)
      .json(createErrorResponse(error, 400, 'RequestValidationError', request));
  }
}
```

Figure 8.21. ErrorFilter.ts

```
import { ApolloError } from 'apollo-server-express';
import { ArgumentsHost, Catch, ExceptionFilter } from '@nestjs/common';
import { createErrorResponse } from '../common/utils/utils';


@Catch()
export class ErrorFilter implements ExceptionFilter {
  catch(error: Error, host: ArgumentsHost) {
    const context = host.switchToHttp();
    const response = context.getResponse();
    const request = context.getRequest();

    // Log error

    // Increment 'request_failures' counter by one
    // with labels:
    // api_endpoint=f'{request.method} {request.url}'
    // status_code=500
    // error_code='UnspecifiedError'

    if (process.env.CONTROLLER_TYPE === 'graphql') {
      return new ApolloError(
        error.message,
        undefined,
```

```
      // This method is specified in utils.ts in GitHub repo
      createErrorResponse(error, 500, 'UnspecifiedInternalError', undefined),
    );
  }

  response
    .status(500)
    .json(
      createErrorResponse(error, 500, 'UnspecifiedInternalError', request),
    );
  }
}
```

The *main.ts* source code files look like the following:

Figure 8.22. main.ts

```
import { ValidationPipe } from '@nestjs/common';
import { NestFactory } from '@nestjs/core';
import { WsAdapter } from '@nestjs/platform-ws';
import { AppModule } from './AppModule';
import SalesItemServiceErrorFilter from './errorfilters/SalesItemServiceErrorFilter';
import { ValidationErrorFilter } from './errorfilters/ValidationErrorFilter';
import { ErrorFilter } from './errorfilters/ErrorFilter';

async function bootstrap() {
  const app = await NestFactory.create(AppModule);

  // This is needed for further WebSocket example only
  app.useWebSocketAdapter(new WsAdapter(app));

  app.useGlobalPipes(
    new ValidationPipe({
      transform: true,
    }),
  );

  // Highest priority global filter is the last one
  app.useGlobalFilters(
    new ErrorFilter(),
    new SalesItemServiceErrorFilter(),
    new ValidationErrorFilter(),
  );

  await app.listen(8000);
}

bootstrap();
```

The above example converted for Express.js is available here[21]. It contains a new controller and Nest.js error filters replaced with Express.js error handlers and Nest.js interceptors replaced with Express.js middlewares.

[21]https://github.com/pksilen/clean-code-principles-code/tree/main/chapter6/salesitemservice_expressjs

8.1.3: GraphQL API Design

Divide API endpoints into queries and mutations. Compared to REST, REST GET requests are GraphQL queries, and REST POST/PUT/PATCH/DELETE requests are GraphQL mutations. With GraphQL, you can name your queries and mutations with descriptive names.

Let's create a GraphQL schema[22] that defines needed types and API endpoints for the *sales-item-service*. After the example, we will discuss the details of the schema below and the schema language in general.

```
type Image {
  id: Int!
  rank: Int!
  url: String!
}
type SalesItem {
  id: ID!
  createdAtTimestampInMs: String!
  name: String!
  priceInCents: Int!
  images(
    sortByField: String = "rank",
    sortDirection: SortDirection = ASC,
    offset: Int = 0,
    limit: Int = 5
  ): [Image!]!
}

input InputImage {
  id: Int!
  rank: Int!
  url: String!
}

input InputSalesItem {
  name: String!
  priceInCents: Int!
  images: [InputImage!]!
}

enum SortDirection {
  ASC
  DESC
}

type IdResponse {
  id: ID!
}

type Query {
  salesItems(
    sortByField: String = "createdAtTimestamp",
    sortDirection: SortDirection = DESC,
    offset: Int = 0,
    limit: Int = 50
  ): [SalesItem!]!

  salesItem(id: ID!): SalesItem!

  salesItemsByFilters(
    nameContains: String,
    priceGreaterThan: Float
```

---

[22]https://graphql.org/learn/schema/

```
  ): [SalesItem!]!
}
type Mutation {
  createSalesItem(salesItem: InputSalesItem!): SalesItem!

  updateSalesItem(
    id: ID!,
    salesItem: InputSalesItem
  ): IdResponse!

  deleteSalesItem(id: ID!): IdResponse!
}
```

The above GraphQL schema defines several types used in API requests and responses. A GraphQL `type` specifies an object type: Its properties and the types of those properties. A type specified with the `input` keyword is an input-only type (input DTO type). GraphQL defines the primitive (scalar) types: `Int` (32-bit), `Float`, `String`, `Boolean`, and `ID`. You can define an array type with the notation: `[<Type>]`. By default, types are nullable. If you want a non-nullable type, add an exclamation mark (!) after the type name. You can define an enumerated type with the `enum` keyword. The `Query` and `Mutation` types are special GraphQL types used to define queries and mutations. The above example defines three queries and four mutations that clients can execute. You can add parameters for a type property. We have added parameters for all the queries (queries are properties of the `Query` type), mutations (mutations are properties of the `Mutation` type), and the `images` property of the `SalesItem` type.

In the above example, I have named all the queries with names that describe the values they return, i.e., there are no verbs in the query names. It is possible to name queries starting with a verb (like the mutations). For example, you can add *get* to the beginning of the names of the above-defined queries if you prefer.

There are two ways to implement a GraphQL API:

- Schema first
- Code first (schema is generated from the code)

Let's first focus on the schema-first approach and implement the above-specified API using the Apollo Server[23] library. The Apollo server below implements some GraphQL type resolvers returning static responses.

Figure 8.23. server.js

```
import { ApolloServer } from '@apollo/server';
import { startStandaloneServer } from '@apollo/server/standalone';

const typeDefs = readFileSync('./schema.graphql',
                              { encoding: 'utf8' });

const resolvers = {
  Query: {
    salesItems: (_, { sortByField,
                      sortDirection,
                      offset,
                      limit }) =>
    [{
        id: 1,
        createdAtTimestampInMs: '12345678999877',
        name: 'sales item',
        price: 10.95
    }],
```

[23]https://www.apollographql.com/docs/apollo-server/

```
  salesItem: (_, { id }) => ({
    id,
    createdAtTimestampInMs: '12345678999877',
    name: 'sales item',
    price: 10.95
  })
},
Mutation: {
  createSalesItem: (_, { newSalesItem }) => {
    return {
      id: 100,
      createdAtTimestampInMs: Date.now().toString(),
      ...newSalesItem
    };
  },
  deleteSalesItem: (_, { id }) => {
    return {
      id
    };
  }
},
SalesItem: {
  images: (parent) => {
    return [{
      id: 1,
      rank: 1,
      url: 'url'
    }];
  }
}
};

const server = new ApolloServer({
  typeDefs,
  resolvers
});

startStandaloneServer(server, {
  listen: { port: 4000 }
});
```

After starting the server with the `node server.js` command, you can browse to *http://localhost:4000* and try to execute some of the implemented queries or mutations. You will see the GraphiQL UI, where you can execute queries and mutations. Enter the following query in the left pane of the UI.

```
query salesItems {
  salesItems(offset: 0) {
    id
    createdAtTimestampInMs
    name
    priceInCents,
    images {
      url
    }
  }
}
```

You should get the following response on the right side pane:

```
{
  "data": {
    "salesItems": [
      {
        "id": "1",
        "createdAtTimestampInMs": "12345678999877",
        "name": "sales item",
        "priceInCents": 1095,
        "images": [
          {
            "url": "url"
          }
        ]
      }
    ]
  }
}
```

You can also try to create a new sales item:

```
mutation create {
  createSalesItem(inputSalesItem: {
    priceInCents: 4095
    name: "test sales item"
    images: []
  }) {
    id,
    createdAtTimestampInMs,
    name,
    priceInCents,
    images {
      id
    },
  }
}
```

Below is the response you would get, except for the timestamp being the current time:

```
{
  "data": {
    "createSalesItem": {
      "id": "100",
      "createdAtTimestampInMs": "1694798999418",
      "name": "test sales item",
      "priceInCents": 4095,
      "images": []
    }
  }
}
```

To delete a sales item, you can issue:

```
mutation delete {
  deleteSalesItem(id: 1) {
    id
  }
}
```

```
{
  "data": {
    "deleteSalesItem": {
      "id": "1"
    }
  }
}
```

Let's replace the dummy static implementations in our GraphQL controller with actual calls to the sales item service:

Source code for the below example is available here[24].

Figure 8.24. GraphQlSalesItemController.ts

```
import { transformAndValidate } from "class-transformer-validator";
import SalesItemService from "../services/SalesItemService";
import InputSalesItem from "../dtos/InputSalesItem";

// In real-life, you might want to put the type definitions
// in a separate source code file
export const typeDefs = `
type SalesItem {
  id: ID!
  createdAtTimestampInMs: String!
  name: String!
  priceInCents: Int!
  images: [Image!]!
}

type Image {
  id: ID!
  rank: Int!
  url: String!
}

input InputSalesItem {
  name: String!
  priceInCents: Int!
  images: [InputImage!]!
}

input InputImage {
  rank: Int!
  url: String!
}

type IdResponse {
  id: ID!
}

type Query {
  salesItems: [SalesItem!]!
  salesItem(id: ID!): SalesItem!
}

type Mutation {
```

[24]https://github.com/pksilen/clean-code-principles-python-code/tree/main/chapter6/salesitemservice_graphql

```
  createSalesItem(inputSalesItem: InputSalesItem!): SalesItem!

  updateSalesItem(
    id: ID!,
    inputSalesItem: InputSalesItem
  ): IdResponse!

  deleteSalesItem(id: ID!): IdResponse!
}
`;

export default class GraphQlSalesItemController {
  constructor(private readonly salesItemService: SalesItemService) {}

  getResolvers() {
    return {
      Query: {
        salesItems: this.getSalesItems,
        salesItem: this.getSalesItem,
      },
      Mutation: {
        createSalesItem: this.createSalesItem,
        updateSalesItem: this.updateSalesItem,
        deleteSalesItem: this.deleteSalesItem,
      },
    };
  }

  private getSalesItems = () => this.salesItemService.getSalesItems();
  private getSalesItem = (_, { id }) => this.salesItemService.getSalesItem(id);

  private createSalesItem = async (_, { inputSalesItem: input }) => {
    const inputSalesItem = await transformAndValidate(
      InputSalesItem,
      input as object,
    );

    return this.salesItemService.createSalesItem(inputSalesItem);
  };
  private updateSalesItem = async (_, { id, inputSalesItem: input }) => {
    const inputSalesItem = await transformAndValidate(
      InputSalesItem,
      input as object,
    );

    this.salesItemService.updateSalesItem(id, inputSalesItem);
    return { id };
  };
  private deleteSalesItem = (_, { id }) => {
    this.salesItemService.deleteSalesItem(id);
    return { id };
  };
}
```

Notice in the above code that we must remember to validate the input for the two mutations. We can do that by using transformAndValidate from the class-transformer-validator[25] library.

Currently our model depends on receiving validated input DTOs. There is even a better approach for validating input DTOs. We can validate them in the entity factory. In this case, we could put the validation of InputSalesItem DTOs into the SalesItem class's factory method, SalesItem.from(inputSalesItem: InputSalesItem). This is a very natural place for validation. Validation is now moved from the input adapter

---

[25]https://www.npmjs.com/package/class-transformer-validator

layer (controllers) to the application core/model. If the validation logic is complex, you should create a separate class, InputSalesItemValidator, that can be used in the entity factory method, SalesItem.from.

We should add authorization, audit logging, and metric updates to make the example more production-like. This can be done by creating decorators, for example (not shown here). The decorators can get the request object from the context:

```
const { url } = await startStandaloneServer(server, {
  context: async ({ request }) => ({
    request
  }),
});
```

GraphQL error handling differs from REST API error handling. A GraphQL API responses do not provide different HTTP response status codes. A GraphQL API response is always sent with the status code *200 OK*. When an error occurs while processing a GraphQL API request, the response body object includes an errors array. You should raise an error in your GraphQL type resolvers when a query or mutation fails. You can use the same ApiError base error class used in the earlier REST API example. As shown below, we need to add an error formatter to handle the custom API errors. The error objects should always have a message field. Additional information about the error can be supplied in an extensions object, which can contain any properties.

Suppose a salesItem query results in an EntityNotFoundError. Then the API response would have a null for the data property and errors property present, as shown below:

```
{
  "data": null,
  "errors": [
    {
      "message": "Sales item not found with id 1",
      "extensions": {
        "statusCode": 404,
        "statusText": "Not Found",
        "errorCode": "EntityNotFound",
        "errorDescription": null,
        "stackTrace": null
      }
    }
  ]
}
```

Below is the code for the *index.ts* module containing source code for the error formatter:

Figure 8.25. index.ts

```
import "reflect-metadata";
import { ApolloServer } from "@apollo/server";
import { unwrapResolverError } from "@apollo/server/errors";
import { startStandaloneServer } from "@apollo/server/standalone";
import GraphQlSalesItemController, {
  typeDefs,
} from "./controller/GraphQlSalesItemController";
import SalesItemServiceImpl from "./services/SalesItemServiceImpl";
import PrismaOrmSalesItemRepository from "./repositories/orm/prisma/PrismaOrmSalesItemRepository";
import SalesItemServiceError from "./errors/SalesItemServiceError";
import { createErrorResponse } from "./utils/utils";


const salesItemRepository = new PrismaOrmSalesItemRepository();
const salesItemService = new SalesItemServiceImpl(salesItemRepository);
const controller = new GraphQlSalesItemController(salesItemService);
```

```
const server = new ApolloServer({
  typeDefs,
  resolvers: controller.getResolvers(),
  formatError: (formattedError, graphQlError) => {
    const error = unwrapResolverError(graphQlError);
    const endpoint = formattedError.path?.[0];

    if (error instanceof SalesItemServiceError) {
      const errorResponse = (error as SalesItemServiceError).toResponse(
        endpoint,
      );

      return {
        message: errorResponse.errorMessage,
        extensions: errorResponse,
      };
    } else if ((error as any).constructor.name === "NonErrorThrown") {
      const errorResponse = createErrorResponse(
        new Error((error as any).thrownValue[0].toString()),
        400,
        "RequestValidationError",
        endpoint,
      );

      return {
        message: "Request validation error",
        extensions: errorResponse,
      };
    } else if (error instanceof Error) {
      const errorResponse = createErrorResponse(
        error,
        500,
        "UnspecifiedInternalError",
        endpoint,
      );

      return {
        message: "Unspecified internal error",
        extensions: errorResponse,
      };
    }

    return formattedError;
  },
});

startStandaloneServer(server, {
  listen: { port: 8000 },
});
```

I apologize for the above code containing *a chain of instanceof checks* code smell. What we should do is to move the formatError code to a factory whose create method we give the error as a parameter.

As an alternative to the described error handling mechanism, it is also possible to return an error as a query/mutation return value. This can be done, e.g., by returning a union type from a query or mutation. This approach requires a more complex GraphQL schema and more complex resolvers on the server side. Here is an example:

```
#  ...

type Error {
    message: String!
    # Other possible properties
}

union SalesItemOrError = SalesItem | Error

type Mutation {
  createSalesItem(inputSalesItem: InputSalesItem!): SalesItemOrError!
}
```

In the `createSalesItem` query resolver, you must add a try-except block to handle an error situation and respond with an `Error` object in case of an error.

You can also specify multiple errors:

```
#  ...

type ErrorType1 {
    #  ...
}

type ErrorType2 {
    #  ...
}

type ErrorType3 {
    #  ...
}

union SalesItemOrError = SalesItem | ErrorType1 | ErrorType2 | ErrorType3

type Mutation {
  createSalesItem(inputSalesItem: InputSalesItem!): SalesItemOrError!
}
```

The above example would require making the `createSalesItem` resolvers to catch multiple different errors and responding with an appropriate error object as a result.

Also, the client-side code will be more complex because of the need to handle the different types of responses for a single operation (query/mutation). For example:

```
mutation {
  createSalesItem(inputSalesItem: {
    price: 200
    name: "test sales item"
    images: []
  }) {
    __typename
    ...on SalesItem {
      id,
      createdAtTimestampInMs
    }
    ...on ErrorType1 {
      # Specify fields here
    }
    ...on ErrorType2 {
      # Specify fields here
    }
    ...on ErrorType3 {
      # Specify fields here
    }
  }
}
```

This approach has a downside: the client must still be able to handle possible errors reported in the response's errors array.

In a GraphQL schema, you can add parameters for a primitive (scalar) property. That is useful for implementing conversions. For example, we could define the SalesItem type with a parameterized priceInCents property:

```
enum Currency {
  USD,
  GBP,
  EUR,
  JPY
}
type SalesItem {
  id: ID!
  createdAtTimestampInMs: String!
  name: String!
  priceInCents(currency: Currency = USD): Int!
  images(
    sortByField: String = "rank",
    sortDirection: SortDirection = ASC,
    offset: Int = 0,
    limit: Int = 5
  ): [Image!]!
}
```

Now, clients can supply a currency parameter for the price property in their queries to get the price in different currencies. The default currency is *USD* if no currency parameter is supplied.

Below are two example queries that a client could perform against the earlier defined GraphQL schema:

```
{
  # gets the name, price in euros and the first 5 images
  # for the sales item with id "1"
  salesItem(id: "1") {
    name
    price(currency: EUR)
    images
  }

  # gets the next 5 images for the sales item 1
  salesItem(id: "1") {
    images(offset: 5)
  }
}
```

In real life, consider limiting the fetching of resources only to the previous or the next page (or the next page only if you are implementing infinite scrolling on the client side). Then, clients cannot fetch random pages. This prevents attacks where a malicious user tries to fetch a page with a huge page number (like 10,000, for example), which can cause extra load for the server or, at the extreme, a denial of service.

Below is an example where clients can only query the first, next, or previous page. When a client requests the first page, the page cursor can be empty, but when the client requests the previous or the next page, it must give the current page cursor as a query parameter.

```
type PageOfSalesItems {
  # Contains the page number encrypted and
  # encoded as a Base64 value.
  pageCursor: String!

  salesItems: [SalesItem!]!
}
enum Page {
  FIRST,
  NEXT,
  PREVIOUS
}
type Query {
  pageOfSalesItems(
    page: Page = FIRST,
    pageCursor: String = ""
  ): PageOfSalesItems!
}
```

Then you can use the *type-graphql* NPM library that allows you to write a GraphQL schema using TypeScript classes Below is the InputSalesItem input type from the earlier GraphQL schema represented as a TypeScript class The *type-graphql* library works with most GraphQL server implementations, like *express-graphql* or *apollo-server*.

Figure 8.26. InputSalesItem.ts

```
import { Field, InputType } from 'type-graphql';
import InputImage from './InputImage';

@InputType()
export default class InputSalesItem {
  @Field()
  name: string;

  @Field()
  price: number;

  @Field()
  images: InputImage[];
}
```

Instead of *type-graphql*, you can use the Nest.js web framework. It also allows you to define a GraphQL schema using TypeScript classes, too. The above and below examples are identical, except that some decorators are imported from a different library.

Figure 8.27. InputSalesItem.ts

```
import { Field, Int, InputType } from '@nestjs/graphql';
import InputImage from './InputImage';

@InputType()
export class InputSalesItem {
  @Field()
  name: string;

  @Field()
  price: number;

  images: InputImage[];
}
```

541

Below is an example of a code-first GraphQl controller implemented for Nest.js. In addition to the controller, certain decorators must be present in DTO classes. We discussed those decorators earlier shortly. Input DTOs must be decorated with `@InputType` and output DTOs must be decorated with `@ObjectType`, and each property must have a `@Field` decorator.

Source code for the below example is available here[26].

Figure 8.28. GraphQlSalesItemController.ts

```
import { Inject, UseInterceptors } from '@nestjs/common';
import { Args, Mutation, Query, Resolver } from '@nestjs/graphql';
import OutputSalesItem from '../../dtos/OutputSalesItem';
import SalesItemService from '../../services/SalesItemService';
import InputSalesItem from '../../dtos/InputSalesItem';
import IdResponse from './IdResponse';
import { GraphQlRequestTracer } from './GraphQlRequestTracer';


@UseInterceptors(GraphQlRequestTracer)
// Resolver decorator is needed to define that this class contains
// GraphQL type resolvers
@Resolver()
export default class GraphQlSalesItemController {
  constructor(
    @Inject('salesItemService')
    private readonly salesItemService: SalesItemService,
  ) {}

  // Query type resolvers must have a Query decorator
  @Query(() => [OutputSalesItem])
  async salesItems() {
    return await this.salesItemService.getSalesItems();
  }

  @Query(() => OutputSalesItem)
  async salesItem(@Args('id') id: string) {
    return await this.salesItemService.getSalesItem(id);
  }

  // Mutation type resolvers must have a Mutation decorator
  @Mutation(() => OutputSalesItem)
  async createSalesItem(
    @Args('inputSalesItem')
    inputSalesItem: InputSalesItem,
  ) {
    return this.salesItemService.createSalesItem(inputSalesItem);
  }

  @Mutation(() => IdResponse)
  async updateSalesItem(
    @Args('id') id: string,
    @Args('inputSalesItem') inputSalesItem: InputSalesItem,
  ) {
    await this.salesItemService.updateSalesItem(id, inputSalesItem);
    return { id };
  }

  @Mutation(() => IdResponse)
```

[26]https://github.com/pksilen/clean-code-principles-code/tree/main/chapter6/salesitemservice

```
  async deleteSalesItem(@Args('id') id: string) {
    await this.salesItemService.deleteSalesItem(id);
    return { id };
  }
}
```

We must add authorization, audit logging, and metrics updates to make our GraphQL controller more production-like. We can use Nest.js interceptors and guards in a similar way as for the REST controller. I have provided one interceptor implementation as an example:

Figure 8.29. GraphQlRequestTracer

```
import {
  CallHandler,
  ExecutionContext,
  Inject,
  Injectable,
  NestInterceptor,
} from '@nestjs/common';
import { Observable } from 'rxjs';
import { Logger } from '../../common/logger/Logger';

@Injectable()
export class GraphQlRequestTracer implements NestInterceptor {
  constructor(@Inject('logger') private readonly logger: Logger) {}

  intercept(context: ExecutionContext, next: CallHandler): Observable<any> {
    const query = context.getArgByIndex(2).req.body.query;
    this.logger.log('TRACE', query);
    return next.handle();
  }
}
```

8.1.4: Subscription-Based API Design

Design a subscription-based API when you want clients to be able to subscribe to small, incremental changes to large objects or when clients want to receive low-latency real-time updates.

8.1.4.1: Server-Sent Events (SSE)

Server-Sent Events[27] (SSE) is a uni-directional push technology enabling a client to receive updates from a server via an HTTP connection.

Let's showcase the SSE capabilities with a real-life example with JavaScript and Express.js.

Source code for the below example is available here[28].

---

[27]https://en.wikipedia.org/wiki/Server-sent_events

The below example defines a *subscribe-to-loan-app-summaries* API endpoint for clients to subscribe to loan application summaries. A client will show loan application summaries in a list view in its UI. Whenever a new summary for a loan application is available, the server will send a loan application summary event to clients that will update their UIs by adding a new loan application summary.

Figure 8.30. server.js

```
import express from 'express';
import bodyParser from 'body-parser';
import loanApplicationSummariesSubscriptionHandler
  from './loanApplicationSummariesSubscriptionHandler.js';

const app = express();
app.use(bodyParser.json());
app.use(bodyParser.urlencoded({extended: false}));

app.get('/subscribe-to-loan-application-summaries',
        loanApplicationSummariesSubscriptionHandler);

app.listen(8000);
```

Figure 8.31. subscribers.js

```
import { v4 as uuidv4 } from 'uuid';

export let subscribers = [];

export function addSubscriber(response) {
  const id = uuidv4();

  const subscriber = {
    id,
    response
  };

  subscribers.push(subscriber);
  return id;
}

export function removeSubscriber(id) {
  subscribers = subscribers.filter((subscriber) =>
    subscriber.id !== id);
}
```

Figure 8.32. loanApplicationSummariesSubscriptionHandler.js

```
import { addSubscriber, removeSubscriber } from './subscribers.js';

export default function loanApplicationSummariesSubscriptionHandler(
  request,
  response,
) {
  // Response headers needed for SSE:
  // - Server sent events are identified with
  //   content type 'text/event-stream'
  // - The connection must be kept alive so that server
  //   can send continuously data to client
  // - Server sent events should not be cached
  const headers = {
    'Content-Type': 'text/event-stream',
    Connection: 'keep-alive',
    'Cache-Control': 'no-cache',
```

[28]https://github.com/pksilen/clean-code-principles-code/tree/main/chapter6/sse_backend

```
    // For dev environment you can add CORS header:
    'Access-Control-Allow-Origin': '*',
  };

  response.writeHead(200, headers);

  // Server sent event must be a string beginning with 'data: '
  // and ending with two newline characters
  // First event is empty
  const data = 'data: \n\n';
  response.write(data);
  const subscriberId = addSubscriber(response);
  request.on('close', () => removeSubscriber(subscriberId));
}
```

The below `publishLoanApplicationSummary` function is called whenever the server receives a new loan application summary. The server can receive loan application summaries as messages consumed from a message broker's topic. (This message consumption part is not implemented here, but there is another example later in this chapter demonstrating how messages can be consumed from a Kafka topic.)

Figure 8.33. **publishLoanApplicationSummary.js**

```
import { subscribers } from './subscribers.js';

export default function publishLoanApplicationSummary(
  loanApplicationSummary
) {
  // Send an event to each subscriber
  // Loan application summary data is converted to JSON
  // before sending the event
  // Server sent event must be a string beginning with 'data: '
  // and ending with two newline characters
  const data = JSON.stringify(loanApplicationSummary);
  subscribers.forEach(({ response }) =>
    response.write(`data: ${data}\n\n`));
}
```

Next, we can implement the web client in JavaScript and define the following React functional component:

Source code for the below example is available here[29].

---

[29]https://github.com/pksilen/clean-code-principles-code/tree/main/chapter6/sse_frontend

Figure 8.34. LoanApplicationSummaries.jsx

```
import React, { useEffect, useState } from 'react';

export default function LoanApplicationSummariesView() {
  const [ loanAppSummaries, setLoanAppSummaries ] = useState([]);

  // Define an effect to be executed on component mount
  useEffect(() => {
    // Create new event source
    // Hardcoded dev environment URL is used here for demonstration
    // purposes
    const eventSource =
        new EventSource('http://localhost:8000/subscribe-to-loan-app-summaries');

    // Listen to server sent events and add a new
    // loan application summary to the head of
    // loanAppSummaries array
    eventSource.addEventListener('message', (messageEvent) => {
      try {
        const loanAppSummary = JSON.parse(messageEvent.data);

        if (loanAppSummary) {
          setLoanAppSummaries([loanAppSummary, ...loanAppSummaries]);
        }
      } catch {
        // Handle error
      }
    });

    eventSource.addEventListener('error', (errorEvent) => {
      // Handle error
    });

    // Close the event source on component unmount
    return function cleanup() { eventSource.close(); }
  }, [loanAppSummaries]);

  // Render loan application summary list items
  const loanAppSummaryListItems =
      loanAppSummaries.map(({id}) =>
          (<li key={id}>{id}</li>));

  return (
      <ul>{loanAppSummaryListItems}</ul>
  );
}
```

8.1.4.2: GraphQL Subscriptions

Let's have an example of a GraphQL subscription. The below GraphQL schema defines one subscription for a post's comments. It is not relevant what a post is. It can be a blog post or social media post, for example. We want a client to be able to subscribe to a post's comments.

```
type PostComment {
  id: ID!,
  text: String!
}

type Subscription {
  postComment(postId: ID!): PostComment
}
```

On the client side, we can define a subscription named postCommentText that subscribes to a post's comments and returns the text property of comments:

```
import { gql } from '@apollo/client';

const POST_COMMENT_SUBSCRIPTION = gql`
  subscription postCommentText($postId: ID!) {
    postComment(postID: $postId) {
      text
    }
  }
`;
```

If a client executes the above query for a particular post (defined with the postId parameter), the following kind of response can be expected:

```
{
  "data": {
    "postComment": {
      "text": "Nice post!"
    }
  }
}
```

To be able to use GraphQL subscriptions, you must implement support for them both on the server and client side. For the server side, you can find instructions for the *Apollo server* here: https://www. apollographql.com/docs/apollo-server/data/subscriptions/#enabling-subscriptions. And for the client side, you can find instructions for the *Apollo client* here: https://www.apollographql.com/docs/react/data/subscriptions/#setting-up-the-transport

After the server and client-side support for subscriptions are implemented, you can use the subscription in your React component:

Figure 8.35. SubscribedPostCommentsView.jsx

```
import { useState } from 'react';
import { gql, useSubscription } from '@apollo/client';

const POST_COMMENT_SUBSCRIPTION = gql`
  subscription subscribeToPostComment($postId: ID!) {
    postComment(postID: $postId) {
      id
      text
    }
  }
`;

export default function SubscribedPostCommentsView({ postId }) {
  const [ postComments, setPostComments ] = useState([]);

  const { data } = useSubscription(POST_COMMENT_SUBSCRIPTION,
                                   { variables: { postId } });
```

```
if (data?.postComment) {
  setPostComments([...postComments, data.postComment]);
}

const postCommentListItems =
  postComments.map(( { id, text }) =>
    (<li key={id}>{text}</li>));

return <ul>{postCommentListItems}</ul>;
}
```

8.1.5: WebSocket Example

Below is a chat messaging application consisting of a WebSocket server implemented with Node.js and the ws[30] NPM library and a WebSocket client implemented with React. There can be multiple instances of the server running. These instances are stateless except for storing WebSocket connections for locally connected clients.

We implement the example using the *clean architecture principle*, as shown in the picture below.

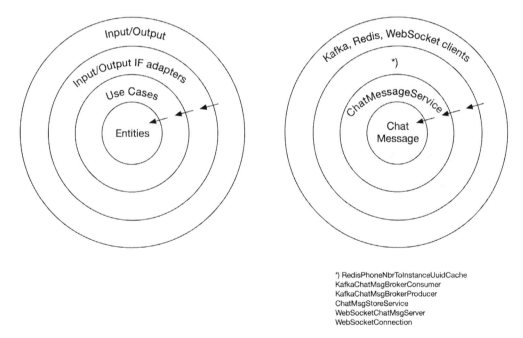

*) RedisPhoneNbrToInstanceUuidCache
KafkaChatMsgBrokerConsumer
KafkaChatMsgBrokerProducer
ChatMsgStoreService
WebSocketChatMsgServer
WebSocketConnection

Figure 8.36. WebSocket Example Clean Architecture

On the interface adapter layer, we have multiple interface adapters:

- RedisPhoneNbrToInstanceUuidCache

[30]https://www.npmjs.com/package/ws

- KafkaChatMsgBrokerAdminClient
- KafkaChatMsgBrokerAdminProducer
- KafkaChatMsgBrokerAdminConsumer
- ChatMsgStoreService
- WebSocketChatMsgServer
- WebSocketConnection

The above classes depend on the microservice model, which consists of `ChatMessageService` and `ChatMessage`. The `RedisPhoneNbrToInstanceUuidCache` implements the `PhoneNbrToInstanceUuidCache` interface and is responsible for storing the chat server instance UUID for each end-user (according to their phone number). The `KafkaChatMsgBrokerAdminProducer` implements the `ChatMsgBrokerAdminProducer` interface and is responsible for sending a chat message to Kafka to be handled by another chat server instance. The `KafkaChatMsgBrokerAdminConsumer` implements the `ChatMsgBrokerAdminConsumer` interface and is responsible for reading chat messages belonging to the particular chat server from the Kafka. The `ChatMsgStoreService` is responsible for contacting a remote *chat-message-store-service* for persistent storage of chat messages. The `WebSocketChatMsgServer` implements a chat message server using WebSocket protocol and is responsible for creating `WebSocketConnection` instances.

First, we list the source code files for the server side.

> Source code for the below example is available here[31].

A new Kafka client is created using the kafkajs[32] NPM library:

Figure 8.37. kafkaClient.ts"

```
import { Kafka } from 'kafkajs';

const kafkaClient = new Kafka({
  clientId: 'app-y',
  brokers: [process.env.KAFKA_BROKER ?? 'localhost:9094'],
});

export default kafkaClient;
```

A new Redis client is created using the ioredis[33] NPM library:

---

[31] https://github.com/pksilen/clean-code--python-code/tree/main/chapter6/chatmsgserver_backend
[32] https://www.npmjs.com/package/kafkajs
[33] https://www.npmjs.com/package/ioredis

Figure 8.38. redisClient.ts

```
import Redis from 'ioredis';


const redisClient = new Redis({
  port: parseInt(process.env.REDIS_PORT ?? '6379', 10),
  host: process.env.REDIS_HOST,
  username: process.env.REDIS_USERNAME,
  password: process.env.REDIS_PASSWORD,
});


export default redisClient;
```

The below `KafkaMessageBrokerAdminClient` class implementing the `ChatMsgBrokerAdminClient` interface is used to create topics in Kafka:

Figure 8.39. ChatMsgServerError.ts

```
export default class ChatMsgServerError extends Error {
}
```

Figure 8.40. ChatMsgBrokerAdminClient.ts

```
export default interface ChatMsgBrokerAdminClient {
  tryCreateTopic(name: string): Promise<void>;
}
```

Figure 8.41. AbstractChatMsgBrokerAdminClient.ts

```
import ChatMsgBrokerAdminClient from './ChatMsgBrokerAdminClient';
import ChatMsgServerError from '../../errors/ChatMsgServerError';


export default abstract class AbstractChatMsgBrokerAdminClient
  implements ChatMsgBrokerAdminClient
{
  static CreateTopicError = class extends ChatMsgServerError {};

  abstract tryCreateTopic(name: string): Promise<void>;
}
```

Figure 8.42. KafkaChatMsgBrokerAdminClient.ts

```
import { Admin, Kafka } from 'kafkajs';
import AbstractChatMsgBrokerAdminClient from './AbstractChatMsgBrokerAdminClient';


export default class KafkaChatMsgBrokerAdminClient extends AbstractChatMsgBrokerAdminClient {
  private readonly kafkaAdminClient: Admin;

  constructor(kafkaClient: Kafka) {
    super();
    this.kafkaAdminClient = kafkaClient.admin();
  }

  async tryCreateTopic(name: string): Promise<void> {
    try {
      await this.kafkaAdminClient.connect();

      await this.kafkaAdminClient.createTopics({
```

```
      topics: [{ topic: name }],
    });

    await this.kafkaAdminClient.disconnect();
  } catch {
    throw new KafkaChatMsgBrokerAdminClient.CreateTopicError();
  }
  }
}
```

Users of the chat messaging application are identified with phone numbers. On the server side, we store the connection for each user in the phoneNbrToConnMap:

Figure 8.43. phoneNbrToConnMap.ts

```
import Connection from './Connection';


const phoneNbrToConnMap = new Map<string, Connection>();
export default phoneNbrToConnMap;
```

Figure 8.44. Connection.ts

```
export default interface Connection {
  send(message: string): void;
}
```

Figure 8.45. WebSocketConnection.ts

```
import WebSocket from 'ws';
import AbstractConnection from './AbstractConnection';


export default class WebSocketConnection extends AbstractConnection {
  constructor(private readonly webSocket: WebSocket) {
    super();
  }

  send(message: string): void {
    this.webSocket.send(message);
  }
}
```

The below WebSocketChatMsgServer class handles the construction of a WebSocket server. The server accepts connections from clients. When it receives a chat message from a client, it will first parse and validate it. If the received chat message contains only sender phone number, the server will register a new user. For an actual chat message, the server will delegate to ChatMsgService that will store the message in persistent storage (using a separate *chat-message-service* REST API, not implemented here). The ChatMsgService gets the recipient's server information from a Redis cache and sends the chat message to the recipient's WebSocket connection or produces the chat message to a Kafka topic where another server instance can consume the chat message and send it to the recipient's WebSocket connection. The Redis cache stores a hash map where the users' phone numbers are mapped to the server instance they are currently connected. A UUID identifies a server instance.

Figure 8.46. WebSocketChatMsgServer.ts

```ts
import WebSocket, { WebSocketServer } from 'ws';
import phoneNbrToConnMap from '../connection/phoneNbrToConnMap';
import { ChatMessage } from '../service/ChatMessage';
import WebSocketConnection from '../connection/WebSocketConnection';
import PhoneNbrToServerUuidCache from '../cache/PhoneNbrToServerUuidCache';
import RedisPhoneNbrToServerUuidCache from '../cache/RedisPhoneNbrToServerUuidCache';
import redisClient from '../cache/redisClient';
import { ChatMsgService } from '../service/ChatMsgService';


export default class WebSocketChatMsgServer {
  private readonly webSocketServer: WebSocketServer;

  private readonly cache: PhoneNbrToServerUuidCache =
    new RedisPhoneNbrToServerUuidCache(redisClient);

  private readonly wsToPhoneNbrMap = new Map<WebSocket, string>();

  constructor(
    private readonly serverUuid: string,
    private readonly chatMsgService: ChatMsgService,
  ) {
    this.webSocketServer = new WebSocketServer({ port: 8000 });

    this.webSocketServer.on('connection', (webSocket: WebSocket) => {
      webSocket.on('message', async (chatMessageJson) => {
        let chatMessage: ChatMessage;

        try {
          // Validate chat message JSON ...
          chatMessage = JSON.parse(chatMessageJson.toString());
        } catch {
          // Handle error
          return;
        }

        phoneNbrToConnMap.set(
          chatMessage.senderPhoneNbr,
          new WebSocketConnection(webSocket),
        );

        this.wsToPhoneNbrMap.set(webSocket, chatMessage.senderPhoneNbr);

        try {
          await this.cache.tryStore(
            chatMessage.senderPhoneNbr,
            this.serverUuid,
          );
        } catch (error) {
          // Handle error
        }

        if (chatMessage.message) {
          await this.chatMsgService.trySend(chatMessage);
        }
      });

      webSocket.on('error', () => {
        // Handle error ...
      });

      webSocket.on('close', async () => {
        await this.close(webSocket);
      });
    });
  }

  closeServer() {
```

```
      this.webSocketServer.close();
      this.webSocketServer.clients.forEach((client) => client.close());
    }

  async close(webSocket: WebSocket) {
    const phoneNumber = this.wsToPhoneNbrMap.get(webSocket);

    if (phoneNumber) {
      phoneNbrToConnMap.delete(phoneNumber);

      try {
        await this.cache.tryRemove(phoneNumber);
      } catch (error) {
        // Handle error
      }
    }

    this.wsToPhoneNbrMap.delete(webSocket);
  }
}
```

Figure 8.47. PhoneNbrToServerUuidCache.ts

```
export default interface PhoneNbrToServerUuidCache {
  retrieveServerUuid(phoneNumber: string | undefined): Promise<string | null>;
  tryStore(phoneNumber: string, serverUuid: string): Promise<void>;
  tryRemove(phoneNumber: string): Promise<void>;
}
```

Figure 8.48. AbstractPhoneNbrToServerUuidCache.ts

```
import PhoneNbrToServerUuidCache from './PhoneNbrToServerUuidCache';
import ChatMsgServerError from '../errors/ChatMsgServerError';

export default abstract class AbstractPhoneNbrToServerUuidCache
  implements PhoneNbrToServerUuidCache
{
  static Error = class extends ChatMsgServerError {};

  abstract retrieveServerUuid(
    phoneNumber: string | undefined,
  ): Promise<string | null>;

  abstract tryStore(phoneNumber: string, instanceUuid: string): Promise<void>;
  abstract tryRemove(phoneNumber: string): Promise<void>;
}
```

Figure 8.49. RedisPhoneNbrToServerUuidCache.ts

```
import Redis from 'ioredis';
import AbstractPhoneNbrToServerUuidCache from './AbstractPhoneNbrToServerUuidCache';

export default class RedisPhoneNbrToServerUuidCache extends AbstractPhoneNbrToServerUuidCache {
  constructor(private readonly redisClient: Redis) {
    super();
  }

  async retrieveServerUuid(
    phoneNumber: string | undefined,
  ): Promise<string | null> {
    let serverUuid: string | null = null;
```

```
    if (phoneNumber) {
      try {
        serverUuid = await this.redisClient.hget(
          'phoneNbrToServerUuidMap',
          phoneNumber,
        );
      } catch {
        // Handle error
      }
    }

    return serverUuid;
  }

  async tryStore(phoneNumber: string, serverUuid: string): Promise<void> {
    try {
      await this.redisClient.hset(
        'phoneNbrToServerUuidMap',
        phoneNumber,
        serverUuid,
      );
    } catch {
      // Handle error
    }
  }

  async tryRemove(phoneNumber: string): Promise<void> {
    try {
      await this.redisClient.hdel('phoneNbrToServerUuidMap', phoneNumber);
    } catch {
      // Handle error
    }
  }
}
```

Figure 8.50. ChatMsgBrokerProducer.ts

```
import { ChatMessage } from '../../service/ChatMessage';


export default interface ChatMsgBrokerProducer {
  tryProduce(chatMessage: ChatMessage, topic: string): Promise<void>;
  tryClose(): Promise<void>;
}
```

Figure 8.51. AbstractChatMsgBrokerProducer.ts

```
import ChatMsgBrokerProducer from './ChatMsgBrokerProducer';
import ChatMsgServerError from '../../errors/ChatMsgServerError';
import { ChatMessage } from '../../service/ChatMessage';


export default abstract class AbstractChatMsgBrokerProducer
  implements ChatMsgBrokerProducer
{
  static Error = class extends ChatMsgServerError {};

  abstract tryProduce(chatMessage: ChatMessage, topic: string): Promise<void>;
  abstract tryClose(): Promise<void>;
}
```

Figure 8.52. KafkaChatMsgBrokerProducer.ts

```ts
import { Kafka, Producer } from 'kafkajs';
import AbstractChatMsgBrokerProducer from './AbstractChatMsgBrokerProducer';
import { ChatMessage } from '../../service/ChatMessage';

export default class KafkaChatMsgBrokerProducer extends AbstractChatMsgBrokerProducer {
  private readonly kafkaProducer: Producer;

  constructor(kafkaClient: Kafka) {
    super();
    this.kafkaProducer = kafkaClient.producer();
  }

  async tryProduce(chatMessage: ChatMessage, topic: string): Promise<void> {
    try {
      await this.kafkaProducer.connect();

      await this.kafkaProducer.send({
        topic,
        messages: [{ value: JSON.stringify(chatMessage) }],
      });
    } catch {
      // Handle error
    }
  }

  async tryClose(): Promise<void> {
    try {
      await this.kafkaProducer.disconnect();
    } catch {
      // Handle error
    }
  }
}
```

The `KafkaMessageBrokerConsumer` class defines a Kafka consumer that consumes chat messages from a particular Kafka topic and sends them to the recipient's WebSocket connection:

Figure 8.53. ChatMsgBrokerConsumer.ts

```ts
export default interface ChatMsgBrokerConsumer {
  consumeChatMessages(topic: string): Promise<void>;
  close(): Promise<void>;
}
```

Figure 8.54. KafkaChatMsgBrokerConsumer.ts

```ts
import { Consumer, Kafka } from 'kafkajs';
import ChatMsgBrokerConsumer from './ChatMsgBrokerConsumer';
import { ChatMsgService } from '../../service/ChatMsgService';

export default class KafkaChatMsgBrokerConsumer
  implements ChatMsgBrokerConsumer
{
  private readonly kafkaConsumer: Consumer;

  constructor(
    kafkaClient: Kafka,
    private readonly chatMsgService: ChatMsgService,
  ) {
    this.kafkaConsumer = kafkaClient.consumer({ groupId: 'chat-msg-server' });
  }
```

```
async consumeChatMessages(topic: string): Promise<void> {
  await this.kafkaConsumer.connect();

  await this.kafkaConsumer.subscribe({
    topic,
    fromBeginning: true,
  });

  this.kafkaConsumer.run({
    eachMessage: async ({ message }) => {
      try {
        if (message.value) {
          const chatMessage = JSON.parse(message.value.toString());
          this.chatMsgService.trySend(chatMessage);
        }
      } catch {
        // Handle error
      }
    },
  });
}

async close(): Promise<void> {
  try {
    await this.kafkaConsumer.disconnect();
  } catch {}
}
}
```

Below is the implementation of `ChatMsgService`:

Figure 8.55. ChatMessage.ts

```
export type ChatMessage = {
  senderPhoneNbr: string;
  recipientPhoneNbr: string;
  message: string;
};
```

Figure 8.56. ChatMsgService.ts

```
import { ChatMessage } from './ChatMessage';


export interface ChatMsgService {
  trySend(chatMessage: ChatMessage): Promise<void>;
}
```

Figure 8.57. ChatMsgServiceImpl.ts

```
import { ChatMsgService } from './ChatMsgService';
import KafkaChatMsgBrokerProducer from '../broker/producer/KafkaChatMsgBrokerProducer';
import kafkaClient from '../broker/kafkaClient';
import { ChatMessage } from './ChatMessage';
import PhoneNbrToServerUuidCache from '../cache/PhoneNbrToServerUuidCache';
import RedisPhoneNbrToServerUuidCache from '../cache/RedisPhoneNbrToServerUuidCache';
import redisClient from '../cache/redisClient';
import phoneNbrToConnMap from '../connection/phoneNbrToConnMap';


export default class ChatMsgServiceImpl implements ChatMsgService {
  private readonly chatMsgBrokerProducer = new KafkaChatMsgBrokerProducer(
```

```
    kafkaClient,
  );

  private readonly cache: PhoneNbrToServerUuidCache =
    new RedisPhoneNbrToServerUuidCache(redisClient);

  constructor(private readonly serverUuid: string) {}

  async trySend(chatMessage: ChatMessage): Promise<void> {
    const recipientServerUuid = await this.cache.retrieveServerUuid(
      chatMessage.recipientPhoneNbr,
    );

    if (recipientServerUuid === this.serverUuid) {
      // Recipient has active connection on
      // the same server instance as sender
      const recipientConnection = phoneNbrToConnMap.get(
        chatMessage.recipientPhoneNbr,
      );

      recipientConnection?.send(JSON.stringify(chatMessage));
    } else if (recipientServerUuid) {
      // Recipient has active connection on different
      // server instance compared to sender
      const topic = recipientServerUuid;
      await this.chatMsgBrokerProducer.tryProduce(chatMessage, topic);
    }
  }
}
```

Finally, we put it all together in the *app.ts* file:

Figure 8.58. app.ts

```
import { v4 as uuidv4 } from 'uuid';
import kafkaClient from './src/broker/kafkaClient';
import KafkaChatMsgBrokerAdminClient from './src/broker/adminclient/KafkaChatMsgBrokerAdminClient';
import WebSocketChatMsgServer from './src/server/WebSocketChatMsgServer';
import KafkaChatMsgBrokerConsumer from './src/broker/consumer/KafkaChatMsgBrokerConsumer';
import ChatMsgServiceImpl from './src/service/ChatMsgServiceImpl';


const serverUuid = uuidv4();
const topic = serverUuid;

new KafkaChatMsgBrokerAdminClient(kafkaClient)
  .tryCreateTopic(topic)
  .then(async () => {
    const chatMsgService = new ChatMsgServiceImpl(serverUuid);

    const chatMsgServer = new WebSocketChatMsgServer(
      serverUuid,
      chatMsgService,
    );

    const chatMsgBrokerConsumer = new KafkaChatMsgBrokerConsumer(
      kafkaClient,
      chatMsgService,
    );

    await chatMsgBrokerConsumer.consumeChatMessages(topic);

    function prepareExit() {
      chatMsgServer.closeServer();
      chatMsgBrokerConsumer.close();
    }

    process.once('SIGINT', prepareExit);
```

```
    process.once('SIGQUIT', prepareExit);
    process.once('SIGTERM', prepareExit);
  })
  .catch(() => {
    // Handle error
  });
```

For the web client, we have the below code.

Source code for the below example is available here[34].

An instance of the `ChatMessagingService` class connects to a chat messaging server via WebSocket. It listens to messages received from the server and dispatches an action upon receiving a chat message. The class also offers a method for sending a chat message to the server.

Figure 8.59. ChatMessagingService.js

```
import store from "./store";

class ChatMessagingService {
  wsConnection;
  connectionIsOpen = false;
  lastChatMessage;

  constructor(dispatch, userPhoneNbr) {
    this.wsConnection =
      new WebSocket(`ws://localhost:8000`);

    this.wsConnection.addEventListener('open', () => {
      this.connectionIsOpen = true;
      this.send( {
        senderPhoneNbr: userPhoneNbr
      })
    });

    this.wsConnection.addEventListener('error', () => {
      this.lastChatMessage = null;
    });

    this.wsConnection.addEventListener(
      'message',
      ({ data: chatMessageJson }) => {
        const chatMessage = JSON.parse(chatMessageJson);

        store.dispatch({
          type: 'receivedChatMessageAction',
          chatMessage
        });
      });

    this.wsConnection.addEventListener('close', () => {
      this.connectionIsOpen = false;
    });
  }
```

```
  send(chatMessage) {
    this.lastChatMessage = chatMessage;

    if (this.connectionIsOpen) {
        this.wsConnection.send(JSON.stringify(chatMessage));
    } else  {
      // Send message to REST API
    }
  }

  close() {
    this.connectionIsOpen = false;
    this.wsConnection.close();
  }
}

export let chatMessagingService;

export default function createChatMessagingService(
  userPhoneNbr
) {
  chatMessagingService =
    new ChatMessagingService(store.dispatch, userPhoneNbr);

  return chatMessagingService;
}
```

Figure 8.60. index.jsx

```
import React from 'react';
import ReactDOM from 'react-dom/client';
import { Provider } from 'react-redux'
import ChatAppView from './ChatAppView';
import store from './store'
import './index.css';


const root = ReactDOM.createRoot(document.getElementById('root'));

root.render(
  <Provider store={store}>
    <ChatAppView/>
  </Provider>
);
```

The chat application view ChatAppView parses the user's and contact's phone numbers from the URL and then renders a chat view between the user and the contact:

Figure 8.61. ChatAppView.jsx

```
import React, { useEffect } from 'react';
import queryString from "query-string";
import ContactChatView from "./ContactChatView";
import createChatMessagingService from "./ChatMessagingService";


const { userPhoneNbr, contactPhoneNbr } =
  queryString.parse(window.location.search);

export default function ChatAppView() {
  useEffect(() => {
    const chatMessagingService =
      createChatMessagingService(userPhoneNbr);

    return function cleanup() {
```

```
      chatMessagingService.close();
    }
  }, []);

  return (
    <div>
      User: {userPhoneNbr}
      <ContactChatView
        userPhoneNbr={userPhoneNbr}
        contactPhoneNbr={contactPhoneNbr}
      />
    </div>
  );
}
```

The ContactChatView component renders chat messages between a user and a contact:

Figure 8.62. ContactChatView.jsx

```
import React, { useRef } from 'react';
import { connect } from "react-redux";
import store from './store';


function ContactChatView({
  userPhoneNbr,
  contactPhoneNbr,
  chatMessages
}) {
  const inputElement = useRef(null);

  function sendChatMessage() {
    if (inputElement?.current.value) {
      store.dispatch({
        type: 'sendChatMessageAction',
        chatMessage: {
          senderPhoneNbr: userPhoneNbr,
          recipientPhoneNbr: contactPhoneNbr,
          message: inputElement.current.value
        }
      });
    }
  }

  const chatMessageElements = chatMessages
    .map(({ message, senderPhoneNbr }, index) => {
      const messageIsReceived =
        senderPhoneNbr === contactPhoneNbr;

      return (
        <li
          key={index}
          className={messageIsReceived ? 'received' : 'sent'}>
            {message}
        </li>
      );
    });

  return (
    <div className="contactChatView">
      Contact: {contactPhoneNbr}
      <ul>{chatMessageElements}</ul>
      <input ref={inputElement}/>
      <button onClick={sendChatMessage}>Send</button>
    </div>
  );
}
```

```
function mapStateToProps(state) {
  return {
    chatMessages: state
  };
}

export default connect(mapStateToProps)(ContactChatView);
```

Figure 8.63. store.js

```
import { createStore } from 'redux';
import { chatMessagingService } from "./ChatMessagingService";

function chatMessagesReducer(state = [], { type, chatMessage }) {
  switch (type) {
    case 'receivedChatMessageAction':
      return state.concat([chatMessage]);
    case 'sendChatMessageAction':
      chatMessagingService.send(chatMessage);
      return state.concat([chatMessage]);
    default:
      return state;
  }
}

const store = createStore(chatMessagesReducer)
export default store;
```

Figure 8.64. index.css

```
.contactChatView {
  width: 420px;
}

.contactChatView ul {
  padding-inline-start: 0;
  list-style-type: none;
}

.contactChatView li {
  margin-top: 15px;
  width: fit-content;
  max-width: 180px;
  padding: 10px;
  border: 1px solid #888;
  border-radius: 20px;
}

.contactChatView li.received {
  margin-right: auto;
}

.contactChatView li.sent {
  margin-left: auto;
}
```

User: 0504877334
Contact: 0501234567

fsfd

111

2222

3333

sdfsdfdsf
fsadfsdafsdfsdafsdafsdf

sdfsdafdsafsda
fsdafsadfsdafsadf s
fsadfsdafas afsdf

| sdfsdfdsf fsadfsdafsdfsdafsd | Send |

Figure 8.65. Chat Messaging Application Views for Two Users

User: 0501234567
Contact: 0504877334

111

2222

3333

sdfsdfdsf
fsadfsdafsdfsdafsdafsdf

sdfsdafdsafsda
fsdafsadfsdafsadf s
fsadfsdafas afsdf

sdfsdafdsafsda fsdafsadfsda | Send

Figure 8.66. Chat Messaging Application Views for Two Users

You can also create a Nest.js WebSocket[35] controller for the *sales item service* API:

Source code for the below example is available here[36].

---

[35] https://docs.nestjs.com/websockets/gateways
[36] https://github.com/pksilen/clean-code-principles-code/tree/main/chapter6/salesitemservice

Figure 8.67. WebSocketSalesItemController.ts

```ts
import { transformAndValidate } from 'class-transformer-validator';
import { Inject, UseFilters, UseInterceptors } from '@nestjs/common';
import {
  MessageBody,
  SubscribeMessage,
  WebSocketGateway,
} from '@nestjs/websockets';
import InputSalesItem from '../../dtos/InputSalesItem';
import SalesItemService from '../../services/SalesItemService';
import { WebSocketErrorFilter } from './WebSocketErrorFilter';
import { WebSocketRequestTracer } from './WebSocketRequestTracer';


@UseInterceptors(WebSocketRequestTracer)
@UseFilters(new WebSocketErrorFilter())
// Defines a WebSocket gateway running on port 8001
@WebSocketGateway(8001, { cors: true })
export default class WebSocketSalesItemController {
  constructor(
    @Inject('salesItemService')
    private readonly salesItemService: SalesItemService,
  ) {}

  @SubscribeMessage('createSalesItem')
  async createSalesItem(@MessageBody() data: object) {
    const inputSalesItem = await transformAndValidate(InputSalesItem, data);
    return this.salesItemService.createSalesItem(inputSalesItem);
  }

  @SubscribeMessage('getSalesItems')
  getSalesItems() {
    return this.salesItemService.getSalesItems();
  }

  @SubscribeMessage('getSalesItem')
  getSalesItem(@MessageBody() data: string) {
    return this.salesItemService.getSalesItem(data);
  }

  @SubscribeMessage('updateSalesItem')
  async updateSalesItem(@MessageBody() data: object) {
    const inputSalesItem = await transformAndValidate(InputSalesItem, data);

    await this.salesItemService.updateSalesItem(
      (inputSalesItem as any).id,
      inputSalesItem,
    );

    return '';
  }

  @SubscribeMessage('deleteSalesItem')
  async deleteSalesItem(@MessageBody() data: string) {
    await this.salesItemService.deleteSalesItem(data);
    return '';
  }
}
```

Here is an example JSON message that a WebSocket client could send to get a single sales item with a specific id:

```
{
  "event": "getSalesItem",
  "data": "48fc99f1-fef6-43d2-afdc-57331a2aad02"
}
```

More examples are available in the GitHub repo in the *salesitemservice_websocket.http* file.

8.2: Inter-Microservice API Design Principles

Inter-microservice APIs can be divided into two categories based on the type of communication: synchronous and asynchronous. Synchronous communication should be used when an immediate response to an issued request is expected. Asynchronous communication can be used when no response to a request is expected or the response is not immediately required.

8.2.1: Synchronous API Design Principle

Use HTTP-based RPC or REST APIs with JSON data encoding, preferably with HTTP/2 or HTTP/3 transport, when requests and responses are not very large and do not contain much binary data. Suppose you have large requests or responses or a lot of binary data. In that case, you are better off encoding the data in Avro binary format (Content-Type: avro/binary) instead of JSON or using a gRPC-based API. gRPC always encodes data in a binary format (Protocol Buffers).

8.2.1.1: gRPC-Based API Design Example

Let's have an example of a gRPC-based API.

Source code for the below example is available here[37].

First, we must define the needed Protocol Buffers types. They are defined in a file named with the extension *.proto*. The syntax of *proto* files is pretty simple. We define the service by listing the remote procedures. A remote procedure is defined with the following syntax: `rpc <procedure-name> (<argument-type>) returns (<return-type>) {}`. A type is defined with the below syntax:

```
message <type-name> {
  <field-type> <field-name> [= <field-index>];
  ...
}
```

[37]https://github.com/pksilen/clean-code-principles-code/tree/main/chapter6/salesitemservice

Figure 8.68. sales_item_service.proto

```
syntax = "proto3";

option objc_class_prefix = "SIS";

package salesitemservice;

service SalesItemService {
  rpc createSalesItem (InputSalesItem) returns (OutputSalesItem) {}
  rpc getSalesItems (GetSalesItemsArg) returns (OutputSalesItems) {}
  rpc getSalesItem (Id) returns (OutputSalesItem) {}
  rpc updateSalesItem (SalesItemUpdate) returns (Nothing) {}
  rpc deleteSalesItem (Id) returns (Nothing) {}
}

message GetSalesItemsArg {
  optional string sortByField = 1;
  optional string sortDirection = 2;
  optional uint64 offset = 3;
  optional uint64 limit = 4;
}

message Nothing {}

message InputSalesItemImage {
  uint32 rank = 1;
  string url = 2;
}

message InputSalesItem {
  string name = 1;
  uint32 priceInCents = 2;
  repeated InputSalesItemImage images = 3;
}

message SalesItemUpdate {
  string id = 1;
  string name = 2;
  uint32 priceInCents = 3;
  repeated InputSalesItemImage images = 4;
}

message OutputSalesItemImage {
  string id = 1;
  uint32 rank = 2;
  string url = 3;
}

message OutputSalesItem {
  string id = 1;
  uint64 createdAtTimestampInMs = 2;
  string name = 3;
  uint32 priceInCents = 4;
  repeated OutputSalesItemImage images = 5;
}

message Id {
  string id = 1;
}

message OutputSalesItems {
  repeated OutputSalesItem salesItems = 1;
}

message ErrorDetails {
  optional string code = 1;
  optional string description = 2;
  optional string stackTrace = 3;
}
```

Below is a gRPC controller for the *sales item service* API:

Figure 8.69. GrpcSalesItemController.ts

```typescript
import { transformAndValidate } from 'class-transformer-validator';
import SalesItemService from '../../services/SalesItemService';
import InputSalesItem from '../../dtos/InputSalesItem';
import { createGrpcErrorResponse } from '../../common/utils/utils';


export default class GrpcSalesItemController {
  constructor(private readonly salesItemService: SalesItemService) {}

  getRequestHandlers() {
    return {
      getSalesItems: this.getSalesItems,
      getSalesItem: this.getSalesItem,
      createSalesItem: this.createSalesItem,
      updateSalesItem: this.updateSalesItem,
      deleteSalesItem: this.deleteSalesItem,
    };
  }

  private getSalesItems = async (rpc, callback) => {
    try {
      callback(null, {
        salesItems: await this.salesItemService.getSalesItems(),
      });
    } catch (error) {
      this.respondWithError(rpc.path, error, callback);
    }
  };

  private getSalesItem = async (rpc, callback) => {
    try {
      callback(null, await this.salesItemService.getSalesItem(rpc.request.id));
    } catch (error) {
      this.respondWithError(rpc.path, error, callback);
    }
  };

  private createSalesItem = async (rpc, callback) => {
    try {
      const inputSalesItem = await transformAndValidate(
        InputSalesItem,
        rpc.request as object,
      );

      callback(
        null,
        await this.salesItemService.createSalesItem(inputSalesItem),
      );
    } catch (error) {
      this.respondWithError(rpc.path, error, callback);
    }
  };

  private updateSalesItem = async (rpc, callback) => {
    try {
      const inputSalesItem = await transformAndValidate(
        InputSalesItem,
        rpc.request as object,
      );

      await this.salesItemService.updateSalesItem(
        rpc.request.id,
        inputSalesItem,
      );
      callback(null, undefined);
    } catch (error) {
```

```
        this.respondWithError(rpc.path, error, callback);
      }
    };

    private deleteSalesItem = async (rpc, callback) => {
      try {
        await this.salesItemService.deleteSalesItem(rpc.request.id);
        callback(null, undefined);
      } catch (error) {
        this.respondWithError(rpc.path, error, callback);
      }
    };

    private respondWithError(endpoint: string, error: Error, callback) {
      // Function createGrpcErrorResponse is implemented in utils.ts file
      // in the GitHub repo
      callback(createGrpcErrorResponse(endpoint, error));
    }
}
```

Below is the gRPC server implementation that dynamically loads Protocol Buffers definition from the *sales_-item_service.proto* file:

Figure 8.70. grpcServer.ts

```
import GrpcSalesItemController from './controllers/grpc/GrpcSalesItemController';
import {
  loadPackageDefinition,
  Server,
  ServerCredentials,
} from '@grpc/grpc-js';
import { loadSync } from '@grpc/proto-loader';
import SalesItemServiceImpl from './services/SalesItemServiceImpl';
import PrismaOrmSalesItemRepository from './repositories/orm/prisma/PrismaOrmSalesItemRepository';


const PROTO_PATH = __dirname + '/controllers/grpc/sales_item_service.proto';

const packageDefinition = loadSync(PROTO_PATH, {
  keepCase: true,
  longs: String,
  enums: String,
  defaults: true,
  oneofs: true,
});

const salesitemservice =
  loadPackageDefinition(packageDefinition).salesitemservice;

const salesItemRepository = new PrismaOrmSalesItemRepository();
const salesItemService = new SalesItemServiceImpl(salesItemRepository);
const grpcSalesItemController = new GrpcSalesItemController(salesItemService);
const grpcServer = new Server();

grpcServer.addService(
  (salesitemservice as any).SalesItemService.service,
  grpcSalesItemController.getRequestHandlers() as any,
);

grpcServer.bindAsync(
  '0.0.0.0:50051',
  ServerCredentials.createInsecure(),
  () => {
    // Handle error
  },
);
```

Below is an example gRPC client to use with the above gRPC server:

Figure 8.71. grpcClient.ts

```typescript
import { credentials, loadPackageDefinition } from '@grpc/grpc-js';
import { loadSync } from '@grpc/proto-loader';


const PROTO_PATH = __dirname + '/controllers/grpc/sales_item_service.proto';

const packageDefinition = loadSync(PROTO_PATH, {
  keepCase: true,
  longs: String,
  enums: String,
  defaults: true,
  oneofs: true,
});
const salesitemservice =
  loadPackageDefinition(packageDefinition).salesitemservice;

const grpcClient = new (salesitemservice as any).SalesItemService(
  'localhost:50051',
  credentials.createInsecure(),
);

grpcClient.getSalesItem({ id: '' }, (error, response) => {
  console.log(error, JSON.stringify(response, undefined, 2));
});

grpcClient.getSalesItems({}, (error, response) => {
  console.log(error, JSON.stringify(response.salesItems, undefined, 2));
});

grpcClient.createSalesItem(
  {
    name: 'Sales item 11',
    priceInCents: 2000,
    images: [{ rank: 1, url: 'http://test.com/images/1' }],
  },
  (error, response) => {
    console.log(error, JSON.stringify(response, undefined, 2));
  },
);

grpcClient.updateSalesItem(
  {
    id: 'b8f691e3-32e4-4971-9a27-8e9b269724f1',
    name: 'Sales item 22',
    priceInCents: 3000,
    images: [{ rank: 2222, url: 'http://test.com/images/1' }],
  },
  (error, response) => {
    console.log(error, response);
  },
);

grpcClient.deleteSalesItem(
  { id: '94d24e8d-2ae3-49b8-844a-29e3031e5d60' },
  (error, response) => {
    console.log(error, response);
  },
);
```

To make the above code more production like, you should add request tracing, audit logging and observability (metrics, like request counts). You don't necessarily need authorization if the gRPC server and clients are running in the backend and the services can trust each other.

8.2.2: Asynchronous API Design Principle

Use asynchronous APIs when requests are request-only (fire-and-forget, i.e., no response is expected) or when the response is not immediately expected.

8.2.2.1: Request-Only Asynchronous API Design

In request-only asynchronous APIs, the request sender does not expect a response. Such APIs are typically implemented using a message broker. The request sender will send a JSON or other format request to a topic in the message broker, where the request recipient consumes the request asynchronously.

Different API endpoints can be specified in a request using a procedure property, for example. You can name the procedure property as you wish, e.g., command, action, method, operation, apiEndpoint, etc. Parameters for the procedure can be supplied in a parameters property. Below is an example request in JSON:

```
{
  "procedure": "<procedure name>",
  "parameters": {
    "<parameterName1>": "parameter value 1",
    "<parameterName2>": "parameter value 2",
    // ...
  }
}
```

Let's have an example with an email-sending microservice that implements a request-only asynchronous API and handles the sending of emails. We start by defining a message broker topic for the microservice. The topic should be named after the microservice, for example, *email-sending-service*.

In the *email-sending-service*, we define the following request schema for an API endpoint that sends an email:

```
{
  "procedure": "sendEmailMessage",
  "parameters": {
    "fromEmailAddress": "...",
    "toEmailAddresses": ["...", "...", ...],
    "subject": "...",
    "message": "..."
  }
}
```

Below is an example request that some other microservice can produce to the *email-sending-service* topic in the message broker to be handled by the *email-sending-service*:

```
{
  "procedure": "sendEmailMessage",
  "parameters": {
    "fromEmailAddress": "sender@domain.com",
    "toEmailAddresses": ["receiver@domain.com"],
    "subject": "Status update",
    "message": "Hi, Here is my status update ..."
  }
}
```

8.2.2.2: Request-Response Asynchronous API Design

A request-response asynchronous API microservice receives requests from other microservices and then produces responses asynchronously. Request-response asynchronous APIs are typically implemented using a message broker. The request sender will send a request to a topic where the request recipient consumes the request asynchronously and then produces a response or responses to a message broker topic or topics. Each participating microservice should have a topic named after the microservice in the message broker.

The request format is the same as defined earlier, but the response has a `response` or `result` property instead of the `parameters` property, meaning that responses have the following format:

```
{
  "procedure": "<procedure name>",
  "response": {
    "propertyName1": "property value 1",
    "propertyName2": "property value 2",
    // ...
  }
}
```

Below is an example where a *loan-application-service* requests a *loan-eligibility-assessment-service* to assess loan eligibility. The *loan-application-service* sends the following JSON-format request to the message broker's *loan-eligibility-assessment-service* topic:

```
{
  "procedure": "assessLoanEligibility",
  "parameters": {
    "userId": 123456789012,
    "loanApplicationId": 5888482223,
    // Other parameters...
  }
}
```

The *loan-eligibility-assessment-service* responds to the above request by sending the following JSON-format response to the message broker's *loan-application-service* topic:

```
{
  "procedure": "assessLoanEligibility",
  "response": {
    "loanApplicationId": 5888482223,
    "isEligible": true,
    "amountInDollars": 10000,
    "interestRate": 9.75,
    "termInMonths": 120
  }
}
```

Below is an example response when the loan application is rejected:

```
{
  "procedure": "assessLoanEligibility",
  "response": {
    "loanApplicationId": 5888482223,
    "isEligible": false
  }
}
```

Alternatively, request and response messages can be treated as events with some data. When we send events between microservices, we call it an event-driven architecture[38]. For event-driven architecture, we must decide if we have a single or multiple topics for the software system in the message broker. If all the microservices share a single topic in the software system, then each microservice will consume each message from the message broker and decide if they should act on it. This approach is suitable except when large events are produced to the message broker. When large events are produced, each microservice must consume those large events even if they don't need to react to them. This will unnecessarily consume a lot of network bandwidth if the number of microservices is also high. The other extreme is to create a topic for each microservice in the message broker. This approach causes extra network bandwidth consumption if a large event must be produced to multiple topics to be handled by multiple microservices. You can also create a hybrid model with a broadcast topic or topics and individual topics for specific microservices.

To solve the problems described above, you can use the claim check pattern[39]. In that pattern, you split a large message into a claim check and the actual payload of the message. You only send the claim check to a message queue and store the payload elsewhere. This protects other microservices from needing to read large messages from the message queue that they don't have to react to.

Below are the earlier request and response messages written as events. Event names are usually given in past tense.

The *loan-application-service* produces the following event:

```
{
  "event": "LoanApplicationCreated",
  "data": {
    "userId": 123456789012,
    "loanApplicationId": 5888482223,
    // ...
  }
}
```

The *loan-eligibility-assessment-service* consumes the above message, processes it and produces a new event:

```
{
  "event": "LoanEligibilityAssessed",
  "data": {
    "loanApplicationId": 5888482223,
    "isEligible": true,
    "amountInDollars": 10000,
    "interestRate": 9.75,
    "termInMonths": 120
  }
}
```

The *loan-application-service* consumes the above event and either continues processing the loan application when isEligible is true or rejects the load application.

[38]https://en.wikipedia.org/wiki/Event-driven_architecture
[39]https://learn.microsoft.com/enus/azure/architecture/patterns/claim-check

8.2.2.3: Asynchronous API Documentation

AsyncAPI[40] provides tools for building and documenting event-driven architectures. Below is an example where two events are defined for the *sales-service*:

```
asyncapi: 3.0.0
info:
  title: Sales Item Service
  version: 1.0.0
channels:
  salesItemService:
    address: sales-item-service
    messages:
      createSalesItem:
        description: Creates a sales item.
        payload:
          type: object
          properties:
            name:
              type: string
            price:
              type: integer
  notifications:
    address: notifications
    messages:
      salesItemCreated:
        description: A Sales item was created.
        payload:
          type: object
          properties:
            id:
              type: string
            name:
              type: string
            price:
              type: integer
operations:
  createSalesItem:
    action: receive
    channel:
      $ref: '#/channels/salesItemService'
  salesItemCreated:
    action: send
    channel:
      $ref: '#/channels/notifications'
```

The service receives `createSalesItem` events on channel `salesItemService` and sends `salesItemCreated` events on the `notifications` channel. The `createSalesItem` event contains the following properties: `name` and `price`. And the `salesItemCreated` event contains an additional `id` property.

8.3: API Design Example

Let's have a concrete example of designing an API for a trip booking service. The first feature, as presented by product management, is for a user to be able to *book a trip*. We do not concern ourselves with frontend development here; we only focus on the backend (API) side.

The team uses domain-driven design and starts with an event-storming session, which results in the following output.

---

[40]https://www.asyncapi.com/

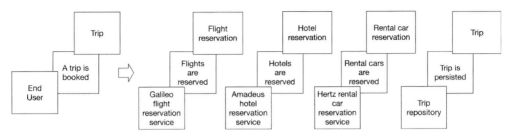

Figure 8.72. Event Storming Result

From the above picture, we can infer our user stories for the backend API:

- As a user I want flight(s) to be reserved for my trip
- As a user I want hotel room(s) to be reserved for my trip
- As a user I want rental car(s) to be reserved for my trip
- As a user I want my trip to be persisted

From the above picture, we can infer our classes and put them in the following directory layout:

```
trip-booking-service
└── src
    └── tripbooking
        ├── model (or core)
        │   ├── dtos
        │   │   ├── InputTrip.java
        │   │   ├── InputFlightReservation.java
        │   │   ├── InputHotelReservation.java
        │   │   ├── InputRentalCarReservation.java
        │   │   ├── OutputTrip.java
        │   │   ├── OutputFlightReservation.java
        │   │   ├── OutputHotelReservation.java
        │   │   └── OutputRentalCarReservation.java
        │   ├── entities
        │   │   ├── FlightReservation.java
        │   │   ├── HotelReservation.java
        │   │   ├── RentalCarReservation.java
        │   │   └── Trip.java
        │   ├── errors
        │   │   ├── TripBookingServiceError.java
        │   │   └── ...
        │   ├── repositories
        │   │   └── TripRepository.java
        │   ├── services
        │   │   ├── FlightReservationService.java
        │   │   ├── HotelReservationService.java
        │   │   └── RentalCarReservationService.java
        │   └── usecases
        │       ├── TripBookingUseCases.java
        │       └── TripBookingUseCasesImpl.java
        └── ifadapters
            ├── controllers
            │   └── RestTripBookingController.java
            ├── repositories
            │   └── MongoDbTripRepository.java
            └── services
                ├── GalileoFlightReservationService.java
                ├── AmadeusHotelReservationService.java
                └── HertzRentalCarReservationService.java
```

Next, we should use BDD and ATDD to define acceptance tests for the trip booking feature. We will skip that step here because it was already well covered in the testing principles chapter.

After we have implemented our acceptance tests, we need to start implementing our API microservice to get those acceptance tests passed. For the implementation, we should use either Detroit/Chicago or London-style TDD. We choose the London style and start from the outer layer, i.e., from the controller. I am not presenting the TDD steps here; I am only presenting the implementation. We have already covered the TDD in several examples. We should use the bounded context-specific ubiquitous language in our code. For example, instead of speaking about creating a trip, we use the term "book a trip". Below are the most important parts of the source written in Java using Spring Boot.

Source code for the below example is available here[41].

The controller method for booking a trip should be simple and delegate to a business use case.

Figure 8.73. **RestTripBookingController.java**

```java
@RestController
@RequestMapping("/trips")
public class RestTripBookingController {
  @Autowired
  private TripBookingUseCases tripBookingUseCases;

  @PostMapping
  @ResponseStatus(HttpStatus.CREATED)
  public OutputTrip bookTrip(@RequestBody InputTrip inputTrip) {
      return tripBookingUseCases.bookTrip(inputTrip);
  }
}
```

Notice below how we put behavior into domain entities, and our use case class is not crowded with business logic code but delegate to entity class and repository to achieve a business use case.

Figure 8.74. **TripBookingUseCasesImpl.java**

```java
@Service
public class TripBookingUseCasesImpl implements TripBookingUseCases {
  @Autowired
  private TripRepository tripRepository;

  @Override
  @Transactional
  public OutputTrip bookTrip(InputTrip inputTrip) {
    Trip trip = Trip.from(inputTrip);
    trip.makeReservations();

    try {
      tripRepository.save(trip);
    } catch (final TripRepository.Error error) {
      trip.cancelReservations();
      throw error;
    }
```

---

[41] https://github.com/pksilen/clean-code-principles-code/tree/main/chapter6/apidesign

```
    return OutputTrip.from(trip);
  }
}
```

Figure 8.75. TripRepository.java

```
public interface TripRepository {
  public static class Error extends TripBookingServiceError {
      public Error(final Exception exception) {
        super(exception);
      }
      // ...
    }

  void save(Trip trip);
}
```

Figure 8.76. MongoDbTripRepository.java

```
@Repository
public interface MongoDbTripRepository
                    extends MongoRepository<Trip, String>, TripRepository {
  // ...
}
```

Below is the code for the domain entities:

Figure 8.77. Trip.java

```
public class Trip {
  private final List<Reservation> reservations;

  public Trip(final List<Reservation> reservations, ...) {
    this.reservations = reservations;
  }

  public static Trip from(final InputTrip inputTrip) {
    final List<Reservation> reservations = new ArrayList<>();

    for (final var flightReservation : inputTrip.getFlightReservations()) {
      reservations.add(new FlightReservation(...));
    }

    // Similar loop as above for hotel reservations and
    // rental car reservations

    return new Trip(reservations, ...);
  }

  public void makeReservations() {
    for (final var reservation : reservations) {
      try {
        reservation.make();
      } catch (final Reservation.MakeError error) {
        this.cancelReservations();
        throw error;
      }
    }
  }

  public void cancelReservations() {
    // In production code, this loop cannot be forever but should be
    // replaced with more robust and complex error handling as described
    // earlier in first chapter when discussing distributed transactions
```

```
    while (!reservations.isEmpty()) {
      for (final var reservation : reservations) {
        try {
          reservation.cancel();
          reservations.remove(reservation);
          break;
        } catch (final Reservation.CancelError error) {
          // Intentionally no operation
        }
      }
    }
  }
}
```

Figure 8.78. Reservation.java

```
public interface Reservation {
  class MakeError extends TripBookingServiceError {
    public MakeError(final Exception exception) {
      super(exception);
    }
    // ...
  }

  class AlreadyReservedError extends MakeError {
    public AlreadyReservedError(final Exception exception) {
      super(exception);
    }
    // ...
  }

  void make();

  class CancelError extends TripBookingServiceError {
    public CancelError(final Exception exception) {
      super(exception);
    }
    // ...
  }

  void cancel();
}
```

Figure 8.79. AbstractReservation.java

```
public abstract class AbstractReservation implements Reservation {
  private Optional<String> maybeId;

  public AbstractReservation(final Optional<String> maybeId) {
    this.maybeId = maybeId;
  }

  public void setId(final String id) {
    this.maybeId = Optional.of(id);
  }

  protected void assertIsNotReserved() {
    if (maybeId.isPresent()) {
      throw new AlreadyReservedError();
    }
  }

  protected void cancelUsing(final ReservationService reservationService) {
    maybeId.ifPresent((id) -> {
      try {
```

```
        reservationService.cancelReservation(id);
        id = null;
      } catch (final ReservationService.CancelReservationError error) {
        throw new CancelError(error);
      }
    });
  }
}
```

Figure 8.80. FlightReservation.java

```
public class FlightReservation extends AbstractReservation {
  private final FlightReservationService flightReservationService;

  public FlightReservation(
    final FlightReservationService flightReservationService, ...
    ) {
    super(Optional.empty());
  }

  @Override
  public void make() {
    assertIsNotReserved();

    try {
      this.setId(flightReservationService.reserveFlight(...));
    } catch (final FlightReservationService.ReserveFlightError error) {
      throw new MakeError(error);
    }
  }

  @Override
  public void cancel() {
    cancelUsing(flightReservationService);
  }
}
```

Figure 8.81. HotelReservation.java

```
public class HotelReservation extends AbstractReservation {
  private final HotelReservationService hotelReservationService;

  public HotelReservation(...) {
    super(Optional.empty());
  }

  @Override
  public void make() {
    assertIsNotReserved();

    try {
      this.setId(hotelReservationService.reserveHotel(...));
    } catch (final HotelReservationService.ReserveHotelError error) {
      throw new MakeError( error);
    }
  }

  @Override
  public void cancel() {
    cancelUsing(hotelReservationService);
  }
}
```

Figure 8.82. RentalCarReservation.java

```java
public class RentalCarReservation extends AbstractReservation {
  private final RentalCarReservationService rentalCarReservationService;

  public RentalCarReservation(...) {
    super(Optional.empty());
  }

  @Override
  public void make() {
    assertIsNotReserved();

    try {
      this.setId(rentalCarReservationService.reserveCar(...));
    } catch (final RentalCarReservationService.ReserveCarError error) {
      throw new MakeError( error);
    }
  }

  @Override
  public void cancel() {
    cancelUsing(rentalCarReservationService);
  }
}
```

Figure 8.83. ReservationService.java

```java
public interface ReservationService {
  class CancelReservationError extends TripBookingServiceError {
    public CancelReservationError(Exception exception) {
      super(exception);
    }
    // ...
  }

  void cancelReservation(final String id);
}
```

Figure 8.84. FlightReservationService.java

```java
public interface FlightReservationService extends ReservationService {
  class ReserveFlightError extends TripBookingServiceError {
    public ReserveFlightError(Exception exception) {
      super(exception);
    }
    // ...
  }

  String reserveFlight(...);
}
```

Figure 8.85. GalileoFlightReservationService.java

```java
public class GalileoFlightReservationService implements FlightReservationService {
  public String reserveFlight(...) {
    // ...
  }

  public void cancelReservation(final String id) {
    // ...
  }
}
```

Figure 8.86. HotelReservationService.java

```java
public interface HotelReservationService extends ReservationService {
  class ReserveHotelError extends TripBookingServiceError {
    public ReserveHotelError(Exception exception) {
      super(exception);
    }
    // ...
  }

  String reserveHotel(...);
}
```

Figure 8.87. AmadeusHotelReservationService.java

```java
public class AmadeusHotelReservationService implements HotelReservationService {
  public String reserveHotel(...) {
    // ...
  }

  public void cancelReservation(final String id) {
    // ...
  }
}
```

Figure 8.88. RentalCarReservationService.java

```java
public interface RentalCarReservationService extends ReservationService {
  class ReserveCarError extends TripBookingServiceError {
    public ReserveCarError(Exception exception) {
      super(exception);
    }
    // ...
  }

  String reserveCar(...);
}
```

Figure 8.89. HertzRentalCarReservationService.java

```
public class HertzRentalCarReservationService implements RentalCarReservationService {
  public String reserveCar(...) {
    // ...
  }

  public void cancelReservation(final String id) {
    // ...
  }
}
```

Let's see how we can further develop the trip booking service. Let's assume that product management requests us to allow users to reserve tours and activities during their trip. We can implement this feature by mostly using the *open-closed principle*. For tour and activities reservations, we should introduce input and output DTO classes, an entity class derived from the Reservation class, and a service class for performing the actual reservations. Then, we only need to modify the Trip class factory method to create instances of the newly created tour and activities reservation entity class.

After booking a trip, product management wants users to be able to modify their reservations, like adding, replacing, and removing reservations. Let's have an example of a feature for adding a rental car reservation to an existing trip.

Figure 8.90. RestTripBookingController.java

```
@RestController
@RequestMapping("/trips")
public class RestTripBookingController {
  // ...

  @PostMapping("/{tripId}/rental-car-reservations")
  @ResponseStatus(HttpStatus.CREATED)
  public OutputRentalCarReservation addRentalCarReservation(
      @PathVariable String tripId,
      @RequestBody InputRentalCarReservation inputRentalCarReservation
  ) {
    return tripBookingUseCase.addRentalCarReservation(
      tripId,
      inputRentalCarReservation
    );
  }
}
```

Figure 8.91. TripBookingUseCasesImpl.java

```
@Service
public class TripBookingUseCasesImpl implements TripBookingUseCases {
  // ...

  @Override
  @Transactional
  public OutputRentalCarReservation addRentalCarReservation(
    final String tripId,
    final InputRentalCarReservation inputRentalCarReservation
  ) {
    // Retrieve the Trip entity
    final var trip = tripRepository.findById(tripId)
              .orElseThrow(() -> new EntityNotFoundError("Trip", tripId));

    // Create RentalCarReservation domain object
    final var rentalCarReservation =
      RentalCarReservation.from(inputRentalCarReservation);
```

```
    trip.add(rentalCarReservation);

    try {
      tripRepository.save(trip);
    } catch (final TripRepository.Error error) {
      trip.remove(rentalCarReservation);
      throw error;
    }

    return OutputRentalCarReservation.from(rentalCarReservation);
  }
}
```

Figure 8.92. TripRepository.java

```
public interface TripRepository {
  // ...

  Optional<Trip> findById(final String id);
  void update(final Trip trip);
}
```

Figure 8.93. Trip.java

```
public class Trip {
  // ...

  public void add(final Reservation reservation) {
    reservation.make();
    reservations.add(reservation);
  }

  public void remove(final Reservation reservation) {
    while (true) {
      try {
        reservation.cancel();
        break;
      } catch (final Reservation.CancelError error) {
        // Intentionally no operation
      }
    }

    reservations.remove(reservation);
  }
}
```

In the above examples, we did not use the convention of adding a *try*-prefix to a method that can raise an error. However, it could have been beneficial in this case due to distributed transactions. *Try*-prefixed methods would have clarified where our distributed transactions can fail and execution of, e.g., compensating actions, is required.

We could add many other features to the trip booking service, like getting trips or a single trip, canceling a trip, making/replacing/canceling various types of reservations, etc. However, we should not put all those features in a single controller, use cases, and repository class. We should implement the *vertical slice architecture* as presented in the earlier *object-oriented design principles chapter*. We should create separate subdirectories for each feature (or feature set or subdomain). Each subdirectory should have a controller, use cases, and repository class containing functionality related to that particular feature (or feature set or subdomain) only. Organizing your code in feature or feature set-specific directories is called *screaming architecture*. The directory layout *screams* about the software component's features.

9: Databases And Database Principles

This chapter presents principles for selecting and using databases. Principles are presented for the following database types:

- Relational databases
- Document databases
- Key-value databases
- Wide column databases
- Search engines

Relational databases are also called SQL databases because accessing a relational database involves issuing SQL statements. Databases of the other database types are called NoSQL[1] databases because they don't support SQL at all or they support only a subset of it, possibly with some additions and modifications.

9.1: Relational Databases

Relational databases are multipurpose databases that suit many needs. Choose a relational database if you are not aware of all the requirements you have for a database now or in the future.

For example, if you don't know what kind of database table relations and queries you need now or will need in the future, you should consider using a relational database that is well-suited for different kinds of queries.

9.1.1: Structure of Relational Database

Data in a relational database is organized in the following hierarchy:

- Logical databases (or schemas)
  - Tables
    * Columns

A table consists of columns and rows. Data in a database is stored as rows in the tables. Each row has a value for each column in the table. A special NULL value is used if a row does not have a value for a particular column. You can specify if null values are allowed for a column or not.

A microservice should have a single logical database (or schema). Some relational databases have one logical database (or schema) available by default; in other databases, you must create a logical database (or schema) by yourself.

---

[1]https://en.wikipedia.org/wiki/NoSQL

9.1.2: Use Object Relational Mapper (ORM) Principle

Use an object-relational mapper (ORM) to avoid writing SQL and to avoid making your microservice potentially vulnerable to SQL injection attacks. An ORM automatically maps the database rows to objects that can be serialized to JSON.

Many languages have ORM frameworks. Java has Java Persistence API (JPA, the most famous implementation of which is Hibernate), JavaScript/TypeScript has TypeORM and Prisma, and Python has the Django framework and SQLAlchemy, for example.

An ORM uses entities as building blocks for the database schema. Each entity class in a microservice is reflected as a table in the database. Use the same name for an entity and the database table, except the table name should be plural.

The domain entity and database entity are not necessarily the same. A typical example is when the entity id in the database entity is numeric, a 64-bit integer (BIGINT), but the domain entity has it as a string so that it can be used by any client (including JavaScript, where the number type is less than 64-bit). Another example is storing the entity id in the database as a binary or special *uuid* type and using the *string* type everywhere else. Yet another example is storing the domain entity id in the _id field in MongoDB. You often benefit from creating separate entity classes for a repository and the domain model. You might want to store domain entities in a database in a slightly different format. In that case, you must define separate entity classes for the domain and the repository. You can name database-related entities with a Db-prefix, e.g., DbSalesItem. In the DbSalesItem class, you need two conversion methods: from a domain entity and to a domain entity:

```
DbSalesItem.from(domainEntity)
// For example
DbSalesItem.from(salesItem)

salesItem = dbSalesItem.toDomainEntity()
```

If you need to change your database, you can end up having mixed format ids (e.g., from a relational database with BIGINT ids to a MongoDB with string-format ObjectIds). If you want uniform unique ids, you must generate them in your software component, not by the database. This might be a good approach also from the security point of view to prevent IDOR[2]. If you generate random UUIDs in your application, and you have accidentally broken authorization (IDOR), it is not possible for an attacker to guess UUIDs and try to access other users' resources using them.

Below is an example of a DbSalesItem entity class:

Figure 9.1. DbSalesItem.java"

```
@Entity
public class DbSalesItem {
  private Long id;
  private String name;
  private Integer price;
}
```

Store DbSalesItem entities in a table named salesitems. In this book, I write all identifiers in lowercase. The case sensitivity of a database depends on the database and the operating system it is running on. For example, MySQL is case-sensitive only on Linux systems.

[2]https://cheatsheetseries.owasp.org/cheatsheets/Insecure_Direct_Object_Reference_Prevention_Cheat_Sheet.html

The properties of an entity map to columns of the entity table, meaning that the salesitems table has the following columns:

- id
- name
- price

Each entity table must have a primary key defined. The primary key must be unique for each row in the table. In the example below, we use the @Id annotation to define the id column as the primary key containing a unique value for each row. The @GeneratedValue annotation states that the database should automatically generate a value for the id column using the supplied strategy.

Figure 9.2. DbSalesItem.java

```
@Entity
@Table(name = "salesitems")
public class DbSalesItem {
  @Id
  @GeneratedValue(strategy = GenerationType.IDENTITY)
  private Long id;

  private String name;
  private Integer price;
}
```

ORM can create database tables according to entity specifications in code. Below is an example SQL statement for PostgreSQL that an ORM generates to create a table for storing SalesItem entities:

```
CREATE TABLE salesitems (
  id BIGINT GENERATED ALWAYS AS IDENTITY,
  name TEXT,
  price INTEGER,
  PRIMARY KEY (id)
);
```

A table's columns can be specified as containing unique or non-nullable values. By default, a column can contain nullable values, which need not be unique. Below is an example where we define that the name column in the salesitems table cannot have null values, and values must be unique. We don't want to store sales items with null names, and we want to store sales items with unique names.

Figure 9.3. DbSalesItem.java

```
@Entity
@Table(name = "salesitems")
public class DbSalesItem {
  @Id
  @GeneratedValue(strategy = GenerationType.IDENTITY)
  private Long id;

  @Column(unique=true, nullable=false)
  private String name;

  private Integer price;
}
```

When you have a DbSalesItem entity, you can persist it with an instance of JPA's EntityManager:

```
entityManager.persist(dbSalesItem);
```

JPA will generate the needed SQL statement and execute it on your behalf. Below is an example SQL statement generated by the ORM to persist a sales item (Remember that the database autogenerates the id column).

```
INSERT INTO salesitems (name, price)
VALUES ('Sample sales item', 10);
```

You can search for the created sales item in the database (assuming here that we have a getId getter defined):

```
entityManager.find(DbSalesItem.class, salesItem.getId());
```

For the above operation, the ORM will generate the following SQL query:

```
SELECT id, name, price FROM salesitems WHERE id = 1;
```

Then, you can modify the entity and merge it with the entity manager to update the database:

```
dbSalesItem.setPrice(20);
entityManager.merge(dbSalesItem);
```

Finally, you can delete the sales item with the entity manager:

```
entityManager.remove(dbSalesItem);
```

The ORM will execute the following SQL statement:

```
DELETE FROM salesitems WHERE id = 1;
```

Suppose your microservice executes SQL queries that do not include the primary key column in the query's WHERE clause. In that case, the database engine must perform a full table scan to find the wanted rows. Let's say you want to query sales items, the price of which is less than 10. This can be achieved with the below query:

```
// final var price = ...

final TypedQuery<DbSalesItem> dbSalesItemsQuery = entityManager
 .createQuery("SELECT s FROM salesitems s WHERE s.price < :price",
            DbSalesItem.class);

dbSalesItemsQuery.setParameter("price", price);

final List<DbSalesItem> dbSalesItems = dbSalesItemsQuery.getResultList();
```

The database engine must perform a full table scan to find all the sales items where the price column has a value below the price variable's value. If the database is large, this can be slow. If you perform the above query often, you should optimize those queries by creating an index. For the above query to be fast, we must create an index for the price column using the @Index annotation inside the @Table annotation:

Figure 9.4. DbSalesItem.java

```
@Entity
@Table(
  name = "salesitems",
  indexes = @Index(columnList = "price")
)
public class DbSalesItem {
  @Id
  @GeneratedValue(strategy = GenerationType.IDENTITY)
  private Long id;

  @Column(unique=true, nullable=false)
  private String name;

  private Integer price;
}
```

9.1.2.1: Entity/Table Relationships

Tables in a relational database can have relationships with other tables. There are three types of relationships:

- One-to-one
- One-to-many
- Many-to-many

9.1.2.1.1: One-To-One/Many Relationships

In this section, we focus on one-to-one and one-to-many relationships. In a one-to-one relationship, a single row in a table can have a relationship with another row in another table. In a one-to-many relationship, a single row in a table can have a relationship with multiple rows in another table.

Let's have an example with an *order-service* that can store orders in a database. Each order consists of one or more order items. An order item contains information about the bought sales item.

```
@Entity
@Table(name = "orders")
public class DbOrder {
  @Id
  @GeneratedValue(strategy = GenerationType.IDENTITY)
  private Long id;

  // Other order fields ...

  @OneToMany(mappedBy="order")
  private List<DbOrderItem> orderItems;
}

@Entity
@Table(name = "orderitems")
public class DbOrderItem {
  @Id
  @GeneratedValue(strategy = GenerationType.IDENTITY)
  private Long id;

  @OneToOne
  @JoinColumn(name = "salesitemid")
```

```
  private DbSalesItem salesItem;

  @ManyToOne
  @JoinColumn(name = "orderid", nullable = false)
  private DbOrder dbOrder;
}
```

Orders are stored in the orders table, and order items are stored in the orderitems table, which contains a join column named orderid. Using this join column, we can map a particular order item to a specific order. Each order item maps to precisely one sales item. For this reason, the orderitems table also contains a join column named salesitemid. Using this join column, we can map an order item to a sales item.

Below is the SQL statement generated by the ORM for creating the orderitems table. The one-to-one and one-to-many relationships are reflected in the foreign key constraints:

- fksalesitem: a salesitemid column value in the orderitems table references an id column value in the salesitems table
- fkorder: an orderid column value in the orderitems table references an id column value in the orders table

```
CREATE TABLE orderitems (
  id BIGINT GENERATED ALWAYS AS IDENTITY,
  salesitemid BIGINT,
  orderid BIGINT,
  CONSTRAINT fksalesitem FOREIGN KEY (salesitemid)
    REFERENCES salesitems(id),
  CONSTRAINT fkorder FOREIGN KEY (orderid)
    REFERENCES orders(id)
);
```

The following SQL query is executed by the ORM to fetch the order with id 123 and its order items:

```
SELECT o.id, s.name, ...
FROM orders o
LEFT JOIN orderitems oi ON o.id = oi.orderid
LEFT JOIN salesitems s ON s.id = oi.salesitemid
WHERE o.id = 123;
```

9.1.2.1.2: Many-To-Many Relationships

In a many-to-many relationship, one entity has a relationship with many entities of another type, and those entities have a relationship with many entities of the first entity type. For example, a student can attend many courses, and a course can have numerous students attending it.

Suppose we have a service that stores student and course entities in a database. Each student entity contains the courses the student has attended. Similarly, each course entity contains a list of students that have attended the course. We have a many-to-many relationship where one student can attend multiple courses, and multiple students can attend one course. This means an additional association/associative table[3], studentcourse, must be created. This new table maps a particular student to a particular course.

---

[3]https://en.wikipedia.org/wiki/Associative_entity

```
@Entity
@Table(name = "students")
class DbStudent {
  @Id
  @GeneratedValue(strategy = GenerationType.IDENTITY)
  private Long id;

  // Other Student fields...

  @JoinTable(
    name = "studentcourse",
    joinColumns = @JoinColumn(name = "studentid"),
    inverseJoinColumns = @JoinColumn(name = "courseid")
  )
  @ManyToMany
  private List<DbCourse> attendedCourses;
}

@Entity
@Table(name = "courses")
class DbCourse {
  @Id
  @GeneratedValue(strategy = GenerationType.IDENTITY)
  private Long id;

  // Other Course fields...

  @ManyToMany(mappedBy = "attendedCourses")
  private List<DbStudent> students;
}
```

The ORM creates the students and courses tables in addition to the studentcourse mapping table:

```
CREATE TABLE studentcourse (
  studentid BIGINT,
  courseid BIGINT,
  CONSTRAINT fkstudent FOREIGN KEY (studentid)
    REFERENCES students(id),
  CONSTRAINT fkorder FOREIGN KEY (courseid)
    REFERENCES courses(id)
);
```

Below is an example SQL query that the ORM executes to fetch attended courses for the user identified with id 123:

```
SELECT s.id, c.id, ...
FROM students s
LEFT JOIN studentcourse sc ON s.id = sc.studentid
LEFT JOIN courses c ON c.id = sc.courseid
WHERE s.id = 123;
```

Below is an example SQL query that the ORM executes to fetch students for the course identified with id 123:

```
SELECT c.id, s.id
FROM courses c
LEFT JOIN studentcourse sc ON c.id = sc.courseid
LEFT JOIN students s ON s.id = sc.studentid
WHERE c.id = 123;
```

In real-life scenarios, you don't necessarily have to or should implement many-to-many database relations inside a single microservice. For example, the above service that handles students and courses is against the *single responsibility principle* on the abstraction level of courses and students. (However, if we created a *school* microservice on a higher abstraction level, we can have students and courses tables in the same microservice) If we created a separate microservice for students and a separate microservice for courses, then there wouldn't be many-to-many relationships between database tables in a single microservice.

9.1.2.2: Sales Item Repository Example

Let's define a `SalesItemRepository` implementation using TypeORM[4] for the *sales-item-service* API defined in the previous chapter. TypeORM is a popular ORM that can be used with various SQL database engines, including MySQL, PostgreSQL, MariaDB, Oracle, SQL Server, CockroachDB, SAP Hana, and even MongoDB. In the below example, we don't need database transactions because each repository operation is a single atomic operation like `save`, `update`, or `delete`. You need a transaction if you need to perform multiple database operations to fulfill a repository operation. Consult your ORM documentation to find out how transactions can be used. In the case of Spring JPA ORM, if your repository extends the `CrudRepository` interface, the repository methods are, by default, transactional. In TypeORM, you need to supply a callback function where you execute database operations:

```
await myDataSource.transaction(async (transactionalEntityManager) => {
    // execute queries using 'transactionalEntityManager'
})
```

Source code for the below example is available here[5].

Let's start by defining the `DbSalesItem`, and `DbSalesItemImage` database entities:

Figure 9.5. DbSalesItem.ts

```
import { Column, Entity, OneToMany, PrimaryColumn } from 'typeorm';
import DbSalesItemImage from './DbSalesItemImage';
import SalesItem from '../../../../entities/SalesItem';

@Entity('salesitems')
export default class DbSalesItem {
  @PrimaryColumn()
  id: string;

  @Column({ type: 'bigint' })
  createdAtTimestampInMs: string;

  @Column()
  name: string;

  @Column()
  priceInCents: number;

  @OneToMany(
    () => DbSalesItemImage,
```

---

[4]https://typeorm.io/

[5]https://github.com/pksilen/clean-code-principles-code/tree/main/chapter6/salesitemservice

```
      (dbSalesItemImage) => dbSalesItemImage.salesItem,
      { cascade: true, eager: true },
    )
    images: DbSalesItemImage[];


    // Factory method for creating a database entity
    // from a domain entity
    // In this example, the domain and database entities
    // contain exact same properties, but that is not
    // always true. This method allows you to make
    // various transformations like adding/dropping properties,
    // type conversions etc...
    static from(salesItem: SalesItem): DbSalesItem {
      const dbSalesItem = new DbSalesItem();
      dbSalesItem.id = salesItem.id;
      dbSalesItem.createdAtTimestampInMs = salesItem.createdAtTimestampInMs;
      dbSalesItem.name = salesItem.name;
      dbSalesItem.priceInCents = salesItem.priceInCents;

      dbSalesItem.images = salesItem.images.map((salesItemImage) => {
        const dbSalesItemImage = new DbSalesItemImage();
        dbSalesItemImage.id = salesItemImage.id;
        dbSalesItemImage.rank = salesItemImage.rank;
        dbSalesItemImage.url = salesItemImage.url;
        return dbSalesItemImage;
      });

      return dbSalesItem;
    }

    toDomainEntity(): SalesItem {
      return SalesItem.from(this, this.id);
    }
  }
}
```

Figure 9.6. DbSalesItemImage.ts

```
import { Column, Entity, ManyToOne, PrimaryColumn } from 'typeorm';
import DbSalesItem from './DbSalesItem';


@Entity('salesitemimages')
export default class DbSalesItemImage {
  @PrimaryColumn()
  id: string;

  @Column()
  salesItemId: number;

  @Column()
  rank: number;

  @Column()
  url: string;

  @ManyToOne(() => DbSalesItem, (salesItem) => salesItem.images, {
    onDelete: 'CASCADE',
  })
  salesItem: DbSalesItem;
}
```

Below is the implementation of the TypeOrmSalesItemRepository:

Figure 9.7. TypeOrmSalesItemRepository.ts

```
import { Injectable } from '@nestjs/common';
import { DataSource } from 'typeorm';
import SalesItemRepository from '../../SalesItemRepository';
import SalesItem from '../../../entities/SalesItem';
import DbSalesItem from './entities/DbSalesItem';
import DatabaseError from '../../../errors/DatabaseError';
import DbSalesItemImage from './entities/DbSalesItemImage';
import { getDbConnProperties } from '../../../common/utils/utils';


@Injectable()
export default class TypeOrmSalesItemRepository implements SalesItemRepository {
  private readonly dataSource: DataSource;
  private isDataSourceInitialized = false;

  constructor() {
    const { user, password, host, port, database } = getDbConnProperties();

    this.dataSource = new DataSource({
      type: 'mysql',
      host: host,
      port: port,
      username: user,
      password: password,
      database: database,
      entities: [DbSalesItem, DbSalesItemImage],
      // Do not use 'true' in production environment,
      // but use migrations when needed
      synchronize: true,
    });
  }

  async save(salesItem: SalesItem): Promise<void> {
    try {
      await this.initializeDataSourceIfNeeded();
      const dbSalesItem = DbSalesItem.from(salesItem);
      await this.dataSource.manager.save(dbSalesItem);
    } catch (error) {
      throw new DatabaseError(error);
    }
  }

  async findAll(): Promise<SalesItem[]> {
    try {
      await this.initializeDataSourceIfNeeded();
      const dbSalesItems = await this.dataSource.manager.find(DbSalesItem);
      return dbSalesItems.map((item) => item.toDomainEntity());
    } catch (error) {
      throw new DatabaseError(error);
    }
  }

  async find(id: string): Promise<SalesItem | null> {
    try {
      await this.initializeDataSourceIfNeeded();
      const dbSalesItem = await this.dataSource.manager.findOneBy(DbSalesItem, {
        id,
      });

      return dbSalesItem ? dbSalesItem.toDomainEntity() : null;
    } catch (error) {
      throw new DatabaseError(error);
    }
  }

  async update(salesItem: SalesItem): Promise<void> {
    try {
      await this.initializeDataSourceIfNeeded();
```

```
    const dbSalesItem = DbSalesItem.from(salesItem);

    await this.dataSource.transaction(async (transactionalEntityManager) => {
      await transactionalEntityManager.delete(DbSalesItem, salesItem.id);
      await transactionalEntityManager.save(dbSalesItem);
    });
  } catch (error) {
    throw new DatabaseError(error);
  }
}

async delete(id: string): Promise<void> {
  try {
    await this.initializeDataSourceIfNeeded();
    await this.dataSource.manager.delete(DbSalesItem, id);
  } catch (error) {
    throw new DatabaseError(error);
  }
}

private async initializeDataSourceIfNeeded() {
  if (!this.isDataSourceInitialized) {
    await this.dataSource.initialize();
    this.isDataSourceInitialized = true;
  }
}
}
```

Here is the implementation of the getDbConnProperties function:

Figure 9.8. utils.ts

```
export function getDbConnProperties() {
  const databaseUrl = process.env.DATABASE_URL;

  if (!databaseUrl) {
    throw new Error('DATABASE_URL environment variable is not set');
  }

  const [, , authAndHost, path] = databaseUrl.split('/');
  const [userAndPassword, hostAndPort] = authAndHost.split('@');
  const [user, password] = userAndPassword.split(':');
  const [host, portString] = hostAndPort.split(':');
  const port = parseInt(portString, 10);
  const database = path;
  return { user, password, host, port, database };
}
```

We can also use Prisma ORM[6] instead of TypeORM. Below is an example of the implementation of the Prisma ORM repository.

Source code for the below example is available here[7].

First, we need to define the database schema:

[6]https://www.prisma.io/docs/orm

[7]https://github.com/pksilen/clean-code-principles-code/tree/main/chapter6/salesitemservice

Figure 9.9. schema.prisma

```
datasource db {
  provider = "mysql"
  url       = env("DATABASE_URL")
}

generator client {
  provider = "prisma-client-js"
}

model SalesItem {
  id                      String        @id @db.VarChar(36)
  createdAtTimestampInMs  String
  name                    String
  priceInCents            Int
  images                  SalesItemImage[]
}

model SalesItemImage {
  id         String     @id @db.VarChar(36)
  rank       Int
  url        String
  salesItem  SalesItem? @relation(fields: [salesItemId], references: [id], onDelete: Cascade)
  salesItemId String?
}
```

And then the repository implementation:

Figure 9.10. PrismaOrmSalesItemRepository.ts

```
import { Injectable } from '@nestjs/common';
import { PrismaClient } from '@prisma/client';
import SalesItemRepository from '../../SalesItemRepository';
import SalesItem from '../../../entities/SalesItem';
import DatabaseError from '../../../errors/DatabaseError';


@Injectable()
export default class PrismaOrmSalesItemRepository
  implements SalesItemRepository
{
  private readonly prismaClient: PrismaClient;

  constructor() {
    this.prismaClient = new PrismaClient();
  }

  async save(salesItem: SalesItem): Promise<void> {
    try {
      const data = PrismaOrmSalesItemRepository.toData(salesItem);
      await this.prismaClient.salesItem.create({ data });
    } catch (error) {
      throw new DatabaseError(error);
    }
  }

  async findAll(): Promise<SalesItem[]> {
    try {
      const dbSalesItems = await this.prismaClient.salesItem.findMany({
        include: { images: true },
      });

      return dbSalesItems.map((item) =>
        PrismaOrmSalesItemRepository.toDomainEntity(item),
      );
    } catch (error) {
      throw new DatabaseError(error);
```

```
    }
  }
  async find(id: string): Promise<SalesItem | null> {
    try {
      const dbSalesItem = await this.prismaClient.salesItem.findUnique({
        where: {
          id,
        },
        include: { images: true },
      });

      return dbSalesItem
        ? PrismaOrmSalesItemRepository.toDomainEntity(dbSalesItem)
        : null;
    } catch (error) {
      throw new DatabaseError(error);
    }
  }

  async update(salesItem: SalesItem): Promise<void> {
    try {
      const data = PrismaOrmSalesItemRepository.toData(salesItem);

      await this.prismaClient.$transaction([
        this.prismaClient.salesItem.delete({
          where: { id: salesItem.id },
        }),
        this.prismaClient.salesItem.create({ data }),
      ]);
    } catch (error) {
      throw new DatabaseError(error);
    }
  }

  async delete(id: string): Promise<void> {
    try {
      await this.prismaClient.salesItem.delete({
        where: { id },
      });
    } catch (error) {
      throw new DatabaseError(error);
    }
  }

  private static toData(salesItem: SalesItem) {
    return {
      id: salesItem.id,
      createdAtTimestampInMs: salesItem.createdAtTimestampInMs,
      name: salesItem.name,
      priceInCents: salesItem.priceInCents,
      images: {
        create: salesItem.images.map((image) => ({
          id: image.id,
          rank: image.rank,
          url: image.url,
        })),
      },
    };
  }

  private static toDomainEntity(salesItemObject: any): SalesItem {
    return SalesItem.from(salesItemObject, salesItemObject.id);
  }
}
```

Before you can use the above repository, you must generate code from the Prisma schema file and create the database tables using the following commands:

```
prisma generate --schema=./src/repositories/orm/prisma/schema.prisma
prisma migrate dev --name init --schema=./src/repositories/orm/prisma/schema.prisma
```

9.1.3: Use Parameterized SQL Statements Principle

If you are not using an ORM for database access, use parameterized SQL statements to prevent potential SQL injection attacks.

Let's use Node.js and the mysql[8] NPM library for parameterized SQL examples. First, let's insert data to the salesitems table:

```
// Create a connection...
connection.query(
  `INSERT INTO salesitems (name, price)
  VALUES (?, ?)`,
  ['Sample sales item', 10]
);
```

The question marks (?) are placeholders for parameters in a parameterized SQL query. The second argument to the query method contains the parameter values. When a database engine receives a parameterized query, it will replace the placeholders with the supplied parameter values.

Next, we can update a row in the salesitems table. The below example changes the price of the sales item with id 123 to 20:

```
connection.query('UPDATE salesitems SET price = ? WHERE id = ?',
                 [20, 123]);
```

Let's execute a SELECT statement to get sales items with their price over 20:

```
connection.query(
  'SELECT id, name, price FROM salesitems WHERE price >= ?',
  [20]
);
```

In an SQL SELECT statement, you cannot use parameters everywhere. You can use them as value placeholders in the WHERE clause. If you want to use user-supplied data in other parts of an SQL SELECT statement, you need to use string concatenation. You should not concatenate user-supplied data without sanitation because that would open up possibilities for SQL injection attacks. Let's say you allow the microservice client to specify a sorting column:

---

[8]https://www.npmjs.com/package//mysql

```
const sortColumn = // Unvalidated data got from client
const sqlQuery =
  'SELECT id, name, price FROM salesitems ORDER BY ' +
  connection.escapeId(sortColumn);

connection.query(sqlQuery);
```

As shown above, you need to escape the sortColumn value so that it contains only valid characters for a MySQL column name. If you need to get the sorting direction from the client, you should validate that value as either ASC or DESC. In the below example, we assume that a validateSortDirection function exists:

```
const sortColumn = // Unvalidated data got from client
const sortDirection = // Unvalidated data got from client

// throws if invalid sorting direction
const validatedSortDirection =
  validateSortDirection(sortDirection);

const sqlQuery = `
  SELECT id, name, price
  FROM salesitems
  ORDER BY
  ${connection.escapeId(sortColumn)}
  ${validatedSortDirection}
`;

connection.query(sqlQuery);
```

When you get values for a MySQL query's LIMIT clause from a client, you must validate that those values are integers and in a valid range. Don't allow the client to supply random, very large values. In the example below, we assume two validation functions exist: validateRowOffset and validateRowCount. The validation functions will throw if validation fails.

```
const rowOffset = // Unvalidated data got from client
const rowCount = // Unvalidated data got from client

const validatedRowOffset = validateRowOffset(rowOffset);
const validatedRowCount = validateRowCount(rowCount);

const sqlQuery = `
  SELECT id, name, price
  FROM salesitems
  LIMIT ${validatedRowOffset}, ${validatedRowCount}
`;

connection.query(sqlQuery);
```

When you get a list of wanted column names from a client, you must validate that each of them is a valid column identifier:

```
const columnNames = // Unvalidated data got from client

const escapedColumnNames =
  columnNames.map(columnName => connection.escapedId(columnName));

const sqlQuery =
  `SELECT ${escapedColumnNames.join(', ')} FROM salesitems`;

connection.query(sqlQuery);
```

9.1.3.1: Sales Item Repository Example

Let's implement the SalesItemRepository for the *sales-item-service* API from the previous chapter using parameterized SQL and the mysql2[9] library:

Source code for the below example is available here[10].

Figure 9.11. ParamSqlSalesItemRepository.ts

```
import * as mysql from 'mysql2/promise';
import SalesItemRepository from './SalesItemRepository';
import SalesItem from '../entities/SalesItem';
import DatabaseError from 'src/errors/DatabaseError';
import SalesItemImage from '../entities/SalesItemImage';
import { getDbConnProperties } from '../common/utils/utils';

interface DatabaseConfig {
  user: string;
  password: string;
  host: string;
  port: number;
  database: string;
  poolSize?: number;
}

export default class ParamSqlSalesItemRepository
  implements SalesItemRepository
{
  private readonly connectionPool: mysql.Pool;

  constructor() {
    const connConfig = ParamSqlSalesItemRepository.tryCreateConnConfig();
    this.connectionPool = mysql.createPool(connConfig);
    this.tryCreateDbTablesIfNeeded();
  }

  async save(salesItem: SalesItem): Promise<void> {
    let connection: mysql.PoolConnection | undefined;

    try {
      connection = await this.connectionPool.getConnection();

      await connection.execute(
```

---

[9]https://sidorares.github.io/node-mysql2/docs

[10]https://github.com/pksilen/clean-code-principles-code/tree/main/chapter6/salesitemservice

```
        'INSERT INTO salesitems (id, createdAtTimestampInMs, name, priceInCents) VALUES (?, ?, ?, ?)',
        [
          salesItem.id,
          salesItem.createdAtTimestampInMs,
          salesItem.name,
          salesItem.priceInCents,
        ],
      );

      await this.insertSalesItemImages(
        connection,
        salesItem.id,
        salesItem.images,
      );

      await connection.commit();
    } catch (error) {
      throw new DatabaseError(error);
    } finally {
      connection?.release();
    }
  }

  async findAll(): Promise<SalesItem[]> {
    let connection: mysql.PoolConnection | undefined;

    try {
      connection = await this.connectionPool.getConnection();
      const [rows] = await connection.execute(
        'SELECT s.id, s.createdAtTimestampInMs, s.name, s.priceInCents, ' +
          'si.id as imageId, si.rank as imageRank, si.url as imageUrl ' +
          'FROM salesitems s LEFT JOIN salesitemimages si ON si.salesItemId = s.id',
      );

      return this.getSalesItems(rows as any[]);
    } catch (error) {
      throw new DatabaseError(error);
    } finally {
      connection?.release();
    }
  }

  async find(id: string): Promise<SalesItem | null> {
    let connection: mysql.PoolConnection | undefined;

    try {
      connection = await this.connectionPool.getConnection();

      const [rows] = await connection.execute(
        'SELECT s.id, s.createdAtTimestampInMs, s.name, s.priceInCents, ' +
          'si.id as imageId, si.rank as imageRank, si.url as imageUrl ' +
          'FROM salesitems s LEFT JOIN salesitemimages si ON si.salesItemId = s.id WHERE s.id = ?',
        [id],
      );

      return this.getSalesItems(rows as any[])[0] || null;
    } catch (error) {
      throw new DatabaseError(error);
    } finally {
      connection?.release();
    }
  }

  async update(salesItem: SalesItem): Promise<void> {
    let connection: mysql.PoolConnection | undefined;

    try {
      connection = await this.connectionPool.getConnection();

      await connection.execute(
```

```
        'UPDATE salesitems SET name = ?, priceInCents = ? WHERE id = ?',
        [salesItem.name, salesItem.priceInCents, salesItem.id],
      );

      await connection.execute(
        'DELETE FROM salesitemimages WHERE salesItemId = ?',
        [salesItem.id],
      );

      await this.insertSalesItemImages(
        connection,
        salesItem.id,
        salesItem.images,
      );

      await connection.commit();
    } catch (error) {
      throw new DatabaseError(error);
    } finally {
      connection?.release();
    }
  }

  async delete(id: string): Promise<void> {
    let connection: mysql.PoolConnection | undefined;

    try {
      connection = await this.connectionPool.getConnection();

      await connection.execute(
        'DELETE FROM salesitemimages WHERE salesItemId = ?',
        [id],
      );

      await connection.execute('DELETE FROM salesitems WHERE id = ?', [id]);
      await connection.commit();
    } catch (error) {
      throw new DatabaseError(error);
    } finally {
      connection?.release();
    }
  }

  private static tryCreateConnConfig(): DatabaseConfig {
    const { user, password, host, port, database } = getDbConnProperties();

    return {
      user,
      password,
      host,
      port,
      database,
      poolSize: 25,
    };
  }

  async tryCreateDbTablesIfNeeded(): Promise<void> {
    const connection = await this.connectionPool.getConnection();

    try {
      const createSalesItemsTableQuery = `
              CREATE TABLE IF NOT EXISTS salesitems (
                  id VARCHAR(36) NOT NULL,
                  createdAtTimestampInMs BIGINT NOT NULL,
                  name VARCHAR(256) NOT NULL,
                  priceInCents INTEGER NOT NULL,
                  PRIMARY KEY (id)
              )
          `;
```

```
        await connection.execute(createSalesItemsTableQuery);

        const createSalesItemImagesTableQuery = `
                CREATE TABLE IF NOT EXISTS salesitemimages (
                    id VARCHAR(36) NOT NULL,
                    \`rank\` INTEGER NOT NULL,
                    url VARCHAR(2084) NOT NULL,
                    salesItemId VARCHAR(36) NOT NULL,
                    PRIMARY KEY (id),
                    FOREIGN KEY (salesItemId) REFERENCES salesitems(id)
                )
            `;

        await connection.execute(createSalesItemImagesTableQuery);
        await connection.commit();
    } catch (error) {
        throw new Error(`Error creating tables: ${error.message}`);
    } finally {
        connection.release();
    }
}

private async insertSalesItemImages(
    connection: mysql.Connection,
    salesItemId: string,
    images: SalesItemImage[],
) {
    const statement =
        'INSERT INTO salesitemimages (id, `rank`, url, salesItemId) VALUES (?, ?, ?, ?)';

    for (const image of images) {
        await connection.execute(statement, [
            image.id,
            image.rank,
            image.url,
            salesItemId,
        ]);
    }
}

private getSalesItems(cursor: any): SalesItem[] {
    const idToSalesItem: Record<string, SalesItem> = {};

    for (const row of cursor) {
        if (!idToSalesItem[row.id]) {
            idToSalesItem[row.id] = SalesItem.from(row, row.id);
        }

        if (row.imageId) {
            idToSalesItem[row.id].images.push(
                new SalesItemImage({
                    id: row.imageId,
                    rank: row.imageRank,
                    url: row.imageUrl,
                }),
            );
        }
    }
    return Object.values(idToSalesItem);
}
}
```

9.1.4: Normalization Rules

Apply normalization rules to your database design.

Below are listed the three most basic database normalization rules[11]:

- First normal form (1NF)
- Second normal form (2NF)
- Third normal form (3NF)

A database relation is often described as "normalized" if it meets the first, second, and third normal forms.

9.1.4.1: First Normal Form (1NF)

The first normal form requires that a single value exists at every row and column intersection, never a list of values. When considering a sales item, the first normal form states that there cannot be two different price values in the `price` column or more than one name for the sales item in the `name` column. If you need multiple names for a sales item, you must establish a one-to-many relationship between a `SalesItem` entity and `SalesItemName` entities. What this means in practice is that you remove the `name` property from the `SalesItem` entity class and create a new `SalesItemName` entity class used to store sales items' names. Then, you create a one-to-many mapping between a `SalesItem` entity and `SalesItemName` entities.

9.1.4.2: Second Normal Form (2NF)

The second normal form requires that each non-key column entirely depends on the primary key. Let's assume that we have the following columns in an `orderitems` table:

- `orderid` (primary key)
- `productid` (primary key)
- `orderstate`

The `orderstate` column depends only on the `orderid` column, not the entire primary key. It is in the wrong table. It should, of course, be in the `orders` table.

9.1.4.3: Third Normal Form (3NF)

The third normal form requires that non-key columns are independent of each other.

Let's assume that we have the following columns in a `salesitems` table:

- `id` (primary key)
- `name`
- `price`
- `category`
- `discount`

Let's assume that the discount depends on the category. This table violates the third normal form because a non-key column, `discount`, depends on another non-key column, `category`. Column independence means that you can change any non-key column value without affecting any other column. If you changed the category, the discount would need to be changed accordingly, thus violating the third normal form rule.

The discount column should be moved to a new `categories` table with the following columns:

---

[11]https://en.wikipedia.org/wiki/Database_normalization

- `id` (primary key)
- `name`
- `discount`

Then we should update the `salesitems` table to contain the following columns:

- `id` (primary key)
- `name`
- `price`
- `categoryid` (a foreign key that references the `id` column in the `categories` table)

9.2: Document Databases

Use a document database in cases where complete documents (e.g., JSON objects) are typically stored and retrieved as a whole.

Document databases, like MongoDB[12], are useful for storing complete documents. A document is usually a JSON object containing information in arrays and nested objects. Documents are stored as such, and a whole document will be fetched when queried.

Let's consider a microservice for sales items. Each sales item contains an id, name, price, image URLs, and user reviews.

Below is an example sales item as a JSON object:

```
{
  "id": "507f191e810c19729de860ea",
  "category": "Power tools",
  "name": "Sample sales item",
  "price": 10,
  "imageUrls": ["https://url-to-image-1...",
               "https://url-to-image-2..."],
  "averageRatingInStars": 5,
  "reviews": [
    {
      "reviewerName": "John Doe",
      "date": "2022-09-01",
      "ratingInStars": 5,
      "text": "Such a great product!"
    }
  ]
}
```

A document database usually has a size limit for a single document. Therefore, the above example does not store images of sales items directly inside the document; it only stores URLs for the images. Actual images are stored in another data store that is more suitable for storing images, like Amazon S3.

When creating a microservice for sales items, we can choose a document database because we usually store and access whole documents. When sales items are created, they are created as JSON objects of the above shape, with the `reviews` array empty and `averageRatingInStars` null. When a sales item is fetched, the

---

[12]https://www.mongodb.com/

whole document is retrieved from the database. When a client adds a review for a sales item, the sales item is fetched from the database. The new review is appended to the `reviews` array, a new average rating is calculated, and finally, the document is persisted with the modifications.

Below is an example of inserting one sales item to a MongoDB collection named `salesItems`. MongoDB uses the term *collection* instead of *table*. A MongoDB collection can store multiple documents.

```
db.salesItems.insertOne({
  category: "Power tools",
  name: "Sample sales item",
  price: 10,
  images: ["https://url-to-image-1...",
           "https://url-to-image-2..."],
  averageRatingInStars: null,
  reviews: []
})
```

You can find sales items for the *Power tools* category with the following query:

```
db.salesItems.find({ category: "Power tools" })
```

If clients are usually querying sales items by category, it is wise to create an index for that field:

```
// 1 means ascending index, -1 means descending index
db.salesItems.createIndex( { category: 1 } )
```

When a client wants to add a new review for a sales item, you first fetch the document for the sales item:

```
db.salesItems.find({ _id: ObjectId("507f191e810c19729de860ea") })
```

Then, you calculate a new value for the `averageRatingInStars` field using the existing ratings and the new rating and add the new review to the `reviews` array and then update the document with the following command:

```
db.salesItems.updateOne(
  { _id: ObjectId("507f191e810c19729de860ea")  },
  { $set: { averageRatingInStars: 5 },
    $push: { reviews: {
      reviewerName: "John Doe",
      date: "2022-09-01",
      ratingInStars: 5,
      text: "Such a great product!"
    }}
  }
)
```

Clients may want to retrieve sales items sorted descending by the average rating. For this reason, you might want to change the indexing to be the following:

```
db.salesItems.createIndex( { category: 1, averageStarCount: -1 } )
```

A client can issue, for example, a request to get the best-rated sales items in the *power tools* category. This request can be fulfilled with the following query that utilizes the above-created index:

```
db.salesItems
  .find({ category: "Power tools" })
  .sort({ averageStarCount: -1 })
```

9.2.1: Sales Item Repository Example

Let's implement the `SalesItemRepository` for the *sales-item-service* API from the previous chapter using MongoDB and the mongodb[13] NPM library:

Source code for the below example is available here[14].

Figure 9.12. MongoDbSalesItemRepository.ts

```typescript
import * as mongodb from 'mongodb';
import SalesItemRepository from './SalesItemRepository';
import SalesItem from '../entities/SalesItem';
import DatabaseError from '../errors/DatabaseError';


export default class MongoDbSalesItemRepository implements SalesItemRepository {
  private readonly client: mongodb.MongoClient;
  private salesItemsCollection: mongodb.Collection;

  constructor() {
    try {
      const databaseUrl = process.env.DATABASE_URL ?? '<undefined database url>';
      this.client = new mongodb.MongoClient(databaseUrl);
    } catch (error) {
      // Handle error
    }
  }

  async save(salesItem: SalesItem): Promise<void> {
    const salesItemDocument = MongoDbSalesItemRepository.toDocument(salesItem);

    try {
      await this.connectIfNeeded();
      await this.salesItemsCollection.insertOne(salesItemDocument);
    } catch (error) {
      throw new DatabaseError(error);
    }
  }

  async findAll(): Promise<SalesItem[]> {
    try {
      await this.connectIfNeeded();
      const cursor = this.salesItemsCollection.find();
      const salesItemDocuments = await cursor.toArray();

      return salesItemDocuments.map((salesItemDocument) =>
        this.toDomainEntity(salesItemDocument),
      );
    } catch (error) {
      throw new DatabaseError(error);
```

---

[13]https://www.npmjs.com/package/mongodb

[14]https://github.com/pksilen/clean-code-principles-code/tree/main/chapter6/salesitemservice

```
    }
  }

  async find(id: string): Promise<SalesItem | null> {
    try {
      await this.connectIfNeeded();

      const salesItemDocument = await this.salesItemsCollection.findOne({
        _id: id as any,
      });

      return salesItemDocument ? this.toDomainEntity(salesItemDocument) : null;
    } catch (error) {
      throw new DatabaseError(error);
    }
  }

  async update(salesItem: SalesItem): Promise<void> {
    const filter = { _id: salesItem.id as any };

    const update = {
      $set: MongoDbSalesItemRepository.toDocumentWithout(salesItem, [
        '_id',
        'createdAtTimestampInMs',
      ]),
    };

    try {
      await this.connectIfNeeded();
      await this.salesItemsCollection.updateOne(filter, update);
    } catch (error) {
      throw new DatabaseError(error.message);
    }
  }

  async delete(id: string): Promise<void> {
    try {
      await this.connectIfNeeded();

      await this.salesItemsCollection.deleteOne({
        _id: id as any,
      });
    } catch (error) {
      throw new DatabaseError(error);
    }
  }

  private async connectIfNeeded() {
    if (this.salesItemsCollection) {
      return;
    }

    await this.client.connect();
    const databaseUrl = process.env.DATABASE_URL ?? '';
    const databaseName = databaseUrl.split('/')[3];
    const db = this.client.db(databaseName);
    this.salesItemsCollection = db.collection('salesitems');
  }

  private toDomainEntity(salesItemDoc: mongodb.Document): SalesItem {
    const { _id, ...rest } = salesItemDoc;
    return { id: _id.toString(), ...rest } as SalesItem;
  }

  private static toDocument(salesItem: SalesItem): Record<string, any> {
    return {
      _id: salesItem.id,
      createdAtTimestampInMs: salesItem.createdAtTimestampInMs,
      name: salesItem.name,
      priceInCents: salesItem.priceInCents,
```

```
      images: salesItem.images.map((image) => ({
        id: image.id,
        rank: image.rank,
        url: image.url,
      })),
    };
  }

  private static toDocumentWithout(
    salesItem: SalesItem,
    keys: string[],
  ): Record<string, any> {
    const fullDocument = MongoDbSalesItemRepository.toDocument(salesItem);

    return Object.fromEntries(
      Object.entries(fullDocument).filter(([key]) => !keys.includes(key)),
    );
  }
}
```

9.3: Key-Value Database Principle

Use a key-value database for fast real-time access to data stored by a key. Key-value stores usually store data in memory with a possibility for persistence.

A simple use case for a key-value database is to use it as a cache for a relational database. For example, a microservice can store SQL query results from a relational database in the cache. *Redis* is a popular open-source key-value store. Let's have an example using JavaScript and Redis to cache an SQL query result. In the below example, we assume that the SQL query result is available as a JavaScript object:

```
redisClient.set(sqlQueryStatement, JSON.stringify(sqlQueryResult));
```

The cached SQL query result can be fetched from Redis:

```
const sqlQueryResultJson = redisClient.get(sqlQueryStatement);
```

With Redis, you can create key-value pairs that expire automatically after a specific time. This is a useful feature if you are using the key-value database as a cache. You may want the cached items to expire after a while.

In addition to plain strings, Redis also supports other data structures. For example, you can store a list, queue, or hash map for a key. If you store a queue in Redis, you can use it as a simple single-consumer message broker. Below is an example of producing a message to a topic in the message broker:

```
// RPUSH command (= right push) pushes a new message
// to the end of the list identified by key _topic_.
redisClient.rpush(topic, message);
```

Below is an example of consuming a message from a topic in the message broker:

```
// LPOP command (= left pop) pops a message from
// the beginning of the list identified by key _topic_
// The LPOP command removes the value from the list
const message = redisClient.lpop(topic);
```

9.4: Wide-Column Databases

Use a wide-column database when you have a large amount of data and know what queries you need to execute, and you want these queries to be fast.

Table structures of a wide-column database are optimized for specific queries. With a wide-column database, storing duplicate data is okay to make the queries faster. Wide-column databases also scale horizontally well, making them suitable for storing a large amount of data.

This section uses Apache Cassandra[15] as an example of a wide-column database. Cassandra is a scalable multi-node database engine. In Cassandra, the data of a table is divided into partitions according to the table's partition key[16]. A partition key is composed of one or more columns of the table. Each partition is stored on a single Cassandra node. You can think that Cassandra is a key-value store where the key is the partition key, and the value is another "nested" table. The rows in the "nested" table are uniquely identified by clustering columns sorted by default in ascending order. The sort order can be changed to descending if wanted.

The partition key and the clustering columns form the table's primary key. The primary key uniquely identifies a row. The order of these components always puts the partition key first and then the clustering columns (or clustering key). Let's have an example table that is used to store hotels near a particular point of interest (POI):

```
CREATE TABLE hotels_by_poi (
  poi_name text,
  hotel_distance_in_meters_from_poi int,
  hotel_id uuid,
  hotel_name text,
  hotel_address text,
  PRIMARY KEY (poi_name, hotel_distance_in_meters_from_poi, hotel_id)
);
```

In the above example, the primary key consists of three columns. The first column (poi_name) is always the partition key. The partition key must be given in a query. Otherwise, the query will be slow because Cassandra must perform a full table scan because it does not know which node data is located. When the partition key is given in a SELECT statement's WHERE clause, Cassandra can find the appropriate node where the data for that particular partition resides. The two other primary key columns, hotel_distance_-in_meters_from_poi and hotel_id, are the clustering columns. They define the order and uniqueness of the rows in the "nested" table.

---

[15]https://cassandra.apache.org/_/index.html

[16]https://www.baeldung.com/cassandra-keys

hotel_distance_fro m_poi	hotel_id	hotel_name	hotel_address
100	3456	Hotel X	...
100	8976	Hotel Y	...
150	11234	Hotel A	...

poi_name
Picadilly Circus
Trafalgar Square
...

hotel_distance_fro m_poi	hotel_id	hotel_name	hotel_address
250	2346	Hotel C	...
300	7865	Hotel B	...
350	14566	Hotel F	...

Figure 9.13. hotels_by_poi Table

The above figure shows that when you give a partition key value (poi_name), you have access to the respective "nested" table where rows are ordered first by the hotel_distance_in_meters_from_poi (ascending) and second by the hotel_id (ascending).

Now, it is easy for a hotel room booking client to ask the server to execute a query to find hotels near a POI given by a user. The following query will return the first 15 hotels nearest to *Piccadilly Circus* POI:

```
SELECT
  hotel_distance_in_meters_from_poi,
  hotel_id,
  hotel_name,
  hotel_address
FROM hotels_by_poi
WHERE poi_name = 'Piccadilly Circus'
LIMIT 15
```

When a user selects a particular hotel from the result of the above query, the client can request the execution of another query to fetch information about the selected hotel. The user wants to see other POIs near the selected hotel. For that query, we should create another table:

```
CREATE TABLE pois_by_hotel_id (
  hotel_id uuid,
  poi_distance_in_meters_from_hotel int,
  poi_id uuid,
  poi_name text,
  poi_address text,
  PRIMARY KEY (hotel_id, poi_distance_in_meters_from_hotel, poi_id)
);
```

Now, a client can request the server to execute a query to fetch the nearest 20 POIs for a selected hotel. (hotel with id c5a49cb0-8d98-47e3-8767-c30bc075e529):

```
SELECT
  poi_distance_in_meters_from_hotel,
  poi_id,
  poi_name,
  poi_address
FROM pois_by_hotel_id
WHERE hotel_id = c5a49cb0-8d98-47e3-8767-c30bc075e529
LIMIT 20
```

In a real-life scenario, a user wants to search for hotels near a particular POI for a selected period. The server should respond with the nearest hotels having free rooms for the selected period. For that kind of query, we can create an additional table for storing hotel room availability:

```
CREATE TABLE availability_by_hotel_id (
  hotel_id uuid,
  accommodation_date date,
  available_room_count counter,
  PRIMARY KEY (hotel_id, accommodation_date)
);
```

The above table is updated whenever a room for a specific day is booked or a booking for a room is canceled. The available_room_count column value is either decremented or incremented by one in the update procedure.

Let's say that the following query has been executed:

```
SELECT
  hotel_distance_in_meters_from_poi,
  hotel_id,
  hotel_name,
  hotel_address
FROM hotels_by_poi
WHERE poi_name = 'Piccadilly Circus'
LIMIT 30
```

Next, we should find hotels from the result of 30 hotels that have available rooms between the 1st of September 2023 and 3rd of September 2023. We cannot use joins in Cassandra, but we can execute the following query where we specifically list the hotel ids returned by the above query:

```
SELECT hotel_id, MIN(available_room_count)
FROM availability_by_hotel_id
WHERE hotel_id IN (List the 30 hotel_ids here...) AND
      accommodation_date >= '2022-09-01' AND
      accommodation_date <= '2022-09-03'
GROUP BY hotel_id
LIMIT 15
```

As a result of the above query, we have a list of a maximum of 15 hotels for which the minimum available room count is listed. We can return a list of those maximum 15 hotels where the minimum available room count is one or more to the user.

If Cassandra's query language supported the HAVING clause, which it does not currently support, we could have issued the following query to get what we wanted:

```
SELECT hotel_id, MIN(available_room_count)
FROM availability_by_hotel_id
WHERE hotel_id IN (List the 30 hotel_ids here...) AND
      accommodation_date >= '2022-09-01' AND
      accommodation_date <= '2022-09-03'
GROUP BY hotel_id
HAVING MIN(available_room_count) >= 1
LIMIT 15
```

A wide-column database is also useful for storing time-series data, e.g., from IoT devices and sensors. Below is a table definition for storing measurement data in a telecom network analytics system:

```
CREATE TABLE measurements (
  measure_name text,
  dimension_name text,
  aggregation_period text,
  measure_timestamp timestamp,
  measure_value double,
  dimension_value text,
  PRIMARY KEY ((measure_name, dimension_name, aggregation_period),
              measure_timestamp,
              measure_value,
              dimension_value)
) WITH CLUSTERING ORDER BY (
  measure_timestamp DESC,
  measure_value DESC,
  dimension_value ASC
);
```

In the above table, we have defined a *compound partition key* containing three columns: measure_name, dimension_name, and aggregation_period. Columns for a compound partition key are given in parentheses because the first column of the primary key is always the partition key.

Suppose we have implemented a client that visualizes measurements. In the client, a user can first choose what counter/KPI (= measure name) to visualize, then select a dimension and aggregation period. Let's say that the user wants to see *dropped_call_percentage* for *cells* calculated for one minute at 2023-02-03 16:00. The following kind of query can be executed:

```
SELECT measure_value, dimension_value
FROM measurements
WHERE measure_name = 'dropped_call_percentage' AND
      dimension_name = 'cell' AND
      aggregation_period = '1min' AND
      measureTimestamp = '2022-02-03T16:00+0000'
LIMIT 50;
```

The above query returns the top 50 cells with the highest dropped call percentage for the givenWe can create another table to hold measurements for a selected dimension value, e.g., for a particular cell id. This table can be used to drill down to a particular dimension and measure values in history. minute.

We can create another table to hold measurements for a selected dimension value, e.g., for a particular cell id. This table can be used to drill down to a particular dimension and measure values in history.

```
CREATE TABLE measurements_by_dimension (
  measure_name text,
  dimension_name text,
  aggregation_period text,
  dimension_value text,
  measure_timestamp timestamp,
  measure_value double,
  PRIMARY KEY ((measure_name,
                dimension_name,
                aggregation_period,
                dimension_value), measure_timestamp)
) WITH CLUSTERING ORDER BY (measureTimestamp DESC);
```

The below query will return dropped call percentage values for the last 30 minutes for the cell identified by *cell id* 3000:

```
SELECT measure_value, measureTimestamp
FROM measurements_by_dimension
WHERE measure_name = 'dropped_call_percentage' AND
      dimension_name = 'cell' AND
      aggregation_period = '1min' AND
      dimension_value = '3000'
LIMIT 30;
```

9.5: Search Engines

Use a search engine if you have free-form text data that users should be able to query.

A search engine (like Elasticsearch[17]) is useful for storing information like log entries collected from microservices. You typically want to search the collected log data by the text in the log messages.

It is not necessary to use a search engine when you need to search for text data. Other databases, both document and relational, have a special index type that can index free-form text data in a column. Considering the earlier example with MongoDB, we might want a client to be able to search sales items by the text in the sales item's name. We don't need to store sales items in a search engine database. We can continue storing them in a document database (MongoDB) and introduce a *text* type index for the name field. That index can be created with the following MongoDB command:

```
sales_items.create_index( { 'name': 'text' } )
```

---

[17]https://www.elastic.co/elasticsearch

10: Concurrent Programming Principles

This chapter presents the following concurrent programming principles:

- Threading principle
- Thread safety principle

10.1: Threading Principle

Modern cloud-native microservices should primarily scale out by adding more processes, not scale up by adding more threads. Use threading only when it is needed or is a good optimization.

When developing modern cloud-native software, microservices should be stateless and automatically scale horizontally (scaling out and in via adding and removing processes). The role of threading in modern cloud-native microservices is not as prominent as it was earlier when software consisted of monoliths running on bare metal servers, mainly capable of scaling up or down. Nowadays, you should use threading if it is a good optimization or otherwise needed.

Suppose we have a software system with an event-driven architecture. Multiple microservices communicate with each other using asynchronous messaging. Each microservice instance has only a single thread that consumes messages from a message broker and processes them. If the message broker's message queue for a microservice starts growing too long, the microservice should scale out by adding a new instance. When the load for the microservice diminishes, it can scale in by removing an instance. There is no need to use threading at all.

We could use threading in the data exporter microservice if the input consumer and the output producer were synchronous. The reason for threading is optimization. If we had everything in a single thread and the microservice was performing network I/O (either input or output-related), the microservice would have nothing to execute because it is waiting for some network I/O to complete. Using threads, we can optimize the execution of the microservice so that it potentially has something to do when waiting for an I/O operation to complete.

Many modern input consumers and output producers are available as asynchronous implementations. If we use an asynchronous consumer and producer in the data exporter microservice, we can eliminate threading because network I/O will not block the execution of the main thread anymore. As a rule of thumb, consider using asynchronous code first, and if it is not possible or feasible, only then consider threading.

You might need a microservice to execute housekeeping tasks on a specific schedule in the background. Instead of using threading and implementing the housekeeping functionality in the microservice, consider implementing it in a separate microservice to ensure that the *single responsibility principle* is followed. For example, you can configure the housekeeping microservice to be run at regular intervals using a Kubernetes CronJob.

Threading also brings complexity to a microservice because the microservice must ensure thread safety. You will be in big trouble if you forget to implement thread safety, as threading and synchronization-related bugs are hard to find. Thread safety is discussed later in this chapter. Threading also brings complexity to deploying a microservice because the number of vCPUs requested by the microservice can depend on the thread count.

10.1.1: Parallel Algorithms

Parallel algorithms are similar to threading. With parallel algorithms, it is a question about implicit threading instead of explicit threading. Threads are created behind the scenes to enable an algorithm to execute in parallel on some data set. You don't necessarily need a parallel algorithm in a cloud-native microservice. You can often run algorithms without parallelization and instead scale out on demand.

Many languages offer parallel algorithms. In Java, you can perform parallel operations with a parallel stream created with the `parallelStream` method:

```
final var numbers = List.of(1, 2, 3, 4);
numbers.parallelStream().forEach(number ->
  System.out.println(number + " " +
                     Thread.currentThread().getName())
);
```

The output of the above code could be, for example:

```
3 ForkJoinPool.commonPool-worker-2
2 ForkJoinPool.commonPool-worker-1
1 ForkJoinPool.commonPool-worker-3
4 main
```

The output will differ on each run. Usually, the parallel executor creates the same amount of threads as there are CPU cores available. This means that you can scale your microservice up by requesting more CPU cores. In many languages, you can control how many CPU cores the parallel algorithm should use. You can, for example, configure that a parallel algorithm should use the number of available CPU cores minus two if you have two threads dedicated to some other processing. In C++20, you cannot control the number of threads for a parallel algorithm, but an improvement is coming in a future C++ release.

Below is the same example as above written in C++:

```
#include <algorithm>
#include <execution>
#include <thread>
#include <iostream>

std::vector<int> numbers{1, 2, 4, 5};

std::for_each(std::execution::par,
              numbers.cbegin(),
              numbers.cend(),
              [](const auto number)
              {
                std::cout << number
                          << " "
                          << std::this_thread::get_id()
                          << "\n";
              });
```

10.2: Thread Safety Principle

If you are using threads, you must ensure thread safety. Thread safety means that only one thread can access shared data simultaneously to avoid race conditions.

Do not assume thread safety if you use a data structure or library. You must consult the documentation to see whether thread safety is guaranteed. If thread safety is not mentioned in the documentation, it can't be assumed. The best way to communicate thread safety to developers is to name things so that thread safety is explicit. For example, you could create a thread-safe collection library and have a class named `ThreadSafeLinkedList` to indicate the class is thread-safe. Another common word used to indicate thread safety is *concurrent*, e.g., the `ConcurrentHashMap` class in Java.

There are several ways to ensure thread safety:

- Synchronization directive
- Atomic variables
- Concurrent collections
- Mutexes
- Spin locks

The subsequent sections describe each of the above techniques in more detail.

10.2.1: Synchronization Directive

In some languages, you can use a specific directive to indicate that a particular piece of code is synchronized, meaning that only one thread can execute that piece of code at a time.

Java offers the `synchronized` keyword that can be used in the following ways:

- Synchronized instance method
- Synchronized static method
- Synchronized code block

```
public synchronized void doSomething() {
  // Only one thread can execute this at the same time
}
public static synchronized void doSomething() {
  // Only one thread can execute this at the same time
}
public void doSomething() {
  // ...

  synchronized (this) {
    // Only one thread can execute this at the same time
  }

  // ...
}
```

10.2.2: Atomic Variables

If you have some data shared between threads and that data is just a simple primitive variable, like a boolean or integer, you can use an atomic variable to guarantee thread safety and don't need any additional synchronization. Atomic variable reads and updates are guaranteed to be atomic, so there is no possibility for a race condition between two threads. Some atomic variable implementations use locks. Consult the language's documentation to see if a certain atomic type is guaranteed to be lock-free.

In C++, you can create a thread-safe counter using an atomic variable:

Figure 10.1. ThreadSafeCounter.h

```
#include <atomic>

class ThreadSafeCounter
{
public:
  ThreadSafeCounter() = default;

  void increment()
  {
    ++m_counter;
  }

  uint32_t getValue() const
  {
    return m_counter.load();
  }

private:
  std::atomic<uint64_t> m_counter{0U};
}
```

Multiple threads can increment a counter of the above type simultaneously without additional synchronization.

10.2.3: Concurrent Collections

Concurrent collections can be used by multiple threads without any additional synchronization. Java offers several concurrent collections in the java.util.concurrent package.

C++ does not offer concurrent collections in its standard library. You can create a concurrent, i.e., a thread-safe collection using the *decorator pattern* by adding needed synchronization (locking) to an existing collection class. Below is a partial example of a thread-safe vector created in C++:

Figure 10.2. ThreadSafeVector.h

```
#include <vector>

template <typename T>
class ThreadSafeVector
{
public:
  explicit ThreadSafeVector(std::vector<T>&& vector):
    m_vector{std::move(vector)}
  {}

  void pushBack(const T& value)
  {
    // Lock using a mutex or spin lock
```

```
    m_vector.push_back(value);

    // Unlock
  }

  // Implement other methods with locking...

private:
  std::vector<T> m_vector;
};
```

10.2.4: Mutexes

A mutex is a synchronization primitive that can protect shared data from being simultaneously accessed by multiple threads. A mutex is usually implemented as a class with lock and unlock methods. The locking only succeeds by one thread at a time. Another thread can lock the mutex only after the previous thread has unlocked the mutex. The lock method waits until the mutex becomes available for locking.

Let's implement the pushBack method using a mutex:

Figure 10.3. ThreadSafeVector.h

```
#include <mutex>
#include <vector>

template <typename T>
class ThreadSafeVector
{
public:
  explicit ThreadSafeVector(std::vector<T>&& vector):
    m_vector{std::move(vector)}
  {}

  void pushBack(const T& value)
  {
    m_mutex.lock();
    m_vector.push_back(value);
    m_mutex.unlock();
  }

  // Implement other methods ...

private:
  std::vector<T> m_vector;
  std::mutex m_mutex;
};
```

Mutexes are not usually directly used because the risk exists that a mutex is forgotten to be unlocked. Instead of using the plain std::mutex class, you can use a mutex with the std::scoped_lock class. The std::scoped_lock class wraps a mutex instance. It will lock the wrapped mutex during construction and unlock it during destruction. In this way, you cannot forget to unlock a locked mutex. The mutex will be locked for the scope of the scoped lock variable. Below is the above example modified to use a scoped lock:

Figure 10.4. ThreadSafeVector.h

```cpp
#include <mutex>
#include <vector>

template <typename T>
class ThreadSafeVector
{
public:
  explicit ThreadSafeVector(std::vector<T>&& vector):
    m_vector{std::move(vector)}
  {}

  void pushBack(const T& value)
  {
    const std::scoped_lock scopedLock{m_mutex};
    m_vector.push_back(value);
  }

  // Implement other methods ...

private:
  std::vector<T> m_vector;
  std::mutex m_mutex;
};
```

10.2.5: Spinlocks

A spinlock is a lock that causes a thread trying to acquire it to simply wait in a loop (spinning the loop) while repeatedly checking whether the lock has become available. Since the thread remains active but is not performing a useful task, using a spinlock is busy waiting. You can avoid some of the overhead of thread context switches using a spinlock. Spinlocks are an effective way of locking if the locking periods are short.

Let's implement a spinlock using C++:

Figure 10.5. Spinlock.h"

```cpp
#include <atomic>
#include <thread>

#include <boost/core/noncopyable.hpp>

class Spinlock : public boost::noncopyable
{
public:
  void lock()
  {
    while (true) {
      const bool wasLocked =
        m_isLocked.test_and_set(std::memory_order_acquire);

      if (!wasLocked) {
        // Is now locked
        return;
      }

      // Wait for the lock to be released
      while (m_isLocked.test(std::memory_order_relaxed)) {
        // Prioritize other threads
        std::this_thread::yield();
      }
    }
  }
```

619

```
  void unlock()
  {
    m_isLocked.clear(std::memory_order_release);
  }
private:
  std::atomic_flag m_isLocked = ATOMIC_FLAG_INIT;
};
```

In the above implementation, we use the `std::atomic_flag` class because it guarantees a lock-free implementation across all C++ compilers. We also use a non-default memory ordering to allow the compiler to emit more efficient code.

Now we can re-implement the `ThreadSafeVector` class using a spinlock instead of a mutex:

Figure 10.6. ThreadSafeVector.h

```
#include <vector>
#include "Spinlock.h"

template <typename T>
class ThreadSafeVector
{
public:
  explicit ThreadSafeVector(std::vector<T>&& vector):
    m_vector{std::move(vector)}
  {}

  void pushBack(const T& value)
  {
    m_spinlock.lock();
    m_vector.push_back(value);
    m_spinlock.unlock();
  }

  // Implement other methods ...

private:
  std::vector<T> m_vector;
  Spinlock m_spinlock;
};
```

Like mutexes, we should not use raw spinlocks in our code; instead, we should use a scoped lock. Below is an implementation of a generic `ScopedLock` class that handles the locking and unlocking of a lockable object:

Figure 10.7. ScopedLock.h

```
#include <concepts>

#include <boost/core/noncopyable.hpp>

template<typename T>
concept Lockable = requires(T a)
{
    { a.lock() } -> std::convertible_to<void>;
    { a.unlock() } -> std::convertible_to<void>;
};

template <Lockable L>
class ScopedLock : public boost::noncopyable
{
public:
  explicit ScopedLock(L& lockable):
    m_lockable{lockable}
```

```
  {
    m_lockable.lock();
  }

  ~ScopedLock()
  {
    m_lockable.unlock();
  }
private:
  L& m_lockable;
};
```

Let's change the ThreadSafeVector class to use a scoped lock:

Figure 10.8. ThreadSafeVector.h

```
#include <vector>
#include "ScopedLock.h"
#include "Spinlock.h"

template <typename T>
class ThreadSafeVector
{
public:
  explicit ThreadSafeVector(std::vector<T>&& vector):
    m_vector{std::move(vector)}
  {}

  void pushBack(const T& value)
  {
    const ScopedLock scopedLock{m_spinlock};
    m_vector.push_back(value);
  }

  // Implement other methods ...

private:
  std::vector<T> m_vector;
  Spinlock m_spinlock;
};
```

11: Agile and Teamwork Principles

This chapter presents agile and teamwork principles. The following principles are described:

- Twelve principles of agile software
- Use an agile framework principle
- Define the done principle
- You write code for other people principle
- Avoid technical debt principle
- Software component documentation principle
- Code review principle
- Uniform code formatting principle
- Highly concurrent development principle
- Pair programming principle
- Mob programming principle
- Ask and offer help principle
- Well-defined development team roles principle
- Competence transfer principle
- Inter-team communication principle

11.1: Twelve Principles of Agile Software

There are 12 principles behind the Agile Manifesto[1] that we will discuss next.

1. **Our highest priority is to satisfy the customer through early and continuous delivery of valuable software.**

Important points to note in the above statement are that customer satisfaction should always be the number one priority. The software has to be valuable for the customer. We have to build software that the customer needs, not necessarily what the customer wants. Valuable software can be built only together with the customer and listening to the customer's feedback. We have to have a continuous delivery pipeline available from the first delivery onwards, and the first delivery should occur as soon as something is ready to be delivered, something that has value for the customer.

2. **Welcome changing requirements, even late in development. Agile processes harness change for the customer's competitive advantage.**

We have to embrace change. If the requirements are changing quickly, use Kanban as the process. When the software is more mature, the requirements tend to change slower. In that case, you can use Scrum and some agile framework like SAFe. We will talk about the agile framework in the next section.

---

[1]https://agilemanifesto.org/

3. **Deliver working software frequently, from a couple of weeks to a couple of months, with a preference for the shorter timescale.**

You must build a CI/CD pipeline to automate the software delivery. Otherwise, you will not be able to deliver working software on a short timescale.

4. **Business people and developers must work together daily throughout the project.**

This means that there should exist a tight feedback loop between developers, product management, and the customer whenever the customer needs and requirements are not clear.

5. **Build projects around motivated individuals. Give them the environment and support they need, and trust them to get the job done.**

The key idea here is that management should offer all the needed tools, support, and trust, not manage the software development project.

6. **The most efficient and effective method of conveying information to and within a development team is face-to-face conversation.**

I know this too well. Information is often shared via email messages or other channels like Confluence. These messages are often left unread or not fully read and understood. F2F communication allows better delivery of the message and allows people to react and ask questions easier.

7. **Working software is the primary measure of progress.**

Working software means comprehensively tested software. You need to define doneness criteria for software user stories and features. Only after the customer's verification can the software be declared fully working.

8. **Agile processes promote sustainable development. The sponsors, developers, and users should be able to maintain a constant pace indefinitely.**

For a development team that measures user stories in story points, this means that each month, the team should be able to produce software worth of the same amount of story points, and this should continue indefinitely.

9. **Continuous attention to technical excellence and good design enhances agility.**

Bad design or lack of design and technical excellence produces software with technical debt that will slow the team down and reduce the team agility.

10. **Simplicity—the art of maximizing the amount of work not done—is essential.**

This is the YAGNI principle we discussed in an earlier chapter. Implement functionality only when or if it is really needed. Simplicity does not mean sloppy design or lack of design.

11. **The best architectures, requirements, and designs emerge from self-organizing teams.**

If the management forces a certain organization, the architecture of the software produced by the teams will resemble the organization of the teams, which means that the management has actually architected the software, which should never be done. Management should not force an organization but let teams organize themselves as they see best.

12. **At regular intervals, the team reflects on how to become more effective, then tunes and adjusts its behavior accordingly.**

Instead of at regular intervals, this can be a continuous thing. Whenever somebody notices a need for fine-tuning or adjustment, that should be brought up immediately. Agile frameworks and scrum have ceremonies for retrospection, but the problem with these ceremonies is that people should not wait until a ceremony to speak up. People quickly forget what they had in mind. It is better to speak up right when an improvement need is noticed.

11.2: Use Agile Framework Principle

Using an agile framework can bring numerous benefits to an organization, including an increase in productivity, improvements in quality, faster time-to-market, and better employee satisfaction.

The above statements come from SAFe customer stories[2] of some companies having adopted Scaled Agile Framework (SAFe)[3].

An agile framework describes a standardized way of developing software, which is essential, especially in large organizations. In today's work environments, people change jobs frequently, and teams tend to change often, which can lead to a situation where there is no common understanding of the way of working unless a particular agile framework is used. An agile framework establishes a clear division of responsibilities, and everyone can focus on what they do best.

In the *SAFe*, for example, during a program increment (PI) planning[4], development teams plan features for the next PI[5] (consisting of 4 iterations, two weeks per iteration, a total of 8 weeks followed by an IP iteration[6]). In the PI planning, teams split features into user stories to see which features fit the PI. Planned user stories will be assigned story points, and stories will be placed into iterations.

> Story points can be measured in concrete units, like person days. Use a slightly modified Fibonacci sequence, like 1, 2, 3, 5, 8, 13, 20, 40, to estimate the size of a user story. The benefit of using the Fibonacci sequence is that it takes into account the fact that the effort estimation accuracy decreases when the needed work amount increases. Story points can also be measured in abstract units of work. Then, you compare a user story to a so-called *golden user story* (a medium-sized user story known to all team members) and assign the effort estimate for the user story based on how much smaller or larger it is compared to the golden user story. When using abstract story points, you can also use a Fibonacci

[2]https://scaledagile.com/insights-customer-stories/
[3]https://www.scaledagileframework.com/
[4]https://scaledagileframework.com/pi-planning/
[5]https://v5.scaledagileframework.com/program-increment/
[6]https://scaledagileframework.com/innovation-and-planning-iteration/

sequence, e.g., 1 (XS), 2 (S), 3 (M), 5 (L), 8 (XL). Let's say you have a medium-sized golden user story with three story points, and you need to estimate work effort for a new user story known to be bigger than the golden user story. Then, you assign either 5 or 8 story points to the new user story, depending on how much bigger it is compared to the golden user story. Similarly, if a new user story is known to be smaller than the golden user story, you assign either 2 or 1 story points to it. If the new user story is roughly the same amount of work as the golden user story, assign three story points to the user story. Remember that a single user story should be completed in one iteration. If you think a user story is bigger than that, it must be split into smaller user stories. Smaller user stories are always better because they are easier to estimate, and the estimates will be more accurate.

There are several ways to estimate story points for user stories:

- If a user story has a single assignee, they can estimate the effort. The assignee might be the person who knows most about the particular user story.
- Team can decide together, e.g., using planning poker[7]
- Lead developer can provide initial estimates, which are gone through with the team

When using concrete story points (person days), the team velocity for an iteration is also calculated in person days. This makes it easy to adjust the iteration velocity based on estimated ad-hoc and maintenance work, as well as public holidays and vacations. If the team uses abstract story points, the team velocity is inferred from past iterations. This method does not allow straightforward adjustments to the velocity due to team size changes, sudden changes in the amount of ad-hoc/maintenance work, and leaves. I like to estimate in person days, because I use time as a unit for anything else I estimate in the world, so why not use time with story points also. I find it difficult to figure out relative estimates in my head. I also feel that estimating in person days allows me to give more accurate estimates. Estimating in person days works best with a team of seasoned developers primarily working on user stories independently and when those user stories are split into small enough.

This planning phase results in a plan the team should follow in the PI. Junior SAFe practitioners can make mistakes like underestimating the work needed to complete a user story. But this is a self-correcting issue. When teams and individuals develop, they can better estimate the needed work amount, making plans more solid. Teams and developers learn that they must make all work visible. For example, reserve time for maintenance activities, reserve time to learn new things, like a programming language or framework, and reserve time for refactoring. When you estimate the effort needed for a user story, you should rather overestimate than underestimate. Let's have an example with a user story measured in concrete units, i.e., person days. If you think you can do it in half a day, assign one story point to that user story. If you think it takes two days, if everything goes well, assign three story points for that user story so that you have some safety margin if things go awry. Being able to keep the planned schedule and sometimes even completing work early is very satisfying. This will make you feel like a true professional and boost your self-esteem.

Teams and individuals estimate their work. There is no management involved. Managers don't tell you how much time you have for something. They don't come asking when something is ready or pressure you to complete tasks earlier than estimated. Also, they don't come to you with extra work to do. All of this will make your work feel less stressful.

My personal experience with SAFe over the past five years has been mainly positive. I feel I can concentrate more on "the real work", which makes me happier. There are fewer meetings, fewer irrelevant emails, and fewer interruptions in the development flow in general. This is mainly because the team has a *product*

---

[7]https://en.wikipedia.org/wiki/Planning_poker

owner and *scrum master* whose role is to protect the team members from any "waste" or "the management stuff" and allow them to concentrate on their work.

If a team has work that does not require effort estimation, Kanban can be used instead of Scrum. For example, in my organization, the DevOps team uses Kanban, and all development teams use Scrum. A Scrum development team can commit to delivering a feature on a certain schedule, which is not possible when using Kanban. Many development teams use Scrum to enable making commitments to the business that can make commitments to customers.

A fast-paced start-up (or any other company) delivering software to production frequently should also use Kanban if it does not need effort estimates for anything. Spending time estimating is not worthwhile if the estimates are not used for anything.

11.3: Define the Done Principle

For user stories and features, define what "done" means.

In the most optimal situation, development teams have a shared understanding of what is needed to declare a *user story* or *feature* done. Consistent results and quality from each development team can be ensured when a common definition of done exists.

When considering a user story, at least the following requirements for a done user story can be defined:

- Source code is committed to a source code repository
- Source code is reviewed
- Static code analysis is performed (No blocker/critical/major issues)
- Unit test coverage is at least X%
- CI/CD pipeline is passing
- No 3rd party software vulnerabilities
- Technical documentation is updated if needed

The product owner's (PO) role in a team is to accept user stories as done. Some of the above-mentioned requirements can be automatically checked. For example, the static code analysis should be part of every CI/CD pipeline and can also check the unit test coverage automatically. If static code analysis does not pass or the unit test coverage is unacceptable, the CI/CD pipeline should not pass.

Some additional requirements for done-ness should be defined when considering a feature because features can be delivered to customers. Below is a non-exhaustive list of some requirements for a done feature:

- Architectural design documentation is updated
- Integration tests are added/updated
- End-to-end tests are added/updated if needed
- Non-functional testing is done
- User documentation is updated and reviewed
- Threat modeling is done, and threat countermeasures (security features) are implemented
- Observability is updated if needed

To complete all the needed done-ness requirements, development teams can use tooling that helps them remember what needs to be done. For example, when creating a new user story in a tool like Jira, an existing prototype story could be cloned (or a template used). The prototype or template story should contain tasks that must be completed before a user story can be approved.

11.4: You Write Code for Other People Principle

You write code for other people and your future self.

The *fundamental theorem of readability* (from the book *The Art of Readable Code* by *Dustin Boswell* and *Trevor Foucher*) states:

> *Code should be written to minimize the time needed for someone else to understand it.*

And in the above statement, that *someone else* also means the future version of you.

Situations where you work alone with a piece of software are relatively rare. You cannot predict what will happen in the future. There might be someone else responsible for the code you once wrote. There are cases when you work with some code for some time and then, after several years, need to return to that code. For these reasons, writing clean code that is easy to read and understand by others and yourself in the future is essential. Remember that code is not written for a computer only but also for people. People should be able to read and comprehend code easily. Remember that code is read more often than written. At best, the code reads like beautiful prose!

11.5: Avoid Technical Debt Principle

Technical debt is the implied cost of future rework/refactoring required when choosing an easy but limited solution instead of a better approach that could take more time.

The most common practices for avoiding technical debt are the following:

- The architecture team should design the high-level architecture (Each team should have a representative in the architecture team. Usually, it is the technical lead of the team)
- Development teams should perform domain-driven design (DDD) and object-oriented design (OOD) first, and only after that proceed with implementation
- Conduct DDD and OOD within the team with relevant senior and junior developers involved
- Don't take the newest 3rd party software immediately into use. Instead, use mature 3rd party software that has an established position in the market
- Design for easily replacing a 3rd party software component with another 3rd party component.
- Design for scalability (for future load)
- Design for extension: new functionality is placed in new classes instead of modifying existing classes (open-closed principle)
- Utilize a plugin architecture (possibility to create plugins to add new functionality later)
- Reserve time for refactoring
- Use test-driven development (TDD)
- Use behavioral-driven development (BDD)

The top reasons for technical debt are the following (not in any particular order):

- Using niche technologies or brand-new technologies that are immature
- Not making software scalable for future processing needs
- When it is not relatively easy to replace a 3rd party software component (E.g., using custom SQL syntax does not allow changing the database, not using the *adapter pattern* with 3rd party libraries)
- Not reviewing the architecture
- Not doing any domain-driven design and object-oriented design before starting coding
- Not engaging senior enough developers in the DDD and OOD phase
- Not understanding and using relevant design principles and patterns

    - Not programming against interfaces
    - Not easy to change a dependency (DI missing)
    - No facades

- Not reviewing code changes
- Not reserving time for refactoring
- Too small work effort estimates
- Time pressure from management
- Management does not understand the value of refactoring
- Postponing refactoring to a time point that never comes
- Forgetting to refactor (at least store the needed refactoring work items in a TODO.MD file in the source code repository)
- No unit tests, harder to refactor
- Not practicing TDD
- Duplicate code
- Not conducting the Boy Scout rule
- Laziness (using what comes first in mind or constantly trying to find the easiest and quickest way to do things)

11.6: Software Component Documentation Principle

Each software component needs to be documented. The main idea behind documenting is quickly onboarding new people to development work.

It is crucial that setting up a development environment for a software component is well-documented and as easy as possible. Another important thing is to let people easily understand the problem domain the software component tries to solve. Also, the object-oriented design of the software component should be documented.

Software component documentation should reside in the same source code repository as the source code. The recommended way is to use a README.MD file in the root directory of the source code repository for documentation in Markdown format[8]. You should split the documentation into multiple files and store

---

[8]https://www.markdownguide.org/basic-syntax/

additional files in the *docs* directory of the source code repository. This way, it is less likely to face a merge conflict if multiple persons edit the documentation simultaneously.

JetBrains offers a new tool called Writerside[9] to author software documentation in Markdown format. This tool will automatically generate a table of contents for you. It allows you to produce diagrams using declarative code (with Mermaid.js[10]) instead of drawing them by hand. It offers tools to generate a documentation website for GitHub Pages[11] or GitLab Pages[12] as part of the software component's CI/CD pipeline.

Below is an example table of contents that can be used when documenting a software component:

- Short description of the software component and its purpose
- Feature list

    - You can provide a link to Gherkin feature files here, and then you don't have to store the same information in two places.

- Architecture (how the software component relates to other software components)
- Data flow diagram
- OOD diagrams describing different subdomains and the interfaces/classes in each subdomain, their relationships, and their main public methods.

    - Explanation of the design (if needed)
    - Don't create or generate a single class diagram for the whole microservice, but create or generate multiple class diagrams for various subdomains

- API documentation (for libraries, this should be auto-generated from the source code)
- Implementation-related documentation

    - Error handling mechanism
    - Special algorithms used
    - Performance considerations
    - Major security features

- Instructions for setting up a development environment

    - The easiest way to set up a development environment is to use a development container, a concept supported by the Visual Studio Code and several JetBrains IDEs. The benefit of using a development container[13] is that you don't have to install development tools locally, and there is no risk of using the wrong versions of the development tools

- Instructions for building the software locally
- Instructions for running unit tests locally
- Instructions for running integration tests locally
- Instructions for deploying to a test environment

---

[9]https://www.jetbrains.com/writerside/

[10]https://mermaid.js.org/intro/

[11]https://pages.github.com/

[12]https://docs.gitlab.com/ee/user/project/pages/

[13]https://containers.dev/

- Configuration

    - Environment variables
    - Configuration files
    - Secrets

- Observability

    - Logging (levels, log format, error codes including their meaning and possible resolution instructions)
    - Metrics/SLIs
    - SLOs
    - Alarms

11.7: Code Review Principle

In a code review, focus on issues a machine cannot find for you.

Before reviewing code, a static code analysis should be performed to find any issues a machine can find. The actual code review should focus on issues that static code analyzers cannot find. You should not need to review code formatting because every team member should use the same code format, which should be ensured by an automatic formatting tool. You cannot review your own code. At least one of the reviewers should be in a senior or lead role. Things to focus on in a code review are presented in the subsequent sections.

An essential part of code review is to ensure that code is readable and understandable because code is read more often than written. You can write code once (assuming perfect code), which can be read by tens or even hundreds of developers during tens of years. When reviewing (reading) code, every misunderstanding, doubt, and WTF? moment reveals that there is room for improvement in the code readability. In a code review, finding bugs can be a secondary target because bugs can be found by a machine (static code analyzers) and with an extensive set of automated tests that should always exist.

11.7.1: Focus on Object-Oriented Design

Before starting coding, it is recommended to design the software: define subdomains, needed interfaces, and classes. The product of this initial design phase should be committed to the source code repository and reviewed before starting coding. This way, correcting design flaws early and avoiding technical debt is easier. Fixing design flaws in a later phase might require significant effort or even a rewrite of the existing code. At least one senior developer should participate in the design.

If a design flaw or flaws are encountered in a review, and there is no time for an immediate fix, a refactoring user story or stories should be added to the team's backlog.

11.7.2: Focus on Removal of Duplicate Information (DRY principle)

The review material might contain duplicate information (code) the author is unaware of. It might be a question about a library that can perform the same operations the author has implemented himself. The author was not aware of the existence of the library.

11.7.3: Focus on Spreading Knowledge

If you are a senior or a lead developer, remember to lead by example. You can use a review of your code as a way to teach clean code principles and practices to your teammates in a very practical manner.

11.7.4: Focus on Function Specification by Unit Tests

To review each public function, the reviewer should start with the unit tests and see if they cover all the functionality. Is there a unit test missing for an error scenario, a security scenario, or an edge/corner case?

11.7.5: Focus on Proper and Uniform Naming

One thing that static code analysis tools can only partially do is ensure proper and uniform naming of things, like classes, functions, and variables. Correct naming is where the focus should be put in a code review. Renaming things is a very straightforward and fast refactoring task that can be performed automatically by modern IDEs.

11.7.6: Don't Focus on Premature Optimization

Do not focus on optimization in regular code reviews. Optimization is usually performed on a need basis after the code is ready and the performance is first measured. Focus on optimization-related issues only when the commit you are reviewing is dedicated to optimizing something.

11.7.7: Detect Possible Malicious Code

Code reviewers must ensure that the committed code does not contain malicious code.

11.8: Uniform Code Formatting Principle

> *In a software development team, you must decide on common rules for formatting source code.*

Consistent source code formatting is vital because if team members have different source code formatting rules, one team member's small change to a file can reformat the whole file using their formatting rules, which can cause another developer to face a major merge conflict that slows down the development process. Always agree on common source code formatting rules and preferably use a tool like *Prettier*, *Black* or *Blue* to enforce the formatting rules.

11.9: Highly Concurrent Development Principle

> *Each team member can work with a piece of code. No one should have to wait long for someone else's work to finish.*

Concurrent development is enabled when different people modify different source code files. When several people need to alter the same files, it can cause merge conflicts. These merge conflicts cause extra work because they often must be resolved manually. This manual work can be slow, and it is error-prone. The best thing is to avoid merge conflicts as much as possible. This can be achieved in the ways described in the following sections.

11.9.1: Dedicated Microservices and Microlibraries

Microservices are small by nature, and it is possible to assign the responsibility of a microservice to a single team member. This team member can proceed with the microservice at full velocity and rest assured that no one else is modifying the codebase. The same goes for libraries. You should create small microlibraries (= libraries with a single responsibility) and assign the responsibility of developing a microlibrary to a single person.

11.9.2: Dedicated Domains

Sometimes, assigning a single microservice or library to a single developer is impossible. It could be because the microservice or library is relatively large and it is not feasible to split it into multiple microservices or libraries. In those cases, the microservice or library should be divided into several subdomains. Each source code directory reflects a different subdomain. It is then possible to assign the responsibility of a single subdomain to a single person. The assignment of subdomains need not be fixed but can and should change as time passes. To distribute the knowledge of different domains in the team, it is advisable to rotate the responsibilities amongst the team members. Let's say you have a team of three developers developing a data exporter microservice consisting of input, transform, and output subdomains. The team can implement the microservice by assigning the responsibility of a single domain to a single developer. Then, all developers can proceed highly independently and concurrently with the implementation. In the early phase, they must collaborate to define interfacing between the different subdomains.

In the future, when new features are developed, team members can take responsibility for other domains to spread knowledge about the microservice in the team.

11.9.3: Follow Open-Closed Principle

Sometimes, you might face a situation where a single subdomain is so large that you need multiple developers. This, of course, should be a relatively rare case. When several developers modify source code files belonging to the same subdomain (i.e., in the same directory), merge conflicts may arise. This is the case, especially when existing source code files are modified. But when developers follow the *single responsibility principle* and *open-closed principle*, they should not change existing classes (source code files) but rather implement new functionality in new classes (source code files). Using the *open-closed principle* enables developers to develop more concurrently because they primarily work with different source code files, making merge conflicts rare or at least less frequent.

11.10: Pair Programming Principle

Pair programming helps produce better quality software with better design, less technical debt, better tests, and fewer bugs.

Pair programming is something some developers like and other developers hate. It is not a one-fits-all solution. It is not take it or leave it, either. You can have a team where some developers program in pairs and others don't. Also, people's opinions about pair programming can be prejudiced. They may have never done pair programming, so how do they know if they like it or not? It is also true that choosing the right partner to pair with can mean a lot. Some pairs have better chemistry than other pairs.

Does pair programming just increase development costs? What benefits does pair programming bring?

I see pair programming as valuable, especially in situations where a junior developer pairs with a more senior developer, and in this way, the junior developer is onboarded much faster. He can "learn from the best". Pair programming can improve software design because there is always at least two persons' view of the design. Bugs can be found more easily and usually in an earlier phase (four eyes compared to two eyes only). So, even if pair programming can add some cost, it usually results in software with better quality: better design, less technical debt, better tests, and fewer bugs.

11.11: Mob Programming Principle

> *Mob programming is a collaborative approach to software development in which the whole team or a group of developers work together in real-time on one task.*

Mob programming is an extension of pair programming where the whole team or a part of it works together using a single computer and screen to produce software. Mob programming brings the same benefits as pair programming, like a shared understanding of the domain and code, better design, less technical debt, and fewer bugs. Mob programming is also an excellent way to teach junior developers software development principles and practices in a very practical manner. Mob programming also completely removes the need for a code review. Mob programming is useful, especially when a team embarks on an entirely new domain with little knowledge beforehand. Not needing code reviews is a real benefit. In code reviews, raising issues regarding major design flaws can be difficult because correcting such flaws can require major rework. Reviewers are sympathetic towards the author and do not bring up such issues as major design flaws.

11.12: Ask and Offer Help Principle

> *Ask for help as soon as possible to speed yourself up. Offer help to your teammates in a proactive manner.*

If a developer faces a problem that is hard to solve, there are typically two schools of people: The ones that ask for help and the others that try to solve the problem themselves, no matter how long it takes. I advise every developer to ask for help when they realize they cannot quickly solve a problem by themselves. It is possible that someone else has pondered the same issue earlier and has the right answer for you immediately available. This will save you from headaches, stress, and a lot of time.

If you are a senior developer, you typically have much more knowledge than the junior developers. Thus, you should make yourself available to the junior developers proactively. If you know someone who does not know something, offer your help immediately. Don't wait until help is asked, but try to be as proactive as possible. You can simply ask: Do you want some help with that thing X?

11.13: Well-Defined Development Team Roles Principle

A software development team should have a well-defined role for each team member.

A software development team does not function optimally if everyone is doing everything or if it is expected that anyone can do anything. No one is a jack of all trades. A team achieves the best results with specialists targeted for different types of tasks. Team members need to have focus areas they like to work with and where they can excel. When you are a specialist in some area, you can complete tasks belonging to that area faster and with better quality.

Below is a list of needed roles for a development team:

- Product owner (PO)
- Scrum master (SM)
- Software developer (junior/senior/lead)
- Test automation developer
- DevOps engineer
- UI designer (if the team develops UI software components)

Let's discuss each role's responsibilities in detail in the following sections.

11.13.1: Product Owner

The product owner (PO) acts as an interface between the development team and the business, which usually means product management (PM). The PO gathers requirements (non-functional and functional) from PM via discussions. The PO is responsible for prioritizing the team backlog according to the PM's guidance and defining user stories with the team. The PO role is not usually full-time, so a single PO can serve two small teams. When the PO gathers requirements (non-functional and functional) from the PM, the PM does not usually list all the requirements, but the PO must determine all the requirements by asking the right questions and discussing them with the PM. The PO should be a technical person and should be able to create, e.g., Gherkin feature file(s) as the acceptance criteria for a backlog feature.

11.13.2: Scrum Master

A scrum master (SM) is a servant leader and a coach for the development team. The scrum master ensures that relevant agile practices and the agile process are followed. They educate the team in agile practices. If the team has a line manager, the line manager can serve as the scrum master, but any team member can be the scrum master. Being a scrum master is a part-time job. The role of the scrum master can also be rotated between the team members.

11.13.3: Software Developer

A software developer is responsible for designing, implementing, and testing software (including unit and, in many cases, integration testing). A software developer is usually focused on one or two programming languages and a couple of technical frameworks. Typically, software developers are divided into the following categories:

- Backend developers
- Frontend developers
- Full-stack developers
- Mobile developers
- Embedded developers

A backend developer develops microservices, like APIs, running in the backend. A frontend developer develops web clients. Typically, a frontend developer uses JavaScript or TypeScript, React/Angular/Vue, HTML, and CSS. A full-stack developer is a combination of a backend and frontend developer capable of developing backend microservices and frontend clients. A mobile developer develops software for mobile devices, like phones and tablets.

A team should have software developers at various seniority levels. Each team should have a lead developer (or staff developer/engineer) with the best experience in the used technologies and the domain. The lead developer has the technical leadership in the team and typically belongs to the virtual architecture team led by the system architect. The lead developer also works closely with the PO to prepare work for the team.

There is no point in having a team with just junior or senior developers. The idea is to transfer skills and knowledge from senior to junior developers. This also works the other way around. Junior developers can have knowledge of some new technologies and practices that senior developers lack. So overall, the best team consists of a good mix of junior, medior, and senior developers.

11.13.4: Test Automation Developer

A test automation developer is responsible for developing different kinds of automated tests. Typically, test automation developers develop integration, E2E, and automated non-functional tests. A test automation developer must be proficient in at least one programming language, like Python, used to develop automated tests. Test automation developers must have a good command of BDD and ATDD and some common testing frameworks, like Behave or Robot Framework. Knowledge of some non-functional testing tools, like Apache JMeter, is appreciated. Test automation developers can also develop internal testing tools, like interface simulators and data generators. Test automation developers should form a virtual team to facilitate the development of E2E and automated non-functional tests.

11.13.5: DevOps Engineer

A DevOps engineer acts as an interface between the software development team and the software operations. A DevOps engineer usually creates CI/CD pipelines for microservices and crafts infrastructure and deployment-related code. DevOps engineers also define alerting rules and metrics visualization dashboards that can be used when monitoring the software in production. DevOps engineers help operations personnel monitor software in production. They can help troubleshoot problems that the technical support organization cannot solve. DevOps engineer knows the environment (=infrastructure and platform) where the software is deployed, meaning that basic knowledge of at least one cloud provider (AWS/Azure/Google Cloud, etc.) and perhaps Kubernetes is required. DevOps engineers should form a virtual team to facilitate specifying DevOps-related practices and guidelines.

11.13.6: UI Designer

A UI designer is responsible for designing the final UIs based on higher-level UX/UI designs/wireframes. The UI designer will also conduct usability testing of the software.

11.14: Competence Transfer Principle

An extreme case of competence transfer happens when a person leaving a company must hand off the responsibility of a software component to another person. Many times, this other person is not familiar with the software component at all or has only little knowledge about it. To ensure a smooth transfer of competence, at least the following must be performed as part of the competence transfer:

- Demonstration of the software component features
- Explaining the architecture of the software component (how it interacts with other software components in the system)
- Explaining the (object-oriented) design of the software component

  - How the software component is split into subdomains
  - Major interfaces/classes

- Explaining the major implementation decisions for the software component:

  - Special algorithms used
  - Concurrency
  - Error handling mechanism
  - Major security features
  - Performance considerations

- Explaining the configuration of the software component
- Setting up the development environment according to the instructions in the README.MD to ensure that the instructions are correct and up-to-date.
- Building the software, executing unit tests, and executing the integration tests
- Deploying the software component to a test environment
- Explaining the CI/CD pipeline (if it differs from CI/CD pipelines of other software components)
- Explaining other possible automated functional and non-functional tests, like E2E tests, performance and stability tests
- Explaining the observability of the software component, i.e., logging, audit logging, metrics, dashboards, and alerts

11.15: Inter-Team Communication Principle

Regardless of whether you have a distributed or modular monolithic software architecture, teams should have a high degree of organizational autonomy. This means self-directed, fast-paced teams with minimal communication overhead with other teams.

Conway's law describes how an organization's communication structure resembles the architectural structure of the produced software. The software architecture can be a big ball of mud-type monolith without a clear organizational communication structure. If teams are siloed, the missing communication between the teams can produce compatibility issues when software components produced by the teams need to work together. A team suitable for a modular monolith or microservices architecture mainly communicates internally but co-operates with other teams to agree upon interfaces (context mapping) between bounded contexts.

Some aspects require coordination between teams. Those are the things that are visible to software's end-users and administrators. Software should look and feel harmonious, not something that is crafted by siloed teams. For example, coordination is needed in UX/UI design, customer documentation, configuration, and observability (logging format, SLIs, metric dashboards, SLOs, and alarms). The team can decide what is best for things that are not visible to customers and users. For example, the team can choose the programming language, framework, libraries, testing methods, and tools. High independence in teams and lack of inter-team communication can result in an inability to follow the *DRY principle*. There should always be enough communication to avoid unnecessary duplicated effort.

12: DevSecOps

DevOps describes practices that integrate software development (Dev) and software operations (Ops). It aims to shorten the software development lifecycle through development parallelization and automation and provides continuous delivery of high-quality software. DevSecOps enhances DevOps by adding security aspects to the software lifecycle.

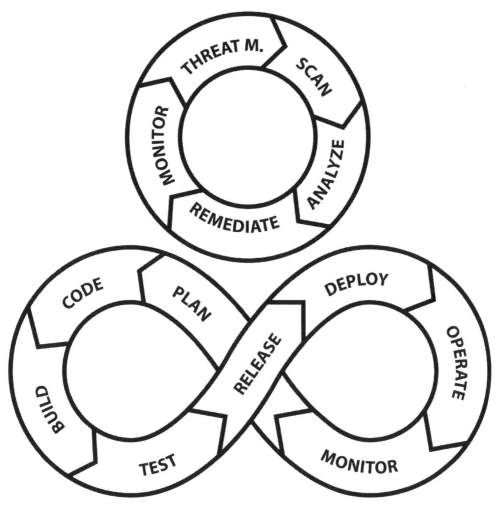

Figure 12.1. DevSecOps Diagram

A software development organization is responsible for planning, designing, and implementing software deliverables. Software operations deploy software to IT infrastructure and platforms. They monitor the deployed software to ensure it runs without problems. Software operations also provide feedback to the software development organization through support requests, bug reports, and enhancement ideas.

12.1: SecOps Lifecycle

The SecOps lifecycle is divided into the following phases:

- Threat modeling

    - To find out what kind of security features and tests are needed
    - Implementation of threat countermeasures and mitigation. This aspect was covered in the earlier *security principles* chapter

- Scan

    - Static security analysis (also known as SAST = Static Application Security Testing)
    - Security testing (also known as DAST = Dynamic Application Security Testing)
    - Container vulnerability scanning

- Analyze

    - Analyze the results of the scanning phase, detect and remove false positives, and prioritize corrections of vulnerabilities

- Remediate

    - Fix the found vulnerabilities according to prioritization

- Monitor

    - Define SecOps-related metrics and monitor them

12.2: DevOps Lifecycle

The DevOps lifecycle is divided into the following phases:

- Plan
- Code
- Build
- Test
- Release
- Deploy
- Operate
- Monitor

Subsequent sections describe each of the phases in more detail.

12.2.1: Plan

Plan is the first phase in the DevOps lifecycle. In this phase, software features are planned, and high-level architecture and user experience (UX) are designed. This phase involves business (product management) and software development organizations.

12.2.2: Code

Code is the software implementation phase. It consists of designing and implementing software components and writing various automated tests, including unit, integration, and E2E tests. This phase also includes all other coding needed to make the software deployable. Most of the work is done in this phase, so it should be streamlined as much as possible.

The key to shortening this phase is to parallelize everything to the maximum possible extent. In the *Plan* phase, the software was architecturally split into smaller pieces (microservices) that different teams could develop in parallel. Regarding developing a single microservice, there should also be as much parallelization as possible. This means that if a microservice can be split into multiple subdomains, the development of these subdomains can be done very much in parallel. If we think about the data exporter microservice, we identified several subdomains: input, decoding, transformations, and output. If you can parallelize the development of these four subdomains instead of developing them one after another, you can significantly shorten the time needed to complete the implementation of the microservice.

To shorten this phase even more, a team should have dedicated test automation developer(s) who can start developing automated tests in an early phase parallel to the implementation.

Providing high-quality software requires high-quality design, implementation with little technical debt, and comprehensive functional and non-functional testing. All of these aspects were handled in the earlier chapters.

12.2.3: Build and Test

The *Build and Test* phase should be automated and run as continuous integration[1] (CI) pipelines. Each software component in a software system should have its own CI pipeline. A CI pipeline is run by a CI tool like Jenkins[2] or GitHub Actions[3]. A CI pipeline is defined using (declarative) code stored in the software component's source code repository. Every time a commit is made to the main branch in the source code repository, it should trigger a CI pipeline run.

The CI pipeline for a software component should perform at least the following tasks:

- Checkout the latest source code from the source code repository
- Build the software
- Perform static code analysis. A tool like SonarQube[4] or SonarCloud[5] can be used
- Perform static application security testing[6] (SAST).

---

[1]https://en.wikipedia.org/wiki/Continuous_integration
[2]https://www.jenkins.io/
[3]https://docs.github.com/en/actions
[4]https://www.sonarsource.com/products/sonarqube/
[5]https://www.sonarsource.com/products/sonarcloud/
[6]https://en.wikipedia.org/wiki/Static_application_security_testing

- Execute unit tests
- Execute integration tests
- Perform dynamic application security testing[7] (DAST). A tool like ZAP[8] can be used
- Verify 3rd party license compliance and provide a software bill of materials[9] (SBOM). A tool like Fossa[10] can be used

12.2.4: Release

In the *Release* phase, built and tested software is released automatically. After a software component's CI pipeline is successfully executed, the software component can be automatically released. This is called continuous delivery[11] (CD). Continuous delivery is often combined with the CI pipeline to create a CI/CD pipeline for a software component. Continuous delivery means that the software component's artifacts are delivered to artifact repositories, like Artifactory[12], Docker Hub[13], or a Helm chart repository[14].

A CD pipeline should perform the following tasks:

- Perform static code analysis for the code that builds a container image (e.g., Dockerfile[15]). A tool like Hadolint[16] can be used for *Dockerfiles*.
- Build a container image for the software component
- Publish the container image to a container registry (e.g., Docker Hub, Artifactory, or a registry provided by your cloud provider)
- Perform a container image vulnerability scan

    - Remember also to enable container vulnerability scanning at regular intervals in your container registry

- Perform static code analysis for deployment code. Tools like Helm's *lint* command, Kubesec[17] and Checkov[18] can be used
- Package and publish the deployment code (for example, package a Helm chart and publish it to a Helm chart repository)

[7]https://en.wikipedia.org/wiki/Dynamic_application_security_testing
[8]https://www.zaproxy.org/
[9]https://en.wikipedia.org/wiki/Software_supply_chain
[10]https://fossa.com/
[11]https://en.wikipedia.org/wiki/Continuous_delivery
[12]https://jfrog.com/artifactory/
[13]https://hub.docker.com/
[14]https://helm.sh/docs/topics/chart_repository/
[15]https://docs.docker.com/engine/reference/builder/
[16]https://github.com/hadolint/hadolint
[17]https://kubesec.io/
[18]https://www.checkov.io/

12.2.4.1: Example Dockerfile

Below is an example *Dockerfile* for a microservice written in TypeScript for Node.js. The Dockerfile uses Docker's multi-stage feature. First (at the builder stage), it builds the source code, i.e., transpiles TypeScript source code files to JavaScript source code files. Then (at the intermediate stage), it creates an intermediate image that copies the built source code from the builder stage and installs only the production dependencies. The last stage (final) copies files from the intermediate stage to a distroless Node.js base image. You should use a distroless base image to make the image size and the attack surface smaller. A distroless image does not contain any Linux distribution inside it.

```
# syntax=docker/dockerfile:1

FROM node:18 as builder
WORKDIR /microservice
COPY package*.json ./
RUN  npm ci
COPY tsconfig*.json ./
COPY src ./src
RUN npm run build

FROM node:18 as intermediate
WORKDIR /microservice
COPY package*.json ./
RUN npm ci --only=production
COPY --from=builder /microservice/build ./build

FROM gcr.io/distroless/nodejs:18 as final
WORKDIR /microservice
USER nonroot:nonroot
COPY --from=intermediate --chown=nonroot:nonroot /microservice ./
CMD ["build/main"]
```

12.2.4.2: Example Kubernetes Deployment

Below is an example Helm chart template *deployment.yaml* for a Kubernetes Deployment. The template code is given in double braces.

```
apiVersion: apps/v1
kind: Deployment
metadata:
  name: {{ include "microservice.fullname" . }}
  labels:
    {{- include "microservice.labels" . | nindent 4 }}
spec:
  {{- if ne .Values.nodeEnv "production" }}
  replicas: 1
  {{- end }}
  selector:
    matchLabels:
      {{- include "microservice.selectorLabels" . | nindent 6 }}
  template:
    metadata:
      {{- with .Values.deployment.pod.annotations }}
      annotations:
        {{- toYaml . | nindent 8 }}
      {{- end }}
      labels:
        {{- include "microservice.selectorLabels" . | nindent 8 }}
    spec:
      {{- with .Values.deployment.pod.imagePullSecrets }}
      imagePullSecrets:
```

```
    {{- toYaml . | nindent 8 }}
{{- end }}
serviceAccountName: {{ include "microservice.serviceAccountName" . }}
containers:
  - name: {{ .Chart.Name }}
    image: "{{ .Values.imageRegistry }}/{{ .Values.imageRepository }}:{{ .Values.imageTag }}"
    imagePullPolicy: {{ .Values.deployment.pod.container.imagePullPolicy }}
    securityContext:
      {{- toYaml .Values.deployment.pod.container.securityContext | nindent 12 }}
    {{- if .Values.httpServer.port }}
    ports:
      - name: http
        containerPort: {{ .Values.httpServer.port }}
        protocol: TCP
    {{- end }}
    env:
      - name: NODE_ENV
        value: {{ .Values.nodeEnv }}
      - name: ENCRYPTION_KEY
        valueFrom:
          secretKeyRef:
            name: {{ include "microservice.fullname" . }}
            key: encryptionKey
      - name: MICROSERVICE_NAME
        value: {{ include "microservice.fullname" . }}
      - name: MICROSERVICE_NAMESPACE
        valueFrom:
          fieldRef:
            fieldPath: metadata.namespace
      - name: MICROSERVICE_INSTANCE_ID
        valueFrom:
          fieldRef:
            fieldPath: metadata.name
      - name: NODE_NAME
        valueFrom:
          fieldRef:
            fieldPath: spec.nodeName
      - name: MYSQL_HOST
        value: {{ .Values.database.mySql.host }}
      - name: MYSQL_PORT
        value: "{{ .Values.database.mySql.port }}"
      - name: MYSQL_USER
        valueFrom:
          secretKeyRef:
            name: {{ include "microservice.fullname" . }}
            key: mySqlUser
      - name: MYSQL_PASSWORD
        valueFrom:
          secretKeyRef:
            name: {{ include "microservice.fullname" . }}
            key: mySqlPassword
    livenessProbe:
      httpGet:
        path: /isMicroserviceAlive
        port: http
      failureThreshold: 3
      periodSeconds: 10
    readinessProbe:
      httpGet:
        path: /isMicroserviceReady
        port: http
      failureThreshold: 3
      periodSeconds: 5
    startupProbe:
      httpGet:
        path: /isMicroserviceStarted
        port: http
      failureThreshold: {{ .Values.deployment.pod.container.startupProbe.failureThreshold }}
      periodSeconds: 10
    resources:
```

```
            {{- if eq .Values.nodeEnv "development" }}
            {{- toYaml .Values.deployment.pod.container.resources.development | nindent 12 }}
            {{- else if eq .Values.nodeEnv "integration"  }}
            {{- toYaml .Values.deployment.pod.container.resources.integration | nindent 12 }}
            {{- else }}
            {{- toYaml .Values.deployment.pod.container.resources.production | nindent 12 }}
            {{- end}}
      {{- with .Values.deployment.pod.nodeSelector }}
      nodeSelector:
        {{- toYaml . | nindent 8 }}
      {{- end }}
      {{- with .Values.deployment.pod.affinity }}
      affinity:
        podAntiAffinity:
          requiredDuringSchedulingIgnoredDuringExecution:
            - labelSelector:
                matchLabels:
                  app.kubernetes.io/name: {{ include "microservice.name" . }}
              topologyKey: "kubernetes.io/hostname"
        {{- toYaml . | nindent 8 }}
      {{- end }}
      {{- with .Values.deployment.pod.tolerations }}
      tolerations:
        {{- toYaml . | nindent 8 }}
      {{- end }}
```

The values (indicated by `.Values.<something>`) in the above template come from a *values.yaml* file. Below is an example *values.yaml* file to be used with the above Helm chart template.

```
imageRegistry: docker.io
imageRepository: pksilen2/backk-example-microservice
imageTag:
nodeEnv: production
auth:
  # Authorization Server Issuer URL
  # For example
  # http://keycloak.platform.svc.cluster.local:8080/auth/realms/<my-realm>
  issuerUrl:

  # JWT path where for user's roles,
  # for example 'realm_access.roles'
  jwtRolesClaimPath:
secrets:
  encryptionKey:
database:
  mySql:
    # For example:
    # my-microservice-mysql.default.svc.cluster.local or
    # cloud database host
    host:
    port: 3306
    user:
    password: &mySqlPassword ""
mysql:
  auth:
    rootPassword: *mySqlPassword
deployment:
  pod:
    annotations: {}
    imagePullSecrets: []
    container:
      imagePullPolicy: Always
      securityContext:
        privileged: false
        capabilities:
          drop:
            - ALL
        readOnlyRootFilesystem: true
```

```
          runAsNonRoot: true
          runAsUser: 65532
          runAsGroup: 65532
          allowPrivilegeEscalation: false
        env:
        startupProbe:
          failureThreshold: 30
        resources:
          development:
            limits:
              cpu: '1'
              memory: 768Mi
            requests:
              cpu: '1'
              memory: 384Mi
          integration:
            limits:
              cpu: '1'
              memory: 768Mi
            requests:
              cpu: '1'
              memory: 384Mi
          production:
            limits:
              cpu: 1
              memory: 768Mi
            requests:
              cpu: 1
              memory: 384Mi
    nodeSelector: {}
    tolerations: []
    affinity: {}
```

Notice the `deployment.pod.container.securityContext` object in the above file. It is used to define the
security context for a microservice container.

By default, the security context should be the following:

- Container should not be privileged
- All capabilities are dropped
- Container filesystem is read-only
- Only a non-root user is allowed to run inside the container
- Define the non-root user and group under which the container should run
- Disallow privilege escalation

You can remove things from the above list only if required for a microservice. For example, if the
microservice must write to the filesystem for some valid reason, then the filesystem cannot be defined
as read-only.

12.2.4.3: Example CI/CD Pipeline

Below is a GitHub Actions CI/CD workflow for a Node.js microservice. The declarative workflow is
written in YAML. The workflow file should be located in the microservice's source code repository in the
.github/workflows directory. Steps in the workflow are described in more detail after the example.

```
name: CI/CD workflow
on:
  workflow_dispatch: {}
  push:
    branches:
      - main
    tags-ignore:
      - '**'
jobs:
  build:
    runs-on: ubuntu-latest
    name: Build with Node version 18
    steps:
      - name: Checkout Git repo
        uses: actions/checkout@v2

      - name: Setup Node.js
        uses: actions/setup-node@v2
        with:
          node-version: '18'
          cache: 'npm'

      - name: Install NPM dependencies
        run: npm ci

      - name: Lint source code
        run: npm run lint

      - name: Run unit tests with coverage
        run: npm run test:coverage

      - name: Setup integration testing environment
        run: docker-compose --env-file .env.ci up --build -d

      - name: Run integration tests
        run: scripts/run-integration-tests-in-ci.sh

      - name: OWASP ZAP API scan
        uses: zaproxy/action-api-scan@v0.1.0
        with:
          target: generated/openapi/openApiPublicSpec.yaml
          fail_action: true
          cmd_options: -I -z "-config replacer.full_list(0).description=auth1
                          -config replacer.full_list(0).enabled=true
                          -config replacer.full_list(0).matchtype=REQ_HEADER
                          -config replacer.full_list(0).matchstr=Authorization
                          -config replacer.full_list(0).regex=false
                          -config 'replacer.full_list(0).replacement=Bearer ZX1K...aGJHZ='"

      - name: Tear down integration testing environment
        run: docker-compose --env-file .env.ci down -v

      - name: Static code analysis with SonarCloud scan
        uses: sonarsource/sonarcloud-github-action@v1.6
        env:
          GITHUB_TOKEN: ${{ secrets.GITHUB_TOKEN }}
          SONAR_TOKEN: ${{ secrets.SONAR_TOKEN }}

      - name: 3rd party software license compliance analysis with FOSSA
        uses: fossas/fossa-action@v1
        with:
          api-key: ${{ secrets.FOSSA_API_KEY }}
          run-tests: false

      - name: Lint Dockerfile
        uses: hadolint/hadolint-action@v1.6.0

      - name: Log in to Docker registry
        uses: docker/login-action@v1
        with:
```

```
      registry: docker.io
      username: ${{ secrets.DOCKER_REGISTRY_USERNAME }}
      password: ${{ secrets.DOCKER_REGISTRY_PASSWORD }}

  - name: Extract latest Git tag
    uses: actions-ecosystem/action-get-latest-tag@v1
    id: extractLatestGitTag

  - name: Set up Docker Buildx
    id: setupBuildx
    uses: docker/setup-buildx-action@v1

  - name: Cache Docker layers
    uses: actions/cache@v2
    with:
      path: /tmp/.buildx-cache
      key: ${{ runner.os }}-buildx-${{ github.sha }}
      restore-keys: |
        ${{ runner.os }}-buildx-

  - name: Extract metadata for building and pushing Docker image
    id: dockerImageMetadata
    uses: docker/metadata-action@v3
    with:
      images: ${{ secrets.DOCKER_REGISTRY_USERNAME }}/example-microservice
      tags: |
        type=semver,pattern={{version}},value=${{ steps.extractLatestGitTag.outputs.value }}

  - name: Build and push Docker image
    id: dockerImageBuildAndPush
    uses: docker/build-push-action@v2
    with:
      context: .
      builder: ${{ steps.setupBuildx.outputs.name }}
      push: true
      cache-from: type=local,src=/tmp/.buildx-cache
      cache-to: type=local,dest=/tmp/.buildx-cache
      tags: ${{ steps.dockerImageMetadata.outputs.tags }}
      labels: ${{ steps.dockerImageMetadata.outputs.labels }}

  - name: Docker image vulnerability scan with Anchore
    id: anchoreScan
    uses: anchore/scan-action@v3
    with:
      image: ${{ secrets.DOCKER_REGISTRY_USERNAME }}/example-microservice:latest
      fail-build: false
      severity-cutoff: high

  - name: Upload Anchore scan SARIF report
    uses: github/codeql-action/upload-sarif@v1
    with:
      sarif_file: ${{ steps.anchoreScan.outputs.sarif }}

  - name: Install Helm
    uses: azure/setup-helm@v1
    with:
      version: v3.7.2

  - name: Extract microservice version from Git tag
    id: extractMicroserviceVersionFromGitTag
    run: |
      value="${{ steps.extractLatestGitTag.outputs.value }}"
      value=${value:1}
      echo "::set-output name=value::$value"

  - name: Update Helm chart versions in Chart.yaml
    run: |
      sed -i "s/^version:.*/version: ${{ steps.extractMicroserviceVersionFromGitTag.outputs.value \
}}/g" helm/example-microservice/Chart.yaml
      sed -i "s/^appVersion:.*/appVersion: ${{ steps.extractMicroserviceVersionFromGitTag.outputs.\
```

```
value }}/g" helm/example-microservice/Chart.yaml

      - name: Update Docker image tag in values.yaml
        run: |
          sed -i "s/^imageTag:.*/imageTag: {{ steps.extractMicroserviceVersionFromGitTag.outputs.value\
}}@${{ steps.dockerImageBuildAndPush.outputs.digest }}/g" helm/example-microservice/values.yaml

      - name: Lint Helm chart
        run: helm lint -f helm/values/values-minikube.yaml helm/example-microservice

      - name: Static code analysis for Helm chart with Checkov
        uses: bridgecrewio/checkov-action@master
        with:
          directory: helm/example-microservice
          quiet: false
          framework: helm
          soft_fail: false

      - name: Upload Checkov SARIF report
        uses: github/codeql-action/upload-sarif@v1
        with:
          sarif_file: results.sarif
          category: checkov-iac-sca

      - name: Configure Git user
        run: |
          git config user.name "$GITHUB_ACTOR"
          git config user.email "$GITHUB_ACTOR@users.noreply.github.com"

      - name: Package and publish Helm chart
        uses: helm/chart-releaser-action@v1.2.1
        with:
          charts_dir: helm
        env:
          CR_TOKEN: "${{ secrets.GITHUB_TOKEN }}"
```

1) Checkout the microservice's Git repository
2) Setup Node.js 18
3) Install dependencies
4) Lint source code using the `npm run lint` command, which uses ESLint
5) Execute unit tests
6) Report coverage
7) Set up an integration testing environment using Docker's `docker-compose up` command. After executing the command, the microservice is built, and all the dependencies in separate containers are started. These dependencies can include other microservices and, for example, a database and a message broker, like Apache Kafka
8) Execute integration tests. This script will first wait until all dependencies are up and ready. This waiting is done running a container using the dokku/wait[19] image.
9) Perform DAST with ZAP API scan[20]. For the scan, we define the URL to the OpenAPI 3.0 specification against which the scan will be made. We also give command options to set a valid Authorization header for the HTTP requests made by the scan
10) Tear down the integration testing environment
11) Perform static code analysis using SonarCloud. You need to have the following file in the root of the source code repository:

[19] https://hub.docker.com/r/dokku/wait
[20] https://www.zaproxy.org/docs/docker/api-scan/

```
sonar.projectKey=<sonar-project-key>
sonar.organization=<sonar-organization>

sonar.python.coverage.reportPaths=coverage.xml
```

12) Check 3rd party software license compliance using FOSSA
13) Lint Dockerfile
14) Log in to Docker Hub
15) Extract the latest Git tag for further use
16) Setup Docker Buildx and cache Docker layers
17) Extract metadata, like the tag and labels for building and pushing a Docker image
18) Build and push a Docker image
19) Perform a Docker image vulnerability scan with Anchore[21]
20) Upload the Anchore scan report to the GitHub repository
21) Install Helm
22) Extract the microservice version from the Git tag (remove the 'v' letter before the version number)
23) Replace Helm chart versions in the Helm chart's *Chart.yaml* file using the Linux *sed* command
24) Update the Docker image tag in the *values.yaml* file
25) Lint the Helm chart and perform static code analysis for it
26) Upload the static code analysis report to the GitHub repository and perform git user configuration for the next step
27) Package the Helm chart and publish it to GitHub Pages. There exists an alternative method: the newest version of the *helm* tool allows you to publish a Helm chart using the `helm push` command

Some of the above steps are parallelizable, but a GitHub Actions workflow does not currently support parallel steps in a job. In *Jenkins*, you can easily parallelize stages using a *parallel* block.

You could also execute the unit tests and linting when building a Docker image by adding the following steps to the *builder* stage in the *Dockerfile*:

```
RUN npm run lint
RUN npm run test:coverage
```

The problem with the above solution is that you don't get a clear indication of what failed in a build. You must examine the output of the Docker build command to see if linting or unit tests failed. Also, you cannot use the SonarCloud GitHub Action anymore. You must implement SonarCloud reporting in the *builder* stage of the *Dockerfile* (after completing the unit testing to report the unit test coverage to SonarCloud).

12.2.5: Deploy

In the *Deploy* phase, released software is deployed to an execution environment automatically. A software component can be automatically deployed after a successful CI/CD pipeline run. This is called continuous deployment[22] (CD). Notice that both *continuous delivery* and *continuous deployment* are abbreviated as CD. This can cause unfortunate misunderstandings. Continuous delivery is about releasing software automatically, and continuous deployment is about automatically deploying released software to one or more environments. These environments include, for example, a CI/CD environment, staging

---

[21] https://github.com/anchore/scan-action
[22] https://en.wikipedia.org/wiki/Continuous_deployment

environment(s) and finally, production environment(s). There are different ways to automate software deployment. One modern and popular way is GitOps[23], which uses a Git repository or repositories to define automatic deployments to different environments using a declarative approach. GitOps can be configured to update an environment automatically when new software is released. This is typically done for the CI/CD environment, which should always be kept up-to-date and contain the latest software component versions. Notable GitOps solutions are, for example, Flux[24] and Argo CD[25].

GitOps can also be configured to deploy automatically and regularly to a staging environment. A staging environment replicates a production environment. It is an environment where end-to-end functional and non-functional tests are executed before the software is deployed to production. You can use multiple staging environments to speed up the continuous deployment to production. It is vital that all needed testing is completed before deploying to production. Testing can take a couple of days to validate the stability of the software. If testing in a staging environment requires three days and you set up three staging environments, you can deploy to production daily. On the other hand, if testing in a staging environment takes one week and you have only one staging environment, you can deploy to production only once a week. (Assuming that all tests execute successfully) Deployment to a production environment can also be automated. Or it can be triggered manually after completing all testing in a staging environment.

12.2.6: Operate

Operate is the phase when the software runs in production. In this phase, it needs to be ensured that software updates (like security patches) are deployed timely. Also, the production environment's infrastructure and platform should be kept up-to-date and secure.

12.2.7: Monitor

Monitor is the phase when a deployed software system is monitored to detect any possible problems. Monitoring should be automated as much as possible. It can be automated by defining rules for alerts triggered when the software system operation requires human intervention. These alerts are typically based on various metrics collected from the microservices, infrastructure, and platform. Prometheus[26] is a popular system for collecting metrics and triggering alerts.

The basic monitoring workflow follows the path below:

1) Monitor alerts
2) If an alert is triggered, investigate metrics in the relevant dashboard(s)
3) Check logs for errors in relevant services
4) Distributed tracing can help to visualize if and how requests between different microservices are failing

The following needs to be implemented to make monitoring possible and easy:

- Logging to standard input
- Distributed tracing

---

[23]https://about.gitlab.com/topics/gitops/
[24]https://fluxcd.io/
[25]https://argo-cd.readthedocs.io/en/stable/
[26]https://prometheus.io/

- Metrics collection
- Metrics visualization
- Alerting

12.2.7.1: Logging to Standard Input

Each service must log to the standard output. If your microservice is using a 3rd party library that logs to the standard output, choose a library that allows you to configure the log format or request the log format configurability as an enhancement to the library. Choose a standardized log format and use it in all microservices. For example, use Syslog[27] format or the OpenTelemetry Log Data Model (defined in a later section). Collect logs from each microservice and store them in a centralized location, like an ElasticSearch database, where they are easily queriable.

12.2.7.2: Distributed Tracing

Integrate microservices with a distributed tracing tool, like Jaeger[28]. A distributed tracing tool collects information about network requests microservices make.

12.2.7.3: Metrics Collection

Define what metrics need to be collected from each microservice. Typically, metrics are either *counters* (e.g., number of requests handled or request errors) or *gauges* (e.g., current CPU/memory usage). Collect metrics to calculate the service level indicators[29] (SLIs). Below are listed the five categories of SLIs and a few examples of SLIs in each category.

- Availability

  - Is the service down?
  - Is a dependent service down?

- Error rate

  - How many times a service has been restarted due to a crash or unresponsiveness
  - Message processing errors
  - Request errors
  - Other errors
  - Different errors can be monitored by setting a metric label. For example, if you have a *request_-errors* counter and a request produces an internal server error, you can increment the *request_-errors* counter with the label *internal_server_error* by one.

- Latency

  - Message or request processing duration

- Throughput

---

[27]https://datatracker.ietf.org/doc/html/rfc5424
[28]https://www.jaegertracing.io/
[29]https://sre.google/sre-book/service-level-objectives/

– Number of messages/requests handled

- Saturation

  – Resource usage, e.g., CPU/memory/disk usage vs. requested amount

Instrument your microservice with the necessary code to collect the metrics. This can be done using a metrics collection library, like Prometheus.

12.2.7.4: Metrics Visualization

Create a main dashboard for each microservice to present the SLIs. Additionally, you should present *service level objectives* (SLOs) as dashboard charts. An example of an SLO is "service error rate must be less than x percent". When all SLOs are met, the dashboard should show SLO charts in green, and if an SLO is not met, the corresponding chart should be shown in red. You can also use yellow and orange colors to indicate that an SLO is still met, but the SLI value is no longer optimal. Use a visualization tool that integrates with the metrics collection tool, like Grafana[30] with Prometheus. You can usually deploy metric dashboards as part of the microservice deployment.

12.2.7.5: Alerting

To define alerting rules, first define the service level objectives (SLOs) and base the alerting rules on them. If an SLO cannot be met, an alert should be triggered, and when the SLO is met again, the alert should automatically cancel. If you are using Kubernetes and Prometheus, you can define alerts using the Prometheus Operator[31] and PrometheusRule CRs[32].

12.2.8: Software System Alerts Dashboard Example

Below is an example of a Grafana dashboard that visualizes active alerts in a software system.

---

[30]https://grafana.com/

[31]https://github.com/prometheus-operator/prometheus-operator

[32]https://github.com/prometheus-operator/prometheus-operator/blob/main/Documentation/user-guides/alerting.md

Alerts Dashboard

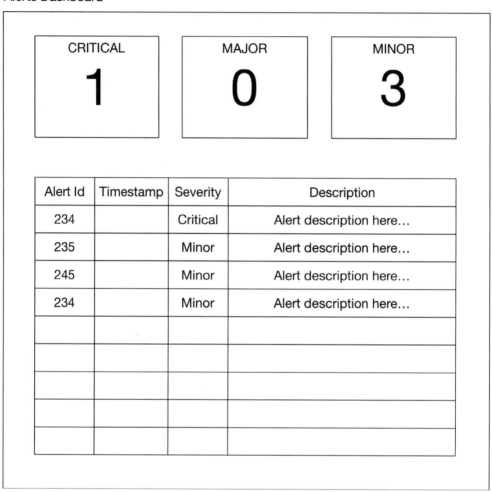

Figure 12.2. Alert Dashboard

12.2.9: Microservice Grafana Dashboard Example

Below is an example of a Grafana dashboard to visualize SLOs and SLIs for a single microservice. SLOs are presented as charts in the topmost section of the dashboard, and below them are five accordions, the first being opened to reveal the charts inside it. When opened, each accordion reveals charts for a particular SLI category. Each chart presents a specific SLI. In the figure below, the SLO 2 is shown in red background, and it could indicate that the number of errors in the last hour is too high, for example.

Alerts Dashboard

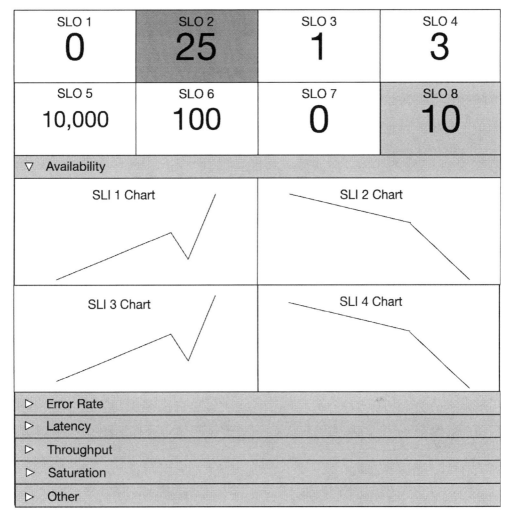

Figure 12.3. Microservice Monitoring Dashboard

Software operations staff connects back to the software development side of the DevOps lifecycle in the following ways:

- Ask for technical support
- File a bug report
- File an improvement idea

The first one will result in a solved case or bug report. The latter two will reach the *Plan* phase of the DevOps lifecycle. Bug reports usually enter the *Code* phase immediately, depending on the fault severity.

12.2.9.1: Logging

Implement logging in software components using the following logging severities:

- (CRITICAL/FATAL)
- ERROR
- WARNING
- INFO
- DEBUG
- TRACE

I don't usually use the CRITICAL/FATAL severity at all. It might be better to report all errors with the ERROR severity because then it is easy to query logs for errors using a single keyword only, for example:

```
kubectl logs <pod-name> | grep ERROR
```

You can add information about the criticality/fatality of an error to the log message itself. When you log an error for which there is a solution available, you should inform the user about the solution in the log message, e.g., provide a link to a troubleshooting guide or give an error code that can be used to search the troubleshooting guide.

Do not log too much information using the INFO severity because the logs become hard to read when there is too much noise. Consider carefully what should be logged with the INFO severity and what can be logged with the DEBUG severity instead. The default logging level of a microservice should preferably be WARNING (or INFO).

Use the TRACE severity to log only tracing information, e.g., detailed information about processing a single request, event, or message.

If you are implementing a 3rd party library, the library should allow customizing the logging if the library logs something. There should be a way to set the logging level and allow the code that is using the library to customize the format in which log entries are written. Otherwise, 3rd party library log entries appear in the log in a different format than the log entries from the microservice itself, making the logs harder to read.

12.2.9.2: OpenTelemetry Log Data Model

This section describes the essence of the OpenTelemetry log data model version 1.12.0 (Please check OpenTelemetry Specification[33] for possible updates).

A log entry is a JSON object containing the following properties:

---

[33]https://github.com/open-telemetry/opentelemetry-specification

Field Name	Description
Timestamp	Time when the event occurred. Nanoseconds since Unix epoch
TraceId	Request trace id
SpanId	Request span id
SeverityText	The severity text (also known as log level)
SeverityNumber	Numerical value of the severity
Body	The body of the log entry. You can include ISO 8601 timestamp and the severity/log level before the actual log message
Resource	A JSON object that describes the source of the log entry
Attributes	Additional information about the log event. This is a JSON object where custom attributes can be given

Below is an example log entry according to the above log data model.

```
{
  "Timestamp": "1586960586000000000",
  "TraceId": "f4dbb3edd765f620",
  "SpanId": "43222c2d51a7abe3",
  "SeverityText": "ERROR",
  "SeverityNumber": 9,
  "Body": "20200415T072306-0700 ERROR Error message comes here",
  "Resource": {
    "service.namespace": "default",
    "service.name": "my-microservice",
    "service.version": "1.1.1",
    "service.instance.id": "my-microservice-34fggd-56faae"
  },
  "Attributes": {
    "http.status_code": 500,
    "http.url": "http://example.com",
    "myCustomAttributeKey": "myCustomAttributeValue"
  }
}
```

The above JSON-format log entries might be hard to read as plain text on the console, for example, when viewing a pod's logs with the `kubectl logs` command in a Kubernetes cluster. You can create a small script that extracts only the `Body` property value from each log entry.

12.2.9.3: PrometheusRule Example

PrometheusRule custom resources (CRs) can be used to define rules for triggering alerts. In the below example, an *example-microservice-high-request-latency* alert will be triggered with a major severity when the median request latency in seconds is greater than one (request_latencies_in_seconds{quantile="0.5"} > 1).

```
apiVersion: monitoring.coreos.com/v1
kind: PrometheusRule
metadata:
  name: example-microservice-rules
spec:
  groups:
  - name: example-microservice-rules
    rules:
    - alert: example-microservice-high-request-latency
      expr: request_latencies_in_seconds{quantile="0.5"} > 1
      for: 10m
      labels:
        application: example-microservice
        severity: major
        class: latency
      annotations:
        summary: "High request latency on {{ $labels.instance }}"
        description: "{{ $labels.instance }} has a median request latency above 1s (current value: {{ \
$value }}s)"
```

13: Conclusion

This book has presented a lot of valuable principles and patterns. It can be challenging to grasp them all at once. For this reason, I suggest you prioritize learning. Topics I have found most important during many years of coding are the following:

- Code is read more often than written principle

    - For this reason, pay attention to the fact that your code is easily readable and understandable. To achieve this, you can use the uniform naming principle and avoid writing comments principle presented in this book

- Prefer object composition over inheritance principle

    - Consider always first if there is a *has-a* relationship between two objects, then use object composition. But if there is not a has-a relationship but a *is-a* relationship, then use inheritance

- Encapsulation principle

    - Don't automatically implement attribute getters and setters in a class. They can break encapsulation. Only implement them when needed. If you have getters and setters for all or most attributes and little other behavior in your class, the class can be an anemic class. You might not be following the don't ask, tell principle, which results in the feature envy code smell.

- Single responsibility principle

    - Whether it is a question about a software component or a class, try to make it have a single responsibility at a certain level of abstraction to keep the software component or class small enough. If the level of abstraction is high, the software component or class can become too large. What you can do is extract functionality from the large class to smaller classes and make the original class use the smaller ones

- Program against interfaces principle

    - This is a necessity if you want to follow the open-closed principle

- Open-closed principle

    - When you put new functionality into new classes, instead of modifying existing classes and their methods, you usually cannot accidentally break any existing functionality

- TDD or USDD

    - When creating new functions, use TDD or USDD to make it less likely to forget to implement some failure scenarios or edge cases. Consider preferring TDD over USDD because of the following additional benefits:

       * Refactoring becomes a norm and helps you achieve a better design
       * Less stress and cognitive load
       * You are bound to write testable code

- Threat modeling

  - Helps you and your team to create more secure software

- Integration testing using BDD and ATDD

  - Define integration tests using BDD and formal specifications and make those integration tests acceptance tests of a feature. This formalized way of specifying a feature makes it less likely not to forget to write integration tests for the features of the software component.

Regarding design patterns, the following two patterns are the most valuable, and you can use them in almost every project. Other design patterns are not necessarily as widely used.

- (Abstract) Factory pattern

  - Use factories to instantiate different implementations of an interface

- Adapter pattern

  - You can create multiple implementations for a common interface using adapter classes that adapt another interface to the common interface

If you want to master more design patterns, I suggest to learn the following:

- Strategy pattern

  - Make the class behavior dynamic by depending on an abstract strategy with multiple implementations. When following this pattern, you implement different behaviors (strategies) in separate classes, making your code follow the single responsibility principle and open-closed principle

- Decorator pattern

  - Augment the behavior of a class or function without modifying the class or function. For functions, this pattern can be implemented using Python function decorators.

- Proxy pattern

  - Conditionally delegate to the wrapped class's or function's behavior. A good example of the proxy pattern is caching. The caching proxy class delegates to the wrapped class or function only when a result isn't available in the cache already. For functions, this pattern can be implemented using Python function decorators. For example, Python has a built-in `@cache` decorator that utilizes the proxy pattern.

- Command/Action pattern

- – Encapsulate functionality with parameters in a command/action object. This pattern allows you to follow the open-closed principle because you can put new functionality in a new command/action class.

- State pattern

  - – Don't treat state as enums. Use objects that have attached behavior related to a particular state. Following this pattern allows you to replace conditionals with polymorphism.

- Template method pattern

  - – Put a common algorithm that calls an abstract method to a base class in a class inheritance hierarchy. This abstract method call in the common algorithm makes the method a template method. The final behavior of the common algorithm is refined by the subclasses that implement the abstract method called from the template method.

To fully embrace a principle or pattern, you need to apply it in real-life projects and see the benefits yourself. When you see the benefits in practice, the value of a principle or pattern becomes more evident and no longer feels like a law imposed by some authority that you are forced to obey.

14: Appendix A

This appendix presents the implementation of an object validation library in TypeScript (version 4.7.4 used). This library uses the validated-types NPM library as a basis.

This object validation library will be able to validate a JSON object whose schema is given in the below format. The schema object lists the properties of the object to be validated. The value of each property is the schema for that property in the object to be validated. In this example, we implement support for validating integers, strings, and nested objects. Validation of other types (e.g., floats and arrays) could also be added.

The schema of an integer property is defined as follows:

```
['int' | 'int?', 'min-value,max-value']
```

The schema of a string property is defined using one of the three syntaxes as shown below:

```
['string' | 'string?', 'min-length,max-length,validator']

['string' | 'string?', ['min-length,max-length,validator',
                        'validator']]


['string' | 'string?', ['min-length,max-length,validator',
                        'validator',
                        'validator']]
```

Below is an example schema object:

```
const schema = {
  inputUrl: ['string', ['1,1024,url',
                        'startsWith,https',
                        'endsWith,com']] as const,

  outputPort: ['int?', '1,65535'] as const,
  mongoDb: {
    user: ['string?', '1,512'] as const
  },
  transformations: [
    {
      outputFieldName: ['string', '1,512'] as const,
      inputFieldName: ['string', '1,512'] as const
    }
  ] as const
};

const defaultValues = {
  outputPort: 8080
};
```

Explanations for individual property schemas from above: - inputUrl * Mandatory string property * Length must be between 1-1024 characters * Value must be an URL and start with 'https' and end with 'com' - outputPort * Optional integer property * Value must be between 1-65535 - mongoDb.user * Optional string property * Length must be between 1-512 characters - transformations[].outputFieldName * Mandatory string property * Length must be between 1-512 characters - transformations[].inputFieldName * Mandatory string property * Length must be between 1-512 characters

Below are the definitions of TypeScript types needed for the library:

```
type ValidationClass<T extends Type, V extends ValidationSpec> = T extends `${infer NullableType}?`
  ? NullableType extends 'string'
    ? VString<V> | null
    : NullableType extends 'int'
    ? V extends string
      ? VInt<V> | null
      : never
    : never
  : T extends `${infer T}`
  ? T extends 'string'
    ? VString<V>
    : T extends 'int'
    ? V extends string
      ? VInt<V>
      : never
    : never
  : never;

type PropertySchema = [Type, ValidationSpec];
export type ObjectSchema = { [propertyName: string]: PropertySchema | ObjectSchema | [ObjectSchema] };

export type ValidatedObject<S extends ObjectSchema> = {
  [P in keyof S]: S[P] extends [ObjectSchema]
    ? Array<ValidatedObject<S[P][0]>>
    : S[P] extends ObjectSchema
    ? ValidatedObject<S[P]>
    : S[P] extends PropertySchema
    ? ValidationClass<S[P][0], S[P][1]>
    : never;
};
```

The below `tryCreateValidatedObject` function tries to create a validated version of a given object:

```
import { VInt, VString } from 'validated-types';
import { DeepWritable, Writable } from 'ts-essentials';
import { ObjectSchema, ValidatedObject } from './ValidatedObject';

function tryCreateValidatedObject<S extends ObjectSchema>(
  object: Record<string, any>,
  objectSchema: OS,
  defaultValuesObject?: Record<string, any>
): ValidatedObject<S> {
  const validatedObject = {};

  Object.entries(objectSchema as Writable<S>).forEach(([propertyName,
                                                         objectOrPropertySchema]) => {
    const isPropertySchema = Array.isArray(objectOrPropertySchema) &&
                             typeof objectOrPropertySchema[0] === 'string';

    if (isPropertySchema) {
      const [propertyType, propertySchema] = objectOrPropertySchema;
      if (propertyType.startsWith('string')) {
        (validatedObject as any)[propertyName] = propertyType.endsWith('?')
          ? VString.create(propertySchema, object[propertyName] ??
              defaultValuesObject?.[propertyName])
          : VString.tryCreate(propertySchema, object[propertyName]);
      } else if (propertyType.startsWith('int') && !Array.isArray(propertySchema)) {
        (validatedObject as any)[propertyName] = propertyType.endsWith('?')
          ? VInt.create<typeof propertySchema>(
              propertySchema,
              object[propertyName] ?? defaultValuesObject?.[propertyName]
            )
          : VInt.tryCreate<typeof propertySchema>(propertySchema, object[propertyName]);
      }
    } else {
      if (Array.isArray(objectOrPropertySchema)) {
        (object[propertyName] ?? []).forEach((subObject: any) => {
          (validatedObject as any)[propertyName] = [
```

```
            ...((validatedObject as any)[propertyName] ?? []),
            tryCreateValidatedObject(subObject ?? {},
                                     objectOrPropertySchema[0],
                                     defaultValuesObject?.[propertyName])
        ];
      });
    } else {
      (validatedObject as any)[propertyName] = tryCreateValidatedObject(
        object[propertyName] ?? {},
        objectOrPropertySchema,
        defaultValuesObject?.[propertyName]
      );
    }
  }
});

  return validatedObject as ValidatedObject<ObjSchema>;
}
```

Let's have the following unvalidated configuration object and create a validated version of it:

```
const unvalidatedConfiguration = {
  inputUrl: 'https://www.google.com',
  mongoDb: {
    user: 'root'
  },
  transformations: [
    {
      outputFieldName: 'outputField',
      inputFieldName: 'inputField'
    }
  ]
};

// This will contain the validated configuration object with strong typing
let configuration: ValidatedObject<DeepWritable<typeof configurationSchema>>;

try {
  configuration = tryCreateValidatedObject(
    unvalidatedConfiguration,
    configurationSchema as DeepWritable<typeof configurationSchema>,
    configurationDefaultValues
  );

  console.log(validatedConfiguration.inputUrl.value);
  console.log(validatedConfiguration.outputPort?.value);
  console.log(validatedConfiguration.mongoDb.user?.value);
  console.log(validatedConfiguration.transformations[0].inputFieldName.value);
  console.log(validatedConfiguration.transformations[0].outputFieldName.value);
} catch (error) {
  // Handle error...
}

// We export the validated configuration object with strong typing
// to be used in other parts of the application
export default configuration;
```

Below is an example schema for a Node.js process.env object:

```
export const environmentSchema = {
  NODE_ENV: ['string', '1,32,isOneOf,["development","integration","production"]'],
  LOGGING_LEVEL: ['string?', '1,32,isOneOf,["DEBUG","INFO","WARN","ERROR"]'],
  MONGODB_PORT: ['string?', '1,5,numericRange,1-65535'],
  MONGODB_USER: ['string?', '1,512']
}

export const environmentDefaultValues = {
  LOGGING_LEVEL: 'INFO',
  MONGODB_PORT: '27017'
}
```

We can create a validated environment from the process.env:

```
import { environmentDefaultValue, environmentSchema } from './environmentSchema';

let environment: ValidatedObject<DeepWritable<typeof environmentSchema>>;

try {
  environment = tryCreateValidatedObject(
    process.env,
    environmentSchema as DeepWritable<typeof environmentSchema>,
    environmentDefaultValues
  );
} catch (error) {
  // Handle error...
}

export default environment;
```

Made in the USA
Columbia, SC
16 May 2025

58048601R00370